LINCOLN COUNTY, TENNESSEE

OFFICIAL

I0091169

MARRIAGE RECORDS

1838 - 1880

Compiled from original Marriage Licenses and Bonds,

Family Records

&

Newspaper Accounts

by

Helen C. Marsh

&

Timothy R. Marsh

Southern Historical Press, Inc.
Greenville, South Carolina

Please direct all correspondence and orders to:
www.southernhistoricalpress.com
or
SOUTHERN HISTORICAL PRESS, Inc.
PO BOX 1267
375 West Broad Street
Greenville, SC   29601
southernhistoricalpress@gmail.com

ISBN #0-89308-571-5

Printed in the United States of America

TAYLOR CRAWFORD
LINCOLN COUNTY JUDGE

Mrs.Helen Marsh
Mr.Timothy Marsh
Authors of this Book

It is my firm belief and conviction that one of the greatest
sins of modern times is our failure to preserve the records
of our Lincoln County history.

We are proud of the Authors of this book and the information
contained within its pages.

I thank God for our ancestors,their lives,the records they
left behind,the pride they took in a history rich and valuable
to their offspring and the generations to come.

Taylor Crawford
LINCOLN COUNTY JUDGE

iii

Clyde Moore

COUNTY COURT CLERK of LINCOLN COUNTY
Fayetteville, Tennessee 37334

The hearts and lives of our earley ancestors have given us the great heritage we possess today. As the years pass, men and women have made great contributions to society in various ways. One of these ways is by preserving the historical records we prize so greatly. The Lincoln County Courthouse holds many of these valuable historical records. During the year 1969 and for two years following, Mrs. Helen Marsh and Mr. Tim Marsh made a diligent search of the oldest Lincoln County records, and compiled them for book printing. Mrs. Helen Marsh worked daily and copied all the old marriage records for the History Books she and Mr. Marsh were compiling. We compliment Mr. and Mrs. Marsh for the interest they have in Lincoln County History, and we Congratulate them for a job well done.

Clyde Moore , Fayetteville, Tennessee
COUNTY COURT CLERK

Wilma J. Moore , Fayetteville, Tennessee
DEPUTY COUNTY COURT CLERK

Doris W. Moore , Fayetteville, Tennessee

Dorothy W. Campbell , Fayetteville, Tennessee

Louise J. Johnston ,

FOREWORD

One who researches the events of the past, whether he be historian or genealogist, faces unavoidable frustration when he confronts a gap in the official records of the community wherein his intrest lies.

So it is that one who has reason to search through the marriage records of Lincoln County, Tennessee will be disappointed to find that the marriages were not officially recorded there until 1838, though the County was formed in 1810. No doubt those pioneer Lincoln Countians were too involved in the mere business of survival and in the structuring of their new community to find time to record all the vital statistics and civil events.

Realizing that the absence of any official recording of marriages during this 28-year span may cause difficulties in genealogical studies, the authors researched area newspapers and family records in order to include an additional list of Lincoln County marriages not officially recorded. This list appears on pages 184-189.

This book is the results of our own interest in genealogical research, but we are indebted to many who have made invaluable contributions to our efforts, we express our appreciation to all.

[No official marriage records were kept by the clerk before 1836, when the Legislature directed the clerks to start recording them.. Eds]

ABBREVIATIONS

Col.--------Colored
J.P.--------Justice of the Peace
M.G.--------Minister of the Gospel
NB----------National Banner
NBNDA-------National Banner & Nashville Daily Advertiser
NBNW--------National Banner & Nashville Whig
NR----------Nashville Republican
NRSG--------Nashville Republican & State Gazette
NW----------Nashville Whig
Obit--------Obituary
RB----------Republican Banner
VDM--------Verbi Dei Ministri or Minister of the Word of
                                                      God.

LINCOLN COUNTY

MARRIAGE RECORDS
1838-1880

A record of Marriage Licenses issued by the Clerk of Lincoln
County Court, Tennessee, after the 1st day of February 1838.
1838
page 1
Feb 3,   Thomas Kirkland to Sally Patterson by A.W.Parks
     3,   Wiley C. Ellis to Peggy Ann Waggoner, by Wm. Timmins,JP
     5,   William Warren to Sarah Wilkerson by John King
     8,   Robert Wood to Mary Mallard by Joel Reece
     8,   William W. Moores to Jane M. Browning by A.B.Gilbert
     7,   William Stephens to Jane Berry by Samuel J. Bland
     6,   William G. Hamilton to Caroline McGaugh by Thomas Chiles
     6,   John Webb to Rebuah Cumberland by John Moorehead, JP
    13,   John Bearden to Mary Warren
    14,   Micajah Clark to Jemima Murrell by John Webb, MG
    15,   David Tipps to Elizabeth Thompson
    18,   Samuel M. Rosebrough to Lucy Brandon
    24,   James Grant to Caroline Hinkle
page 2
    22,   Benjamin D. Hancock to Fenetta Lyon by Henry Turney, JP
Mar 7,   Wiley Ware to Fanny R. Carithers by Davis Smith, JP
     5,   Thomas Criner to Sarah Walker by Robert Monday, MG
    11,   Alexander M. Galloway to Nanct Wiley
    14,   David B. Smith to Martha Gunter by Thomas Chiles, MG
    12,   Sandford Dunson to Martha Ann Forbes by J.K.Blair, JP
    13,   Henry Snow to Polly Eslick
    15,   John A. Tuley to Sally McGaugh
    14,   Lewis Wamack to Ellenor Campbell by John Gilbert
    22,   Abram Cunningham to Mary Wiles by Samuel Boone, JP
    22,   Tarply Flynt to Eliza M. Claiborn
    22,   Jackson C. Davis to Caladoni Husband
    22,   Hugh Watson to Ellen McMillen by John Lanier, JP
page 3
    25,   John Michael to Elizabeth McClure by Wiley C. Newman, JP
    27,   Arnold Brine to Parthena Culberson by C.W. McGuire, JP
    27,   William G. Spain to Mary E. Logan
    29,   William B. Sanders to Martha Driver by Wm. Timmins, JP
    29,   Archibald Baxter to Jane B. James
Apr 1,   Richard M. Rolin to Eliza Ann Holman
     3,   Alexander Brady to Polly Milstead by Isaac Conger
    12,   Nathaniel Steed to Martha Brady by Samuel Boone, JP
     3,   Jonas Byans to Malinda Hall by Stephen Walker, JP
     4,   William Tripp to Drury Pritchett
    24,   James D. Morris to Sarah Robinson by Wm. Timmins, JP
     5,   Armstead Pamplin to Cynthia Ann Raney by B.F.Clark, JP
    10,   Singleton Sikes to Margaret Hilton by Wm. Timmins, JP
    12,   William H. Tuley to Adaline Buchanan
page 4
May 3,   Henry Coble to Sarah Brady by Davis Smith, JP
     3,   A.J.Clark to Ellenor B. Clift by G.W.C.Edmiston, JP
    15,   John F. Walker to Elizabeth Pack by G.B.Allison, JP
    13,   Manuel Alstead to Nicey Hogue
    23,   James Carbo to Betsey Nicholas by John King, JP
    20,   George C. McClain to Louisa Smith by Jefferson Kelso, JP

1838

May	20,	William Lyles to Eliza Christian by John Walker JP
	24,	Curral Lee to Elizabeth Latham by John C. Wear MG
	31,	Samuel T. Crenshaw to Milly Watson by John Lanier JP
Jun	5,	Hampton Sims to Mary Ann Brown
	24,	Samuel Isaacs to Rebecca Oliver by Wm. Spencer JP
	18,	Manuel Roberts to Carolin Calhoun
	21,	Isham Smith to Elsey Oliver
	24,	William S. Bowers to Cynthia Winters by Samuel T. Bland JP

page 5

Jul	28,	James A.G.Ely to Eliza Batie by J.R.Brown
	12,	Henry Waggoner to Frances Hulsey by G.B.Allison JP
	11,	Felix Grundy McGaugh to Minerva Jane Whitaker
	17,	James S. Culberson to Abigail Kennedy by C.W.McGuire JP
	17,	Jeremiah Sulivan to Lucinda Leach by Samuel Boone JP
	19,	William W. Reese to Frances J. Halbert by Pleasant Halbert
	21,	James S. Davis to Nancy E. Turner by John Lanier JP
	26,	William W. Tucker to Martha Marler by A.B.Gilbert
	22,	Richard McNatt to Sophia McNatt by Robert M. Whiteman
	23,	Thomas H. Glidewell to Lethe A. Simmons
	31,	Leroy Luker to Susannah P. Jennings by David Crook MG
	24,	Martin Wright to Frances Massey by J.L.Stone JP
Aug	7,	John Caldwell to Mary Timmins by Henry Turner JP
	9,	Roling Smith to Elizabeth Henry

page 6

	9,	Thomas L. Samson to Mary Renegar
	14,	David Rorex to Sarah Ann Wilkinson
	15,	Bluford P. Nowlin to Margaret Phagan
	16,	John M. Van Hoozer to Agatha Isaacs by Wm. Anderson JP
	19,	Hiraim January to Sarah Williams by Wm. Spencer JP
	18,	James Sorrells to Minerva Frame
	21,	Isham G. Bailey to Susan B. Smith by A.W.Parks JP
	22,	Moses Bradley to Jenny Boren
	23,	James Vincent to Sarah Parrish by Stephen Walker JP
	26,	John Bethune to Polly Ann Cole by W.P.Pulliam JP
	30,	Edward G.G.Beanland to Mary L. Moores by John Bell MG
	30,	Hugh Randolph to Loucinda Milam by Samuel J. Bland JP
	29,	John Abbot to Rebecca Hayes
Sep	2,	Littleton M. Stovall to Emily Gray by Samuel J.Bland JP

page 7

	3,	Samuel Hawkins to Edy Wilkins by Sam. J. Bland JP
	3,	Jonathan O. Thompson to Loucinda Hall by James R. Brown
	3,	Wiley C. Newman to Polly Bethany
	5,	Green D, Smith to Martha Halbert by Davis Smith JP
	10,	Harrison Wells to Mary Bryant
	10,	Absalom M. Reid to Sabry Lemmons by Davis Smith JP
	13,	William H. Rees to Mary M. Whitaker by A.B.Gilbert
	15,	Moses Sweaton to Julia Ann Gray by George W. Dennis JP
	13,	Preston Hampton to Rachel Malier by B.F.Clark JP
	14,	Preston Burke to Rhoda Dallas by Wm. Timmins Jp
	18,	Asa Jones to Feriby Philips by Samuel J. Bland JP
	15,	Isaac Collins to Mary Frances Brown
	17,	Matthew T. Cole to Hannah Ritta Petty
	18,	Jacob Hasch to Martha Caroline Rowel by J.K.Blair JP

page 8

	18,	John Hamilton to Nancy Van Hoozer by Wm. Anderson JP
	18,	James D. Smith to Narcissa Davis by Davis Smith JP
	20,	Morris Carpenter to Mary Swanner by Pleasant Halbert JP
	20,	E. Blankenship to E. Blankenship by Samuel J. Bland JP
	20,	Hosea Fuller to Sarah Ann Willett by A.B.Gilbert Jp

```
     1838
     20,    Wilson Woodard to Sally Polk
     26,    John W. Dobbs to Naomi Bowman by Samuel Bland JP
     24,    David B. Cooper to Mary A. Mitchel
     27,    James G. Harrison to Susannah J. Small by A.B.Gilbert
     26,    Peter Weaver to Priscilla Driver
     30,    Preastley Ruckers to Margaret Cunningham by Henry Turney
Oct   2,    Ervin Stephens to Emily Wheeler by S.J.Bland JP
      1,    William Clark to Elizabeth Ruth by B. Wilson JP
      1,    A. Vincent to Mary Ann Parrish
page 9
      4,    Benjamin T. Parks to Martha Thomison by Geo. W. Dennis JP
      4,    William H. Sims to Mary Sims
      6,    John Emmons to Delila Robinson
      9,    G.L.Taylor to Peggy Hindman by T.S.Williams JP
     16,    J.L.Bedford to Emeline Roter by Joseph Smith
     13,    William Bedford to Mary Jones by A.W.Parks JP
     14,    Nathan Perry to Evaline Mitchel by John Lanier JP
    -18,    James E. Curry to Matilda Massey by A.W.Parks JP
     18,    William Merrill to Charlotte Grant by C.W.McGuire JP
     23,    Sirah Taylor to Elizabeth Puryear
     23,    Byrd Douglas to Martha R. Bright by M. Marshall
     29,    Isreal Morris to Linney Couch by T.S.Williams JP
Nov   4,    Bedford Hopkins to Nancy Neeley by S.J.Bland JP
      3,    Benjamin D. Nabers to Rebecca A. Mason
page 10
      8,    William W. Davis to Margaret Johnston by John Gilbert
     15,    William Thomison to Jane Bailey by Thomas Chiles MG
     13,    James Cowley to Mariah Duke
     14,    Mark McClure to Charlotte Lynn
     15,    Isaac S. Porter to Emeline Dennis
     20,    John Williams to Martha Buchanan by B.F.Clark JP
     21,    James Campbell to Mahala Hambrick
     25,    Joseph Ellerson to Margaret Couch by Wiley C. Newman JP
     23,    Erasmus Ward to Mary King
     25,    Nathan P. Harden to Martha Jane Wells by J.L.Stone JP
     24,    Henry L. Smith to Elizabeth A. Wanslow
     26,    William Abbot to Margaret McCalister by Robt. Drennon JP
     29,    Jarrel J. Burrow to Matilda Madison
Dec  11,    William Wright to Mary McNatt by J.H.Leftwich
page 11
      4,    John Grigory to Mary Gaddy
      6,    James Rutledge to Mary Ann Ready by A.B.Gilbert
      5,    Alexander Beard to Nancy Clark
      8,    Joseph Clark to Jane E. Massey by B.F.Clark JP
     13,    Thomas Davidson to Margaret Jane Hudson by John Gilbert
     13,    John H. Frame to Mary Dennis by William Spencer JP
     13,    Allen Smith to Milisa Lock by J.K.Blair JP
     16,    William M. Davis to Sally Davis by Davis Smith JP
     20,    Wilbourn Beck to Dorcus Allsup by Pleasant Halbert JP
     18,    Lodawick Archer to Sally Ann Goff by Robt. Drennon JP
     18,    Joel Wright to Peggy Jane Prosser by A.B.Gilbert
page 12
     19,    Montgomery English to Sarah Bell
     19,    Perry Wells to Eliza L. Willet
     25,    Daniel Farrar to Nancy C. Shipp by C.W.McGuire JP
     25,    L.B.Cole to Assena H. Stovall by S.J.Bland JP
     27,    Joseph Row to Susan Wagoner by Samuel Boone JP
```

4

pg 13

1839
Feb 30, Jesse Norman to Martha King by John Moorehead JP
Jan 8, A.D.Summerford to Lucy E. Small by A.B.Gilbert
     3, William Jean to Susan Warren by T.S.Williams JP
     3, William D. Moorhead to Mariah Cunningham by Woodruff
                                                         Parkes Esq
     4, John Mays to Pamela Anthony by John Walker JP
     6, Jackson Berry to Frances Carson by John King JP
     9, Calvin Beck to Mary Crowder
     8, John Rodgers to Martha Hancock by Wm. P. Pullian JP
     9, John George to Perona Stanford

pg 13

    12, Jackson Bramcon to Nancy A. Revis
    12, S.D.Buchanan to Celia A. Kennon
    14, Alexander Hayes to Mary Strong
    15, David M. Wise to Emily Smith by A.B.Gilbert
Feb 9, John McCown to Tibitha Coleman by Samuel Bland JP
Jan 15, Drury M. Perkins to Sarah H. Bonner by Pleasant Halbert JP
    17, James Harrison to Anna Pigg by Henry Turney JP
    17, James Ellis to Irena Ellis
    22, E.T.Cashion to Mary Shelton by W.C.Newman Esq
    22, James B. Dillender to Mary Brewer by C.W.McGuire JP
    23, Joseph Johnston to Keriah Jane Penick
    30, Samuel Fannon to Elizabeth Gray by John King JP
    31, Lamuel Todd to Ann G. Dick by M. Marshall
Feb 3, Green B. Russell to Margaret Brannon by Boone Wilson JP

pg 14

     2, Robert M. Harwell to Parthena P. Smith
     3, James A. Stone to Milly Reese by Robert M. Whitman
     3, William Hale to Amanda Staton by John Walker JP
     4, John H. Reed to Margit Grigg
     5, James Darnell to Nancy Merrill by Wm. Anderson JP
     6, William Kidd to Sarah Dale
     6, John Thompson to Loucinda Easlick
     7, Burrel Hale to Mary Ann Murry by A.B.Gilbert MG
    14, David Allen to Sarah Martin by Joel Reese
    14, David Ramsey to Mary Ann Cunningham
    18, Jonathan A. Taylor to Betsey A. Wilson by Davis Smith JP
    12, William J. Hopkins to Marget Neely by Samuel Blair JP
    21, William P. Bright to Amanda M. Medcalfe by M. Marshall

pg 15

    26, Andrew J. King to Ibby Mitchell
    27, Morgan W. Hinkle to Cyntha Douthit by J.W.Holman JP
    26, William F. Smith to Mary Jane Todd by M. Marshall
    28, Wm. Gunter to Mary A. Crowder by Boone Wilson JP
    28, Joseph Stewart to Martha Williamson
    28, S.A.M.Hart to Emily G. Motlow by A.W.Parks
Mar 8, William A. Morgan to Mary Davidson by T.H.Leftwich MG
     7, John Foreman to Prudence Mansfield by John Moorhead JP
     7, Josiah M. Norwood to Sarah A. Ramsey
     7, James Taylor to ___ Brown
    11, Hollis T. Allen to Eliza Sharp by John Walker JP
    11, Joseph Burt to Eliza Thomas
    12, Moses H. Bonner to Ann F. Robertson
    19, Eliphas Shelton to Mary Hardin by W.C.Newman JP

pg 16

    28, Richmond P. Reed to Polly Marlow by Ira McKinney JP
    30, Eli Moores to Agnes Broadway by Tho Chiles

1839

31, Walter E. Jewell to Frances A. Broadway by Stephen
Walker JP
31, Martin K. Shofner to Martha Burnett by W.C.Newman JP
Apr 2, Williamson Matney to Sarah Frances Bedford by Wm.Timmins JP
3, Thomas Atwood to Nancy Kearn by Tho Childs
13, Isaac J. Curry to Mary M. Enochs by Wm. Timmins JP
16, Robert C. McEwen to Mary E. Greer by M. Marshall
17, Drury M. Connally to Dianna Payne by John Moorhead JP
18, Wm. T. Wilson to Rebecca J. McCormack
24, James Wright to Eliza J. McLemore by T.H.Leftwich
pg 17
May 7, Elisha Bagley to Elizabeth Todd by M. Marshall
9, Allen Pool to Rebecca Rhodes by Samuel J. Bland JP
15, Abner Guy to Eveline F. King by Stephen Walker JP
15, John C. Corder to Sarah Mangum
22, William W. Ferwault to Mary Commons by John Lanier JP
30, James H. Gray to Mary E. Russell
Jun 7, Daniel E. George to Julia Snoddy by John Copeland
18, Moses Buchanan to Judith Moffett by John Lanier JP
24, H.H.Neese to Margaret Carns by J.H.Leftwich MG
23, A.C.Ogletree to Melissa Monday by A. Alexander JP
24, John W. Flemming to Polly Moore
25, James A. Burnett to Matilda Shofner by Wm.C.Newman JP
25, James W. McClung to Margaret E. Patrick by M. Marshall
26, Elijah Davis to Rosanna Temple by B. Wilson JP
pg 18
26, James J. Burnett to Matilda H. Shofner
Jul 3, James Wiley to Mary M. Galloway
4, F.R.Moore to E.W.Wynn by Tho Whitaker JP
8, Miles H. McCown to Mary L. Rowland by J.K.Blair JP
9, Wm. Cashion to Elizabeth Gattis by John Moorehead JP
10, John H. Mills to Louisa Buntley by Samuel Boone JP
13, Charles Merrell to Lydia Massay by John Webb
13, George Gaddy by Sally Reeves
15, Jefferson Duke to Elizabeth Ramsey by Tho Whitaker JP
18, George Milstead to Ruth Rutledge by Samuel Boone JP
18, Wm. H. Moores to Elizabeth H. Sugg by Pleasant Halbert JP
19, Wm. W. Pruitt to Mary Ann Young by Stephen Walker JP
pg 19
23, Wm. McCormack to Mary Hughey
30, Wm. A. Murry to Parthenia Hail by A.B.Gilbert
30, James J. Pigg to Mary J. Mason by J. Moore JP
30, A.J.Carloss to Mary Ann Franklin by M. Marshall
31, Robert Edmiston to Sophia Blackamore
Aug 1, John Mayfield to Lucentha Watson by Wm. Gattis JP
1, J.W.Martin to Mary Johnston by Samuel Boone JP
4, William H. Russell to Elizabeth Dyer by B. Wilson JP
3, Ridley B. Wynn to Rebeccah B. Hopkins
7, Benjamin T. Cowley to Margaret Elizabeth Ann Nicks
10, John Mills to Malinda Taylor by John King JP
18, J.B.Bristow to Sarah Mathews by Joel Reese JP
13, Nicholas Burns to Mary Warner by J.H.Leftwich MG
14, Alfred West to Eunicey Robinson
15, George Copeland to Nancy Braden by John King JP
pg 20
14, Meredith Pearson to Ann J. Moore
17, Isham Perry to Sarah Hodges
27, Milton Buchanan to Sirrah A. Marrs by J. Lanier Jp

6

1839

<pre>
          27,   John F. Black to Jane M. Petty by G.W.Puckett
     Sep 2,   Alfred Blyth to Nancy Webb by Wm. Martin MG
          2,   George Webb to Sarah Jones by Wm. Martin MG
          9,   Andrew Hendrick to Tempey Williams
         11,   John A. Dewoody to Mary E. Tool by John Bell MG
         12,   Thomas Justice to Nancy Blakes
         14,   George Copeland to Nancy Braden
         14,   George W. Smith to Elizabeth Fortune
         23,   Jacob Vance to Mary Ann Eddins by J.K.Blair JP
         16,   Robert R. Graves to Esther Hinkle
         25,   Eli Barnes to Talitha Owden by Ira McKinney JP
     pg 21
         19,   Dempsey Pace to Polly Pruitt
         23,   Benjamin Couch to Rebeciah Casey
         25,   Daniel M. Tucker to Nancy Y. Higgins by J.H.Leftwich MG
         26,   Edward Butler to Cardine McDaniel by Ira McKinney JP
         29,   Robert Cook to Rachel Long by Wm. C. Timmins JP
         30,   Malaciah Lusk to Sarah McDugal
     Oct 2,   John T. Balch to Sarah R. Blakmore
          5,   Loderick Robertson to Nancy Waggoner
          9,   Hial S. Woodard to Martha Haley by Pleasant Halbert JP
     Nov 4,   Jacob A. Keller to Laurret Walker by A.W.Parks JP
     Oct 10,   John Litch to Susannah A. Miller by Levi Vickory JP
     Nov 7,   Wm. Bearden to Nancy Hobbs by H. Turney JP
     Oct 14,   Lewis Sexton to Rachel Moore by Wm. Anderson JP
     Dec 16,   Thomas Manifer to Catherine Bowers by Stephen Walker JP
     pg 22
     Oct 17,   John W. Blair to Eliza J. Rowell by J.K.Blair JP
         19,   John Rigg to Sally Durham
         21,   Gilbert K. Adams to Caroline McKinney
         22,   Andrew Waggoner to Betsey Hulsey by Woodruff Parks JP
         23,   Ephraim Riddle to Rachel Smith
         24,   Harmon Riddle to Marget Hurt
         27,   Tho. McAfee to Martha Rosson by John Gilbert
         31,   David L. Gray to Mary Moorehead by Woodruff Parks JP
     Nov 8,   Alexander Waggoner to Cyntha Roe by Samuel Boone JP
         12,   James M. Bell to Catherine K. McDaniel by W.H.Baldridge MG
         13,   Joel P. Bryant to Susan Alexander
         13,   John M. Patterson to Ruth K. Browning by W.H.Baldridge MG
         15,   Jonathan Harden to Mariah Wilson by J.L.Stone JP
         18,   Jefferson Parham to Betsey Beavers
     pg 23
         26,   John B. Tucker to Nancy A. Townsand by W.H.Halcumbe
         24,   Lewis B. Morgan to Burnetta Hurt by Joel Rees JP
         29,   James J. Blackmore to Martha L. Hays by John Bell
     Dec 12,   William C. White to Polly M. Nixon by Wm. Gattis JP
          6,   Joshua Stroud to Nancy Mills
         10,   Nicholas N. Welch to Asena Beavers
         12,   Wm. Gleghorn to E.H.Wilson by Samuel S. Ralston MG
         12,   Elijah Gleghorn to S.C.Wilson by Samuel S. Ralston MG
         12,   Richard Hill to Louisa Litterill
         12,   Wm. M. Davis to Amelia A. Turney
         15,   John G. Enochs to Susan G. Enochs by Josiah Smith MG
         18,   Hugh M.C.Epps to Elizabeth Epps by A.B.Gilbert
         19,   Benjamin G. Burow to Adaline Wright by David Crook
         18,   Allen Jones to Mary Ann Sanders by Stephen Walker JP
     pg 24
         23,   John Hurt to Parthena Ann Dennis by Tho. Whitaker JP
</pre>

```
         23,   William E. Gibbs to Anna Majors
         24,   Alfred Nixon to Elizabeth Fannon by W.S.Williams JP
         23,   Alfred Evans to Sady Hilton by A.W.Parks JP
         24,   G.M.Steel to Mary Robertson
         25,   Allen L. Anderson to Elizabeth C. Fullerton
         26,   Martin Finley to Mary Meek by J.K.Blair JP
         31,   James Burton to Nancy Moss by Wm. P. Pulliam JP
         28,   Zachariah Simons to Betsey Riddle
         28,   Mathew Hasty to Charlotte Jones
         31,   Moses Cruise to Catherine Johnston by James Rorex JP
1840
Jan  1,   John Harper to Malinda Norman by John King JP
pg 25
          2,   Robert S. Strong to Margaret Penny by J.K.Blair JP
          2,   John F. Shelton to Martha P. Milam
          3,   Benjamin Ramey to Elizabeth Parker
          5,   Andrew King to Elizabeth Hobbs by W.C.Newman JP
         15,   W.W.Gill to Sarah Ann Whitaker by J.H.Leftwich MG
          6,   J.M.Dean to Ann Rountree by A.W.Parks JP
          6,   Wright P. Collins to Elizabeth Davis by Davis Smith JP
          7,   David Polly to Lucinda Simmons
          9,   William Price to Rebeccah Gore by W.C.Timmins JP
          9,   John Franklin to Elizabeth Neely by J.K.Blair JP
         13,   James Woodward to Rebecah Roane
pg 26
         13,   Greenwood Nichols to Rebecah Nix
         16,   Isaac C. Hall to Marget S. Campbell by Woodruff Parks JP
         16,   Joel Reese to Patience Ede by Joseph Smith
         18,   Jonathan B. Dildine to Malinda Hunts
         19,   Newberry James to Catherine Wright by A.B.Gilbert
         20,   William Pilant to Nancy Campbell by Levi Vickory JP
         22,   Joshua Smith to Jenetta Claunch
         23,   David R. Smyth to Jane C. Greer by M. Marshall
         24,   Elias McDaniel to Mary George
         30,   Henry Sulivan to Celia Wiles by A.B.Gilbert
Feb  2,   James McCowley to Mary Beggerley by Stephen Walker JP
pg 27
Jan 28,   James Seaton to Mary Ann Mims
         29,   Solomon Mason to Elizabeth Land
         29,   John Stewart to Nancy Abernathy
Feb 11,   William Cone to Elizabeth Wright by John Gilbert
          3,   John A. Johnson to Eliza Moffett by James Rorex JP
          4,   Edmond Boaze to Elizabeth Hoots by James Rorex JP
         11,   Campbell Douthit to Margaret M. Stegall by J.W.Holman JP
          6,   Bolin Clark to Sarah Blyth
          6,   Isaiah King to Catharin Hulsey by Woodruff Parks JP
         13,   Thomas H. Armstrong to Charlotta Cone by John Gilbert
         13,   Wm. D. Lackey to Mary W. Hinkle
         20,   Thomas W. Bell to Mary Damron by James Alexander
pg 28
         18,   Willis B. Stovall to Elizabeth Felps by Stephen Walker JP
         20,   Jesse Shelton to Betsey Shaw by Robert Drennon JP
         23,   James Clark to Susan Williams by Wm. R. Jones JP
         27,   David Hines to Eliza Ann Kymes by Joseph Smith
Mar  1,   William McKenney to Elizabeth Wakefield by Henry Turney JP
          5,   Leonard H. McKenney to Elzera Woodard by B.F.Clark JP
          5,   William Craig to Louisa Pickett by T.S.Williams JP
          5,   Richard W. West to Ruth Sulivan by Ira McKinney JP
         10,   Hiram Epps to Fenetta Weaver by John Weaver MG
```

8

11,   Jacob Hayes to Prudence Hamilton by Ira McKinney JP
12,   John McRee to Frances M. Hayes by Henry Turney JP
pg 29
11,   Daniel B. Ward to Elizabeth Land by Wm. Gattis JP
10,   Robert Edmiston to Martha Wise
12,   Isaac Green to Mary Beasley by Tho. S. Williams JP
11,   James C. Pace to Amanda Clanton
17,   John Reese to Dorinda Davis by H. Birmingham JP
19,   Harrison C. Taylor to Candass D. McCoy by H. Turney JP
19,   Austin G. Smith to Mary E. Clanton
15,   William Dollar to Eliza Ann Levan by G.W.Prichett
21,   William Watson to Sarah McAfee
25,   Berry Hobbs to Nancy Owens by Pleasant Halbert JP
25,   James M. Birmingham to Mary A. Cocks by H. Birmingham JP
pg 30
26,   Samuel C. Miles to Martha White by Woodruff Parks JP
26,   Isaac N. Wright to Jane T. Downing by Ira McKinney JP
Apr 1,   Eppey Harden to Minerva Reese by H. Birmingham JP
2,   James Towry to Drucilla Moss by Wm. P. Pullen JP
2,   Abraham Washburn to Sarah Ann M. Gray by M. Marshall
12,   Hezekiah Smith to Sarah King by Wiley C. Newman Esq
9,   Thomas Childs to Sarah Williams by B.F.Clark JP
12,   William P. Loyd to Thursay Ann Martin by John Moorhead JP
18,   John S. Baggett to Elizabeth Mahala Jones
22,   Robert Honey to Eveline White by A.W.Parks JP
23,   Jeremiah Sullivan to Catharine O'Quin by Samuel Boone JP
pg 31
22,   Leander Speck to Polly Mason
May 2,   William S. Woodward to Nancy R. Bruce by C.W.McGuire JP
5,   Stephen Riddle to Jensey Tucker
11,   George Coleman to Hannah Patterson
14,   Benjamin Hawood to Esther H. George by John Moorhead JP
21,   Alexander H. Gill to Nancy Leftwich
26,   Joseph Donaldson to Susannah W. Brown by John Lanier JP
27,   Mansel Bartlet to Ritta C. Richardson by J.H.Leftwich MG
28,   Wm. Turley to Martha Mitchell by L. Williams JP
30,   John Swenea to Betsey Oliver
Jun 3,   Oliver C. Holmes to Henryetta Crawford
pg 32
11,   William Gaddy to Martha Ann Reevis by Pleasant Halbert JP
18,   Jonathan Couch to Sarah Nowell by David Snoddy JP
21,   John Ray to Margaret Jane Epps by G.W.C.Edmiston JP
18,   Augustus Steed to Mary Brady by Joseph Smith
Jul 7,   James T. Childress to Elizabeth D. Hughey by C.W.McGuire JP
8,   Charles D. Eddington to Mary Ledbetter
16,   Wiley Hill to Malinda King by A.B.Gilbert
21,   James D. Hays to Rebeca Hays by Henry Turney JP
14,   John Swinford to Arena Abbott
16,   William Timmins to Martha Julia Martin by Rev. Joseph Smith
21,   William H. Gibson to Elizabeth Freeman
pg 33
Aug 4,   Henry Waggoner to Julian Johnston by James Rorex JP
5,   Joel Halbert to Lethe Harrison
6,   William T. Hamlin to Eliza McLin by M. Marshall
6,   Linville P. Shephard to Rutha Broadway by Tho. Chiles
20,   Wilson Gray to Rosannah Clark by A.W.Parks JP
26,   John A. Pearce to Emily Sanderson by Stephen Walker JP
26,   William W. Delany to Eliza Jane Martin by Wm.P.Pullen JP

```
          1840
          26,    Haslip Goforth to Labrary Bland by C.W.McGuire JP
      Sep 17,    Josiah O'Quinn to Louisa Lane by Samuel Boone JP
           3,    Hugh P. Mooney to Caroline T. Roan by C.W.McGuire JP
           3,    Michael Lincoln to Mary Ann Marshall by T.S.Williams JP
      pg 34
          10,    Isaac N. Gattis to Leuticie Cashion by T.S.Williams JP
          10,    Richard Stephens to Lucinda Frost by J.W.Holman JP
          16,    William Givens to Margaret Wiley by James Pressley
           9,    Charles H. Whitaker to Harriet Evans
          19,    Isham J. Walker to Polly Arnold by Wm. C. Jennings JP
          16,    Shaddrick A. King to Mary McAdams
          24,    David D. Rosebrough to Ann T. Eastland by Benj. F. Clark JP
          23,    John Neive to Nancy Landers by Stephen Walker JP
          28,    Joel L. Reese to Mary L. Solomon by John Bell
          28,    William Davis to Nancy Gavin
          28,    Benjamin McClusky to Sarah Howard by Stephen Walker JP
      pg 35
      Oct  1,    Silas C. Ross to Matilda Ayers by C.W.McGuire JP
           4,    William W. Vaughn to Fanny Pool by Wm. P. Pullen JP
           1,    Samuel C. McCoy to Susan E. Hampton by C.W.McGuire JP
           1,    Matthew H. Campbell to Mary A. Hampton by C.W.McGuire JP
           5,    Henry Warren to Mary Bright
      pg 36
          14,    William A. Pruitt to Mary McDougal by J. Kelso JP
          14,    James Hamilton to Elizabeth S. McGaugh by B.F.Clark JP
          14,    Alexander McAdams to Nancy A. Nelson
          15,    Joseph Wright to Hetty Goode
          15,    John McCullough to Ducinda Bynum by Thomas Chiles MG
          18,    Thomas Holman to Permelia Johnson by James Rorex JP
          24,    James G. Hays to Martha S. Raymond by Wm. R. Jones JP
          25,    Henry T. Dennis to Martha Caroline Hobbs by John King JP
          29,    Andrew Cashion to Catharine Renegar by Wm. Gattis JP
          29,    Philip Cooper to Nancy Sanders by John Moore JP
          29,    Peter Cunningham to Sarah Mills by John Weaver MG
      pg 37
          29,    Lewis C. McCowen to Cassena Blair by J.K.Blair JP
      Nov 12,    Charles Price to Elizabeth Ann Frame by David Snoddy JP
           5,    Pleasant Oliver to Lucinda Smith by W.P.Pulliam JP
          10,    Umstead George to Cena West by Tho. Chiles MG
          11,    Constant T. McMillen to Malinda Ann Isham
          12,    William H. Bryant to Martha Crabtree
          18,    Lewis H. Little to Nancy A. Randolph by W.P.Pulliam JP
          22,    Moses Cook to Martha Beard by Davis Smith JP
          26,    Samuel M. Rowell to Matilda W. Lay by J.K.Blair JP
          26,    John Wood to Jane J. Dobbins by Henry Turney JP
      pg 38
          26,    David B. Guinn to Narcissa Owen by Pleasant Halbert JP
          26,    Anderson Tucker to Nancy Story
          27,    Jesse Preston to Mary Aldridge by W.C.Newman JP
      Dec  1,    Argyle Wells to Sarah Oliver by W.P.Pulliam JP
           2,    John A. Browning to Mary Ann Ruth Dollar by John Bell MG
           3,    Thomas Huff to Nancy Couch by W.C.Newman JP
           3,    Young S. Taylor to Caroline Marshall by Woodruff Parks Esq
           8,    Henry C. Gault to Mary Ann Gleghorn by Samuel S. Ralston MG
           8,    Newton Harris to Theodosia Hampton by B.F.Clark JP
          10,    Franklin A. Campbell to Elvira Husbands by John Bell MG
      pg 39
          14,    A.C.Small to Keziah A. George
          14,    Alvin M. Dean to Ann S. Parks
```

16,   James Caughran to Jane Wilson
17,   Alexander G. Dickson to Sarah Hinkle by H.S.Porter MG
18,   Isiah R. Jackson to Adaline Taylor
24,   Joseph W. Trigg to Nancy Robertson by Aaron Alexander
23,   Simeon Rhodes to Mary Forbes by J.K.Blair JP
24,   Wm. Norman to Sarah Lemonds(Leonards) by John King JP
22,   James R. Rogers to Catharine E. Tiller by T.S.Williams JP
23,   John P. Cole to Susan M.C.Leonards
24,   James E. Seymore to Matilda Craig by C.W.McGuire JP

pg 40
1841
Feb 4, William Ashby to Nancy Ashby by John Weaver MG
Jan 11, James M. Arnold to Elizabeth Walker by W.C.Jennings JP
   7, Charles M. Crawford to Mary Brown by A.W.Parks JP
   5, Starkie Robertson to Catharine Robertson by Stephen
                                           Walker JP
   7, George Oliver to Jane Campbell by M. Marshall LDM
   7, Charles L. Smith to Mary Stanley by B.F.Clark JP
   8, Earl Rains to Lera Smith by Wm. Spencer JP
   8, Robert J. Tate to Eliza Jane Ramsey by Thomas Chiles MG
  11, William J. Teagey to Emily J. Chambless by A.F.Driskill MG
  14, Squire Pickle to Martha Harris by B.F.Clark JP
  13, Robert Durham to Elizabeth Riggs

pg 41
  14, Samuel Hogan to Elzira Robinson by Davis Smith JP
  14, James H. McKinney to Lydia Ann Watson by B.F.Clark JP
  17, William Hamilton to Emeline Hobbs by John King JP
  19, Joseph G. Smith to Rosannah M. Edmiston by M. Marshall VDM
  20, Alexander Philpot to Mary Renegar
  21, William Fife to Elizabeth Caughran by Robert Drennon JP
  21, James R. Hallam to Clarina M. Bailey by M. Marshall VDM
  26, John Hopper to Martha Dooley by Thomas Chiles MG
  28, John Hobbs to Elly Michael by Wiley C. Newman JP
  28, Casey P. Smith to Cynthia M. Walker by G.W.Dennis JP
  28, William R. Warren to Harriet E. Stuart by Samuel Boone JP

pg 42
  28, John G. McClellan to Eliza J. McClellan by G.W.Dennis JP
Feb 2, Brice D. Shelton to Jane Styles by W.C.Jennings JP
   4, Asa Smith to Nancy Perry by Wm. Spencer JP
   7, William P. Neeld to Mary Smith by M. Marshall VDM
   8, John F. Cowden to Elizabeth Price
   8, Isaac Parkes to Viannus Mullins by A.W.Parks JP
   9, John B. Hay to Sabra Elston
  14, John Smith to Ibby Couch by T.S.Williams JP
  18, Oliver D. Tankesly to Malissa Arnold by W.C.Newman JP
  14, John S. West to Elizabeth Rayburn by Thomas Chiles MG
  15, Mark H. Pickett to Catharine Shelton by W.C.Newman JP

pg 43
  16, John B. Foster to Sarah L. Bryant by Henry Turney JP
  16, Allen Davis to Lucy Lazenby
  23, Calvin Stone to Elizabeth Kizer by T.W.Griffin ECC
  25, Archibald B. King to Sceny Morris by T.S.Williams JP
  25, William S. Gill to Salina Evans by S.M.Cowan, Min.
  25, Jackson Champion to Angelina Upton by Stephen Walker JP
  24, John Parker to Matilda Hawkins by J.K.Blair JP
  24, Daniel Hawkins to Margaret Ables by J.K.Blair JP
  25, William Wiseman to Lucinda Evans by J.W.Holman JP
  27, Hugh Parkinson to Martha Morton

pg 44
Mar 4,   Richard L. Cox to Sarah C. Birmingham by G.W.Puckett
     4,   Wm. D. McKinney to Sarah N. Wear by S.M.Cowan MG
     4,   James E. Travis to Elizabeth Ann Scivally by W.Jenkins VDM
     7,   Alfred Felps to Jane Spry by Joel Rees JP
     9,   Norbourne Cook to Amanda Clayton by A.G.Gibson MG
     9,   Lewis G. Sanderson to Eliza Jane Maloney by C.W.McGuire JP
     9,   Holloway Powers to Narcissa Bates by W.C.Jennings JP
    11,   John Crabtree to Nancy Pigg by Henry Turney JP
    11,   James Russ to Margaret E. Laird
    13,   Milton A. Edmiston to Minerva L. Kimes
pg 45
May 3,   George W. Tuck to Maleria Timmins by A.W.Parks JP
Mar 25,   Nathaniel Conally to Virginia A. Channing by W.C.Newman JP
    27,   Thomas George to Mary Colbert by T.S.Williams JP
    29,   Wm. H. Hall to Elizabeth Marbery by John Moore JP
Apr 1,   Miles R. Sherrell to Elizabeth H. Sharp by M. Marshall VDM
Mar 31,   David Thompson to Lucinda Tucker by Wm. Gattis JP
Apr 1,   Henry C. Dickson to Eveline Reed by Davis Smith JP
     4,   Robert S. McDonald to Maria McDaniel by Stephen Walker JP
     7,   Charles Martin to Hetty West by Robert M. Whitman
pg 46
     9,   William Wamack to Rebecca Thurman by Robert Drennon JP
     9,   Thomas Jenkins to Nancy Adcock
    16,   Nathaniel Bradford to Anna Blackshear
    22,   Allen Johnston to Sudy D. Browning by Samuel Boone JP
    19,   William C. Bryant to Sarah Buchanan by C.W.McGuire JP
    22,   Wm. K. Simpson to Eliza Smith
    29,   Davidson Holly to Sally Roe by Joel Rees JP
May 2,   Thomas B. Eastland to Sarah S. Crawford by B.F.Clark JP
    13,   Allen G. Waggoner to Catharine Cole by Wm. Gattis JP
    12,   Williamson Haggard to Frances A. Parkes
    16,   Vardy M. Rhyme to Mary Trailor by Pleasant Bearden JP
pg 47
    19,   Jonathan Fisher to Ann Tucker
    23,   John L. Gobbell to Elizabeth Riley by T.L.Long MG
    27,   Mial Ramsey to Belinda Commons
    29,   James D. Jarnett to Susannah Edmondson by Pleasant Halbert
Jun 1,   H.L.Todd to Mary L. Crows by J.A.Summers JP
    11,   John Cretchett to Letha Freeman
    15,   Abner Scoggins to Elizabeth McCurdy by W.R.Jones JP
    16,   Elijah Dollar to Elizabeth C. Haley by G.W.Puckett
    24,   Francis M. Jeans to Elizabeth Nixon by David Snoddy JP
Jul 1,   Enoch D. Fox to Sarah F. Moorehead by J.W.Holman JP
    24,   John Bond to Harriet Withers by G.W.C.Edmiston JP
pg 48
Jul 7,   Manson G. Pearson to Nancy Cowson
    13,   Alexander Felps to America Spry by Joel Rees JP
    22,   Peter J. Hamilton to Cordela Mary Whitaker by P. Halbert JP
    19,   Reddin B. Mattox to Susannah L. Reeves by C.W.McGuire JP
    19,   Peter Shelton to Sarah Keith by J. Copeland MG
    20,   Beckwith J. Tiller to Sarah Ramsey by Woodruff Parks Esq
    29,   John Washburn to Sarah M. Bell by A.G.Gibson MG
    27,   Benjamin B. Bryant to Jane Parr
    27,   Milton Walker to Fennetta T. Smith
    29,   William Springer to Rachel Wells by Major M. Bedwell
    28,   Wm. Thronton to Lucinda McBride
pg 49
    28,   Richard Cottrell to Jane Crouch by Jno Moore JP

12

1841
Aug 1,   Wm. Stafford to Mary Robertson by A.W.Parks JP
     10,   Isham Hambrick to Martha Walker by W.R.Jones JP
Oct 27,   Duncan Dollar to Rachel Jones by W.R.Jones JP
Aug 3,   James M. Matthews to Rachel Foster by M.M.Bedwell
     12,   Augustus Furgerson to Mary Lope by A.G.Gibson MG
     11,   Levi Pritchard to Jermima Oliver by Wm. Gattis JP
     16,   Oliver P. Griffis to Dessey Evans by Robert Drennon JP
     19,   John W. Pulliam to Martha R. Marshall by Wm. R. Jones JP
     15,   Green Miles to Elizabeth McWhorter by John Moorehead JP
pg 50
     17,   Daniel J. Whittington to Caroline J. Beaty by Henry Turney
     24,   George Reid to Jane White by H. Birmingham JP
     27,   Aquilla Arnold to Elmira Langston by W.C.Newman JP
     30,   Wm. Pamplin to Lucy Hanks by Isaac Conger
     29,   Wm. M. McMillin to Lucinda McDaniel by W. McKinney JP
Sep 13,   James Hightower to Polly Jones by Samuel Boone JP
      2,   Samuel Jones to Arena Philips by W.R.Jones JP
      9,   Mitchel Pool to Anna S. Wallace by W.P.Pulliam JP
      2,   Tillman Finley to Elizabeth Sanders by Henry Turney JP
      2,   James Dunlap to Elizabeth Pollard by C.W.McGuire JP
pg 51
      2,   Alfred Smith to Mary M.B.Rhea
      4,   Stephen M. Lewis to Sarah M. Franklin
     12,   Robert B. Southern to Mary Van Hoozer by G.W.Puckett
      9,   David F. Hobbs to Sarah Shipp by C.W.McGuire JP
     10,   Daniel H. Gowen to Mary Ann Myrick by John Moore JP
     13,   Richard Hill to Sarah Hobbs by John Lanier JP
     14,   Francis Wells to Louisa G. Drake by John Moore JP
     16,   George McWhorter to Fanny Ledford by John Moorehead JP
     19,   Hezekiah Brown to Elizabeth Mallard by M.M.Bedwell
     16,   Jesse Malone to Penina Robertson
     16,   John N. Owen to Nancy P. Noah by Davis Smith JP
pg 52
     16,   Robert Lauderdale to Rachel P. Surber
     18,   John D. Hall to Prescious G. Smith
     16,   William C. Andrews to Mary Ann Darnell by Thomas Chiles MP
     23,   William Crabtree to Mary A. Foster
     30,   John McGee to Mary Taylor by Samuel Boone JP
     30,   Joseph B. Hodge to Rachel Forman by W.C.Timmins JP
Oct 4,   John J. Sexton to Angeline E. Yeager by Wm. R. Jones JP
     14,   Thomas H. Freeman to Martha A. Whitaker by W.C.Timmins JP
      5,   Harrison H. Hughey to Elizabeth B. Hampton by Pleasant
                                                         Halbert JP
      7,   Lemuel Rhodes to Jane McCan
pg 53
      8,   Benjamin Jeffers to Clarrisa Jones by Isaac Conger MG
     12,   John Satterfield to Letty Philips by W.M.Jones JP
     13,   John A. McPhail to Mary E. Gilliland by M. Marshall VDM
     14,   Isaac N. Sledgpath to Margaret Reeves by Pleasant Halbert JP
     19,   Robert A. Hamilton to Mary J. McMillin
     19,   Wm. H. Griffis to Elizabeth Evans
     20,   Ephraim F. Christie to Sarah A. Saunders
     21,   Wm. B. Smith to Catharine Brandon by J.W.Holman JP
     22,   Hardy H. Smith to Susan A. Young
     26,   Sterling McLemore to Margaret Ward
     26,   Lewis Shipp to Elizabeth McElroy by Pleasant Halbert JP
pg 54
     29,   Elijah Majors to Maudana M. Pulliam by W.P.Pulliam JP

31,	Job K. Boles to Martha Powers by Levi Vickery JP
Nov 2,	James S. George to Margaret Stewart by C.W.McGuire JP
2,	John M. Commons to Mary McElroy by B.F.Clark JP
4,	Stephen Porter to Jemima Quarles by R. Ellis MG
11,	John L. Ashby to Eliza Mills by John Weaver MG
7,	Willford Nickson to Narcissa Petty by T.S.Williams JP
9,	Charles McIntosh to Margaret Land by John Lanier JP
21,	Samuel Stiles to Mary Cashion by John Moorehead JP

pg 55

21,	Reid Hopper to Jane Rich by Ira McKinney JP
23,	Benjamin F. Bearden to Susan M. Blake
24,	King David Bradford to Winney McCoy by John Moore JP
25,	George W. Beasley to Sarah Stanley by G.W.C.Edmiston JP
25,	James M. Spencer to Mary Copeland by J.W.Holman JP
25,	Thomas W. Brents to Angeline Scott by J.W.Holman JP
30,	William Kennon to Nancy Pack
Dec 1,	Pleasant M. Ellis to Nancy Patterson
9,	John Barnes to Polly Ann Millikin by Ira McKinney JP
5,	Anderson Billings to Fereby Melson by J.A.Simmons JP

pg 56

16,	Samuel M. Hedgpeth to Sarah Wilson by C.W.McGuire JP
9,	Joel Wooley to Mariah Parker by G.W.Puckett
10,	Jacob Van Hoozer to Nancy Majors by Wm. Anderson JP
9,	Samuel J. Isaacs to Amanda J. Robertson
17,	Ezekiel McAfee to Mary Faulkner by John Weaver MG
21,	John Dyer to Susan Payne by Wm. Gattis JP
16,	Calvin Koonce to Sarah Clounch by G.W.Dennis JP
15,	Jesse Blacksher to Sally Massey
18,	William Cooper to Susannah McClure by W.C.Newman JP
22,	Miles Gibbs to Jane Meeks by Wm. Anderson JP

pg 57

21,	John M. Clark to Catharine Raney by Joseph H. Holloway MG
23,	John Patterson to Eliza Hinds by A.M.Pickens MG
22,	Hardy C. Coleman to Margit J. Hodge by Robert Drennon JP
22,	Andrew J. Berry to Nancy Shelton by John Moorehead JP
23,	Dempsey Pace to Delila Hanks by J.Thos.S. Young MG
23,	John T. Wilson to Ann E. Davis by Davis Smith JP
23,	John G. Eslick to Sarah Gregory by G.W.Dennis JP
25,	Sample Orr to Patience O.B.Houston
28,	William Davidson to Martha Brandon by T.S.Young MG

pg 58
1842

Jan 2,	Matthew Carter to Cynthia Noles by Wm. Gattis JP
2,	William F. Sanders to Martha Houston by T.S.Williams JP
5,	Albert Speck to Nancy Ward by Wm. Gattis JP
6,	Avery Stewart to Sophia A.E.Stewart by C.W.McGuire JP
9,	Samuel Morris to Nancy Massey by Wm. Martin MG
13,	James Harris to Louisa Buchanan by A.G.Gibson MG
9,	David Boren to Clementine Bradly by John King JP
11,	John W. Kenedy to Mary A.B.Corley by Wm. Anderson JP
8,	Coleman Wells to Eliza Tucker
13,	Moses Park to Mary A. Davis by Pleasant Bearden JP
11,	Russell Hughes to Elvina Staten by B.F.Clark JP

pg 60

13,	John Kimes to Margaret Millard by A.M.Pickens MG
15,	Edward McBay to Jane Cumberland by Wm. Gattis JP
13,	Robert Ross to Julia Roper by Wm. Neeld JP
15,	William D. Roper to Mary E. Harris

```
         20,   Samuel T. Nicks to Malinda C. Gilbert by J.A.Simmons JP
         20,   Abner Freeman to Drucilla Glidewell by J.A.Simmons JP
         19,   John T. Curtis to Elizabeth C. Franklin
         20,   Othneil Rice to Mary Mooney by John Moore JP
         24,   Ruffin Stricklin to Mary Ann Butler by Stephen Walker JP
         25,   William Rees to Susan Burrow by J.H.Leftwich MG
         29,   James Mills to Elinor P. Welder by Samuel Boone JP
pg 61
         25,   Martin Flynt to Mary R. Estill
         26,   Napoleon B. Clayton to Mary Trentham
         27,   Daniel Holman to Mary Anderson by Woodruff Parks Esq
         27,   William Hall to Sarah Leonard by W.C.Jennings JP
         29,   Daniel F. Freeman to Catharine J. Simmons
         31,   James Gerelds to Drucilla Greer
Feb   2,   Jackson Rogers to Mahaley Gray by John King JP
      2,   John Huey to Eliza J. Greham by Matt Marshall
     10,   Clesbey Ellis to Nancy Snow by Thomas Chiles MG
      5,   Arnold Blades to Ann Jackson
     13,   John G. Wells to Susan Harris by A.G.Gibson MG
pg 62
      7,   Brown Gregory to Mary Ann McClellan
Sep 25,   Berry Cole to Melissa Coleman by Henry Turney JP
Feb 13,   Thomas McClure to Mary M. Dickson by W.C.Newman JP
     21,   Alexander S. Rives to Mary Felps
     22,   Byars Logan to Sarah Felps by Joel Rees JP
     22,   David Blackshear to Elizabeth Carter
     24,   Edwin S. Douglass to Louisa M. Bell
     24,   James Williams to Caroline Neal
Mar  1,   John H. Fox to Mary Waggoner by T.S.Young MG
      3,   David Carden to Susan Colvit by G.W.Jones JP
      7,   Andrew J. Smith to Elizabeth Oliver by W.P.Pulliam JP
pg 63
      9,   Hiram W. King to Susan McAdams
     10,   Carter T. Crawford to Elizabeth Hill by A.W.Parks JP
     11,   Coleman Runnells to Martha Runnells
     12,   William Curtis to Margaret McAfee
     14,   Peter Gilley to Eliza Witt by Levi Vickory JP
     15,   John Crammer to Mary Sewell by Wm. Neeld JP
     17,   Thomas H. Moore to Maria E. Bright by M. Marshall VDM
     24,   William McAfee to Lydia E. Hedgepeth by Ira McKinney JP
     19,   John A. Silvertooth to Mahala S.D.Gibson by A.W.Parks JP
     31,   Allen Parks to Mary Gregory by Woodruff Parks Esq
     31,   William Preston to Unice Morris
pg 64
Apr  3,   Thomas Moore to Ann Fox by J.W.Holman JP
      3,   Charles L. Walker to Mary E. Smith by G.W.Dennis JP
      7,   Albert Bryant to Mary Street by David Snoddy JP
      9,   Samuel McCalla to Elizabeth Brown by John H. Taylor JP
      9,   Patrick H. Wanslow to Elizabeth C. Brown
     14,   John Crane to Rebecca Wade by Isaac Conger
     12,   Owen Colvert to Malinda Saunders by T.S.Williams JP
     13,   Daniel Leatherman to Sally Dobbins
     21,   William Marshall to Margaret Ann Gray by Stephen Walker JP
May 10,   William T. Crenshaw to Esther Wright by John Weaver MG
      5,   John Mullins to Julia Ann Gray by David J. Rowell JP
pg 65
     15,   Charles Wiles to Hannah Mills by John Weaver MG
     10,   Michael Seagraves to Sarah Ann E. Couch by Wm. Pryor JP
```

1842
- 12, Ebnezer Pickett to Mary Graham
- 19, Andrew J. Pickett to Margaret Wilkerson by T.S.Williams JP
- 21, John Frost to Hannah Whitworth by John H. Taylor JP
- 22, Jasper P. Hammonds to Mary E. Jones by W.B.Rhea JP
- Jun 9, John G. Crawford to Rhoda Ann Malier by A.G.Gibson MG
- 7, William Wright to Elizabeth Mitchell by James R.Chilcoat JP
- 8, William Martin to Eliza Jane Martin
- 16, Anderson Fitch to Elizabeth Roch by T.S.Williams JP
- 15, Aaron McDugal to Rachel Sims by Hiram Buchanan JP

pg 66
- 21, Edward G. Johnson to Sarah Ann Davis by W.B.Rhea JP
- 21, Wilson C. Pruitt to Elizabeth K. Moore by J.H.Taylor JP
- 30, Samuel Solomon to Martha Fleming by Robert M.Whitman
- Jul 2, Drury J. Smith to Siambra Westerman
- 4, William V. White to Delitha Kernel by S. Leatherwood JP
- 6, Elisha E. Desmukes to Sarah C. Lay by A.G.Gibson MG
- 13, Vincent Mullins to Mary McCan by S.J.Bland JP
- 15, Benjamin H. Berry to Ann Dean
- 21, John Harbin to Margaret Lincoln by David Snoddy JP
- 21, Nimrod W. Watson to Mary B. Randolph

pg 67
- 26, Jesse McClure to Jane McClure by W.C.Jennings JP
- 26, Jeptha Yarbrough to Julia A. Campbell by T.S.Williams JP
- Aug 19, Samuel Little to Jane Jones by Stanford Lasater JP
- Jul 28, Hardy H. Logan to Harriet Motlow by Joel Rees JP
- 30, William M. James to Julia Ann Solomon
- Aug 4, John Sumerford to Mary C. Parkes by Woodruff Parks Esq
- 16, William T. Childress to Mahulda Pebby by James R.Chilcoat
- 4, Samuel D. Collins to Rebecca J. McMillin by Davis Smith JP
- 4, William Dooley to Sarah Massey by Thomas Childs
- 11, Jesse W. Hobbs to Louisa George by C.W.McGuire JP
- 7, Amzi Anthony to Amanda Parks by A.W.Parks JP

pg 68
- 7, Harvey Damron to Mary Parks by A.W.Parks JP
- 9, James L. Campers to Isabella Edmondson by Pleasant Halbert
- 12, William R. Akin to Mary Creasey by Cornelius McGuire MG
- 12, David S. Enochs by Martha A.E.Dance by T.L.Young MG
- 15, Henry A. Gilliams to Susan Nelson by B.M.Allsup JP
- 21, Michael Holt to Matilda Long by A.W.Parks JP
- 20, John D. Mitchel to Susan Fox
- 30, Robert Warren to Temperance Wilkerson by Levi Newsom JP
- 25, William Warren to Elizabeth Burrus by Levi Newsom JP
- 30, James B. Maloney to Eleanor C. Thompson by C.W.McGuire JP
- Sep 1, Wiles A. Grizzard to Susan E. Whitaker by Joel Rees JP

pg 69
- 1, Felix Waggoner to Mahuldah M. Dusenberry by W. Jenkins VDM
- 1, William Perry to Elizabeth M. Allen by J.H.Taylor JP
- 1, Wiley K. Hardin to Sarah M. Edmiston by J.G.Green MG
- 2, James Parrish to Sarah Vincent by W.R.Jones JP
- 5, Charles S. Howell to Julia Ann McKinney
- 6, David K. Weaver to Belinda Renegar by John Moorehead JP
- 8, Joel B. Kaar to Mary Renegar by John Moorehead JP
- 8, William B. Walker to Narcissa Ellis by S.M.Cowan MG
- 11, Benjamin Whitaker to Susan W. Fox by J.H.Holman JP
- 11, James Cunningham to Susan D. Griffis by A.L.Randolph JP
- 15, Joseph P. Williams to Elizabeth Williams by J.B.Hollis MG

pg 70
- 15, Lenzy C. Harper to Cassa Coble by J.H.Taylor JP

13, John W.C.Cunningham to Mary A. Buchanan by Wm. Harris
14, James Davidson to Mary M. Fulton by Wm. Neeld JP
14, James Nees to Ermin Leftwich by R.M.Whitman
14, Charles H. Bethany to Delila Couch by W.C.Jennings JP
14, John T. Gordon to Louisa Buchanan
15, John W. Gregg to Martha J. Reed
17, William Faulkner to Elizabeth Bandy by John Weaver MG
Oct 4, Hawley Williamson to Elizabeth Beachboard by Hiram
                                             Buchanan JP
Sep 27, Michael Lincoln to Mary Jane Cooper by T.S.Williams JP
    29, Thomas H. Bledsoe to Permelia Nelson by R. Ellis
pg 71
Oct 6, Samuel D. Brown to Phebe Rutledge by John Weaver MG
     3, Ambrose H. Pierce to Sarah Williams by J.W.Holman JP
Sep 29, Charles Bethume to Elizabeth Cole by Wm. Neeld JP
Oct 5, Joseph Sexton to Margaret Williams by J.P.Williams G.P.
     6, John M. Buchanan to Elizabeth A. Crawford by A.G.Gibson MG
     8, Moses Curtis to Elizabeth Blacksher
    13, Elisha M. Brewer to Mary Ann Ryals by J. Kimes JP
    20, James Monks to Tabitha Brown by D. Jacks MG
    20, William Wood to Nancy Collins by Ira McKinney JP
    20, William C. Frost to Angeline Bert by J.H.Taylor JP
    18, Jacob Barnes to Salina J. Merrell by Spencer Leatherwood JP
pg 72
    19, William Allbright to Mary Arrendale by Robert Drennon JP
    20, Emory M. Posey to Susan P. Smith by W.B.McLaughlin JP
    27, James Luttrell to Frances Taylor by Wiley M. Newman JP
Nov 1, Harrison Smith to Margaret McWhorter
     3, Isaac Rutledge to Martha J. Waggoner by John Copeland MG
    22, William Bullock to Mary M. Bridges by E.B.King JP
     8, Carleton Davidson to Loucinda Flack by J.H.Leftwich MG
    13, Alfred Douthit to Amanda Dillander by Pleas. Halbert JP
    10, John L. Scott to Harriet Chapman by Wm. Harris
    10, John R. Toole to Matilda G. Kennon by A.G.Gibson MG
    10, Thomas McAfee to Elizabeth McRee by Henry Turney JP
pg 73
Dec 10, Thomas M. Newman to Rinah McGehee by John King JP
Nov 17, John M. McFerrin to Margaret Hughy by W.R.Jones JP
    16, General W.C.Edmiston to Sally Dobbins by M. Marshall VDM
    17, Thomas A. Paysinger to Mary A. McRee by Henry Turney JP
    24, Francis Suttle to Frances A. Wilson by T.L.Young MG
    24, Daniel Ortner to Hannah Harris by Joel Rees JP
    27, Douglas Harper to Martha J. Brown by Wm. Gattis JP
    26, Ralph Petty to Minerva Myrick by Wm. Pryor JP
    27, Benjamin Bryan to Mary Ann Hicks by D.J.Rowell JP
    28, Cornelius Johnson to Cressy Philips
    30, William Latham to Mary Ann Campbell
pg 74
Dec 1, Joseph Gibson to Sarah Kelso by W.R.Jones JP
     8, William Smith to Susannah Beachboard by L. Walker JP
     8, Brice P. Gray to Elizabeth Jennings by John Moorehead JP
     8, Henry Paysinger to Elizabeth B. Leatherwood by D.J.Rowell
     8, James Hill to Majesary Abbott by Robert Drennon JP
    12, Ezekiel Baker to Susan Carrie by J.H.Taylor JP
    15, Robert B. Burton to Sarah Murphy by S.J.Bland JP
    15, John W. Wright to Sarah Elizabeth Lenard by E.B.King JP
    22, William S. Evans to Elizabeth Waggoner by W. Jenkins VDM

```
      16,    John Marberry to Rachel Isom by D.J.Rowell JP
      20,    Arthur A. Goodin to Martha B. Wilson by H.B.Warren MG
pg 75
      19,    Andrew Roberts to Elizabeth Dickey
      20,    Reubin B. Ramsey to Matilda B. Kennedy
      22,    James B. Gill to Tallafar Robertson by C.W.McGuire JP
      22,    Harry C. Cowan to Agness B. McDaniel by C.B.Farris MG
      22,    James J. Tate to Isabella Casey
      23,    William Tucker to Nancy Eslick by John King JP
1843
Apr 25,    William S. Buchanan to Martha A. Timmins by Stanford
                                                           Lasater
1842
Dec 22,    William W. McNeely to Lucinda C. McKinney by A.G.Gibson MG
      25,    Benjamin B. Brandon to Lucinda Williams by L.S.Woodward JP
      29,    Robert S. Woodward to Mary McKinney by David Smith JP
      27,    James M. George to Jane Farrar by C.W.McGuire JP
pg 76
      27,    James C. Birmingham to Eliza Eagan by S. Leatherwood JP
1843
Jan  3,    Green C. Gattis to Mary Ann Marshall by Wm. Gattis JP
1842
Dec 29,    Charles Wiles to Emeline Wade by John Weaver MG
1843
Jan  1,    Elijah F. Wade to Caroline Crane by John Weaver MG
1842
Dec 29,    Alexander Williams to Maria Foster by T.S.Williams JP
1843
Jan  1,    William Riddle to Nancy C. Gattis by Wm. Gattis JP
1842
Dec 29,    Hugh M. Smith to Eliza Ann Smith by W.B.McLaughlin JP
                        194 Licenses issued in 1842
pg 77
1843
Jan  4,    John E. McWhorter to Sarah E. Noe by Robert Drennon JP
      12,    Wm. A. Moore to Elizabeth Waggoner by S. Boone JP
      10,    Daniel Bethume to Lucinda Rawles by S.J.Bland JP
      16,    Daniel Blakemore to Ann M. Chitwood by J.W.McDaniel PGC
      12,    Andrew W. Stroud to Sarah Rhodes by S.J.Bland JP
      15,    Daniel Smoot to Ann Shaw by John H. Taylor JP
      18,    Andrew M. Wilson to Nancy A. Dobbins by H.B.Warren MG
      19,    Henry Robinson to Mildred Crowder by David Smith JP
      24,    Andrew Drake to Nancy Hazelwood by J.H.Taylor JP
      24,    Wilson Smith to Elizabeth Cruse by W.C.Jennings JP
      26,    Newton McQuiddy to Nancy A. Shofner by W. Jenkins V.D.M.
pg 78
      26,    Joseph Montgomery to Mary A. Mansfield by J.B.Hudson JP
      28,    George King to Susannah Lathaim
Feb  6,    John Reid to Elizabeth Cashin
       9,    Samuel Roan to Elizabeth DeJarnett by J.R.Chitcoat JP
       9,    Claborn Isham to Parthenia Turker by Woodruff Parks Esq
       7,    Jacob Siler to Louisa Hunt by W.C.Jennings JP
       9,    Matthew Allbright to Hester Ann Smith by Robert Drennon JP
      14,    Matthew Waggoner to Catharine Waggoner by W. Jenkins VDM
      13,    David B. Walker to Lavoy Erwin
      14,    Charles Mitchell to Mary J. Cooper by Bradley Kimbrough MG
      14,    George Gant to Eliza Ann Garner
```

pg 79
```
     18,    Massey Copeland to Mahalla Eslick
     20,    Peter A. Dale to Mary G. Phagan
     20,    William Lenard to Elizabeth C. Cole by B.Kimbrough MG
     22,    Benjamin Warren to Emily Parks by Woodruff Parks Esq
     23,    John W. Nichol to Minerva S. Kimes by Henry Turney JP
     23,    Wm. R. Warren to Mary J. McFarland by John Warren MG,Esq
     23,    Manly M. Hairston to Martha P. Koonce
Mar   2,    Patrick H. Wanslow to Elizabeth A. Rhoten by J.H.Taylor JP
      2,    William Sorrells to Eleanor M. King by E.B.King JP
      2,    William Malone to Louisa Luttrell by W.C.Jennings JP
      5,    Harrison W. Kyser to Maranda Stone by Joel Rees JP
```
pg 80
```
      7,    John Roach to Martha D. Parkes by W.B.Rhea JP
     11,    Jacob D. Drake to Martha Jane Hemphill by Wm. Pryor JP
     12,    John Blue to Clementine J. Roberts by J. Bland JP
     16,    William W. Cobble to Elizabeth Brown by J.H.Taylor JP
     16,    Benjamin K. Daniel to Sarah J. Baxter by S. Woodward JP
     13,    John Chastine to Sarah White by S. Leatherwood JP
     16,    Theophilus Harris to Sinai A. Buchanan by Joseph Smith
     21,    Joseph Taylor to Caroline George
     23,    Spartin G. Crane to Jane Steelman by John Weaver MG
     23,    George Bower to Winney West by W.R.Jones JP
     22,    K.H.Burford to Elizabeth K. Baxter
```
pg 81
```
     16,    David M. McClure to Sarah Collier by Lewis Newsom JP
     16,    Alexander Allbright to Harriet Hamblin by Robert Drennon JP
Apr  11,    William G. Mackey to Martha Rives by J.H.Leftwich MG
      3,    William Moffett,Jr. to Rebecca K. Buchanan by W.B.Rhea JP
      6,    James W. Walker to Lavina Flack by J.H.Taylor JP
      4,    Jesse Warren to Rebecca Bedwell by J.R.Brown
      5,    George Broadway to Frankey West by John McDaniel JP
      6,    William J. Stockston to Margaret Moffett by C.H.Edmondson
      8,    Ruffin C. Stennett to Sarah A. Flannagan by Wm. Neeld JP
      8,    Pleasant Mullins to Milly Locke by David J. Rowell JP
      9,    Edwin T. Thomas to Jane Moore by A.W.Pickens MG
```
pg 82
```
     11,    George Bates to Susan J. Roach by John Weaver MG
     12,    George F. Renegar to Sarah Cashion by J. Copeland
     13,    John K. Moore to Elizabeth Gray by W.B.Jones JP
     14,    Anderson Cashion to Polly Taylor by T.S.Williams JP
     13,    Samuel H. Hall to Mary A. Ramey by Joseph Smith
     20,    Thomas P. Summers to Eliza L. Drinkard by Davis Smith JP
     19,    Isaac Parks to Mary F. Collins by S. Woodard JP
May   2,    Alexander Forester to Minerva Eaton by Samuel Boone JP
Apr  22,    Thomas J. Cotten to Lucinda Nelson
     23,    Henry A. Lazenby to Sarah Seagraves
```
pg 83
```
     29,    Milton A. Edmondson to Mary A. Williams by J.Kimes JP
May   4,    John S. McCarver to Eliza A. Clark by Benjamin Butler JP
      7,    William Upton to Eliza Watson by W.B.McLaughlin JP
     18,    Matthew Price to Jemima G. Gore by A.W.Parks JP
     20,    William C. White to Elizar Wilkerson by John King JP
     25,    Isaac Kelso to Cynthia Jones by W.R.Jones JP
     30,    John Latham to Sarah Sweeny
Jun   4,    William J. Thompson to Ellender J. Ezell by S.Leatherwood
      1,    Madison Beatie to Martha A. Cunningham by A.M.Pickens MG
      4,    Constantine A. Hall to Martha J. Raney by Joseph Smith
```

1843   19

| Jul | 3, | Presly Rucker to Lavina Jones by Benj. Butler JP |

pg 84

	6,	James L. Keith to Margaret B. Clark by H.B.Warren MG
	4,	Moses McWhorter to Matilda Watson by W.B.McLaughlin JP
Mar	2,	Henderson Harris to Martha Harris (Col) by Wm. Neeld JP
	5,	John Whitworth to Frances M. Bailey by J.H.Taylor JP
Jul	18,	Thomas Kelso to Eliza Dean by W.R.Jones JP
	18,	Jesse M. Roland to Mary Cole by Benjamin Butler JP
	19,	Joseph Boyd to Lucretia Webb
	20,	John Burns to Nancy McNatt by M.M.Bedwell
	27,	Mortimor Hurst to Sarah A. Jarred by Joel Rees JP
	23,	C.W.Montgomery to O.F.Moon by Bradley Kimbro MG
	23,	N. Tolly to G.E.Landess

pg 85

	27,	William Sanders to Sarah Wheeler by W.R.Jones JP
Aug	6,	Samuel Crabtree to Nancy Bradford by E.B.King JP
	6,	Edward Gobble to Emeline Clay by L.S.Woodward JP
	13,	J.A.Laws to Syntha Steed by A.W.Parks JP
	10,	Robert P. Garman to Julina Sanders by Wm. Pryor JP
	7,	Austin Morgan to Adeliza Isaacs
	7,	James M. Moors to Sarah Harper
	8,	Isham Sorrels to Penena Pylant by J.A.Simmons JP
	10,	Joel M. Dollins to Margaret Summerford by A.G.Gibson MG
	10,	Jesse P. McGeehee to Susan Waggoner by Samuel Boone JP
	17,	Peter C. Webster to Narcissa Nickson by Wm. Pryor JP

pg 86

	13,	Marion Dodd to Emily West by W.R.Jones JP
	12,	William Huffman to Narcissa Braden
	17,	Joseph Holman to Irena L. Quarles by Woodruff Parks Esq
	16,	George W. Clements to Luvina Wright by E.B.King JP
	24,	David B. Dollins to Elizabeth Tucker by Amos Small JP
	28,	Willis Gattis to Mary J. White by Wm. Gattis JP
	31,	Ephraim Weaver to Sarah C. Sullivan by Samuel Boone JP
	31,	Thomas Hampton to Martha Smith by D. Smith JP
Sep	3,	Charles Bethany to Margaret Williams by David Snoddy JP
	7,	John Armstrong to Mariel McCollum by A.G.Gibson MG
	6,	John Brown to Lucretia Shuffield by D.J.Rowell JP

pg 87

	6,	Solomon Blades to Rachel Woody by T.W.Ledbetter JP
	13,	Hardy Sanders to Susan Crabtree by T.W.Ledbetter JP
	14,	John G. Troup to Martha A. Sumners by Davis Smith JP
	13,	William Kidd to Margaret Nowlan
	14,	William O. Barnes to Martha A. Beasley by D.Smith JP
	14,	Jonathan N. Davis to Elizabeth F. Tatum byJ.McDaniel JP
	19,	David McClusky to Elizabeth Damron by Wm. Pryor JP
	19,	Joseph Gray to Susan Mullins
	27,	Joseph Hitchcock to Nancy Inman by W.B.McLaughlin JP
	25,	John L. Martin to Louisa J. Bailey by E.B.King JP
	28,	Berry Norman to Hetty McVay by T.S.Williams JP

pg 88

Oct	5,	L.L.Cole to Elizabeth H. Small by S. Wood
	3,	T.M.Ledbetter to Frances N. Moores by A.G.Gibson
	4,	Ludy C. Byram to Susan King by W.R.Brice JP
	3,	Samuel S. Morrow to Jane E. Moore by W.B.Rhea JP
	3,	Kiser Mullins to Mary Harrison by W.R.Brice JP
	8,	James M. Buchanan to Elzira Ramsey by Jas Smith
	10,	Elijah Norman to Malinda Broyles

20

11,   Charles Dellender to Brunetta Wilson
         8,   James Andrews to Nancy Griffis by D.J.Rowell JP
        12,   Lewis F. Arney to Catharine W. Butts by John McDaniel JP
        15,   James Simmons to Martha A. Mullins by W.R.Bruch JP
pg 89
Oct 16,   William Crawford to Nancy R. Gibson by A.G.Gibson
        17,   Jesse M. Cole to Jane B. Kelly by S.J.Bland JP
        17,   Benjamin M. Land to Elizabeth A. Wells by Lee Walker JP
        22,   Levi Smith to Elizabeth Malone by Wm. Pryor JP
        24,   Spencer Williams to Rebecca Jones by E.B.King JP
        27,   Randolph Houge to Eliza Wanslow by J.H.Taylor JP
        26,   Peter Ashby to Mary Jane George by John Weaver MG
Nov 3,   William Langston to Lydia McClure to H. Buchanan JP
         6,   James A. Walker to Catharine J. Chambers by D.Jacks
         7,   John M. Hill to Burchet R. Campbell by A.G.Gibson
        16,   George Small to Naomi Steed by T. Ledbetter JP
pg 90
         8,   James Parrish to Catharine Pruitt by W.R.Jones JP
         8,   Emaziah Denison to Martha Wilkins by D.J.Rowell JP
        18,   F.M.Bearden to Lucinda Burrow by Lewis Newsom JP
        23,   John L. Brown to Susan Williams by Lemuel Bearden MG
        23,   R.S.Brown to Elizabeth McClure by Wm. Pryor JP
         5,   James Bates to Caroline Wallace by W.R.Jones JP
        30,   James G. Woods to Susan J. Boyce by Matt Marshall VDM
        23,   Lorenzo D. Jones to Polly Sandland
        28,   James Gattis to Sarah McCullum by John Moorehead JP
        28,   John A. Bruce to Clarinda J. VanHooser by S. Leatherwood JP
        28,   Zebulon Vickers to Mary Mullins
pg 91
        30,   David M. Beatie to Mary Motlow
        30,   James M. McFarlin to Riney Ann Deal by W.B.Rhea JP
Dec 3,   Newell Ingle to Martha Ann Glidwell by H.A.Simmons JP
         6,   Penuel Ramsey to Eleanor Eveline Rosebrough
         7,   James M. West to Elizabeth Sullivan by A.M.Pickens MG
        13,   William Jeffers to Eliza Pamplin by Woodruff Parks
        13,   Barney Albright to Susannah Evans by Robert Drennon JP
        14,   Wm. C. Woods to Sarah A. Boyce by M. Marshall VDM
        21,   Zachariah Kelso to Gelina Forbus by David J. Rowell JP
        19,   John Rogers to Julia Smith by John Weaver MG
        20,   Richard A. Fitch to Nancy Fuller
pg 92
        22,   Enoch Hamilton to Anna D. Stewart by J.W.Holman JP
        21,   Peter W. Morgan to Mary Smith by C.H.Edmondson JP
        28,   William Polk to Sarah Warren by J.A.Simmons JP
        31,   W.B.Early to Catharine Harris by Wm. Neeld JP
1844
Jan 6,   John Kimes to Mary Ann Chapman by J. Kimes JP
         5,   James H. Bray to Sarah Fackenton
         5,   Harvy Eslick to Lucinda McGehee
        11,   Erestus Lock to Louiza Mullins by D.J.Rowell JP
        16,   George Sanders to Minerva Claunch by Lee Walker JP
        23,   John M. Cobble to Sophia R. Tensley by John H. Taylor JP
pg 93
        18,   John H. Heflin to Mary Eliza Hester by T. Smith JP
        25,   John H. Steelman to Emily Warden by John Weaver MG
        25,   Joshua Yates to Sarah J. Pibus
        29,   Isaac W. McCown to Isabella Jackson
Feb 1,   Wilson B. Shofner to Mary Snoddy by W.C.Jennings JP

1,   William C. Gray to Catharine L. Hague by B.Kimbrough JP
1,   Charles L. Goodrum to Mary Ann Clark
6,   Joseph G. Smith to Frances M. Dooley by Wm. Harris JP
8,   Alfred Nichols to Martha Waters by Wm. Harris JP
12,   Isaiah Hamilton to Eliza Stone by D. Jacks MG
12,   Daniel Westerman to Sarah Freeman
pg 94
13,   James H. Taylor to Martha Simmons
15,   John M. Winstead to Matilda Gavin by Lewis Newsom JP
20,   M.R.Williams to Amanda Tanksley by J.P.Williams JP
21,   John M. Read to Eliza C. Summers by Davis Smith JP
28,   Daniel Marsh to Elizabeth A. Leach by John Weaver MG
26,   William Staton to Letitia Beasley
Mar 2, (issued)2nd Joseph Buchanan to Cyntha Bryant by David Rowell
                                   Jul 21,1844
12,   Montgomery Carter to Ann Cunningham by Henry Turney JP
12,   Robert Martin to Mary A.C.Smith by Bradly Kimbro MG
20,   Thomas Warren to Ann Bedford by Lewis Newsom
21,   James Henderson to Rutha Haggard
pg 95
26,   Elihu McGeehee to Polly A. Leach by John Woodruff
28,   John Hancock to Elizabeth Hamilton by Henry Turney JP
28,   Martin Harbin to Louisa J. Couch by T.S.Williams JP
Apr 3, John B. Milam to Mary Stray by W.R.Jones JP
1,   John D. Stewart to Eliza E. Wells
3,   William W. Gavin to Jane Merril by Woodruff Parks JP
4,   Thomas Moore to Annia M. Bell by A.G.Gibson MG
6,   Isaac Melson to Elizabeth Beard
8,   George Carter to Cintha Hill by W. Bridges JP
8,   Washington Rogers to Mary Martin by Lewis Newsom
11,   Thomas Boteler to Mary C. Hague by A. Bradshaw MG
pg 96
11,   T.U.Stephenson to Margaret Crafford by A.G.Gibson MG
11,   Lemuel T. Sikes to Catharine Fox
19,   William H. Muse to Martha A. Echols by Wm. Neeld JP
25,   David Counts to Sarah Yarbrough by D. Jacks MG
May 2, Robert Buchanan to Mary Cunningham by Henry Turney JP
3,   John Carter to Elizabeth Cunningham by Henry Turney JP
5,   Joseph Scott to Sarah E. Smith by Philip Rowe MG
16,   Ronnie Leatherwood to Barbary A. Randolph by G.W.Puckett M
16,   William H. Cimmons to Easter C. Harkins by J.D.Cole MG
24,   Wm. Hardin to Liza J. Woodbay by S. Leatherwood JP
pg 97
Jun 4, John M. Beaty to Catharine Edmondson by A.G.Gibson MG
4,   Wm. H. Marshall to Delina Childress
6,   Edward A. Brown to Elizabeth D. Solomon by Thomas
                                       Williams JP
6,   Andrew J. Hallum to Harriett Solomon by T. Williams JP
6,   William Murphy to Tullilon Mitchell
13,   Littlebery Stroud to Samantha Heflin by D.J.Rowell JP
24,   John Joins to Christiana Nix by B. Clark JP
12,   Mathew Massengale to Mahaly Reed by D.J.Rowell JP
27,   David M. Cordal to Nancy J. Sewal by Wm. Neeld JP
30,   John Fitch to Malinda Kerbo by T.S.Williams JP
pg 98
Jul 3, William Raby to Mary Holt by W.R.Jones JP
11,   George W. Mullikin to Mary Clark by Henry Turney JP

17,	Thomas A. Owings to Safronia M. Russell by A.G.Gibson MG
18,	Green Bevil to Minerva Qualls by B.F.Clark JP
25,	Robert Wm. Burton to Octavo Whitlock by J.H.Taylor JP
26,	John Roan to Nancy Deshaser by W.R.Jones JP
26,	Abraham Vinson to Nancy Hall by W.R.Jones JP
Aug 6,	Wiley Worley to Louisa H. Trimble by D. Smith JP
Jul 29,	Gabriel Pylant to Nancy Tucker by John Kimes JP
Aug 1,	Bazel Muse to Sarah Foster by R. Anderson MG

pg 99

2,	Smith Lee to Partheny Dunson by D.J.Rowell JP
1,	Hardy F.M.Ramsey to Martha Wickes by J.H.Daniel JP
1,	Lorenzo D. Aikin to Elizabeth J. Foster by J.P.Campbell
6,	Thomas Gray to Martha Night by J.W.Holman JP
8,	Andrew Davidson to Elmyra A.E.Farrar by J.H.Leftwich MG
8,	Samuel Rutledge to Louisa Daniel by J.W.Holman JP
12,	Samuel Gaddy to May A. Bolton by W.R.Bruce JP
13,	James M. Crofford to Cintha A. Philips by B. Butler JP
15,	Alexander Lewis to Jane Lewis
21,	James Stevenson to Elizabeth Griffin
21,	John Turner to Lydia A. Parish by G. Walker JP

pg 100

29,	William S. Curtis to Margaret J. Russell by A.M.Pickens MG
29,	Harrison S. Wilson to Ann Shufford by A.M.Pickens MG
Sep 3,	Elias Neely to Emily Buchanan by S.J.Bland JP
10,	William Davis to Nancy E. Hancock
12,	(Issued and returned) John L.McCowan to Elizabeth A. Jackson
12,	Peter C. Taylor to Lucinda Taylor by T.S.Williams JP
20,	Zachariah Little to Lydia Swinford
24,	John L. Rosebrough to Sarah A. Smith by B.F.Clark JP
26,	Christopher Boyd to Mary Fincher by H. Philips JP
Oct 1,	Stephen C. Butler to Elizabeth Y. Lackey by B.Butler JP

pg 101

6,	Thompson Sullivan to Rachel Wiles by Jesse Neese JP
9,	Obediah Swanner to Rutha Barns by B. Butler JP
3,	Hardin Warden to Eliza P. Ruth by John Weavwe JP
3,	Albert G. King to Fenetta Whitaker by W.B.Rhea JP
3,	George W. Davidson to Margaret S. Norwood
Dec 13,	David O. Lingo to Abetha Simmons by W.R.Bruce JP
Oct 11,	Solomon Wamack to Lucinda Ervin
15,	Wm. R. Hurley to Elizabeth Johnson by A.M.Pickens MG
17,	Henry Spray to Mary Ann Abbott by Robert Drennon JP
Nov 7,	John S. Sneed to Ann Eliza Webster by J.F.Buckner JP

pg 102

Oct 29,	Stanford M. McElroy to Louisa A. Smith by A.G.Gibson MG
29,	Eli George to Mary Brown by G. Walker JP
31,	James L. Reaves to Lucinda J. Carrithers by B.Butler JP
31,	John W. Michael to Martha A. Philips by Amos Small JP
Nov 4,	John H.B.Watson to Martha Moore by John F.Buckner JP
Dec 5,	Jonathan E. Prosser to Epsey Johnson by Jesse Nees JP
Nov 7,	Samuel Kennedy to Mary A. Smith by H. Philips JP
14,	William W. Carpenter to Sarah W. Maddox by C.W.McGuire JP
14,	Joseph Clark to Emeline E. Brown by Jesse Graham MG
14,	George W. Brown to Cisa Ann Small by John Weaver JP
21,	Jacob Locke to Manda S. Mullins by D.J.Rowell JP

pg 103

21,	John C. Saint to Mary H. Kiser by Jesse Nees JP

```
       20,    Alexander Sevier to Martha Ward by H. Philips JP
       28,    James W. Brown to Mary Myrick by C.H.Edmondson JP
Dec   2,    Edward Blades to Mary Ann Bevil
       9,    Thomas Hammons to Elizabeth T. Wilson
       9,    Felix Douthit to Nancy Ellis by Thomas Childs MG
      12,    Wm. W. Reese to Nancy T. Calhoun by J.H.Leftwich MG
      11,    John Dale to Elizabeth A. Phagan
      12,    Young T. Taylor to Catharine Spencer by J. Copeland MG
      19,    Thomas Franklin to Elizabeth Forbes by G.W.Puckett MG
pg 104
      13,    Hiram Franklin to Louisa P. Ship by S.J.Bland JP
      19,    Willis VanHoosier to Nancy C. Webb by G.W.Puckett MG
      15,    James Irvin Neeld to Sarah P. Wallace by Joseph Smith JP
      16,    William H. Hall to Amilla Smith by A.S.Randolph JP
      17,    Hugh B. McWhorter to Eliza Lodderdale
      19,    Samuel Fife to Margaret Jane Towery by Robert Drennon JP
      26,    John Ashby to Lucy C. Waggoner by John Weaver MG
      23,    David S. Patterson to Elizabeth R. Cheatham by C.W.
                                                       McGuire JP
      23,    Bennet Solomon to Elizabeth A. Wear
      25,    Levin G. Ready to May Bates by Amos Small JP
pg 105
      25,    Richard C. Barnes to Desina Halbert by Thomas Childs
      26,    William H. Hazzlewood to Margaret Rhea by John Kimes JP
      29,    Mathew Mullins to Susan Simmons by W.R.Bruce JP
      29,    George W. Wood to A. Caroline Harden
      30,    E.R.Kilpatrick to Sopha R. Brown
1845
Jan   1,    Benjamin E. Spencer to Mary T. Waggoner
       5,    William Howard to Sarah Stiles by John Moorehead JP
       7,    Paul A. Shaw to Mary S. Turner by Robert Drennon JP
       9,    Solomon Gilly to Euticia Witt by John Buckner JP
       9,    Lemuel H. Ventress to Mary Parker by Woodruff Parks JP
pg 106
      13,    John Nance to Elizabeth Walker by S.J.Bland JP
      13,    George Thompson to Leafly Polly by Wm. Gattis
      19,    Elijah T. Williams to Nancy M. Steber by J.H.Taylor JP
      22,    Leander Locke to Catharine Mullins
      18,    John Scales to Martha King by B.F.Clark JP
      22,    Robert Frame to Nancy Ervin
      30,    Peter W. Walton to Missouri A. Collins by John McDaniel JP
      29,    William Hail to Louisa F. Taylor by David Snoddy JP
      31,    Augustus M.B.Alley to Elizabeth B. Taylor
Feb   3,    Leroy Edwards to Louisa Grant by Wm. Pryor JP
pg 107
       4,    John H. Gamblin to Cintha M.Johnson by Richard Anderson MG
May   6,    Henson Picket to Mary Shelton by George Arnold JP
Feb 19,    Thomas M. Hudson to Sarah Boone by Joseph Smith MG
      18,    William B. Smith to Isabella J. Wyatt by Thomas Childs MG
      25,    Ellis Renegar to Susan McGee by Wm. Gattis JP
      27,    Isam Kent to Elizabeth Goff by Travis Ashby JP
      26,    George W. Brown to Elizabeth Wilkins by Isaac Conger MG
Mar   6,    James E. Brown to Delila Brown by Isaac Conger MG
       4,    Berry Duke to Emeline Beasley by Wm. Gattis JP
       9,    John M. Lewis to Josephine Hickman by Jesse Nees JP
pg 108
      13,    James W. Davis to Hannah P. Damsel by M.A.Alexander JP
      13,    James Fanning to Sarah Honey by Wm. Gattis JP
```

19,   John B. Bedwell to Phebe An Rhea by J.H.Leftwich MG
20,   Sandy Henderson to Nancy Land by Wm. Pryor JP
26,   Robert A. Taylor to Sarah Eslick by J. Copeland MG
26,   William Smith to Eliza Gunter by T. Childs MG
Apr 6, Absalom G. Runnels to Kissiah A.M. Guslay by A.W.Parks JP
1,   George W. Reese to Harriet P. Garner
3,   George G. Woodruff to Elizabeth Summerford by Amos
                                                   Small JP
8,   Wm. P. Smith to Martha Jane Wilson by A.M.Perkins MG
pg 109
8,   Charles Bright to Frances D. Robinson by A.G.Gibson MG
9,   Cornelius Harmon to Sarah A.H.Withers by A.G.Gibson MG
10,   John Surber to Cyntha Rees by A.G.Gibson MG
16,   Westly Smith to Rachel E. Lemmonds by D. Small JP
15,   Simpson Buchanan to Sarah Commons
22,   James Woodall to Sarah Ann Stephenson by John Moore JP
22,   Francis W. Little to Florida M. Rousot
24,   William Harbin to Elizabeth Norman by D.S.Gray JP
23,   George Mills to Sarah Griffin by W.R.Bruce JP
May 8, James G. Damron to Teny G. Hamilton by A.Alexander MG
pg 110
15,   John Chapman to Eliza J. Baker by Lemuel Brandon JP
10,   Henry Moore by Dicy King
Jun 2, William C. Prewitt to Elizabeth R.Prewitt by A.W.Parks JP
11,   Alexander McCulloch to Barthena Bell
12,   Thomas J. Shelton to Mary Wilson by Mathew Wilson JP
15,   James M. Eaton to Tabitha Forrester by John Weaver MG
18,   David S. Hobbs to Nancy Heath by Willis Bridges MG
16,   Cornelius Hughs to Roznell Nipp
18,   Leroy W. Woodall to Elizabeth Ann Pitts by John Moore JP
24,   George W. Moyers to Susannah Trantham by D. Smith JP
pg 111
26,   James Campbell to Martha Gamill by Jesse Rees JP
24,   Thomas Gattis to Eliza Waggoner
26,   William Olliver to Mary Radican by S.W.Arnold JP
25,   Samuel M. Cooper to Louisa Waggoner by W.B.Rhea JP
30,   Franklin Gunter to Elizabeth Crowder by Thomas Childs JP
Jul 17, Joab Heflin to Nancy Walker by G.W.Pucket MG
6,   Hardin H. Landreth to Elizabeth Pully by Wm. Gattis JP
16,   Edward Summerford to Martha Allen by Jesse Nees JP
10,   Wiley M. Newman to Elizabeth Parker by W.C.Jennings JP
12,   John G. Gledwell to Frances Freeman
pg 112
17,   Wilson L. Westerman to Malinda M. Robertson by J.Nees JP
24,   Alexander G. Noah to Rebecca Gunter by John McDaniel JP
23,   Silas Michael to Martha P. Hobbs by W.C.Jennings JP
26,   Thomas R. Wind to Martha A. Beaty
29,   Samuel R. Farris to Monica Tate
Aug 5, Carrol Evans to Milly Pearce by J.W.Hamilton JP
3,   Samuel L. English to Hannah Hall
5,   Wm. W. Parks to Sophia A. Koonce by W.B.Rhea JP
5,   Henry Brown to Nancy Ann Smith by C.H.Edmondson JP
6,   Jacob C. Gobble to Tabitha Thompson by L.S.Woodward JP
pg 113
7,   David G. Davis to Amanda Harris by D. Smith JP
7,   Wm. Thompson to Louisa Rorex by Woodruff Parks JP
10,   Benjamin Hill to Clarissa Dorsey by W.C.Jennings JP

14,   James T.S.Dance to Susan F.B.Landess by J.H.Taylor JP
 9,   Samuel H. Sloan to Martha J. McCalla
21,   Jesse L. Bryant to Fenetta B. Leftwich by Jesse Nees JP
20,   William Hanks to Franky McClure by W.C.Jennings JP
26,   Wilkerson W. Rees to Mary J. Smith by Jesse Rees JP
26,   Stephen D. Loyd to Sarah C. Watson by Wm. Gattis JP
28,   Thomas H. Holland to Narcissa J. Bridges by Wm. Dyer JP
pg 114
29,   Obediah C. Echols to Milly Mullins by Absolum Forbes JP
Sep 9,   William A. Hicks to Nancy Blair by Absolum Forbes JP
 7,   William Jones to Mary L. Bland by W.R.Jones JP
11,   John H. Huckabee to Mary Coble by D. Smith JP
14,   John Warren to Margaret Gibson by H.C.Cowan JP
18,   Green B. Duke to Eliza Ledford by Wm. Gattis
23,   Samuel McDonald Woodward to Sarah Caroline Frame by Rev.
                                                    John Scivally
Oct 14,   Bens Ledford to Cyntha White by Wm. Gattis JP
 3,   Joseph Petty to Emeline Keller by J.T.Buckner JP
 9,   John Allen to Sarah Ann Foster by Jesse Nees JP
 8,   Stephen M. Farmer to Sarah A.B.Clift by D. Smith JP
pg 115
 8,   Robert Daniel to Rebecca Logan
 9,   Henry Heathcoat to Martha Michael by Lee Walker JP
14,   James M. Davis to Nancy Rainey by T.B.Clark JP
13,   Exekiah L. Barnes to Susannah Reeves by C.W.McGuire
16,   Calvin L. Hodge to Manerva Templeton by J. Blair JP
23,   David L. Biggers to Caroline Street by J.P.Bland JP
14,   John R. Wood to Priscilla Beavers by H.C.Cowan JP
14,   Jefferson D. Long to Eliza P. Young by J.W.Arnold JP
14,   Anthony Hensley to Rebecca Ward by Hiram Philips JP
30,   Henton Hill to Mary Ann Sewel by T. Griffin MG
20,   John O. Tucker to Ruth Honey by Wm. Gattis MG
pg 116
24,   Ansel W. Irvin to Narcissa N. Davis by C.W.McGuire JP
26,   John H. Hamlet to Sabra Goforth by W. Jones JP
20,   Henry H. Rieves to Nancy Buchanan by D.L.Michael
30,   John Evans to Malinda Hamilton by Rev. John Scivally
Nov 5,   William G. Commons to Mary M. Boone by J.H.Leftwich MG
 3,   Henry Hawkins to Caroline Marshall by W.R.Jones JP
 5,   Ewing Graham to Sarah C. Nicar by Henry Larkins MG
 6,   James W. Perry to Sally Ann Gattis by D. Gray JP
 5,   William N. Collins to Mary J. Clift by Davis Smith JP
11,   William Holt to Anne S. Sandlin by W.R.Jones JP
pg 117
10,   Samuel Merrell to Murina Whitaker
Dec 21,   John King to Rhoda Eslick by W. Tucker JP
Nov 13,   William C. Sikes to Sarah S. Enochs
18,   Isaac W. King to Hetty S. Scott by G.B.Kimbrough MG
18,   Nicholas Renegar to Selina Stone by T.S.Williams JP
18,   Isaac Weeks to Mary Shinalt by Hiram Philips JP
23,   Thomas Bailey to Amanda Shofner by Jesse Nees JP
22,   William J. Pool to Lavina McCown
24,   Daniel McCollum to Sarah B. Tatum
24,   Joseph Bunch to Mary B. McCollum
30,   John F. Ervin to Narcissa Wanslow by Lewis Ashby JP
pg 118
26,   John B. Wright to Nancy Castleman by Amos Small JP

	26,	David C. Finney to Elephia Critchet
	28,	Jesse Scoggins to Louisa J. Epps by B.F.Clark JP
	27,	Joseph T. Landess to Amerrilda M. Howel by C.H.

Edmondson JP

Dec	1,	William B. Baxter to Martha Snoddy
	4,	John R. Moore to Mary E. Malier by A.G.Gibson MG
	11,	Currin D. Benson to Narcissa E. Hayes by C.W.McGuire JP
	7,	William W. Majors to Mary Paysinger by J. McDaniel JP
	9,	Thomas W. Muse to Jane Nichols by Richard Anderson MG
	18,	James Sullinger to Caroline Eslick by Wm. Gattis JP

pg 119

	9,	William T. Staton to Margret E. Wersham by C.A.French JP
	9,	John W. Brundrige to Sarah Young by S. Yarbrough MG
	11,	William S.Cooper to Caroline A.P.Enochs
	17,	George W. Campbell to Keziah Williams by J.F.Buckner JP
	13,	Harmon Franklin to Phebe Fannon
	15,	William Posey to Rachael Durham by John Moore JP
	18,	Absalum Setliff to Margret E. Norris by John F. McCutchen
	16,	Augustus T. Echols to Mary Anderson
	17,	Alexander M. Endsly to Margret J. Peyton by Thomas Childs
	18,	James W. Broadway to Nancy A. ·Motlow by S. Boone JP
	18,	George W. Swinbroad to Charlotta Keith by Wm. Burgess

pg 120

	16,	Willis H. Holman to Ann Rebecca Rutledge
	18,	Thomas Taylor to Mary W. Hill by Wm. Thomison JP
	23,	Hiram H. Cooper to Mary S. Landreth by Wm. Gattis JP
	24,	Peter T. Walker to Rebecca J. Walker by G.W.Puckett MG
	24,	Charles W. Timmins to Eliza Jane Gregg by D.R.Hooker JP
	26,	James Harris to Elizabeth Yarbrough by T.J.Buckner JP
	28,	Eppe Sullivan to Elizabeth Wisham by John Weaver MG
	29,	Felix G. Parks to Margret Ann Hague by G.B.Kimbrough MG

1846

Jan	5,	John Stephens to Caroline Wheeler by W.R.Jones JP

1845

Dec	30,	Josiah T. Webb to Margret J. Gilliland

pg 121

	31,	John C. Rogers to Eliza Jane Fulton by A.G.Gibson MG

1846

Jan	1,	John M. Edens to Mary Blyth
	1,	Thomas R. Ramsey to Jane R. Smith by S.S.Yarbrough MG
	11,	James George to Jane Walker by W.R.Jones JP
	6,	Anderson C. Martin to Louisa Buchanan by A.G.Gibson MG
	8,	John Shapard to Nancy E. Street by W.R.J.Husband MG
	20,	Joel C. Higgins to Mary S. Smith by G.W.Puckett MG
	14,	Asbery J. Hampton to Alader Collins by W.B.Bruce JP
	15,	Lossen P. Whitaker to Eliza J. King by W.B.Rhea JP

pg 122

	16,	Isaac W. Holman to Mary H. Higgins by Hiram Philips JP
	14,	Jacob C. Beard to Sarah Birmingham
	18,	Lewis C. Blair to Martha C. Hosch by S.J.Bland JP
	19,	Samuel M. White to Mary Crenshaw
	22,	Cyrus Eastland to Mary Tranthaim by B.F.Clark,JP
	22,	Samuel N₀ White to Emeline Sanders by Wm. Gattis JP
Feb	1,	Nathaniel R. Hill to Amanda Pack by W.B.Rhea JP
	2,	John W. Gunter to Sarah Holt by W.R.Jones JP
	9,	John Hicklin to Malissa Evans by Robert Drennon JP
	19,	William R. Smith to Prudence E. Johnson by Woodruff

Parks JP

pg 123
  19,   John Collins to Susan A. Edmondson by A.W.Parks JP
  19,   Joel L. Cole to Nancy Woodruff by Amos Small JP
  22,   William Heraldson to Matilda Pool by S.J.Bland JP
  25,   Washington Foster to Annilda J. Allen by Jesse Neese JP
  24,   William L.McMilican to Matilda Clark
  24,   Doct. Earley Huff to Mary F. Huchison by W.D.Shadick MG
  25,   John O. Cole to Nancy Templeton by Robert Drennon JP
  26,   John Vickers to Fanny M. Martin
Mar 5, Otho H.Moores to Sarah F. Grizard by A.M.Pickens MG
  4,   Joseph Broyles to Keziah M. Hague by S.S.Yarbrough
pg 124
  8,   William Webb to Anny L. Calhoun by Lewis Newman JP
  10,   Henry Beck to Louisa C. Barns by Mathew Wilson JP
  12,   George W. Smith to Martha Ann Tunes by H.Philips JP
  12,   John C. Summers to Mary Cunningham
  12,   J. Charles N. Woody to Nancy Ann Dawes by C. Smith JP
  18,   William V. Foster to Cintha J. Anderson
  19,   Alvis Flack to Susan A. Harkins by D.F.Mitchel,Min.
  26,   William E. Hunter to Adaliza T. Smith by H.C.Cowan JP
  19,   Elliot Moffett to Nancy A. Jones by W.B.Rhea JP
Apr 10, Willis M. Milam to Margret Beard by G.W.Puckett MG
pg 125
Mar 30, Joseph T. Land to Margret A. Williams by A.S.Randolph JP
Apr 2, Albin P. Davis to Hellen M. Drinkard by J.McDaniel JP
  4,   William B. McLaughlin to Sinia S. Hart by S.S.Yarbrough
  9,   George W. Crunk to Margret Buchanan by A.G.Gibson MG
  11,   Jesse Leatherwood to Malinda G. Milam by G.W.Puckett MG
  7,   David Bradley to Margaret Cunningham by Davis Smith JP
  15,   John Scott to Elleny Manley by W.R.J.Husband MG
  23,   Samuel Cunningham to Mary Ellis by W.B.Rhea JP
  25,   Zachariah Walker to Polly Ann Lesley by D.S.Gray JP
  30,   John Davis to Nancy F. Owen by John McDaniel JP
pg 126
May 27, Thomas J. Whitaker to Elizabeth M. Moore by A.M.Pickens,M
  12,   Isaac S. Graves to Mary Gatlin by H.C.Cowan JP
  14,   Alexander P. Smith to Mary Allen by A.G.Gibson MG
  20,   Asa L. Sanford to Sarah Jean by T.S.Williams JP
  28,   Willis G. Rives to Eliza J. Hall by David L. Michael MG
  26,   Thomas McQuiston to Ann Garmon by G.W.N.Moore JP
Jun 31, Washington Davis to Ann Lauderdale by H.C.Cowan JP
May 28, Issued:Francis M. Wright to Lucinda Whittington and
        Solomized: 8th May(June) by Thomas Childs MG
Jun 8, James H. Shaw to Elizabeth V. Motlow
  14,   John Forrester to Nancy Mansfield by Travis Ashby JP
pg 127
  25,   Jonas L. Wilson to Dotia Ann Daves by Willis Burgess MG
  25,   Lewis Morgan to Samantha Hopkins by Lewis Newsom JP
  30,   Edward Hardens to Nancy Whittington by Henry Turney JP
Jul 2, David C. Mitchell to Martha A. Blake by A.G.Gibson MG
  1,   Macon Franklin to Louisa Carloss by A.G.Gibson MG
  2,   James Olliver to Barbery Hamilton by J.W.Hamilton JP
  9,   Charles F. Moore to Sarah Freeman by G.W.Moore JP
  4,   George W. Philips to Mahala Hamilton
  9,   William P. Toole to Elizabeth Gray by W.C.Dunlap MG
  16,   Eli L. Hodge to Martha C. Griffis by S.P.Bland JP

pg 128
22,   Morgan H. Higgins to Bethena Butler by W.R.Bruce JP
18,   William C. Smith to Docia Millard by Jno Kimes JP
23,   Henry Clinton to Ann Jane Sloan by C.W.McGuire JP
21,   Andrew J. Vann to Martha E. Hunt by W.R.Jones JP
22,   Willis C. Higgins to Nancy A. Williams by G.W.Puckett MG
23,   William R. Waggoner to Nancy A. Moorehead by Wm.Gattis JP
23,   Lemuel G. Mead to Martha Ann Isham by W.B.Rhea JP
30,   Newton B. Westerman to Frances M. Saintclair by Jesse Nees
Aug 2,   Robert T. Eaton to Martha A.E.Childs by D. Smith JP
Jul 30,   William Cashion to Elizabeth Shelton by T.S.Williams JP
pg 129
Aug 6,   Jesse L. Bryant to Nancy M.A.Buchanan by G.W.Puckett MG
1,   Burrel W. Cooper to Ann Chamberlain by A.W.Parks JP
4,   John Birmingham to Nancy A. Moore by S. Leatherwood
6,   Thomas Roe to Amy M. Brown by John Weaver MG
3,   Joseph W.C.Gray to Martha J. Hazzard by Lee Walker JP
4,   Thomas Hazzard to Pelelope W. Allen by Lee Walker JP
6,   John Crawford to Sarah E. Blake by Albert G. Gibson MG
6,   George W. Timmins to Candess C. Edde by Jeremiah Dean MG
6,   William Orrick to Martha Jones by John Weaver MG
23,   Stephen Freeman to Ellen King by G.W.R.Moore JP
pg 130
10,   Philip J. Hall to Martha L. Hicks by Hugh P. Penny
13,   Henry L. Deavers to Nancy Finney by John Daniel JP
13,   John W. Buchanan to Cynthia J. Kimes by D.L.Mitchel MG
15,   Pinkney J. Bolin to Elizabeth Beddingfield by C.W.McGuire
18,   Samuel Y. McCalla to Catharine B. Parkerson
21,   William Simmons to Nancy A. Laird by Wm. Pryor JP
25,   Hiram Tucker to Elizabeth Tangsley by D.S.Gray JP
21,   Leambros Stafford to Emeline Brown by A.W.Parkes JP
31,   Green Watkins to HarietGarmon by Wm. Pryor JP
Sep 1,   George Gray to Nelda J. Brown by S.W.Arnold JP
2,   William Damron to Susan Parkes by A.W.Parkes JP
pg 131
3,   Thomas Vance Greer to Elizabeth A. McMullin by W.C.
                                                  Dunlap MG
7,   Benjamin Brannon to Phireba J. Moore
13,   Jesse M.C.Burke to Susan Tucker by D.S.Gray JP
13,   Shady D. Hopper to Elizabeth R. Lemonds by John W.McDaniel
13,   Joseph H. Lemonds to Emily R. McRee by John McDaniel JP
10,   Caleb Smith to Lydia Lock by Hugh P. Penny JP
13,   Thomas Boaz to Manerva Germley by J.H.Taylor
14,   Jefferson Mullins to Martha Jane Gray by H.P.Penny Esq
15,   Hardy C. Holman to Sarah T. McConnel by J.W.Holman MG
18,   William Billions to Nancy McCollister by W.R.Jones JP
pg 132
Dec 24,   Carroll McRee to Barshaby Paysinger by Henry Turner JP
Sep 22,   John M. Alexander to Sarah R. McCollum
24,   William H. Lay to Judith L. Conaway by W. Husband MG
29,   Samuel D. Durham to Permelia Ray by N.L.Brims JP
Oct 1,   William E. Carter to Amanda Dyer
1,   Solomon S. Yarbrough to Martha B. Hines by John Sherrill,M
7,   Jonathan Frazier to Sarah Cole by Hugh Parkerson Esq
6,   Nicholas H. McRee to Sarah A. Davis by John McDaniel JP
5,   Miles H. McCowan to Sophina C. Lee
6,   Joseph Fritts to Emily Gattis by A.W.Parkes JP

```
        8,    Daniel B. Shields to Mary W. Clarke by A.G.Gibson MG
pg 133
       10,    John Michael to Adeline Thompson by L.S.Woodward JP
       15,    James C. Beeler to Sarah L. McGuire by Daniel Farrar JP
       17,    Spencer N. Laws to Sintha Westerman by A.W.Parks JP
       21,    William Brown to Sarah Taylor by Wm. Thomison JP
       20,    Alexander A. Greer to Elzira R. Todd by W.C.Dunlap MG
       27,    John W. Watt to Narcissa Givens by Daniel Farrar JP
       22,    George A. Crawford to Martha J. Wilson
       29,    Thornton Luttrell to Sophia E. Heath by S.W.Arnold JP
Nov  3,       James Bates to Cyntha Bostic by Martin Towery
Oct 23,       Needam Sorrels to Mary Morton
pg 134
Nov  1,       Willis Reeves to Lerony Jette by S.J.Bland JP
      3,       John J. Bryan to Mary E. Seamoore by J.C.Stevenson
      5,       Laben A. Webb to Rebecca J. Fox by J.W.Holman MG
      5,       Wormley Bruce to Martha Mosley by C.W.McGuire JP
      8,       Ruel Lothrop to Mary Broadaway by H. Philips JP
      9,       Baker Luttrell to Elizabeth Brady
     12,       Burrel Bobo to Margret M. Wilson by Daniel Farrar JP
     15,       John Sanders to Sarah Sanders by L. Walker JP
     17,       Spencer M. Laws to Leotha Westerman by A.W.Parks JP
     23,       Thomas Lock to Margaret Goode by S.J.Bland JP
     24,       Rodderick Barns to Amanda F. Keith by Willis Burgess MG
pg 135
     26,       Robert Moore to Margret Jane Strong by H. Parkerson
     26,       James H. Pamplin to Mary M. Mulden by B.F.Clark JP
     29,       James McClure to Sarah McBay by D.S.Gray JP
Dec  1,       William S. Lackey to Nancy Mosely by J.C.Stevenson
      1,       William P. Land to Eddey Henderson by Wm. Pryor JP
      2,       William D. Grigory to Amanda Harrison by W.R.Bruce JP
      2,       Joseph Shaw to Mary L. Harper by Thos. Childs
      6,       at 3½ o'clock in the morning: Owen Forester to
              Elizabeth Guin by Amos Small JP
      8,       Larkin Johnson to Harret Walker by J.W.Holman MG
      8,       Thomas J. Jones to Lucy M. Graves by A.J.Stewart MG
pg 136
     22,       Thomas Washburn to Mary Jane Dollins by Amos Small JP
     16,       John Parkerson to Mary Ann McCalla
     16,       Isaac J. Holman to Letha B. Fuller
     22,       Thomas Tucker to Margret A. Pilate by Amos Small JP
     24,       Thomas F. Mitchel to Sarah H. Mosely by C.W.McGuire JP
     21,       Jacob L. Waggoner to Mary Ann Brown by A.W.Parkes JP
     24,       John Green to Martha Taylor by S.W.Arnold JP
     22,       Arabiam Graves to Elizabeth V. Solomon by W.J.H.Martin MG
1847
Jan  5,       William T. Grigory to Rebecca L. Hawes by E.N.Osburn ECC
1846
Dec 24,       Daniel Brazelton to Elinor N. Alexander
pg 137
     25,       Henry Smith to Alvessa Gunter
     30,       Solomon Brown to Catharine Daniel by Wm. Neeld JP
     31,       William W. Woodward to Susannah Hobbs by C.W.McGuire JP
     30,       Alfred Heathcock to Rebecca B. Watson by S.J.Bland JP
     30,       John C. Stephenson to Parthena E. Parker
     30,       Thomas C. Harper to Maryan A. Wilhoit by A.W.Parks JP
     31,       Hugh T. Kenedy to Jane West
```

```
        31,   James Spray to Lucinda Abbot
        31,   Joseph Wanslow to Mary Adkin
        31,   Watson Floyd to Ann R. Price
pg 138
        31,   Absolum Beard to Malinda E. Echols by H. Philips JP
1847
Jan  5,   William Cole to Mary Ann Rawles
     8,   Wm. J.A.Tapley to Mary N. Freeman by S.J.Bland JP
    25,   Turner B. Watson to Margret Ann Moores by Henry Turney
    14,   Eponetus Seamore to Elizabeth Temple by J.C.Stevenson
    15,   Lorenzie Harrison to Lucinda Smith by D. Jacks MG
    15,   George Dempsey to Cyntha Roach by Robert Drennon JP
    14,   James J. Gault to Mary Leonard by W.C.Jennings JP
    14,   John T. Leonard to Harriet Drinkard
pg 139
    14,   David W. Beck to Sarah Trantham
    14,   Richard Colvit to Sarah Brown by C.H.Edmondson JP
    21,   John Bradford to Martha C. Roach
    16,   Linley Couch to Selina Norman by S.W.Arnold JP
    16,   Hugh C. Gault to Jane Luttrell by W.C.Jennings JP
    19,   Robert B. George to Manerva Cole by D. Farrar JP
    20,   Andrew Loyd to Mary Ann Dukes
    21,   Solomon B. Sisk to Elviry Jane Hedgepeth by D. Farrar JP
    27,   Thomas W. Clarke to Mary Swinebroad by W. Burgess MG
    21,   Andy Cavin to Nancy Chapman
pg 140
    27,   Charles B. Hays to Sarah C. Blake by A.G.Gibson MG
    25,   Alfred M. Spencer to Nancy A. Call by J. Copeland MG
    26,   Robert L. Templeton to Elizabeth Snoddy
    26,   James C. Burton to Nancy F.S.Whitlock by A.W.Parkes JP
    26,   Joshua D. Brown to Sarah Anderson
    28,   Samuel R. Brown to Frances S. Ashby by John Weaver MG
    28,   William Eslick to Rosannah Shelton
Feb  5,   Stephen M. Bedford to Mariah C. Clay
     5,   Wiles J. Heathcock to Emily Parrish by S.J.Bland JP
     6,   William Austin to Nancy C. Martin
pg 141
     7,   Bennet Solomon to Clarinda Williams by Wm. Neeld JP
     8,   Jesse W. Martin to Sarah Millard
     8,   Martin Shipman to Cincinatta Sikes by John Bryan MG
    28,   George W. Street to Mary Ann Brown by S.W.Arnold JP
    18,   James A. Yergen to Mary E. Beggerly by W.R.Jones JP
    17,   John Burgess to Manerva Gess
    19,   Chesley Hamby to Eliza Carter by W.B. Rhea JP
    18,   William A. Walker to Mary A.M.Robertson by Martin
                                                  Towry MG
    25,   Richard Smith to Margret C. Fackener by S.W.Arnold JP
    26,   Thomas Larwood to Harriet McAfee by John McDaniel JP
pg 142
Mar  1,   George W. Puckett to Martha E. James
     2,   James C. McClelland to Sarah Beavers by B.F.Clark JP
     4,   Wm. N. Moore to Martha Johnson by W.C.Dunlap
     3,   Thomas J. Wells to Elizabeth J. Wells by John Weaver MG
     4,   Benjamin Buchanan to Elizabeth Smith by W.R.Bruce JP
     4,   Mathew T. Wilson to Elviry Jane Hughey by A.M.Pickens MG
    11,   Francis P. Drinkard to Josephine T. McMullin by John
                                               McDaniel MG
```

```
      15,    George W. Glasscock to Lucy C. Hanes by J. Ray MG
      12,    John Cravener to Amanda J. Swinford by J.D.Brown JP
      14,    Elijah Merrell to Lucinda Cook by Jeremiah Dean MG
pg 143
      14,    George R. Cowan to Julia A. Thomison by H.C.Cowan JP
      16,    William Cole to Jania Reddeck by D. Farrar JP
      16,    Joseph D. Dickson to Nancy M. Wear by Wm. D. Chadick MG
Apr 19,    William Harris to Mary C. Yerger by W.R.Jones JP
Mar 23,    George W. Wright to Elizabeth Bridges by Amos Small JP
      30,    James Martin to Lucinda Coffee by J. Dean MG
Apr  1,    John McNatt to Mary S. Winstead by Jesse Neese JP
       5,    issued: Robert Montgomery to Sarah Broadway by H.P.Penny JP
      15,    Joseph Stubblefield to Irena Scott by D.S.Gray JP
      20,    Green A. Pylant to Sarah Tucker by Amos Small JP
pg 144
      15,    William Good to Rachel Findley by W.R.Jones JP
      15,    Francis M. Ventress to Susan C. Parkes by Woodruff Parkes JP
      17,    Charles N.P.King to Eliza Smith by J. Dean MG
      21,    William M. McCallister to Verlenia McWhorter by A.S.
                                                          Randolph JP
May  1,    issued: Zangy McCastney to Elizabeth Gregory,
             returned: Apr 4th (should May 4) by A.G.Smith MG
       6,    William George to Nancy Perry by Wm. Gattis JP
       9,    Samuel Fanning to Sarah A. Ally by T.S.Williams JP
      12,    Fielding L. Butler to Louisa Gregory by W.R.Bruce JP
      13,    William Olliver to Caroline Jared by Wm. Neeld JP
      15,    John Luttrell to Almyra Couch by W.C.Jennings JP
pg 145
      20,    George W. Wilkins to Lucinda Weshshawn by John Weaver MG
      21,    Daniel J. Martin to Charlotte Black by Wm. Neeld JP
      24,    Ransom Ables to Sarah Sinkton by Wm. Neeld JP
      27,    Cullen C. Blades to Mary J. Moore by B.F.Clark JP
      31,    Robert H. Wheeler to Elizabeth L. Pinkerton by W.R.Jones
Jun  2,    A.C.Ross to Nancy A. Elam
       5,    Wm. R. Straton to Martha J. Smith by B.F.Clark JP
      16,    Henry Easley to Martha Davis by L.S.Woodward JP
       7,    Joel Bruice to E.A.Moore
      11,    Thomas H. King to Nancy A. Allison by Travis Ashby MG
pg 146
      12,    James E. Story to Sarah Story by Wm. Gattis JP
      14,    Wm. Bristen to Mary Heraldson by D. Farrar JP
Jul  1,    Francis W. Thompson to Susan J. Mead by Woodruff Parks JP
Jun 22,    John Hunt to Rachael Edens by J.R.McClure MG
      27,    James M. Crostwait to Jane Enochs by L.S.Woodward JP
      27,    Jesse Freeley to Elizabeth Crofford by S.T.Bland JP
      29,    Albert Bennet to Elizabeth Abbot by J. Dean MG
      29,    Garner M. McConnico to Jane H. Weare by W.D.Chaddrick MG
Jul  1,    Ahiagy B. Carter to Eliza B. White by T.S.Williams JP
       7,    James Sikes to Nancy Parker by A.W.Parkes JP
pg 147
       8,    William G. Roundtree to Mary E. Mayfield by A.W.Parkes JP
      29,    Wm. B. Allison to Susan C. Swinford by R.S.Brown JP
      29,    Wm. S. Murphy to Elizabeth L.A.McCoy by W.R.Bruce JP
Aug 10,    Bennet Whitaker to Margret Ann Ellis by W.H.Moores JP
      10,    Joseph V. Cowan to Nancy B. Webb
      10,    James Cunningham to Elizabeth Vaughn by A.S.Randolph JP
      12,    Francis M. Wade to Rosannah Wiles by Jesse Neese JP
```

1847

12,   Parker Campbell to Sarah Ann Womack by Alphus Merrell MG
14,   Abner S. Woodward to Caroline Clarke
26,   John Hamilton to Sarah Ann Medcalf by J.W.Hamilton JP
pg 148
21,   issued: Claibourn Harris to Alvelena Moore and
     returned: Aug 8 (should be Sep 8) by Alphus Merrell MG
24,   John W.M.Wham to Elizabeth M. Wilson
26,   Jenial P. Robinson to Catharine Emmons by Davis Smith JP
26,   Henry Sanders to Nancy M. Keller by Lee Walker JP
26,   Stephen A. Walker to Rebecca Jane Harris by W.R.Jones JP
Sep 1,   John W. Jean to Elizabeth Little by W. Parks JP
2,   Benjamin A. Beach to Mary Echols by G.R.Sloan JP
2,   George Whitaker to Ann Jane Higgins by Mat Hillman MG
2,   Hardy D. Turner to Della C. Good by W.R.Jones JP
2,   Quintin Marshall to Eliza Hill by A.G.Smith MG
pg 149
4,   Neill McCollum to Rebecca Dobbins
9,   Jesse Pearce to Elizabeth Rogers by J.W.Hamilton MG
9,   Michael Garrett to Martha Gibson by A.G.Gibson MG
9,   John Clark to Eliza C. Robertson by W.C.Dunlap MG
12,   John L. Pitts to Rachel J. Womack by W.B.Rhea JP
13,   James Arendale to Mahaley Heathcock by A.S.Randolph JP
16,   John R. Heathcock to Adeline Heathcock by A.S.Randolph JP
16,   John Turner to Spicy Colvit by Lee Walker JP
14,   Thomas J. Cummins to Margret Jane Rhea by G.W.R.Moore JP
14,   George W. Sawyers to Eliza Smith by B.F.Clark JP
pg 150
14,   Thomas W. Parkerson to Grissilda B. Sloan
16,   Wm. G. Hancock to Elizabeth Hudson
17,   Solomon B. Smith to Martha J. McElroy by S.J.Blair JP
16,   Elliot F. Moffett to Catherine Stewart by W.B.Rhea JP
23,   William Crownover to Rebecca Ann Hamilton by J.W.
                                        Hamilton JP
19,   Urias A. Wilson to Rebecca Price by J.A.Zivley JP
23,   Thomas Clark to Elizabeth Myers by Lee Walker JP
27,   Jasper N. Turner to Elizabeth McCan by N.P.Penny
26,   Joseph H. Greer to Mary M. Edmiston by W.C.Dunlap
28,   Benjamin Olliver to Elizabeth Peach by W.R.Jones JP
pg 151
30,   Andrew H. Armstrong to Mary Thomas by W.C.Dunlap MG
28,   Joseph A. Blakemore to Elizabeth T. Blakemore by
                                        D.L.Mitchel
Oct 3,   John Warden to Rachael Ashby by John Weaver MG
5,   Valentine C. Isom to Mary Camel by Woodruff Parkes JP
4,   John Vining to Ann S. Carty by W.D.Chadrick MG
12,   Charles B. Oliver to Esther E. McWhorter by Alphus Mizell
16,   Edward A. Isom to Eliza McAfee by Woodruff Parkes JP
14,   Sanford Renegar to Ruhama McCollum by Wm. Gattis JP
17,   James Hair to Nancy Sullivan by John Weaver MG
21,   Wm. S. Waggoner to Nancy C. Scivally by W. Jenkins VDM
pg 152
24,   William Wilson to Elizabeth Moores by C.W.McGuire JP
27,   Wm. H. Rosebrough to Frances N. Slack by Lemuel Brandon M
27,   Wm. Cobble to Mary Brazier by J.W.Holman
28,   John W. Wilhoit to Caroline Morris by Wm. Neeld JP
28,   John D. Gillam to Mary B. Holman by Woodruff Parkes JP
29,   Wm. Beavers to Charlotte Davis by John Kimes JP
Nov 2,   Arthur B. Shuffield to Sarah J. Sloan

4,	James A. Warren to Nancy McCarley by Wm. Neeld JP
4,	James Caughran to Fanny Campbell by David Farrar JP
16,	Francis M. Tucker to Nancy McClure by Wm. Gattis JP

pg 153

7,	Wm. Ashworth to Penolope Hardin by John Moores JP
12,	Green P. Rice to Sarah Ann Baptist by J.A.Zivley JP
14,	Micajah Ezell to Emily Green by Spencer Leatherwood JP
16,	James J. Allbright to Martha Hamlin by Robert Drennon JP
18,	Jackson Luttrell to Julia Ann Webb by John Weaver MG
25,	Harvey Green to Caroline Myrick by T.L.Williams JP
24,	Walker Jones to Mary B. Coulter by John Weaver MG
22,	Thomas Webb to Julia A. Harrel by J.J.Brown JP
25,	John Felps to Malinda Wright by G.W.B.Moore JP
24,	James Marr to Martha Richardson by J. Weaver MG
25,	Thomas R. Tucker to Roda Easlick

pg 154

27,	Wm. C. Jackson to Samantha E. Franklin
Dec 22,	James J. Owen to Mary Ann Moore by J. McDaniel JP
9,	James D. Dollins to Sarah E. Harbin by Amos Small JP
9,	Newton Luttrell to Juliana Howard by T.S.Williams JP
14,	Jesse Graves to Ellen Hiat by Wm. Gale MG
16,	Wm. J. Mattox to Martha Lee by B.G.Alsup JP
16,	Montgomery C. Forbes to Jane McDaniel
23,	Robert Templeton to Nancy Meeks by A.S.Randolph JP
20,	Wm. Goldsby to Nancy C. Adkins
21,	James G. Harrison to Jane K. Hudson by Amos Small JP

pg 155

28,	Wm. Richardson to Nancy Raney by John Weaver MG
26,	Robert Boyce to Rachel Holman by Wm. Neeld JP
25,	James W. Troup to Sarah Louisa Blades by C. Smith JP
27,	Wm. C. Sanders to Mary Ann Porch by W. Dyer JP

1848
Jan 4, Samuel Bates to Mary Ann Bostick by Martin Towry
1847
Dec 30, Robert Jacobs to Mary Jane Morris by B.F.Clark JP
1848
Jan 2,	Elsworth R. Kennon to Nancy C. Murdock by W.J.H.Martin MG
3,	George W.N.Moore to Martha King
4,	Hugh Parkerson to Lucinda E. Sloan
5,	Levi Benson to Susan Howell by Lee Walker JP

pg 156

7,	Starlin A. Warren to Celia Pulley by Wm. Gattis JP
6,	James E. English to Margaret Caughran
9,	Abraham James to Susannah M. Walker by Martin Towry
9,	Albert S. Anderson to Rebecca E. Enochs by L.S.Woodward JP
8,	Joshua McDaniel to Mary C. Anderson by G.W.Puckett MG
10,	C.W.Westmoreland to Margaret E. Davis
19,	George W. Scott to Elizabeth Stone
13,	James R. Reese to Elizabeth Reese by John Weaver MG
13,	Henry Jones to Margaret Johnson by J.F.Buckner JP
13,	James Henderson to Mary Monks by Martin Towery

pg 157

13,	John L. Cochran to Mary T. Wiley
17,	Bartin W. Heathcock to Jincy D. Cannon by A.S.Randolph JP
20,	John Foster to Mary E. Nichols by G.W.R.Moore MG
17,	John H. Jobe to Nancy P. Gleghorn
20,	Henry Beasley to Rachel M. Corder by T.L.Williams JP

34   1848

|---|---|
25,	Thomas C. Loyd to Emeline Warren by Wm. Gattis JP
27,	Wm. T. Smith to Catharine E. Brown by J.E.Douthit MG
24,	David C. Hall to Jane Russell
25,	Theopelus Harris to Eliza E. Stewart by D.L.Mitchel MG
27,	James L. Hogan to Loumanda P. Wright by Davis Smith JP

pg 158

29,	Wm. Allen to Elizabeth Ann Rhea by Stephen M. Dance MG
27,	Noah Gold to Sarah E.C.Ellis by G.W.R.Moore JP
27,	Henry J. Barnes to Nancy S. Gilliam by Thos. Childs
27,	Eli K. McCollough to Catharine Holt by W.R.Jones JP
29,	Massey Copeland to Eade E. Tucker by J.W.Holman JP
Feb 1,	James H. Kidd to Monica Tate
2,	Francis M. Hamilton to Elizabeth Ramsey by S.Leatherwood JP
4,	Andrew J. Cox to Mary Stone by D. Jacks MG
3,	Isaac L. Moyers to Lavina VanHoozer by G.W.Puckett MG
3,	George L. Cunningham to Elizabeth Dudley by L.S.Woodward

pg 159

4,	James Dennis to Elizabeth McCollough by W.C.Jennings JP
22,	Nathan F. Gibson to Elizabeth A. Sorrells by G.W.R.Moore
10,	James Rutledge to Sarah Bandy by John Weaver JP
10,	Robert T. Proctor to Margaret L. Thomas by W.C.Dunlap MG
10,	Wm. Howard to Sarah Jane Stegall by M.Henry Sumner MG
8,	Wm. P. Moore to Margret Buchanan by A.G.Gibson MG
8,	Thomas L.D.Parks,Jr. to Rebecca Gray
17,	Henry C. Judy to Nancy E. Clarke by B.M.G.Alsup JP
10,	Wm. Smith to Huldy W. Lunsford by Wm. Gattis JP
17,	Winfield S. Honeycut to Lucinda Smith by Wm.Levesgul MG

pg 160

14,	Gedion Prince to Mary Russell by Wm. Neeld JP
14,	Martin Massey to Nancy Abbot by J. Dean MG
24,	David Waggoner to Jane Felps by Samuel Boone JP
24,	Wm. Nichols to Phebe Massey by G.W.R.Moore JP
24,	Philip T. Phagan to Martha Ann Taylor
24,	George Kirklin to Susan Patterson by L.S.Woodward JP
26,	John Edmiston to Mary E. Fullerton by W.J.H.Martin MG
28,	W.J.Gallaway to Mary Ann Lindsley
Mar 8,	Ezekiah H. Ervin to Sarah Rainey by L.S.Woodward JP
9,	Samuel Martin to Martha Marova by A.S.Randolph JP

pg 161

8,	James H. Pope to Elsina J. Stephenson by G.W.Puckett MG
9,	James Rutledge to Martha Jane Hulsey by Woodruff Parkes JP
10,	Wm. Petty to Ann Roberta Ricks
11,	Austin A. Shipp to Sarah Ann McElroy
14,	Aaron Alexander to Elizabeth M. Shook by A.G.Gibson MG
17,	Wm. T. Runnels to Elizabeth Gamble
21,	Wm. L. Alexander to Elizabeth Steelman by Woodruff Parks
21,	Andrew Fleming to Louisa Hoots by Woodruff Parks JP
22,	John H. Stewart to Mary A.O.McNeil
Apr 1,	Calvin Lee to Clarissa H. Hanks by B.M.G.Alsup

pg 162

13,	Newton F. Neil to Virginia Marshall by W.C.Dunlap MG
14,	Ambrose James to Jane McBride by Spencer Leatherwood JP
17,	Washington Wilson to Mary Hughey
20,	John Sims to Martha A. Wicks by John Moore JP
23,	Nicholas Burns to Elizabeth Wilson by John Weaver MG
26,	Wm. M. Phillips to Mary Walker by Martin Towery MG
27,	James J. Finney to Martha P. Cole by Daniel Farrar JP

May 1,   Wm. A. Hopper to Julian Paysinger
    15,   John C. Ennis to Parthenia Hughey
    16,   John V. Copeland to Mary Potter
pg 163
    21,   Temple Taylor to Jane Shelton by T.S.Williams JP
    25,   Hardin Hampton to Delia E. Pigg
    27,   Ephraim B. Bryan to Susan Shipp
    31,   James A. Prosser to Rebecca W. Bagley by Lewis Newsom JP
Jun 6,   John Sherrell to Martha A.L.Moore by A.G.Gibson MG
    20,   T.S.Corder to Julia Ann Corder by T.S.Williams JP
    28,   Josiah Ellis to Sarah Bradford by G.W.R.Moore JP
Jul 6,   F.A.Dickinson to Amanda J. Smith by W.C.Dunlap MG
     6,   John Coleman to Elizabeth Kensley
     9,   John G. Glidwell to Sarah Durham by G.W.R.Moore JP
pg 164
    11,   John R. Austin to Nancy E. Barns by G.W.R.Moore JP
    12,   Wm. C. Fanning to Martha Luttrell by T.S.Williams JP
    13,   Austin Eslick to Caroline Wilkerson by Young T. Taylor JP
    14,   Hugh W. Thompson to Sarah A.E.Nowls by Young T. Taylor JP
    19,   Joab Moore to Martha Webster by J.H.Buckner
    18,   James Miller to Elizabeth Soronipshear by Wm. Neeld JP
    18,   Pearson Milton to Nancy Huckabee by B.M.G.Alsup JP
    18,   Robert K. Pitts to Elizabeth A. Locker by W.W.Parks JP
    19,   Samuel L. Wilson to Lucretia H. Randolph by A.S.Sloan MG
    20,   Wm. Broadway to Lucinda Polly by Martin Towery MG
pg 165
    27,   Solomon George to Mary Gray by A.Downing JP
    25,   Charles T. Reese to Eliza Delana
    29,   James C. Simmons to Martha Jane Davidson by G.W.R.Moore JP
    27,   Wm. H. Bagley to Martha A. Leftwich by R.M.Whitman Min.
    26,   Thomas Chasteen to Sarah Brinage by D.S.Gray JP
Aug 2,   Nicholas M. Evans to Martha Pierce by D.S.Gray JP
     1,   Robert B. Nelson to Mary Nelson by M.D.Chaddock MG
     3,   James B. Armstrong to Manerva Jane Bonner by G.W.R.Moore
     3,   Mathew M. Cowley to Caroline Warren
     9,   Wm. W. Mullins to Emily Locke
pg 166
    14,   Wm. A. January to Emeline Gibson by D.S.Gray JP
    15,   John B. Bandy to Elizabeth Adcock by Woodruff Parks JP
    13,   Andrew Burns to Eveline Perry by G.W.R.Moore JP
    13,   Williamson Rich to Mary F. Brown by Joseph Dameron JP
    15,   Jasper N. Felps to Caroline Anthony by R.M.Whitman
    16,   Wilson P. Sawyers to Elizabeth Whitaker
    17,   Jacob T. Wright to Judith Buchanan by A.J.Gilmore MG
    20,   George P. Hunter to Cincinnata Howard by T.S.Williams JP
    21,   Neil McCollum to Eliza Neill
    23,   Josiah Wells to Elmyra Trail by Samuel Barns JP
pg 167
    22,   Thomas M. Story to Lucy Cunningham
    24,   Wm. J. Brown to Elizabeth Sullivan by Woodruff Parkes JP
    25,   Jeremiah L. Daughtery to Minney Hardin
    29,   Wm. J.W.Dollinson to Elizabeth E. Gibson by G.W.R.Moore JP
    31,   Anthony Bates to Harriet C. Rutledge by John Weaver MG
Sep 7,   James R. Smith to Malinda Copeland
     7,   John N. Brown to Eliza Solomon by W.W.Parkes JP
     5,   Wm. McGowen to Lucinda Clarke by W.A.Gill MG
     5,   John F. Jenkins to Mariah Haley by Martin Towery

	7,	Thomas H. McGaugh to Mary V. Houston by A.G.Smith JP
	7,	Norman H. Whittenberg to Malvira C. Cunningham by
		Swenson MG

pg 168

	7,	John Holly to Susan K. King
	7,	Henry A. McLin to Katharine Toole by A.G.Gibson MG
	7,	Charles Miller to Mary Ann Hamby
	19,	David Tripp to Nancy A. Braden by Rev. J. Scivally
	13,	Robert M. Shelton to Nancy A. Hughs by A.J.Gilmore MG
	14,	Robert M. Hague to Cordelia J. Alexander by Matt Marshall
	20,	Thomas J. Carter to Margret M. Neeld by A.J.Gilmore MG
	21,	Zachariah Arnold to Sarah C. Hunt by J.W.Holman MG
	25,	Wm. M. Spencer to Elizabeth Jane Frame by J.W.Holman MG
	28,	Ezra Cole to Elizabeth Cole by Daniel Farrar JP
Nov	13,	John Clinto to Arletia Jarvis by John Weaver MG

pg 169

Oct	2,	J.C.McElroy to Sinthey S.A.Smith
	5,	John Baker to Mary Jane Brim by Lewis Newsom JP
	10,	Wm. Bearden to Nancy Glidewell by G.W.R.Moore JP
	5,	J.W.M.Dance to Mary C. Baxter by S.C.Dickson MG
	5,	Wm. W. Wilson to Manerva Ann Whiteside by D. Farrar JP
	12,	David Rudd to Emily Stone by Dempsey Sullivan JP
	10,	Alexander P. Groce to Nancy Spence
	12,	Alfred J. Partin to Mary Alsup by T.P.Sumners JP
	15,	Felix M. Cook to Virginia Chamberland by J. Saintclair JP
	15,	Wm. J. Hughs to Margret A. Cowan by John Davis MG

pg 170

	23,	Robert Norvill to Martha M. Morris by Ira E. Douthit MG
	24,	Jacob W. Moore to Frances G. Hardy by J.W.Ogden MG
	24,	Logan Carpenter to Mary McDaniel
	26,	Thomas Gold to Mary Bradshaw by G.W.R.Moore JP
	26,	Edward Snow to Mahaly Mattox
	30,	Anderson Davis to Martha Ann Warren by Lewis Newsom JP
	28,	Anthony Crawford to Elizabeth Cashion by J.W.Holman JP
Nov	2,	Wm. M. Scivally to Malinda Gray by J.A.Saintclair JP
Oct	31,	Drury Leatherwood to Elizabeth Leatherwood
Nov	2,	George Gant to Emeline Rosebrough
	2,	Joseph Scott to Emily Price

pg 171

1849

Jan	4,	Wm. H. Bailey to Eliza Reese by Samuel Boone JP
	4,	Wm. B. Cole to Mary Ann Armstrong by Amos Small JP
	4,	Charles M. Collier to Elvira Borough by John Weaver MG
	4,	John Clanton to Elizabeth Houston by A.G.Smith MG
	11,	Young A. Taylor to Elizabeth E. Stiles by Young T.Taylor
	10,	Wm. R. Shaw to Louisa E. Parkes
	11,	Felix McP. Crawford to Martha M. Malier by A.G.Gibson MG
	14,	Elijah Warren to Elizabeth Rainey by Dempsey Sullivan
	11,	Hiram T. Hunnicut to Pharaba Yorke by Wm. Laresgen MG
	18,	George W. Maderas to Sarah C.E.Blakemore by Wm.A.Gill MG

pg 172

	15,	Mathew Raiburn to Manerva Bevil by John Kimes JP
	17,	Samuel Webb to Henretta Nicks
	23,	Andrew C. Gleghorn to Sarah C. White
	25,	Nathan Petty to Louisa Sanders by Wm. Dyer JP

	24,	George W. Reese to Manerva C. Hedgepeth
	25,	Wm. H. Webb to Mary Brown
	25,	Edmond D. Larwood to Louisa Murdock by P.W.Walton JP
	30,	Joseph W. Trigg to Eliza Robertson by Wm. Gale MG
	31,	Wm. H. Wade to Margaret A. Mills by John Weaver MG
Feb	4,	John M. Renegar to Sarah Ann Franklin by T.S.Williams JP

pg 173

	3,	Anderson Fitch to Nancy Crabtree
	7,	James A. Silvertooth to Sarah A. Waggoner by J.Brandon
	14,	John A. Woodall to Delilah Langston by John Moore JP
	12,	John Oldfield to Abegail Stone
	13,	Jesse L. Jean to Mary Jane Jones by John Mathews JP
	22,	Stephen L. Wiles to Elizabeth A. Mills by John Weaver MG
	15,	Wm. M. Hardin to Margaret M. Killpatrick by D. Jacks MG
	15,	Alexander F. Collins to Sarah A. Sanders by P.W.Walton JP
	14,	Arch A. Johnson to Mary A. McKinney
	22,	Rederick P. Taylor to Tempy Marshall by Woodruff Parks JP

pg 174

	25,	Joseph George to Elizabeth Mullins
Mar	1,	Henry S. Blakemore to Martha M. Pratt by Wm. A. Gill MG
Feb	28,	George P. Mooney to Lucy Wofford by D. Farrar JP
Mar	1,	George Gant to Catharine Withers by M. Marshall
May	4,	John A. Porch to Calledona Caudle by Wm. Dyer JP
Mar	14,	Archibald S. Sloan to Elizabeth J. Sloan by H.Bryson MG
	17,	Thomas G. Bracken to Martha A. Crawford by John Kimes JP
	17,	Caswell Birmingham to Nancy E. Weaver
	27,	Lewis C. Williamson to Martha J. Bonds by J.C.Stevenson
	27,	Martin L. Forehand to Manerva A. Ezell by J.C.Stevenson

pg 175

	28,	Andrew S. Montgomery to Lavina G. Tate
	28,	Williamson Colier to Jane Rainey by Lewis Newsom JP
Apr	3,	James McNatt to Louisa Prosser by John Weaver MG
	10,	Andrew J. Solomon to Elizabeth Ann Young by A.S.Randolph JP
	19,	John H. Price to Chaney S. Blakemore by Wm.A. Gill MG
	23,	James W. Bruce to Mary Ann Saintclair
May	2,	A.J.Beaver to Martha Hampton
	9,	Willis D. Cole to Nancy J. Phillips by A.G.Downing JP
	27,	John B. Copeland to Elizabeth Michael by John Rees JP
	14,	Elihu Gleghorn to Mary Ann Smith

pg 176

	15,	Wm. Philpot to Mariah B. Webb
	16,	John H. Drenan to Maria E. Yeager by A.S.Sloan
	18,	Franklin A. George to Elizabeth J. Allison by J.N.George
	24,	John R. Ransom to Susannah J. Wiley by A.S.Sloan
	31,	Lilburn L. Clark to Margaret Buchanan by A.G.Smith
Jun	3,	Morgan Reavis to Mary Moore by G.W.R.Moore JP
	3,	Joseph Scott to Rebecca Brim by John Mathews
	5,	Eldrige S. Williams to Elizabeth J. Lee by J.N.George JP
	4,	Alexander M. Bedford to Elizabeth Warren by Lewis Newsom
	9,	Jasper R. Bates to Eliza J. Williams by Wm. Dyer JP

pg 177

	13,	George V. Webb to Jane Yell by John Mathews
	14,	George W. Moyers to Susan McClain
	21,	Thomas R. Robinson to Sarah B. Hamilton by H. Larkin
	24,	Eli Trip to Mary Jane Young by Wm. Gale MG
	24,	Ive Jefferson Harrel to Sarah Forrester by John Weaver JP
	26,	Robert N. Whitaker to Cornelia S. Grantland by J.W.Holman

Jul 4,   Thomas B. Pitts to Sarah Ann E. Coulter by W.B.Rhea JP
    10,   Jacob B. Corder to Sarah McClure by T.S.Williams JP
    10,   Joseph H. Renegar to Nancy E. Taylor by Young T.Taylor JP
    14,   John Brown to Sarah Price by John Weaver MG
pg 178
    15,   Allen McElroy to Luticia Mayfield by W.J.Saintclair JP
    19,   Jacob Wagoner to Louisa Logan by Dempsey Sullivan JP
    17,   Nathaniel Hobbs to Margret Hampton by J.N.George
    19,   James Bradley to Elizabeth Cunningham by Robert Drennon JP
    19,   Stephen Chinnault to Sarah C. Cox by S. Leatherwood JP
    19,   Ruben Stuman to Leah Jane Scivally by Wm. Gale MG
    19,   James McCollister to Eliza Ann McWhorter by A.S.Randolph
    25,   Joseph P. Allison to Margret A. McKenzie by D.L.Mitchel
    31,   David Jones to Sarah Colbert by W.R.Jones JP
Aug 5,   Samuel Stafford to Elizabeth Chapman by D.S.Gray JP
pg 179
     6,   Joel J. Jones to Sarah F. Hall by W.A.Gill MG
     9,   Robert A. Irvin to Nancy H. Brown
     9,   Bryant Hinkle to Jamima Pritchett by J.W.Holman JP
     9,   Wm. A. McClelland to Martha S. Randolph by R. Drennon JP
    14,   James S. Moore to Sarah J. Simpson by L. Brandon MG
    19,   James R. Morris to Emily Pruitt by W.C.Jennings JP
    19,   Calvin Street to Sarah C. Bland by W.R.Jones JP
    18,   Thomas Franklin to Nancy Stubblefield
    20,   Woodroof Parkes to Dovey Cashion by M.J.Copeland MG
    21,   John C. Mottox to Tabitha J. Davis by J.C.Reeves JP
pg 180
    30,   Martin L. Parkes to Malindy M. Timmons by Ira E. Douthit
    21,   Ambrose L. Parkes to Nancy M. Walker
    23,   Wm. S. Hess to Eliza M.J.Edwards by John Mathews
    25,   Benjamin F. Hudson to Rebecca D. Dobbins by John McDaniel
    26,   Zachariah J. Arnold to Martha C. Smith by W.C.Jennings JP
    26,   John March to Nancy H. Price by A.G.Smith
    28,   Crofford Carter to Elizabeth Noblin by Martin Towery MG
    28,   A.E.Moore to N.J.Motlow
    30,   George F. Smith to Judith A. Metcalfe by S.R.Chaddick MG
    31,   John W. Pool to Mary Williams by Robert Drennon JP
pg 181
Sep 4,   John E. Gore to Jane M. Cunningham by Ira E. Douthit
Aug 31,   Benjamin M.Eddens to Pauline D. Blythe
Sep 4,   Benjamin F. Solomon to Nancy H. Whitaker by W.B.Rhea JP
     5,   General S. Marcom to Minerva Hedgepeth by Matthew Wilson JP
     7,   James N. George to Nancy H. McGuire by D. Farrar JP
    13,   Spencer G. Rogers to Lucy A. Hill by Rev. J. Scivally
    13,   Wm. Parks to Elizabeth Phillips by W.B.Rhea JP
    14,   James M. Gold to Harriet E. Bradshaw by Jacob Gillespie JP
    13,   Mitchell Edde to Eliza J. Jenkins by J.W.Holman MG
    13,   James Blythe to Candis C. Timmins by J.W.Holman MG
pg 182
    30,   George W. Fluty to Nancy E. Trimble by T.P.Sumners JP
    20,   James Yates to Almeta Lopey by Martin Towery MG
    20,   Wm. P. Beck to Lucy J. Hughs by John Mathews MG
    20,   John R. Smith to Martha Moyers by A.S.Randolph
    26,   Wm. M. Lemonds to Louisa Kincaide by Mathew Trantham MG
    27,   Nathaniel Hopper to Elainor B. Clark by B.F.Clark JP
    27,   Wm. M. Browning to Rachel M. Simpson by J.W.Spearman MG
    25,   John P. Holman to Elizabeth G. Wilson by Woodroof Parkes JP

        27,   Brice C. Martin to Frances R. Moores by W.C.Dunlap
        27,   Hugh Moore to Mary Ann Steed by W.C.Dunlap
pg 183
        29,   Joseph C. Whitaker to Sarah Jane Moores
Oct 3,   Calvin Jeans to Louisa McCown
         6,   Wm. Cunningham to Emariah Brown
         9,   Daniel H. Bearden to Mary Ann Blake by A.G.Gibson MG
        11,   James S. Findley to Lucy J. Lemonds by P.W.Walton JP
         9,   Daniel Maddox to Mary Jane Eddings
         9,   Allen Stevenson to Nancy M. Sumners by J.W.Holman MG
         9,   Benjamin Handcock to Elizabeth Hay by A.G.Smith
         9,   James L. Spence to Mary Ann McCormack
         9,   John M. Hopper to Martha A. Ramsey by Thomas Childs
pg 184
         9,   James F. Renfrow to Esther Moore by W.C.Dunlap
        10,   Sander Taylor to Charlotte Simmons by W.C.Jennings JP
        16,   Isaah Hancock to Martha E. Haley by A.F.Driskell
        14,   Wm. F. Steed to Emaline Ward by A.J.Saintclair JP
        18,   Benjamin Sullivan to Emeline Marrs by John Weaver MG
        15,   R.J.Nelson to Mary F. McKennon
Nov 1,   Smith Scoggins to Eleanor Holt by Martin Towery
Oct 18,   Philip Bolick to Elizabeth McCown
        24,   Stephen C. Smith to Elizabeth Ellis by John Kimes JP
        25,   Ephraim C. King to Sarah Jane Bagley by H.H.Rives JP
pg 185
        24,   Stephen B. Wilson to Rebecca E. Wamack by J.A.
                                                    Saintclair JP
        23,   James M. Wickes to Mary Ann Hays by Wm. Dyer
Nov 1,   Franklin Stevenson to Elizabeth A. Norwood by A.G.Gibson
Oct 29,   Haisting Roane to Eliza Deshager by W.R.Jones JP
        31,   Wm. D. Brown to Mary C. Wordlow by John Weaver MG
        31,   Jesse Austin to Mahala Brim by G.W.R.Moore JP
Nov 1,   Joseph M. Robertson to Nancy Ann E. Williams by T.S.
                                                    Williams
Oct 31,   George W. Brown to Catharine Maroney by A.S.Randolph JP
Nov 5,   Wesley Bresten to Nancy Noblin by Martin Towery
         4,   Wm. Moffett, Jr. to Susan E. Clift by John Kimes JP
         5,   Mathew Wilson to Jane Gragg by D.S.Hobbs JP
pg 186
         6,   James N. Blackwell to Elizabeth Scott
        14,   John F. Floyd to Aremantha T. Cole by D.L.Mitchell MG
        13,   Robert Crofford to Mary M. Phillips by John Kimes JP
        14,   Joseph Baker to Martha Brown
        18,   Isaac M. Jones to Elizabeth S. Lane by J.D.Davis MG
        18,   John Wagoner to Nancy C. Wagoner by D.B.Cooper JP
        19,   Thomas B. Buffalo to Martha R. Turner
        19,   John A. Carter to Nancy A. Gibson by A.G.Gibson MG
        22,   Isaac N. Siler to Charlotte M. Jennings by S.W.Arnold JP
        27,   Henry M. Morris to Elizabeth Parkes
pg 187
        27,   Alfred N. Mosley to Mary Franklin
        27,   Samuel A. Slaughter to Martha Claborn by S.R.Chaddick MG
        29,   Jacob Lock to Sarah Mullins by A.G.Downing JP
Dec 4,   H.W.Shuffield to Elizabeth M. Bland by W.R.Jones JP
         6,   Wm. A. Parker to Martha Sullivan by John Weaver MG
        10,   Wm. B. Griffin to Louisa J. Martin by G.W.R.Moore JP
        11,   Jefferson L. Rhea to Frances E. Cox by John Corder JP

```
        11,    Robert A. Overby to Mary M. Brown
        11,    James A. Cooper to Eliza H. Colman by M. Wilson JP
        12,    John Ramsey to Elen P. Hopper by B.F.Clark JP
  pg 188
        13,    Henry Trantham to Emmy E. Rice by J.C.Reeves JP
        13,    John Weaver to Mary B. Swanner by John Weaver MG
        13,    Pleasant Marberry to Selina A.S.Hall by John Moore JP
        18,    Richard Forbes by Elizabeth Montgomery
        18,    Andrew A. Dollins to Sarah J. Armstrong by A.G.Downing JP
        20,    Amon A. Williams to Mary T. George by J.N.George
        23,    John Mitchel to Margaret Smith by J.N.George
        19,    Joel R. Bruce to Sarah Coal(Cole)
        19,    George Perry to Eliza Duke
        20,    Wm. S. Raymond to Nancy J. McCalla by A.S.Sloan
  pg 189
        20,    A.J.Gillmore to Louisa J. Franklin by G.W.Winn MG
        23,    Wm. D. Baldin to Nancy C. McWhorter by A.L.Randolph JP
        21,    Wm. C. West to Julia Ann Taylor
        24,    Wm. R. Collins to Annice M. Parkes by Ira E. Douthit MG
        25,    Samuel P. McCullough to Eliza Strong by A.S.Sloan
        22,    Michael Miller to Jane M. Jennings by S.R.Chaddick MG
        24,    Washington Aikins to Lucinda Scott
        28,    Thomas J. Parham to Louisa B. Davis by Thomas Childs MG
        27,    Willis A. Carter to Elizabeth M. Strong by D.B.Cooper JP
        27,    Lewis A. Cameron to Susan C. McMillen by A.S.Sloan
  pg 190
        28,    Green Bolin to Luvena Miars by John C. Reeves JP
        29,    George J. McCarver to Mary Ann Lee
        31,    Daniel Carmicle to Susan S. Dandrige by A.G.Downing JP
  1850
  Jan  1,    Wm. McCartney to Milley Parrish by W.R.Jones JP
        2,    Elijah Pamplin to Sarah R. Hall by D.S.Hobbs JP
        2,    Asa Smith to Rhodica Perry
        2,    George W. Lewis to Ruthy Church
        2,    John H. Sullinger to Penny Ann Carter by D.B.Cooper JP
       10,    Henry J. Rich to Celia E. Damron by Wm. Gale MG
        7,    Albert W. Cheatam to Sarah E. Kennon by A.W.Smith Esq
  pg 191
       10,    Henry A. Grigg to Mary Moore by John Weaver MG
       10,    Samuel B. Grigg to Elizabeth Moore by John Weaver MG
        9,    Westly Franklin to Eliza Jane McCarver
       10,    James N. Powel to Mary C. Davis by H.C.Cowen JP
       17,    Kennelen T. Harrison to Sarah Jane Duke by Young T.
                                                        Taylor JP
       17,    E.N.Crawford to Mary J. McElroy by H.C.Cowen JP
       17,    Robert Fullerton to Mary P. Lauderdale by A.W.Smith
       22,    Calvin Graham to Mary S. Wicks by H. Larkin
       24,    Willis H. Echols to Elizabeth D. Smith by W.H.Moores JP
       24,    Doke Hoots to Manda J. McAfee by Woodroof Parkes JP
  pg 192
       31,    James P. Curry to America Jane Walker by Ira E. Douthit
       31,    Samuel C. Strong to Sarah E. Carter by D.B.Cooper JP
       30,    Robert M. McMullin to Matilda Woodroof by A.S.Sloan
  Feb  3,    Jesse Michael to Mary Warren by G.W.R.Moores JP
        4,    George Sanders to Elizabeth Clouch by Lee Walker JP
        7,    Wm. Duncan to Margaret F. Yeates by W.R.Jones JP
       19,    Allen Parker to Emily E. Crawford by H.C.Cowen JP
```

```
        13,   Robert C. Davis to Narcissa C. Mills by John Kimes JP
        14,   Silvester McKinney to Margret A. Roan by W.W.Parker JP
        16,   John M. Smith to Elizabeth Snoddy
pg 193
        21,   John W. Fanning to Elizabeth Snoddy by John Corder JP
        21,   Samuel Weaver to Letty B. Swanner by J.C.Reeves JP
        28,   David P. Tooly to Emily C. Wright by Wm. Dyer Esq
Mar  4,   Zebuda Mulder to Eliza J. McCowen
        10,   Charles Rayerster to Mary Jane Gibson by A.G.Gibson MG
        13,   Edmond G. Runnels to Lucy Gamell by J.A.Saintclair JP
        12,   James C. King to Sarah Evans by G.W.R.Moore JP
        14,   Henry Snow to Martha Ann Partin by J.W.Holman MG
        19,   Baily Rains to Sarah Mallard
        31,   Wm. D. Bates to Editha Nicks by Amos Small JP
pg 194
Apr  1,   John J. Gassaway to Elizabeth Landreth by D.B.Cooper JP
         7,   A.J.Childress to Margaret George by A.G.Downing JP
        17,   Wm. N. Jester to Mary E.A.Wells by W.A.Gill MG
        16,   S.G.McLeroy to Lucy Ann Woodard by A.G.Smith MG
        17,   John Clarke to Mary Ann Sullivan by W.H.Moores JP
        19,   Lemuel P.M.Dennis to Alpha A. McGee by W.H.Moores JP
        22,   Wm. R. Hudlow to Elizabeth M. Gabner
        25,   James D. Campbell to Mary Jane Faulkner by Woodroof
                                                                  Parkes MG
        24,   John Smith to Rebecca Rogers by Leroy Jones MG
        30,   A. Sanford to Martha A. Jeans by W.B.Rhea JP
pg 195
May  3,   Wm. Stone to Sarah Gore
         4,   James C. Lee to Penina E. Williams by J.N.George JP
         9,   Henry Nichols to Malinda Sorrels by John Wagster MG
        18,   Bryant Taylor to Nancy Hughs by Mathew Wilson JP
        23,   Wm. A. Brown to Margret A. Keith by John Weaver MG
Jun  2,   John W. King to Caroline Johnson by D.B.Cooper JP
         4,   Mitchel Collins to Mary A. Thompson by J.A.Saintclair JP
         9,   Johnathan Langston to Eliza Woodall by John Corder JP
         9,   Paschal White to Malissa Arnold by John Corder JP
         8,   James T. Clark to Sarah Webb
        10,   L.P.Johnson to Nancy Martin
pg 196
        19,   James M. Stephenson to Jaily Whitworth by Lee Walker JP
        19,   Benjamin March to Sarah E. Wilson
        23,   James P. Holman to Emily P. Price by A.W.Smith
Jul  1,   James C. Reece to Louisa McAfee by J.C.Reeves JP
         3,   Caleb Z. Webb to Eliza Jane Kilpatrick
         5,   John Nichols to Malinda Pearce by Young T. Taylor JP
         4,   John R. Smith to Margret E. Endsly by Thomas Chiles MG
        11,   George W. Higgins to Sarah L. Stone by W.H.Moores JP
        18,   George O. McDaniel to Minerva Dillon by Martin Towery MG
        15,   Wm. A. Philips to Martha A. Burr by Lewis Newsom JP
pg 197
        16,   James E. Smith to Nancy Raney by D. Sullivan JP
        18,   Wm. McClusky to Nancy A. Towery by Wm. Pryor JP
        22,   Jesse L. Grammer to Rachel Price by D. Sullivan JP
        23,   James M. Barham to Mary Jane King by G.W.R.Moore JP
        25,   Wesley Lock to Emily Miller by P.P.Riddle JP
        25,   Benjamin Rowe to Matilda Smith
Aug  1,   Wm. Steelman to Ann Miles by Woodroof Parks JP
```

```
        2,    Samuel Shelton to Sarah Cooper by John Moore JP
        1,    Campbell F. Edmiston to Margaret E. Buchanan by
                                        Jacob Gillespie JP
        7,    Abel R. Smith to Nancy K. Reese by John Weaver MG
pg 198
        8,    James C. Robison to Martha Hopper
       13,    Wm. M. Smith to Emeline Koonce by W.W.Parks JP
       17,    Amon Heirs to Denoah Myers by John Weaver MG
       18,    James M. Smith to Nancy E. Michael by D.S.Gray JP
       22,    Wm. E. Bradford to Mary Reece by B.F.Clark JP
       22,    Samuel S. Smith to Cintha A. McElroy by A.G.Smith MG
Sep 11,    Wm. H. Smith to Amanda S. Norris by W.J.Mitchell JP
        1,    Wiley Cunningham to Jane Smith by J.N.George JP
        3,    Milton N. Moore to Elizabeth L. Moore by I.E.Douthit MG
       22,    Jesse Eaton to Sarah Cox by John Bryson MG
pg 199
        6,    Silas Bryant to Tabitha Harris by Joseph Scott JP
        7,    Wm. A. Morrison to Mary Hardy
       11,    Stephen G. Tankersly to Manerva Graham by H. Larkin
       11,    James A. Tankersly to Sarena Graham by H. Larkin
       12,    John F. Robertson to Margaret A. Dameron by H. Larkin
       10,    Thomas Roland to Permelia Smith by Y.T.Taylor JP
       12,    Jordin C. Holt to Jane Waggoner by Samuel Boone JP
       12,    Dolphus A. Stone to Dorthaney Strong
       22,    Reubin G. Bryant to Jane Logan by L. Sullivan JP
       16,    James Edens to Mary R. Landers
pg 200
       16,    Horace L. Benedict to Nancy Hobbs
       22,    Andrew J. Davidson to Mary E. Abbot by J. McDaniel
       24,    Wm. R. Duke to Mary Panther
       24,    Elisha Bobo to Oliva Wilson by Daniel Farrar JP
       26,    James Sullivan to Jane Wishon by John Weaver MG
Oct  3,    Wm. J. Hulsey to Sarah A. Waggoner
        3,    Israel P. Dennis to Sarah E. Patrick by W.W.Parks JP
        4,    George Carter to Martha Warren
       10,    Wm. Stanley to Polly A. Chitwood by Wm. Dyer JP
       10,    George W. Pilant to Barthena E. Sharp by John Corder JP
pg 201
        8,    Joseph O.Dellmon to Eliza Jane Beard by D. Farrar JP
        8,    Johnson J. Gleghorn to Margret Jones by W. Dyer JP
       10,    John F. Wilkins to Jeffries E. Landess
       13,    James F. Pool to Eliza Isom by W.R.Martin JP
       16,    Moses Temple to Eliza Reeves by J.N.George JP
       16,    James C. Green to Lavina Smith by John Weaver MG
       14,    George W. Reese to Cordelia A. Pratt by W.H.Moores JP
       18,    Stephen A. White to Martha A. Jones by W.H.Moores JP
       20,    Samuel Perry to Elizabeth Tennison by Y.T.Taylor JP
       21,    Redorick Price to Elizabeth Ann Busby by W.B.Rhea JP
pg 202
       22,    Wm. H. Bryan to Julia A.J.E.Smith by D. Farrar JP
       20,    George Freeman to Sophia E. Walker by Ira E. Douthit MG
       24,    Eli A. Lackey to Elizabeth C. West by J.C.Stevenson
       24,    Charles A. Robinson to Martha A. Bell by A.G.Smith
       27,    Mathew P. Gowan to Leoma Mullins by Leroy Jones MG
       26,    Archibald V. McDaniel to Mary F. McKee
       28,    Charles Adkins to Mary Surber by A.G.Smith
       31,    Wm. Petty to Cincinnatta F. Sullivan by P.W.Walton JP
       29,    Nicholas J. House to Malinda Cook
```

30,   Joseph L. Shull to Martha E. Patterson by James
                                        Kirkland MG
pg 203
Nov 5, H.N.Maulding to Mary L. Sullivan by Wm. Dyer JP
     7, Mark H. Cole to Lucinda L. Hedgepeth
     7, Gabriel Davis to Dicy King by G.W.R.Moore JP
    10, Jonathan Smith to Febe Jane Rainey by Samuel Boone JP
    10, James Rainey to Nancy Smith by Samuel Boone JP
    14, A.M.Prosser to America Sullivan by Samuel Boone JP
    14, James M. Hanks to Elizabeth J. Brady by B.M.G.Alsup JP
    12, Henry Jacobs to Tursey A. Tate by Wm. Dyer JP
    12, James Brady to Polly Roberson by W.H.Moores JP
    18, Wm. Smith to Amanda Fackenter by W.C.Jennings JP
pg 204
    24, George Fanning to Martha Ann Smith by Y.T.Taylor
    25, James Bowling to Mary Moyers by J.N.George JP
    28, John W. Bland to Martha E. Blair by Wm. E. Mitchel JP
Dec 2, Wm. L. James to Presilla Ann Moore by A.G.Downing JP
    10, A.A.Bell to C.E.Biggers by A.G.Gibson MG
    10, George Pingram to Mary Ann Stephens
    10, James Daniel to Catharine Wagoner
    11, Phillip Cooper to Lucinda McNeace by W.N.Moores JP
    12, John W. Clark to Martha J. Buchanan by A.G.Smith
pg 205
    12, David R. Hamilton to Sarah F. Moore by A.G.Smith
    13, Joseph George to Eldender H. Burton by Wm. J. Mitchell JP
    17, Wm. Montgomery to Nancy R. McNeil by A.G.Smith
    16, Epp Harden to Clarinda C. Webb
    19, E.F.Berry to Elizabeth Eaton by Woodroof Parks JP
    24, Wm. Upton to Ellen Crawford by John Kimes, Sr. JP
    19, Josiah A. Norris to Mary E. Raymond by A.S.Sloan
    24, Charles G. Crump to Lucinda Davidson by A.G.Gibson MG
    19, John Mason to Elizabeth Smith by Martin Towery
    23, Manson Albright to Martha A. Jewell by Robert Drennon JP
pg 206
    24, Wm. Vickers to Rebecca Vickers by R. Drennon JP
    22, Thomas Easlick to Sarah Taylor by T.S.Williams JP
    24, Davis M. Holloway to Amandia C. Randolph by A.G.Downing JP
    24, Wright H. Watson to Charlott M. Hedgepeth by Wm. Dyer JP
    24, James H. Jones to Frances E. Smith by A.G.Smith MG
    24, James H. Harrison to Margaret J. Moyers by S. Record MG
    25, Wm. J. Rainey to Elizabeth Shipp
    26, Robert Jacobs to Elizabeth McCree by Wm. Dyer JP
    29, Allen Smith to Arrena Owen by W.R.Martin JP
1851
Jan 2, John A. Norwood to Elizabeth Inman by W.B.Rhea JP
pg 207
1850
Dec 29, Edward Taylor to Eliza Forester by Woodroof Parks JP
    29, John Armstrong to Margaret J. McCollum by H.C.Cowan JP
    29, Thomas Holman to Mary Perry by John Kimes JP
1851
Jan 2, Hardy H. Cotton to Margret J. Dollins by A.G.Gibson MG
    31, Newton W. Howell to Nancy J. Wiles by Samuel Boone JP
1850
Dec 31, Arthur Washburn to Mary G. Hodges
1851
Jan 1, Austin Eslick to Martha J. George

44

1,	C.G.Tucker to Nancy W. Turney by P.W.Walton JP
6,	Norris Flint to Sarah Ann Jennings
7,	Lee Smith to Elizabeth A. McNeece by A.G.Smith

pg 208

8,	Henry Shelton to Leah Shelton by T.S.Williams JP
8,	Obadiah Clark to Louisa N. Canada by J. McDaniel JP
8,	Marshall Ceatty to Elizabeth Gragg by A.G.Smith MG
14,	Beriah Lackey to Martha Evans by Rev. T. Scivally
Mar 3,	Archibald L. Moyers to Margret M. Alsup by J.C.Reeves JP
Jan 11,	Henry Taylor to Mary Smith
16,	Elisha Leatherwood to Mary E. Smith by John L. Henderson JP

1852
| Dec 12, | James Culbreath to Elizabeth A. Owenby by L.M.Dance MG |

1851
| Jan 15, | John W. Cole to Elizabeth Panter |
| 16, | Elisha Bryant to Phebe Taylor by W.C.Jennings JP |

pg 209
Mar 5,	Wm. M. Cook to Adaline Trimble by T.P.Sumners JP
Jan 28,	F.C.A.Troop to Mahala Jane Cummins by Jacob Gillespie JP
27,	Eli Evans to Mary Ann Massey
30,	Thomas B. McClure to Mary Smith by D.L.Gray JP
Feb 4,	James A.J.Alexander to Sarah P. Jorden by Y.T.Taylor JP
2,	Thomas J. Reese to Pertesia Ann Reese by Dempsey Sullivan JP
4,	McDonald Tucker to Elizabeth Ann Duke
13,	Joel Cunningham to Susan E. Myrick by John Moores JP
6,	Philip McBray to Harriet A. Walker by W.M.Newman JP
4,	Robert Hill to Mary E. McConnell by W.C.Dunlap MG

pg 210
5,	Wm. J. Stephens to Elizabeth E. Eddington
9,	Wm. S. Hill to Margret Pullam by W.H.Moores JP
25,	Simon A. Pearce to Letty Cashion by W.M.Newman JP
15,	Floodle Michael to Drucillar Jane Bledsoe by H.N.Bray MG
12,	John Chapman to Elizabeth A. Graves by Lemuel Brandon
13,	James W. Solomon to Mary Taylor by Y.T.Taylor JP
18,	W.Y.Chesser to Martha Scott by John Weaver MG
20,	John F. Baxter to Hannah A.E.Robertson by J.A.Saintclair
18,	Joseph T. Hopper to Louisa Sawyers by J. McDaniel JP
20,	David P. Cooper to Eliza J. Clark by Allison Akin MG

pg 211
20,	Wm. B. Martin to Levina Ann Solomon by W.B.Rhea JP
22,	Enoch G. Baker to Sarah Fuller
29,	Benjamin Nerrin to Elizabeth West by Rev. J.B.Warren
25,	Mathew Bethume to Sarah Jane Sanders by A.G.Downing JP
27,	James M. Roughton to N.C.Womack by J.A.Saintclair JP
26,	Jasper Rowe to Jane McGee by Dempsey Sullivan JP
Mar 6,	Drury C. Wheeler to Mary C. Cole
12,	John P. McGee to Sarah Jane Rutledge by W.H.Moores JP
Apr 10,	James M. Sims to Jemima E. Green by Allison Eakin MG
Mar 23,	Bailey E. Lane to Levina J. Ashby by John Weaver MG

pg 212
27,	John M. Smith to Mary E. Berry by J.A.Saintclair JP
Apr 3,	Robert B. Young to Elizabeth A. Owens
10,	Francis M. Bryant to Susan D. Williams by Robert Drennon JP
5,	Wm. M. Woodward to Elizabeth McElroy
7,	Wm. H. Stephenson to Frances Luna by Wm. Dyer JP

```
        10,   Josiah S. Thompson to Dulsena Stephenson by A.G.Gibson,M
        16,   Nathan McCalister to Catharine Scott
        24,   Halifax A. Steelman to Nancy Warden by Woodroof Parks JP
Jul 10,   Richard Smith to Anna Faulkner by John Corder JP
Apr 25,   James Watson to Martha J. Edmiston
pg 213
May  1,   Nepoleon Benson to Mary Doss by W.H.Moore JP
     1,   John H. Scott to Mary Ann Chesser by Wm. Dyer JP
     4,   Stephen Patterson to Lillian Patterson by J.E.Douthit MG
     5,   James A. Grill to Julia Ann Cunnungham by W.M.Newman JP
    16,   Robert Patterson to Elizabeth N. Shull by W.H.Moore JP
    18,   John B. Harris to Nancy J. Forrester by S. Boone JP
    18,   Albert G. Wheeler to Elizabeth Philpot by J.N.George JP
    22,   Simpson Abbot to Nancy K. Dickey by Robert Drennon JP
Jun 12,   M.R.Shull to Eliza A. Pemberton
    12,   Wm. D. Prosser to Mary Melson by John Wagster MG
pg 214
    13,   Alfred W. Williams to Nancy Stephens by D. Jacks MG
    17,   Stephen Hart to Catharine V. Beaty by A.F.Driskill
    20,   James S. Davis to Jane Davis by J.W.Holman MG
    24,   Peter Hamilton to Sarah Cunningham
    29,   Peyton Foyester to Claskey Jane Guinn by S. Boone JP
Jul  1,   Willis H. Foster to Mary Lambert by J.O.Cole MG
     7,   Thomas B. Hicks to Elizabeth W. Alexander by R. Drennon
    13,   Wm. H. Sparks to Mary C. Walton by J.McDaniel JP
     3,   Willis F. Cobbert to Mary Ann Saunders by A.A.Bell MG
     6,   John L. Pylant to Elizabeth W. Ford by D.L.Mitchell
pg 215
     9,   James Kirkpatrick to Josephine Bearden
    14,   George Cumberland to Elizabeth Lindsey
    16,   Wm. L. McCann to Mary Jane Rawls by W.R.Martin JP
    17,   John H. Morrison to Martha Jane Davidson
    20,   Adolphus B. Hollaway to Martha J. Fanning by W.H.Moore JP
    23,   Tilman L. McGee to Margret R. Taylor by S. Boone JP
    21,   James D. Paddie to Nancy Ann Broadway
    27,   M.D.Carpenter to Sarah McNatt by D. Sullivan JP
    29,   E.W.Moore to Martha Jane Gross by Woodroof Parks JP
    31,   Joseph A. Casey to Eliza Ann Barker by Wm. C. Jennings JP
pg 216
    30,   Wm. C. Luna to Sarah Jane Chitwood by John Weaver MG
    28,   John W. Carmicle to Jane Bush
    30,   Thomas M. Benefield to Letty Reeves by J.N.George JP
Aug  7,   Henry Luttrell to Sarah L.Templeton by W.C.Jennings JP
     4,   Enoch Warren to Malinda C. Carter
     4,   Samuel Warren to Martha Pamplin
     6,   Wm. J. Grills to Sarah P. Heath by W.M.Newman JP
     5,   Wm. Kelly to Sarah McClure by John Corder JP
     7,   Decatur Barnes to Margarett J. Halbert by Thomas Childs,M
    11,   James Satterfield to Caroline Hankins
    11,   Henry C. Hamilton to Nancy Martin by I.E.Douthit MG
pg 217
    12,   Samuel C. Holman to Sarah Lindsey
    12,   Samuel V. Commons to Sarah Isom
    14,   Wm. Waterman to Sarah L. Commins by W.C.Dunlap MG
    19,   Elisha Shelton to Elizabeth Hooper
    25,   Martin Trantham to Nancy F. Moyers by J.C.Reeves JP
    21,   Elijah Parker to Martha R. Crawford by A.G.Smith MG
    21,   Noah W. Cooper to Lucy H. Webster
```

24,	Samuel J. Howell to Cynthia Ann Steelman by John Weaver MG
24,	A.Y.Nicks to Jane M. Wright by A.G.Smith MG
27,	James B. Stone to Elizabeth C. Medkiff by J.N.George JP

pg 218

28,	Robert A. Morrison to Rachael J. Scott
30,	Peter Cunningham to Mary A. Grills by W.M.Newman JP
29,	August Hess to Priss Prosser by Lewis Newsom JP
31,	Wm. F. Jarred to Mildred Davidson by D. Sullivan JP
Sep 2,	Alexander D. Ferguson to Margaret M. Baxter by B. Kimbrough MG
4,	Wm. Metcalf to Elizabeth F. Cole by J.N.George JP
11,	Barksdale Neece to Sarah Eaton by D. Sullivan JP
16,	John A. Greer to Cynthia Eaton by John Weaver MG
10,	Charles S. Rutledge to Sulthany Wade by S. Boone JP
11,	Samuel P. Smith to Pelina Colman by W.R.Martin JP

pg 219

11,	Charles McCartney to Lucy Coil by A.G.Downing JP
22,	Jeremiah M. Faulkenberry to Mary Ann Caughran by A.J.Childress JP
10,	Benjamin L. Commons to Elizabeth King by W.C.Dunlap MG
15,	Henry H. Winkler to Mary Ann Jones by W.C.Jennings JP
11,	George M. Martin to Caroline Wilkins by Robert Drennon JP
11,	John C. Marony to Nancy Jane Jewell by Robert Drennon JP
15,	John W. Walker to Nancy A. Hamilton by D. Jacks MG
16,	Wm. McClure to Susan E. Cox
16,	Wm. P. Conner to Manerva Gold
17,	James W. Brown to Eliza Summers

pg 220

18,	Henderson Barnes to Parmelia A. Compton by J. McDaniel JP
18,	Wm. M. Thompson to Louisa Jane Bedwell
20,	Benjamin Boone to Sarah Jane Parker
26,	Simca Clarke to Mary M. Patton by A.G.Gibson MG

1852
| Feb 2, | Wm. H. Blue to Nancy Anderson by G.W.Puckett MG |

1851
Sep 23,	George Hanes to Nancy M. Brown
23,	Samuel G. Arwine to Martha C. Gray by J.W.Holman MG
24,	Madison Rozel to Sarah Jane Branson by W.H.Moore
24,	James R. Butler to Nancy A. Ables
25,	R.W.Bryant to Frances C. McKinzie by D.L.Mitchell MG

pg 221

25,	John A. Gilham to Mary F. Dallas by A.G.Smith
Oct 27,	Enoch E. Harbin to Ann E. Sneed by T.S.Williams JP
Sep 29,	Thomas B. Eastland to Sarah Pearson by J. McDaniel JP
29,	Silas Stephenson to Charlotte Bradford
Oct 2,	Hugh B. Wallace to Rebecca VanHoozer
5,	David C. Moyers to Sarah Trantham by J.C.Reeves JP
11,	James T. Emmons to Maulday O. Carithers by J.C.Reeves JP
9,	David M. Tafts to Nancy M. Smith by W.R.Martin JP
14,	John Lock to Nancy Raney by D. Sullivan JP
14,	Henry Austin to Mary Borrow by John Wagster MG

pg 222

15,	Wilson Thompson to Sarah Sullinger
16,	James J. Davis to Nancy Brimm by John Wagster MG
16,	Samuel D. Hope to Eliza M. Cummins by A.G.Gibson MG
20,	Andrew J. Jones to Harriet E. Mitchell by J.E.Douthit MG
21,	Wm. Lipscomb of Davidson Co. to Sarah A.Fulgham by S.E. Jones MG

26,   Tandy W. Ford to Mary R. Armstrong by J.W.O'Keller MG
23,   Milton Parks to Emily A. Raines by Woodroof Parkes JP
25,   H.T.Pettitte to Martha Ann Koonce (license returned)
29,   Craven W. Nees to Rebecca Allen by D. Sullivan JP
28,   A.J.Nichols to Susanah Parish by A.J.Childress JP
pg 223
30,   John P. Turney to Louisa Beck by Thomas Childs MG
30,   Marshall Bruice to Matilda E. Campbell by J.S.Saintclair
Nov 2,   Doctor John D. Whitaker to L.L.Todd by W.H.Moores JP
5,   Wormly R. Bruice to Mary F.E.McCoy by J.C.Stevenson
5,   Robert McGehey to Elizabeth Shelton by T.S.Williams JP
6,   Wm.H. Peyton to Rosanah A. Jackson by Thomas Childs MG
7,   Wm. J. Cole to Martha K. Cole
11,   Wm. F. Cole to Martha Reece
13,   Isaac R. Cole to Mary J. Farrar by J.N.George JP
10,   Joshua D. Gray to Elizabeth Moorehead by W.M.Newman JP
pg 224
13,   B.F.Dennis to Samy Andrews
13,   Mark Colier to Virginia Reese by R.M.Whitman
20,   Wm. C. Dunham to Frances E. Pullam by J.L.Thompson JP
20,   Josiah P. Wallace to Mary Ann Joins by A.J.Childress JP
21,   James Daves to Margret Holley
23,   James N. Ford to Sally S. Green by John Weaver MG
27,   Joshua Phillips to Elizabeth Waggoner by S. Boone JP
26,   D.P.C.Allen to Emeline McAfee
27,   Samuel Heathcock to Caroline Isham by R. Drennon JP
27,   Wm. T. Lauderdale to Margret A.E.Fullerton by A.G.Smith,M
pg 225
29,   Samuel G. Beard to Julia Ann McKinney by Rev. W.W.Beard
Dec 4,   John G. McClellan to Caroline E. Stonebraker by Wm.Gayle
5,   Jesse A. Shand to Mary Hathcock
8,   Westley Luttrell to Lucillar Pruitt
9,   Allen C. Jones to Sebra Powers by Martin Towery MG
9,   Emanuel Runnels to Louisa J. Moore by John Weaver MG
11,   Jesse W. Parkes to Mary A. Snoddy by Woodroff Parkes JP
11,   G.W.Owen to Kanzetty Forbes
11,   Joseph C. Wiley to Racheal Sloan by J.C.Reeves
pg 226
17,   Alfred R. Smith to Mary E. Steadman by A.S.Randolph JP
16,   James A. Wilson to Sara W. Caughran by A.S.Sloan
18,   Henry H. Dunn to Averalah Cothrun by S. Boone JP
17,   Daniel Warren to Elizabeth Felps
18,   Alfred W. Smith to Nancy Ann Clift by B.F.Clark JP
22,   Ira W. Beard to Racheal M. Martin by T.P.Sumners JP
22,   Aaron D. Trimble to Mary E. Whitman by B. Kimbrough MG
22,   Alfred O. Birmingham to Elvira Jane Ayers by J.N.George JP
25,   Wm. B. Roughton to Eliza A. McGee by I.A.Saintclair JP
24,   Elijah C. McLaughlin to Sarah A. Hart
pg 227
25,   Elisha S. Brown to Artimsey J. Brown by S. Boone JP
27,   John Warren to Sarah Prosser
30,   Thomas C. Markes to Emmaranda J. Robinson by D.D.Harwell
29,   Wm. W. Johnson to Mary Marrs
31,   Charles V. Fortune to Mary M. March by Alexander Smith,M

1852
Jan 1,   Benjamin Marshall to Hannah G. Ashby by John Weaver MG
     1,   Wm. Moseley to Mary Keton by Daniel Farrar JP
     4,   Wm. Buntley to Mary Forester by Amos Small JP
     8,   Jackson C. Finly to Mary Ann Murdock by Wm. Dyer JP
     11,   David Smith to Elizabeth Creacy by J.C.Stevenson
pg 228
     12,   John N. Moorehead to Mary E. Wagoner
     12,   John Cole to Nancy Reeves
     12,   Richard T. Marshall to Sarah C. Grills
     15,   P.L.Twitty to Eveline Templeton by A.G.Smith MG
     15,   George W. Sanders to Mary C. Floyd by A.S.Randolph JP
     16,   Wm. C. Bates to Margret E. Moyers
     24,   Silvester H. Wright to Amanda M. Swinebroad
     22,   Wm. W. Fautner to Henretta Smith by Jeremiah Dean MG
     27,   Jesse Fraley to Sarah Ann Jackson
     28,   Alfred W. Dooley to Ana Hudson by A.G.Gibson MG
pg 229
Feb 4,   Joe B. Smith to Leah C. Scoggins by B.F.Clark JP
     2,   Wiley G. Burrow to Mary A. Crane
     3,   Elephaz Bearden to Celia Cunningham
     5,   John Good to Elizabeth Hays by A.S.Sloan
     4,   Joseph W. Wanslow to Martha Warren
     6,   Shepard Rogers to Elizabeth Hester by John Wagster MG
     9,   Joseph C. Hendrick to Martha A. Gill by W.C.Dunlap
     5,   John D. White to Martha Gibson
     10,   Alexander Daves to Hannah Simmons by G.W.R.Moore JP
pg 230
     11,   Brice M. Abbott to Mary J. Decker by R. Drennon JP
     14,   Robert J. Lively to Sarah Ann Good
     19,   Jacob VanHoozer to M.A.J.Ballow by B.G.W.Puckett MG
     19,   James Phillips to Martha Pinkerton by A.G.Downing JP
     21,   Nicholas Copeland by Rhoda Easlick
     25,   Wm. McGee to Mary Ann Rhoten by S. Boone JP
     23,   James Sanders to Frances Vickers
     23,   Wm. F. Taylor to Almeda E. Eaton by J.W.Holman MG
     24,   John Spray to Nancy Sandlin
     24,   Temple Lackey to Elizabeth Taylor
pg 231
     24,   George W. Posey to Margaret Wiley
     29,   Jacob Cruise to Elizabeth C. Smith by W.C.Jennings JP
Mar 2,   Wm. Y. Taylor to Jensey Scott by Thos. Williams JP
     4,   Josiah Armstrong to Elizabeth Cook by A.G.Gibson MG
May 1,   Lewis L.W.Setliff to Malinda Morris by J.P.Williams MG
Mar 5,   Charles W. Hodge to Susan F. Parkes
     10,   Thomas L.D.Medkiff to Mahaly Snow
     11,   John Montgomery to Melinda Jane Vickers by Wm.R.Martin JP
     11,   Garrett Merrell to Anna Walker
     14,   Thomas H. Rawls to Alzny Moore to John Moore JP
     18,   Alfred S. Templeton to Mary Hobbs by M.Henry Sumners MG
pg 232
     18,   James Jewell to Martha Gilliland by Wm. R. Martin JP
     25,   Muntford R. Townsen to Rilla T. Randolph by A.G.Downing JP
     23,   Manson H. Caughran to Julia Buchanan by A.S.Sloan
     25,   Drury P. Land to Nancy R. Howell by Wm. Pryor JP
     24,   Samuel H.A.Roan to Lydia McDaniel by F.M.Ventress JP
     25,   Robert McElvany to Emeline Cox

       30,   F.M.Dillon to Sarah C. Hancock by A.G.Gill MG
Apr 1,   W.W.Templeton to Lucy J. Bland by Robert Drennon JP
       1,   M.G.Williams to Sarah Ann Gunter by T.S.Williams JP
pg 233

              George Cunningham, Clerk County Court of Lincoln County,
              Sworn and Entered upon the Duties of his Office the 5th
              April 1852
       7,   John F. Armstrong to Martha J. Hardy by A.Walker
                                                    Morison MG
       8,   Pleasant Halbert to Emily Buchanan by A.G.Smith MG
       18,   Simon Hart to Vianna Bailey by Rev. J. Scivally
       29,   Isham Wells to Nancy Ann Stanly by T.P.Sumners JP
       20,   Charles W. Marshall to Martha Sanders by A.G.Downing JP
       20,   Calvin Y. Douthit to Mary Jane Dunlap by J.N.George JP
       21,   Samuel J. Wakefield to Nancy E. Peyton
       28,   James R. Steelman to Mary Jane Whitaker by Amos Small JP
       27,   John L. Jones to Miriah L. Wiley by W.H.Moores JP
pg 234
       29,   Thomas Howell to Rosena Shephard by Wm. Land MG
       30,   Bartlett Hindman to Sarah Pittman
       30,   Peter Warren to Eliza Wilkerson by Lewis Newsom JP
May 2,   John H. Roden to Mary M. Watson by T.P.Sumners JP
       1,   F.G.Landess to Matora Luck
       4,   Tillman Davis to Margaret Bailey by J.S.Saintclair JP
       6,   Wm. Claunch to Mary White by Wm. H. Moores JP
       12,   David M. Gray to H. Caroline King by M.M.Marshall
       20,   John G. Enochs to Margret F. Blackwell by W.G.Hensley,M
       20,   James Claunch to Mary Jeans by John Moores JP
pg 235
       23,   Wm. B. McKee to Bettie F. Gill by Allison Akin MG
       27,   James S. Brown to Sarah Orick by Amos Small JP
Jun 5,   Wm. C. Solomon to Harriet Harrison
       10,   Joseph Surber to Rebecca K. Crawford
       13,   Henry P. Mills to Martha M. Pamplin by J.L.Rosebrough JP
       13,   James W. Mills to Sarah M. Wade by Travis Ashby JP
       17,   Walker Fox to Elizabeth Harper by Lemuel Brandon
       21,   Francis M. Beard to Emily A. Cook
       22,   Andrew H. Bishop to Louisa Clark
       22,   Riley W. Pitts to Susan F.C.George by John Wagster MG
pg 236
       22,   Robert Boyd to Elizabeth Adcock by F.M.Ventress JP
       23,   Wm. M. White to Margaret A. Buchanan by A.G.Smith MG
       28,   Reuben Runnels to Elizabeth Sikes
Jul 6,   A.W.Morrison to Julia Ann Hardy by Rev. James Watson
       8,   Wm. D. Gill to Jane Braden by John C. Reeves JP
       6,   Bryant Moyers to Tempsey Bates by Francis Ashby JP
       7,   A.V.Mills to Nancy Griffin by James N. George JP
       8,   Thomas Couch to Huldy Jane Taylor by W.C.Jennings JP
       9,   America F. Stone to Nancy E. Bostick by D. Jacobs MG
       8,   Huston Hill to Rebecca A. Thurman by W.B.Rhea JP
       8,   James A. Templeton to Mary Ann Dennis by F.M.Ventress JP
pg 237
       9,   Wm. H. Reese to Hannah Dunn by Dempsey Sullivan JP
       10,   Wm. Pearce to Mahala E. Coffee
       13,   Alfred Kiblecason to Mary Ann Adaline William by
                                                    A.G.Downing JP
       12,   Allen Davis to Elizabeth Phillips by John Cary JP
       15,   Jasper Ellis to Elizabeth A. McElroy by H.C.Cowen JP

1852

18,	Mathias Rickets to Mary E. Harbin by Wm. Grills JP
14,	Wm. Faulkner to Elizabeth Smith
21,	William G. Motlow to Sarah E. Gray by J.W.Holman MG
21,	Asa Smith to Martha J. Perry
22,	Edward M. Hicks to Louisana Williams by R. Drennon JP

pg 238

27,	Thomas J. Scott to Elizabeth Jones Hester by G.W.R. Moore JP
28,	Francis M. McHaffy to Martha A. Smith by A.F.Driskill
29,	James R. Fullerton to Sarah A. Kennedy by T.W.Parkison
Aug 1,	Wm. George to Mary A.E.D.Luttrell by T.S.Williams JP
Jul 31,	Joseph G. Pullen to Martha A. Dyer
Aug 3,	Wm. B. Fonville to Martha W. Blackwell by D.L.Mitchell,M
24,	Drury M. Perkins to Mariah H. Sherrell by Matt Marshall,M
5,	Logan Owen to Sina Franklin by Amos Small JP
4,	John Wadkins to Permela Burton
5,	Isaac R. Pitts to Rebecca M. Ashby by A.S.Slone
8,	Robert P. Garman to Arretter Bailey by John Wagster MG

pg 239

6,	Wm. H. Gattis to Mary S. Brown by J.W.Holman MG
6,	Joseph Hopper to Milly Eaton
8,	James Roane to Jane M. King by J.D.Cole MG
12,	James McBride to Rachael Roughton by J.E.Douthit MG
14,	Henry Halloway to Mary Marshall by A.G.Downing JP
19,	Thomas J. Spencer to Amanda West by Martin Towery MG
19,	Joseph George to LouVena Lackey by J.N.George JP
19,	Galen A. McKinney to Martha J. Wright by Wm. Dyer JP
23,	Daniel J. Watson to Mary Ann McAfee by Woodruff Parks JP
25,	Wm. C. Blackwell to Catharine D. Blake by D.L.Mitchell,M

pg 240

24,	Wm. A. Robertson to Sophia S.F.Emmons
30,	Wm. Smallman to Permelia Williamson
Sep 6,	James Shelton to Syntha Story by Thomas Childs MG
7,	John M. Buchanan to Nancy E. Weaver by J.N.George JP
9,	James H. Wright to Anna Trantham by S.M.Emmons MG
9,	Giles Davis to Elizabeth Warren
13,	John L. Dusenberry to Susan J. James by J.W.Holman MG
15,	Byram L.R.Clun(Chem) to Martha E. Gillum by D. Jacks,M
23,	P.G.Prosser to America Pruitt by Dempsey Sullivan JP
27,	James H. Rhea to Elizabeth Jenkins

pg 241

9,	Giles Davis to Elizabeth Warren by R.M.Whitman MG
Oct 3,	Samuel Hawkins to Minerva Williams by A.G.Downing JP
Sep 30,	Samuel Wakefield to Malinda James by Wm. Dyer JP
Oct 4,	A.S.Boone to Avarilla E. Shapard by A.F.Driskill
6,	Robert Stevenson to Nancy Jeans by J. Moore JP
7,	Wm. Sumners to Sarah Camper
7,	Wm. Grammer to Frances L. Burton
8,	Wm. Snoddy to Clarinda Mason by Wm. Dyer JP
14,	Anderson Robertson to Mary Looney by John Weaver MG
11,	James Pearce to Mary Lindsey
11,	Martin L. Parks to Elizabeth A. Edens
18,	A.M.Gallaway to Martha Spence
21,	John H. Timmins to Susan E. Whitaker by C.S.Knott MG
24,	John A. Bruce to Louisa Jane Coats by Wm R. Martin JP

pg 242

25,	Wm. J. Howard to Nancy P. Pruitt
Nov 2,	Wm. H. Ashby to Mary E. Ramsey by W.B.Rhea JP

```
        3,    Alexander Bradey to Amanda M. Gattis by J.W.Holman MG
       10,    Wm. M. Parr to Louisa Bailey by J.W.Holman MG
       11,    John Mills to Nancy K. Reese
       15,    John Motlow to Elvina J. Green by J.W.Holman MG
       18,    John L. Mitchell to Nancy J. Pardon by John Reed JP
       17,    John A. Motlow to Eliza C. Womack
       18,    Wm. H. Malden to Martha C. Tooley by Wm. Dyer JP
       21,    Wm. Eakes to Jane George
pg 243
       23,    Samuel Edmiston to Margaret F. Robinson by T.W.Randle
       23,    J.H.Jobe to Sarah E. Scott
       25,    David Farrar to Nancy Jane Owen by J.N.George JP
       25,    Jefferson Phelps to Sarah Warren by D. Sullivan JP
       25,    James R. Williams to Rebecca J. Watson by Martin
                                                    Towery MG
       28,    Needham George to Emeline R. Coleman by J.N.George JP
       25,    Joseph Cashion to Catharine Parkes by J.W.Holman MG
       26,    John R. McCombs to Susan C. Sorrells
       29,    Robert H. McMillen to Amanda J. Fulgham
Dec  1,    George W. Blake to Henrietta Metcalf by D.L.Mitchell,M
pg 244
Nov 30,    Wm. C. Solomon to Susan McLaughlin by W.B.Rhea JP
Dec  2,    James D. Cooper to Caroline Marr by John Moore JP
      2,    Wm. Crabtree to Nancy Foster by W.P.Gill JP
      6,    Alexander Timmons to Martha J. Parks
      9,    Davidson Renegar to Sarah Buchanan by Wm. Halbert JP
      9,    Wm. C. Ray to Matilda Stegall by Stephen M. Dance MG
     11,    Leroy Carpenter to Evaline Mattox
     16,    Wm. T. Mosley to Eliza J. Abernathy by J.C.Stevenson
     16,    Wiley J. Pitts to Mary Ann Allbright by A.S.Randolph JP
     23,    Abner S. McGee to Mary A. Marshall by S. Boone JP
pg 245
     23,    D.B.Shull to Sarah L. Higgins by R.B.McGaugh MG
     23,    James P. Forsyth to Margaret McBay by John Reed JP
     23,    George A. Craig to Jane Murphy by G.W.R.Moores JP
     26,    Thomas Norman to Julia Lindsey by John Corder JP
     28,    C.T.Cates to Jane Rives
     29,    Samuel D. Pruitt to Catharine A. Dempsey by J.L.
                                                  Thomson JP
     28,    Lovel C. Hardin to Phinas Ann Counts by J.P.Williams
     30,    James Cox to Sarah Renegar by S. Boone JP
     30,    David S. Buchanan to Nancy Douthit by Thomas Childs MG
1853
Jan  6,    Robert D. Hardin to Eliza M. Ewing by Rev. James
                                                  Kirkland
      1,    Wm. F. Lynch to Frances E. Woodward
      4,    A.G.Sawyers to Eliza Whitaker by B.F.Clark JP
      7,    Stephen F. Spencer to Margaret J. Smith by John Copeland,M
pg 246
      6,    Francis M. Fannon to Elizabeth J. Echols by Y.T.Taylor,JP
      6,    Harrison Hanks to Malinda Upton by R. Farquharson JP
      9,    Jacob Buntly to Elizabeth Forester by John Wagster MG
      8,    Jasper Tankersly to Harriett Raney
     11,    James Price to Sarah E. Faulkenberry by A.S.Randolph JP
     13,    Wm. D. Chick to Sarah E. Summerford by John Wagster MG
     24,    Nathan J. Thompson to Charity J. Noles by Y.T.Taylor JP
     20,    R.N.McClure to Martha J. Lesley by John Reed JP
```

1853

	23,	Peter Ellis to Diana Rickets by John Moore JP
	26,	John H. Mills to Tempy Mansfield by D. Sullivan

pg 247

	27,	John C. Hanks to Delina Buchanan by R. Farquharson JP
	31,	Thomas M. Lane to Elizabeth E. Cannon by J.W.Holman MG
Feb	3,	Ervin M. McAdams to Elizabeth S. Sanders by John McDaniel
Mar	24,	Wm. Smith to Cassena McFarin by A.S.Sloan
Feb	15,	Wm. P. Caughran to Luvina E. Drennon by A.S.Sloan
	14,	Willis L. Bedwell to Sisly Ann Davis by John Wagster MG
	16,	Isaac Hays to Delina A. McRee by T.W.Walton JP
	17,	David L. Smith to Louisa Smith by A.S.Randolph JP
	17,	Hardy Reavis to Elizabeth Brown by J.W.Tarant MG
	19,	E.S.N.Bobo to E.G.Landess by J.W.Holman MG

pg 248

	21,	Wiley A. Hobbs to Amanda Eddens by J.W.Holman MG
	23,	James Wilburn to Nancy C. Walker by Wm.A.Gill MG
	23,	Wm. Prosser to Elizabeth Creson by D. Sullivan JP
	27,	B.F.Smith to Nancy King by T.P.Sumners JP
	27,	James W. Laten(Luter) to Martha Jane Irvin by H.R.Bray,M
Mar	3,	Nathan Curry to Sarah Chapman by L. Brandon
	3,	Elijah A. Bray to Mary I.J.Barker by W.C.Jennings JP
	8,	George W. Sims to Martha Land by Wm. Pryor JP
	8,	John Merrell to Margaret R. Anderson
	10,	Daniel T. Wilburn to Mary E. Tate by Rev. J. Kirkland

pg 249

	15,	Wm. M. Freeman to America Fannon by Woodruff Parkes JP
	13,	Wm. F. Williams to Rebecca Nepp by T.W.Walton JP
	16,	Sebron Evans to Jane Wilkins by R. Drennon JP
	21,	Asa S. Reddick to Martha A. Glidwell by R. Whitman MG
	24,	Rufus A. McGee to Eliza Locker by F.M.Ventress JP
Apr	5,	Joel B. Smith to Elizabeth Yell by S.M.Cowan V.D.M.
	7,	David J. Revis to Clarasa Brown by J.W.Tarrent MG
	12,	Wm. M. Todd to Mary O. Bagley by W.C.Dunlap MG
	19,	David Parker to Susan E. Grisard by C.H.Remington MG
	21,	Daniel Warden to Mary Little by J.W.Tarrent MG

pg 250

	24,	S.H.Kimes to S.A.Sawyers by A.G.Gibson MG
	30,	Brice Dillingham to Sarah M. Woodward
May	1,	James M. Davis to Mary J. Bradford by A.G.Smith
	8,	Wm. Melson to Mary E. Freeman by John Wagster MG
	12,	C.H.Remington to Mary F. Ellis by J.W.Holman MG
	19,	Luther M. Pilant to Caladonia Fowler
	24,	Alvin Tucker to Susannah George by J.N.George JP
	22,	Hiram Commons to Mary M. Woodward by John Cary JP
	29,	Freeman Burrow to Louisa C. Nichols by G.W.R.Moore JP
Jun	7,	John W. Webb to Margaret A. Philpot by J.N.George JP

pg 251

	7,	A.S.Duval to Mary Ringo by M. Marshall MG
	16,	Wm. Thompson to Nancy Ann Fox by F. Motlow JP
	16,	James C. Pylant to Lydia R. Bonner by M. Marshall
	20,	John H. Bray to Elizabeth Shires by S.M.Emmons MG
	23,	Drury Richardson to Mary J. Wade by D. Sullivan JP
Aug	2,	Patrick Thompson to Mary Pully by T.H.Freeman JP
Jun	26,	Wm. S. Harris to Nancy Ann Pickle by T. Hill JP
	26,	F. Ennis to Mary E.Walace by S.M.Cowan VDM
	29,	Wm. Steelman to Nancy B. Bearden by John Wagster MG
	30,	Jacob R. Wright, Jr to Harriett Collins by B.M.G.Alsup JP

53

pg 252   1853
30,   Pleasant H. Tucker to Margaret J. George by John W.
Braden JP
30,   Thomas P. Roughton to Sarah T. Landers
30,   Joseph S. Clark to Laura Ann Walker by Wm. Dyer JP
Jul 4,   G.B.Keller to J.C.Blackburn by John Corder JP
5,   Joseph L. Moore to Nancy Ann Ashby by S. Boone JP
10,   James W. Smith to Marilda E. Fox by Lemuel Brandon MG
13,   Jacob Blue to Sealy Abel by R. Drennon JP
21,   John C. Stacy to Sarah Jane Sullivan by Lewis Newsom JP
23,   S.P.Vess to Frances Joiner by T.H.Freeman JP
26,   James Broadway to Martha Caskey by Wm. Dyer JP
pg 253
28,   Theodore G. Smith to Elizabeth McElroy by R.Farquharson
28,   T.M.McHaffey to Martha A. Smith
Aug 4,   R.H.Mitchel to Eliza C. Hamilton by Jacob Nare JP
4,   Asa Oliver to Mary Eadens by D. Sullivan JP
7,   James Dooley to Mary Washburn by A.G.Gibson MG
8,   Daniel B. McAnn to Martha Ann Hunt by W.R.Martin JP
10,   Archibald Johnson to Emily H. Pamplin by Woodruff Parks
11,   Angus D. Johnson to Elizabeth J. Alexander by Woodruff
Parks JP
11,   Jerome B. Brady to Nancy E. Owen by W.R.Hedgepeth
11,   David J. Heflin to Maranda C. Hester by G.W.R.Moore JP
pg 254
11,   John S. Dickey to Elizabeth B. Gleghorn by T.W.Parkerson
21,   Andrew Morgan to Polly Ann Raney by J. Dean MG
11,   James Forester to Rebeca Taylor by D. Sullivan JP
16,   Samuel B. Gallaway to Jane McCown
24,   John Smith to Nancy M. Cunningham by O.P.Hill JP
22,   Wm. W. Butler to America J. Gibbs
Sep 10,   Daniel Harrison to Eliza E. Cunningham by J.N.George JP
Aug 24,   Richard O. Hooper to Minerva Dildine by David Gillespie JP
24,   Calvin W. Drenon to America Abbott by A.S.Randolph JP
25,   Mark Purdom to Eglentine Neece by D. Sullivan JP
pg 255
26,   Wm. Edmiston to Mary M. Kilpatrick by Y.T.Taylor JP
Sep 6,   Thomas Lock to Nancy Jane Stephens by A.G.Downing JP
6,   Marcus C. Taylor to Lettitia L. Raymond by A.S.Sloan
8,   A.J.McCollum to Mary A. Buchanan by A.G.Gibson MG
8,   Thomas H. Clark to Mary Ann Brown by Amos Smith JP
15,   George W. Milliken to Caroline Reed by T.P.Sumners JP
12,   Henry Jacob to Martha E. Harper by Thos. Childs MG
15,   Wm. H. Ellis to Jennett Pigg by Wm. Dyer JP
15,   T.R.W.Crane to Susan C. Sorrells by G.W.R.Moore JP
18,   D.F.Smith to Mary M.J.Miller by F. Motlow JP
pg 256
20,   Benjamin B. Ingle to Martha A. Dusenberry by S.Boone JP
22,   Jasper S. Holman to Margaret A.E.Gibson by S.M.Cowen VDM
25,   Isaac VanHoozer to Nancy Ann Simpson by Jacob Nare JP
25,   Nelson Yarborough to Sarah McWhorter by T.S.Williams JP
26,   John W. Allen to Tennessee W. Campbell
26,   S.B.Sisk to Catharine E. Reid by S.M.Emmons MG
27,   Thomas N. Ashby to E. Tennessee Conaway
29,   Francis T. Fulton to Martha Edmiston by M. Marshall MG
29,   Absolum M. Brown to Nancy J. Hudson by R.B.McGaugh MG
Oct 2,   John Dillingham to Lucy E. Woodward by L. Brandon MG

pg 257 1853
3, John M. McFarin to Mary A.G.Spence
6, W.J.Wamack to Elizabeth Ward by J.E.Douthit MG
4, Robert Davis to Rutha Lee by B.M.G.Allsup JP
4, issued: A.S.Boone to Avarila E. Shepard (see Oct 1852.)
6, Alexander Smith to Mary Rone by F.M.Ventress JP
9, Absolum Beard to Sarah Marshall by John Moore JP
10, David G. Butler to Mary J. Merrell by J.N.George JP
12, John S. Deal to Eliza A. Marlow by John Copeland
13, Wm. Y. Nix to F.A.Pierce by Y.T.Taylor
13, Wm. E. McHaffy to Caroline Satterfield
18, Basdel C. Cothrin to Rebeca A. Duncan by Travis Ashby JP

pg 258
22, Franklin D. Branson to Frances Vickers by A.S.Randolph JP
27, Wm. A. Walker to Mary E. Hamilton by A.J.Steel MG
27, James H. Armstrong to Susan P. Hudson by Howell Harris JP
27, Wm. T. Moyers to Martha J. Rowe by M. Marshall MG
30, Nathaniel Taylor to Martha Brown by S. Boone JP
30, Morgan H. Conaway to Martha A. Ashby
Nov 2, Wm. Askins to E.A.Whitaker by A.S.Sloan
Oct 31, J.A.Burton to T. Cavet by H.C.Holman JP
Nov 4, Henry T. Fason to Martha A. Browning by G.W.Puckett MG
2, Wm. J. Lively to Sally T. Floyd by H.C.Cowen JP

pg 259
3, John N. Pigg to Mary Ramsey by Osin P. Hill JP
6, John E. Neece to Elizabeth Steelman by L. Newsom JP
10, Thomas Stovall to Maulda P. Smith by Jacob Nave JP
7, E.A.Call to Susan A. Timmins
9, J.D.Reed to P.J.Williams by A.H.Bishop MG
10, John Felps to Luretha A. Winstead by S. Boone JP
10, John Colman Boyles to Martha J. Leatherwood by Jacob
Nave JP
10, Thomas A. Hazelwood to Mary J. Crenshaw
17, James B. Price to Mary C. Gore by Ira E. Douthit MG
14, Thomas H. Bledsoe to Elizabeth S. Hamilton by A.G.Smith,M

pg 260
15, George W. Alexander to Mary J. Shores by S.M.Cowen VDM
17, A.D.Anderson to Sarah Ann Bledsoe
20, Hiram F. Freeman to Delia A. Wakefield by Wm. Dyer JP
23, Francis A. Thompson to Paralee Jane Strong by Y.T.Taylor
22, Wm. C. Brantley to Sarah Ann Crunk by D.L.Mitchell MG
24, John M. Smith to Elizabeth A. Gracey by M. Marshall MG
30, Wm. A. Rhodes to Josephine Smith by W.R.Martin JP
30, Wm. Gattis to Mary Burton
Dec 3, George N. Tankesly to Caroline Jane Bowles
4, Gideon J. Hamby to Rebecca Warren by S. Boone JP

pg 261
8, Elijah Floyd to Martha E.D.Phillips by H.C.Cowen JP
12, A.J.Renegar to Martha J. Thompson
15, Malichi B. Land to Emeline Cole by Amos Small JP
17, Newton Hamilton to Lucinda C. Abernathy
19, Wm. B. McMillin to Nancy M. Spence
20, Jackson Smith to Caladonia Cowen by F.M.Ventress JP
22, Thomas Timmins to Susan A. Hamilton by John Mathews
22, Dozier T. Weaver to Alice M. Beddingfield by John W.
Braden JP
22, Henry L. Smith to Amanda M. McClure

```
        22,    Austin Easlick to Ann Cashion by W.M.Newman JP
pg 262
        22,    N.P.Hedgepeth to Catharine Strong by W.R.Hedgepeth JP
        29,    James S. Sumners to Martha Wright by Jacob Nave JP
        29,    Newton Dickey to Amanda Abbott by Robert Drennon JP
        29,    Wm. R. Smith to Martha Jane Shull by John Mathews MG
1854
Jan  4,    Levi W. Hazzellwood to Amanda M. Duke
     7,    George W. Trim to Caroline Foster
    12,    R.B.Gibson to Jane Rebecca Malier by A.G.Gibson MG
    13,    James F. Forsyth to Sarah Snow
    17,    James S. Maupin to America W. Whitaker
    18,    David Luttrell to Eliza Jane Blackwell by L.H.Freeman JP
pg 263
    19,    Jesse Marbery to Nancy Catharine Elam by R. Drennon JP
    23,    James McCoy to Elizabeth Riles by Jacob Gillespie JP
    26,    Alfred Williams to Minerva E. Bowels by J. Dean JP
Feb 18,    Wm. T. Darnell to Mary Ann Rhodes by G.W.Puckett MG
    12,    Milton A. Edmiston to Susan K. Williams by Wm. Dyer JP
     1,    Wm. E. Hunter to Sarah Ann Ellis by Orrin P. Hill JP
     5,    Wm. W. Eaton to Sarah Ann Little by S. Boone JP
     6,    Jesse Claunch to Nancy Wamack
     7,    John T.A.Coble to Martha Ann Smith by John Corder JP
     7,    George W. Murry to Charity Burrow by G.W.R.Moore JP
    11,    George Brewer to Louisa Tucker by H.C.Cowan JP
pg 264
    14,    Wm. H. Taylor to Mary Jane Kennedy by T.W.Parkerson
    16,    James H. Deford to Margaret Jane Allen by T.W.Parkerson
    16,    Jesse J. Price to Mary A.W.Gray by J.L.Thompson JP
    16,    Holly R. Williamson to Susan D. Petty by Wm. Pryor JP
    15,    Hugh P. Penny to Mary B. Morton by T.W.Parkerson
    16,    Cyrus L. Cathy to Eliza Russell by Matt Marshall MG
    16,    Wm. E. McHaffy to Sarah Cason by Wm. Land
    19,    Drewry Wells to Jane Scott by H.H.Rives JP
    23,    Wiley G. Milam to Martha E. Bland by Wm. R. Martin JP
    22,    N.O.Green to Martha A. Fulton by S.M.Cowen VDM
Mar  1,    Thomas Y. Wallace to Mary E. Wiley by A.H.Bishop MG
pg 265
     2,    David C. Craig to Martha P. Greer by M. Marshall MG
     2,    George T. Price to Sarah A. Hatchett by H.C.Holman JP
    26,    Joab Neal to Cyntha A. Smith by Y.T.Taylor JP
     6,    Jonathan E. Spencer to Nancy Ann Waggoner by John
                                              Copeland MG
    14,    Thomas B. Lackey to Sarah Ann Stewart
    15,    J.C.Irvin to Josephine Davis by J.B.Warren MG
    19,    Andrew J. Fannon to Malissa Noles by Y.T.Taylor JP
    18,    James L. Beach to Mary E. Swinford by A.H.Bishop MG
    27,    Benjamin J. Noles to Martha E. Noles by Y.T.Taylor JP
    22,    Calvin Smith to Dessa Cannon by R. Drennon JP
Aug 23,    Joseph Holt to Mary Jenkins by John Bramblet
pg 266
Mar 28,    Isaac R. Pitts to Elvira Reese by G.H.R.Bray MG
    28,    Wm. R. Wamack to Catharine S. Bailey
    29,    John McClure to Susan Hunt by Wm. C. Jennings JP
    30,    Eli Townsend to Susan E. McKee by Wm. A. Gill MG
    30,    Greek P. Rice to M.J.Irvin by M. Marshall MG
Apr  3,    Edward Smith to Margaret Ann Gray
```

6,	John W. Franklin to Delpha Ann Fannon by W.E.Carter JP
6,	Jacob Renegar to Sarah C. Taylor by C.B.White JP
6,	Thomas Whitaker to Martha Shofner
6,	Lewis Spray to Eliza Billens by John Caughran JP

pg 267

8,	David Whitt to Susan J. Browning by G.W.Puckett MG
11,	Joel S. Brewer to Nancy R. Pamplin by H.C.Holman JP
15,	James W. Pamplin to Nancy Ann Pamplin by M.W.Yant JP
20,	John B. Hardy to Pheobe C. Norwood by A.G.Gibson MG
20,	V.M.Rhyne to Joseph Duckworth by Jacob Gillespie JP
23,	J.G.Prosser to Martha Jane Barham by G.W.R.Moore JP
26,	B.E.Melear to Elizabeth E. Kimes by J.B.Warren MG
Jun 11,	Thomas M. Blakemore to Virginia F. Smith by H.H.Rives JP
Apr 27,	Calvin Harris to Amanda Jane Vinson
30,	G.F.Isom to Syntha C. McAfee by M.W.Yant Esq
May 2,	George W. Gattis to Mary Jane Mitchell by Wm. Gattis JP

pg 268

11,	Wm. F. Watson to Mary Ann Gillaim by John Roach
16,	Wm. G. Sexton to Mary Ann Sanderson by G.W.Puckett MG
16,	George Edmison to Ann Eliza Bagley by W.P.Holman JP
27,	Hardin Warden to Mary Keith by Joseph Smith MG
25,	James N. Bland to Permelia S. Smith by Wm. Gayle
30,	W.L.Shelton to Sarah E. Whitworth by Smith L. Walker JP
29,	Wm. R. Faulkenbury to Jane Billions by John Caughran JP
Jun 6,	H.F.Dusenberry to Ann James by Lemuel Brandon MG
4,	F.A.Fencher to Tennessee Forester by M.W.Yant Esq
3,	E. Wamack to Lauret Keller

pg 269

4,	N.B.Pierce,MG to Margaret V. George by John Copeland MG
16,	Elisha Wamack to Laurett Keller by L. Motlow JP
4,	C.J.McKinney to S.E.Reid by B.M.Alsup JP
4,	James B. Carty to S.E.W.Elliott by Wm. Pryor JP
4,	J.R.Marshall to Bethune Pitts by M.W.Yant JP
6,	Wm. W. Stringer to Barbary Parrish
18,	Eli Evans to Mary M. Waggoner by John L. Ashby JP
18,	Alexander Hamilton to Syntha A. Boles by D. Jacks MG
17,	Wm. Heathcock to Elmira Heathcock
24,	Campbell Douthett to Elizabeth Fox by J.W.Holman MG
25,	James H. Sanders to Louisa J. Hedgepeth by Henry Turney

pg 270

Jul 23,	David J. Kimes to Mary L. McDaniel
27,	Lewis A. Colbert to Martha E. Jones
29,	Alexander Edmunson to Catharine Alley by B.Christian JP
Aug 3,	Noris Flynt to Sophronia Easlick by B. Christian JP
3,	J.E.Humphrey to M.E.Cummins by A.G.Smith MG
5,	Samuel Smith to Sarah Mitchell
7,	S.A.Slaughter to Josephine Edmiston by S.M.Cowen VDM
16,	John M. Buchanan to Eliza J. Williamson by S.M. Emmons MG
15,	James L. Moorehead to Mary Spencer by John Copeland MG
23,	Joseph Holt to Mary Jenkins

pg 271

24,	James T. Dickson to Martha Barker by B. Christian JP
29,	John Luttrell to Mandana E. Cox by B. Christian JP
Sep 10,	Wm. B. Roughton to Martha C. Pegram by D. Sullivan
1,	Wm. A. Findley to Isabelle Murdock by W.H.McGee MG
30,	issued: James Land to Martha Cunningham by Orrin P. Hill Solemized 30 Apr 1854 ?

Sep 4,   Wm. M. Scott to Virginia P. Wells by Jacob Gillespie JP
     4,   J.W.Raney to Lyda J. Coller by R.M.Whitman
     7,   Rufus K. Smith to Unice C. Casey by B. Christian JP
     9,   Thomas D. Aderton to Nancy E. Rhea by Jason Ray MG
     8,   John Bonner to Mary Jane Clark by Wm. N. Hicks JP
pg 272
     9,   John R. Johnson to Rebecca Ann Buchanan by A.G.Smith MG
    10,   Nathan Boone to Orpha Johnston by J. Smith MG
    13,   Wm. A. Brown to Milly A. Landess by John A. Jones MG
    21,   Thomas P. Arnold to Mariah Stanley by B. Christian JP
    12,   L.L.Leftwich to Elizabeth Reese
    13,   John R. Hague to Margerett S. McGhee by B. McGaugh MG
    14,   Henry Green Swinebroad to Martha Ann Wilson by J.B.
                                                      Warren MG
    20,   A.G.H.Brandon to Hester R. Simpson by J.M.Holman MG
    21,   Samuel Crabtree to Charlotte Stephenson by Roach JP
Oct 2,   George P. Stephens to Nancy Wells by Rev. John Smith
pg 272
Sep 23,   Alvin Bates to Elizabeth Gail by R.D.Hardin JP
    22,   James Roland to Nancy Miles (License returned but not
           endorsed by any person)
    24,   Daniel B. McCann to Mary Ann Maroney by R.D.Hardin JP
    25,   James McCartney to Mary E. Dillen
    28,   Samuel C. McCollum to Elizabeth Armstrong by Howell
                                                      Harris JP
    27,   James B. Sanford to Elizabeth Smith by R. Drennon JP
    27,   Solomon Mason to Mary E. Scoggins by John Caughran JP
Oct 1,   Davis Smith to Elinor M. Robeson by B.M.G.Alsup JP
    10,   Joseph N. Wakefield to Elizabeth S. Wright by B.F.Ments LD
     5,   Martin Smith to Elizabeth Majors by D.S.Patterson JP
pg 273
     7,   Daniel W. Sanders to Louisa Jane Griffin by W.L.Reese JP
    11,   Jasper Dickey to Pheby E. Bradford by A.H.Bishop MG
    12,   John Hill to Catharine McGeehee by Nicholas Copeland JP
    18,   David F. Brown to Altalitha C. Howell by S.L.Walker JP
    13,   A.J.Hamilton to Narcissa Stone
    19,   Robert Searcey to Martha Gregory by Alex. Smith MG
    24,   Thomas C. Ray to Elizabeth J. Adkins by T.B.White MG
    26,   David M. Smith to Martha Jane Cowden by T.W.Brents MG
    26,   Wm. Summerford to Sarah E. Allen by Jacob Gillespie JP
    26,   Samuel Hall by Rachel A. Pitts by J.B.Warren MG
pg 275
Nov 2,   John Noah to Nancy J. Roberts by S.M.Emmons MG
Oct 31,   Charles G. Taylor to Alley Leonard by B. Christian JP
Nov 3,   Joseph M. Rich to Sarah E. Brown by D. Jacks MG
     2,   Isaac Majors to Rhody Paysinger by D.S.Patterson JP
     2,   Wm. Bunn to Mary A. Bryant by C.B.McDaniel JP
     3,   Roger Foster to Letha King by G.W.R.Moore JP
     5,   Dennis Fowler to Mary Ann Bevels by D.S.Patterson JP
    10,   Reuben Seamore to Norah Heirs
    15,   David Sanders to Mary Jane Watt by John Roach JP
    30,   John D. Sexton to Terresa C. Land by Wm. Pryor JP
pg 276
    22,   Clarence Grant to Sarah Commons by Moses Yant Esq
    23,   W.D.Moore to Susan Dance by L. Brandon
    29,   N.C.Ward to Anna Brown by W.A.Hobbs Esq
    24,   Wm. Copeland to Mary Ann George by J.W.Holman MG
    26,   F.M.Banks to A.J.Sykes by W.A.Hobbs Esq

25, John Warren to Louisa Ables by W.L.Reese JP
26, John Wood to Mary Russell by James Kirkland
28, Daniel Tucker to Margaret Heirs
30, George Moyers to Martha Easlick by J.L.Ashby JP

pg 277

Dec 3, James Brents to Stacy Ellis by J.B.Warren MG
21, Jacob B. Pitcock to Martha Ann Rich by D. Jacks MG
7, John D. Campbell to Sally Ann Been by D. Jacks MG
10, C.C.Eaton to Martha M. McLain by D. Sullivan JP
14, James H. Culbreath to Caroline R. Owensby by W.A.Hobbs Esq
19, John W. Watson to Sarah F. Steelman by Wm. N. Hicks Esq
19, Joseph A. Nicks to Ann Land by Wm. Pryor JP
27, Alexander Scroggins to Eliza Rhodes by R.S.Hardin JP
21, Jonathan Sandlin to Elizabeth M. Smith
28, Wm. N. Wright to Mary Buchanan by S.M.Cowen V.D.M.
28, J.L.Lively to Mary Ann Brown by J.G.Harrison JP

pg 278

1855

Jan 2, Jesse L. Jones to Martha Hawkwood by T.H.Freeman JP
2, Hopson Lewis to Sarah Ann Umphrey by S.M.Cowen VDM
2, Benjamin F. Martin to Martha J. Ewing by S.E.Douthit MG
2, F.P.L.Parr to Rebecca E. Sawyers by James C. Elliott MG
30, Wm. P. Wright to Elizabeth Swan by John Wagster MG
4, John G. McCalla to Lydy L. Boman by A.S.Sloan
4, Wm. M. Smith to Amanda Tucker by B. Christian JP
3, Temple Scott to Nancy Roane by A.S.Moore JP
4, W.W.Haithcock to Sarah L. Franklin by Wm. Hicks Esq
7, J.E.McWhorter to Frances Noe by A.G.Smith MG

pg 279

7, Wm. H. Thompson to Jane Howard by Wm. Gattis JP
7, G.M.Sawyers to Sarah E. Wakefield by J. Kirkland MG
7, Alexander Waggoner to Mary E. McGee by Moses Yant Esq
9, J.H.Malden to Nancy J. McKinney by Henry Turney JP
9, Henry Carty to Margaret E. Blake by M. Marshall MG
11, Samuel A. Hopkins to Elizabeth Petty by Wm Pryor JP
10, A.J.Whitaker to S.J.McMillen by R.B.McGaugh MG
14, Wm. Stanley to Martha C. Arnold by W.P.Holman JP
14, Joel K. Pamplin to Cynthia E. Yant by H.C.Holman JP
16, James M. Smith to Lelia J. Dameron

pg 280

25, Robert Gillespie to Elizabeth Copeland by Rev. J. Scivally
20, John Miller to Jane Tucker
25, A.F.D.Goodwin to Mary Jane Hailey by A.F.Driskill
25, John W. Armstrong to Nancy Jane Dollins by R.B.McGaugh,M
31, A.M.Collins to Sarah J. Allsup by J.M.Emmons MG
29, Larkin A. Smith to Cynthia Landess
Feb 1, James A. Franklin to Lovina Heathcock by Wm. Hicks Esq
3, George Church to Sarah Dameron
5, George T. Martin to Mary J. Wright by Wm. Hicks Esq
6, John H. Coats to Nancy J. Hartgrass by G.W.Puckett MG
7, Wilkinson Reese to Martha Wagster by W.W.Arnold MG

pg 281

13, Lewis Fleming to Salina R. Ashby by M. Marshall MG
12, Benjamin F. Wamack to Susan E. Green by J.W.Holman MG
14, K.A.McKenzie to Susan E. Higgins by W.E.McKenzie MG
19, James Bean to Jane Crane by D. Sullivan JP
20, Thomas B. Clift to Parthena C. Swinebroad by J.Kirkland,M

```
        22,     E.H.Steadman to Mary Bland by Hugh Parkinson JP
        22,     Wm. Patrick to Margaret Ann George by A.S.Moore JP
        25,     Robert T. Collins to Lucy C.A.Clark by Henry Turney JP
Mar  1,         Robert F. Gattis to Harriet Raney by W.A.Hobbs Esq
         4,     Joseph Jones to Elizabeth M. Beard by A.S.Moore JP
pg 282
        20,     Joseph W. Draper to Lillian Kavanaugh by J.G.Woods JP
        22,     Joseph Jeans to Martha L. Pamplin by J.W.Cullum MG
        29,     Felix Clounch to Bertha Koonce by Smith Walker, JP
Apr  1,         James N. Clift to Manerva L. Swinebroad by L.J.Neeley MG
         4,     Henry B. McDaniel to Louisa A. Jefferson
         8,     Wm. Shapard to Elizabeth V. Grills by J.E.White MG
        18,     George M. Strong to Margarett B. Moore by J.C.Elliott MG
        30,     David Sims to Angeline Green
May  2,         Nathaniel Mills to Susanah Conaway by Rev. Wm. Land
         3,     Brown Parkerson to L.C.C.Bearden by A.S.Sloan
         6,     Wm. D. Walker to Nancy E. Culberson by Rev. Wm. Tillery
pg 283
         7,     Henry M. Powell to Becky Ann Pollock by Wm. F.
                                                      Zimmerman JP
         8,     A.P.Clift to Elizabeth Epps by J.G.Harrison JP
         8,     James M. Taylor to Elizabeth R. Hawkings by A.J.Childress
        27,     J.W.Perry to Nancy White by T.H.Freeman JP
        17,     George W. Allison to Ann Ramsey by C.B.McDaniel JP
        22,     James R. Routt to Mary J. Wells by M. Marshall MG
        28,     G.W.Stephenson to Martha J. Sharp by C.W.McGuire JP
        22,     Robert McMullen to Rebeca E. Holt
        23,     Angus N. Bryan to Frances A. Martin by B.F.Clark JP
        29,     James Bates to Mary Ann Gale
Jun  7,         Jacob B. Allison to Nancy R. Thompson by T.H.Freeman JP
pg 284
         7,     N.O.Wallace to M.E.McKinney by Rev. S.M.Cowan
        20,     Wm. L. Allison to Loucinda E. Thompson
        24,     A.J.Ivy to Malinda Roland by W.A.Hobbs Esq
        27,     Wm. H. Shelton to Mary E. Smith by B. Christian JP
        28,     Virgil A. Dudley to Mary Beavers by J. Dean
        28,     William Cross to Malinda Hickson by W.A.Hobbs Esq
        28,     L.J.E.Bearden to Martha E. Wells by M.M.Marshall DD
        28,     John T. Phillips to Mary L. Cole
Aug 17,         Wm. L. Youngblood to Martha J. Hooper by Howell Harris JP
Jul 10,         Wm. Ashworth to Mary R.E.McKee by Joseph White MG
pg 285
         8,     Wm. R. Jester to Elizabeth Ann Wells by J. Rouch JP
        10,     Wm. A. Watson to Jane Holley
        12,     Wm. G. Gillam to Agness J. Tate by Thos. A. Parkinson
        12,     James H. Smith to Margaret L. Majors by O.S.Patterson JP
        13,     John C. Arnold to Martha J. Taylor by B. Christian JP
        16,     F.W.Waggoner to Susan F. Ingle by J.W.Holman MG
        18,     Green B. Casey to Elizabeth L. Hill by B.Christian JP
        18,     James D. Smith to Mary C. Casey by B. Christian JP
        18,     Francis M. Edens to Pheby S. Overby by J.W.Holman MG
        22,     Wm. R. Evans to Frances L. Waggoner by J.L.Ashby JP
        24,     J.H.Lock to Drulina Renfro by D. Sullivan JP
pg 286
        24,     James G. Land to Nancy L. McDugal
        26,     Benjamin F. Odell to Mary Ann Towery
        30,     John P. Turney to Tabithia J. Compton by Thos. Childs
```

```
        31,    Wm. Dossey to Piety Weaver by John L. Gordon JP
Aug  4,    Wm. Buffalo to L.J.Majors by G.W.Puckett MG
     6,    A.M.Brown to E.C.Russell by J.H.Steelman JP
    18,    Wm. Eddens to Martha Ann Allen by W.A.Hobbs Esq
     8,    Francis Hudson to Elvira Coulter by J.H.Steelman
     9,    A.J.Gulley to Lucinda Gulley by G.W.R.Moore JP
    13,    A.M.Anderson to Isabella Edmonson by Wm. Gale MG
    13,    John Owens to Elizabeth Brown by J.W.Holman MG
pg 287
    19,    Wm. W. Hindman to Susan A. Wright by D. Sullivan JP
    18,    Wm. C. Fincher to Fanny B. Reese
    20,    John S. Wiseman to Julianne Cartright
    21,    Isam Wells to Eliza Stanley by W.S.Bachman LD,M.E.S.
    23,    Mathew N. Grinnette to Ruth Hambrick by D. Jacks MG
    23,    James W. Hatchett to Elizabeth Webster by J.L.Gordon JP
    30,    Wm. W. Childs to A.A.Dennis by J.G.Woods JP
Sep  2,    James P. Doss to Martha E. McLin by Matt Marshall,Min.
     2,    Francis H. Bell to Mary C. Grizard by T.I.Neeley, Min.
     5,    John M. Cook to Nancy Ann Smith by S.M.Emmons MG
     9,    Isaac Grammer to Margarett Ann Bruce by John L. Ashby JP
pg 288
     9,    Wm. J. Jefferies to Lucinda Pamplin by I.W.Collum Off Min.
     6,    A.M.Brown to E.C.Russell
     9,    James R. Smith to Nancy Brown by Wm. Gattis JP
     9,    Travis A. Yant to Permelia A. Holman by J.W.Cullum, Min.
     2,    F.M.Pratt to Elizabeth Edde by F. Motlow JP
     9,    John Street to Martha E. Stanley by W.P.Holman JP
    11,    James W. Hester to Mary Ann Scott by Jacob Gillespie JP
    12,    John E. Spencer to Alley J. Waggoner by John Copeland MG
    18,    Rufus C. McElroy to Amanda A. Smith by A.G.Smith MG
    20,    Isaac Keller to Elizabeth McClure by S.L.Walker JP
pg 289
    23,    L.H.Fortner to Synthy E. Smith by J. Daniel MG
    21,    James L. Jordon to Aetsy Luttrell by W.T.Holman JP
    23,    James H. Forkner to Virginia(Viney) E. Jackson by Rev.
                                                     Wm. Tilby
    20,    Green W. Nichols to Sarah E. Price by W.W.Arnold MG
    23,    Samuel Eaton to Jane C. Glasscock
    21,    Ruffus Harris to Nancy E. Blake by S.M.Cowan VDM
    25,    C.B.Carty to Martha Johnson by S.M.Cowan VDM
    28,    Galen P. Wilson to Malinda Jane Hill by J.N.George JP
    27,    John B. Cole to Emily Street by Rev. R.D.Hardin
Oct  4,    Wm. W. Rogers to Martha Jane Petty by W.A.Gill MG
     3,    Dillard Deal to Martha Ann Hall by J.W.Cullam MG
pg 290
     4,    Wm. J. Miller to Louisa Southworth by Joseph E. White MG
     7,    Wm. Gold to Sarah Ann Cummins by G.W.R.Moore JP
     9,    John W. Braden to Sarah A. Taylor by C.W.McGuire JP
    11,    James E. Randolph to Louisa Street by Rev. D. Hardin MG
    10,    E.W.Ellis to Elizabeth McCoy by G.W.R.Moore JP
    18,    S.D.Ellis to Mary E. Cummins by G.W.R.Moore JP
    11,    Wm. M. Henderson to Martha J. Whitworth by J.P.McGee JP
    13,    George W. Summers to Mary Amanda Frances Pamplin by
                                                  T.H.Freeman JP
    19,    Thomas J. Whitworth to Mariah A. Brass
    20,    R.C.Blackwell to Juliana Davidson by J.B.Warren MG
pg 291
    25,    Wm. J. King to Mary G. Russell by M.M.Marshall MG
```

31,   Phillip Cooper to Elizabeth Cooper by Wm. J. Grill JP
27,   Thomas Spelce(Spence) to Catharine Baker by A.J.Steel,M
28,   John Warden to Martha Ann Dunkin by M.W.Yant JP
28,   Andrew Waggoner to Hester Baxter by D. Sullivan JP
31,   Reuben W. Wells to Mary D. Ashby by M.W.Yant JP
Nov 1,   Thomas F. Moore to Elizabeth Blair by T.W.Parkerson
1,   Theodore Smith to M.V.Moores by A.H.Berry
6,   J.A.Martin to Mary Holt by J. Dean MG
4,   Robert Fackender to Mary Ann O'Quinn by D. Sullivan JP
7,   M.J.Clunn to L.T.Robertson by D. Jacks MG
pg 292
7,   Henry B. McCown to Elizabeth McCormack
8,   R.M.Carter to Mary J. Davidson by J.C.B.White JP
15,   Stephen Cole to Sarah Ann Leatherwood by S.M.Emmons MG
14,   James M. Price to Frances E. Woodard by A.G.Smith MG
15,   James Mims to Julia Ann Wells by R.B.McGaugh MG
15,   Shepard Hunter to Mary E. Goodrich by S.M.Cowan VDM
21,   Benjamin Bedford to Nancy Ann Gowan by R.M.Waggoner MG
21,   G.W.Hanvy(Harvey) to Nancy E. Gulley by R.B.McGaugh MG
21,   H.H.Sugg to Sarah Bruce
27,   John H. Hutcherson to Margarett E. Meeks by John Caughran
29,   Pleasant D. Noah to Mary A. Roberts by S.M.Emmons MG
pg 293
27,   Wm. L. Carty to Sarah Jane Moore
29,   Silas Luttrell to Parmela Taylor by W.P.Holman JP
29,   Theodore J. Prichett(Pickett) to Nancy L. Sanders by
                                                W.P.Holman JP
Dec 1,   George Wadkins to Martha Jane Hedrick
11,   Benjamin W. Murphy to Elizabeth Jane Ewing by J.C.Elliott,M
6,   W.P.Wood to Lucinda E. Chitwood by S.M.Emmons MG
6,   James Evans to Elizabeth M. King by D.L.Mitchell MG
7,   James A. George to Jane Cunningham
11,   James Philpot to Martha J. Brown by J.G.Elliott MG
15,   A.J.Minatree to Mary A. Clark
20,   John Price to Mary Mason
pg 294
25,   F.M.Cole to Delila Ellis by J.B.Warren MG
27,   Wm. Fonville to Mary K. Old by John W. Ogden MG
26,   Stephen B. Nelson to Sarah H. Anderson
27,   Moses H. Hawkins to Julia A. Surber by A.G.Smith MG
28,   F.H.Lewis to Matilda Dunn
1856
Jan 3,   James B. Wyatt to Mary E. Wilson by T.W.Parkenson
3,   Lemuel D. Sugg to Margaret E. Halbert by S.M.Cowan VDM
3,   Willis M. Holman to Martha D. Higgins by R.B.McGaugh MG
6,   John White to Elizabeth Lackey
6,   Jesse Prosser to Mary Jackson by D. Sullivan
6,   James Massey to Margaret Cunningham by J.L.Ashby JP
9,   Demarcus P. Cunningham to Prescilla A. Allsup by W.M.
                                                McKinney JP
11,   Wm. M. Becket to Eugenie C. Hague
13,   Wm. G. Pylant to Drusilla Ann Young by G.W.R.Moore JP
13,   Joshua Saunders to Lucinda Tucker by J.G.Woods JP
14,   Martin F. Hampton to Mary E. Abernathy
15,   Albert Caten to Sarah Hobbs by W.R.Martin JP
15,   Robert Land to Elizabeth Pigg by J. Roach, Esq
15,   A.H.Bell to Martha E. McGee by Wm. Pryor JP
16,   Wiley Spray to Nancy J. Abbot

1856

16,   Wm. Becket to Eugine C. Hague (see Jan 11,1856) by
                                            M.M.Marshall VDM
pg 296
16,   Thomas Nichols to Elizann Wagster
17,   Hicks Bennett to Fanny Ann McChristian
20,   John B. Daniel to Emaline Parrish by J.P.McGee JP
20,   Jasper Renegar to Mary J. Buchanan by W.R.Martin JP
20,   Ruben Golden to Anna Stone by D. Jacks MG
22,   John M. Shaw to Mary E. Evans by Wm. N. Hicks JP
23,   Wm. H. Luttrell to Luzanna A. Sanders by W.F.Holman JP
24,   James O. Rees to Nancy Jane Freeman by John Wagster MG
27,   Thomas Jean to Martha Emily Ruthledge by Rev. R.B.McGaugh
Feb 3,   A.C.James to Margaret McBride by S. Leatherwood JP
5,   John Leonard to Sarah E. Templeton by W.C.Jennings JP
pg 297
Jan 31,   A.F.Stone to Susan F. Haskins by John L. Ashby JP
Feb 7,   James Henderson to Nelly E. Harbin by W.J.Grills JP
4,   Wm. M. Franklin to Mary Jane Renegar
18,   P.G.Gilbert to Delila J. Edde by J. Smith MG
11,   Charles M. Beard to Clerasa J. Locker by J.G.Wood JP
12,   R.F.Evans to Julia E. Greer
14,   Joseph C. Wallace to Catharine B. Wiggins by D.S.Patterson
14,   Esson C. Loyd to Sarah Catharine Gattis by Wm. Gattis JP
14,   James A. Moore to Sarah L. McDaniel by T.W.Parkinson MG
14,   James T. Woodward to E.A.Conaway by S.D.Ogburn MG
17,   Edmond C. Jones to Mary L. Demasters by John L. Gorden,JP,
pg 298
18,   Boyers S. Pollock to Martha Renegar by W.L.Neese JP
19,   John Panter to Elizabeth Story by F. Motlow JP
26,   J.E.Coldwell to Amanda F. Yeats by R.B.McGaugh MG
20,   Cornelius B. Adams to Martha E. Jones
28,   Josiah J. Land to Mary E. Pickett by S.L.Walker JP
Mar 6,   Hardin J. Gulley to Susanah Bradford by G.W.R.Moore JP
Feb 26,   Joseph Cole to Sarah Jane Armstrong by Howell Harris JP
Mar 5,   C.M.Wilson to Elizabeth Ann Womack by L. Brandon
4,   Robert A. Shaw to Millie Connelly by L.M.Cowan VDM
5,   Bennet W. Childs to Fannie A. Boon by B.C.Chapman MG
pg 299
5,   Francis M. Moyers to America H. Tucker by J.L.Ashby JP
11,   H.C.Whitaker to L.L.Whitaker by J.W.Holman MG
20,   Josephus West to Manerva J. West by T.W.Parkinson MG
17,   J.W.Wilson to A.J.Tate
19,   David Laws to Mary Painter by L. Brandon
24,   John M. Hutchison to Mary C. Carn by G.W.R.Moore JP
23,   Hickman M. Koonce to Helen M. Dennis by Wm. Pryor JP
20,   Absolum Webster to Rebeca Adcock
27,   Johnson Warren to Egletine Freeman by John Wagster MG
27,   Wm. Tafts to Frances Carpenter by Wm. R. Martin JP
27,   James C. Ellis to Nancy D. Pigg by John Roach JP
pg 300
Apr 3,   J.C.Parr to Eliza Ann Bonner by D.C.Patterson JP
3,   James W. Mitchell to Susan E. Gattis by John Copeland MG
3,   James Richeson to Jane Sorrells by G.W.R.Moore JP
6,   John H. Kay to S.A.E.Pamplin by J.H.Steelman JP
7,   Joseph H. Pollock to Sarah P. Dillingham
8,   Richard S. Williamson to Martha Jane Waldrop by M.W.Yant
10,   John Halflack to Mary C. Anderson by Wiley A. Hobbs JP
8,   M.M.Caldwell to Julia Ann Alexander by S.M.Cowan VDM

```
        17,  Wm. J. Scroggins to Elizabeth Good by R. Drennon JP
        17,  John Sims to Rebecca Pylant by Wm. Pryor JP
pg 301
        22,  Benjamin Fannon to Julia Yarbrough by W.E.Carter JP
        21,  James E. Bray to Mary C. Shappard
        24,  Samuel H. Rhone to Nancy Brown by J.P.McGee JP
        27,  John C. Carter to Sarah P. Stone by D. Jacks MG
        21,  J.S.Hambrick to Emily Pennington
        28,  Wm. Hise to Cynthia J. Abbott by W.A.Hobbs Esq
Jun  6,  Wm. Gattis to Martha Ann VanHooser by G.W.Puckett MG
May  1,  Jefferson Flippo to Susan Ann Jane Simmons by W.A.
                                                    Hobbs Esq
         7,  James M. Curtis to Lydia F. Lankston by Green Nichols MG
        16,  Chesbey Hanvey to Margaret E. Warren
        20,  Ebenezer Hill to Ruth A. Gregory by A.A.Bell MG
pg 302
        23,  G.M.Steele to Louisa Whitaker by M.M.Marshall MG
        22,  Jasper Williams to Jane Counts by John Corder JP
        22,  Jacob C.B.Runnels to Elizabeth Catharine Simmons by
                                                    W.A.Hobbs Esq
Jun  1,  George W. Posey to Sarah Jane Stewart by J.H.Steelman Esq
        15,  Pleasant W. Beavers to Priscilla E. Heath by J.L.Ashby JP
        25,  T.D.Hill to Julia F. Whitaker
         4,  Charles L. Waggoner to E.M.Spencer by John Copeland MG
        29,  James M. Johnson to Sarah H. Jones by M.W.Yant Esq
Jul  6,  Thomas Holley to Edde Emeline Wright by G.W.R.Moore JP
         3,  John W. McClure to Rebecca D. Mitchell by S.F.Spencer JP
         3,  John M. Alford to Frances Ann Lusk by S.D.Ogburn MG
        13,  W.C.Bray to Susan Alexander by Wm. Gale
pg 303
         8,  Isaac N. Eslick to Martha E. Taylor by S.F.Spencer JP
        13,  Wm. H. Hester to Margaret S. White by D.L.Mitchell MG
        17,  James A. Hedrick to Margaret C. Harkins by G.W.R.Moore JP
        17,  John H. Lane to Elizabeth Johnson by M.W.Yant JP
        16,  Thomas J. Stovall to Selia Dameron
        18,  James H. Campbell to Amanda C.R.Sloan by J.N.George JP
        17,  E.J.Phillips to Martha Ann Neaves by J. Caughran JP
        17,  Wm. Roe to Sarah Ann Campbell by Henry Henderson JP
        20,  James C. Beck to Syntha A. Wilson by S.D.Ogburn MG
        20,  David G. Smith to A.H.Whittington by B.M.G.Alsup JP
        20,  Cornelius B. Adams to Martha E. Jones
pg 304
        24,  Bennett Solomon to Nancy P. Stubblefield by J.H.Eslick JP
        26,  Thomas B. Whitworth to Ziephy Billings
        31,  Bennett B. Merritt to Elizabeth McDaniel by H.W.Overall,M
Aug  4,  Zebulon Parr to Dona E.D.Swinebroad by S.E.Wilson MG
Jul 29,  John W. Cashion to Charlotte J. Arnold by W.C.Jennings
Aug  7,  Francis M. Williams to Susan Coleman by Wm. Gayle MG
         4,  Daniel Cole to Mary Jane Nelson by J.W.Holman MG
         5,  John Y. Gill to Mary E. Rodgers by John Caughran JP
         7,  James M. Sorrells to Martha Ann Armstrong by G.W.R.
                                                    Moore JP
         8,  Peter J. Anderton to Nancy M. Cox
pg 305
        14,  J.W.Hodge to Perthena Bledsoe by G.W.Puckett MG
        14,  F.M.Colter to Martha A. Nicks by J.H.Steelman JP
        17,  Joel B. Raney to Huldah Neese by J. Wagster MG
        18,  Josiah A. Biggs to Frances H. Andrews by R.Farquharson JP
```

28, A.J.Mullins to Martha Ann Vickers by W.N.Hicks Esq
25, George W. Fields to Nancy M. Bailey
25, David C. Jean to Mary E. Jones by M.W.Yant Esq
27, Thomas Lock to Margret Ann Marshall by W.N.Hicks Esq
27, Wm. Martin to Ann Forsyth by J.H.Eslick Esq
Sep 3, A.C.Freeman to Mary Ann Perry by Green Nichols MG
pg 306
7, Martin V. Pope to Hester Ann M. Brasier by Henry
                                        Henderson JP
5, John M. Routt to Louisa J. Kelso by W.A.Gill MG
11, James M. Wells to Isabella McKinney by J.P.McGee JP
14, J.L.Burgess to Lucretia McLaughlin by John Wagster MG
13, James Gullett to Maurning Ann Shields
14, Robert Boyd to Cynthia Adcock by R. Farquharson JP
16, S.E.H.Dance to M.A.Berry by T.S.Petway
18, J.M.Bates to Lucinda J. Jenkins by J.S.Ashby JP
15, M.M.Young to Malinda Jones by Green Nichols MG
19, John Petty to Eliza Ann Walker by J. Caughran
pg 307
17, Joseph Brooks to Artenia Reese by D. Sullivan JP
18, Wilson R. Call to Martha J. Waggoner by J. Scivally
20, W.H.Sanders to Nancy Warren
22, issued: E.G.Bevill to Lucinda E. Holt by S.M.Emmons
     Solomized:Sep 6th 1856(Could be Oct 6th)
23, F.L.Ezell to Mary J. McCracken by M.L.Bobo VDM
22, Thomas J. Clark to Mary E. Rodgers by W.F.Blake JP
25, David George to Martha C. Hampton by J.N.George JP
Oct 1, Wm. B. McKenzie to Ann E. Sherrill by W.E.McKenzie MG
6, James B. Wilson to M.A.Whitaker by S.M.Cowan VDM
pg 308
7, Joel Steelman to Belinda Freeman by Green Nichols MG
8, J.P.Williams to Sarah Ann Foster
12, C.G.Spillman to Molly Ann Gill by W.A.Gill MG
13, Ambrose Holt to Martha Webster by J. Caughran JP
15, James C. Cobb to Emeline Petty
18, David M. Wilson to Melinda J. Mullins by W.R.Martin JP
19, Jesse M. Loveless to Eleanor A.E.Nave by W.H.Riggan MG
22, James T. Clark to Susan R. Smith by S.M.Cowan VDM
26, Joseph D. McLelland to Mary A. Stonebraker by B.C.
                                        Chapman MG
25, Wm. Chapman to Nancy Jones
pg 309
30, Elijah B. Brown to Sarah C. Mitchell by M.W.Yant Esq
Nov 4, Sylvester Pinkney to Mary J. Benningfield by John Walton
5, F.E.Fleming to N.A.Niell by S.M.Cowan VDM
12, Benjamin A. Beard to Hetty F. Moyers by J.P.McGee JP
13, James A. Panter to Armacinda Miles by C.B.White JP
13, F.M.Couch to Sarah J. McClure by S.F.Spencer JP
16, James M. Brown to Susan C. Carrigan by W.A.Hobbs JP
19, Daniel G. Story to Nancy L. Stewart by W.F.Zimmerman JP
20, James B. Pigg to Martha J. Morton by O.P.Hill JP
27, John Braidy to Lucinda Williams by B.M.G.Alsup JP
pg 310
25, Robert Hughy to Sarah Tate by Alexander Smith MG
26, James W. Berry to Laurit M. Motlow
26, Isham J. Towery to Celia Raney by J. Caughran JP
26, Hiram H. Reese to Nancy Phelps

```
        26,    J.W.Muse to Martha Nichols by G. Nichols MG
        30,    James K. Moores to M.L.Smith by A.G.Smith MG
Dec      2,    John Yeates to Amanda Yarbrough by W.E.Carter JP
         4,    L.M.Patterson to Lucy A.P.Leatherwood by S.M.Emmons MG
         3,    C.A.Diemer to Rebecca J. Green by M.M.Marshall MG
         8,    James R. Bradford to Elizabeth L.A.Dickey by R. Drennon
pg 311
1857
Jan      3,    J.J.Gulley to Almedia D.Y.Pitts
pg 312
1856
Dec      6,    R.M.Taylor to Eliza C. West
        11,    N.M.Jenkins to Elizabeth E. Nicks by John Caughran JP
        11,    James R. Chilcoat to Susan Flack by A.M.Cowan VDM
        11,    Samuel A. Thompson to Melvina L. Tucker by C.B.White JP
        11,    M.H.Roberts to Sarah L. Waterman by James R. Chilcoat
                                                              Judge
        18,    John J. Bonner to Elizabeth Smith by W.N.Hicks Esq
        18,    B.F.Whitaker to Manerva A. Buchanan by A.G.Smith MG
        23,    Wm. F. Nave to Martha F. Stewart by C.B.McDaniel JP
        20,    Henry McNeece to Martha Wilkins
        21,    Samuel Hanie to Anna Moore by Amos Small JP
pg 313         -Blank-
pg 314
        22,    M.C.Story to Mary E. Ship
        25,    Wm. M. Walker to Martha A.E.Walker by Wm. Pryor JP
        25,    Wm. B. Roseboro to Ann E. Harven by W.T.Grills JP
        28,    Thadeus White to Nancy A. Smith by W.E.Carter JP
1857
Jan      1,    A. Millikin to Mary Rees by A.G.Smith MG
1856
Dec     31,    George F. Gaddis(Gattis) to Susan Hill
1857
Jan      1,    George W. Rudd to Martha J. Cummins by S.M.Cowan
         5,    Wm. J. Rodgers to Frances A. Smith
        12,    John K. Patterson to Sarah P. Beavers by J. Dean MG
        13,    O.P.Owen to Mary Ann Rowell by R.D.Hardin JP
pg 315
        13,    Wm. P. White to Mary Ann Blackwell by C.B.White JP
        13,    Albine Roden to Elizabeth Lewis by W.M.McKinney JP
        16,    Isaac A. Cole to Nancy A. Buchanan by W.F.Zimmerman JP
Jun 11,        Alfred Holt to Mary C. Edgeman by Martin Towery MG
Jan 21,        Johnathan W. Rowell to Lucinda C. Smith by A.F.Driskill,M
        22,    Thomas Bryant to Nancy J. Pickle by J. Roach JP
        22,    Wm. B. George to Hester M. Stubblefield by S.L.Walker JP
        22,    Wm. S. Moores to Nancy A. Bunn by J.G.Woods JP
        31,    J.C.Ewing to Nancy C. Grubbs
pg 316
        25,    Samuel B. Roseborough to Mary C. Snoddy by W.E.Carter JP
        24,    Wm. P. Lemmonds to N.J.Woodard
        26,    James H. Hamlin to Emily D. Glen by J.W.T.Lee
        29,    James T. Currin to Arabella J. Franklin by S.L.Walker JP
        31,    John L. Tennison to Susan Jane Stubblefield
Feb      4,    Joel R. Neece to Sarah E. Jones by D. Sullivan JP
         2,    John Jones to Emily Pennington
         5,    Henry S. Clift to Sarah J. Pigg by John Roach JP
        10,    Andrew J. Patrick to Eliza Marshall by T.H.Freeman JP
         9,    Wiley Langston to Martha Bragg by John Corder JP
```

1857

2,	J.C.Ewing to Nancy C. Grubbs by J.C.Elliott MG

pg 317

10,	John Collins to Mahala Carpenter by W.M.McKinney
17,	John A. Silvertooth to Marilda Cox by Joseph Smith MG
11,	Martin Smith to Rhoda Eslick by S.F.Spencer JP
12,	James W. Dyer to Narcissa J. Woodard by O.P.Hill JP
Mar 1,	Benjamin F. Cochran to Louisa J. Pickett by D.H.Jones MG
Feb 18,	Enoch N. Bradley to Helen Boren by Isaac H. Eslick JP
22,	John Little to Martha Howard by C.B.McDaniel JP
26,	R.L.Thornton to Eliza J. Snoddy by W.E.Carter JP
26,	James B. Lamb to Elizabeth F. Bonner by C.D.Elliott MG
Mar 5,	Daniel B. Downing to Margarett Templeton by J. Caughran JP

pg 318

5,	Wiley Bunn to Rebecca Wells by J.T.Gordon JP
5,	J.W.Dryden to Arabella C. Bradshaw by W.F.Blake JP
5,	Solomon Roland to Sarah Womack by W.A.Hobbs JP
11,	Wm. Lindsey to Margarett Ann Shackleford by C.B.White JP
11,	Samuel McCalister to Malinda Walker by J. Caughran JP
12,	W.W.McDaniel to Susan Carpenter by W.T.Martin JP
23,	R.K.Hill to Caroline King by J.W.Holman MG
27,	George W. Sumners to Lyda C. Brotherton by W.M.McKinney
Apr 9,	James S. Keith to Mary Ann Sims by Amos Small JP
12,	Henry Williams to Mary Ann Pigg by Zebulin Parr MG
12,	John S. Haskins to Nancy M. Collins by J. Dean MG

pg 319

15,	Wm. V. Tate to R.K.Alexander by Alex. Smith MG
22,	Reece Williams to Elizabeth Watson by W.N.Hicks Esq
May 8,	M.G.Waggoner to Frances Hensley by John Copeland
Apr 23,	W.A.Wright to Susan C. Hamilton by A.G.Smith MG
May 7,	John W.M.Dance to Sarah E. Price by W.A.Hobbs Esq
5,	D.L.Harris to Julia Conaway by Rev. R.D.Hardin
7,	Thomas H. Boles to Eliza Bunn by M.W.Yant JP
12,	Willis White to Martha E. Arnold by W.E.Carter JP
13,	George L.Beck to Amanda S. Rowell by W.R.Martin JP
14,	John Reese to Nancy Allen by D. Sullivan JP

pg 320

18,	Hillory Mosely to Parthenia Chilcoat by M.M.Marshall VDM
20,	Joseph Dean to Catharine McClure by I.A.Eslick
Jun 1,	H.W.Hamblin to Mary A. Bright
8,	Bascom Beverly to Eliza P. Sexton by W.A.Gill MG
9,	John M. Brown to Nancy P. Kelly by S.L.Walker JP
7,	Smith L. Walker to Susan J. Stubblefield by Wm. Pryor JP
12,	Jesse Reynolds to Evicy T. Hamilton by D. Jacks MG
11,	George Saunders to Alphia P. Pope by H. Henderson JP
11,	S.J.Gilliland to Sarah Jane Alsbrook by J.T.Landers JP
16,	S.M.White to Sarah Owens by T.H.Freeman JP
18,	Hunter Hill to Martha Jane Adcock by R.Farquharson

pg 321

26,	Hamilton White to Nancy Brown by C.B.White JP
24,	Wm. P. Lindsey to Martha J. Wiley by A.S.Sloan
Jul 3,	George Campbell to Emeline Campbell by John Corder JP
9,	Charles Cunningham to Sarah Willis by J.N.George JP
9,	Samuel Mason to Mary E. Delaney by L.B.Wiley Esq
14,	Wm. Y. Lackey to Mary Jane Cox by W.E.Carter JP
20,	Elijah Edgemon to Isa Hensley by T.H.Freeman JP
21,	Alfred Walker to Martha Walker by J. Caughran JP
23,	Wm. Williams to Sarah Jane Shaw by R. Drennon JP
29,	James L. Thompson to Matilda Ann Strong by C.B.McDaniel

Aug 28, 1857 pg 322	Samuel W. Browning to Margret M. Smith by Rev R.D. Hardin
Jul 29,	Francis A. Thompson to Frances A. Noles by C.B.McDaniel
30,	A.B.Scott to Mary Jane Ford by Jacob Gillespie JP
Aug 1,	Samuel McNatt to Jane Watson by M.W.Yant Esq
2,	J.V.Allsup to Mary Elizabeth Wright by S.M.Emmons MG
11,	M.T.Noles to Caroline Payne by C.B.McDaniel JP
9,	M.V.Riddle to Catharine L. Tucker by John Copeland
10,	James A.C.Millikin to Margaret C. Barnes by B.F.Clark JP
13,	James B. Taylor to Nancy Ann McClure by W.T.Holman JP
13,	James H. Darnal to Delia Margarett Scott by G.Nichols MG
20,	Gray J. Pylant to Ann E. Adkins by Rev. A. Tribble
Apr 20, pg 323	Thomas B. McElroy to Frances E. Smith by Rev.R.D.Hardin
Aug 23,	James R. Gunter to Martha Pigg by B.F.Clark JP
25,	Wright W. Tooley to Louisa J. Collins by W.M.McKinney
26,	John H. Bryan to Martha Jane Blue by Rev. R.D.Hardin
26,	P.S.Hanks to Mary Riddle
27,	Wiley Jean to Mary E. Bunn by C.B.McDaniel JP
30,	John Jean to Lucinda Hazelwood by Wm. Gattis JP
Sep 3,	Milton S. Ray to Mary Emery by Jeremiah Dean MG
1,	Jesse Ortner to Elizabeth Cates by W. Rees JP
3,	Henry P. Pitts to Harriett S. Albright by A.S.Sloan
6,	Eli Brown to Elvira Duke by Wm. Gattis JP
7, pg 324	Joseph Sebastian to Rebecca Bledsoe by J.W.Holman MG
10,	Thomas B. McGeehee to Mary Jane Rutledge by John Copeland
8,	George Brewer to Emeline Martin by R. Farquharson JP
10,	T.F.Mitchell to E.M.J.Grant by J.C.Stevenson
10,	James W. Braden to Sarah B. Gill by James C. Stevenson
11,	Wm. Anderson to Emeline E. Bagley by J.T.Gordon JP
11,	Jackson Richardson to Susan C. Duncan by D. Sullivan JP
15,	John V. McKinney to Mary E. Thomison by John Harris
17,	Joseph S.H.Gillian to Rebecca S. Pigg by John Roach JP
17,	John Rogers to Julia Ann Camper by Martin Towery MG
20,	Robert F. Fox to Eliza Jane Harrison by Amos Small JP
20, pg 325	Moses W. Yant to Eliza E. Bunn by John Copeland
24,	John P. Shires to Molly Ann Jackson by Wm. F. Zimmerman
24,	James D. Evans to Martha E. Darnal by J.L.Ashby JP
24,	Benjamin Jackson to Eliza Bryant by John Milton
25,	R.H.Berry to Louiza Burnes by Hugh Thomison JP
27,	John D. Harris to Eliza C. Woodward by J.C.Stevenson
27,	Middleton McGeehee to Louisa Dennis by J.H.Eslick JP
27,	John W. Moore to Martha H. Redd by G.W.R.Moore JP
30,	John J. Grayham to Susan M. Barker by W.P.Holman JP
21,	John Mason to Sarah Boyd by S.L.Walker JP
Oct 3,	James M. Brady to Mary A. Sumners by W.M.McKinney JP
4, pg 326	Joseph Mansfield to Margarett Daniel by J.H.Steelman JP
6,	P.H.Reeves to Caroline Felps by T.J.Wells MG
6,	Samuel H. Locker to Elizabeth M. Rowe by Henry Henderson
19,	Thomas R. Carter to Frances E. Wright by Green Nichols,M
7,	H.S.Davis to Fannie P. Strong by A.A.Bell MG
13,	J.W.Cullum to Mary B. Isom by M.M.Marshall MG
15,	D.M.Patterson to Bettie Woodruff by M.M.Marshall MG

15,   W.H.Rees to Susan Sullivan by J.H.Steelman JP
15,   Wm. Ables to Jane Brown by S.H.McCord JP
17,   James Foster to Mary Jane Lambert
21,   Wm. Hamilton to Elizabeth E. Wyatt by A.S.Sloan
pg 327
22,   R.W.Long to Tabitha Bledsoe by J.S.Davis MG
23,   Wiley Bunn to Elizabeth Rowlin by J.T.Gordon JP
22,   Samuel Hall to Sarah Ann Henderson by Isaac R. Nelson JP
27,   E.S.Wilson to Mary L. Kimes by M.M.Marshall MG
26,   C.B.Oliver to Elizabeth Tucker by J.T.Gordon JP
25,   John Jones to Mary Boyd by J.T.Gordon JP
28,   Martin Bryant to Susan E. Branham by W.C.Jennings JP
28,   John T. Bennet to Melissa Couch(M) by W.C.Jennings JP
28,   Nicholas Sandlin to Susanah Womack by J. Caughran JP
29,   M.M.Story to Lucinda C. Braden by James C. Stevenson
30,   John V. Moyers to George Ann Weigart by J.T.Gordon JP
pg 328
Nov 2,   Reuben Echols to Mary E. Benson by W.E.Carter JP
3,   H.C.Luna to Sarah E. Blakemore by C.R.Darnell MG
4,   W.P.Childs to Mary W. Glenn by J.W.T.Lee MG
5,   A.W.Tripp to Susan E. McClure S.F.Spencer JP
4,   Drury M. Winns to Martha M. Wisner by A.G.Smith MG
8,   George W. Tipps to Lucinda Lambert by J. Caughran JP
7,   W.H.Riley to Nancy Jane Stovall by E.D.Hardin MG
8,   Allen Elston to Manerva Gibson by A.G.Smith MG
10,   B.W.L.Rives to H.E.Flynt by L.D.Mitchell MG
12,   J.T.McGuire to Rachel J. Allsup by W.F.Zimmerman JP
10,   Stephen Sawyer to Sarah George by Martin Towery MG
pg 329
11,   Drury M. Mims to Martha M. Wisner by A.G.Smith MG (see
                              Nov 4, 1857)
19,   Zero Sawyers to Elizabeth Hensley by John Copeland MG
17,   J.W.Hester to Sarah A. Stephenson by J.S.Davis MG
17,   J.C.Goodrich to C.H.Massey by M.M.Marshall MG
20,   David Jean to Elizabeth Bryant by W.P.Holman JP
23,   Hiram Cole to Cleressa Smith by W.N.Hicks JP
26,   John R. White to R.S.C.Smith by J.S.Freeman MG
26,   John E. Brown to Mary A. Brown by R.M.Haggard MG
29,   Samuel Clark to Fennetta Rowlin by J.T.Gordon JP
30,   Robert Taylor to Sarah Jenkins
pg 330
Dec 2,   Wm. Noles to Prudy McWhorter by C.B.McDaniel JP
3,   James H. Phagan to Martha A. Strong by A.S.Sloan
3,   Patrick Ray to Dicy Evans by W.R.Waggoner JP
8,   James Pigg to Elizabeth S. Patterson by Howell Harris JP
8,   P.T.Murray to C.J.Morgan by M.M.Marshall MG
15,   Robert Reese to Mary J. Puckett by A.G.Smith MG
17,   Rev. T.D.Jones to Sarah A. Kimbrough by A.D.Trimble MG
14,   Wm. Michael to Elizabeth Cox
15,   Wm. Posey to Martha Warren by T.H.Freeman JP
16,   C.A.McDaniel to Margaret Buchanan by M.M.Marshall MG
pg 331
17,   Jeremiah Prince to Mary A. Rolin by W.A.Hobbs Esq
17,   Alexander S. Lee to Frances M. Vickers by S.L.Walker JP
20,   Wm. Smith to Susanah Woodard by J.N.George JP
22,   Gilbert Stovall to Sarah A. Sanderson by W.R.Martin JP
23,   E.W.Stone to Mary Gore by W.A.Hobbs Esq
24,   D.J.Hill to P.E.Rowel by J. Caughran JP

```
24,  Isaac Williamson to Rhoda Ann Oldham by J.T.Gordon JP
31,  Henry A. Waggoner to Emeline Tucker by W.R.Waggoner JP
1858
Jan 5,  Nathanial Mallard to Manerva S. Nichols by M.M.
                                              Marshall MG
    6,  H.J.Renegar to Louisa Stubblefield by Wm. Gattis JP
pg 332
    6,  Elifus G. Shelton to Mary A. Luttrell by W.E.Carter JP
    7,  T.R.Nelson to Jane Turney by J.B.Warren MG
   12,  Andrew J. Wright to Sarah J. Lauderdale by A.G.Smith MG
   17,  N.A.Bailey to Ann B. Hester by Bradley Kimbrough MG
   19,  Wm. R. Metcalf to Mary Ann Pitcock by S.L.Walker JP
   20,  Miles J. Reeves to Tempa A. Melton by S.M.Emmons MG
   19,  James Hailey to Sarah A. Wright by R.D.Hardin MG
   21,  John Clark to Sarah Gully by J.B.Warren MG
   19,  Hyson M. Howell to Sarah Smith by S.L.Walker JP
   20,  Charles Smith to Elizabeth Isom by T.H.Freeman JP
pg 333
   20,  James Hamilton to Mary Ann Smith by D.S.Patterson JP
   21,  Anderson W. March to L.M.McDaniel by D.R.Marshall MG
   22,  Jasper N. Perry to Elizabeth Tennison by J.L.Gordon JP
   27,  H.D.A.Thomas to Cynthia Millard by M.M.Marshall MG
   27,  R.D.McMillen to Mary Jane Millard by M.M.Marshall MG
   25,  Isaac M. Holman to Susan Nix by J.H.Eslick Esq
   26,  W.S.Sherrell to Permelia T. George by G.W.Puckett MG
   26,  G.W.Massey to Mary Ann Sawyers by W.R.Waggoner JP
   28,  Charles B. Browning to Sarah F. Grubbs by W.A.Gill MG
   26,  Wm. Donald to Polly Brazier by W.R.Waggoner JP
pg 334
   27,  Nicholas Evans to Martha Chapman by J.W.Holman MG
   27,  George Burrough to Ritty C. Bartlet by W. Rees JP
   28,  Wm. C. Tripp to Martha Ann Shelton by S.F,Spencer JP
   31,  Wm. A. Pitts to Polly Ann Wyles by R. Drennon JP
Feb 1,  Isaac Evans to Elizabeth Massey by J.L.Ashby JP
    4,  John Coleman to Sarah Patterson by S.A.Sloan
    4,  Henry S. Commons to Jane Griffis by B.F.Clark JP
    4,  J.H.McAdams to Mary L. Paton
    9,  J.W.Nelson to Sarah E. Watt by J.B.Warren MG
    9,  Jacob Gillespie to Julia Butler by M.M.Marshall MG
pg 335
    9,  James H. Castleman to Catharine Carty by G.W.Martin MG
   11,  James H. Heralson to Martha J. Webb by W.N.Hicks JP
   11,  T.M.Bell to S.J.Pearson by W.A.Gill MG
   11,  Emery M. Posey to Martha Stewart by J.H.Steelman JP
   16,  T.J.Russell to Mary E. Cathy by Matt Marshall MG
   18,  Noah H. McElvy to Jane Edins by W.A.Hobbs Esq
   16,  Elisha Hicks to Frances Raines by W.L.Rees JP
   18,  Kelly Norman to Sarah Cobb by R.B.McGaugh MG
   23,  John H. Taylor to Martha C. Styles by J.H.Eslick Esq
   18,  Anderson Cole to Lucy E. Cummins by J.B.Warren MG
pg 336
   25,  W.B.Hamilton to Harriet M. Smith by A.G.Smith MG
Mar 2,  Samuel Hill to Martha Porter by J.T.Gordon JP
    2,  Joel E. Yowel to Martha E. Halbert by G.W.Martin MG
    3,  W.W.McCloud to Mary A. Shook by Henry Larkin
    4,  Wm. B. Taylor to Angeline O. Scott by J.H.Eslick JP
   10,  Jackson O. Mitchel to Rutha Swanner by S.M.Emmons MG
Apr 5,  Claiborn Harris to Mary Moore by Henry Turney JP
```

Mar 10,	Reubin J. Stone to Elizabeth M. Haskins by J.L.Ashby JP
Feb 11,	E.M.Posey to Martha Stuart by J.H.Steelman JP
Mar 11,	John Commons to Elizabeth Ellis by G.W.R.Moore JP
14,	John T. Renegar to Lucinda Stubblefield by J.H.Eslick

pg 337

15,	John Strickland to Martha E. Abbott by S.H.McCord JP
18,	W.A.Horton to M.A.Waggoner by W.M.Shaw MG
25,	Presley R. Johnson to Martha J. Paysinger by D.S. Patterson JP
23,	Francis M. Gatlin to Martha M. Nelson by John A. Milhous
21,	Peterson Grammer to Mary Ann Evans by W.R.Waggoner JP
Apr 4,	Henderson Speck to Racheal Davis by Wm. Gattis JP
Mar 23,	John B. Derick to Martha Jane Jennings by R.B.McGaugh,M
25,	E.Y.Solomon to H.C.Taylor by J.W.Holman MG
28,	John C. Walker to Nancy M. Walker by John A. Milhous
29,	W.L.Mitcalfe to Elizabeth B. Pitcock

pg 338

Apr 1,	Thomas J. Gaddy to Martha J. Maddox by J.C.Stevenson
Mar 30,	A.A.Tate to Jane C. Galoway by J.H.Bryson
Apr 15,	Edward B. Dunn to Sarah E. Womack by J.L.Gordon JP
19,	L.C.Blair to Julia Ann Luttrell by W.N.Hicks Esq
21,	Milton Ervin to Mary Ann Morris by W.A.Hobbs Esq
17,	Allen Coble to C.A.W.Bradey by W.M.McKinney JP
17,	Tilman Towry to Nancy Burns
20,	C.T.Chesor to Mourning Washburn by J.B.Warren MG
25,	Jackson Whitlock to Nancy C. Davis by J.L.Ashby JP
24,	J.F.Wakefield to Nancy E. Chesser by B.F.Clark JP

pg 339

28,	John Porter to Lou M. Doss by G.W.Martin MG
May 4,	J.P.Pinkerton to M.R.Templeton by J. Caughran JP
6,	James J. Alexander to Louisa McMullin by J.H.Bryson
10,	Henry Burn to C.H.Yant by J.T.Gordon JP
13,	J.B.Davis to Mary Ann Smith by W.M.McKinney JP
13,	J.T.Maxvill to Elizabeth Gaddy by J.T.Gordon JP
16,	George Bolin to Elizabeth Miles by W.A.Hobbs Esq
27,	James C. Flynt to Lizzie P. Buchanan
Jun 15,	Isaac H. Gray to Sarah Miller by W.E.Carter JP
18,	Wm. R. Rison to Mariah L. Jones by R.Farquharson JP
23,	John D. Carter to M. Annie Neeld by G.W.Martin MG

pg 340

24,	John W. Smith to Susan Young Smith by S.F.Spencer JP
24,	N.J.Wells to A.F.Downing by W.A.Gill MG
28,	Moses C. Freeman to Martha Jane Prosser by G.W.Nichols MG
30,	Wm. F. Neece to Martha M. White by R.Farquharson JP
Jul 1,	John Copeland to Rutha Watson by J.F.Spencer JP
1,	David H. Coble to Juley Ann Coble by W.M.McKinney JP
1,	M.M.Hairston to Eliza Bell by Martin Towery MG
11,	E.L.M.Shelton to Elizabeth Hunt by W.C.Jennings JP
Jun 28,	John R. Williams to Elizabeth Beavers by J. Dean MG
Jul 5,	George S. Wright to Z.C.Hill by Joseph Dameron JP
4,	Stephen Touchstone to Mary E. Hayes by John Cary JP
4,	Henry Henderson to Sarah E. Crawford by J.H.McCord JP

pg 341

7,	Robert F. Wicks to Phebe E. Rees by John Carey JP
13,	A.G.Downing to Catharine Gray by J. Caughran JP
8,	Wm. J. Melson to Jane E. Haskins(Harkins) by G.W.R. Moore JP
10,	Thomas L. Dougan to Henretta Coleman by J.Dameron JP

```
        13,   Elijah L. Hester to Mary Ann Ingle by N.A.Bailey MG
        14,   James Corder to Sarah Ann Cummins by C.B.McDaniel JP
        18,   J.E.Spencer to C.J.Wade by S.F.Spencer JP
        18,   James D. Stedford to Elizabeth C. Luttrell by W.E.
                                                    Carter   JP
        19,   Luke W. Marbary to Jane Hill by R. Drennon JP
        20,   Wm. Buchanan to Ann Thomison by A.G.Smith MG
        22,   James M. Bright to Elizabeth E. Stephens by A.S.Sloan
pg 342
        25,   Abner S. Woodward to Elizabeth A. Young by W.F.
                                                    Zimmerman JP
        29,   Caleb Smith to Palmyrah E. Byrns by Wm. Land MG
        26,   Abraham Simmons to Elizabeth Brady by W.M.McKinney JP
        27,   John George to Catharine Allison by J.C.Stevenson
        29,   Jesse M. George to Mary J. Ashby by J.H.Steelman JP
        29,   C.L.Smith to Mary Majors
Aug  1,   George W. Lesley to Nancy E. Owens by Samuel Stiles JP
Jul 31,   Briggs Nichols to Alsy Foster by W.W.Arnold MG
Aug  5,   Charles A. Rees to Sarah Milliken by John Carey JP
        11,   Erastus Taylor to F.L.Randolph by A.S.Sloan
pg 343
        12,   A.T.Delaney to Bettie L. Pearson by M.H.Bone MG
        12,   Wm. P. Hobbs to Mary Ann Harris by J.C.Stephenson
        19,   Eli Simmons to Sarah C. Riley by Rev. R.D.Hardin
        18,   J.D.Hardin to Elizabeth Fox by R.L.McCree MG
        20,   James L. Dyer to V.T.Nelson by J.G.Bledsoe MG
        19,   Wm. J. Coldwell to Nancy Simmons by S.M.Cowan VDM
        20,   Charles W. Smith to Mary Ann Dunn
        22,   John L. McCoy to Lucinda Rowe by J.C.Stevenson
        26,   Benjamin F. Fannon to Syntha F. Thompson by J.H.Eslick
        28,   George W. Dunn to Sarah Ann Smith by W.N.Hicks Esq
pg 344
Sep  1,   John W. Franklin to Lucy Ann Haithcock by W.N.Hicks Esq
Aug 31,   Calvin Gilbert to Tranquila R. Gracy by Rev.R.L.McElvie
Sep  4,   James C. Clark to Bettie A. Allison
         7,   Robert Farquharson to Sarah A. Burke by A.S.Sloan MG
         8,   John B. Luttrell to Caroline Duke
         9,   John C. West to Elizabeth J. Taylor
         9,   J.M.Kerbo to Susan Sulenger by T.H.Freeman JP
        14,   James P. McCown to J.A.McDill
        16,   Wilford Abbott to Caroline Dickey by R. Drennon JP
        18,   John W. Howard to Nancy Ann Rudd by D. Sullivan JP
pg 345
        24,   John Blackwell to Agness Rorex by Wm. Gattis JP
        23,   Joseph Simpson to Elizabeth Jane Banks by Lemuel Brandon
        23,   Wm. C. Sugg to Mary S. Wood by A.H.Berry MG
        28,   Rufus Harris to Susan Ann Blake by D.L.Mitchell MG
        30,   George W. Waggoner to Martha Ann Gattis by G.W.Holman MG
        27,   John C. Birdsong to Eliza Cail by Rev. R.D.Hardin
        29,   Isaac Rutledge to R.A.Johnson by J.W.Holman MG
        30,   John F.M.Haithcock to Eliza Ann Delia VanHoozer by
                                                    W.N.Hicks Esq
        30,   Wilson Ashby to Cynthia E. Pitts by N.A.Bailey MG
        30,   Adam Landess to Manerva Williamson by T.H.Freeman JP
        30,   Wm. Knight to Elizabeth Asa by R. Farquharson JP
pg 346
Oct  3,   W.J.Bryant to Mary Jane Fitch by W.E.Carter JP
```

	2,	John S. Sanders to Surfrona Pope by T.H.Freeman JP
		(T.H.Freeman has cancelled all information out)
	3,	Franklin A. Hughey to Sarah Morgan Smith by A.C.Dickey JP
	5,	James Howard to Huldah Thompson by C.B.McDaniel JP
	4,	Silvannes Sullivan to Palina A. Reese by J.H.Steelman JP
	6,	Robert W. Wilson to Mary Elizabeth Hughey
	6,	Wm. Epps to Frances Richerson by W.L.Rees JP
Nov	7,	John J. Rhea to Catharine E. Ward by N.A.Bailey MG
Oct	8,	S.A.Bond to Mary Milton by B.M.G.Allsup JP
	11,	Z.R.Dotson to Sarah Ann Radegan by S.H.McCord JP
	12,	Benjamin Howard to Mary Jane Gattis by J.W.Holman MG

pg 347

	12,	Eli Abbott to Sarah E. Weaver by R. Drennon JP
	12,	Nathaniel Tucker to Martha Speck by T.H.Freeman JP
	19,	George W. Waggoner to Lutishia A. McAfee by J.H.Steelman
	14,	James R. Brewer to Sue E. Rives by N.A.Bailey MG
	14,	Wm. F. White to Adaline Dickson by T.H.Freeman JP
	14,	James Massey to Mary Holley by Green Nichols MG
	21,	John C. Crabtree to Mary Spencer by Elder John Copeland
	23,	Andrew M. Harbin to Vina E. Fowler by George W. Carmichael MG
	26,	E.P.Gibbs to Syntha O. Smith by Rev. R.D.Hardin
	19,	J.B.Tigert to Margaret A. Crawford by J.B.Warren
	20,	Benjamin F. Womack to Mildred H.F.Green by J.W.Holman MG
	21,	G.H.Ray to Sarah Ann Couser by W.A.Hobbs JP

pg 348

	24,	C.C.Rousseau to Bethenia Dobbs by W.E.Carter JP
	26,	J.W.Causby to Mahala Panter by G.W.R.Moore JP
	23,	H.H.Logan to Sallie K. Caldwell by J.W.Holman MG
	26,	Joseph H. Baxter to Samantha J. Guthrie by W.A.Hobbs Esq
	28,	James F. Byers to Eliza J. Grubbs by W.A.Gill MG
	31,	Fleming J. Sisco to Mary Elizabeth Hill by W.E.Carter JP
Nov	4,	Michal Sulivan to Joannah Sulivan by H.V.Brown,C Priest
	3,	George W. Steelman to Viletia A. Fleming by T.H. Freeman JP
	9,	Thomas M. Harkins to Elizabeth M. Davidson by G.W.R. Moore JP
	10,	W.D.Yant to Sarah E. Cummons by R.L.McElvie MG
	11,	Carrol Commons to Elizabeth W. Harrelson

pg 349

	10,	John R. McCown to Martha K. Taylor by Henry P. Turner MG
	12,	Bolen Merrett to Mary Birdsong by J. Caughran JP
	11,	Moses S. Story to Susan Zimmerman by G.E.Eagleton VDM
	25,	Wm. M. Spencer to Martha L. Haiselwood by W.R.Waggoner JP
	16,	Hestarpas Stewart to Naomi E.J.Stinson by Martin Towery,M
	16,	John H. Keneday to Isabell C. West
	11,	Francis D. Epps to Sarah Frances Moore by Thomas Childs,M
	18,	John J. Rowell to Elizabeth Griffis by R.D.Hardin MG
	25,	Solomon Smith to Louiza Henslee by John Copeland MG
	26,	R.M.Brown to M.E.V.Bearden by A.S.Sloan MG
	24,	R.L.McElvie to Mary E. Smith by S.E.Wilson MG

pg 350

	25,	John F. Gregory to Mary Cruse by R.L.McElvie MG
Dec	2,	Amasa Flynt to Mariah W. Clarke by Rev. N.T.Powers
	6,	Wm. R. Lee to Sarah Stallcup by W.E.Carter JP
	8,	James J. McCann to Sarah F. Webb by W.N.Hicks Esq
	7,	Daniel T. Norman to Sarah Brown by R.B.McGaugh MG
	8,	Samuel Holt to Angaline Stewart by J. Caughran JP

9,   J.H.Southworth to Mattie J. Stonebraker by J.C.
                                              Elliott MG
12,   J.C.Brown to A.L.Hamilton by B.M.G.Allsup JP
14,   Willis Blankenship to Martha J. Thomison by E.Strode MG
14,   James A. Byers to Leah A. Jeffiers by J.T.Gordon JP
14,   Manson E. Rowell to Nancy M. Smith by W.N.Hicks JP
pg 351
16,   Theophelus Pepper to Jane Carpenter by W.R.Martin JP
16,   A.H.Robinson to E.A.Emmons by G.S.Marcum MG
16,   Charles Fowler to Hannah Harbin by W.E.Carter JP
19,   Joseph S. Rowe to Mary E. Farrar by J.N.George JP
16,   W.T.Armstrong to M.A.McKenzie by M.W.Yant JP
21,   G.W.Jones to Elizabeth Whitaker by Bradley Kimbrough MG
20,   Thomas Hale to Emeline Barnes by G.W.R.Moore JP
23,   G.A.Robertson to Martha F. Parkes by R.B.McGaugh MG
20,   Marcus D. Motes to Emily F. Nelson
21,   James W. Newsom to Sarah C.H.Overby by W.L.Rees JP
22,   Joseph G. Carrigan to Fannie E. Higgins by N.A.Bailey MG
pg 352
23,   Wm. A. Lee to Marcia Ann Cox by T.S.Corder JP
23,   Andrew Waggoner to Emily Jane Edens by W.A.Hobbs JP
22,   Thomas J. Coats to Mary A. Stewart
22,   J.W.Lemmon to Martha C. Pigg by J.B.Warren MG
25,   Isaac F.McElyea to Mitta C. Woodward by J.N.George JP
23,   George R. Allen to Isabella Strong by A.S.Sloan MG
23,   Wm. M. Woodard to Eveline P. Grills by J.H.Bryson MG
26,   David M. Tafts to Sarah A.F.Powell by J.A.Milhous
26,   M.C.Ratliff to Sarah C. Richy by W.E.Carter JP
25,   A.J.Waggoner to Susan Hensley by John Copeland MG
1859
Jan 8,   J.M.Smith to Mary E. Evans by S.F.Spencer JP
pg 353
1858
Dec 30,   James C. Halbert to Frances E. Gibson by A.G.Smith MG
30,   John Minger to Margarett V. Grisard by J.T.Gordon JP
1859
Jan 4,   I.A.Benson to Ruth J. Harbin by T.S.Corder JP
6,   Samuel Stallcup to Julia Ann Hunter by W.L.Rees JP
4,   Hamilton Gowen to Frances Prosser
7,   J.W.Forsythe to Isabella C. Lesley by John Copeland MG
10,   Spencer C. Dodson to Permelia Ratiken by John Copeland,M
12,   Joseph Lock to Jane Rhodes by W.R.Martin JP
18,   Nathan Moore to Alsa Couser by W.A.Hobbs JP
17,   John F. Redd to Eliza A. Burns by G.W.R.Moore JP
13,   Cullen Bailey to S.A.Holman by J.W.Holman MG
pg 354
12,   J.H.Milliken to D.A.Anderson
13,   A.M.Walker to A.M.Gibson by A.F.Rankin MG
18,   John Hoots to Hattie N. Hill by J.W.Holman MG
21,   Wyatt Jean to Susanah Bryant by T.S.Corder JP
27,   Thomas Daniel to Nancy Billings by J. Caughran JP
29,   James M. Rowell to Sarah J. McKinney by W.R.Martin JP
Feb 3,   Benjamin F. McAfee to Sarah J. Bates by J.L.Ashby JP
1,   C. Forrester to Sarah B. Taylor by Bradley Kimbrough MG
1,   W.F.Stockstill to Nancy Ashby by W.R.Waggoner JP
3,   Wm. Cobb to Sarah Norman by R.B.McGaugh JP
8,   R.L.Holman to A.E.Shofner by John Copeland MG

pg 355   1859
   8,   Millford Grammer to Eliza Ann Lock by J.L.Ashby JP
  10,   Champion Smith to Frances E. Smith by S.F.Spencer JP
  17,   Samuel Price to Sarah L. Call by C.B.McDaniel JP
  22,   James Kirkland to Susan Bowers by J.S.Davis MG
  24,   James Parkinson to Mary Pinkerton by A.S.Sloan MG
Mar 10,   W.B.Smith to Sarah E. Vaugh by W.B.Martin JP
  10,   Wm. R. Bonner to Sarah T. Moodey by D.S.Patterson JP
  10,   Wm. Scott to Carlotta Daniel by J. Caughran JP
  13,   M.A.Prosser to L.J.Leftwich by W.E.Jewell MG
  17,   W.W.James to S.V.Freeman by J.W.Holman MG
  22,   E.H.Brewer to R.J.Smith by Bradley Kimbrough MG
pg 356
  30,   Wm. T. Thomas to Elizabeth B. Clerk(Clark) by G.E.
                                Eagleton VDM
  31,   W.W.McNelly to Mary A. Johnson by W.L.Tarbet MG
Apr 5,   Thomas H. Silvester to Mary Merrell by G.S.Marcom MG
   7,   F.E.B.Stevenson to M.L.Franklin
   7,   R.M.Dunlap to Mary E. Cole by W.F.Zimmerman JP
  11,   Leonard Marberry to Mary Dosier by R. Drennon JP
  19,   Samuel E. Gowen to Mary E. Prosser by G.W.R.Moore JP
  13,   Alexander Thompson to Mary Jane Bradford by T.L.Clark JP
  17,   Bennet Whitaker to Sarah Shipp by Wm. Pryor JP
  16,   Rowlin Newsom to B.A.Jackson
  21,   James B. Armstrong to Mary E. Sharp by G.W.R.Moore JP
pg 357
  28,   Wm. C. Yeates to Sarah J. Fincher by J.A.Edmondson MG
May 2,   Charles B. Metcalf to Sarah Rives by W.R.Smith JP
   3,   Wm. R. Brown to Sophy A. Metcalfe by W.A.Hobbs Esq
   3,   D.O.Hicks to Mary Ann Holder by Amos Small JP
  15,   John R. Hamilton to Sarah H. Smith by J.B.Tigert MG
  17,   James Shires to Manda Huckabee by B.M.G.Allsup JP
  19,   Henry H. Sugg to Elvira Allen by A.H.Berry MG
  22,   John Holly to Nelly Sorrels by G.W.R.Moore JP
  26,   Archibald Davis to Margaret Massey by J.L.Ashby JP
pg 358
  29,   B.F.Holley to Mary Ann Simmons by G.W.R.Moore JP
Jun 5,   Maxfield Henslee to Nancy A. Haizlewood by W.L.Waggoner
   2,   Robert W. Williamson to Louisa Thompson by T.H.Freeman JP
   9,   Joseph H. Ringo to Martha E. Gillespie by M.M.Marshall MG
  12,   T.M.Ramsy to Mary Ann Elizabeth Jean by C.B.White JP
Jul 3,   Kennett M. Loyd to Martha Jane Allen by W.A.Hobbs Esq
Jun 30,   issued: M.A.Wisner to E.O.Sawyers by A.H.Berry MG
Jul 4,   Lorenzo Dow to Mary E. Price by J. Caughran JP
   5,   Levi Michael to Melissa Tankersley by Samuel Stiles JP
   7,   John A. Gracey to Frances M. Smith by R.L.McGeehee MG
   9,   Alfred D. Stovall to Jane Maroney
pg 359
  10,   James J. Pitts to Martha Jane Albright by N.A.Bailey MG
   9,   Lewis G. James to Syntha Ann Taylor
  13,   M.A.Edmondson to Charlotta H. Foster by John Roach JP
  14,   Joseph L. Hudson to Easther H. Moore by M.W.Yant JP
  14,   R.F.Weaver to Mary Randolph by C.B.McDaniel JP
  18,   Patrick Snow to Sarah Jean by T.S.Corder JP
  20,   James T. Thompson to Jane Washburn by Amos Small JP
  21,   Gabriel Young to Adaline Sorrells by Green Nichols MG
  23,   J.L.Burrow to Margaret Bingham
  25,   David Jolly to Sarah A. Bryant by T.S.Corder JP

pg 360 1859
 26, J.P.Ensley to Julia Clift by W.M.McKinney JP
 28, John W. Hobbs to Martha Ann Roe
Aug 1, Wm. C. Taylor to Elizabeth Jean by S.F.Spencer JP
 2, James Steelman to Mary E. Newsom by W.T.Rees JP
 1, Joseph R. Nichols to Pantha R. Owenby
 7, Wm. H. Brown to Frances J. Martin by W.H.Hobbs JP
 2, John H. Cox to Elizabeth A. King by A.C.Dickey JP
 3, J.E.Runnels to Mary F. Rees
 4, A.J.Fitch to Nancy J. Webster by T.S.Corder JP
 7, Joseph D. Webster to Frances A. Stephenson by G.W.Puckett
 16, Wm. E. Moore to Eliza Stockstill by Hugh Thomison JP
pg 361
 28, John A. Reavis to Susan C. Byrum by Jeremiah Dean MG
 23, Henry J. Pamplin to Mary E. McLaughlin by R.M.Haggard,M
 24, George P. Landman to Mary Frances Scivally by J.A.
               Edmondson MG
 25, Wm. Street to Mary Louisa Jones by Henry T. Turner MG
Sep 6, Ethelbert Palmer to Mary Lucinda Hardeman by Wm. J.
                Buckman MG
 6, Colman Roggers to Lyddia Polly
 6, James A. Shoemake to Nancy Cole by J.S.Davis MG
 7, John R. Austin to Elizabeth Partin
 8, W.R.Driver to Margaret A. Cox by J. Dean MG
 11, Thomas Dickey to Elvira A. McGeehee by T.H.Eslick JP
 11, H.H.Hunter to Elvira Powers by Samuel Stiles JP
 11, H. McKee to Sally Campbell to D. Jacks MG
pg 362
 14, Brown Pinkerton to Narcissa Hedgepeth by H.Parkinson JP
 15, J.B.Bedwell to Sarah A. Wells by R.M.Haggard MG
 14, Wm. F.M.Oliver to Louisa J. Perry by J.T.Gordon JP
 19, D.M.Holloway to Phebe Elizabeth Clark by A.H.Perry MG
 21, Joel T. Pigg to Martha Elizabeth Sullivan by John
                Roach JP
 22, James Tucker to Amy Speck by I.H.Eslick JP
 28, James Clark to Sarah Gulley by Wm. R. Smith JP
 29, Reubin Webster to Amanda M. Myrick by S.L.Walker JP
Oct 3, Pleasant A. Randolph to Lucinda J. Caruthers by J.M.
                Brown MG
 4, James M. Clift to Martha L. Hughey by H.M.McKinney JP
 4, Wm. C. Murdock to Minerva A. Rees by R.L.McGee MG
pg 363
 4, R.A.McDonald to Martha Cordelia McKinney by M.B.Dewitt,M
 5, Henry W. Hamblin to Elizabeth Hall
 6, Thomas B. Hicks to Louisa Ann Williams by R. Drennon JP
 6, Solomon E. Keith to Rebecca E. Ashby by R.M.Haggard MG
 10, G.M.Steele to Martha Craig by M.M.Marshall MG
 11, John D. Moore to Lucy Ann Coldwell by M.B.Dewitt MG
 13, James Bevels to Elizabeth Ross by G.S.Marcom MG
 16, C.B.White to Elizabeth Watson by W.E.Carter JP
 18, E.L.Patton to Mary Bryson by R.B.McMullin MG
 17, S.W.Foster to Martha P. Pinkerton by A.S.Sloan MG
 18, W.S.Curtis to Narcissa Oliver by A.S.Sloan MG
pg 364
 26, Joseph H. Good to Sarah J. Spence by A.S.Sloan MG
 28, A.D.Smith to M.M.Kennedy by S.M.Howell MG
 30, Wm. Norman to L. Dobbs by W.E.Carter JP
 27, A.J.Alford to Margarett A. Russell by M.D.Dewitt MG

```
Nov  1,    John F. Montgomery to Susan H. Askins
     5,    Newton W. Findly to Harriet Ann Brown by W.H.McRee
     8,    N.S.Rees to Nancy Johnson by Wm. W. Anthony
    11,    John H. Walker to Nicey J. Crawley by D. Jacks MG
    10,    Wm. Grant to Sarah Frances Donaldson by R.J.Scivally
    15,    R.L.Whitworth to Malissa Woodall
    17,    J.F.Webb to Mary Ann McCown by Wm. N. Hicks JP
pg 365
    23,    S.M.Conger to R.C.C.Beall Norton by J.C.Putman MG
    24,    G.W.Hopper to E.J.Hedgepeth by S.M.Emmons MG
    23,    John H. Scott to Susan Ann George by W.R.Bledsoe JP
    24,    John W. Cunningham to Revy Waggoner by J.H.Steelman JP
    24,    F.G.Cole to Amanda Hosch by Wm. N. Hicks JP
    26,    Wm. Williams to Charlotta Watson by J. Roach JP
    29,    Wm. H. Myers to Amanda J. Wright by F.L.Ezell JP
    29,    E.F.M. Grace to Susan M.Cluts
Dec  3,    W.R.Presswood to Elizabeth Ratlif by J.T.Gordon JP
     7,    Carrell Williams to Catharine Bowels by A.J.Steel MG
    10,    Shadrack Holly to Mahala F. Simmons by G.W.R.Moore JP
pg 366
    10,    Wm. Ables to Mary Jane Elizabeth Rebecca Dempsey by
                                        M.W.Yant Esq
    12,    Wm. T. Gill to Mary Finer Lloyd by Wm. A. Gill MG
    12,    James Pigg to Emeline P. Jeter by J. Roach JP
    22,    James M. Lewter to Caroline York by J.L.Colman
    15,    W.Z.Jennings to Margaret A. Stiles by W.E.Carter JP
    15,    J.R.Smith to Nancy Stafford by J.T.Ashby JP
    17,    Wm. R. Smith to Martha E. Koonce
    20,    L.W.Gale to Caroline Bates by H.Parkinson JP
    22,    J.F.Ledford to Louisa Lund by John Roach JP
    23,    R.E.Gilliland to M. Addie Drake by M.M.Marshall MG
    25,    A. Sutliff to Nancy S. Shaw by J.W.Holman MG
pg 367
    24,    John W. Hazelwood to Mary Ann Jenkins by Wm. Gattis JP
    27,    F.M.Baldwin to Letisha C. Barham by G.W.R.Moore JP
    26,    H.C. Shaw to Mary Jane Mullins by R. Drennon JP
    27,    Wm. J. Grills to Sarah Smith by Wm. A. Gill MG
1860
Jan  1,    Joseph Luttrell to M. Ann Cox by S. Stiles JP
     2,    Wm. Buchanan to Susan Boling
     5,    Wm. W.S.Lester to Elizabeth C. Bledsoe by A.H.Brown MG
    11,    J.H. Walker to Nancy E. Maben by John Milton
     3,    Wm. R. Ellis to Louisa Jane Rowell by R.M.Haggard MG
     5,    Thomas J. Rich to Clarissa Hill by J. Dameron JP
     5,    James Jolly to Margaret Ward by W.L.Rees JP
pg 368
     5,    G.H.Renfrow to Nancy C. Cates by D. Sullivan JP
     5,    Wm. A. Sloan to Martha J. Moore by A.S.Sloan
     8,    Henry Marr to Jane Warren by W.L.Rees JP
    12,    John P. Stewart to Eliza Lindsey by A.S.Sloan MG
    12,    Jesse Rochel to Margaret Hays by A.S.Sloan MG
    16,    Willis Stephens to Cyntha Stephens by T.S.Corder JP
    16,    R.M.Rambo to Elizabeth Jackson
    17,    Martin Van Clark to Mary A.C.Gully by L.L.Clark JP
    18,    James A. Clark to Mary E. Hunter by W.M.McKinney JP
    19,    Alexander Riddle to Jane Dean by J.H.Hobbs MG
    18,    A.H.Gill to Martha Taylor by W.F.Rees JP
```

```
pg 369    1860
    19,   Wm. A. Sullinger to Nancy Ward by J.H.Eslick JP
    18,   James S. Conner to M.E.Daniel
    20,   John W. Hampton to Nancy Jane Farrar
    26,   J.H.Dobbs to L.H.Hill by J.W.Holman MG
    26,   John Vickers to Martha Catharine Swinford by R.Drennon
    28,   Wm. W. Cannon to Nancy E. Claunch
    31,   J.R.Hinson to N.M.Smith by Rev R.D.Hardin
Feb  2,   Harris Tucker to Adaline Wright by S.M.Emmons MG
Jan 31,   W.N.Taylor to L.M.Wiseman
Feb  2,   J.A.Stiles to Maria Payne by J.H.Eslick JP
     1,   R.M.James to Eliza Jane Taylor
pg 370
    12,   Daniel Warren to Priscilla Jackson by W.L.Rees
    12,   John Dobbs to Presilla Jane Stanley by W.E.Carter JP
    12,   H.P.McElyea to Frances A. Pitcock by D.L.Mitchell MG
    20,   R.E.Buchanan to M.A.Horton by J.T.Gordon JP
Mar  1.   F.M.Snoddy to Martha G. Howard by W.E.Carter JP
Feb 28,   Enoch Cunningham to Nancy K. Noah by A.C.Dickey JP
    27,   Wm. N. Young to Nancy M. Woodall
    28,   A.M.Whitworth to Alpha N. Chiles by S.L.Walker JP
Mar  1,   Wm. Pigg to Sarah M. Dyer by John Roach JP
     8,   John N. Helton to May Ramsey Read by G.W.Nichols MG
    26,   Wm. Stubblefield to Martha Carter by J.H.Eslick JP
pg 371
    29,   James A. Albright to Susanna M.E.Baxter by S.L.Walker
    29,   Wm. C. Ward to Sarah R. Moyers by J.H.Eslick JP
    30,   John L. Clark to Julia M. O'Neal by M.B.Dewitt MG
Apr  1,   Thomas A. Maddox to Sarah J. Pamplin by B.F.Clark JP
     2,   William Williams to Casey Ann Pylant
    12,   James E. Green to Mary F. Bonner by G.W.Puckett MG
    15,   Little Wilson Beck to Angeline Chick by J.T.Gordon JP
    16,   Jesse L. Jean to Cyntha Caroline Boyd by S.H.McCord JP
    18,   Wm. A. Walker to Nancy C. Koonce
    19,   Elisha M. McClure to Susan Catharine Brown by J.H.Eslick
pg 372
    21,   Wm. T. Cartright to Fannie Catharine Hill by J.H.Eslick
May  9,   G.W.Higgins to Sue Carrigan by J.B.Warren MG
    24,   Wm. T. Baldwin to Adeline Daniel by Wm. R. Waggoner JP
    17,   R.U.McEntire to A.A.Franklin by Z.T.Ezell JP
    23,   Anderson Davis to Manerva Bartlett by J.A.Prosser JP
    24,   Wm. Cannon to Nancy Claunch by Martin Towry MG
    31,   M.P.Russell to Margaret M. Gibson by J.G.Bledsoe MG
Jun 14,   H.M.Bledsoe to Sarah Bond by R.D.Hardin MG
    27,   Thomas Connelly to Mary Nealy by M.B.Dewitt MG
    28,   John L. Steelman to Mary Steelman by James B. Hudson JP
    28,   Thomas J. Tucker to Jane Caroline Armstrong
pg 373
Jul  1,   Nathan Gairy to Patsey Smith by W.W.Wilson JP
     3,   George W. Whitworth to Priscilla Nancy Adeline Dempsey
                                              by J.B.Hudson JP
     3,   Thomas Hart to Sarah E. Hunter by Joseph Damons JP
    10,   J.P.Kent to Ruth E. Thompson by Benjamin Fox JP
    24,   Benjamin Gattis to Nancy Howard by J.H.Eslick JP
    17,   M.J.Beddingfield to Elizabeth R. Mitchell by Z.T.Ezell
    19,   S.R.Reynolds to Julia A. Street by W.C.Solomon JP
    24,   R.D.C.McMillin to Faner Howard by J.H.Eslick JP
    26,   Thomas B. Strong to Willie E. Ezell by R.Farquharson JP
```

78

Aug 2,   John Moore to Nancy E. Kiser by J.L.Bryant JP
pg 374 1860
Jul 29,   Josephus Miles to Polly Pearce by W.R.Waggoner JP
    30,   John Honey to Lydia E. Whitworth
Aug 2,   Joseph H. Pigg to Delinda L. Pamplin by J. Roach JP
     2,   D.R.Holloway to Elizabeth Spence by A.S.Sloan MG
     5,   Thomas B. Lee to Priscilla L. Peoples by F.L.Ezell JP
     7,   John Hill to Mary Ann Yarbrough
    17,   John Wilson to Mary M. Kiser by Robert M. Whitman JP
    12,   James Brown to Sarah E.F.Enoch by Samuel Bobo JP
    14,   Wm. M. Smith to Mary E. Hardin by Wm. A. Rhoden JP
    16,   George H. Wagoner to Ann Parks by J.L.Ashby JP
    16,   Martin V. Howell to M.H.Womack by A.G.Smith JP
    16,   John P. Keith to E.S.Yant by J.B.Hudson JP
pg 375
    23,   Wm. Moyers to Mary Wise by S. Bobo JP
    23,   Dudley Tipps to Jane R. Tipps by W.R.Waggoner JP
    21,   James W. Wise to Mary Ann Baily by S. Bobo JP
    26,   John B. Gray to Mary Womack by S. Bobo JP
    24,   M.A.Clifford to Elizabeth Solomon
    28,   Wm. Mullins to Selome Sanders by Martin Towry MG
Sep 4,   W.B.Hedgepeth to Harriet Luna by John Roach JP
     4,   George H. Britton to Mary Elizabeth Rice
     6,   Eli Barns to Ellen Ramsy by B.F.Clark JP
     6,   Jackson Smith to Elzada Hall
    14,   Charles Moore to Mary F. Gully by Martin Towry MG
pg 376
    13,   Wm. M. Phagan to Nancy V. Moore by A.S.Sloan
    25,   Aaron Parks to Angeline McNeece by W.H.Thompson JP
    19,   James T. Coop to Virginia A. Webb by W.E.Carter JP
    19,   Pallis Griffin to Elizabeth Pitcock by D.L.Mitchell MG
    20,   James M. Coats to Orlena B. Shipp by Wm. Tillery MG
    20,   Benjamin F. Clark to Sarah Jane Sanders by David G.
                                                      Smith JP
    25,   Morgan Carter to Elizabeth Davidson by Wm. D.Moorhead
    25,   Jerome B. Williams to Rutha E. Barley
    30,   Wm. Ray to Manerva Dennis by John D. Smith JP
Oct 4,   Hiram Howard to Elizabeth Rudd by J.L.Bryant JP
     4,   John C. Mills to Margaret Rutledge by J.B.Hudson JP
pg 377
    10,   Jacob Mitchel to Letha Ann Elizabeth Tripp by J.B.
                                                      Smith JP
    11,   C.W.Lucas to J.L.Motlow by J.W.Holman MG
    11,   C.H.Cunningham to S.N.Story by W.W.Wilson JP
    12,   Daniel Thompson to Artimesa Clifford by J.A.Prosser JP
    12,   Wm. Dawson to Pheba T. Sawyers by A.G.Smith MG
    14,   James C. Stuart to Margret R. Patrick by Needham
                                                      Koonce JP
    14,   James Roden to Susan Y. Abbott by David G. Smith JP
    14,   N.J.Smith to Sopha S. Robertson by W.W.Wilson JP
    22,   Wm. J. Harris to Jane Mosely
    22,   Lewis Sandlin to Elizabeth Howell by John Caughran JP
pg 378
    23,   Amos Small to Elizabeth M.G.Clark by J.B.Hudson JP
    25,   Thomas Groce to Mary M. Creason by Wm. Ashby JP
    28,   W.M.Tucker to Amanda Jane Tankerster by J.H.Eslick JP
    27,   James H. Majors to Martha Miles
    27,   Wm. Harrison to Martha E.Cunningham by S.M.Hampton JP

	29,	L.A.Patillo to Fanny Jane Hale by D.L.Mitchell MG
	30,	Micajah L. McElroy to Martha Whitaker by A.G.Smith JP
Nov	1,	John Mills to Margret Jane Sanders by L.L.Cole JP
	6,	Wm. Carter to Lucretia Jane McCowen by Rev. John Milton
	12,	Isaac J. Smith to L.Z. Hall by A.T.Nicks JP

pg 379

	14,	John H. Dyer to Dillia E. Chitwood by Wm. R. Smith JP
	14,	Moses Fisk to Mary S. Jones
	14,	Oliver Street to Hester D. Haley by A.F.Driskill JP
	17,	John W. Tillery to Nancy Elizabeth McKinney by J. VanHoozer JP
	22,	William Roland to Tabitha Elizabeth Locker
	22,	D.J.Noblett to S. Boon by J.L.Bryant JP
	25,	James H. Hanes to Martha P. Riddle by John H. Holt MG
	25,	James F. Cathy to Sarah A. Hughey by G. Eagleton VDM
	27,	Wm. H. Ingle to Mary Catharine Bell by E.L.Hester MG
	28,	George A. Anderson to Nancy G. Jones

pg 380

	Dec 2,	Thomas P. Sumners to Sarah E. Brotherton by D.G.Smith JP
	4,	B.F.Tiller to Louisa Thompson by Wm. Ashby JP
	6,	G.W.Stephenson to Judia L. Gay by A.G.Smith MG
	11,	James S. Merrell to Loisa Josephine Reed by J. Van-Hoozer JP
	11,	G.W.Merrell to Martha S.A.Reed by J. VanHoozer JP
	4,	Thomas M. Rowell to Isabellia E.McCawley by Rev. R.D. Hardin
	5,	Henry Rutledge to Rachel Thompson by Wm. Ashby JP
	6,	W.J.Davidson to Elizabeth A. Smith by M.B.Dewitt MG
	6,	D.M.Armstrong to Martha E. King
	11,	John H. Brewer to Margaret E. Denham

pg 381

	11,	John W. Kelly to T.C.Moores by H.H.Brown
	12,	John F. Fly to Sarah Glen McLaughlin by A.T. Rankin MG
	13,	Samuel R. Murdock to Sarah Patterson by A.G.Smith MG
	13,	Joseph C. Stephens to Mary Jane Raney by A.J.Childress
	24,	T.D.Moore to Mary Frances Buchanan by A.T.Rankin MG
	20,	James N. Epps to Hessey Prosser by J.B.Hudson JP
	20,	J.W.Randolph to Hanah J. Thermon by E.L.Hester MG
	20,	E.L.Bray to Joanah McCray by R.B.McGaugh MG
	20,	Robert W. Locker to Rachel T. Rowe
	24,	James C. Epps to Julia Ann Taylor by B.F.Clark JP

pg 382

	24,	J.M.Brown to Amanda Shull by A.T.Rankin MG
	24,	John Smith to Mary M. Caton by R.D.Hardin MG
	28,	Smith Ceton to Mary Frances Smith by F.L.Ezell JP
	30,	William Bartlett to Fanny Farris by J.A.Prosser JP
	30,	William Thomas Clanton to Nancy Honney by W.E.Carter JP
	31,	J.E.Bailey to Nancy Catharine Nash
	31,	John Stubblefield to Letisha A. Claunch

Lincoln County Marriage Records
Book # B

1861

pg 1

	Jan 1,	Berry Macberry to Mary Jane Davis
	2,	Thomas J. Spencer to Hanah C. Chapman
	4,	Daniel Chambers to Sarah Brown by John L. Ashby JP
	3,	James B. Drake to Martha McEwen by M.M.Marshall MG

1861

	3,	F.S.Clark to Mollie McGee by Needham Koonce JP
	3,	Charles H. Locker to Mary J. Roland

pg 2

	5,	F.M.Cashmons to Nancy Smith
	6,	C.M.Banton to Margret E. Small by Wm. A. Rhodes JP
	10,	Henry Bateman to Elizabeth C. Ashby by Wm. Ashby Esq
	8,	F.M.Martin to S.S.Melton by J. Vanhoozer JP
	17,	Pleasant N. Bryan to Paullina Jane McCown by W.A. Rhodes JP
	11,	James D. Stone to Sue Shull by J.B.Warren MG

pg 3

	14,	Bradley White to Susan Caroline Perry by T.H.Eslick JP
	13,	R.A.Wallace to Mary Adeline Martin by F. Motlow JP
	14,	Barney Nelson to Margret E. Paradice by M.M.Marshall,M
	17,	Joseph Cunningham to A.E.Cruse by J.T.Gordon JP
	17,	George E. Bates to C.L.Scivally by J.T.Gordon JP
	18,	Wiley Jeans to Rosana Webb by T.S.Corder JP

pg 4

	22,	Newton Thompson to Fanny Duke by W.H.Thompson Esq
	21,	Benjamin Westly Norris to Nancy Bennett
	24,	Wm. B. Whitaker to Nanny Kimbrough by T.G.Jones MG
	24,	H.H.Berch to Eveline Elam by O.T.Griffis JP
	27,	Howell H. Bledsoe to Frances M. Chitwood by J.B.Warren,M
	30,	Lewis Newsom to Elizabeth Nicks by J.L.Bryant JP
Feb	7,	Thomas J. Bennett to Martha Robertson by G.S.Marcom MG

pg 5

Jan	31,	John A. Pamplin to Lucy C. Johnson by W.L.Alexander JP
Feb	7,	O.D.Evans to Ellen Wilson by M.B.Dewitt MG
	13,	Wm. C. Lesley to Elizabeth Ann Arnold by J.D.Smith JP
	14,	Robert A. Allison to Belle Kelso by W.M.Reed MG
	14,	Charles W. Womack to Malinda Panter by F. Motlow JP
	18,	James H. Wakefield to Mary Damron by N.J.Powers MG

pg 6

	21,	John H. Little to Sarah Ann Cocks by T.S.Corder JP
	21,	Jefferson Lenord to Milly Barker by W.E.Carter JP
	21,	James C. Saunders to Lucretia Dyer by J.B.Stephens MG
	27,	F.A.Thorton to Lucinda Randolph by W.C.Solomon JP
Mar	3,	George T. Price to Susan Patrick by W.A.Gill MG
	3,	Stephen P. Brown to Vinetta Moyers by J.A.Prosser JP
Feb	28,	Andrew Hudlow to Martha Thomas by J.L.Bryant JP
Mar	6,	Wm. J. Taylor to Sarah E. Waggoner by W.R.Waggoner JP

pg 7

	7,	Harris J. Wadkins to Amandy C. Cayton by J. Vanhoozer
	7,	James M. Koonce to Susan Rowland by S.L.Walker JP
	12,	Wm. D. Wright to Lucy J. Hicks by N. Koonce JP
	18,	Smith Sanders to Ann Dosier by O.P.Griffis JP
	19,	Young A. Taylor to Martha McClure by I.H.Eslick JP
	20,	G.C.Gattis to Ellen J. Wade by Wm. R. Waggoner JP

pg 8

	21,	Thomas R. Riley to Mary Ann E. Smith by S. Stiles JP
	23,	G.C.Church to Lindia A. Damron by S. Stiles JP
	26,	William Brown to Camile Cayton by G.W.Puckett MG
	25,	John Adkins to Elizabeth Gore
	27,	H.A.Reeves to Sarah Eliza Simmons
Apr	4,	James W. Hardin to Mary Jane Brooks by W.A.Rhodes JP

pg 9

	1,	Willis D. Bentson to Jane Faulkiner by W.E.Carter JP
	4,	Martin V. Groce to Mary J. Ashby by John L. Ashby JP

     9,   L.S.Farrar to M.C.Rowe by F.L.Ezell JP
    11,   J.P.Fox to Permelia Ann King by E.L.Hester MG
    18,   Anderson Bonner to Malinda Bryant by W.A.Rhodes JP
    15,   Robert Daniel to Martha Ann Blankingship
pg 10
    16,   G.W.Fox to Sarah A. McClure
May 2,   H.B.McCown to Jane Fife by A.S.Sloan MG
    30,   James F. Smith to Sarah E.T.Neece by A.F.Driskill
     2,   Isaac W. Grisard to Lucy A. Farrar by W.W.Wilson JP
     8,   D.W.Scivally to A.E.Pierce by I.H.Eslick JP
    14,   Eli R. Calloway to Sarah Duckworth by W.C.Solomon JP
pg 11
    16,   Samuel P. Hamilton to Sarah J. Hamilton by A.S.Sloan MG
    20,   Calvin G. Candiff to Sarah C. Jones by Ben Fox JP
    24,   L.A.J.Bedwell to Mary E. Stewart
    24,   W.A.Collins to Sarah E.R.Tooley by D.G.Smith JP
Jun 3,   Franklin Warden to Loucretia Cunningham by L.L.Cole JP
May 31,   Wm. G. Dunlap to Martha E. Bright by G.W.Puckett MG
pg 12
Jun 3,   Joseph M. Gragg to Elizabeth Jane Wiley by A.S.Sloan MG
    16,   James G. Tafts to Mary E. Powell by G.W.Puckett MG
    15,   E.B.Pitts to Mary L. Albright
    27,   Edward Blankingship to Louisa Jones by J. Caughran JP
Jul 4,   Benjamin F. Reece to Sarah Isabella Young by Henry
                                                          Bryson
     4,   William P. Holman to Eliza Allison
pg 13
    17,   Samuel Watson to Martha J. Rowell by A.R.Smith JP
     7,   Joseph W. Laughlinghouse to Laurana Dalton by S.L.
                                                      Walker JP
     9,   W.B.Beatie to Harriet F. Logan by R.B.McGaugh MG
    11,   Thomas M. Edmondson to Susan S. Deford by B.F.Clark JP
    13,   J.H.Armstrong to Mary M. Smiley by J.B.Warren MG
    20,   Benjamin Vines to Lucinda Preston by W.E.Carter JP
    18,   N.J.Pearson to Sarah C. Armstrong by J.A.Prosser JP
pg 14
    20,   Joel Richardson to Christianna T. Redd
Aug 1,   Taylor Smith to Nancy L. Ayers by S.M.Hampton JP
    11,   William Orick to Amandy M. Wright by J.B.Hudson JP
    15,   Ephraim B. Bryan to Margaret L. McCoy by S.M.Hampton JP
    18,   Calvin McEwen to Susan Wallace by M.M.Marshall MG
    24,   L. Hamilton to Sarah Damron
pg 15
    24,   George J. McNeece to Delia A. Freeman
    24,   Joshua P. Gammill to Martha E. Raby
Sep 1,   James M. Barham to Mary A. Davidson by J.A.Prosser JP
     2,   C.M.Mitchel to Elizabeth C. McElyea
     4,   Milage Birdsong to Angeline Neely by Wm. A. Gill MG
     4,   S.S.McCown to Maggi J. Wyatt
pg 16
     4,   Joseph S. McMinn to M.E.D.Carter by A.S.Sloan
     5,   Wm. Y. Sorrels to Martha Creason by J.A.Prosser JP
     7,   B.F.Harkins to Mary Pruitt
    11,   James Pinkerton to Elizabeth A. Anderson by J. Caughran
    12,   George Mullins to Martha Elizabeth Wilson by A.R.Smith JP
    17,   George E. Suttle to Theodosia O. Green by W.E.Caldwell
pg 17
    19,   John Bland to Eliza Jane Kelly(no marriage)License returr
                                                 ed by John Bland

```
        29,    J.T.Patrick to Augustus A. Holt by N.J.Powers MG
 Oct   3,    Squire Pickle to Harriet Scott by A.C.Martin
        3,    William G. Moore to Mary R. Dollar
        9,    W.T.Collins to Sarah A. McCracken
       15,    Wm. S. Towery to Nancy Jane Warren by A.J.Childress JP
 pg 18
       17,    John B. Smith to Sarah Elizabeth Hamilton by D. Jacks
       23,    Wm. H. McCann to Sarah Ann McDill by A.S.Sloan MG
 Sep 12,    Hiram A. Johnson to Nancy A. Paysinger by J.C.Prosser JP
 Oct 24,    Martin Harbin to Martha Rickets by S.M.Emmons MG
       28,    T.W.Bledsoe to H.E.Blake by A.T.Rankin MG
 Nov  2,    W.J.C.Britton to J.M.Webb
 pg 19
       10,    George W. Brady to Rachel E. George by Martin Towery MG
       12,    E.R.Kilpatrick to Mary L. Patterson by John Moore JP
       21,    C.S.Wilson to Mary E. Lauderdale by A.S.Sloan MG
       26,    J.H.George to M. Jane Halbert by J.B.Tigert MG
       27,    George B. Boyles to M.M.Gillespie by G.E.Eagleton MG
       30,    Bedford Lackey to E.D.Cane
 pg 20
 Dec 12,    John J. Shuffield to Margaret J. Watson by Wm. A. Gill MG
       12,    Wm. R. Smith to Mollie Thompson
       14,    R.A.Foster to Louisa Jane Swinney
       17,    Wm. G. Seaton to Mary S. Jolley by J.B.Hudson JP
       20,    John M. Dickey to Louisa E. McGee
       26,    J.P.McGee to Eliza N. Koonce by F.M.Ventress JP
 pg 21
       26,    B.F.Thomas to Polly A. Fox by J.W.Holman MG
       29,    Wm. H. Hester to Sarah Ann Welch by J.B.Stephens MG
       31,    Joel Foster to Charlotta A. Rees by J.A.Prosser JP
 1862
 Jan  9,    M.V.Brown to Martha A. Beasley by J.B.Hudson JP
       20,    J.F.Wiseman to Margaret J. Allen
       23,    H.H. Beech to Evaline Elam
 pg 22
       28,    John Phagan to Arminta M. Spence by A.S.Sloan
       29,    Samuel Weaver to Mary Miller by O.P.Griffis JP
       29,    Thomas B. Abbott by Lucinda Bradford by O.P.Griffis JP
       30,    James Armstrong to Elizabeth McKinney by J.B.Warren MG
 Feb 22,    John E. Bobo to A.E.Pratt
       27,    F.A.Thurman to Loucinda Randolph by Wm. C. Solomon JP
 pg 23
 Mar  2,    George T. Price to Susan A. Patrick by Wm. A. Gill MG
       13,    W.C.Andrews to Sarah E. Roach by Wm. S. Findley MG
       12,    R.C.Rives to R.J.Gillum by J.B.Warren MG
       15,    John Bradly to Martha Marshall by J. Caughran JP
       24,    A.B.Whitt to Mary E. Simmons by W.A.Gill MG
 Aug 25,    A.J.Brown to D.A.Davidson by J.A.Prosser JP
 pg 24
 Sep  9,    R.D.Hardin to Ann Sawyers by J.B.Tigert MG
 1863
 Apr 27,    James M. Prosser to F.C.Martin by J.A.Prosser JP
 Jun 25,    H.H.Fauch to Mary A. Steelman by J.A.Prosser JP
 Oct  9,    H.B.Talley to E.J.Kimes by J.B.Tigert MG
 Nov  1,    M.D.Warren to Canada Noblet by J.A.Prosser JP
 Dec 25,    Rev. A.P.Copeland to Ann Moling Bright by G.W.Puckett,M
```

pg 25
1864
Jan 15,   Calvin Rawls to Martha A. McAnn by G.W.Puckett MG
    28,   James Sims to Cassanda Sumford by J. Caughran JP
     8,   W.J.Edwards to Milly J. Roper by G.W.Puckett MG
1862
Feb 29,   Simpson Abbott to Martha A. Albright by C.P.Griffis JP
Nov 19,   W.C.Mills to Mary E. Marberry by Samuel Bobo JP
1863
Jan 1,   James T. Sanford to Martha Mills by T.S.Corder JP
     4,   James Mills to Amanda Abernathy by J. Caughran JP
    15,   G.W.Thomas to Lunna J. McMullin by L.L.Clark JP
Apr 9,   A.J.Crunk to M.D.Blakemore by C.R.Daniel MG
Aug 7,   W.R.Smith to S.A.Merrett by J.B.Warren MG
Oct 15,   John Davis to Mary Hamby by J.B.Warren MG
Nov 24,   John F. Brewer to T.C.Gulley by J.B.Warren MG
pg 27
Nov 26,   E.W.Ford to Mattie E. Brewer by J.B.Warren MG
1864
Jan 14,   H.C.McKenzie to Esther Thomas by J.B.Warren MG
Mar 4,   J.D.Armstrong to Mary J. Pearson by J.B.Warren MG
1863
Sep 29,   Phillip S. Bruce to Nancy C. Grammer by J.L.Ashby JP
Jun 22,   Charles May to Manadora Butler by S.M.Emmons MG
Nov 5,   Joseph N. George to Miss M.P.McGuire by J.C.Stevenson,M
     5,   Lewis B. Brown to Elizabeth A. Renegar by J.B.Hudson JP
pg 28
Oct 15,   Timothy Crane to Elizabeth Bedwell by J.B.Hudson JP
Sep 30,   H.M.Largen to Mary A. Keith by J.B.Hudson JP
1864
Mar 31,   George Tiller to Martha Groce by J.B.Hudson JP
1863
Nov 1,   James J. Gulley to Nancy A. Ables by J.B.Hudson JP
1864
Mar 3,   Alexander A. McAfee to Elizabeth Groce by J.B.Hudson JP
    24,   B.W.Pamplin to Mary Ele Moore by J.B.Hudson JP
pg 29
1863
Jan 14,   Wm. H. Brown to Mary M. Pamplin by J.B.Hudson JP
Jun 24,   John W. Beasley to Sarah E. Keith by J.B.Hudson JP
Oct 15,   John Fincher to Paralee Hall by J.B.Hudson JP
1864
Mar 17,   G.W.McAfee to Derinda Harden by J.B.Hudson JP
Sep 1,   B.L.Clements to Mary J. Rickey by Wm. Largen MG
Dec 13,   B.H.Berry to Harriet Johnston by F. Motlow JP
pg 460   (cont'd)
1864
Jan 14,   Samuel D. Brown to Margaret Brown by W.R.Waggoner JP
Feb 11,   Lodrick Robinson to Viana Hart by F. Motlow JP
1863
Dec 8,   W.E.Freeman to Susan E. Harkins by G.W.Nichols MG
Feb 27,   John Willett to Jane Hale by G.W.Nichols MG
1864
May 30,   S.J.Smith to Mary C. Smith by R.D.Hardin MG
    24,   Isaac Mason to Sarah Roughton by R.D.Hardin MG
pg 30
Apr 5,   Samuel McCracken to Mrs. A.M.Emmons
     7,   John W. McAfee to Rachell McRee by Samuel Hall JP

```
        7,    James Taylor to Elizabeth Crabtree by Alexander Smith,M
        9,    James M. Luna to Lucinda Sanders
       13,    Patrick Boyle to Mary L. Yant by W.L.Alexander JP
       21,    H.L.Howell to Nancy A. Cole
pg 31
       28,    John W. Bernet to Martha Roper by J. Melton MG
May  8,       Armstead Hatshet to Sarah A. Jeffers by W.A.Brown JP
        3,    George Stovall to Elizabeth J. Daniel
        5,    Thomas P. Phagan to Mary A. McFerrin by J. Caughran JP
        5,    James L. Foster to Amanda A. Easlick by W.R.Waggoner JP
       10,    W.T.Blackwell to Nancy Riley by R.D.Hardin MG
pg 32
       31,    S.Y.McCalla to Martha J. Stone by A.P.Copeland MG
1865
May  5,       Joel T. Dollar to Elizabeth D. Orrick by J.B.Warren MG
1864
May 17,       James Smith to Mary Mullins by R.D.Hardin MG
       20,    Bennett Solomon to Mary Renegar by J.H.Eslick JP
       17,    Aron Glidewell to Caroline Noles
       18,    James H. Fulgham to Susan A. Washburn
pg 33
       19,    James P. Hudson to Mary S, Gross by W.A.Brown JP
       22,    F.P.L.Parr to Nancy J. Higgins by R.D.Hardin MG
       24,    Robert H. Askins to Nancy D. Hairston by A.P.Copeland,M
       26,    Vincen Mullins to Jane Jones by R.D.Hardin MG
       26,    J.S.Hines to Louisa A. Pylant by J.B.Tigert MG
       29,    Isaac H. Eslick to Catharine Ratliff by S.D.Loyd MG
pg 34
       30,    M.E.Bunn to M.J.Morgan
Jun  2,       Henry J. Harper to M.J.Lock by J.T.Ashby JP
        5,    Hillery W. Brown to Margaret E. Jolly by J.B.Hudson JP
       16,    John Slaton to Manerva A. Franks by Sam Hall JP
       23,    David A. Franklin to Malissa A. Fannin by J.H.Eslick JP
       22,    James Honey to Mrs. Edie Land
pg 35
       29,    Wm. H. Medcalf to Mrs. Jane Hampton by J.R.Abernathy MG
       29,    Robert A. Davidson to Mary A. Solomon by S.D.Loyd MG
Jul  5,       Wm. R. Wyatt to Sarah L. McCown by A.S.Smith MG
        5,    John L. McGehee to Sarah J. Alley by J.H.Eslick JP
        7,    John S. Morton to Catharine Wagoner
        7,    James C. Hague to Mary A. Wakefield by J.W.Holman MG
       17,    Alexander Hobbs to Emeline Lynn by W.F.Zimmerman JP
       17,    William Lynn to Sarah A. Hamilton by W.F.Zimmerman JP
       17,    T.A.Stewart to E.C.Story by Wm. D. Cherry MG
Aug  3,       Ely Lane to Eveline Hudson by W.A.Brown JP
        3,    Robert McWhorter to Serena Miller
       11,    Joel J. Pitts to Martha C. Little by W.L.Alexander JP
pg 37
       11,    Richard Hall to Jane Jolly by J.B.Hudson JP
       14,    John H. Chaffin to Sarah Johnson by W.M.Hailey MG
       13,    W.B.Morrison to Nancy E. Epps by J.B.Warren MG
       14,    F.M.Pamplin to Cinthia E. Pitts by W.L.Alexander JP
       15,    Jacob Hamilton to Unice C. Smith
       18,    W.H.Sorrels to S.E.Scott by J.G.Bledsoe MG
pg 38
       18,    William F. Keith to S. Pamplin by W.A.Brown JP
       18,    Presley A. Keith to Mary J. Pamplin by W.A.Brown JP
       18,    Joseph R. Clift to Eliza N. Taylor by J.B.Tigert MG
```

	27,	B.F.Burgess to Jane F. George by W.F.Zimmerman JP
	21,	W.F.Ragsdale to Mary M. Locker by J.L.Jean JP
	21,	Henry Sulser to N.C.E.Martin by R.D.Hardin MG

pg 39

Sep	17,	H.D.V.Benson to Sarah P. Barker
	1,	W.J.Brazier to Martha L. Spencer by W.R.Waggoner JP
Aug	31,	Marion Bennet to Nancy Caldwell
	31,	Willis Arnold to Elizabeth Taylor by S.H.Taylor JP
Sep	4,	James Trader to Sarah McCown by John Carey JP
	9,	Joseph A. Jackson to C.E.Worthy by W.T.Andrews MG

pg 40

	10,	T.W.Thompson to Lucinda Preston by W.H.Thompson JP
	12,	M.T.Wilson to Jane C. Tate by A. Smith MG
	12,	Thomas M. Reece to Catharine A. Petty
	15,	M.D.L.Hanby to Susan C. Swinford by W.L.Alexander JP
	18,	W.B.Cole to Martha H. Hughy by J.G.Stephenson MG
	17,	B.R.Floyd to C.E.Cooley

pg 41

	21,	William A. Meeks to Caledonia V. Davis by Alexander Smith MG
	22,	Joseph Moore to Tursey B. Thurman by W.L.Alexander JP
Oct	1,	S.C.Evans to Eliza Jefers by W.A.Brown JP
Sep	26,	E.M.Ousley to Elizabeth Whiteman
	28,	Sanford Renegar to Thussey A. Martin
Oct	6,	Patrick H. Puckett to Sarah Jane Kidd by John Carey JP

pg 42

	4,	James A. Rowe to Elizabeth Corpier by J.C.Stephenson MG
	13,	Hilton Hill to M.M.V.Hambrick
	18,	Ephraim Hovis to Margaret C. Collins by W.W.Wilson JP
	18,	Robert R. Anderson to Louisa Patterson by Alexander Smith MG
	18,	James Langston to Angeline McNeil
	19,	Calaway Sherley to Nancy E. Wakefield by J.R.Nelson JP

pg 43

Dec	4,	A.H.Summers to Amanda McAfee by S.M.Emmons MG
Oct	20,	John Nichol to Frances J. Freeman by G.W.Nichols MG
	29,	John Dyer to Jane R. Fuller by J.B.Warren MG
	31,	John C. Anderson to Mary E. McCown by Alexander Smith,M
	31,	H.W.Thompson to Mary E. McGhee by S.D.Loyd MG
	31,	P.W.Thompson to Elizabeth McWhorter by W.H.Thompson JP

pg 44

Nov	6,	John G. Millard to Tennessee Blake by J.B.Tigert MG
	6,	W.D.Price to Huldar Neece by H. Tartar MG
	6,	Richard Cunningham to Sarah South by R. Martin MG
	7,	Manning Dean to Nannie Reece
	13,	Lafayette F. Barnes to Amanda S. McCracken by J.C. Stevenson MG
	12,	Henry B. Love to Louisa Virginia Fielding

pg 45

	22,	William F. Tucker to N.L.Story by W.G.Cherry MG
	18,	Matthew M. Shelton to Mary Jane Michael
	20,	William Butler to Catharine Pruitt by J.B.Hudson JP
	23,	Charles Gray to Eliza A. Birdthrone by J. Caughran JP
	24,	Berry Hall to Nancy Franklin by W.A.Gill MG
	27,	W.M.D.Prosser to Martha A. Redd by G.W.Nichols MG

pg 46

	28,	F.M.Raney to Matilda Raney by J. Caughran JP
Dec	23,	Thomas A. Paysinger to Ferdonia E. Merrell by G.W. Puckett MG

```
          1,   R.N.Dunlap to Sarah A. Bonner by R.D.Hardin
Nov 27,   Thomas Price to Sarah A. Hatchett by W.A.Brown JP
Dec  1,   Marcus Marrs to Sally M. Buchanan by J.B.Tigert MG
Nov 30,   J. Patterson to Ann Griffin
pg 47
Dec  6,   Joseph M. Gragg to Lucy A. Brown by J.H.Bryson MG
     5,   James P. Gray to Sophrona J. Holman
     5,   Francis Crabtree to Ellen Finch by Alexander Smith MG
    11,   A.Y.Pool to Margaret Marberry by L.L.Cole JP
     8,   James Roper to Emily Mulder by G.W.Puckett MG
     8,   Thomas Fox to Margaret Parham by J.B.Tigert MG
pg 48
    13,   James Gulley to Elizabeth Hopkins by W.M.Hailey MG
    14,   T.A.Gray to F.W.A.Marshall by L.L.Cole JP
1865
Jan  5,   Frank Arney to Elizabeth McWhorter by W.W.Wilson JP
1864
Dec 20,   Hugh Randolph to Martha E. Brooks by A.P.Copeland MG
    23,   Silas Dollar to Martha Stovall by G.W.Puckett MG
    21,   W.M.C.Gather to Hulder G. Robinson by W.H.Thompson JP
pg 49
    22,   J.W.McDougall to Mary A. Geralds
    22,   J.J.Stevenson to Mary J. Walker
    26,   W.L.Bankstone to Malissa Jones by R.D.Hardin MG
    29,   M.S.Simmons to Emma Jackson by S.M.Emmons MG
1865
Jan  3,   J.C.Harrison to D.F.Mitchell by J.C.Stevans MG
     5,   G.W.Steadman to Mary J. Marshall by L.L.Cole JP
pg 50
     5,   Andrew Cowen to Mary J. Graves by J.L.Ashby JP
     4,   William Andrews to Elizabeth Rochel by L.L.Cole JP
     4,   William Warren to Nancy Jackson by G.W.Nichols MG
     6,   William Armstrong to Sarah Katon by W.A.Bryan JP
     8,   William Cobb to Jane Norman by D.L.Mitchell MG
     6,   John H. Davis to Mary E. Mays by W.H.Thompson JP
pg 51
     8,   J.H.Woodard to M.E.Butler by J.C.Stephens MG
     6,   John Connally to Miss E. Booth by W.A.Gill MG
     7,   Alexander Taylor to Eliza E. Faulkes by W.D.Price JP
    10,   R.N.Burton to M.E.Randolph by J. Caughran JP
     9,   D.R.Ecklberger to A.B.Wormack by W.A.Gill MG
    12,   Lafayette Swanner to Margaret Willis by J.C.Stevenson,M
pg 52
    12,   John McDaniel to Mary Jane Smith by R.D.Hardin MG
    12,   John G. Davidson to Martha E. Freeman by J.A.Prosser JP
    11,   Jesse C. Webb to Sarah C. Marshall
    20,   Temple W. Taylor to Lucy A. Womack by D.L.Mitchell MG
    24,   William P. Lee to Susannah Counts by David Jacks MG
    24,   Isaack Sawyer to Sarah C. Joiner by W.R.Waggoner JP
pg 53
    24,   Lewis Sweden to Sarah H. Evans by A.P.Copeland MG
    26,   William H. McCown to Mary E. Wyatt by Alex. Smith MG
    25,   William Locker to Margaret M. Holt
    19,   Thomas Fanning to Mary E. Shelton
Feb  8,   Richard Hall to Louisa J. Neeld by G.W.Puckett MG
     5,   Joseph Philpot to Rebecca A. George by G.W.Puckett MG
pg 54
     8,   J.J.Summerford to M.E.Smith by L.L.Cole JP
```

```
       9,   J. Grammer to Mary A. Lock by J.T.Ashby JP
       7,   John W. Lauderdale to Nancy M. Turley by Alex. Smith MG
      16,   G.T.Roper to E.J.Bond by G.W.Puckett MG
      14,   A.B.Bell to Martha A. Randolph by L.D.Jones MG
      16,   J.T.Pamplin to Rebecca Yant by W.L.Alexander JP
pg 55
      19,   Wm. Harelston to Caroline Hathcoat by L.L.Cole JP
Mar  1,    J.N.Sullivan to Susan Elizabeth Logan by E.L.Hester MG
Feb 20,    William McCants to Frances Holley
      25,   Alexander Lasenberry to E.S.Wilson by John Carey JP
Mar  2,    A.J.Ledbetter to Elizabeth Joins by W.A.Bryan JP
       2,   James W. Ellis to Fannie E. Kimes by J.B.Tigert MG
pg 56
Feb 24,    Henry Casey to Ann Shanks by W.A.Bryan JP
      22,   John Corder to Mary Pilant by W.E.Carter JP
      28,   A.J.Young to M.A.Coleman by J. Carey JP
Mar  7,    James Harrison to C.C.Grant by W.D.Cherry MG
       7,   James E. Mills to Elizabeth Lane by J.B.Hudson JP
      21,   David G. Smith to Amanda C. Cole by R.D.Hardin MG
pg 57
      22,   John M. McKinney to Mary J. Smith by J. Caughran JP
      25,   John C. Spencer to Martha J. Ward by J.H.Eslick JP
      21,   H.B.McCalla to Martha A. Sloan by A.P.Copeland MG
      23,   Win J. Mills to Mary M. Roden by L.L.Cole JP
      28,   J.G.Beard to Bethena Bond by G.W.Puckett MG
Apr 11,    T.B.Yates to Melinda Jennings by D.L.Mitchell MG
pg 58
Mar 28,    E.F.Brown to Bethiah E. Warden by J.B.Hudson JP
Apr  2,    J.J.Donaldson to Nancy E. Taylor by J.H.Eslick JP
Mar 30,    Samuel M. Hill to Mary E. Hambrick by T.D.Jones MG
Apr  5,    D. Hood to Margaret J. Hobbs by J.C.Stevenson MG
       4,   C.M.Sims to Louisa J. Frame by J.D.Smith JP
       9,   Mikel McGrath to Elizabeth Brotherton by W.W.Wilson JP
pg 59
      10,   W.S.Butler to Martha E. Welch
Feb 25,    O.C.Talent to Jane Marly
Apr 20,    M.W.Cooley to Martha Myrick by G.W.Carmickel MG
      19,   S.D.Brown to Ann W. Marlor by J.D.Smith JP
      24,   Thomas B. Eastland to Florinda Hopkins
      27,   T.M.Harkins to Ariva J. Allbright by J.A.Prosser JP
pg 60
May  4,    Alexander Stone to Vina Martin by S. Womack MG
Apr 27,    Taylor Cogwell to Sarah J. Scott by Hiram Tartar MG
May  2,    C.W.Williams to Martha Lindsey
       4,   W.N.Boaz to Lucy S. Thurman by W.L.Alexander JP
      14,   William Tafts to Mary Hovis by R.D.Hardin MG
       7,   M.C.Harris to S.M.Stanford by T.D.Jones MG
pg 61
      11,   H.H.Neece to F.B.Reece by T.D.Jones MG
       9,   James P. Howell to Lamira Touchstone by W.P.Price JP
      14,   G.W.Williams to Lilly Campbell by A.J.Steel MG
      18,   John E. Broyles to Agnes A. McLaughlin by T.H.Woodard,M
      22,   N.S.Hudson to Tennessee C. Roughton by J.L.Ashby JP
      23,   G.L.Cashion to Sarah Ann Walker
pg 62
      25,   Frederick Wagoner to Margaret Larson by J.W.Holman MG
      30,   W.L.Silvester to E.J.Jibbs by G.W.Puckett MG
      30,   John W. Revis to Mary E. Dyer by John Roach JP
```

1865

	31,	Thomas W. Gibson to Sarah C. Sorrells by G.W.Nichols MG
Jun	3,	H.B.Chilcoat to Sallie C. Whitaker by Elder T.D.Jones
	6,	Thomas P. Arnold to M.M.Stublefield by J.D.Smith JP

pg 63

6,	Wyatt T. Woodruff to Mary C. Price by Wm. Dawson MG
8,	William Duke to Melissa C. Cunningham by Bradley Kimbrough MG
11,	Levi Latham to Margaret E. Lesley by I.H.Eslick JP
11,	William Williams to Elizabeth Hill by D.L.Mitchell MG
13,	Isaac Rice to Sarah J. Markum
13,	Wright Looney to Minerva Markum by S.M.Emmons MG

pg 64

15,	Peter Foster to Sarah Morton by G.W.Nichols MG
15,	J.J.Cummins to Fannie Blake by J.B.Warren MG
17,	A.S.Moore to Jane Moore
19,	Davis Drake to Mrs. C.M.Hillum by W.A.Bryan JP
20,	Henry H. Brock to Lavina J. Hathcock by A.P.Copeland MG
21,	John J. McAdams to Frances C. Heflin by J.B.Warren MG

pg 65

21,	M.C.Anderson to Margaret R. McCown by J.B.Tigert MG
22,	John T. English to Sarah E. Tate by A.P.Copeland MG
25,	Benjamin B. Chapman to Nancy Tillery by J.C.Stevenson,M
29,	William Wade to Susannah Brown by J.D.Smith JP
27,	Cornelius Hedgepeth to Mary E. Nerrin
28,	Aaron McDaniel to Nancy C. Cunningham by W.F.Zimmerman

pg 66

	29,	W.H.Carrigan to Catharine Summerford by Elder T.D.Jones,M
	30,	Joseph Sanders to Jane Frayley by Alexander Smith MG
Jul	2,	S.J.Gilliland to Mrs. R.L.Locker by A.J.Childress JP
	5,	W.H.Cunningham to Louisa A. Whited by J.D.Sullivan MG
	3,	J.M.Bratton to E.F.Reynolds
	5,	J.R.Brown to N.M.Morgan by J.A.Prosser JP

pg 67

5,	David L. Smith to Emeline McKinney by A.S.Randolph JP
6,	J.M.Hambrick to Lucy A. Solomon by Eld. T.D.Jones MG
9,	Isaac Mason to Mary J. Allbright by A.P.Copeland MG
9,	Wm. H. Gunter to Amanda M. Owen by W.W.Wilson JP
8,	James F. Spencer to Susan J. Foster by J.T.Gordon(Not Solemized)
11,	James G. Fowler to Eliza E. Reed by G.W.Puckett MG

pg 68

11,	George W. Daniel to Eliza Pigg by A.C.Martin JP
13,	L.C.Mitchell to Sallie Hamilton by G.W.Puckett MG
12,	Thomas Cobb to Milly Melson (col)
12,	K.J.Pearson to E.C.Farrar
13,	Thomas J. Boggs to Cansada C. Pearson by R.Martin MG
14,	John Crunk to Caroline Allen (col) by S.W.Brookins

pg 69

15,	Alfred Askins to Cassanda Bonner (col) by Lewis Neal,M
16,	J.H.Reynolds to P.E.Bearden by Martin Towery MG
20,	Isaac Crouch to Elizabeth J. Lovelace by W.C.Fletcher
23,	James W. Rawls to Susan Griffis by A.P.Copeland MG
25,	W.J.Couch to Emeline P. Noles by W.M.Becket JP
25,	John Wilson to Martha A. Holt by S.L.Walker JP

pg 70

	25,	Ben A. Shelton to Mary E. Thompson by W.M.Becket,Esq
Aug	27,	J.W.Farnsworth to Parmelia Williamson by W.O.Price JP

Jul 27,   H.C.Lambert to Nancy S. Muse by Green Nichols MG
    26,   A.J.Radican to May J. Hunt
    27,   James M. Short to A.D.Smith by M.M.Marshall MG
    28,   Wm. Sutherland to Sally Swinger by J.B.Hudson JP
    29,   James Threet to Fannie Drake (col) by S. Askins MG
    29,   John T. Daniel to Lucy J. Brazier
    29,   Alfred White to Margaret Ann Poorstone (col)
Aug 6,   Thomas C. Eason to Cynthia A. Murdock by J. Roach JP
     2,   John S. Askins to M.A.Harston by A.P.Copeland MG
     1,   Calvin M. Decobb to Nancy A. White by J.D.Smith JP
pg 72
Sep 24,   Charles Gant to Sarah Burns (col) by J.M.Dyer JP
Aug 3,   John J. Paysinger to Orleany B. Coats by G.W.Puckett,M
     3,   James H. Campbell to Margaret E. Meeks by Ransom
                                                 Martin MG
     6,   Antoney Nelson to Lucy A. Gibson (col) by Hector
                                                 Warren MG
     8,   James Fulgham to Grazilder Meeks by W.A.Gill MG
     6,   James Cox to Martha Boggs by Alexander Smith MG
pg 73
     9,   Elija Phelps to Harriet Logan (col) by Amos Hop MG
     9,   Isaac A. Lincoln to Jane English by S.W.Brookins JP
     9,   Wm. R. Hubble to Lutitia Reece
    12,   John T. Gattis to Vincy Stubblefield by J.H.Eslick JP
    16,   Jackson Ostrander to Polly J. Posey by J. Roach JP
    14,   S.W.Robertson to W.P.Robertson by B. Christian JP
pg 74
Sep 3,   Nedd Hayse to Easter McKinney (col) by W.O.Price JP
Aug 22,   William McWhorter to Jane Cooper by W.E.Carter JP
    20,   James J. Emmons to M.L.Hedgepeth by W.W.Wilson JP
Oct 27,   Peter Broadaway to Anica Buchanan (col)by Hector
                                                 Warren MG
    27,   Cassan Buchanan to Jane Warren (col) by Hector Warren,M
Nov 12,   Samuel Wilson to Mary Wilson (col) by S. Askins MG
pg 75
Aug 24,   John Sawyers to Iba(Ida) Mitchell by J.D.Smith JP
    24,   R.M.Bearden to Mary Cunningham by J.O.Sullivan MG
    24,   Marion J. Delaney to M.R.Allbright by A.P.Copeland MG
    23,   Henry H. Sugg to Sallie E. Yowell by S.E.Wilson MG
    24,   L.A.E.Bearden to Cynthia H. Webb by W.A.Gill MG
    25,   James C. Maynard to E.C.Dennison by W.O.Price JP
pg 76
    25,   Wm. M. Holly to Mary Welch by W.C.Fletcher JP
    26,   Robert Brandon to Adaline Spencer
    30,   D.W.Ellis to C.D.Roughton by J.W.Holman MG
Sep 3,   Lewis Koonce to Nancy Price (col) by W.O.Price JP
Aug 30,   D.B.Gattis to M.J.Bray by B. Christian JP
    28,   Charles Diemer to Susan Diemer (col)
pg 77
    30,   John D. Bryant to Susan Ann Fitch by W.E.Carter
    29,   Henry F. Taylor to Mary E. Smith by J.B.Tigert MG
Nov 20,   Tom Bright to Easter Bright (col) by S. Askins MG
Sep 1,   Andrew B. Edmison to Mary A. Owen by John Carey JP
     6,   James H. Burnam to Mary E. Robison by M.B.Dewitt MG
     5,   A.M.Noles to Frances Eslick by W.H.Thompson JP
pg 78
    10,   James Lay to Harriet Lay (col)
     4,   A. Bennet to Virginia Holt

1865

6,   Sanders T. Nix to Martha A. Moorehead by I.H.Eslick JP
5,   Wm. A. Rutledge to Susan A. Waggoner by W.O.Price JP
5,   Henry McDaniel to Angeline Key
7,   W.S.Fox to E.A.Hinkle by J.W.Holman MG
pg 79
6,   J.R.(P) Donaldson to Mariah Denison by N.T.Powers MG
7,   Isaac Morton to Nancy Foster by G. Nichols MG
10,   John D. Massey to Louisa J. Sawyers by W.R.Waggoner JP
Sep --,   Thomas B. Harris to R.E.Lesley
Sep --,   Samuel C. Carver to Mary C. Hudson by John E. Frost MG
Sep 11,   Alick Eastland to Ann Clarke (col)
pg 80
13,   M.P.Caughran to Sarah A. Taylor by A.S.Montgomery MG
14,   W.T.Dale to Lucy J. Marshall by A.P.Copeland MG
14,   Samuel B. Gault to Martha E. Hines by J.B.Tigert MG
17,   Alexander Smith to Emily E. Wright by J.B.Tigert MG
26,   Wesley Whitt to Astelia Delapp by Samuel Bond JP
17,   S.M.Griffeth to Sarah E. Franklin by S. Walker JP
pg 81
19,   James L. Spence to Jane Lindsey
21,   George W. Hale to Susan C. Scott by Green Nichols MG
21,   Walton Hiles to Nannie S. Thomison by T.J.Shaw MG
24,   E.S.Harralson to Malinda Ann Maddox by W.D.Cherry MG
24,   John A. Cowley to Rachel Warren (col) by D.L.Mitchell,M
28,   B.F.Martin to M.J.Phelps by J.E.Frost MG
pg 82
28,   James R. Stevenson to Sarah E. Walker
28,   Lesell Marr to Nancy A.E.Williams by W.L.Rees JP
31,   Thomas Clark to Patsey Kelso (col)
Oct 2,   James C. Shofner to Mary A. Rutledge
2,   W.M.Guerin to J.L.Lock by W.A.Rhodes JP
3,   Wiley Gross to Cynthia Waggoner by J.B.Hudson JP
pg 83
6,   James B. McCracken to Maggie Tharp by J.O.Sullivan MG
8,   Samuel Roe to Mary F. Isom by W.L.Alexander JP
5,   James K. Hicks to Martha A. Webb by J.B.Hudson JP
22,   Cyrus Edwards to Levina Allen (col) by Lewis Neal MG
11,   T.J.Allison to Sallie Elmore by J.W.Holman MG
9,   J.C.McGee to Manervy A. Tucker
pg 84
10,   Allen Taylor to Mrs. Mary Reece by E.S.Patton MG
12,   L.J.Whitaker to Bettie M. Mosely by T.D.Jones MG
12,   Wm. E. Turley to Margaret E. Lauderdale by Wm. Dawson,M
12,   Joel S. Brewer to Ann Allison by W.L.Alexander JP
13,   Elmore Marshall to Agy Bonner (col)
15,   James A. Hunt to Martha J. Smith by B.Christian JP
pg 85
14,   Hiram J. Daniel to Nancy A. Tharp
21,   Aaron Cole to Amanda Cannon (col) by J.B.Hudson JP
Nov 5,   Cezar Clark to Susan Allen (col) by Lewis Clark MG
Oct 16,   J.S.Ray to Mary T. Couser
19,   J.F.Moore to Mary E. Wanslow by J.W.Holman MG
19,   Johnson Riddle to Nancy J. Swinford by John Caughran JP
pg 86
22,   John N. Williams to Jane Williams by A.J.Steel MG
23,   John H. Lewis to Syntha J. Malier by J.D.Smith JP
Nov 5,   Harrison Kercherval to Brancee Allen (col) by L.Neal,M
Oct 26,   T.E.Turner to Mary E. Scivally by W.R.Waggoner JP

26,   Charles F. Blackwell to Martha J. Mitchell by T.D.
                                          Jones MG
24,   James Williams to Virginia Key by Ransom Martin MG

pg 87
Nov 28, Henry Harris to Jane Slone (col) by J.B.Hudson JP
Oct 29, L.W.Gayle to Mrs. Mary E. Drennon by R.D.Hardin MG
Nov 23, Hiram Bright to Rebecca Bright (col) by M.M.Marshall,M
5, Charles Bright to Mary Allen (col) by Lewis Neal MG
Oct 28, Abraham Clark to Easter Clark (col)
Nov 2, James Gore to Mary Hobbs by D.L.Enoch JP

pg 88
2, Elisha J. Parks to Mary A. Alexander by J.W.Holman MG
Oct 31, Jason Billins to Sarah Clark by J. Caughran JP
Nov 1, H.C.Buchanan to P.J.Kimes by J.B.Tigert MG
3, J.T.Ratliff to M.C.Webb by J.H.Eslick JP
2, Thomas M. White to Sina Woodard by J.B.Tigert MG
1866
Mar 11, Marcus Neil to May Parks (col) by Lewis Neal MG

pg 89
1865
Nov 3, J.G.Askins to C.C.Randolph by A.P.Copeland MG
3, Van Parks to Mary Parks (col) by J.M.Groce MG
3, Harry Hardin to Mary Johnson (col) by J.M.Groce MG
4, Abram Gill to Amanda Cole (col) by J.B.Hudson JP
5, B.H.Hobbs to Sarah Farrar by W.F.Zimmerman JP
3, Henry Parks to Fanny Parks (col)

pg 90
23, Abb Todd to Emily Alexander (col) by M.M.Marshall MG
12, Mike Stone to Polly Stone (col) by J.B.Hudson JP
12, Newton Slone to Emily Slone (col) by J.B.Hudson JP
1866
Jan 21, George DeKins to Louisa Moyers (col) by A.Woodfolk MG
1865
Nov 4, William Morgan to Clarinda White (col)
27, Elliott Martin to Nancy Thomison (col) by J.B.Hudson JP

pg 91
12, Dan Norris to Mary Holdin (col) by J.B.Hudson JP
1866
Jan 8, Dick Smith to Malinda Smith (col) by Singer Askins MG
1865
Nov 11, Amos McDaniel to Julia McDonald (col) by Singer
                                      Askins MG
11, Hugh McDonald to Fanny McDonald (col) by Singer Askins,M
12, Monroe Thomison to Narcissa Thomison (col) by J.B.
                                      Hudson JP
12, Lack Thomison to Maria Stone (col) by J.B.Hudson JP

pg 92
4, Moses Martin to Judith Martin (col)
5, Cicero Allen to Caroline Allen (col) by Lewis Neal MG
5, Wm. Bonner to Nancy Bonner (col) by Lewis Neal MG
6, Edmond E. Hester to Emily Bonner (col) by Lewis Neal,M
8, Josiah Hobbs to Nancy Vessor by M. Emmons MG
7, Wells Robinson to Susan Robinson by J.B.Hudson JP

pg 93
11, Cass McDonald to Mary McDonald (col) by Singer Askins,M
12, G. Small to Lucy Summerford by J.B.Hudson JP
9, John Thomas to Martha Dollins by J.B.Hudson JP
9, Bob Dollins to Ronia McKenzie by J.B.Hudson JP

```
        12,    G. Campbell to Mariah Cannon (col) by J.B.Hudson JP
        16,    Aron Lamb to Delda McDonald (col) by Singer Askins,M
pg 94
         9,    J.P.Manly to Martha Mason by John Milton MG
Dec  1,        William Stone to Elizabeth Stone (col) by W.E.Carter JP
Nov  7,        John Ezell to Doncilla Henderson
        28,    Anderson Redick to Jane Redick (col) by Lewis Neal MG
        28,    Sam Hickman to Sarah Jackson (col) by Lewis Neal MG
        11,    Lewis Neal to Betty Allen (col) by Singer Askins MG
pg 95
        11,    Washington Neal to Laura Bright (col) by Lewis Neal MG
        11,    Ben Bright to Amanda Bonner (col) by Lewis Neal MG
         8,    S.M.McDonald to Nancy Mason by J. Moore JP
         8,    A.L.Walker to M.A.Mason by J. Moore JP
         8,    John P. Smith to Sarah E. Honey by Needham Koonce JP
        15,    E.G.B.Lee to Mrs. Lucy A. Grisard by L.D.Howell MG
pg 96
        11,    Alford McDonald to Melia McDonald (col) by Singer Askins,M
         9,    John Bland to Nancy Nelson by W.D.Smith JP
         9,    Abe Millikin to Catharine A. Edmondson by John Carey JP
        10,    W.M.Stephenson to M.J.Hampton by W.F.Zimmerman JP
        16,    Dennis Higgins to Charry Ashworth (col) by Rev.W.W.
                                                            Hailey
         9,    John L. Mitchell to Mrs. Darcus Hall by A.C.Martin JP
pg 97
        10,    Wm. A. Thompson to Arriva Cunningham by J.A.Prosser JP
        11,    Daniel McDonald to Amy McDonald (col) by Singer Askins,M
        11,    Kiah Kimes to Mary McDonald (col) by S. Askins MG
        11,    John Neeld to Edna Harris (col) by Lewis Neal MG
         9,    R.J.Yarbrough to Elvira Cruse by T.H.Woodard MG
        10,    Sidney Gaines to Harriet Buchanan (col)
pg 98
        11,    G.W.McDonald to Margaret McDonald (col)
        16,    Wilson Askins to Easter Hester (col) by S. Askins MG
1866
Jan 19,        Singer Askins to Violet Askins (col) by A. Woodfolk MG
1865
Nov 16,        George Pitts to Sarah Askins (col) by S. Askins MG
        12,    James Isom to Malinda J. Warden by J.B.Hudson JP
1866
Jan 20,        Harry Bagley to Ann Bagley (col) by A. Woodfolk MG
pg 99
1865
Nov 12,        Robert Landess to Susan Epps (col) by J.B.Hudson JP
        11,    Harry Landess to Ellen Bobo (col)
        12,    B.F.Dyer to D.E.Dyer by J.B.Warren MG
        27,    Robert McElroy to Priscilla Cowan (col) by J.B.Hudson
        12,    James Sugg to Hetty S. Dunlap (col) by Lewis Neal MG
        11,    Abe McConnell to Anna Phelps (col)
pg 100
        24,    Enoch Harston to Nora Harston (col) by S. Askins MG
        11,    Fred Harston to Alsy Harston (col) by S. Askins MG
        11,    G. Thomison to Mary McDonald (col) by S. Askins MG
        11,    Andy McDonald to Mariah McDonald (col) by S. Askins,M
        12,    Isaac McElroy to Ann Buchanan (col)
        16,    Thomas W. Twitty to Mary M.J.Emmons by W.W.Wilson JP
pg 101
        15,    Samuel Walker to Sarah E. Cashion by J.D.Smith JP
```

```
        23,   Isaac Ashby to Sopha Ashby (col) by W.H.Thompson JP
        15,   Allen Lamb to Martha Lamb (col) by S. Askins MG
        14,   David Witt to Charlotte M. Williams by W.W.Wilson JP
        16,   John Rice to Mary J. Miller by W. Smith JP
        15,   James M. Bell to Mrs. Ann Armstrong by J.B.Warren MG
pg 102
        16,   Franklin F. Mitchell to Elizabeth Brown by J.D.Smith JP
        27,   Henry Cowan to Sebra Smith (col) by J.B.Hudson JP
        14,   Frank Wiley to Fanny Lamb (col) by S. Askins MG
        15,   J.F.Goodrich to Sallie Clarke by John Carey JP
Dec 10,   Berry Zimmerman to Marinda Zimmerman (col) by S.Askins
Nov 15,   Jack Dismukes to Betsey Dismukes (col)
pg 103
        16,   Hary Sherrell to Elza Henderson (col)
        16,   Wm. H. Jones to Mary C. Little by Robert R. Jones MG
        16,   Henry Williams to Victoria Street by J. Roach JP
        19,   James K. Marrs to Emily B. McElroy (col) by S. Askins,M
Dec 12,   Manuel Crawford to Jane Gibson (col) by A.C.Martin JP
        18,   Henry Crawford to Catharine Massey (col) by J.B.Tigert,M
pg 104
        18,   Samuel Crawford to Rebecca Bryson (col) by S. Askins MG
Nov 18,   Esek McDonald to Delilah Hairston (col) by S.Askins MG
        18,   Ned Timmins to Sally Timmins (col) by S. Askins MG
        18,   Milton Timmins to Rachel Timmins (col) by S. Askins MG
Dec 10,   Charley Fullerton to Mary Clanton (col) by S. Askins MG
         5,   Willis Bland to Catharine Bland (col) by Lewis Neal MG
pg 105
Nov 18,   Nelson Kimes to Syntha Small (col) by J.B.Hudson JP
Dec  1,   Dick Kelso to Celia Kelso (col) by W.E.Carter JP
         1,   Matt Woods to Emeline Kelso (col) by W.E.Carter JP
         1,   Ben Garner to Patsey Kelso (col) by W.E.Carter JP
         1,   Clinton Hall to Nancy Kelso (col) by W.E.Carter JP
        30,   Coleman Bonner to Jane Bonner (col) by Lewis Neal MG
pg 106
Nov 29,   Robert McDonald to Emily McDonald (col) by S. Askins MG
Dec  1,   Carol Kelso to Emily Kelso (col) by W.E.Carter JP
         3,   Robert Moore to Sarah Moore (col) by Lewis Neal MG
Nov 27,   Peter Disonbry to Catharine Bledsoe (col) by M.T.
                                                  Griswell JP
        26,   Daniel Robinson to Mary McClelland (col) by Needham
                                                   Koonce JP
        20,   Arch King to Lucinda Nichols (col)
pg 107
Dec  1,   Bob Desmukes to Milly Kelso (col) by W.E.Carter JP
Nov 22,   Woodson Douglas to Mary McClelland (col) by Lewis Neal,M
        20,   Berrell Hampton to Mariah Halbert (col)
        20,   Thomas Patterson to Silva Farrar (col) by J.R.Abernathy,M
Dec  3,   Adam Bonner to Mary E. Smith (col) by Lewis Neal MG
Nov 20,   Arthur Benton to Leona Robinson (col)
pg 108
        20,   Jacob Pamplin to Nancy Pamplin (col)
        20,   John Dobbins to Celia Clanton (col)
        20,   Wm. A. Clarke to Angeline Smith (col)
        20,   Wm. Buchanan to Polly Smith (col)
        21,   J.B.Stegall to M.L.Shofner by Elder T.D.Jones
        20,   Junurs Bonner to Juda Bonner (col)
pg 109
        23,   James H. Holman to Lizzie C. Kimbrough by Eld. T.D.Jones
```

```
          23,    Cullen Bailey to Kate Kimbrough by Eld. T.D.Jones
     Dec 10,    Frank Pamplin to Susan Kimes (col) by S. Askins MG
     1866
     Mar 22,    J.R.Wilson to Mary K.A.Ruth by J.O.Sullivan MG
     1865
     Nov 21,    W.P.Isom to Martha E. Pigg by J. Roach JP
          23,    Lenard Marbery to Rachel A. Scrogins by L.L.Cole JP
     pg 110
          22,    Daniel Lamb to Lucinda Douglass (col) by S. Askins MG
          22,    Daniel Weigart to Rachel L. Rowlin by W.L.Alexander JP
          25,    Manuel White to Allice Savish (col) by S. Askins MG
     Dec  3,    Harrison Moore to Cela Sugg (col) by Lewis Neal MG
     Nov 25,    Gilbert Wilson to Della Wilson (col)
     1866
     Mar 31,    Peter Smith to Mary Clark (col) by S.H.Taylor JP
     1865
     Nov 25,    Spencer Clarke to Cyntha Clark (col)
          26,    J.W.Hardin to W.C.Warren by W.L.Reese JP
          29,    Peter Galloway to Harriet Givens (col) by S.Askins MG
          29,    Marion M. Bedford to Ann Sutliff
          30,    Ephraim Mitchell to Corilla Brown by R.D.Hardin MG
          30,    J.P.Buchanan to M.E.Martin by A.A.Bell MG
     pg 112
     Dec  1,    Nathaniel M. Riddle to S.E.J.Young by S.D.Smith JP
     Nov 30,    John M. Blair to Sarah E. Phagan by L.L.Cole JP
          30,    William L. Bobo to Mary E.C.Shaw by T.W.Brents MG
     Dec 24,    Jack Dusenberry to Jane V. Whitaker (col) by M.T.
                                                    Greswell JP
     Nov 30,    Martin Bright to Charlotte Buchanan (col)
     Dec 14,    W.W.Hailey to Mrs. Nancy A. Templeton by A.F.Driskill MG
     pg 113
           5,    Neeld Bonner to Martha Bright (col) by Lewis Neal MG
           3,    W.A.Gilbert to Margaret Sorrells by Green Nichols MG
          20,    Arch Turley to Martha Brysent (col)
           7,    Dan N. Waggoner to Ann C. Cashion by J.W.Holman MG
           5,    Thomas N. Bledsoe to Fannie M. Prosser by W.R.Hannaway JP
           5,    R.F.Bell to Mary A. Edmondson by M.M.Marshall MG
     pg 114
           6,    W.D.Wade to Louisa J. Clift by J.B.Tigert MG
           7,    James T. Barker to Louisa G. Jordan by W.E.Carter JP
           6,    D.J.Kimes to R.H.Sawyers by William Dawson MG
           7,    James M. McFreean to Nancy M. Jones by R.D.Hardin MG
           6,    Jo McMullen to Agnes McMullen (col)
           7,    W.J.Raney to Sarah M. McMillen
     pg 115
          14,    George Woodwin to Frances Smith by G.W.Puckett MG
          14,    Solomon Brandon to Elizabeth Dean by J.S.Ervin MG
          14,    Anthony White to Mary Gregory (col) by S. Askins MG
          14,    W.H.Tripp to Elizabeth J. Little by J.D.Smith JP
          18,    R.G.Deford to Nancy A. Farrar by S.H.Taylor JP
          17,    James W. Hampton to Sarah A. Cunningham by W.E.Caldwell,M
     pg 116
          19,    G.L.Hughey to Mary M. Hampton by Newton Hamilton MG
          18,    J.F.Clarke to Mary J. McFarren by A.S.Sloan MG
          20,    Davis W. Clark to Lucy G. Carter by A.A.Bell MG
          21,    Henry Craig to Jane Stone by S. Wormack MG
          30,    Charles Perkins to Lottie Dobbins (col) by N.Hamilton MG
          19,    James T. Gray to M.J.Davis by D.M.Gross MG
```

pg 117
25, W.T.Cummins to Margaret E. Allison by R.R.Jones MG
24, M.H.Hicks to Lucinda C. McGuire by W.A.Bryant JP
21, John A. McElroy to M.A.Goodwin by J.O.Sullivan MG
24, J.C.Raney to Molly J. Raby by W.S.Rees JP
24, John W. Malone to Millie A. Harbin by W.E.Carter JP
23, James Milton to Mary J. Owen
pg 118
24, S.M.Moore to Mrs. E.C.Lewter by Henry P. Turner MG
24, W.B.Prosser to Catharine Holley by W.S.Rees JP
25, Prince Griffis to Mary Sugg (col)
25, Jack Whitaker to Fannie Whitfield (col) by M.T.Greswell
26, W.B.Blair to M.J.Phagan
28, John D. Floyd to Susan B. Motlow by J.E.Frost MG
pg 119
27, Barton Kimes to Amanda Halbert (col) by J.O.Sullivan MG
28, John Lindsey to M.J.Caughran by A.S.Sloan MG
28, John Jean to Lucy A. Barker by W.E.Carter JP
29, Charles Blake to Alice Kimes (col) by J.B.Hudson JP
28, William Floyd to Angeline Lively by J.B.Hudson JP
27, J.W.Patterson to Eliza L. Lewis by Jeremiah Dean MG
pg 120
1866
Jan 4, Wiley B. Daniel to Susan E. Waggoner by J.E.Frost MG
1865
Dec 29, Henry Clark to Sarah Jones (col)
27, Ned Gregory to Mary Wiseman (col) by M.T.Greswell JP
30, Mack Bonner to Eliza Ann Bonner (col) by Lewis Neal MG
30, Hardy Kelso to Sarah Kelso (col) by W.E.Carter JP
31, Samuel Pitts to Nancy Washburn (col) by J.B.Warren MG
pg 121
30, G.W.Hunt to Mary E. Norman
31, John Gray to Margaret Bates by W.O.Price JP
1866
Jan 4, Dave Crawford to Mira Wright (col) by W.P.Price JP
2, W.H.Tipton to Frances E. Jolly by T.D.Jones MG
4, Jackson Wilson to Mary Dean by J.S.Ervin MG
Mar 20, Joshua Lazenbery to Amanda J. Swinford by S.H.Taylor JP
Jan 3, Wm. Reagor to Mrs. Anna E. Holman by J.E.Frost MG
5, J.G.Waggoner to M.A.Crawford by J.S.Ashby MG
3, Ephraim Stone to Mrs. Fannie J. Fuller
4, James Cunningham to Anna Rowe by J.B.Hudson JP
9, G.W.J.Lenard to Martha R. Griffin by W.M.Beckett JP
9, W.M.Easlick to Caroline Carter by W.H.Thompson JP
pg 123
9, W.J.Howard to Sarah Carter by W.H.Thompson JP
6, Henderson A. Shelton to Mary Thompson
6, S.C.Birdwell to Mary F. Bruce
7, Brice Martin to Rena Beggerly (col) by Rev. W.W.Hailey
7, Archibald Henson to Margaret E. Woodard by Samuel Hall JP
14, William Gatlin to Eliza Hathcock by R.D.Hardin MG
pg 124
15, Green Moore to Sarah Howard (col) by W.H.Thompson JP
9, L.L.C.Neece to Frances A. Hodge by L.L.Cole JP
8, James Garner to Mariah Kelso (col)
13, G. Cunningham to E. Cunningham (col) by J.B.Hudson JP
11, Wm. Freeman to Lura Faulkenberry by J. Caughran JP
11, George Milstead to Sally Faulkner by J.T.Dusenberry JP

pg 125 1866

11,	George W. Towery to Mary J. Monks
15,	John Patterson to Maria Stephens (col) by Lewis Neal MG
13,	Ben Conger to Tempa Cunningham (col) by J.B.Hudson JP
28,	Dary Dunlap to Edith Perkins (col) by N. Hamilton MG
13,	James B. Marshall to Sarah A. McDaniel

pg 126

16,	P.A.Raby to Annie Sebastian by Bradly Kimbrough MG
18,	Jesse Steed to Mrs. Elizabeth Webb by J.B.Hudson JP
18,	Nathan Smith to Mary L. Maddox by R.D.Hardin MG
18,	Barrett Merritt to Fannie Edmondson (col)
18,	J.R.Ashby to Elizabeth C. Milstead by J.T.Dusenberry JP
18,	E.R.Lusk to Mary Short by W.O.Price JP

pg 127

25,	Charles Sexton to Mary A. Woodard by J.R.Abernathy MG
21,	Benjamin Smith to Milly F. Haynes by J.E.Frost MG
21,	L.N.McGehee to Sarah E. Weeks by J.H.Eslick JP
21,	Washington Bullard to S.E.Bledsoe by Needham Koonce JP
21,	S.M.Wright to Jane Spray by A.S.Randolph JP
21,	S.M.Walker to Martha E. Frame by J.D.Smith JP

pg 128

21,	P.H.Edwards to Nancy R. Locker by N. Koonce JP
23,	Wm. B. Falkner to Charlotte Taylor by W.M.Beckett JP
23,	Isaiah Taylor to Susan A. Hamilton by W.F.Zimmerman JP
May 5,	Arch Sherrell to Suiah Stone (col) by N. Hamilton MG
Jan 23,	Wiley Turner to Sarah Staton (col) by J.O.Sullivan MG
23,	John McKinney to Ann Lee

pg 129

26,	W.G.M.Ray to M.A.J.Byrons by J. Dean MG
31,	R.N.Compton to Permelia Bryant by W.F.Zimmerman JP
Feb 1,	John W. Hobbs to Elizabeth Hogan by W.F.Zimmerman JP
Jan 27,	Robert Carter to Rosa Kelso (col)
28,	J.B.Coats to Sarah E. Henderson by W.A.Rhodes JP
30,	G.M.Bevels to Mary Beddingfield by F.L.Ezell JP

pg 130

28,	S.A.McGee to Hannah Taylor by J.H.Eastland JP
30,	Andrew Duke to Mary Jane Elizabeth Hazelwood by W.R. Waggoner JP
Feb 1,	J.W.Dandridge to M.J.Stewart by A.S.Sloan MG
1,	Jeff Austin to Susan Shaw (col) by Benj. Womack MG
Jan 30,	George W. Albright to Harriet Hamilton
Feb 1,	I.B.Benson to Rosa A. Luttrell by J.D.Smith JP

pg 131

1,	Joseph F. Dunn to Mrs. M.C.Mitchell by Samuel Hall JP
8,	Jefferson Polly to Jane Cross by J.R.Abernathy MG
4,	Allen Stephens to Charry Bonner (col) by L. Neal MG
1,	Thomas P. George to Sarah J. Land by J. Moore JP
1,	T.M.Quick to Mahala H. Land by J. Moore JP
Jan 31,	John V. Bates to Sarah J. Abel

pg 132

Feb 17,	Alex Burns to Joanna Groce (col) by N. Hamilton MG
24,	Thornton Russell to Jane Pamplin (col) by J.B.Hudson JP
5,	John D. Dennis to Mary E. Norman by J.E.Frost MG
7,	James Ellis to T.J.Beddingfield by F.L.Ezell JP
8,	W.B.Alexander to Adeline Randolph by Wm. Dawson MG
10,	Stephen Wiles to Martha Newsom by H.C.Furgarson

pg 133

13,	M.W.Hinkle to Matilda Daniel by J.L.Ashby JP

         14,   W.H.Hughey to M.G.Cunningham by J.O.Sullivan MG
         14,   Jasper N. Armstrong to Julia A. Dollins by J.B.Warren,M
         13,   D.R.Bedford to A.E.Moore by D.L.Enochs JP
         14,   C.G.Key to H.L.Wallace
         15,   James Blythe to Sarah E. Edde by D.L.Enochs JP
pg 134
         14,   W.A.Millhous to Sue Holman by Elder T.D.Jones
         15,   Stephen Johnston to Martha Bright by J.E.Frost MG
         15,   A.J.Foster to M.J.Moore by F. Motlow JP
         17,   James Burton to Mary A. Roulin
         18,   James Warden to Elizabeth Sims by J.B.Hudson JP
         21,   H.M.Carter to Mary E. Miles by W.H.Thompson
pg 135
         20,   David C. Sanders to Rebecca M. Steelman
         27,   D. Bledsoe to Judith Beatie (col) by S. Hall JP
         22,   James J. Conaway to Martha A. Bray by W.L.Alexander JP
         27,   S.W.Buchanan to Sarah J. Yarbrough by F.L.Ezell JP
         26,   Stephen Eddins to Mariah Leatherwood (col)
Mar   3,   H.T.Thomas to Julia A. Robinson (col) by S. Askins MG
pg 136
Feb 27,   James M. Ayres to Sarah E. Dunivan by W.F.Zimmerman JP
Mar   4,   Hiram Anderson to Rutha C. Scivally by W.R.Waggoner JP
Feb 28,   James D. Tillman to Mary F. Bonner by M.M.Marshall MG
Mar   1,   E. Vickers to Mary C. Durham by L.L.Cole JP
         5,   Thomas Jenkins to Eliza A. Venson by W.E.Carter JP
         6,   Archy Holman to -------Phelps (col) by Bradley Kimbrough,M
         5,   E.R.Kilpatrick to Martha S. Lankford
         8,   A.R.Patton to E.A.Jones by W.R.Waggoner JP
         10,   J.A.Quick to Elizabeth Fitch by W.E.Carter JP
         8,   J.W.N.Gray to E.M.Locker by S.H.McCord JP
         11,   W.A.Tucker to M.J.Copeland by T.H.Eslick JP
         11,   James M. Grammer to Susan E. Sawyers by W.R.Waggoner JP
pg 138
         15,   M.E.Franklin to Hannah Crabtree by P.B.Marsh JP
         17,   Benjamin C. Smith to Jane Story by I.H.Easlick JP
         17,   Daniel March to Lucy Wilson (col)
         31,   Ike Bright to Emily Edmonson (col) by S.H.Taylor JP
         25,   John Dobbs to Sarah Jane Carson by W.E.Carter JP
         22,   J.W.Bridgeforth to Ann J. Moore by M.L.Whitters MG
pg 139
         22,   Elias A. Ashby to Martha A. Ashby by J.B.Hidson JP
         25,   M.R.Cobb to Nancy Lewis by J. Dean MG
Apr 19,   Wm. C. Norman to Lucinda Griffin by W.M.Beckett JP
Mar 28,   Andrew J. West to Harriet M. Hamilton by L.L.Cole JP
         28,   G.W.Smith to Margaret A. Birdwell by W.A.Rhodes JP
Jun   1,   Milton Smith to Rebecca Clark (col) by J. Sullivan MG
pg 140
Apr   5,   J.L.Baxter to Mary J. McDaniel by S.S.Walker JP
         5,   B.M.Satterfield to Fannie V. Harris by J.B.Tigert MG
         8,   James N. Yarbrough to Mary E. Blair by W.A.Rhodes JP
         10,   Matthew Wise to Mary O. Patterson by J. Dean MG
         12,   Wiley A. Hobbs to Amanda J. Woodard by D.L.Enochs JP
         15,   Charles M. Beard to Sarah Raney by W.O.Price JP
pg 141
         15,   Alfred Imessan to Rachel Glover (col) by Alex. Smith MG
         22,   Ben Solomon to Lucinda Mead (col) by H. Tartar MG
         18,   F.M.Dorning to Elizabeth Neely by Hugh Parkerson JP
         19,   Henry Hamilton to Drusilla Cannon by W.F.Zimmerman JP

```
        18,    Prince Sugg to Sally Moore (col)
        22,    Perry Wells to Minerva J. Wells by W.C.Jennings JP
pg 142
        29,    John Thomas Pamplin to Sarah Lucreecy Caroline Pamplin
                                              by W.F.Alexander JP
May 10,        Iverson M. Coop to Mary J. Revis by J. Dean MG
         6,    Wm. D. Moore to Martha J. Deal by J. Melton MG
         5,    J.W.Edmondson to Martha A. Clark (col) by S. Askins MG
         9,    J.W.Blair to Mrs. Sarah J. Carty by John Sherrell MG
         9,    J.A.Walker to Charity C. Rosebrough by A.S.Sloan JP
pg 143
         9,    T.A.McKinney to C.H.Whitworth by T.S.Corder JP
        14,    William Ayres to Sarah Reece by John Carey JP
        13,    John Eslick to Mary E. Duke by J.H.Eslick JP
        21,    James C. McCown to Elizabeth J. Smith by W.A.Rhodes JP
        24,    Jonny Fulton to Frances McErin (col) by S. Askins MG
        25,    Jerry Timmins to Mollie Commons (col) by S. Askins MG
pg 144
        29,    DeWitt C. Young to M.A.Bryson by T.S.Corder JP
        31,    J.W.Woodard to Mary E. Hampton by J.B.Stevenson JP
        26,    Abe Thomas to Ann Cunningham (col) by J.B.Hudson JP
        27,    W.B.Rudd to Parmelia Sullivan by W.L.Reese JP
        29,    Robert R. Hananady to Fannie W. Wynns
        29,    S.H.Smith to Parmelia Tripp
pg 145
Jun  3,        Isaac Ballard to Ann E. Bailey by J.L.Ashby JP
      3,        Fulton Patton to Mary George by A.A.Bell MG
      3,        J.C.Goodrich to A.A.Finney by C.R.Darnell MG
     10,        Napoleon Hall to Elizabeth T. Benson by W.M.Beckett JP
      8,        Thomas J. Neeld to Sarah E. Mitchell by Eld. D. Jones
      7,        James M. Sawyers to Louisa V. Buchanan by J.B.Tigert MG
pg 146
     13,        Wilson Holder to Mrs. Eliza Jane Crook by D.T.Enochs JP
     17,        C.M.M.Tuley to Sarah L. Finley by J.R.Nelson JP
     17,        S.B.Durham to Catharine Davis by G.W.Puckett MG
     19,        H.F.Dusenberry to Martha James by Elder T.D.Jones
     20,        John Steed to P.R.Brown by J.B.Tigert MG
     21,        Henry Hamilton to Amanda Bonner by G.W.Puckett MG
pg 147
     24,        Jasper Vanhoozer to Susan E. Darnell by S. Hall JP
     24,        Thomas O. Brown to Julia Bradford by J.B.Hudson JP
     27,        Marion Williams to Nancy Yarbrough
     28,        James R. Feeney to Sallie C. Edwards by J.H.Bryson MG
     30,        John Kelso to Polly Kelso (col)
Jul  1,        George W. Hazelwood to Louisa Smith by W.R.Waggoner JP
pg 148
Jun 30,        Alfred Bright to Lizzie George (col)
Jul  5,        T.D.Griffis to Bettie M. Johnson by W.A.Gill MG
      9,        Wm. Tyler to Ellen McKinney (col) by L. Neal MG
     10,        T.M.Sylvester to Emeline Peebles
     12,        W.W.Hobbs to Josephine Ross by W.F.Zimmerman JP
     18,        Thomas W. McCown to Margaret L. McDill by Henry Allen,M
pg 149
      5,        J.A.Davis to E.A.Stewart by J.B.Tigert MG
      7,        George White to Molly Lamb (col) by S. Askins MG
     15,        A.J.Wright to Milly R. Hankins by W.A.Gill MG
     11,        John Wade to Margaret Creason by J.A.Prosser JP
     12,        James Damron to C.A.Daves
```

      15,   Wm. F. Hamilton to M.A.Hampton by J.O.Sullivan MG
pg 150
      18,   J. Brown to Molly Robinson (col) by S. Askins MG
      19,   James C. Pitts to M.E.Hague by J.O.Sullivan MG
      24,   G.W.Hilliard to Delilah Leonard by W.M.Beckett JP
      26,   Isaac T. Gatlin to Sarah A. Smith by G.W.Puckett MG
      26,   Parker Durham to Emily Campbell by L.L.Cole JP
      26,   Elisha Wiseman to M.J.Price by J.S.Ervin MG
pg 151
      24,   Wm. G. Newton to Eliza A. Coleman by A.S.Stone MG
      25,   George T. Cobb to Mary E. Price by W.O.Price JP
      25,   Robert Bright to Lou Freeman (col) by S. Askins MG
      26,   Isom Wells to Mrs. Margaret Jolly by J.B.Hudson JP
      26,   John Melson to Susan E. Redd by W.L.Reese JP
      31,   A.H.Russell to Mrs. M.E.Dooley by W.O.Price JP
pg 152
Aug 2,   W.C.Thomas to Martha E. Grubbs by R.D.Hardin MG
      1,   Joseph Broughton to Jane Phelps by W.L.Reese JP
      1,   Robert M. Davis to Mrs. E.C.Harris
      2,   William Daniel to Sallie Randolph
      5,   John M. Manly to Margaret Gilliland by Samuel Hall JP
      11,   Wilson Motlow to Sarah Berry (col) by B. Womack MG
pg 153
      6,   A.J.Cashion to Mary A. Dennis by W.R.Waggoner JP
      6,   H.A.Steelman to Melvina Pluss(returned Aug 7, not
            Executed) by H.A.Steelman
      8,   Abe McGaugh to Alcy Todd (col) by S. Askins MG
      9,   A.J.Benson to Mary E.L.Lenard by W.M.Beckett JP
      9,   F.M.Pack to Mary M. Moore by J.B.Hudson JP
      9,   C.M.Massey to Martha J. Dennis
pg 154
      9,   M.T.Cannon to Elizabeth Mason by A.S.Randolph JP
      11,   A. Deal to Cyntha A. Lewis
      15,   F.M.Alexander to Sarah E. Neece by W.O.Price JP
      15,   Alexander Hall to Mary Jane E. Dupree by R.Drennon JP
      19,   Thomas J. Noah to C.A.McDaniel by W.W.Wilson JP
      23,   M.M.Emmons to Margaret M. Allsup by W.W.Wilson JP
pg 155
      21,   Robert Boyd to M.F.Hannah by W.W.Hailey MG
      21,   John Bryant to Sally Marr
      29,   John Oldfield to M.L.Sisk by W.L.Reese JP
      23,   T.R.Garrett to Nancy E. Tillery by G.W.Puckett MG
      23,   Dink Wales to Martha Sandlin by S.M.Emmons MG
Sep 8,   John N. Jackson to Susan N. Wright by J.O.Sullivan MG
pg 156
      1,   Richard Green to Fannie Daniel (col) by Berry Wamack,M
Aug 26,   Enoch F. Jones to Hannah E. McCluskey by W.A.Bryan JP
      25,   Isaac Hudson to Carrie Scales (col)
      26,   Washington Glenn to Sarah Ann Atchinson (col) by
                                                Charles Laxen
      26,   Willis H. Foster to Martha Lambert by J.A.Prosser JP
      30,   John N. Jones to Sarah Bradford by W.W.Hailey MG
pg 157
      30,   James S. Crenshaw to Sarah Eaton by W.A.Wood JP
Sep 9,   Peter Marks to Margaret Myers (col) by F.L.Ezell JP
      2,   J.M.Stephens to Julia A. Mauldin by R.M.Haggard MG
Aug 30,   James G. Woods to Lou S. Webb by M.B.DeWitt MG
      31,   David Wise to Dyca J. Gunter

1866

Sep 6,   John A. Hogan to Mary F. Ross by W.F.Zimmerman JP
pg 158
     2,   James H. Smith to C.C.Markham by W.W.Wilson JP
     6,   Rufus Oliver to Ann McCracken (col) by F.L.Ezell JP
     5,   A.J.Parks to Martha Gore by D.T.Enochs JP
     5,   George Mullins to Rebeca Kemps by L.L.Cole JP
     6,   J.P.Ellis to M.F.Brown by W.R.Waggoner JP
     9,   Martin V. Rees to N.J.Foster by J.A.Prosser JP
pg 159
    12,   Thomas Gore to Mary Moorehead by W.S.Findley MG
    13,   Wm. B. Carter to Artemisia A. Thompson by J.H.Eslick JP
    13,   Francis M. Wade to Martha Rives by J.A.Prosser JP
    13,   James Massey to Martha M. Durham by A.C.Martin JP
    20,   T.N.Craig to Frances Manier by A.A.Bell MG
    18,   C.C.Groves to Ann Fox by S.D.Loyd MG
pg 160
    18,   J.T.Hardin to Harriet E. Robinson by A. Allsup JP
    21,   Nelson Myers to Rutha Smith (col) by F.L.Ezell JP
    20,   J.M.George to Sarah Harper by J.H.Eslick JP
    22,   William Sullivan to Ellen Motlow (col) by W.S.Findley MG
Oct 15,   Flenn Greer to Margaret Buchanan (col) by H. Warren MG
Sep 25,   John Bartlett to Mariah Warren by J.A.Prosser
pg 161
    26,   Robert Gatlin to Laura Elizabeth Sandlin Holloway by
                               G.W.Puckett MG
    26,   Samuel McWhorter to Elizabeth Carter
Oct 7,   F.M.Baldwin to Ella Burrough by Rev. N.D.Crawford
     3,   Spencer F. Leatherwood to Fanie E. Bledsoe by J.Milhous,M
Sep 29,   Thomas Gray to E.V.Dorning by A.S.Randolph JP
Oct 4,   Texas P. Dennwitt to Mary C. Corder by T.S.Corder JP
pg 162
     2,   J.C.Fergason to Nancy C. Sorrells
     4,   G.M.D.Wiley to Sarah E.J.Martin by M.M.Marshall MG
     4,   Joseph Cruse to Julia Ann Caudle by T.P.Dennis JP
     7,   Peter Phillips to Eglentine Warren by J.A.Prosser JP
    14,   W.J.Runnels to Elizabeth Brown by R.R.Jones MG
Sep 6,   Thomas W. Crenshaw to Margaret E. Forrester by J.T.
                               Dusenberry JP
pg 163
Oct 7,   Samuel M. Story to Mary C. Gill by W.D.Smith JP
    18,   Wm. F. Dunn to Ann E. Ray by Samuel Bond JP
     9,   P.L.Shofner to H.M.Brown by J. Dean MG
    10,   Hezekiah Gore to Sarah Brown by J. Dean MG
    10,   Robert N. Freeman to E.C.Moorehead by Alexander J.
                               Whitaker JP
    11,   F.H.McDonald to Mary Majors by R.D.Hardin MG
pg 164
    11,   Mathew Eslick to Cordelia Sullenger by J.H.Eslick JP
    11,   Wm. Daniel to F.J.Smith by D.L.Mitchell MG
    11,   D.A.McWhirter to C.A.Wells by A.S.Randolph JP
    14,   W.P.Campbell to Nancy Williams by A.J.Steel MG
    14,   Samuel Johnson to A.F.Bennett
    18,   A.L.Glaze to Martha J. Stone by W.E.Coldwell MG
pg 165
    18,   H.N.T.Shipp to Mary Pink Allen by Alex. Smith MG
    18,   P.L.Boazs to Parmelia Ann Harpe by John Carey JP
    21,   T.P.Gilliam to May E.C.Cowan by F.L.Ezell JP
    23,   J.H.Hamilton to Mary E. McDill by Alex. Smith MG

```
        25,   J.W.Steelman to Nancy Land by J.A.Prosser JP
        25,   A.D.Kelso to Jennie Chilcoat by M.B.DeWitt MG
pg 166
        28,   Young Taylor to Mrs. Martha Waggoner by E.H.Eslick JP
        30,   E.J.King to E.P.Small by Rev. N.D.Crawford
Nov  3,   J.C.Williams to Mary S. Anderson by G.W.Puckett MG
         1,   Joseph C. West to Amanda Jones by L.L.Cole JP
         3,   William H. Warren to Lucretta B. Hamilton
         3,   Robert Russell to Mary Jordin (col) by S. Askins MG
pg 167
         4,   Isaac A. Crowder to Rebecca N. Sawyers by W.W.Wilson
         6,   Thomas B. Pitts to Medora M. Sanders by R.D.Hardin MG
         6,   W.B.Pulliam to S.E.Christian
         8,   Solomon Honea to Sarah F. Fergason by S.L.Walker JP
         8,   James H. Vaughan to Amanda Smith by J.W.Cooper JP
         8,   Jasper Billings to Margaret L. Caughran by A.S.
                                                 Randolph JP
pg 168
Mar  6,   Robert P. Harriston to Mary E. Hamilton by J.B.Warren,M
Nov 11,   Elias M. Scott to Margaret Chitwood by S.M.Emmons MG
        10,   Richard Shelton to Tempa Scott (col)
        11,   Lary F. Epps to Mary M. Mason by S.L.Walker JP
        15,   Jacob Wilbanks to Viana E. Wilbanks by A.F.Driskell,M
        12,   B.C.Smith to Celina A.E.Walker by A.S.Moore JP
pg 169
        12,   W.M.Hodge to Sarah A. Stroud by R.D.Hardin MG
Mar 13,   Wm. E. McKinney to Amanda Crenshaw by G.W.Puckett MG
Nov 12,   Harrison Mosley to Sarah E. Hughey
        13,   Henry C. Brown to Martha J. Brown
        14,   F.M.Barnes to Amanda M. Cunningham by W.W.Wilson JP
        14,   Thomas A. Wilson to Lucy C. Hopper by J.O.Sullivan MG
pg 170
        15,   James M. McAfee to Mrs. Eliza A. Robison by W.W.Wilson
        17,   Sharper Mead to Roda Pamplin (col) by H. Tartar MG
        15,   James Sanders to Margaret Tate by Alex. Smith MG
        15,   C.M.Pearson to F.O.Hays by Alex. Smith MG
        16,   Andrew Talley to Harriet Harstin (col) by S.Askins,M
        19,   David H. Smith to Mary Walls by E.H.Bennett MG
pg 171
        18,   James M. Coker to Nancy E. Boyd by S.L.Walker JP
        18,   John Massey to Jennie Bonner (col) by S. Askins MG
        19,   A.J.McCown to Sarah E. Hays by William Dawson MG
        19,   Benjamin Freeman to E.J.Harwell by A. Allsup JP
        20,   Z.H.Grubbs to Susan F. Bledsoe by R.D.Hardin MG
        20,   Jeptha Towery to Elvira Phillips
pg 172
        22,   Andrew J. Warren to Mary J. Brown by S.L.Walker JP
        21,   E.F.Story to S.F.Hampton
        22,   Wm. W. Sneed to Sarah A. Nelson by A.J.Steel MG
        22,   Pleasant W. Halbert to Sallie E. Beatie by J.B.Tigert,M
        22,   John J. Short to Mary A. Kimes by J.B.Tigert MG
        29,   Willis M. Smith to Aulina C. Reed by G.W.Puckett MG
pg 173
        25,   Charles Moore to Laura Moore
        25,   George Bean to Malinda George (col) by A.A.Bell MG
        29,   Zadock Motlow to Nancy H. Bobo by T.J.Shaw MG
        27,   B.H.Berry,Jr. to Mary B. Motlow by T.J.Shaw MG
Dec  4,   H.W.Mullins to Lucretia Vickers by R.D.Hardin MG
```

Nov 30,   J.B.Berrier to Ruth A.E.Martin by S.L.Walker JP
pg 174
      29,   George L. Tipps to Virginia Clark by J.B.Hudson JP
Dec   2,   Emanuel Carpenter to Sarah E. Rowell by R.D.Hardin MG
       1,   Jack Vance to Polly McDaniel (col) by S. Askins MG
       1,   Berry Mathis to Violet McDaniel (col)(not properly
                                                       formed)
       6,   Leander Brown to Nancy J. Reynolds by J.L.Dusenbery JP
       3,   Robert P. Smith to Molly A. Allsup by J.O.Sullivan MG
pg 175
       4,   J.E.Smith to Sarah A. Wilson by J.O.Sullivan MG
       6,   W.J.Gunter to F.F.E.McCracken by S.M.Emmons MG
       3,   George Love to Clarrinda Buchanan (col) by S. Askins MG
       3,   H.A.Steelman to Bettie Milton by J.B.Hudson JP
       5,   J.W.Blair to M.L.Steadman by L.L.Cole JP
       6,   James A. Chitwood to Isola A. Kimes by J.B.Tigert MG
pg 176
       6,   John Francis Marion Shaddy to Susan Ann Bledsoe by
                                                   A.C.Martin JP
       6,   John W. McClenny to Maud Amy Harvey by W.L.Alexander JP
       8,   William Davis to Nancy A. Cobb by J. Dean MG
       7,   Newton Lamb to Sarah Ann Smith (col) by S. Neal MG
       9,   Dave M. Sanders to Martha J. Watson by Wm. Dawson MG
       9,   Thomas B. Cox to Margaret Fauch by John Milton MG
pg 177
       9,   Ben Hamlet to Lousa Scales (col) by C. Laxen
       9,   Wiley B. Ellis to H.L.Chitwood by J.B.Tigert MG
       8,   Jordan Connell to Susan Waggoner (col) by Bradley
                                                   Kimbro MG
      12,   M.N.Parks to F.M.Womack by T.J.Shaw MG
      13,   W.A.Thompson to Martha C. Davidson by I.H.Eslick JP
      11,   Washington Carroll to Susan Morrow by A.J.Whitaker JP
pg 178
      13,   George W. Syler to Samantha Jennings by W.M.Beckett JP
      15,   Marcus L. Smith to Mary C. Alexander by M.M.Marshall MG
1867
Feb 13,   Wm. Montgomery to Eliza J. Carrigan by J.L.Dusenbery JP
1866
Dec 13,   Samuel T. Farrar to Delia O. Bearden by Y.H.Davenport,M
      13,   John P. Baker to Lydia Hanna Cannon by A.S.Randolpn JP
      13,   James P. Rogers to Susan McMullin by W.W.Wilson MG
pg 179
      18,   George W. Gattis to Julia A. Brown by W.R.Waggoner JP
      15,   John H. Delk to Letha E. Foster by G. Nichols MG
      16,   H.F.White to Elizabeth Landers by J.H.Eslick JP
1867
Jan 10,   W.A.Williams to Sarah J. Burns by J.S.Erwin MG
1866
Dec 17,   R.L.Newman to Emily Stone
      18,   Isaac N. Workman to Martha A. Jenkins by S.L.Walker JP
pg 180
      20,   M.D.Hutchison to Martha J. Johnson by Wm. Dawson MG
      19,   W.M.Riddle to M.C.Bryson
      29,   Washington Sugg to Lottie Wilson (col) by W.F.Zimmerman
      20,   Milton Bledsoe to Isabella Burford (col) by S. Bond JP
      20,   James Tucker to Malinda A. Tooley by J.R.Nelson JP
      19,   G.W.Crabtree to Mary D. Cunningham by A.C.Martin JP

pg 181
20,   Joel A. Pitts to F.E.Solomon by S.L.Sanford MG
20,   G.J.Stonebraker to Lottie C. Renegar by J.B.Tigert MG
20,   J.A.Edmonston to N.C.Cunningham by John Carey JP
20,   H.W.Gunter to L.S.Clark by John Carey JP
20,   Wm. A. Miles to Mattie A. Woods by M.M.Marshall MG
20,   W.T.Haggard to Bettie Groce by W.A.Gill MG
pg 182
22,   George W. Prince to Nancy A. McElyea by A.J.Steel MG
22,   W.G.Maddox to N.R.Steadman by W.A.Bryan JP
22,   Freeman Chappell to Lizzie Smith (col)
23,   W.W.Bonner to Mariah L. Clark (col) by W.A.Bryan JP
25,   John Pannaqula to Mrs. Susan A. Holley by W.F.
                                          Zimmerman JP
28,   Gilford Kerr to Candis Hopkins (col) by D.R.Robertson,M
pg 183
25,   Robert Westbrook to Laura A. Bright (col) by Dock
                                          Robertson MG
22,   Alexander Coats to Lizzie Green (col) by S. Askins MG
26,   Henry Lay to Anna Robertson (col) by D.R.Robertson MG
26,   Wm. T. Garrett to Sarah A. Childs by Alexander Smith MG
26,   W.S.(L) Davis to Sarah Jackson by John Milton MG
27,   Jesse Whitaker to Mariah Bright (col) by A.J.Whitaker JP
pg 184
26,   Isaac Bonner to Rachel Massey (col) by S. Askins MG
26,   Thomas Moore to Judea Sawyers (col) by W.W.Wilson JP
27,   R.A.Jones to Henrietta Cooley by J.W.Holman MG
27,   Phillip Rees to Louisa Dance (col) by D.S.Enochs JP
27,   Wm. C. Stewart to Mary A. Manley by R.D.Hardin MG
1867
Jan 21,   John Buchanan to Rena Buchanan (col) by Dock Robertson,M
pg 185
1866
Dec 28,   Wm. Fearrson to Samira Higgins (col) by D. Robertson MG
27,   Jacob Halbert to Cary Ann Staton (col) by F.W.Clark JP
27,   Joseph A. White to Sofa Rees
28,   Samuel Franklin to Lucy A. Griffis (col) by L. Neal
27,   Dunkin Griffis to Judia Potts (col)
29,   Wm. McMullin to Charlot McDaniel (col) by S.S.Clark JP
pg 186
29,   H. Hedgepeth to Creacy Wilson (col) by W.F.Zimmerman
29,   M.C.Eslick to M.E.Parks by W.O.Price JP
30,   M.T.Buchanan to M.A.Gardner by J.B.Tigert MG
31,   Henry Small to Martha King (col) by J.B.Hudson JP
1867
Jan 3,   Samuel Thomison to Catharine Barnes (col) by Loderick
                                          Robertson
1866
Dec 31,   Edmond Whitaker to Violet Grantlin (col)
pg 187
1867
Jan 1,   M.C.Atkinson to A.J.V.Sherrell by M. Marshall MG
Sep 1,   John M. Pinky to Mary J. Head by J.A.Prosser JP
Jan 1,   N.H.Marbry to Rebecca Neece
3,   Felix R. Evans to Rebecca J. Waggoner by W.R.Waggoner JP
3,   Dick Waggoner to Martha Tucker (col) by Bery Womack MG
5,   Edmond Pigg to Jane Harper (col) by J.O.Sullivan MG
pg 188
3,   Anderson Fitch to Sarah A. Jolly by T.S.Corder JP

21,   Wesley Buchanan to Harriett Dodson (col) by Dock
                                          Robertson MG
6,   William Cox to Esther George by A.C.Martin JP
9,   R.P.Lackey to Sarah A.E.Smith by T.S.Corder JP
8,   John Robinson to Molly Bonner (col)
10,   Isaac M. Jones to Lucy S. Walker by R.D.Hardin MG
pg 189
9,   H.M.Martin to Eliza J. Koonce
10,   Alexander Strong to Lucy Smith (col) by F.L.Ezell JP
13,   H.Y.Carter to Mary A. Lock by G.W.Puckett MG
9,   William H. Davis to Martha C. Runnells
20,   Burrell Landess to Hetty Gracey (col) by J.B.Hudson JP
10,   H.B.Dillingham to C.J.Farrar
pg 190
10,   Peter Langly to Sallie Scott by A.S.Randolph JP
10,   James H. Webb to Henrietta M. Waterman by Ulysess Bates,M
13,   R.H.Wright to S.N.Ellison by W.A.Bryan JP
12,   Grif Shelton to Angeline Taylor (col) by S.D.Loyd MG
15,   Sam Huddspeth to Lindy Henderson (col) by W.A.Bryan JP
24,   George Armstrong to Mary Williams (col) by Dock
                                          Robertson MG

pg 191
23,   J.R.Mullins to Elizabeth Bell by J.S.Erwin MG
16,   M.A.Beard to M.F.Gray by W.A.Gill MG
17,   Wm. A. Caton to Sarah M. Donald by F.L.Ezell JP
16,   Thomas Sawyer to Mary E.B.Donalson
16,   J.R.King to Cordelia A. Rutledge by W.O.Price JP
17,   Gress Clark to Elinor Scott (col) by E.M.Bennett MG
pg 192
17,   Wm. S. Hays to Nancy P. Cole by R.D.Hardin MG
17,   Ely Wright to Sarah J. Parr (col) by W.D.Smith JP
17,   J.R.Woodard to Sarah E. Rowell by J.B.Abernathy MG
1866
Dec 27, Henry C. Brown to Mary Buchanan (col) by H. Warren
1867
Jan 19, Jerry Askins to Mary Akin (col)
21,   Elbrady Buchanan to Fannie Smith (col) by D. Robertson,M
pg 193
23,   L.W.Davidson to A.R.Rives by J.H.Prosser JP
23,   C.C.Pearce to S.A.Woodard
25,   James Brown to Margaret Best (col) by Berry Womack MG
23,   John F. Davis to L. Waggoner
24,   J.H.Woods to Nannie Whittington by A.A.Bell MG
26,   Dock Bonner to Lou Carloss (col) by Dock Robertson MG
pg 194
27,   Alexander Ezell to Lusina Benson (col) by F.L.Ezell JP
27,   Stephen Touchstone to Sarah Newton by J. Carey JP
27,   J.W.Robinson to M.F.Silvertooth by D.L.Enochs JP
Feb 21, James Jean to Mary Boman by W.R.Waggoner JP
Jan 29, J.W.Daniel to Mary J. Jenkins by A.S.Moore JP
Feb 1, Scott Hampton to Caroline Douthit (col) by Wade Staten,M
pg 195
Jan 30, James T. Farrar to Sallie L. Fullerton
31,   Morris Jones to Jane Cathey (col) by Eli Bennett MG
Feb 3, A.C.Green to Mary E. Hannah by L.L.Cole JP
1,   George W. Payne to Nancy N. Renegar by J.H.Eslick JP
8,   Joe McDonald to Ann Thomison (col) by S.H.Taylor JP
3,   W.D.Jones to Elizabeth Smith by W.A.Bryan JP

pg 196   1867
     5,   J.B.Clift to Mary Jane Hogan by W.W.Wilson JP
     7,   George W. Mullins to Nancy A. Nichols by James M.Dyer JP
May 18,   R.F.Hamilton to Josephine Jones by J.B.Hudson JP
Feb 4,   Preston Riggs to E. Thompson (col)
     4,   Martin R. Gross to Mary Moore by J.B.Hudson JP
    12,   Isaac B. Madox to Amanda Blue by R.D.Hardin MG
pg 197
     7,   H.B.Wallace to Burline Genavia Buffalo by S. Bond JP
     5,   John Eslick to Frances E. Radigan
     6,   A.V.Boyd to Nancy C. Moore
     6,   Robert T. Griffis to Maggie E. Hampton
     7,   J.H.Southworth to Mrs. E.O.Wisener by J.B.Tigert MG
     6,   Wiley Driver, of Bedford County,Tenn to D.J.Gunter by
                                                    John Carey JP
pg 198
     7,   John T. Cox to Sophronia C. Green
    15,   Benjamin Melton to M.J.Marsh by J.A.Prosser JP
    14,   Sanford Renegar to Julia Smith by A.J.Whitaker JP
    14,   James Brock to Elizabeth Randall
    12,   J. Brasleton to E.J.Price by J.S.Erwin MG
    14,   Hiel A. Moore to Mrs. Minerva A. Murdock by A.S.Sloan MG
pg 199
    14,   William Rorax to Lucy Johnston by W.S.Alexander JP
Jun 15,   Simon Farmer to Sallie McCoy (col) by Eli H. Bennett MG
Feb 15,   Willis S. Herelston to Casanda Hearthcock by W.A.Bryan JP
    14,   H.S.Zimmerman to Maggie Cunningham by J.O.Sullivan MG
    14,   Wm. R. Duncan to Mollie E. Waggoner by J.S.Dusenbery JP
    17,   Thomas R. Steadman to Mary A. Phagan by L.L.Cole JP
pg 200
    17,   John Williams to Nancy R. Wright by W.W.Wilson JP
    21,   B.F.Winford to Mary M. Ward by A.J.Whitaker JP
    21,   J.B.Thomison to Adelia Kimbro by T.D.Jones, Elder
    21,   Harey Whitaker to Caroline Whitaker (col) by A. Whitaker JP
    24,   George R. Dunkin to Nancy J. Keda by J.B.Riley JP
    28,   C.A.P.Shelton to Caledonia Eslick (col) by Berry Womack,M
pg 201
    28,   Josiah Seeth to Terrissa Orr by A.J.Steel MG
    28,   Richard Moore to Laura Moore (col) by S.H.Taylor JP
    28,   H.M.Carrigan to Fannie Mead by W.L.Alexander JP
Mar 6,   Albert Hill to Margret Bonner (col) by Dock Robinson MG
     3,   Samuel Forrest to Julia Allen (col) by W.O.Price JP
     2,   James E. Hanes to Malinda C. Wamack
pg 202
     5,   Jack Travis to Ester Scivally (col)
     7,   Paskel Crenshaw to Manurvy McGee
    11,   Jack Smith to Mariah Ashby by H. Tartar MG
    10,   Edd Suggs to Lucinda Vents (col) by Charles Laxen
     9,   B.A.Stevenson to Nancy A. Bray
    14,   John Davidson to E. Hopkins by J.A.Prosser JP
pg 203
    12,   S.S.Scruggs to Mary Mullins by R.D.Hardin MG
    14,   Wm. M. Forester to Nancy Rowe by J.B.Hudson JP
    14,   Thomas Boaz to S.A.Thomison by W.L.Alexander JP
    14,   Isaac Edmondson to Easter Patterson (col)
    21,   Thomas M. Horton to Ann R. Pryor by A.F.Driskell MG
    20,   W.C.Green to A.L.Tyner by D. Jacks MG

pg 204   1867
   21,   E.F.Spray to Nancy J. Wright by A.S.Randolph JP
   21,   Wm. D. Sims to Cynthia E. Pamplin by J.B.Hudson JP
   20,   W.D.Holman to Sallie Murphy by U.S.Bates MG
   23,   William Gulley to Sarah A. Thompson
   23,   Starlin Justin to Jane O'Neal (col)
Apr 4,   Sack Baget to Amanda Purkins (col) by C. Laxen
pg 205
Mar 28,   George W. Hunt to Frances R. McGehee by N.B.Pearce MG
Apr 1,   Jack Halaway to Rachel Clark (col) not properly found.
    4,   Andy Moore to Susan Scott (col) by S.H.Taylor JP
    4,   A.F.Riley to Martha Roper by R.D.Hardin MG
    2,   J.O.Bryant to Martha A. Carpenter by S.M.Emmons MG
    3,   Carrol Henry to Cordelia Tucker by S.D.Loyd MG
pg 206
    1,   A.B.Nelson to Mary Carter
Apr 4,   Andy Wakefield to Martha Gilbert (col) by W.O.Price JP
    5,   A. McDaniel to Ann Chilcoat (col)
    7,   B.F.Lynch to Emeline Bradford by John J. York MG
    7,   John E. Howe to Elinor T. Gray by W.O.Price JP
  11,   S.W.Gleghorn to Sarah S. Gleghorn by A.S.Sloan MG
pg 207
  12,   Thomas Warren to Artemicia Williams by John Milton MG
  14,   Thomas B. Hobbs to Harriette Ruthe by W.W.Wilson JP
  18,   W.S.Beavers to Jocie C. Wells by J.B.Tigert MG
  22,   Enoch Hooper to Harriette A. Philpott
  24,   John M. Pilant to Nancy Gray by T.S.Corder JP
  27,   James Jones to Hanah Warren
pg 208
May 2,   Jacob Strong to Elizabeth Fanning by I.H.Eslick JP
    5,   Charly Parks to Mariah Nelson (col) by J.R.Nelson JP
    6,   Tim Denver to Emily Clark (col) by Dock Robinson MG
    9,   Felix W. Motlow to Rebecca A. Rutledge by J.E.Frost MG
    9,   J.B.Smith to Fannie Simms by R.D.Hardin MG
    9,   David Jeans to Anna E. Neeld by T.S.Corder JP
pg 209
    9,   James Cole to Mary Street by R.D.Hardin MG
  15,   Buck Patterson to Ella Sherell (col) by Eld. G.W.Puckett
  12,   Thomas H. Harris to Mary C. Massey by J.L.Sewell MG
  13,   George W. Twitty to Lou Wilson by R.D.Hardin MG
  26,   Thomas Clark to Jane Fox (col) by E.H.Bennett MG
  19,   C.M.Tucker to Sarah R. Hague by S.L.Sanford MG
pg 210
  26,   Munroe R. Lusk to Patience E. Brown by J.B.Hudson JP
  25,   Stephen Daniel to Harriet Swinford by A.S.Randolph JP
  30,   John Sartin to Elizabeth Wilks
Jun 1,   J.W.Billions to Elizabeth Daniel by A.S.Randolph JP
    2,   John Beason to Lizzie White (col) by T.W.Clark JP
    6,   M.L.Whitaker to Martha R------ by S.L.Sanford MG
pg 211
    8,   G.L.Green to Angeline Heathcock by L.L.Cole JP
  10,   Dennis Mead to Julia James (col) by D. Robinson MG
    8,   Manuel Harvey to Fanny Hunter (col) by W.M.Beckett JP
  15,   Orange Mead to Hannah Cannon (col) by J.B.Hudson JP
  22,   Ben Benson to Fany Buchanan (col) by D. Robinson MG
  17,   Eliza Hart to Lucy Jolley (col)
pg 212
  18,   J. Sumford to Cordelia Sims by A.S.Randolph MG

19,	James B. Freeman to Martha J. Rees by J.A.Prosser
19,	William Massey to Mary Woodard
19,	Jo. Tolley to Martha Bailey (col)
19,	Wm. S. Martin to M.E.Johnson by J.B.Tigert MG
23,	L.N.Carpenter to Mary E. Gady by W.W.Wilson JP

pg 213

22,	Isaac Litcher to Winney Simmons (col) by D.Robinson MG
Jul 6,	Reubin Massey to Rachel Clark (col) by S.H.Taylor JP
Jun 30,	C.C.Street to Nannie H. Timmins by Robert R. Jones MG
Jul 4,	L.P.Gilliam to Bettie C. McLaughlin by W.C.Jennings JP
1,	George W. Pilant to Julia Ann Seal
1,	Columbus Dyer to Lizzie E. Gibson

pg 214

1,	R.V.Drake to Octava Smith
18,	J.H.Gray to Emmarandi C. Brazier by W.R.Waggoner JP
4,	John T. Kirsey to Sarah E. Payne by Newton Hampton MG
4,	J.B.Pitts to Laura A. McLain by S.L.Sanford MG
9,	Wm. H. Metcalf to Nancy M. Sylvester by N.Hamilton MG
7,	John C. Johnson to Isabella Buchanan by J.B.Tigert MG

pg 215

9,	J.B.Hedricks to Mary Harkins by J.A.Prosser JP
16,	Wade McKnight to Marinda Dunkin by W.W.Wilson JP
10,	Richard J. McDaniel to Lavina C. Butler by J.W.Cooper JP
10,	J.M.Lemming to R.A.Broadaway
18,	J.H.Thrasher to Nancy E. McCallister by J.P.Dennis JP
21,	Columbus Dyer to Elizabeth E. Gibson by J.A.Prosser JP

pg 216

24,	Hiram Winkers to Elizabeth Bradford by Thomas Corder JP
25,	William Ashby to Elizabeth E. Ridings by J.B.Hudson JP
25,	W.P.Cobb to Mary Flemimg
26,	James Simmons to Susan Harkins
31,	Wm. A. Spencer to P.J.Crabtree by Wm. S. Findley MG
30,	B.S.Ervins to Elizabeth Shaw by R. Drennon JP

pg 217

31,	Henderson Johnson to Nancy Manon
Aug 2,	John A. Jackson to Mrs Louvina Bolden by W.F.Zimmerman JP
3,	Abb Webb to Elzira Kelsoe (col) by S.D.Loyd MG
3,	Spencer Gardner to Lucy Jennings (col) by S.D.Loyd MG
4,	Isaac N. Maddox to Mary Ann Hamilton by S. Hall JP
7,	J.A.Coble to Sarah A. Coble by S.M.Emmons MG

pg 218

8,	Elijah J. Runnels to Louisa Honey by T.W.Clark JP
6,	Isaac Marrs to M.L.Buchanan by J.B.Tigert MG
8,	Samuel Gillespie to Nancy A. Clark by A.S.Sloan JP
8,	Gilbert Moore to Elizabeth-------
8,	T.G.McCalley to M.L.Martin
14,	H.H.Warnick to Sarah Scruggs by G.W.Puckett MG

pg 219

11,	Wm. C. West to Mrs. Nancy J. Deford by B.F.Hudson JP

1868

Apr 4,	John Jones to Jane Blunt (col) by R.Robertson MG

1867

Aug 11,	A.J.Fincher to Mrs. T.W.Fincher by T.L.Clark JP
12,	W.T.Furguson to Sarah Brown by Alex. Whitaker JP
15,	James Walls to H.A.Nearin by Eli H. Bennett MG
Oct 22,	George Shaw to Sallie Rives (col) by Berry Womack MG

pg 220

Aug 14,	Grandville Harvy to Gracy Greer (col)

15,   John W. Smith to Mary Freeman by J.A.Prosser JP
15,   James M. Owen to Rebeca E. Clark by T.W.Clark JP
15,   James F. Byers to A.E.Grantlin by Henry P. Turner MG
16,   Dr. S.H.Hines to N.A.Merrell by F.L.Ezell JP
24,   George Bledsoe to Anna Braden (col) by Samuel Hall JP

pg 221
17,   Thomas W. Fears to Nancy J. Lesley
18,   Thomas B. Thompson to Hannah M. Carter by J.H.Eslick JP
20,   Houston Campbell to Janie Whitaker (col)
22,   Will H.Clerckman to Annie E. Roberts by T.S.Corder JP
21,   J.B.Gibson to Mary J. Edge
Sep 22,   Jack Clark to Mag Wright (col) by E.H.Bennett MG

pg 222
Aug 21,   Jacob Ellis to Luddy Bonner (col)
25,   J.F.Ray to Mrs. S.J.Roden by T.W.Clark JP
25,   James Rains to Sallie Murphy (col) by W.M.Beckett JP
24,   G.J.Alexander to Ida Thomison by S.L.Sanford MG
Sep 1,   Jesse C. Turner to America E. Davidson by T.W.Clark JP
Aug 29,   Edward Everage to Mary E. Lenard by J.B.Riley JP

pg 223
29,   Hillsman Bledsoe to Nancy R. Freeman by J.A.Prosser JP
29,   Argile Brewer to Parthena Massey by D.L.Mitchell MG
Sep 1,   Isham Staten to Mary P. Clark (col) by A.H.Bishop MG
1,   Wiley Clark to Caroline March (col) by Archey Staton MG
10,   W.W.Gilbert to Martha Nichols by J.A.Prosser JP
5,   Ashbery Ashby to Rachel E. Pitts by W.L.Alexander JP

pg 224
8,   W.F.Gunter to L.F.Emmons by W.W.Wilson JP
8,   J.W.McCracken to A.O.Emmons by W.W.Wilson JP
7,   Henry Floyd to Sinda Mullins (col) by R. Drennon JP
10,   Alford Burns to Victory J. Reaves by J.A.Prosser JP
12,   T.N.Brazier to Lucy C. Kelley by W.R.Waggoner JP
12,   Aqueller Derrer to Hulda N. Howard by A.J.Whitaker JP

pg 225
12,   Thomas N. Bledsoe to Hessey Cummins by G.W.Nichols MG
19,   Anderson Hall to Rebeca E. Brewer by D.L.Mitchell MG
25,   Tillman Bledsoe to Harriet Anderson (col) by S. Bond JP
17,   James Cheatham to Mary Ann Hall by L.L.Cole JP
18,   Edward H. Kyle to Laura V. Tucker by S.H.McCord JP
19,   James M. Franklin to Emma C. Darnell by D.L.Mitchell MG

pg 226
18,   W.B.English to Sarah J. Puckett by A.B.Coleman MG
19,   James C. Hodges to Virginia C. Canady by F.L.Ezell JP
19,   Richard Wright to Mrs. Nannie S. Whitaker by J.W.
                                     Holman MG
19,   Perry Hariston to Elizabeth M. Scott (col) by W.H.
                                     Reid MG
22,   J.W.Dement to Loucinda Maddox by Samuel Hall JP
21,   G.H.M.Briton to Martha M. Mooney

pg 227
25,   James Hicks to Nancy L. Dennis by F. Motlow JP
26,   Joe Robinson to Celia Leatherwood (col) by W.A.Bryan JP
25,   Y.U.Pinkerton to Hettie V. McCown by Henry P. Turner MG
30,   G.W.Lovelace to Josephine Tucker by N.D.Crawford MG
25,   Richard Marr to Mary M. Williams
26,   James P. Morrison to E.C.Carty by Ulysses Bates MG

pg 228
29,   W.F.Temple to Laura A. York by E.H.Holland MG

```
        28,   John M. Pierson to Sallie G. Gill
        29,   P.G.Smith to Nancy E. Floyd by W.O.Price JP
        29,   M.H.Dollar to Cordelia McCown by Newton Hamilton MG
Oct  1,   Alfred G. Thomas to May(Mary) J. Summerford by N.D.
                                              Crawford MG
Sep 30,   Jacob Wadkins to D.E.Faulkner by J.N.Dyer JP
pg 229
Oct  2,   James P. McGee to Eliza A. Pitts by A.S.Randolph JP
     3,   B.M.Delk to Martha A. Pylant by N.D.Crawford MG
     2,   Wesley McElroy to Ann McPhail (col) by Lewis Neal MG
     2,   James G. Hamilton to Nancy L. Woodard by J.B.Tigert MG
     4,   Isham Hampton to Mary J. McDonald (col) by L. Neal MG
     6,   Ruben Phelps to Sarah A. Newsom (col)
pg 230
     8,   E.P.Solomon to Mollie Elmore by S.L.Sanford MG
     9,   W.S.Woodard to Mary Denison
    17,   George B. Paynne to Sarah Franklin by N. Hamilton MG
    17,   Green A.F.Pylant to Rachel E. Moore by J.B.Tigert MG
    21,   W.B.Jennings to Mrs. Susan A. Bray by J.B.Riley JP
    20,   B.F.Donivan to Nancy Burton by J.L.Ashby JP
pg 231
    20,   Sandy Myers to Silva Pentecost (col) by F.L.Ezell JP
    19,   H.P.Rowell to Mary C. Blair by H.P.Turner MG
    24,   Presley O. George to Pheby E. Rutledge by J.B.Hudson JP
    25,   R.H.Crawford to M.C.Laws by R. Farquharson JP
    26,   Dock King to Margaret Leatherwood (col) by S.H.Taylor
    27,   Jesse Bowden to Emmaline Campbell by W.D.Smith JP
pg 232
    27,   George W. Rees to Mary J. Farley by John Y. York MG
    27,   R.S.Douthit to Mary A. Noblett by C.L.Randolph MG
1868
Jun 13,   G.A.Dockins to Elizabeth Rutledge (col) by R.Robertson,M
1867
Nov  4,   Ethelvin McKinney to Mrs. Mary Bledsoe by G.W.Puckett,M
Oct 31,   Joseph Clark to Hannah B. Spence by A.S.Sloan MG
    31,   James Hatley to Dicey J. Temple by James S. Cran MG
pg 233
Nov  4,   E.S.Terry to V. Whitaker by J.E.Frost MG
    12,   Allen Spencer to Elinora Massey (col) by L. Neal MG
     5,   Elijah W. Walker to Mary F. Mead by W.L.Alexander JP
     4,   Timothy Beggerly to Mariah Wilburn (col) by W.W.
                                              Hailey MG
     7,   Robert H. Pitts to Lizzie P. Rees by S.L.Sanford MG
     6,   J.H.Bledsoe to R.L.Jones by G.W.Nichols MG
pg 234
     7,   Henry H. Bell to Sarah E. Harden by W.W.Wilson JP
     7,   A.A.Wright to Anna McPhail
    10,   Zekiel York to Eliza Weaver (col) by S. Bond JP
    10,   Allen Norris to Mary Campbell (col) by W. Green MG
    17,   Jacob March to Rose A. Halbert (col) by S.H.Taylor JP
    10,   Wm. Brett to Lucy A. Howard by S.D.Loyd MG
pg 235
    13,   John B. Corn to Virginia Wicks by R.D.Hardin MG
    12,   A.T.Sikes to Bettie Whitaker by S.L.Sanford MG
    14,   W.B.McAdams to Nancy E. Mitchell by G.W.Nicholas MG
    14,   J.H.Thompson to E.C.Wiley by A.S.Sloan MG
    13,   F.F.Crabtree to M.B.Welch by A.C.Martin JP
```

110

14,   Jas. Fortenberry to Nancy E. Faulkinboro by S.L.
                                            Sanford MG
pg 236
14,   Wm. Styles to Udora Flynt by N.B.Pearce MG
14,   W.A.Thornton to Josia A. Smith by J.B.Tigert MG
1868
Mar 6,   George Love to Caroline Bennett (col) by R.Robertson,M
1867
Nov 21,   John Moore to Tabitha Cowan by F.L.Ezell JP
16,   James K. Scott to Martha Chitwood
24,   Edmond Jacobs to Crica Cooper (col)
pg 237
17,   F.E.Fleming to Mrs. Susan F. McErvin by S.H.McCord JP
21,   J.S.Smiley to Becca Thomas by N.D.Crawford MG
21,   Thomas Brazel to Elizabeth Goosby by Jones G. Erwin,M
24,   John A. Whitworth to Roena J. Waters by J.N.Dyer JP
24,   Samuel Campbell to Eliza J. Hilliard by W.M.Beckett JP
25,   W.A.Chesney to L.J.Cashion
pg 238
28,   Smith Thomas to Mary C. Lucas by J.E.Frost MG
26,   Dr. Allen Parks to Mary E. Keller by Thomas J. Shaw MG
26,   W.S.Alexander to J.R.Kelso by M.B.Dewitt MG
28,   W.L.Ward to Milley Pearson by S.L.Sanford MG
28,   Thomas H. Tripp to Samantha J. McClure by J.H.Eslick JP
28,   G.W.Hamilton to Susanah A. Tripps by F.L.Ezell JP
pg 239
26,   A.F.Seaton to Rachel M.A.Corder by T.S.Corder JP
28,   Dr. G.W.Blake to Eliza H. McCord
Dec 1,   Felix G.G.Pylant to Canthus V. Dyer by N.D.Crawford MG
1,   C.M.Dozier to Mariah N. McCalley by R.D.Hardin MG
1,   Henry W. Watson to Tabitha Howard by S.L.Loyd MG
1868
Apr 10,   Fred Smith to Judy Battle (col) by R. Robertson MG
1867
pg 240
Dec 3,   J.G.Burt to Mary Davidson by S.L.Sanford MG
2,   Asa Street to Mrs. Martha M. Anderson
5,   S.H.Estill to Mary M. Whitaker by S.L.Sanford MG
4,   W.C.Wilson to Mary C. Barnes by W.W.Wilson JP
4,   Nathaniel H. Whitaker to Elmira H. Perkins by C.S.Rand-
                                            olph MG
4,   Fernando R. Dobbs to Nancy S. Bates
pg 241
5,   Elijah Warren to Lizzie Street
5,   James M. Payne to Sarah Hopper by S.M.Emmons MG
13,   John B. Sullivan to Bettie A. Ashby by J.B.Hudson JP
5,   James S. Hill to Frances J. Davis by R. Drennon JP
5,   Wyatt Vance to Frances Diemer (col) by L. Neal MG
6,   John R. Sneed to Nancy J. Webb
pg 242
8,   W.J.Lancaster to Elizabeth C. Epps by S.M.Emmons MG
8,   James Thompson to Mary Duckworth by W.L.Alexander JP
10,   G.W.Porter to Eliza A. Patrick by S.N.McCord JP
12,   James S. Camron to Lucy A. Lazenberry by W.F.Zimmerman
12,   W.W.Finley to Martha J. Isom by W.H.Dixon MG
12,   W.P.Starnes to Caroline Winford by A.J.Whitaker JP
pg 243
12,   J.H.McCown to Cordelia McGuire by W.A.Bryan JP

15,	James L. Mitchell to Mary E. Payne by W.F.Zimmerman
17,	Thomas W. Smith to Cintha B. Thomas by S.L.Sanford MG
17,	E.N.Crawford to Elizabeth Smith by J.B.Tigert MG
19,	Dr. Grandville B. Lester to Rebecca S.C.White by M.M. Marshall MG
16,	I.P.Dismukes to Virginia Fulton

pg 244
18,	Wm. Simmons to Catharine Noles by S.D.Loyd MG
19,	T.L.Darnell to Anna E. Watson by D.L.Mitchell MG
19,	Lewis R. Massey to Mary C. Brazier by W.R.Waggoner JP
19,	J.T.Kidd to M.A.Galoway by A.S.Sloan
19,	H.D.Cummins to Cincinnatti Sullivan by S.L.Sanford MG
23,	Amos Speck to Anna Lenard by J.B.Riley JP

pg 245
19,	W.J.Bingham to Angeline Reeves
19,	Daniel Warren to Cammilla McCary by John Milton MG
22,	E.P.Gatlin to Martha J. Turner by R.D.Hardin MG
21,	James Barker to Cemantha Lenard
21,	Joseph Scales to Caroline Massey (col) by S.H.Taylor JP
23,	Thomas B. George to Sarah Taylor

pg 246
24,	John W. King to M.I.Fortenberry by A.C.Martin JP
26,	Benjamin Yates to Bird Heart (col) by Berry Womack MG
26,	Erwin Harvey to Anna Greer (col) by Hester Warren MG
24,	John W. Gatlin to Mrs. Lucy Ann Franklin by Isaac Gatlin,M
24,	Wm. Vandever to Anna E. Taylor by S.D.Loyd MG
24,	Wm. Hulsey to Mariah Roughton by Lewis Neal MG

pg 247
26,	John A. Stiles to Sarah C. McDaniel by S.D.Loyd MG
26,	James Cashion to Malinda A. Benson by W.M.Beckett JP
26,	Isaac R. Lambert to Susa A. Scivally by Rev. R.M.Stephens
25,	Charles Staton to Susan Halbert (col)
25,	Polk Staton to Mary F. Wilson (col)
25,	Alford Noble to Judy Stacy (col)

pg 248
25,	Ruben Hall to Mary E. Cluts
26,	J.R.Small, Sr. to Mrs. Virginia Rives by S.L.Sanford,M
26,	John H. George to Mary Lively by T.S.Corder JP
26,	Wm. Todd to Rosa Williamson (col) by L.Neal MG

1868
Jan 18, Henry Vance to Jane Waggoner (col) by S.H.Taylor JP
1867
Dec 26, Thomas J. Price to Sarah C. Formwalt by J.B.Tigert MG
1868
Jan 2, Robert H. Ray to Perlina Dyer by D.L.Mitchell MG
1867
Dec 29, J.T.McCauley to Mary L. French by S.L.Sanford MG
30,	Wyatt Bonner to Allice Bonner (col) by L.Neal MG
30,	James Buchanan to Louvenia Vance (col) by L.Neal MG
31,	Henry Harper to Jane Nearren (col) by A.H.Bishop MG
31,	F.B.Terry to Mattie Landess by J.E.Frost MG

pg 250
30,	Marion McNatt to Fannie Bryant
30,	Samuel J. Melton to Amanda J. Thompson
30,	Wiley Commons to Martha Burke (col) by L. Neal MG

1868
Jan 1, Thomas B. Moore to Mary M. Whitaker by A.S.Moore JP
1, G.B.Bedwell to Fannie M. Dunkin by J.B.Hudson JP

1867
Dec 31,   Wm. F. Haley to Amanda A. Smith
pg 251
1868
Jan 2,   J.J.C.Drennon to Frances J. Dale by A.B.Coleman MG
1867
Dec 31,   Henry C. Childs to Sally C. Taylor
1868
Jan 2,   James M. Hamilton to Parthenia Payne by W.F.Zimmerman
    1,   Nelson Johnson to Mariah Porter (col) by D.Robertson
    2,   H.B.N.Thomison to Margaret Beverly by A.F.Driskell MG
    1,   E.H.Brandon to Miss Sidney Miller
pg 252
    1,   Hill E. Wells to Fannie R. Moores by J.B.Tigert MG
    5,   James S. McGuire to Jennetta M. Farrar by F.L.Ezell JP
    5,   Wm. Owen to Susanah Coble by A.Alsup JP
    5,   Wesley Proctor to Mary Smith (col) by A.H.Bishop MG
    5,   R.F.Hamilton to Josephine Jones by W.F.Zimmerman JP
    7,   W.A.Woodard to Elizabeth Mayfield by J.E.Frost MG
pg 253
    7,   James H. Clark to Sarah E. Finley
    8,   Angus A. Johnson to Rebecca A. Duckworth by W.L. Alexander JP
  12,   Nelson F. Bonner to Martha A. Cowan by F.L.Ezell JP
   8,   John H. Smith to Maving A. Hogan by T.W.Clark JP
   9,   F.W.Buchanan to Ellen C. McKinney by C.L.Randolph MG
   9,   George R. Blacknell to Eliza Warren by C.L.Randolpn MG
pg 254
   9,   Samuel Maples to Sarah Smith (col)
   9,   M.B.McLaughlin to Leoma Moyers by F.L.Ezell JP
  12,   D.C.Myers to M.G.Russell by W.D.Smith JP
  11,   W.P.Myers to Milly Harris (col)
  15,   Wm. Womack to Jennie Shaw (col) by B. Woamck MG
Feb 6,   Jacob Brandon to Mary Gray by B. Woamck MG
pg 255
Jan 16,   Wm. Damron to E.E.Walker by D. Jacks MG
  16,   John P. Arnold to Mary E. Wicks by J.B.Riley JP
  14,   W.T.McDaniel to Fannie E. Lauderdale
  14,   J.L.Rodgers to Mary M. Gant by J.R.Thompson MG
  15,   J.M.Sims to C.E.Puckett
  16,   James Reece to Fannie Martin by S.L.Sanford MG
pg 256
  16,   Joseph N. Neely to Sarah A. Downing by A.S.Randolph JP
  16,   W.R.Noah to Mary F. Arney by W.W.Wilson JP
Feb 9,   G.A.Watson to Sophia Curtis by J.W.Cooper JP
Jan 15,   Peter Smith to Jane Felps (col) by Bradly Kimbro MG
  16,   B.F.Walls to Margaret McWhorter by W.W.Wilson JP
  16,   W.F.Robertson to Sarah Morris by D.L.Emmons JP
pg 257
  18,   Reuben Moorehead to Hester Phillips (col) by S.D.Loyd,M
  18,   John W. Ashworth to Adelia F. Crawford
  19,   B.W.Rives to Mrs. C.H.Rives by D.L.Mitchell MG
  23,   Isaac V. Gattis to Mary F. Read by W.R.Waggoner JP
  22,   Thomas M. Slone to Mary E. Moore by A.S.Sloan MG
  22,   Wm. J. Echols to Frances C. Barns by A.S.Sloan MG
pg 258
  22,   Robert Bates to Lucy Burts
  22,   Davy Bright to Sarah Jones (col)

23,   J.H.Halbert to Martha J. Barns by B.F.Hudson MG
22,   John Williams to Nancy C. McCrary by R.B.Riley JP
23,   Henry Sherrell to Amanda Henderson (col) by W.F.
                                    Zimmerman JP
27,   J.W.Bates to Sarah T. Manly by W. Kincade
pg 259
28,   W.H.Waller to Martha A. Tripp by W.F.Findley MG
30,   Henry McDaniel to Lou Harris (col) by A.H.Bishop MG
Feb 3, R.D.Bagley to N.C.Davidson by G. Nichols MG
 4,   Larry Thompson to Nancy Pierce by F. Motlow JP
 6,   Dave F. Grable to Ruth Stephens by D.L.Enochs JP
 4,   Robert Johnston to Lucy T. Inman by T.W.Clark JP
pg 260
 4,   James A. McKinney to Martha J. Nicks by A.S.Randolph JP
 4,   James P. Hamilton to Sally E. Desmukes
 6,   Minos A. Cannon to Martha J. Colter by N.D.Crawford MG
 9,   John Helms to Jane Blair by W.M.Beckett JP
12,   Isaac B. Moore to Mrs. L.C.C.Parkinson by A.S.Sloan MG
13,   W.A.Barnes to R.A.George by W.W.Wilson JP
pg 261
15,   C.D.Hankins(Harkins) to S.S.Birdsong by Hugh Parkerson
13,   A.L.Cooper to S.M.Finney to F.L.Ezell JP
12,   John C. Smith to L. McLaughlin by W.A.Wood JP
14,   W.H.Morgan to S.L.Damron by D. Jakes MG, don't publish
        until after 4th Sunday.
12,   J.L.Harris to E.K.Stanley
13,   Hugh Porter to Jane Twitty (col) by G.W.Puckett JP
pg 262
16,   Seaborn Stiles to M.A.Franklin by N.B.Pearce MG
14,   Abram Conwell to Mary Logan (col)
18,   William Holt to Sue V. Motlow by T.S.Shaw MG
18,   E.P.Bobo to Bettie Broadway by T.J.Shaw MG
16,   J.T.Weaver to Nancy A. Buchanan by Rev. Wm. J. Hailey
18,   Henry Wilson to Agnes Black by R. Farquharson JP
pg 263
19,   W.K.Boyd to Mary J. Allen by A.B.Coleman MG
20,   Manuel Riddell to Sidney Pearson by Jason Ray MG
22,   Turnie Wyatt to Martha Benson (col) by J.W.Cooper JP
19,   W.M.Gross to Julia A. Thompson by W.A.Wood JP
19,   F.M.Gross to Mary J. Thompson by W.A.Wood JP
20,   Louis Walker to Margaret Perkins (col) by W.A.Bryan JP
pg 264
20,   Mikel Luttrell to Susan J. Cashion by W.M.Beckett JP
23,   Wm. Short to Nancy Hines (col) by A.C.Martin JP
Mar 6, Hamilton Hunter to Mary J. McClure by J.B.Riley JP
14,   Solomon Perkins to Polly Perkins (col) by N. Hamilton,M
Feb 22, Enos T. Fielder to Nancy L. Lewis by J.M.Dyer JP
24,   Robert Gill to Anny Prosser (col)
pg 265
26,   J.W.Perkins to M.J.Cummins by P.B.Marsh JP
27,   G.D.Haloway to Jane Baker by Martin Towry MG
26,   J.H.Milliken to M.A.Cooper by A.S.Sloan
27,   J.H.Taylor to Susan E. Corder by Thomas S. Corder
27,   George C. Carmack to Susan E. Warren by D.L.Mitchell MG
Mar 1, J.H.O.Caldwell to E.M.Ward by J.H.Eslick JP
pg 266
 3,   Isaac W. Sullivan, of Madison County Alabama to
        Mary A. Byers by R.D.Hardin MG

4,   Harris Holoway to Victora Smith (col) by A.H.Bishop MG
4,   Young Stiles to Martha A. McGhee by J.H.Eslick JP
4,   Clabren A. Finly to M.L.Pigg by W.H.Dickson MG
5,   George C. Gillespie to Mattie D. Blake by D.L.Mitchell,M
5,   Jasper Jones to Tilda Taylor by W.F.Zimmerman JP
pg 267
5,   W.C.Corder to R.A.Wilkerson by L.L.Cole JP
Jun 5,   W.W.Thompson to Jo Celia Scott by J.B.Tigert MG
Mar 10,   F.M.Birdsong to Mrs. Angeline Birdsong by A.S.Randolph
10,   N.J.Grizzard to Sue Ann Rice by S.H.McCord JP
12,   E.C.McLaughlin to Mrs. Sallie Logan by S.T.Sanford MG
18,   John L. Payne to Lucinda C. Haynes by W.L.Alexander JP
pg 268
19,   Milton N. Rowell to Nancy A. Martin by R.D.Hardin MG
29,   M.R.Cobb to Clementine Cates by J.S.Erwin MG
24,   Samuel Maples to Ann Curtis (col) by J.M.Lock MG
28,   Bill Faning to Flora Pryor (col) by T.S.Corder JP
25,   M.M.Corder to Elizabeth Sanders
31,   W.T.Henderson to Jennie Whitaker by S.L.Sanford MG
pg 269
Apr 1,   Samuel T. Lauderdale to Georgia Ann Phagan by J.Carey JP
5,   A.W.Feenney to Mary E. Meadaris by T.W.Brents MG
8,   W.M.Crabtree to Mary J. Hill by D.L.Mitchell MG
9,   A.C.Martin to Mrs. Mary Hedgepeth by J.B.Tigert MG
8,   W.P.Prosser to Mary E. Broadway
12,   George Sanders to L.P.Hogan by E.H.Bennett MG
pg 270
11,   Abraham M. Haynes to Sarah A. Panter by J.S.Erwin MG
14,   James C. Pylant to Emily Thomas by N.D.Crawford MG
20,   Cezar Henderson to Martha Bryson (col)
22,   John Jackson to Isabella Mansfield
May 30,   George A. Cross to Jane Buchanan (col) by R.Robertson MG
Apr 24,   Bonner Goodrich to Fanny Kelso (col)
pg 271
22,   J.W.Hazlewood to Matilda S. Farris by J.B.Hudson JP
30,   J.P.Cooley to Sarah J. Locker by A.S.Randolph JP
30,   James M. Davis to Lenizetta A. Woodard
May 1,   Wm. Scott to Sarah Haynes (col)
5,   Edmen Ellison to Sophia Stewart (col)
8,   A.C.Beasley to Mary E. Wells by J.B.Warren MG
pg 272
7,   John Hariston to Margaret Bryson (col)
7,   R.M.Brown to Mary J. Thomas
7,   William Bonner to Susan Bonner (col) by R.Robertson MG
28,   Frank Stoneman to Nancy A. Sanders by W.R.Waggoner JP
12,   S.P.Duckworth to Mary R. Gravet by T.S.Corder JP
16,   Wiley Ashby to Martha E. Baker by T.S.Corder JP
pg 273
Jun 1,   J.H.Phillips to Eliza A. Wood by J.P.Dennis JP
7,   J.H.Fuller to M.E.A.Tallent
8,   Thomas Dailey to Hanah Fowler by W.M.Beckett JP
9,   Jesse L. Muse to Sarah E. Reece
11,   James M. Cooper to Sue E. Peach by D.L.Mitchell MG
11,   John T. Middlebrooks to Tempy Elizabeth Junior by S.H.
                                                    Taylor JP
pg 274
16,   W.T.Neeld to Luvenia M. Wiley by A.S.Randolph JP
21,   Wm. R. Harper to Sarah A. Huffman by John L. Ashby JP

    20,   Nick Woods to Margaret Rhea (col)
    23,   Grose Prosser to Nancy Jane Dyer
    24,   F.M.Smith to P.G.Grimes by L.L.Cole JP
    27,   Martin Kimes to Manerva Pitts (col) by J.B.Hudson JP
pg 275
    25,   Wm. M. Anderson to Clarrissa Jane Thompson by W.O.
                                                        Price JP
    28,   O.J.Bailey to M.M.Morris by D.L.Enochs JP
Jul 1,   A.J.D.Middleton to Cordelia J. Hague by J.W.Holman MG
     1,   J.M.Kent to Manda Polston
     1,   William Ratliff to Nancy Honey
     2,   James K. Warren to Nancy J. Davidson
pg 276
     2,   Archabald Tanner to Sarah Nevels by Martin Towry MG
     2,   Pleasant Halbert to Martha V. Smith by J.B.Tigert MG
     4,   George Campbell to Ditha Tallent
     5,   Wiles Wilson to Sarah Young (col) by W.D.Smith JP
     6,   John W. Warren to Martha Hall by John R. Thompson MG
     6,   J.A.F.Whitworth to Rachel E. Deal by J.B.Hudson JP
pg 277
     8,   John L. Abbott to Thursa A. Weeks by E. Kenady MG
    11,   Inez Ringo to Sarrah Smith (col)
    13,   Wm Ashby to Elizabeth Redings by S.N.McCord JP
    13,   James Bird to Sally Dance by D.L.Enochs JP
    15,   Rufus D. Flautt to Mrs. E.C.Cathy by J.B.Tigert MG
    17,   A.J.Mullins to Margarett Taylor by W.F.Zimmerman JP
pg 278
    16,   A.R.Long to Louisa E. Warren by L.L.Cole JP
    16,   issued: James Calvin Phillips to Susanah Nelson NOTE:
          Note on this case was unproperly found. by E.T.Reynolds
    18,   Dewell Trigg to Mahala Haley (col)
    26,   Essex McDonald to Ann Hariston (col) by A.S.Randolph JP
    22,   Wm. Taylor to Nancy H. George by W.M.Beckett JP
    21,   John Carlton to Rebecca J. Bradford by S.L.Walker JP
    23,   Lafayett Miller to Jane Walden by John G. York MG
    23,   J.T.Flynn to Mattie J. Windborn by A.S.Sloan
    22,   Newton Dickey to Mrs. Susan A. Timmons by L.L.Cole JP
    28,   Primus Vaughn to Caroline Hester (col) by L.L.Cole JP
    28,   Thomas C. Nearen to Eliza Jane Perryman by B.F.Hudson,M
    30,   Wm. Yarborough to Amanda A. Tipps by F.L.Ezell JP
pg 280
    30,   Robert R. Davis to Mattie Harden by W.W.Wilson JP
Aug 2,   M.A.Bryant to M.A.McGeehee by J.W.Holman MG
Jul 31,   Thomas Scott to Larza Wilson (col)
Aug 2,   Jessie L. Wisdom to Mary R. Whitworth by P.B.Marsh JP
     1,   G.W.Martin to Jane Thompson
     2,   Rufus Dodson to Catharine Bowlen by Charles Laxon MG
pg 281
     1,   Isaac Diemer to Frances Bonner (col)
     9,   Allen Huff to Angeline Conger (col) by J.B.Mims JP
     5,   James Green to Elizabeth McLemore by R. Drennon JP
     9,   James A. Jones to Mary E. Marbary by W.A.Bryan
     4,   David B. Smith to Jane E. McWhorter by A. Allsup JP
     6,   A.B.Johnson to S.J.Hedgepeth by W.W.Wilson JP
pg 282
    11,   Thomas Carpien to Nancy Justice (col) by F.L.Ezell JP
     6,   B.J.Chafin to S.K.Ramsey by J.R.Thompson MG
     8,   Thomas Bennet to Sarah J. Couser

```
        9,   W.D.Bryan to Martha E. Wright by L.L.Cole JP
       12,   C.A.J.Enochs to Sallie Ann Jones by R.P.Garraway MG
       13,   A.J.Hill to Lucy A. Gunter by B.F.Hudson JP
pg 283
       13,   Jacob Bradford to Nancy Jane Vaughn by T.S.Corder JP
       16,   James Wade to Cyntha Taylor by W.M.Beckett JP
       27,   James Brown to Lucy Dye by L. Henry Grubbs MG
       20,   J.T.Hutcherson to Sarah M. Smith by A.S.Randolph JP
       20,   W.R.Oldham to S.J.Clark by B.F.Hudson JP
       24,   J.W.Damron to Elizabeth Bridges by A.J.Steele MG
pg 284
       25,   B.C.McKinney to R.L.Gilliam by S.M.Emmons MG
       26,   W.E.Sively to Casenia George by T.S.Corder JP
       27,   Jerry Stephens to Hannah Hopkins (col) by A.D.Trimble,M
       27,   Lewis Hopkins to Fanny Whitaker (col) by A.D. Trimble,M
       30,   J.B.Rozell to Eliza Beverly by A.F.Driskell MG
       29,   J.S.Heard to M.C.Talley
pg 285
       30,   D.F.Moore to Caroline Mills by J.B.Hudson JP
       31,   Wm. A.H. Delap to Margaret A. Largen by Isaac Gatlin
Sep  1,   Thomas L. Sanders to Sarah E. Cowen by W.F.Zimmerman JP
       3,   G.W.Enocks to Fanny Sullivan by S.L.Sandford MG
       3,   John Stephens to Eddy Brison (col)
       5,   Robert Corder to Sarah A. King
pg 286
       10,   Thomas E. Turner to A.E.Teal by T.W.Clark JP
        6,   James Bradford to Frona Sims
        6,   William Weaver to Nancy J. Bradford
        8,   Goodwin Batt to Martha Oliver (col) by F.L.Ezell JP
       10,   Arch Womack to Lucy Allen (col) by Berry Womack MG
       10,   G.D.Miles to A.A.Loyd by A.J.Whitaker JP
pg 287
       11,   John A. Sorrells to Susan Edge by G. Nichols MG
       13,   P.R.Powell to Margaret A. Dobbs by T.S.Corder JP
       12,   Benjamin Vance to Marriah Woodard (col) by Alexander
                                                      Smith,M
       14,   T.J.Rives to A.A.Peach by D.L.Mitchell MG
       20,   M.L.Steadman to A.E.Bryan by L.L.Cole JP
       20,   Henry Thornton to Bettie Ann Hickman by Dock Robertson,M
pg 288
       24,   Henry Dillard to Sallie Heals (col) by Archey Staton,M
       24,   J.K.P.Damron to Sarah E. Huffman by J.L.Ashby JP
       24,   H.L.Dever to Annie Jane Harris by W.W.Wilson JP
       24,   Green B. Evans to Julia McCanless by S.L.Sanford MG
       24,   Jordon Whitaker to Martha Berry (col) by Berry Womack,M
       24,   William Dyer to Sarah E. Woodard by J.R.Nelson JP
pg 289
       27,   James R. Shelton to Mary V. Smith by J.R.Thompson MG
       27,   James S. Herrings to Margaret E. Nelson by A.J.Steele,M
Oct  1,   Henry Bonner to Luveney Shuffield (col) by G.W.Puckett,M
Sep 28,   C.L.Smith to Margaret S. Mealer by A.S.Randolph JP
Oct  1,   James W. Burton to Mary C. Bruce by R.M.Stephens MG
Sep 29,   F.M.Stephenson to Amanda Bray
pg 290
       29,   Lewis W. Bray to Mollie C. Canady
       30,   J.C.George to Eliza E. Dollar
Oct  1,   Thomas Shields to Frances Childress (col) by B.F.Hudson,M
Sep 24,   Daniel Sisk to Elizabeth Webb by W.O.Price JP
```

Oct 1,   James Anderson to Lucy Cunningham (col) by J.B.Hudson JP
     8,   James N. George to Netie J. Douthit by J.R.Abernathy MG
pg 291
     7,   Andrew M. Holt to Amanda Downing by S.M.Emmons MG
     6,   H.D.Wright to A.E.McWhorter by J.B.Hudson JP
     7,   W.H.Sims to S.J.Bell by Henry P. Turner MG
     6,   W.M.Smith to Elizabeth Bailey by S.L.Sandford MG
     6,   James K. Neece to Mary Martin by S.L.Sandford MG
     8,   Elisha E. Brown to Cyntha C. Orr by J.B.Hudson JP
pg 292
    12,   Bryant Carnes to Ann Collins (col) by Archy Staton MG
    11,   J.R.Lenard to Maggie J. Blakemore by C.L.Randolph MG
    15,   J.R.Steelman to Elizabeth Jenkins by R.W.Stephens MG
    14,   Wm. T. Richardson to Eliza Street by W.A.Bryan JP
    15,   J.R.Walker to Sarrah C. Myrick by A.S.Moore JP
    16,   John Carey to Nancy C. Davis by Alexander Smith MG
pg 293
    16,   Thomas B. Stubblefield to Martha J. Vann
    16,   Major Dangerfield to Martha Cathey (col) by Archy
                                                          Staton MG
    17,   D.G.Harden to Linsey B. Turner
    20,   J.H.Hill to A.C.Curtis by D.L.Mitchell MG
    22,   John D. Wells to Margaret A. Templeton
    22,   J.G.Webb to Martha J. Reedy
pg 294
    22,   Edmund Cooper to Lucy Bonner by Rev. C.H.Coley
    24,   Manson Shuffield to Jane Oliver by F.L.Ezell JP
    24,   Jorden Bright to Allis Whitaker
    28,   Eli Taylor to Sarah Elizabeth Gauthy by W.W.Wilson JP
    27,   W.H.H.Ward to Susan Melton by S.M.Emmons MG
    29,   W.W.Hampton to Eudonia D. Bearden by J.B.Tigert MG
pg 295
    29,   W.J.Ventress to Mary F. Koonce by A.S.Randolph JP
Nov 5,   J.F.Moore to Mary E. Forrester by J.L.Ashby JP
     5,   J.V.McKinney to Dana Kelso by A.S.Sloan MG
     8,   Tobe Martin to Martha Jane Brown (col)
    12,   J.A.Newman to Mary Sisk by A.C.Martin JP
    10,   J.T.Benington to Margaret A. Welch by B.F.Hudson MG
pg 296
    10,   B.W.Rhoten to Sarrah J. Moore by D.L.Enochs JP
    10,   G.W.Anderson to Louisa Setliff by D.L.Enochs JP
    11,   F.M.Williams to Josephine Howard
    12,   George Cunningham to Hanah D. Evans by J.L.Ervine MG
    14,   Wm. Bruce to Elizabeth West by F.L.Ezell JP
    12,   J.H.Crabtree to S.A.Hester by D.L.Mitchell MG
pg 297
    12,   Thomas R. Pickett to Mary E. Porter by A.S.Randolph JP
    12,   John Tanner to Emaline Seaton by A.J.Childress JP
    13,   Newton Kelso to Julia Sanders by A.S.Randolph JP
    16,   Thomas A.J.Harshaw to E. Jane Hall by D.L.Enochs JP
    15,   Thomas W. Kent to Ann R.L.Toon by P.B.Marsh
    19,   A.J.Tipps to M.A.Moore by John L. Ashby JP
pg 298
    18,   James T. Cowen to Adaline Sanders by J.G.Erwin MG
    17,   George W. Cunningham to Kate S.J.Whitlock by J.L.Ashby
    19,   A.B.Culloms to G.E.Tulley by B.F.Hudson MG
    19,   William Yarley to Eliza Jane Kent by J.B.Hudson JP
    19,   Daniel Sanders to Sarah Ann Edgeman by A.J.Childress

```
        20,    Benjamin Ashby to Joanna Bradford by Ezekiel Kennady MG
    pg 299
        24,    Wm. A. McDonald to Mary A. Thompson by R.D.Hardin MG
        22,    Claiborn Vaughn to Mary Marbery by L.L.Cole JP
        24,    A.G.March to Sallie Cathey by W.E.Coldwell MG
        25,    Milton Pamplin to Mary A. Boyle by J.B.Tigert MG
        26,    F.M.Waggoner to Mary C. Spencer by J.W.Holman MG
        24,    Nulen T. Jackson to Juley Ann Epps by W.O.Price JP
    pg 300
        25,    T.F.George to Lizzie P. Thorpe
        26,    M. Hensley to Rhodie Elizabeth Eastlick by W.R.Waggoner
        26,    J.M.Harris to N.H.Stephenson by J.B.Tigert MG
        26,    Moses Whitaker to Catharine Parks (col) by David
                                                    Whitaker MG
        26,    W.W.McClelland to M.E.Martin by J.B.Tigert MG
        26,    James B. Hill to Maggie Bearden by A.S.Sloan MG
    pg 301
    Dec  1,    B.H.Whitfield to Martha Jane King by David Jacks MG
         2,    C.O.Wilbur to Jane Renegar by Alex. J. Whitaker JP
         1,    Robert G. Fullerton to Lucy A. McDaniel by Henry Bryson,M
         3,    C.C.Hamilton to Bettie Moody by Samuel Hall JP
         3,    H.B.Morgan to Mary Jane Reese by T.J.Shaw MG
         2,    John T. Rowe to Sarah A. Woodard
    pg 302
         2,    John P. Funk to Medora A. Woodard
         3,    J.J.Rawls to Madeline Bearden by A.S.Sloan MG
        28,    Stephen McGee to Sarah Massey (col) by Rev. W.W.Hailey
        28,    Jack Holloway to Jane Massey (col) by Rev. W.W.Hailey
        10,    Annanias Watkins to Martha E. Wray by S. Bond JP
        10,    J.J.Newman to Mary E. Smith by W.R.Waggoner JP
    pg 303
        10,    Enoch Stephens to Elizabeth Beech by L.L.Cole JP
         9,    Childress Brady of Sardis, Miss. to Sarah J. Childress
                                              by T.L.Ervin MG
        10,    A.H.Turney to Mary C.E.Tate by B.F.Hudson MG
        10,    T.C.Little to Agnes Goodrich by James Watson MG
        10,    J.W.Turner to Margaret Jane Barnes by T.W.Clark JP
        10,    Abner Moore to Mary Ann Jean
    pg 304
        10,    A.M.Templeton to Mary A.V.Couch by J.B.Riley JP
        13,    Dave H. Pitman to Sarah A. Bledsoe by E.H.Holland MG
        12,    Henry Smith to Ann Vance (col) by Alex. Smith MG
    1869
    Jan  8,    Monroe Bright to Ann Bonner (col) by D.Robertson MG
    1868
    Dec 15,    Hilliard Raby to Julia Scales (col) by R.D.Hardin MG
        17,    D.J.Waggoner to Ann E. Rhoten by J.L.Ashby JP
    pg 305
        16,    W.H.H.Moore to M.C.Moore by A.S.Sloan MG
        17,    John Ward to Mary Thompson by W.B.Pearce MG
        17,    Martin Edwards to Emily Roper by G.W.Puckett MG
        16,    M.R.Luna to M.E.Roach by A.C.Martin JP
        17,    James Cunningham to Sarah Kilpatrick by Ezekiel
                                                    Kennady MG
        17,    L.C.Rodin to M.A.Abbot by B.F.Hudson JP
    pg 306
        20,    G.W.Adams to Martha McCord by J.S.Erwin
        25,    John Wells to Sarah Smith (col) by F.L.Ezell JP
```

```
20,    W.P.Oliver to Nancy C. Gore by D.L.Enocks JP
21,    I.F.Bobo to Mariam Shaw by D.L.Enocks JP
18,    Calvin Clark to Maria Myers (col) by T.A.Shells MG
20,    N.C.Hodge to Sarah Hedricks by S. Hall JP
```
pg 307
```
21,    W.W.Adcock to Nancy Davis by Jacob Gray MG
22,    H.C.Higgins to Fanny A. Stone by John M. Gold MG
21,    Felix Motlow to Netie J. Daniel
24,    R.F.Darnall to Ellender E. Moore by T.J.Shaw MG
23,    Joshua Y. Price to Sallie P. Bird by D.L.Enocks JP
24,    John Scott to Susan McDaniel (col) by Dock Robertson,M
```
pg 308
```
22,    J.S.Alexander to Florinda Smith by J. Watson MG
24,    W.J.Ward to Mary J. Warren by W.F.Zimmerman JP
23,    Bracken Roper to Sarah Edwards
31,    L.S.Barnett to Eliza Roper by G.W.Puckett MG
23,    D.L.Gray to Mary A. Crawford by J.B.Tigert MG
24,    J.W.Crawford to Emma Harris by J.B.Tigert MG
```
pg 309
```
23,    Rufus Mitchell to Belle Moore (col)
17,    Wilson Bailey to Lily Parks (col) by David Whitaker MG
24,    Wm. A. Pitts to Mattie J. Brown by Rev. M.R.Tucker
24,    John A. Formwalt to M.D.Murphy by James Watson MG
24,    Guss Herren to Sally Drake (col)
25,    John McEwing to Betty Millins (col)
```
pg 310
```
26,    Jery Thompson to Mary Woodard (col) by A. Smith MG
```
1869
```
Jan  3,    S.R.Chilton to A.E.Mayes by G.W.Jackson MG
```
1868
```
Dec 28,    John S. Grant to Nancy Beddingfield
28,    George Ragins to Milley Sims (col)
29,    Nelson Stephens to Nancy E. McDougal
30,    Josiah P. Wallace to Mary Fowler by W.A.Bryan JP
```
pg 311
```
30,    A.B.Coleman to H.B.Taylor by Alex. Smith MG
31,    B.T.Cole to Mollie Ann Rhodes by R.D.Hardin MG
30,    Joe Bright to Nancy Love (col)
30,    J.M.Morgan to Louisa Miller, returned on the 20th day
       of June 1869 without being solomized.
```
1869
```
Jan  3,    David A. Laws to Mary Jane Neece by W.O.Price JP
```
1868
```
Dec 30,    Thomas F. Williams to Nancy C. Thompson
```
pg 312
```
31,    W.P.Clift to H.P.Wright by W.J.Brown MG
30,    Ben Duncan to Mary Anderson (col)
31,    Samuel Burget to Margaret Grimes
31,    Tillman Black to Martha Walker (col)
```
1869
```
Jan  3,    James B. McNatt to Ann E.B.Raby by G. Nichols MG
6,    Peter Stephens to Eliza Taylor (col) by S.L.Lloyd MG
```
pg 313
```
20,    Neil S. Hamilton to Mollie E. Chitwood by W.A.Bryan JP
7,    A.J.Fuller to Virginia A. Dillon by Martin Towry MG
8,    I.V.Forrester to Jennie E. Jackson by Alex. Whitaker JP
7,    A.H.Nelson to Barbara Walden by A. Allsup JP
7,    John P. Oliver to Sarah J. George by N.B.Pearce MG
```

                7,   R.W.Bearden to Nancy J. Watt by W.W.Wilson JP
        pg 314
                6,   A.A.Gill to Minerva Wiles
               24,   Nelson Edmondson to Alice Bonner (col) by D.Robertson,M
                7,   Fountain Townsend to Kitty Pryor (col) by T.S.Corder JP
               10,   Norris Franklin to Easter Vance by S. Hall JP
                7,   Benjamin F. Davis to Margaret M. Adcock by A.L.Bates,M
                7,   N.P.Smith to Emaline Koonce by A.S.Randolph JP
        pg 315
                7,   Cuff Merry to Martha Wells (col) by B.F.Hudson MG
               10,   J.R.Thompson to Jane E. Williams by J.B.Hudson JP
               10,   Willis Benson to Donnda Swinebro (col) by W.W.Wilson JP
               11,   G.W.Newton to Sarah C. West by M.H.Dixon MG
               14,   Nathaniel Hutchinson to Lou F. Cole by J.B.Hudson JP
               14,   F.M.Waggoner to Mary J. Waggoner by J.L.Ashby JP
        pg 316
               13,   K.J.Bobo to Sue Robertson by D.L.Enocks JP
               14,   George Templeton to Sarah Jane Dismukes (col) by A.B.
                                                          Coleman MG
               19,   J.J.Waggoner to Louisa V. Cunningham by W.R.Waggoner JP
               16,   Sam McBay to Olive Rattler
               20,   Nathan Harris to Celia Ann Harper (col) by Thomas
                                                          Shuld MG
               20,   Henry W. Griffith to Nannie E. George by T.L.Ezell JP
        pg 317
               18,   Alex Woods to Alice Black (col)
               21,   Robert Gatlin to Sarah Simmons by R.D.Hardin MG
        Feb 10,   Lewis Nevils to Adeline Wilson (col) by D.Robertson MG
        Jan 21,   Daniel Stephens to Charlotte Snoddy (col) by G.S.
                                                          Corder JP
               22,   J.P.Faulkner to Mary L. Damron by David Jakes MG
               21,   C.H.McGee to Margaret Steelman by J.B.Hudson JP
        pg 318
               21,   W.A.Story to Sarah L. Myers by F.L.Ezell JP
               27,   Spence Brown to Mahala Berry (col) by B. Womack MG
               26,   George Carlos to Clary Edmondson (col) by D.Robertson,M
               23,   W.T.Mangrum to Milly Riddle by J.S.Erwin JP
               24,   Nathaniel Reed to Lutetia Ward by W.B.Pearce MG
               24,   George Goodwin to Mary McQuary by W.M.Beckett JP
        pg 319
        Feb 8,   John F. Haywood to Sallie Bolden (col) by D.Robèrtson,M
        Jan 28,   M.V.Tucker to Mary Easlick by W.B.Pearce MG
               28,   B.W.Smith to Mary Ann Hale
               28,   Jonathan McCurry to Sarah E. Cannon by M. Towry MG
               28,   E.F.Brown to B.T.Orr by J.B.Hudson JP
               28,   Wm. Dismukes to Frances Moore (col)
        pg 320
               28,   Robb Dismukes to Rebecca Scott (col)
               30,   Felix Green to Laura Brown (col)
        Feb 2,   W.O.Read to Kate Edmondson by B.F.Hudson MG
                8,   Charles Perkins to Maggie Kye (col) by D.Robertson MG
                3,   R.H.Templeton to Frances C. Walker by J.B.Riley JP
                4,   Thomas Sullenger to Jane McGehee by J.H.Easlick JP
        pg 321
                4,   Price M. Snoddy to Maggie J. Reed by J.W.Holman MG
               10,   M.O.Clark to S.E.Ayers by H. Bryson MG
               10,   Samuel J. Dollar to Sarah Jane Hopkins by A.S.Randolph
               10,   John Pool to Elizabeth Scoggins

```
    10,    Josephus Berry to Maggie Cannon (col)
    11,    George M.D.Creson to Mary Wade by J.B.Hudson JP
pg 322
    11,    Randol Perkins to Maria Dangerfield (col) by T.S.
                                                    Childs MG
    11,    G.F.Perry to Mary Frances Holman by S.H.Taylor JP
    14,    Wm. B. Wright to S.C.Smith by B.F.Hudson MG
    16,    James M. Holt to Sarah E. Gregory
    18,    John T. Corder to Margaret M. Weeks by T.S.Corder JP
    18,    R.S.Walker to Mary J. Hedgepeth by J.B.Tigert MG
pg 323
    18,    Harrison C. Wray to Mary A. Rheyer by S. Bond JP
    18,    John Shelton to Mary J. Tripp
    19,    William G. Howell to Ella Benson
    21,    J.B.Upton to Jane Fenley by N.D.Crawford MG
    22,    John Henry Bonner to Brancy Ann Townsend (col)
    24,    James J. Sweeny to Artelia Foster
pg 324
    27,    James H. Campbell to Mary M. Griggs
Mar  4,    J.B.Mullins to Susan Savannah Nichols by J.W.Dyer JP
     2,    W.B.Taylor to Susan T. Keller by J.W.Holman MG
     2,    Wm. D. Hughes to Margaret F. Fox by Newton Hamilton MG
     4,    J.H.Hardin to Margaret A. Pickett by E. Kenedy MG
     5,    E.F.Tucker to Emily Sullenger
pg 325
     7,    Jo Short to Rutha Jane Rawson (col) by A.C.Martin JP
    11,    Daniel Fuller to Elizabeth Scoggin by S.H.Taylor JP
     9,    Oliver Cowan to Sarah Bryson by J.H.Bryson MG
     9,    H.B.McCowan to Fenica J. Phagan by A.B.Coleman MG
    11,    J.J.Hanvy to Sarah Jane Clark by S.L.Sanford MG
    11,    Ery Taylor to Mary Ann Galtna by W.F.Zimmerman JP
pg 326
    11,    D.B.D.Davis to Ellender Dambron by H.H.Harton MG
    11,    Isaac Williams to Ellen Todd (col)
    16,    Patrick Driver to Amanda Kizer (col)
    18,    W.A.Williams to Matilda Beasley by A.B.Coleman MG
    24,    Martin L. Parks to Frona Edens by D.L.Enocks JP
    20,    George Kimes to Susan Woods (col) by A.C.Martin JP
pg 327
    22,    James F. Pierce to Louella Coldwell by T.S.Corder JP
    25,    Mart. Morehead to Margaret Jennings (col) by S.D.Lloyd,M
    24,    F.R.Wallace to Sarah J. Hickland by A.S.Randolph JP
    25,    James H. Dale to Mary E. Marshall by R. Drennon JP
    28,    James A. Foster to Mollie E. Barnes by L.L.Clark
Apr  1,    J.J.Golden to Sarah A. Arnold by J.B.Rily JP
pg 328
     1,    John George to Lizzie Griffis by W.F.Zimmerman JP
     1,    T.W.Andrews to Lavonia Denham by T.W.Clark JP
     6,    S.M.Clayton to Naomi Halbert by J.B.Tigert MG
     7,    George Eaton to Sarah Hale (col)
     8,    E.A.Braxton to Margaret J. Epps by P.B.Marsh JP
    13,    E.T.Beavel to Serena Walker
pg 329
    18,    A.P.Simmons to Sallie Sanders by J. Erwin MG
    18,    G.R.Jenkins to Narcissa Clark by B.F.Hudson MG
    17,    George Weeks to Lizzie Harris (col)
    27,    Henry J. Barnes to L.A.Milliken by B.F.Hudson MG
    28,    Wm. H. McDaniel to Nancy M. Sanderson by S. Hall JP
```

1869

May 2,   Andrew Fulton to Martha Cunningham by J.C.Mills MG
pg 330
      3,   Robert Hunt to Martha C. Stevens by A.S.Sloan MG
      6,   Berry Williams to Caroline Pitts (col) by H.Lasters,M
      8,   Joseph Lambert to Martha C. Griffis
     11,   T.H.Parkes to Emily Taylor by J.W.Holman MG
     11,   John B. Smith to Gabrilla L. McCord by Wm. Hutchen MG
     10,   John W. Denham to Mary F.E.Ray by L.L.Cole JP
pg 331
     13,   George L. McDougal to Eady V. Mason
     16,   Anderson Whitaker to Mary Mitchell (col) by A.J.
                                                   Whitaker JP
     16,   Calvin Pursin to Nancy Hall (col) by D.L.Mitchell MG
     17,   J.D.Leonard to Lucinda Cox by J.B.Riley MG
     20,   Gustavus A. Jarvis to M. Lula Greer by F.L.Ewing MG
     20,   Oscar Wood to Eliza M. Renegar by A.J.Whitaker JP
pg 332
     23,   John A. Taylor to Mary Jane Hamilton by W.F.Zimmerman
     26,   Calvin Gracy to Mary Kelso (col) by Rev. D.Robertson
     25,   Samuel A. Hill to Eliza J. Mosely by Charles Laxton,M
     29,   Henry Leatherwood to Susan McDaniel (col) by W.A.Bryan
     31,   Nathan Jones to Nancy Ann Pylant by E. Kennedy MG
Jun 1,   George W. Johnson to Martha A. Puckett
pg 333
      3,   E.A.Walker to Nancy C. Cooley by E. Kennedy MG
      3,   Joseph Walworke to Julia Jones by J. Watson MG
      3,   David McElroy to Lou Hoskins by S.H.McCord JP
      6,   James Cameron to Elizabeth Hamilton by W.F.Zimmerman
      6,   W.F.Collins to Mary J. Wakefield by S.M.Emmons MG
     10,   John P. Bennett to Laura A. Berry by T.J.Shaw MG
pg 334
     14,   John Williams to Margaret E. Wright by W.W.Wilson JP
     15,   J.F.Goodrich to Maria R. Landess by J.E.Frost MG
     17,   Eli Sawyers to Nancy Virginia Davidson
     24,   Archibald Ellet to Mary Ann Timmons by D.L.Enocks JP
     23,   W.J.Pitts to Mary E. Hill by L.L.Cole
     24,   Ben McDaniel to Sarah Jane Stonebraker (col) by Wm.
                                                   Mitchell MG
pg 335
     27,   William Bowling to Jane E. Smith by Charles Laxton MG
     26,   James T. Workman to Letty C. Koonce
Jul 1,   Joseph Burt to Milly Morgan by J.A.Prosser JP
Jun 29,   Joseph G. Street to Ida L. Hall by D.L.Mitchell MG
Jul 1,   Alvin M. Grammer to Selina Harper by J.L.Ashby JP
Jun 30,   Wm. C. Stewart to M.A.Damron by David Jakes MG
pg 336
Jul 3,   William Norvell to Mattie Carrigan
      8,   James Tiller to Susan Rowe by J.B.Hudson JP
      8,   J.C.Stubblefield to Fanny P. James by J.B.Riley JP
      8,   Daniel V. McWright to Mary Jane Thacker
     18,   Pleasant Mayes to Mary Jackson by A.C.Martin JP
     17,   J.L.Bledsoe to Mary E. Hopper
pg 337
     21,   J.R.Dyer to Amanda Wright by W.W.Wilson JP
     22,   James Simmons to Eliza Jane Towery by Hugh Parkerson
     22,   John Jones to Sarah Mullins by W.F.Zimmerman JP
     25,   John Berry to Lucinda White by S.D.Lloyd MG
     22,   William Moody to Rhodia A. Wells by N.D.Crawford MG

29,   Jefferson Polly to Nancy Bryant by W.F.Zimmerman JP
pg 338
26,   William E. Harris to Susan Jane Bagley (col)
27,   David Cox to Missouri Myers by W.O.Price JP
29,   John Bowden to Mary E. Lock by W.O.Price JP
Aug 1,   Hiram Franklin to Manerva Vance (col) by S. Hall JP
Jul 31,   O.A.Parker to M.E.Harper
31,   Henry F. Williams to P.J.Harper
pg 339
Aug 3,   D.M.Summers to M.C.Stewart by Charles Laxton MG
4,   Thomas J. Russell to Lebrewster Dawston by B.F.Hudson
4,   John B. Clark to Caroline McDonald by B.F.Hudson MG
4,   J.S.Albright to M.C.Davidson
5,   James A. Warren to Mary Elizabeth Dale
5,   J.H.Erwin to Elizabeth Clark by J.B.Tigert MG
pg 340
8,   George Thomas to Ann McLemore by L.L.Cole JP
9,   Hardy Gill to Jose Harden (col)
15,   J.D.Neeld to L.C.Medearies by J.L.Sewell MG
16,   George Clark to Mary T. Ely (col)
18,   Charley Dangerfield to Indiana Claresly (col) by D.
Robertson MG
17,   E.H.Allen to T.M.Roughton by D.L.Enochs JP
pg 341
17,   Samuel H. Walker to Rose E. Bostick (did not marry)
18,   J.W.Mullins to Eliza McMillen by A.S.Randolph JP
18,   W.R.Woodward to Margarett Arnold
20,   Silas McGraw to Elizabeth Bonner (col)
21,   Alfred Allen to Susan Maples (col)
23,   W.A.Britton to Susan J.C.Sneed
pg 342
24,   Wm. Sanders to Eliza Galbreath by W.F.Zimmerman JP
26,   John A. Wicks to Mahaley Hopkins by E. Kennedy MG
28,   Samuel Briggs to Dariah Epps (col) by P.B.Marsh JP
26,   William Lee to Martha Jane Bradford by T.S.Corder JP
26,   Wm. R. Honey to Louisa E. Woodall by A.L.Bates MG
Oct 28,   A.H.Grammer to M.A.Renfro by R.M.Stephens MG
pg 343
Aug 31,   Robert C. Haskins to Ann M. Bright by S.L.Sandford MG
Sep 1,   L.B.Rogers to A.M.Weaver by W.W.Wilson JP
2,   John C. Brown to Mary E. Pitts by S.L.Sandford MG
3,   James Cooper to Lucy Jane Vinson by W.A.Bryan JP
7,   M.A.L.Enochs to Lizzie Lucus by T.J.Shaw MG
6,   James Raney to Eliza A. Howard
pg 344
7,   Lee A. Jones to Ellen Harrison by B.F.Hudson MG
8,   William Miles to Mary Kirkland by J.L.Ashby JP
9,   J.P.Everett to C.S.Hampton by W.W.Wilson JP
9,   William Prints to Caroline Lyon by W.J.Tipps MG
9,   Charles Eaks to Sallie M. Sherriff by W.O.Price JP
11,   Charles Bright to Fannie Orrick (col)
pg 345
12,   John R. Duncan to Louisa O. Hester by J.B.Warren MG
14,   Thomas M. Harper to D.F.Turney by F.R.McGaugh MG
14,   Anthony Moore to Frances Hasket (col)
18,   Lewis Mullins to Hanah Rawls (col)
21,   Hugh L. Patterson to Mary S. Patterson by W.E.
Coldwell MG

20,   George Davidson to Mary Rieves

pg 346

22,   R.E.Lazenberry to S.A.McMullin by B.F.Hudson MG
29,   J.R.Baxter to Elizabeth Stone by D.L.Enochs JP
Dec 19, James S. Bedford to Jane Eaton by D.L.Enochs JP
Sep 22, James Mitchell to Mary Ann Mullins by Frank L. Ezell
21,   J.E.Haugh to Emily A. Hill by M.B.Dewitt MG
23,   J.A.Henderson to Emaranda McCowen by R.D.Hardin MG

pg 347

23,   Orlando Duke to Mary S. Ward by I.H.Eslick JP
26,   A.J.West to E.D.Spurlock by W.A.Bryan JP
29,   Thomas W. Little by Harriet V. Waters by J.B.Warren,M
26,   George Price to Ellen Crabtree by W.O.Price JP
28,   Stephen L. Quick to Elizabeth D. Simms by A.S.Moore JP
29,   J.R.Raby to Mary J. Bagley

pg 348

29,   Henry Patterson to Ann Benson (col)
30,   Rufus Easlick to Mary Rowland by I.H.Easlick JP
30,   James M. Picket to S.J.Hester by J.B.Warren MG
Oct 3, John Pheares to Winey Donaldson by J.H.Eslick JP
2,   Duke Johnson to Viney Todd (col)
6,   John Hill to Matilda Anderson

pg 349

9,   Wm. P. Dollar to America J. Lightfoot by A.S.Randolph
14,   Joseph G. Roseborough to Julia Smith (col) by Hester
                                              Warren MG,
14,   D.W.Scivally to Sarah E. Grant by W.R.Waggoner JP
12,   J.B.Stewart to Jose Sloan by A.S.Sloan MG
14,   James S. Woodward to Mary Smith by Samuel Bond JP
19,   Henry L. Martin to Mattie J. Childress by F.R.McGaugh,M

pg 350

18,   J.T.Renegar to Nancy Hall
19,   James M. Baker to Sarah M. Roughton by D.L.Enochs JP
20,   A.P.Stephens to Susan S. McCown by W.A.Gill MG
21,   J.W.McGuire to Jane VanHooser by S. Hall JP
21,   W.T.Ramsey to M.F.Franklin by Alex. J. Whitaker JP
21,   A.M.Davis to Edy Bates by J. Gray MG

pg 351

27,   Richard Williams to Louisa Renegar
27,   J.L.A.Anthony to Mattie F. Bruce
28,   W.R.Bailey to M.M.Grammer by J.L.Ashby JP
28,   Wm. A. Tucker to Levina A. Wickes by J.B.Hudson JP
Nov 1, John H. Bonner to Susan Clinton (col)
2,   D.T.Harding to B.E.Pasinger by S.M.Emmons MG

pg 352

4,   John Kimes to Mary A. Cowen by J.B.Tigert MG
2,   G.B.Bruce to Ella Dickey by W.W.Wilson JP
3,   Newton F. Thomas to Nancy Watson by E.J.McGerry JP
6,   Robertson Smith to J.A.Wilson by W.W.Wilson JP
8,   John Jones to Harriet Caughran (col) by D.Whitaker MG
11,   Frank Green to Louisa Kimes (col) by H. Warren MG

pg 353

10,   Andy Tolly to Mary Motlow (col) by Berry Womack MG
11,   Wm. Nichols to Nancy J. Scott by J.M.Dyer JP
14,   William Noah to Susan Arney by W.W.Wilson JP
16,   Samuel A. Jobe to Nancy A. Butler by R.M.Haggard MG
16,   Thomas Pulliam to Sarah Hall by J.B.Riley JP
Dec 18, L.P.Myrick to Elizabeth J. McGuire by A.S.Moore JP

pg 354   1869
Nov 17,   James W. Goodwin to Molly Sumner by B.F.Hudson MG
    18,   Lacy L. Bobo to Sarah J. Gore by D.L.Enochs JP
    18,   Richard W. West to Mary E. Welch by B.F.Hudson MG
    17,   Arch Bonner to Jane Moore (col) by W.O.Price JP
    21,   Nelson A. Patterson to E.C.Endsley by Jesse Childress,M
    20,   William Howard to Margaret Ray by W.M.Becket JP
pg 355
    24,   P(T).A.Edminson to L.J.West by R.M.Haggard MG
    24,   Kenney McDonald to T.A.West by R.M.Haggard MG
    24,   Henry S. Gault to Tabitha E. Busbee by J.B.Riley JP
    24,   John J. Easlick to Emily C. Snow by Wm. S. Findley MG
    28,   Thomas J. Anderson to Mary E. Maddox by S. Hall JP
    25,   Daniel M. Jenkins to Martha E. Shofner
pg 356
    30,   John K. Breast to Vadora E. Gillespie by A. Eaton MG
Dec 1,   James Wilson to Darah Ruth by W.W.Wilson JP
     2,   Jasper Whitaker to Sarah Waggoner (col) by D. Whitaker,M
     1,   J.C.Stephenson to Amanda Sawyers by J.B.Tigert MG
     2,   John R. Branson to Eliza Rodgers by T.J.McGerry JP
    21,   Calvin Wright to Amanda Bonner (col) by A. Allsup JP
pg 357
     5,   Abner Sebastian to Sarah Solomon (col) by M.R.Tucker,M
     7,   Wm. J. Evans to Lucy L. Clark by W.R.Waggoner JP
     9,   F.B.Crawford to Ruth E. Evans by W.R.Waggoner JP
     8,   Thomas B. Tipps to A.M.Wheeler
     9,   R.M.James to Sarah Jane Crabtree by S.A.McCord JP
     9,   Andrew Holman to Milly Bright (col)
pg 358
    10,   William Cooper to Susan Waggoner by W.S.Findley MG
    12,   George W. Berry to Mary E. Harbin by T.S.Corder JP
    11,   David Miliam to Margaret Simmons (col)
    14,   W.J.Scoggins to Martha Jane Pamplin by S.H.Taylor JP
    14,   P.L.Bledsoe to M.E.Melson
    15,   John Allen to Faney Benson by W.G.Coldwell MG
pg 359
    15,   W.S.Cole to M.A.Bagerly
    16,   Henry W. Hampton to Susan Talley by G.Lipscomb MG
    16,   James Gulley to Harriet M. Hamby by W.G.Alexander JP
    16,   Martin Taylor to Vicy Jane Busby by J.B.Riley JP
    19,   Terry Zolicofer to Jane Allen by D.L.Enochs JP
    19,   E.M.Ross to M.A.McEwen by D.L.Mitchell MG
pg 360
    20,   Jesse Neece to M.A.Reese by S.L.Sanford MG
    20,   Z. Taylor Bland to Mary L. Coble by A. Allsup JP
    22,   James Hopkins to Culpurna Dollar
    29,   J.T.Singleton to Margaret T. Phillips by S. Hall JP
    23,   S.W.Gleghorn to M.L.Poindexter by J.B.Tigert MG
    30,   D.G.Walker to Allice M. Fraily by W.J.Brown MG
pg 361
    23,   W.W.Ervin to Addie Woods by J.B.Tigert MG
    22,   George W. Stiles to Mary E. Easlick by W.R.Waggoner JP
    23,   J.H.King to Isabella Curtis by W.E.Coldwell MG
    30,   G.W.Luttrell to Martha J. Ramsey by Alex. J. Whitaker
    23,   James A. Hasty to Mary Jane Warden by J.B.Hudson JP
    23,   William Lamb to Dealie Gustus (col)
pg 362
    24,   Charles McDonald to Etna Neeld (col) by D.Robertson,M

26,   Robert Bennett to Margaret Elizabeth Snow by I.H.
Easlick

26,   John C. Lincoln to Pamphilla Pitts by R. Drennon JP

26,   Ross McPherson to Martha E. Cannon by A.S.Randolph JP

26,   Edmon Whitaker to Violet Grantlet (col) by A.J.
Whitaker JP

29,   Morgan Baluglass to Sarah Rosborough (col) by L.L.
Clark JP

pg 363

30,   Ned Waggoner to Margaret Parks (col) by B. Womack MG

28,   Arch Cashion to Nancy Benson by W.M.Becket JP

29,   Wm. Thomas to Caroline Dangerfield (col) by B.F.
Hudson MG

30,   Daniel Holman to Ellen Carter (col) by D. Whitaker MG

29,   Luther Sugg to Amanda Sugg (col)

29,   James Robinson to Martha Whitaker (col) by D.Whitaker,M

pg 364

29,   Wade Hampton to Maggie Buchanan (col) by L.L.Clark JP

29,   J.M.Wisdom to Emaline Land by P.B.Marsh JP

30,   W.H.Snow to Martha A. Campbell by J.H.Easlick JP

31,   Patrick Holt to Mary Green (col) by W.D.Smith JP

30,   Wm. Whitaker to Mary Keith (col) by D.Whitaker MG

31,   Neeley Bonner to Mary Todd (col)

pg 365

31,   George Bright to Emaline Moffin (col)

31,   Andy Whitaker to Ann Carter (col)

31,   Scott Diemer to Mariah Dodson (col)

1870

Jan 2,   James Perry to Mary F. Hicks by J.B.Hudson JP

2,   Jacob Sanders to Sarah Ferrin by S.H.McCord JP

5,   T.J.Shaw to Mattie Milton by D.L.Enochs JP

pg 366

9,   W.H.Hutchinson to Eliza Owen by B.F.Hudson MG

6,   J.H.Dunnary to P.J.Grimes by W.F.Zimmerman JP

5,   Nath Berry to Lucinda Bailey (col)

6,   Merdica Reed to Frances Gowen by E.M.Brown MG

6,   D.F.Moore to Fanny Epps by Rev. N.D.Crawford

6,   Henry M. Renegar to Martha Jane Taylor by J.H.Eslick JP

pg 367

9,   J.R.Brown to Amanda Silvertooth by I.J.Shaw MG

6,   George Perkins to Caroline Hester (col)

8,   Antney Nelson to Rivey Felips (col)

11,   R.H.Campbell to Mary C. Smith by T.S.Corder JP

11,   Augustus T. Ackes to Sarah E. Patterson by A.S.Sloan,M

13,   Thomas McFerrin to Hellena F. Dale by A.S.Sloan MG

pg 368

12,   George W. Heath to Mrs. Martha Ann Smotherman by D.L.
Enochs JP

11,   J.H.Cooley to Bettie Neeld by M.W.Gray MG

13,   G.W.Denham to Nancy J. Barnes by W.W.Wilson JP

27,   Henry Whitaker to Nancy Eddens (col) by D. Whitaker MG

12,   M.J.Allison to L.L.McGuire

13,   Wm. Ward to Jerusha Melton by S.M.Emmons MG

pg 369

13,   J.W.B.Davis to Sarah J. Robinson by A.Allsup JP

13,   Thomas N. Jeffers to Sarah C. Bates

13,   T.W.Childs to Sarah Johnson by N.T.Powers MG

15,   John Thermon to Clersa Dunson by W.L.Alexander JP

```
    18,    T.H.Kenedy to Amanda Allsup by A.M.Ezell MG
    20,    A.R.Hinkle to M.E.Pattie by D.L.Enochs JP
pg 370
    18,    Parks Townsend to Rosa Wilson by T.S.Corder JP
    20,    H.F.Durham to Elizabeth Smith by T.S.Corder JP
    21,    H.F.Woodard to S.F.Hobbs by D.L.Enochs
    19,    Charles Wilson to Ann McDaniel (col)
    19,    Calvin Little to Jane Dodson (col)
    20,    G.W.D.Porter to Mattie R. Beanland
pg 371
    22,    David Turner to Jane Berry (col)
    23,    Nathaniel Bradford to Amanda Dempsey by J.B.Hudson JP
    25,    Charles J. Yaunt to Martha Perry by S.H.Taylor JP
    27,    J.Y.Hobson to Hantipie Wilson by W.E.Coldwell MG
    27,    Wm. M. Armstrong to Nancy J. Cole by Rev. N.D.Crawford
    27,    Flenn Green to Easter Short (col) by D.L.Mitchell MG
pg 372
    29,    William D. Bledsoe to C.A.Moore
    30,    Thomas F. Key to Elizabeth Key by Rev. A.J.Steele
Feb 10,    Henry Bowden to Harriet Patton (col) by S.H.Taylor JP
Jan 30,    Wm. W. Langston to Mary Elizabeth Bragg by J.B.Riley JP
Feb  3,    Jerry Hutson to Julia Diemer (col)
     5,    John R. Strong to Mary Jane George by S.D.Lloyd MG
pg 373
     6,    John Thomison to Elizabeth Langston by E. Canada MG
     7,    John Warren to Mary E. Brewer by M.W.Gary MG
     7,    George B. Bates to Sarah E. Gray by T.S.Corder JP
     8,    John Young to Sarah M. Bradford by T.S.Corder JP
    10,    Joseph T. Vickers to O.C.Gillery by S. Bond JP
     9,    E.A.Berry to Susan Jane Martin
pg 374
    13,    Wm. Little to Janie Rosborough (col) by D. Whitaker
    17,    George Washington Mullins to Mary Jane Hamilton by
                                                    S. Hall JP
    17,    G.W.Lane to Sallie M. Holman
    23,    James Sublet to M.J.Bevell
    24,    George W. Martin to Elizabeth M. McClelland by W.A.Gill
    29,    Henry Berry to Mary Moore (col) by John Moore MG
pg 375
    25,    William Womack to Eliza Smith (col) by John Moore MG
    28,    John F. Tipps to Mary Dilleha by W.A.Bryan JP
    26,    M.M.Thomison to Sarah A. Benson by J.B.Riley JP
    26,    William Weaver to Scula A. Clark
Mar  4,    James Bailey to Julia McClelland (col) by John Moore MG
     2,    T.H.Clark to Sallie E. Hudson by R.M.Hagger MG
pg 276
     3,    C.M.Buchanan to Sallie Sumner by B.F.Hudson MG
     2,    N.N.Davis to Elizabeth Miller
     6,    George W. Buchanan to Emily Waggoner (col) by J.B.
                                                    Tigert MG
     9,    E.J.West to Sarah E. Whitlow by Rev. W.W.Hailey
     8,    Benjamin Couch to Palina Couch by A.S.Moore JP
     9,    R.W.Gray to Mary J. Wiseman
pg 377
    13,    E.D.Hawkins to Mary E. Gunter by J.B.Riley JP
    12,    Thomas Lamb to Ellen Henderson (col)
    15,    John Fulton to Inda Hunter (col) by D.Robertson MG
    16,    Robert S. Hereford to Bettie McCrackin by W.E.Coldwell,M
```

128

1870

17, John W. Blair to Zerilda E. Shuffield by Henry P.
Turner MG

17, W.H.Hovis to Sarah A. Hoper by S.M.Emmons MG

pg 378

15, Jacob Douglass to Caroline Renfor (col) by D.Robertson

30, John B. Love to Flora D. Pryor by H.P.Turner MG

26, William Sharp to Elizabeth Parkes (col)

27, Westley Smith to Harriet Womack (col)

Apr 1, Bailey Griffin to Martha Jane Scivally by Rev.R.M.
Stephens

4, John A. Taylor to Martha S. Crowson by W.W.Wilson JP

pg 379

3, Henry Hampton to Fanny Bonner (col) by D.Robertson,M

3, James Hill to Lousania Claresbery (col) by D.
Robertson MG

3, Edmon Dangerfield to Frances Brown (col) by D.Robertson,M

5, D.H.Durham to Nancy Jane Smith by Ezekiel Kenedy MG

4, G.W.Pickett to N.A.Walker by J.B.Riley JP

5, Harris Smith to Frances Womack (col)

pg 380

7, Jerry Askins to Mary S. Scott (col)

10, H.P.Womack to Ruth Ann Berry by W.M.Beckett JP

12, J.W.Swanner to Nancy A. Hope by W.W.Wilson JP

13, C.C.Sheppherd to Mrs. Margret A. Wells by T.S.Corder JP

May 14, Thomas McAnn to Eliza Hobbs by W.A.Bryan JP

Apr 23, Joseph Smith to Amery Wherey (col) by Elder L.L.Cole JP

pg 381

17, Wm. Buchanan to Sarah Ann Haywood by J.C.McKinney JP

28, Abraham Nelson to Westhey Kemp by W.J.Brown MG

Sep 21, Henderson Tague to Selena Panther by D.L.Enochs JP

Apr 18, Edward McBay to Sarah McCulley

19, J.J.Gambil to Martha Anderson by W.O.Price JP

23, William Bray to Susan H. Toon by S.D.Lloyd MG

pg 382

22, S.M.Gray to Casey Pylant

23, E.H.Heath to Mary P.E.Lewis

25, Ronald Carter to Dore Benson (col)

28, James Hill to Polly Price by R.H.Askins JP

28, S.P.Hamilton to Ellie Desmukes by W.M.Gray MG

May 3, Jackson Renegar to Rebecca Waddle by W.M.Gray MG

pg 383

4, W.J.Markham to Sallie E. Sumners by B.F.Hudson MG

13, H.P.Caughran to Catharine C. Fife by A.S.Randolph JP

14, Elijah Waggoner to Milley Pigg (col)

16, John Allen to Amanda Ashby (col) by G.B.McKenzie JP

17, William A. McGee to Mary J. Morris by L. Motlow JP

19, Joseph M. Marshall to Parthenia E. Davis by L.L.Cole JP

pg 384

22, J.T.McGhee to Martha E. Stubblefield by J.H.Easlick JP

25, Harrison McLaughlin to Charity Burn by J.A.Prosser JP

26, R.W.Stewart to Mary M. McCown by Hugh Parkerson JP

28, N.S.Forrester to M.A.Jackson

Jun 4, Wm. C. Boles to Sarah L. Langston by A.S.Moore JP

9, Joseph Meeks to Frances A. Baker by M.W.Gray MG

pg 385

6, Joseph Rowe to Nancy A. Fowler

6, Americus Bibb to Anna Holt (col)

9, Asbery Thompson to Nancy Jane Morrow by E.H.Brown MG

1870

      17,   John Kelly to Eliza Whit by Charles Laxton
      15,   William Oakly to Phobe C. Easlick
      19,   W.H.Merritt to Ella D. Peach by J.B.Warren MG
pg 386
      19,   F.M.Allen to M.M.Hopwood by Granville Lipscomb MG
      21,   W.A.Buchanan to Mattie S. Revis by Rev. N.D.Crawford
      23,   Henry W. Boggs to Wennie E. Hogan by J.K.Moore JP
      23,   Bud Gilbreath to Frances A. Proctor (col) by J.W.
                                                  Goodwin JP
      26,   S.M.Gray to S.M.Musgraves by John Clark JP
      28,   John Smith to M.A.McCown by W.A.Bryan JP
pg 387
      27,   S.R.Davis to Garbrell Harden by J.C.McKinney JP
Jul   6,   Jack Thornton to Dinah Hilton (col) by D.Whitaker MG
      2,   John McKeon to Elizabeth A. Little by W.O.Price JP
      2,   John Durham to R.S.Jones by J.G.Laxton
      7,   J.S.Estus to Maggie A. Martin by J.M.Groce MG
      6,   A.H.Morris to Mary J. Phillips
pg 388
      7,   R.A.Gentry to Amanda C. Murdock by B.F.Hudson MG
      10,   Wm. H. Patterson to Mary R. Jenkins by J.W.Goodwin JP
      7,   Thomas D. Sims to Ann E. Harden
      10,   F.M.Bonner to N.C.Barham by J.A.Prosser JP
      10,   A.H.Sanders to Elizabeth Taylor by G.B.McKenzie JP
      14,   P.H.Freeman to M.A.Rees by J.A.Prosser JP
pg 389
      18,   Wm. J. Bowlin to Cordelia Sanders by L.L.Cole JP
      24,   H.A.Flynn to B.J.Bland by A.S.Randolph JP
      26,   John A. Corder to Hanah E. Corder by T.S.Corder JP
      26,   E.A.Strong to Sallie Reese by M.W.Gray MG
      28,   Wm. Robertson to T.A.Noah by W.W.Wilson JP
Oct 28,   O.G.Harrison to E.A.George by R. Haggard MG
pg 390
Jul 27,   Wm. H. Talley to Sue Yowell by W.H.Dixon MG
Aug   1,   A.B.Shuffield to Nancy V. Phagan by A.S.Sloan
      3,   David L. Harris to Sarah J. Bray by J.M.Groce MG
      1,   George K. Cornwell to Martha E. Davidson
      7,   S.W.Allen to Sarah Brazier by D.L.Enochs JP
      5,   Archa Womack to Lucie Porter (col) by B.Womack MG
pg 391
      3,   W.H.Bedford to Margaret A. Campbell by J.L.Ashby JP
      7,   Wm. Smith to Lucy Smith (col) by Wiley Johnson
      3,   Thomas U. Pinkerton to Elizabeth F. Milam by R.H.Askins
      11,   Charley Scott to Fanny Bryson (col) by A.C.Martin JP
      6,   Gabriel M. Pylant to Sallie J. Sorrels by Rev.N.D.
                                                  Crawford
      7,   J.B.Dollar to Sarah Wallace by S. Hall JP
pg 392
      9,   Isham Pamplin to Mary Pamplin (col) by John Moore JP
      13,   James Shelton to Mary Gault by J.B.Riley JP
      14,   H.D.Griffis to Josephine McLemore by L.L.Cole JP
      14,   William Clark to Margarett Scott (col) by L.L.Clark
      17,   W.G.Counts to Eliza A. Pulliam by T.S.Corder JP
      18,   Richard W. Cashion to Mary E. Johnson by W.M.Beckett JP
pg 393
      18,   W.F.Carpenter to Mary E. Matlock by S.S.Cole JP
      17,   W.F.Williams to M.E.Russell
      18,   W.H.Hazelett to Mary J. Sorrells by Rev. N.D.Crawford

1870

17,	Joseph S. Burton to Louisa C. Fowler by S. Hall JP
20,	William Bates to Matilda Powers by A.S.Randolph JP
20,	G.W.Hall to Margaret E. Cranshaw

pg 394

27,	Henry Clark to Mary Burgess (col)
28,	F.M.White to Mary Jane Smith by W.S.Finley MG
30,	W.F.Locke to S.E.Stephens by D.L.Enochs JP
Sep 1,	W.A.Barnes to Sarah A. Denham by W.W.Wilson JP
1,	Pleasant Hobbs to S.G.Halbert by J.B.Tigert MG
1,	S.B.Ramsey to Sallie B. Renegar by M.R.Tucker MG

pg 395

1,	S.M.Wamack to Jane Rogers by -.C.McKinney JP
1,	Alex. Edmondson to Susan Bright (col)
7,	W.H.Stone to E. Nelson by W.E.Coldwell MG
6,	B.D.Lenard to Martha A. Smith by W.S.Findley MG
8,	John R. Muse to Mary F. Jones by J.A.Prosser JP
10,	William Goosby to Catharine Stephens by W.A.Bryan JP

pg 396

8,	J.H.Bryan to C. Oliver by D.L.Smith MG
8,	W.H.Newman to C.E.Waggoner by J.L.Ashby JP
11,	Temple Taylor to Martha J. White by J.T.Barker JP
11,	J.W.M.Short to Malinda P. Tillery by F. McGow LE
11,	Jack Dyer to Emaline Halbert (col) by Josephus Dunnigan MG
14,	J.G.Brandon to J.C.Newman by M.R.Tucker MG

pg 397

13,	Isaac Stone to Fannie Benson by J.T.Barker JP
13,	J.M.Newman to M.S.Turner
15,	Gabriel Tanner to Frances E. Bradley by L.L.Cole JP
15,	Turner Evans to Sarah Jane Greer by W.L.Alexander JP
15,	James R. Brown to Nancy Jane Warren
15,	W.H.Halbert to S.J.Beatie by J.B.Tigert MG

pg 398

15,	Richard Smith to Hannah Holman (col) by Cold. Preacher
18,	W.H.Counts to Margarett A. Lindsey by L.P.Myrick JP
18,	Thomas O. George to Mary Ann Hill by L.L.Clark JP
18,	J.A.Reeves to M.F.Burns by L.C.Butler JP
20,	John Compton to Susan Elizabeth Gunter
25,	W.H.Gibbs to Emily Jane Hamilton

pg 399

25,	W.F.Sweeney to D.C.Ramsey by W.W.Wilson JP
28,	John Wesley Speck to Eliza J. Church by J.B.Riley JP
27,	J.H.Beanland to Sallie A. Pitts by N.D.Crawford MG
28,	John Clayborn to Catharine Stonebraker (col)
Oct 2,	James D. Hampton to Frances Stovall by S.M.Emmons MG
Sep 28,	John J. Martin to Mary E. Blair

pg 400

29,	Elias Dusenbery to Jane Waggoner (col) by J.W.Smith
Oct 1,	Wm. Womack to Mary Smith (col) by Alex. J. Whitaker JP
6,	Wallace Cathy to Alcy McKay (col)
8,	Jones H.Hinton to Martha J. Towry
9,	James M. Sanders to Mat. McAfee by W.W.Wilson JP
10,	William E. Evans to Sarah E. Belle Brown

pg 401

12,	R.B.Mason to Mollie P. Garrett by James Watson
15,	W.H.Gray to Elizabeth Halbert by J.B.Tigert MG
13,	Thomas E. Dryden to B.A.Woodard by N.D.Crawford MG
13,	S.P.Hamlin to M.J.McGee by S.L.Sandford MG

1870

14,	John J. Griffin to Mary Bartlett by J.A.Prosser JP
18,	Mack Bryant to Jennie Talley (col) by John Moore

pg 402

15,	P.C.Pylant to L.C.Armstrong
19,	M.S.Shaw to Nellie Smith by F.R.McGaugh LE
18,	Reuben Thomas Redman to Margaret Carmack McEwen by T.D.Wadlow
19,	Samuel Oldham to M.E.Templeton by F.M.Ventress JP
20,	W.T.Benson to Sarah Ann Fitch by T.S.Corder JP
22,	W.R.Burton to N.R.Chapman

pg 403

26,	Jackson Reese to Milly Motlow (col) by Berry Womack
25,	John J. Gulley to Mary C. Randolph by Martin Towry MG
26,	John B. Wakefield to Mary E. Warren by M.R.Harp MG
30,	Peter Driver to Eliza Greer (col) by W.R.Moore JP
31,	Thomas Groce to Susan R. Creason by J.A.Prosser JP
29,	William Bright,Jr. to Martha Johnson (col)

pg 404

30,	Abram McGown to Hanah Burk (col) by Edmond Cockrell MG
30,	H.H.Alexander to L.A.Randolph by A.S.Sloan MG
Dec 9,	John W. Smith to Nancy Scrugg by J.G.Laxton JP
Nov 10,	Wm. R. Bedford to Ann McCullough by John W. Martin JP
9,	David Bradley to Harriet Hall (col)
10,	W.C.Goodrich to Lizzie Dollins

pg 405

13,	James J. Holman to E.D.Thompson by W.A.Bryan JP
16,	James Hatchett to Linda Jeffers
20,	B.F.Griffis to Louisa McClaren by R.H.Askins JP
20,	Dennis Fowler to Sarah Edwards by S. Bond JP
21,	J. Porter Clark to Rebecca McClain
22,	Green Womack to Elizabeth Shelton by J.T.Barker JP

pg 406

22,	George W. Ashby to Christine Collins by D.J.Nobblet JP
24,	E.M.Crawford to Mary Jane Whittington by J.B.Tigert MG
23,	Jesse N. Gill to Pamela Creason
27,	David A. Jeans to Lathie Tucker by S.D.Lloyd MG
27,	Jack Wilson to Anna Lloyd (col) by Edward Cockrell MG

1871

Feb 3,	R.A.Drennon to Martha Satterfield by A.S.Randolph JP

pg 407

1870

Nov 27,	Solomon Mason to Manda Stricklin by R.H.Askins JP
26,	Pearse Howell to Lou Goodrich (col) by John Moore
30,	Wm. R. Bledsoe to Sarah Jane Williams by G.W.R.Moore JP
Dec 1,	Joe Zimmerman to Eliza Henderson (col) by James K. Meres JP
Nov 30,	James M. Buchanan to Martha Alford by Mark H. Gray MG
Dec 1,	James P. Edwards to Bettie Warren by N.J.P--- MG

pg 408

1,	S.M.McCalister to Sarah Daniel by A.S.Randolph JP
6,	Hugh A. Dollins to Margret Armstrong by G.W.R.Moore JP
1,	Toney Farquharson to Mollie Goodrich (col)
3,	Green Neeld to Charlotte Berks (col)
6,	B.E.Forbes to Jane Brown Beanland by N.T.Powers MG
15,	John A. Taylor to Mary E. Runnels by S.D.Lloyd MG

pg 409

8,	G.A.George to N.A.Norwood by Hugh Parkinson JP
8,	C.M.Martin to M.J.Weeks by J.K.Moore JP

1870
12,   George Harbin to Frances R. Powers by J.M.Groce MG
11,   Silas M. Dodson to Martha A. Ratiken by W.A.Bryan JP
15,   Benjamin M. Blanton to Fannie E. Bray by B.F.Duggan MG
1871
Feb 18, Jefferson Neil to M.V.Davidson (col) by Lon Yowell MG
pg 410
1870
Dec 15, S.W.Bruce to Frances O. Pitts by L.L.Cole JP
15,   James H. Brown to Pheby C. Bradford
18,   G.W.White to Josephine Stanley by J.T.Barker JP
17,   J.A.Cambron to S.J.Walker by J.S.Moore JP
21,   B.M.Hopper to M.O.Hamilton by J.K.Moores JP
1871
Feb 22, Benton L. Towry to Emaline D. Land by Isaiah Hancock JP
pg 411
1870
Dec 21, William N. Lock to Sarah Durham by S.G.Laxon
21,   Hiram Dollar to Sarah Stovall
22,   S.J.Henderson to Margaret S. Smith by W.A.Bryan JP
22,   Thomas Gray to Nancy Ellen Harbin by J.M.Groce MG
22,   Harrison Edmondson to Caroline Spencer (col) by E.
                                                Cockrill MG
24,   Jack Harden to Ann Waggoner (col) by D.J.Noblett JP
pg 412
24,   George Henderson to Manerva Zimmerman (col)
24,   George Dollins to Sallie Kimes (col) by W.F.Cole JP
28,   William R. Mullins to Mary F. Nichols by L.C.Butler JP
27,   T.F.Small to M. Fannie Blake by J.B.Tigert MG
26,   Joe Wallace to Mag. Brown (col) by Joseph Stephens MG
26,   Ford Washington to Caroline McPhail (col)
pg 413
27,   B.M.McCaulley to M.L.Sheffield by A.S.Sloan MG
28,   John W. Toon to Mollie A. Mullins by A.J.Whitaker JP
27,   Bob Williamson to Julia Gammels (col)
27,   Edwin Green to Caroline Smith (col)
27,   issued: Ben Ford to Caroline Smith (col), Not properly
        found, returned Dec 28, 1870.
28,   Charles Calstore to Mary Jane Mitchell by J.K.Moores JP
pg 414
28,   Lafayette Duke to Susan McGehee
28,   Johnson Higgins to Mollie Roper (col) by D.L.Mitchell,M
1871
Jan 1, W.C.Maddox to Martha Strand by S. Bond JP
1870
Dec 31, John H. Sullivan to Caldonia Falkner by D.J.Noblett JP
30,   Dave Nicks to Patience Phelps (col)
1871
Jan 1, Benjamin Rhea to Mattie Sebastian (col) by D.J.Noblett
pg 415
2,   George Scott to Nancy Diggins (col) by Edmond Cockran,M
3,   B.L.Wright to M.M.Clift by J.M.McAfee JP
2,   George Harriston to Selia Keith (col) by Josephus, MG
16,   Wm. Newton Cates to Dilly Ann Woodard by J.S.Enochs MG
9,   Thomas P. Stewart to Sarah Jane Land by Wm. A. Gill MG
4,   Jarmon Porter to Sarah Whitaker (col)
pg 416
5,   George T. Webb to Bettie Nix by G.W.Jackson MG
5,   D.C.Boon to Mary Gordon by S.L.Sandford MG

5,   Nelson Patterson to Martha Edmondson (col) by E. Cockrill

5,   Noah Edmondson to Milly Ann Patterson (col) by E.
                                             Cockrill,M

8,   Barnett F. Allison to Rebecca C. Estes by J.M.Groce MG

8,   R.A.Thorp to M.S.Tranthram by S.M.Emmons MG

pg 417

7,   W.P.Forbes to L.E.Philpot

9,   P.C.Love to Mary Bradford by W.A.Bryan JP

8,   John A. Green to M.V.Thurmon by L.M.Jackson MG

9,   George Prosser to Amanda Harden (col)

10,   J.W.Carpenter to Elizabeth Taylor by W.W.Wilson JP

pg 418

Feb 15,   Charles Sumner to Rosanna Oliver (col) by C. Laxon MG

Jan 12,   W.C.Hall to Mary Lou Graham by Jacob Gray MG

11,   J.M.Menefee to Mattie Cast(Cost) by L.C.Butler

12,   Anderson Wagoner to Mary E. Smith

18,   Alexander Freeman to Dianna Dillingham by J.S.Ewen MG

15,   Wm. Blackburn to Mrs. Martha F. Gault by J.B.Riley JP

pg 419

17,   W.T.Gault to Catharine A. Taylor by A.B.Coleman MG

19,   Samuel Boyd to Sarah Smith by R.H.Askins JP

19,   James Caudle to Casena Raney by A.S.Randolph JP

29,   Thomas Sumners to Ann Williams by W.W.Wilson JP

19,   J.H.Landess to H. Bettie Shofner by J.E.Frost MG

24,   George H. Coble to Mary A. Sumner by S.M.Emmons MG

pg 420

22,   G.W.Arnold to Martha White by J.B.Barker JP

21,   Samuel Wilson to Cyntha Staton (col)

Feb 4,   George Sullivan to Harriet Cole (col) by C. Laxton MG

25,   Wm. Miles to Jane George by L.P.Myrick JP

Jan 25,   Green Dye to Mat. Mitchell (col)

Feb 21,   J.B.Ramsey to Julia F. White by Thomas J. McCaudle MG

pg 421

Jan 25,   E.F.Maddox to Martha McCown by W.A.Bryan JP

25,   Henry Whitaker to Fannie Ann Summers (col) by W.W.
                                            Wilson JP

27,   R.F.Waggoner to Mary C. Parks by J.L.Ashby JP

26,   Henry Hunter to Mariah Hickman (col) by J.Cephas MG

28,   Thomas C. Sullinger to Edie E. Tucker

28,   G.M.March to S.A.Gordy

pg 422

Feb 2,   George M. Riley to Margaret Moore by A.S.Sloan MG

Jan 31,   Joseph H. Kennard to Savanah McDill by A.B.Coleman MG

Feb 2,   John W. Merrett to Martha Luttrell by J.T.Barker JP

1,   W.M.McClure to Rebecca Gill

2,   Richard Allen Anderson to Nancy Ann Love by Alex.
                                            Smith MG

2,   Franklin Mitchel to Easther Whitaker (col)

pg 423

--,   J.B.Shaw to Frances C. Evans by W.A.Bryan JP

9,   Henry Hasket to Corda Commons (col) by W.A.Bryan JP

7,   J.J.Delk to Eliza Jane Kirk (King) by Rev. N.D.Crawford

6,   Henry Allen to Ellen Nelson (col)

8,   Wm. Henry Roan to Josephine Edgeman by T.J.Jones MG

16,   George Coble to Susan Virginia Freeman by S.M.Emmons,M

pg 424

9,   Robert Smith to Mary L. Hobbs by J.G.Laxon JP

9,   Walker Johnson to Amanda Sebastian (col) by F.G.Buchanan

134

14,   H.H.Smith to Josephine Buchanan (col) by A.C.Martin JP
12,   James Henry Honey to Martha J. Wicker by R.N.Bevers JP
13,   Charles Duglass to Sallie Monney (col) by A.J.
                                           Whitaker JP
15,   James Bray to Mary Ann Lively by J.T.Barker JP
pg 425
Feb 16, John J. Norman to Julia Ann Cashion by J.B.Riley JP
21,   H.C.McKinney to Mrs. Henrietta Hines by J.L.McCutchen MG
16,   C.M.Ready to Orpha Waggoner by M.R.Harp MG
17,   J.E.Broadway to Fannie Bunn
25,   Daniel Chalk to Fanny Henderson (col) by L.L.Cole JP
18,   Alson Bright to Martha Fulton (col) by A.J.Whitaker JP
pg 426
20,   Henry Burns to Magie Wright by J.A.Prosser JP
20,   Clark Howell to Amanda Conger (col)
22,   J.S.Carriger to H.A.Sullivan by John E. Ford MG
24,   Burrel Small to Susan Kimes (col) by A.J.Whitaker
23,   J.C.Pitts to Mary Fannie Forrester by M.R.Harp MG
23,   John H. Cowan to Sarah Ann Hopkins by J.K.Myers JP
pg 427
25,   J.M.Morgan to Frances Louisa Miller by J.A.Hall JP
27,   James Cole to India McKinney (col) by W.F.Cole JP
28,   Louis Crabtree to Martha Smith by J.E.Spencer JP
Mar 2, Thomas Rose to Jennie Winkler by L.M.Jackson MG
2,   E.B.Nevels to Sarah Bersheba Lucinda Smith by W.W.Wilson
2,   Wm. L. Hasty to Martha E. Bates by Rev. W.W.Hailey
pg 428
3,   Edward Fox to Julia Whitaker (col) by A.J.Whitaker JP
9,   J.A.Franklin to S.C.Stroud by John Abernathy MG
9,   Jarred S. Taylor to Mollie McLaughlin by J.B.Riley JP
9,   Wm. A. Copeland to Harriet C. Stubblefield by J.B.Riley
9,   Aleck Kimes to Hesiah Buchanan (col) by A.C.Martin JP
9,   Lonie Clark to Elizabeth Marshall (col) by A.Enloe MG
pg 429
13,   Bill Chrisman to Katie Motlow (col) by B. Womack
16,   Thomas Bledsoe to Nancy Jane Flax (col) by J.A.Prosser JP
16,   Norman Steel to Jocie Spur (col) by G.W.R.Moore JP
19,   Robert Fulton to Susan Herrington by L.P.Myrick JP
16,   Wm. A. Walker to Martha E. Land by Josiah Handcock JP
17,   Cornelius Buchanan to Caroline Gillespie (col) by D.L.
                                           Mitchell MG
pg 430
16,   James P. Stovall to Nancy N. Cashion
17,   Davis Tipps to L.A.Brown
19,   Matt Cortner to Bettie S. George by Rev.T.D.Jones
21,   Thomas Bowers to Louisa A. Pierce by J.W.Martin JP
23,   James D. Hunter to Sarah A. Golden by T.S.Corder JP
25,   William Womack to Susan Whitaker (col)
pg 431
28,   James K. Sawyers to Martha E. Evans by J.E.Spencer JP
31,   Preston Hamilton to Frances Stonebraker (col) by G.B.
                                           McKenzie JP
Apr 2, Andrew Kelso to Edith Strong (col) by E. Cockrill MG
9,   Samuel Pitts to Harriett Ann Watson (col) by S.Whitaker MG
11,   Wiley Jones to Cassa Ann Pilot by S. Cross L.D.
13,   Alexander Harbin to Mary Odom by N.J.Wells JP
pg 432
12,   R.B.Johnson to Nancy Jane Sheriff by Martin Towry MG

1871

	23,	W.W.Hobbs to Selina Pearson by Alex. Smith
	23,	William Holman to Mrs. Martha Jane Cobb by J.G.Barker
	25,	Judge Josiah Swain of Franklin County,Tenn. to Nancy Williams by J.H.Laster MG
May	1,	Zack Budgett to (first Name omitted) Sugg (col)
	2,	T.H.Fuller to Mattie Stone by N.D.Crawford MG

pg 433

	4,	W.F.Hulme to Nancy O. Smith by G.B.McKenzie JP
	4,	J.C.Stephenson to M.J.Cambron by J.B.Riley JP
	5,	A.C.Nix to Eliza Jane Hoots by A.J.Whitaker JP
	7,	John Hainey to Mary Allen by J.W.Martin JP
	8,	S.B.Garland to M.C.Bailey by A.S.Moore JP
	10,	W.F.Jarrett to Amanda White by G.W.Jackson MG

pg 434

	11,	Joel Rees to Ermine McNatt by S.L.Sanders MG
	11,	S.W.Carmack to Mattie G. Ross by M.M.Marshall MG
	14,	J.P.Thorp to R.O.Gill by W.W.Wilson JP
	22,	Charles Commons to Louisa Stone (col) by D.J.Noblett JP
	18,	James Whorton to Caroline Todd (col) by E. Cockrill MG
	20,	F.M.Cambron to M.A.Kelly by A.S.Sloan JP

pg 435

Jun	24,	J.R.Hanaway to Mahalia J. Gibson by Rev. N.D.Crawford
May	27,	G.C.Logan to Lizzie C. Parkes by J. Campbell MG
	31,	James A. Talley to M.A.Dickey by W.H.Dixon MG
	30,	L.W.Nelson to J.E.King by J.K.Moores JP
Jun	1,	Z.T.Brazier to M.E.Newman by J.L.Ashby JP
	1,	John H. Scott to Susan P. Winsett by A.S.Randolph JP

pg 436

	1,	John Branch to Josephine Landis by J.W.Martin JP
	1,	W.S.Ross to Annie H. Miller by M.M.Marshall MG
	4,	Joshua Benet to Nancy W. Sanders by J.W.Martin JP
	4,	Humphrey Walker to T.J.Bostick by J.A.Hall JP
May	1,	W.M.Blye to M.J.Daniel
Jun	8,	William Williams to Catharine Ratliff by S.L.Walker JP

pg 437

	18,	William Lazenberry to Mary M.A.Isabel by A.Enloe MG
	16,	D.S.Womack to Caladonia Blackenship by J.T.Barker JP
	17,	Brice M. Clem to Jane Maddox
	22,	George Pitts to Sarah Clark (col) by J.G.Laxon JP
	23,	W.A.Rachiells to Sarah Emma Williamson by J.W.Morton JP
	27,	Hiram Winkley to Elizabeth Baker by J.W.Martin JP

pg 438

	28,	W.H.Hamilton to C. Darnald by J.K.Moore
	29,	Joe Hampton to Mary Galaway (col) by A.B.Coleman MG
Jul	3,	James P. Moore to Anna P. Fraily
	3,	George Webb to Julia Sea (col)
	9,	J.M.Timmons to Sarah A. Evans by T.J.Shaw MG
	10,	William N. Bonner to Sarah E. Wagster

pg 439

	12,	Ervin Wright to Leann Staten (col) by J.M.McAfee Esq
	13,	James G. Fisk to Malissa C. Jones by W.A.Gill MG
	12,	L.A.Webb to Susan E. Cebring by H. Parkenson JP
	15,	Luke Flemings to Millie A. Bonner (col) by D.Whitaker,M
	15,	Dr. Richard A. McWherter to Samathia E. Dickey by by W.D.Moorehead JP
	23,	A.L.White to Ollie Campbell by James Henderson JP

pg 440

	18,	S.T.Stevenson to A.N.Wright

1871

19, James R. Rambo to Amanda McKinney by J.M.McAfee Esq
20, D.N.Gray to Maggie A. Bowers by N.B.Pearce MG
20, L.J.McCaudliss to Addie Griffis by S.L.Sanford MG
20, Wash Taylor to Emaline Edy (col) by B. Womack MG
22, Henry Isom to Meah Conger (col)

pg 441

25, George Mills to Julia Ann Holman by M.R.Harp MG
26, John Hill to Eliza Shelton by J.B.Riley JP
28, Abe McKinney to Caroline Hudson (col) by D. Whitaker MG
28, George Robertson to Lucy Clunn (col) by Bedford Greer,M
27, William Chunn to Amy Mock (col) by S. Hall JP
Aug 1, John Pitcock to Elizabeth Cashion by J.T.Barker JP

pg 442

3, Wilson Lacy to Caroline Abernathy (col) by J.W.Cooper JP
3, Thomas F. McAfee to Caldonia Gunter by W.W.Wilson JP
3, E.M.C.Dickey to Malvina F. Moorehead by G.W.Jackson MG
6, William Jones to Mary A. Mays by J.T.Barker JP
10, J.T.Gattis to Tilda Spencer by S. McElroy MG
9, J.A.Smith to Louella Brown by J.W.Martin JP

pg 443

10, George Bledsoe to Mariah Hampton (col) by L.C.Butler JP
10, Dick Harris to Tilda Hunter by S. Hall JP
9, N.M.Welch to H.C.Isom by A.C.Martin JP
12, Sam Benton to Henritta Dyer (col) by D. Whitaker MG
13, Thomas Y. Butler to Susan C. Bruce by A.A.Williamson JP
15, E.G.Burton to M.E.Cunningham by A.S.Randolph JP

pg 444

16, George E. Small to Josie Felps by S.L.Sanford MG
16, Sidney L. Diemer to S.M.Martin by W.A.Gill MG
20, M.B.Sims to Lucy Green to J.W.Holmes MG
20, A.D.Blythe to Lucy A. Merrell by G.W.R.Moore JP
21, David A. Walden to Ruthia Miller by W.D.Frailey JP
22, Moses Wagoner to Sallie E. Hodge by S. Hall JP

pg 445

26, John Henry Jackson to Caroline Wright (col) by A.C.
                                              Coleman
23, John Harris to Lizzie Scoggins by John Clark JP
24, Anthony Sugg to Lucinda Oliver (col) by J.K.Moores JP
Sep 1, George Stamps to Elvira Rigney (col) by W.D.Frailey JP
Aug 27, Thomas Swinford to Julia Noles by W.D.Moorehead JP
21, Sanford Martin to Ann Brown (col) by J.G.Laxon JP

pg 446

29, Columbus Miller to Lou Guest
29, Thomas Whitaker to Amanda Whitaker (col) by S. Hall JP
28, John D. Hunter to Elizabeth Oxoudince by A.S.Randolph JP
31, W.H.Dawson to Mary F. King
Sep 3, John Evans to Margaret Davis by N.B.Pearce MG
5, David M. Venable to Mary Susan Gibson by S. Hall JP

pg 447

6, John H. Perdue to Martha C. Brown (col)
7, J.M.Tate to M.J.Gault by A.S.Sloan
10, Green Stewart to Docia George by J.K.Moores
9, Milton Bonner to Sally Ann Marshall (col) by J.A.Prosser
10, Benjamin Wells to Susan Ann McClelland (col) by T.S.
                                              Corder JP
15, Newton Hopkins to Nancy P. Hambrick by Isaiah Hancock JP

pg 448

17, David L. Parks to Mary Ann Walker by J.W.Martin JP

1871
14, S.P.Helton to Polly Allen by J.G.Ervin MG
14, J.T.Reeves to Parmelia G. Richardson by D.J.Noblett JP
17, Samuel Jackson Purdy to Perlina Elizabeth Kennedy by
                    Jacob Gray MG
16, John P. Pruitt to Nancy Ann Key by Smith L. Walker JP
19, Thomas C. Harris to M.C.Sheriff by Martin Towry MG
pg 453 (no pages omitted just misnumbered)
20, Mathew M. Wright to Sarah E. Bryant by L.L.Cole JP
21, John T. Mason to Mary A. Young by S.L.Walker JP
20, J.L.Spray to Nancy Boyd by A.S.Randolph JP
20, G.W.Berry to Rebecca E. Berry by W.D.Moorehead JP
21, W.R.Loving to Mattie Old by C.L.Randolph MG
23, Ben Bright to Lorra Bright (col) by J.M.McAfee Esq
pg 454
22, Richard Allen, Jr. to Florence Kelso by Alex. Smith MG
Oct 5, Isaac Ferrell to Jane Merrit (col) by Wm. Cunningham
Sep 26, Isaac L. Jones to Rebecca Burns by W.A.Gill MG
27, Joseph H. Ferguson to Frances Ann Whitt by Isaac Gatlin
28, C.T.Koonce to Martha J. Fitch by S.L.Walker JP
28, John D. Green to Mary Farris by Jacob Cowan MG
pg 455
28, W.R.Carter to Henrietta Noles by W.D.Moorehead JP
28, James Bartlett to Elvira Foster by J.A.Prosser JP
30, Bonner Goodrich to Jenie Allen (col) by J.A.Barbee MG
Oct 1, M.M.Dean to Ida Neeld by W.A.Gill MG
5, Warren Guyer to Nancy Standback by L.P.Myrick JP
4, Madison Eslick to Sarah Arnold
pg 456
4, Jasper King to Mrs. Olley Ann King by Solomon Cross MG
10, Dr. Josiah W. Pearce to Vedora Ann Greer by J.B.Bryson,M
9, Woodson Douglas to Delphia Cunningham (col) by G.B.
                    McKenzie JP
10, James Whitaker to Sally Neeley (col) by D. Whitaker MG
11, C.C.McLemore to Mary D.C.Green by J.E.Frost MG
11, Crawford Woodson to Hettie Halbert (col) by B.F.Hudson,M
pg 457
12, J.N.Hobbs to M.M.Stephens
15, T.J.Richardson to Louisa Kincade by J.A.Prosser JP
12, H.L.Hampton to M.E.Jones by J.C.Stevenson MG
13, William Clark to Joanna McDonald (col)
14, Harry Coppage to Sarah Ann Hines (col) by A.C.Martin JP
Dec 31, Alexander Campbell to S.J.Vickers by A.J.Steel MG
pg 458
1868
May 6, Arthur Taylor to Lizzie Helton by Dock Robertson
Mar 5, W.W.Thompson to Jocelia Scott by J.B.Tigert MG
Jul 2, William Ratliff to Nancy Honey by J.H.Eslick JP
May 6, Charley Woodly to Martha Smith (col) by D. Robertson
1867
Dec 31, Wm. F. Haley to Amanda A. Smith by A.F.Driskill MG
1868
May 31, John Greer to Ellen Smith (col) by Hicks Warren
pg 359
1865
Mar 18, Newton Smith to Elema Graves by R.D.Hardin MG
1863
Mar 18, W.H.Gibson to Sarah Catharine Eddy by R.D.Hardin MG
1864
Mar 30, A.J.Dunn to Margaret Smith by R.D.Hardin MG

138

```
1863
Jun 25,   J.N.Gattis to E.V.Payne by J.H.Easlick JP
Sep 13,   James L. Miles to Mary Ramsey by J.H.Eslick JP
1868
Apr 22,   John Jackson to Isabella Mansfield by J.B.Hudson JP
pg 460
1864
Jan 14,   Samuel D. Brown to Margaret Brown by W.R.Waggoner JP
Feb 11,   Lodrick Robinson to Viana Hart by F. Motlow JP
1863
Dec  8,   W.E.Freeman to Susan E. Harkins by G.W.Nichols MG
Feb 27,   John Willett to Jane Hale by G.W.Nichols MG
1865
Mar 30,   S.J.Smith to May C. Smith by R.D.Harden MG
1864
Mar 24,   Isaac Mason to Sarah Roughton by R.D.Hardin MG


          MARRIAGE RECORD BOOK "C"

1871
pg 1
Oct 14,   Stephen Carter to Sarah Ann Sanders by J.W.Rawls
    15,   John M. Wright to F.A.Hurley by J.M.McAfee JP
    18,   Alfred Johnson to Jodie Hairston (col) by Joseph Stephens
    17,   Thomas Juber to Hannah Spencer (col) by Edward Cockrill
    19,   T.S.Raby to S.J.Wiles
    19,   Jordon Whitaker to Caroline Waggoner by D.J.Noblett JP
    22,   J.J.Martin to C.C.Woodard by J.R.Abernathy MG
    21,   J.T.Orrick to F.J.Hall by J.A.Prosser JP
    23,   O.G.Smith to Ella H. Smith
    26,   James Griffin to Docia Ann Bryant by J.B.Riley JP
pg 2
    26,   T.B.Daniel to Mattie J. Renfoe by D.L.Mitchell MG
    26,   G.L.Gibson to M.A.McDonald by James K. Moore JP
    26,   P.H.Smith to A.J.Thomas by N.D.Crawford MG
    26,   J.W.Griffis to Mollie Lambert by T.J.McClendles MG
    26,   M.W.Woodard to Ida Lou Hatcher by A.S.Sloan MG
    28,   James Bonner to Percy Bonner (col)
Nov  1,   Robert C. Patterson to Martha J. Durham by E. Kennedy MG
     2,   W.E.Templeton to Nannie C. Spencer by J.E.Spencer JP
    13,   J.M.Hill to Mattie A. Kinney by J.H.Eslick JP
     2,   Robert J. Small to Allice R. Shofner by J.E.Frost MG
pg 3
     1,   Henry F. Simmons to Mary E. Newman
     2,   David F. McDougal to Mary Ann Devins by W.A.Gill MG
     2,   Carrol E. Payne to Mary C.D.Radican by S. Hall JP
     2,   Wiley D. Bradford to Malissa C. Brown by T.M.Jackson MG
     7,   Samuel McKelvy, Sr. to Margaret J. Spence by J.E.
                                                   Spence JP
     7,   Garret Mansfield to Nancy Ashby by D.J.Noblett JP
     6,   Lewis Pitcock to Milly Cashion
     9,   R.M.Meek to Abigail Myers by A.C.Martin JP
     9,   James Noble to Margaret Driver (col) by J.M.McAfee JP
     9,   W.B.French to Sallie E. Summerford by N.D.Crawford MG
pg 4
     7,   A.S.Thomas, Esq to Jennie F. McKennie by M.H.Bone MG
     9,   John N. Epps to Sarah E. Cole by R.N.B---- JP
```

1871

9, W.C.Callicott to Lizie A. Solomon by S.L.Sanford MG
8, F.W.Smith to Sarah Murrah by L.L.Cole JP
12, T.T.Davidson to Mollie Hopkins by S.L.Walker JP
15, John H. Ervin to Lucinda Cooly (col) by W.D.Moorehead JP
16, David Chalk to Eveline Hairston (col) by Josephus MG
11, John Russel to Ivson Parks (col)
16, Wiley Hopkins to Mary McDougal by W.A.Gill MG
16, H.P.George to Susan A. McLaughlin by C.L.Randolph MG
pg 5
21, W.A.Woodard to L.A.Brown by J.E.Frost MG
23, P.M.Harper to Susan Rhoda Brotherton by C.Laxson MG
21, Bery Boner to Ellen Conger (col) by D. Whitaker MG
26, Burrick Merrit to Fannie Edmiston (col) by Thomas Ward MG
23, E.T.Hampton to N.V.Wright by J.B.Tigert MG
23, Alfred Johnson to Hester Ann Hamilton (col) by J. Stephens
23, Wm. N. Webb to Sallie Sullivan by D.J.Noblitt JP
30, Rufus Jones to Elizabeth Brown (col) by Rev. Edward
                                                    Cocker
27, Lucius Gentry to Sarah Gains by Rev. G.S.Stiles
Dec 1, J.J.Ervin to S.A.L.Pigg by A.S.Sloan JP
pg 6
Nov 28, James K. Raby to Laura C. Sebastain by S.L.Sanford MG
30, Mark L. Gill to Eliza Ann Langston by J.B.Riley JP
30, E.B.Summerford to Adaline Menafee by L.C.Butler JP
30, John D. McWhirter to Lizzie C. Formwalt by Rev. G.L.
                                                    Staley
Dec 7, Thomas Guyer to Mary Jane Rickey
6, James Kidd to Mrs. Ellen J. Smith by Alex. Smith MG
7, G.A.Norwood to N.A.Ellison by J.R.Abernathy MG
7, George Morrison to Eliza J. Mason
12, Josephus Owens to Sarah McDonald by S. Hall JP
11, N.S.Smith to Mary Ann J. Young by Wm. D. Frailey JP
pg 7
11, John D. Smith to Ella J. Walden by W.D.Frailey JP
10, Ned Bonner to Mary Broffett (col) by S. Hall JP
11, W.T.Hardy to F.E.Moore by A. Ensloe MG
9, Marion Grizard to Margaret Whitaker (col)
10, Newton Ratliff to Caladonia Solomon by G.W.Jackson MG
10, Wm. Hairston to Parelee Shepherd by J.T.Alexander JP
14, Wm. McKee to Martha Ann Richie by L.P.Myrick JP
13, J. Knox Moore to Annie B. Mills by I.F.Catchan MG
14, P.D.Boyce to Kate W. McKinney by M.H.Bone MG
19, J.R.Waggoner to L.A.Moore by T.J.Shaw MG
pg 8
29, Nat Fowler to Laura Davis (col) by J.G.Askins JP
21, John Massey to E.J.Nelson by F.R.McGaugh LE
21, Samuel M. Jordon to Tabithia Steed by W.A.Woods JP
25, Samuel Branch to Sallie Smith by John W. Corpier JP
21, Robert Koonce to Mary J. Stiles by W.A.Gill MG
20, Jesse M. Shelton to Sarah J. Hill
20, Robert M. Wilson to Henrietta Kirkpatrick by G.L.
                                                    Staley MG
21, Jacob Anthony to Mollie E. Sugg by J.F.Catchan MG
22, Follin Bailey to Lacy Newsom (col)
22, William Waggoner to Emily Whitaker (col)
pg 9
24, George B. Seaton to S.E.Williams by J.M.Groce MG
22, Wyatt Clemons to Martha Bonner (col) by D. Whitaker MG

1871

24, John Nelson to Selah Martin (col) by D.J.Noblitt JP
25, George Hardin to Jennie Camel (col) by D.J.Noblitt JP
27, G.W.Cowan to Jennie Crenshaw by J.W.Corpier JP
25, Dan Olliver to Ann McCrackin (col)
25, Amos Turner to Lucy Ann Robinson (col) by Ed.Cockrill
26, T.L.Daniel to Rebecca M. Clark by A. Enloe MG
28, J.E.M.Enochs to Sena Daniel by Bradley Kimbrough MG
27, John Cox to Martha Shepherd by J.T.Alexander JP

pg 10

26, James S. McCandless to F.J.Allison by J.A.Barbee MG
27, James H. Pack to Nettie Reece by J.A.Prosser JP
28, W.W.Manley to Mrs. Mary Jane Stephens by W.A.Gill MG
28, T.J.Menefee to Mary F. Pylant by Rufus Harris JP
27, George Smith to Ann Bagley (col) by E. Cockrill
28, Wm. S. Owens to Narcissa McGuire by J.W.Corpier JP
28, Pat. H. McElroy to Ellen Johnson (col) by D.Whitaker MG
29, Stewart Herd to Olla Hopkins (col) by G.B.McKenzie JP

1872

Jan 3, Logan Ray to Caldonia Morrison by J.T.Alexander JP

1871

Dec 31, Wm. M. Coble to Sarah T. McKinney by J.M.McAfee JP

pg 11

31, George Cowan to Tenny Sutton (col)

1872

Jan 1, R.A.Morrison to E.J.Connel
11, Daniel Bonner to Mary Wiley (col) by Ed. Cockrill MG
1, R.K.Paul to Annie Guy by J.C.McKinney JP
4, John Clark to Cinda Mullins (col) by J.R.Abernathy MG
4, Lewis Mullins to Sarah Bonner (col) by J.R.Abernathy MG
2, G.W.Bright to Tempy Smith (col)
3, B.A.Clark to Nancy McClain by A.S.Sloan MG
4, W.P.Bledsoe to M.A.Hampton by J.B.Tigert MG
9, T.D.Newman to Allice Wilson by A.W.Young

pg 12

4, Daniel Warren to Julia Drennon by A.S.Randolph JP
4, James Sugg to Malinda Smith (col)
4, Robert Vance to Annie Buchanan (col)
9, James A. Bramlet to Eliza V. Hill by R.P.Davis LD
7, Daniel McDougal to Vienna Ellen Land by A.L.Bates MG
8, Wm. B. Bailey to Jame Gray by J.C.McKinney JP
9, George G. Crawford to Fanny E. Kimes by J.B.Tigert MG
10, John B. Baggerly to Fannie A. Grantland by J.R.Abernathy
11, Henry Loyd to Cynthia A. Carter by W.D.Moorehead JP
11, T.M.Wilson to Margaret M. Hayes by A.S.Sloan MG

pg 13

11, G.W.Gunter to D. Adaline Williams by R.R.Davis JP
11, James D. Bowden to Nancy A. Webb by G.B.McKenzie JP
14, W.M.Shofner to Emma L. Smith by D.L.Mitchell MG
16, Robert Bright to Frances Franklin (col) by E. Cockrill
16, Elijah D. Sumners to Sarah E. Williams by S.M.Emmons,M
17, Isom Newton McCluskey to Lettie Stephens by Isiah
Hancock JP
17, Rev. B.F.Hudson to Adaline K. Sumner by J.H.S., MG
18, H.D.McAteer to E.R.Beverly by Charles Laxson MG
18, F.M.Tripp to Sarah J. Cashion by J.E.Spencer JP
21, P.A.Cline to Martha Moore by J.A.Hall JP

pg 14

21, Wm. Blankenship to Mary Jones by J.T.Barker JP

21,   Andrew Buchanan to Julia Ann Hairston (col) by W.F.
                                                Cole JP
22,   James D. Gowan to Maggie Daniel by J.G.Ervin MG
23,   W.T.Menefee to Sarah M. Summerford by L.C.Butler JP
23,   C.W.Waid to Mollie V. Morrison by N.J.Wells JP
25,   C.C.Wood to Nannie Winfred by W.D.Moorehead JP
25,   Joseph M. Patterson to Josie L. Cole by S.L.Sanford MG
25,   J.R.Badget to A.A.Alexander by M.R.Harp MG
26,   James Whorley to Nancy Parks (col) returned not properly
                                                    found
28,   James T. Rowell to Mattie Hobbs by J.G.Askins JP

pg 15

28,   Neeley Tucker to Mary Dyer by J.W.Corpier JP
30,   Archibald Cashion to E.J.Taylor by Felix G.Buchanan JP
31,   D.S.Porter to Endora Seaton by W.A.Gill MG
Feb 1,   J.A.Gunter to Manervia Owen by D.M.Hollaway JP
1,   W.F.Watson to J.R.Singleton by S. Hall JP
2,   Reuben Kelso to Delpha Murdock (col) by F.G.Buchanan JP
1,   Riley Felps to Frances Howard (col)
10,   Bozwell Butler to Julia Simms (col) by J.C.McKinney JP
8,   D.W.Holman to Fannie E. Landess by J.W.Holman MG
9,   William Wise to Martha Woodard by W.L.Rees JP

pg 16

10,   P.S.Lovett to Martha F. McAdams by N.D.Crawford MG
11,   Ephraim H. Gregory to Matilda C. Towns by Rev. W.W.Hailey
15,   J.N.Taylor to Carrie B. McClelland by W.H.Dixon MG
14,   A.O.Edwards to Elizabeth H. Pryor by G.L.Staley MG
15,   Fredrick Hill to L.C.Busby by J.B.Riley JP
15,   J.F.Smith to Nancy Jane Templeton by J.B.Riley JP
15,   Joseph N. Renegar to Martha E. Gattis by A.J.Whitaker JP
16,   Booker Reece to Susan Boon (col) by J.G.Ervin MG
18,   A.D.O.Benson to S.P.Luttrell by T.S.Corder JP
21,   Thomas Bagley to Lucy Smith (col) by Rev. Edward Cockrill

pg 17

21,   William Hall to Vicy Malear (col) by B.F.Hudson LE
21,   James Rice to Sallie Caruthers (col) by Rev.E.Cockrill
23,   Sandy Wilhoit to Mary Alsup (col)
21,   James C. Little to Nancy J. Faning by I.H.Eslick JP
27,   J.E.Bagley to Florinda J. Petty by W.L.Rees JP
Feb 27,   J.T.Smith to Mary V. Petty by W.L.Rees JP
27,   A.D.Stovall to Mary J. Riley
Mar 5,   Wm. R. Rucker to Elizabeth Searcy Smith by Alex. Smith
Feb 29,   Wm. D. Beech to Amanda M. Hall by L.L.Cole JP
29,   Dr. James A. Collett to Sallie Gattis by Rev. J.C.Mials

pg 18

Mar 7,   John Patterson to Mary Jane Williams by E. Kenedy MG
2,   Reuben Hampton to Lucy Gray (col) by W.D.Moorehead JP
4,   W.J.Haithcock to Martha Arnold by D.M.Holloway JP
2,   James W. Yarbrough to Mary E. Yarbrough by J.A.Hall
7,   W.E.Summerford to P.O.Reece by T.J.McCandless MG
7,   M.A.Mitchell to M.A.Holman by J.H.Eslick JP
14,   J.G.Franklin to S.G.Darnell by W.T.Gill MG
14,   R.W.Kelso to Martha A. Corrine by J.R.Abernathy MG
14,   J.S.Crawford to Elizabeth Pamplin by M.R.Harp MG
14,   John Whitaker to Mary Bonner (col)
17,   J.J.Goosby to Mary Malier by J.C.Stevenson MG

pg 19

17,   William Boyce to Elizabeth Hayes by J.T.Barker JP

1872

17,	Caleb Ransom to Jane Little (col) by Rev. E.Cockrill
20,	W.C.Tucker to Tennie Parks by J.A.Barbee MG
20,	George E. Barnes to Susan Collins by J.M.McAfee JP
24,	S.W.Fagan to Mary Hitt by A.L.Bates MG
24,	Robert Lane to Melvina Dyer by J.C.Alexander JP
31,	J.V.Brown to Matilda Kirkland by J.W.Martin JP
30,	C.C.Graves to Tennessee Hall
Apr 1,	George Brewer to Nancy A. Pearson by J.A.Prosser JP
4,	William Busby to Nancy Preston by J.T.Barker JP

pg 20

11,	Wm. S. Raymond to Susan McFerrin by A.S.Sloan MG
21,	Mastin Bonner to Mary Parks (col) by F.G.Buchanan JP
25,	Robert A. Stewart to T.J.Scruggs by Wm. A. Gill MG
25,	George R. Lynch to Margaret E. Bradford by L.D.Harwell
28,	Jordon Edmondson to Lou Jenkins (col) by J.G.Askins JP
May 7,	J.B.Mitchell to Ann E. Williamson by J.A.Milhous MG
2,	James Mullins to Sarah Ann Mitchell by J.W.Corpier JP
5,	S.N.Cash to Lucy Marshall by Rufus Harris JP
1,	N.C.Ward to Finette Edens by J.W.Martin JP
2,	James H. Hampton to Mary L. Reeves by J.K.Moores JP

pg 21

3,	J.W.George to Lucy A. Thomas
5,	Bob Walter to Charlotte Cole (col) by J.G.Askins JP
7,	Jasper N. Wilson to Martha A. McCallister by W.O.Price
9,	Reuben A. Bryant to Louisa J. Roberson by D.M. Callaway JP
9,	A.C.Sheriff to Frances J. Shelton by A.L.Bates MG
9,	Peter Hinebough to Virginia Higgins by N.D.Crawford,M
10,	Samuel Driver to Mary E. Hayes (col) by B.B.Bradford
13,	Peter L. Whittenburg to Vina C. Mitchell
15,	Nathaniel Troop to Mary Oliver by J.T.Barker JP
17,	Daniel B. Dodson to Manda Jane Jarret by J.C.McKinney

pg 22

19,	P.F.Patterson to S.E.Rowe by J.C.Stevenson MG
19,	Robert Pentecost to Laura McClarren (col) by J.W. Corpier JP
26,	James Rodgers to Mahala Pruitt (col) by J. Stephens MG
18,	Adam James to Betsie Chisam (col) by D. Whitaker MG
23,	Joseph Ellerson to Mrs. Sarah J. Hollaway by S.M. Emmons MG
22,	L.M.Shofner to Georgia E. Rochelle by S.L.Sanford MG
23,	Richard Routt to Kate Pierce by J.W.T.Smith MG
29,	J.T.Swann to L.C.Barnes by J.M.McAfee JP
29,	William L. Gore to Sarah E. Baxter
30,	R.A.Neeld to Frances McKinney by D.L.Mitchell MG

pg 23

30,	Wright Gillespie to Bettie Wakefield (col) by L.C. Butler JP
Jun 2,	John D. Smith to Mrs. Amanda E. Lyle by L.C.Butler JP
1,	Wm. Young Lackey to Margaret Corder
5,	Andrew J. Burns to Maggie Gilbert
6,	H.H.Talley to S.J.Murdock by W.C.Dixon MG
10,	Bartley Garrett to Fannie Smith (col) by S. Hall JP
13,	Allen Colter to Ann Goodrich (col) by T.M.Jackson
12,	John Bowden to Jane Spray by J.C.McKinney JP
13,	M.V.King to L.T.Vining by W.O.Price JP
20,	Henry R. Cooper to H.D.F.Harrington by G.B.McKenzie JP

pg 24 1872
23, Garrison King to Caroline Melton (col) by Joseph
                                        Cephus MG
24, Thomas Holman to Sallie Pamplin by W.O.Price JP
26, Charley Bagley to Sarah Simmons (col)
30, George Griffis to Kasiah Wilson (col) by J.W.Rawls JP
Jul 2, John W. Reed to Eliza J. Collins by J.M.McAfee JP
4, Smith Ray to M.E.Saunders by T.S.Corder JP
3, Thomas Diemer to Sarah J. Landess (col) by E.Cockrill
4, R.T.Fagan to Martha A. Bullard by N.J.Wells JP
4, Robert Bullard to Icy Dora Wellman by N.J.Wells JP
12, Robert Edmiston to Kate Clark (col) by E. Cockrill
pg 25
16, A.J.Tosh to S.L.Boland by A.A.Williams JP
14, Jessie Edmiston to Sarah Pruitt (col) by W.D.Moorehead
17, John Hobbs to Margaret George by A.A.Williams JP
18, John Shephard to Vicy Hollensworth by J.S.Alexander JP
22, Henry Moore to Mrs. S.E.Cox by R.R.Davis JP
21, A.J.Turner to S.J.Billians by T.J.Jones MG
25, Mack Marks to Harriet George (col) by W.F.Cole JP
26, James Campbell to Sallie Norris
28, Marion Holman to M.M.Mitchell by J.B.Riley JP
27, Nelson Whitaker to Louisa Bonner (col)
pg 26
Aug 1, Daniel Harper to Mary Ann Wilson (col) by J.F.McCutchen
1, John Stone to Amanda J. Benson by J.T.Barker JP
1, James Koonce to Ann McClelland (col) by E. Cockrill
1, George Smith to Hettie Whitaker (col)
4, James M. Lankester to Sarah E. George by A.C.Martin JP
6, R.W.Turan to A.C.Ellerson by J.R.Abernathy MG
6, Levy Talman to E.J.King by W.A.Wood JP
6, William Gully to Martha Hamby
7, R.M.Holman to Rosanna Whitaker by J.W.Holman
8, A.E.Smith to D.C.Orr by D. Tucker MG
pg 27
8, Benjamin W. Knowles to Cyntha M. Renegar by W.D.
                                        Moorehead JP
Sep 8, M.T.Cartright to Ella Thomison by S.L.Sanford MG
Aug 8, J.P.McFerrin to N.J.Sanders by A.S.Sloan MG
8, William Wicks to Elizabeth Thompson by J.T.Barker JP
8, James M. Swinford to Rena A. Daniel by A.S.Sloan MG
10, Joseph W. Burns to Sarah P. Whittington by J.B.Tigert,M
11, W.F.Watson to Lucy Anabella West by J.M.McAfee JP
12, Leander Etheridge to Ellen Damron by J.B.Riley JP
14, F.M.Smith to Martha A. Echols by A.S.Sloan MG
13, F.H.Brazier to Nannie Lee by D.M.Hollaway JP
pg 28
16, Wm. T. Green to Sarah Elizabeth Webb by Charles Kelly JP
14, Charles Gant to Martha Landess (col) by E. Cockrill MG
15, Joseph Moore to Anna Pitts by R.N.Beavers JP
15, Doak Boaz to Louiza Buntley
15, John McMullins to Ora Davis (col) by D.L.Mitchell
18, W.P.Fowler to Martha E. Harden by S. Hall JP
20, John R. Smith to Susan L.A.Walker by A.L.Bates
22, James P. Jones to Nancy E. Sanders by J.W.Rawls JP
21, J.C.McClelland to M.E.Flynt by D. Tucker MG
22, D.M.Little to Sarah Jane Taylor by J.H.Eslick JP

pg 29 1872
21,   P.C.Askins to M.N.Caughran by A.S.Sloan MG
22,   J.R.Ratley to Nancy Malissa Abbott by A.S.Randolph JP
22,   T.W.Caughran to Amanda Jane Askins by A.S.Sloan MG
22,   Simon Smith to Amanda Hague (col)
22,   James M. Hall to Martha Bradford by J.W.Rawls JP
22,   Wm. Arnold to Frances Rowland by S.M.Emmons MG
24,   Wm. Buchanan to Milley Milambes (col) by W.A.Gill MG
28,   James T. Williams to Harriet Compton by Charles Kelly JP
25,   Martin L. Dickey to Sarah Nix
29,   J.W.Dempsey to M.J.Bagwell by J.C.Stevenson MG
pg 30
29,   J.D.Ventress to Lou M. Tucker by W.A.Gill MG
31,   Peter Wadkins to Jocie Crawford (col) by Rev. Joseph
                                                    Cephus
Sep 1,   Edmond Snow to Mary E. Crabtree by A.A.Williams JP
     2,   George Baker to Cyntha A. Allen by J.T.Alexander JP
     3,   Albert Campbell to Charlotte Ragsdale by A.S.Moore JP
     5,   J.W.Smith to F.E.Martin by J.W.Rawls JP
     4,   Calvin Galloway to Lucretia Kenedy by A.B.Coleman MG
     6,   Ed. Hayes to Ella Buchanan (col) by Rev. E. Cockrill
     7,   A.W.Honea to Mary E. Slaughter by Isaac Gibb MG
     6,   Robert R. Turner to Polly Ann Hobbs
pg 31
     8,   John H. Spurlock to Martha A.E.Evans by J.W.Rawls JP
     8,   H.H.Sullivan to Jane Tool by J.K.Moore JP
    13,   Calvin A. Miles to Rebecca L. Bynum by J.T.Barker JP
     9,   J.P.Miles to Malinda Carter by A.J.Whitaker JP
    11,   J.W.Braden to E.L.Williams by D.M.Halloway JP
    13,   James Hopkins to Sarah Tabitha Simmons by W.A.Gill MG
    19,   T.J.Monks to Elizabeth Faulkner by P. Hall MG
    12,   J.F.Bland to M.E.Collins by J.W.McAfee JP
    15,   J.D.Bledsoe to S.A.E.Muse by N.D.Crawford MG
pg 32
    14,   James Whitaker to Julia McCollum (col)
    18,   Thomas N. Jeffers to Lucy A. Crawford by M.R.Harp MG
    18,   J.T.Renegar to Mary Elizabeth Neeld by W.D.Moorehead JP
    20,   Izarel Bonner to Mary Johnson (col)
    21,   T.C.Chisom to Faney Carpenter by E.H.Stedman JP
    22,   J.A.Henderson to Elizabeth A. Wilson by J.G.Askins JP
    25,   R.J.Simpson to M.H.Hammond by Rev. J.W.Haite
    24,   T.R.Moore to I.V.Smith by N.D.Crawford MG
    25,   John M. Morgan to Nancy M. Hall by S.P.Myrick JP
    26,   Alfred Woodard to Harriet Wright (col) by S.R.Stormony,M
pg 33
    29,   George C. Durham to Mary Frances Smith by S.P.Myrick JP
    29,   R.A.Holman to Lizzie Carlin by W.T.Gill MG
Oct 3,   David Jones to Anna Hathcock by J.R.Abernathy MG
     3,   James H. Moore to Nancy J. Whitaker by W.A.Wood JP
    10,   Harris Austin to Celian Robinson by B.B.Bradford JP
     8,   N.S.B.Rieves to Eliza J. Dollins by J.B.Warren MG
     8,   George Thomison to Lou Eddins (col)
    10,   W.S.Robinson to M.A.Gill by D.M.Hollaway JP
    10,   Superior Goodner to Louisa J. McCollum by J.B.Tigert MG
     9,   J.S.Woodard to Rachel Pitts
pg 34
     9,   Lewis Hopkins to Catharine Robinson (col) by D.Robertson
    11,   Landen Wood to Mirah Harber (col) by A.B.Coleman MG

145

1872 13,   B.J.Arnold to Sue Couch by J.B.Riley JP
21,   James H. Edmondson to Mary Jane Rutledge by T.M.Jackson
23,   Jacob Lewter to Martha Hayes (col) by A.B.Coleman MG
24,   Thompson Sloan to Nora Sloan by A.S.Sloan MG
24,   J.S.Bryant to Mrs. E.L.Bevels by J.K.Moores JP
24,   J.M.McAdams to C.M.Kimes by J.B.Tigert MG
27,   Wm. N. Martin to Frances A. Smith by J.R.Abernathy MG
27,   George W. Mason to Martha E. Floyd by A.S.Randolph JP

pg 35
27,   Wesley Campbell to Lucretta I. Davis by N.J.Wells JP
31,   Joel Drake to Catharine Leatherwood (col) by Rev. E. Cockrill

31,   Wiley Smart to Margaret Ann Stewart by J.Williams JP
Oct 1,   Bob McDonald to Polly Scott (col) by A.B.Coleman
31,   J.H.J.Britton to M.E.Nevels by R.R.Davis JP
Nov 30,   H.C.Whitworth to Elizabeth Brotherton by S.M.Emmons MG
6,   James Brown to Jane Pamplin (col) by S.R.Stormont MG
3,   Calvin Dollar to Caroline Hickland by S. Bond JP
2,   O.A.White to D.F.White
3,   W.F.Gordy to M.A.Hays by J.H.Rawls JP

pg 36
7,   Robert Moore to Maude Bonner (col) by S.R.Stormont MG
8,   John Kimes to L.J.McAdams by A.C.Martin JP
13,   Jarrett Whorley to Silva Farrar (col) by Balos Johnson,M
6,   James K. Moore to Mrs. Dora I. Wilson by J.B.Tigert MG
7,   Richard Coppage to Manda Jane Coppage (col) by Alex. Smith MG

7,   H.G.Gates to Margaret Daniel by T.J.Jones MG
12,   M.J.Bedwell to Sallie Donkins(Dollins) by W.F.Cole JP
12,   W.S.Gauthney to Nannie E. Newman by J.H.Alexander MG
15,   James M.D.Wilson to Maggie B.Cunningham by J.Campbell,M
14,   J.C.Brewer to Mattie Menefee by L.C.Butler JP

pg 37
14,   J.A.Clark to Catharine Phagan by H. Tarter MG
14,   John F. Cole to Mary A. Sherwood by D.L.Mitchell MG
14,   William Merritt to Mrs. Martha Moore by H. Parkinson JP
24,   Wm. Kinnells to Rosala Edmondson by A.C.Martin JP
14,   George Gully to Martha Childress by Martin Towry MG
17,   H.S.Crabtree to Mandy McWhorter by J.W.L.Smith MG
17,   Willis Holman to Mollie Barnes by J.R.Abernathy MG
19,   Lewis B. Wiley to Jocie Scott by A.S.Sloan MG
20,   Wm. P. Galloway to Martha J. Caughran by A.S.Sloan MG
20,   J.M.Fight to Fannie Lineberger by J.B.Tigert MG

pg 38
21,   W.V.Diemer to Mary S. Hastin by W.O.Price JP
21,   Taylor Compton to Fanny Murphy by D.M.Holloway JP
26,   N.G.Gatlin to S.B.McRee by J.W.W. MG
24,   Sacratees Riley to Sarah Thompson by Isaiah Hancock JP
27,   H.H.Mosely to Sallie Zimmerman by J.K.Moore JP
25,   Henry J. Smith to H.E.Williamson
26,   M.L.Kimes to S.H.Ashby by C.L.Randolph MG
26,   W.A.Malone to Mollie A. Beatie by J.B.Tigert MG
27,   Cicero Reynolds to Sarah J. Finney by D. Tucker MG
27,   W.A.Hine to Kaye K. Kelso by A.N.Cunningham DD

pg 39
27,   D.W.Byers to L.V.Petty by J.R.Abernathy MG
27,   Berrill Landess to Lucy Carty
29,   John Craig to Susan Lancaster by A.C.Martin JP

146

1872
Dec 4,   William Mason to Jane George by Martin Towry MG
     5,   D.L.Nearin to Mary Jobe by B.F.Hudson MG
     4,   John L. Kidd to Mary Jane Fullerton by A.S.Sloan MG
     5,   W.A.Reives to Mrs. Jane Wilson by J.K.Moores
     6,   J.D.R.Brashier to B.E.Nabors
     8,   John Martin to Amanda J. Spray by A.S.Randolph JP
    12,   John R. Marshall to B.J.McDaniel by J.P.O. MG
     8,   Thomas H. Ellison to Elmira McAnn by J.R.Abernathy MG
pg 40
    10,   J.W.Hudson to Mary Martha Walker by A.J.Moore JP
    12,   William A. Tate to Sarah A. Gault by A.S.Sloan MG
    14,   G.D.Wicks to A.L.Crawford
    17,   M.E.Buffalo to M.E.Turner by J.R.Abernathy MG
    20,   W.A.Dooley to Mrs. M.J.Bohannon by Rev. T.D.Jones
    22,   T.A.Harbin to Martha Ann Hardin by D. Tucker MG
    22,   Joseph Alsup to Sarah Cowan (col) by R. Davis JP
    21,   J.M.D.Elzy to Tabitha A. Dyer
    23,   Noah Cooper to Mary Killingsworth by J.T.Alexander JP
    25,   A.W.Davis to Mrs. Mary I.(J) Mitchell by J.W.Corpier JP
pg 41
    24,   John F. Ward to Mrs. Fannie V. Satterfield by J.D.Barbar
    24,   Travis D. Ashby to Nancy Jane Cunningham by C.L.
                                          Randolph MG
    24,   Ned Gregory to Pink Bonner (col)
    24,   W.H.Coleman to M.A.Boggs
1873
Aug 17,   John H. Coppage to Isabela Rossan (col) by S.C.Martin JP
1872
Dec 24,   Thomas Cason to Emily McKinney (col) by D. Whitaker MG
    25,   L.L.McCourt to E.L.A.Porter by W.A.Gill MG
    25,   Squire Broadway to Clemie Clark (col) by Alex. Britton,M
    26,   Dock King to Sarah Jane Chism (col) by Ed. Cockrill MG
    27,   Henry Bonner to Clarinda Buchanan (col) by F.G.
                                          Buchanan JP
pg 42
    26,   J.E.Holland to M.E.Cheatham by E.H.Stedman JP
1873
Jan 5,   William Bently to Mary Jane McCarver by J.R.Abernathy MG
1872
Dec 26,   Henry Blackshire to Margaret Morrison
    26,   Anthony Gaines to Manerva Buchanan (col) by Rev. J.Cephus
    29,   James Thornton to Amanda Ellen Mullins by A.A.Williams JP
1873
Mar 2,   J.W.Linton to Sarah Thomas by W.O.Price JP
1872
Dec 29,   Talton Thomas to Crecy Shuffield (col) by J.H.Smith JP
    29,   Pryor Clark to Caroline McClure (col) by B.B.Bradford JP
    29,   Andrew Barker to Vicy Todd (col) by Rev. E. Cockrill
    31,   Edmon Smith to Fannie Wadkins (col) by E.H.Stedman JP
pg 43
    31,   James Cashion to Margaret Benson by L.P.Myrick JP
1873
Jan 2,   C.L.Coleman to M.J.Rowell by J.R.Abernathy MG
     1,   J.A.Smith to Margaret J. Young
     1,   John Robinson to Julia Robinson (col) by Rev. E. Cockrill
     2,   George McCaw to Liza Clark (col) by B.F.Hudson LE
     2,   T.H.Warren to M.E.Tucker by W.R.Harp MG
     3,   Alexander Freeman to Fannie Reese

1873

3,   William F. Jeans to Caladonia Campbell
8,   M.H.Tafts to Elizabeth Satterfield by J.R.Abernathy MG
5,   Johnson Brewer to Mary Hazlewood by T.M.Jackson

pg 44

8,   Solomon C. Bledsoe to Nannie M. Vance by J.D.Barbar MG
9,   T.R.Hays to S.A.Martin by J.R.Abernathy MG
8,   James J. Bland to Mary Walton by B.B.Bradford JP
9,   Marion Bates to Loutenny Jenkins by M.R.Harp MG
9,   William Paul to Millie A. Jones
12,   John Wadkins to Vincy Patterson (col) by J.R.Abernathy,M
11,   Johnson Clark to Angeline Smith
11,   Bill Stone to Mandy Cannon (col) by D. Whitaker MG
17,   Thomas Hall to Eldonia Jackson (col) by A.C.Martin JP
15,   J.C.Reynolds to Mattie Lou Groce by F.G.Buchanan JP

pg 45

19,   John H. Perkins to Louiza I. McLean by J.W.Corpier JP
16,   J.S.Hobbs to Culpernia Leatherwood by J.R.Abernathy MG
16,   James H. Swinford to Manervy George by Silas Bruce MG
18,   David Fowler to Dinah Smith (col) by J.G.Askins JP
22,   William E. Shelton to Jaala Kelly by Jacob Gray MG
23,   James Bailey to Milly Thomison by J.B.Riley JP
23,   James M. Owen to Eliza A. Jones by T.W.Clark JP
21,   Andrew J. Chrisman to E.P.Alexander by A.N.Cunningham DD
23,   Thomas Pruitt to L. Elizabeth Henderson by S.L.Walker JP

pg 46

20,   Alfred Weeks to Ana Stone (col) by D. Whitaker MG
24,   Thomas McGee to Martha Holman (col) by H.E.Bryant MG
26,   Joseph Epps to Sallie F. Taylor by R.N.Beavers JP
26,   William T. Tanner to Catharine Bates by Rev. W.W.Hailey
25,   Charles Moore to Hailey Whitaker (col) by H.E.Bryant MG
30,   John Morrow to Lucinda Fennel (col) by Alex. Smith MG
26,   A.J.Commons to Sarah E. Clark by J.G.Askins JP
27,   William F. Moss to Jane Sanders to S.L.Walker JP
29,   W.H.Barnes to Lucinda E. Moore by F.R.McGaugh MG
30,   Lewis Murphy to Margarett Carnes (col) by J.M.McAfee JP

pg 47

30,   Benjamin Greer Corder to Ruth Raney by J.M.Groce MG
29,   William T. Holman to N.E.Hoskins by J.S.Alexander JP
29,   Henry Smith to Edy Williams (col)
30,   M.W.Webb to Mary Ann Gillams by A.J.Randolph JP
29,   Samuel Buchanan to Frances Meddearis (col)
Feb 4, J.P.Holloway to Martha A. Gatlin by Isaac Gatlin DD
6,   M.W.Carter to Martha M. Thompson by W.D.Moorehead JP
6,   John Griffis to M.E.Byers to J.R.Abernathy MG
20,   Wilson Bonner to Julia Zimmerman (col) by L.L.Cole JP
10,   James Lee to M.E.Davis by A.A.Williams

pg 48

13,   O.R.Hatcher to Mary E. Woodard by J.D.Barbee MG
13,   William Wilson to Mary Ann Cheatham by L.L.Cole JP
15,   Stephen Wood to Rhoda Woodard (col)
19,   John Murrah to Martha A. Bradley by L.L.Cole JP
20,   W.E.Hopewood to Susan V. Franklin by Isaac Gatlin DD
20,   G.W.Collins to A.E.Tuley by J.M.McAfee JP
20,   Peter Halbert to Nancy Staton (col) by J.M.McAfee JP
20,   J.F.Barnes to Isabel Josephine Moores by F.R.McGaugh,M
20,   John Harbin to Mary Jane Land by T.S.Corder JP
20,   D.M.Perkins to Mrs. Susan A. Fletcher by J.W.Holman MG

pg 49 1873

20,	W.Y.Bryan to Sarah Love by L.L.Cole JP
20,	G.M.Hicks to Frances Moore by L.L.Cole JP
23,	J.M.M.George to Mary E. Sims by J.M.Groce MG
23,	George E. Brother to Maggie E. Ray by J.S.Alexander JP
27,	Robert McDonald to Chaddy Roberson (col) by J.G.Askins JP
Mar 6,	Robert Roberson to Ella Henderson (col) by E.H.Steadman
Feb 27,	S.H.Sloan to Mrs. M.A.C.Stewart by A.S.Sloan MG
25,	J.L.Lewis to Mollie Curtis
27,	Henry Bonepart Coble to Martha Ann Huckabee by J.M. McAfee JP
27,	Solomon Cooper to Mary Vickers

pg 50

Mar 1,	Benjamin B.D.Smith to Lucy Coffie (col) by Baylor Johnson
6,	Madison N. Gillbreath to Sallie Hays
6,	R.M.McCarry to Sarah Ann Wells by A.S.Randolph JP
9,	J.M.Wright to Caladonia Bryan by E.H.Steadman JP
13,	William Hickman to Elizabeth Cheatham (col) by B.Johnson,
13,	Andrew T. Hobbs to Allie M. Hastie by A.A.Williams JP
12,	Bob Wiley to Mary Bonner (col) by Rev. E. Cockrill
19,	John Joiner to Mary Walls by John Carey JP
20,	Jake Rees to Emily Felps (col)
20,	John McElroy to Ann Buchanan by S.R.Stewart MG

pg 51

20,	Benjamin Vickers to Caroline Cowan
May 13,	Fred Land to Manerva Hughlin by W.B.M. JP
Apr 3,	Clus Grau to Narcissa Gustus (col)
3,	Peter Bright to Addie McElroy (col) by E. Cockrill MG
4,	Lewis Hailey to Elizabeth C. Gully (col) by I. Hancock JP
6,	Henry R. McClane to Mary C. Little by W.O.Price JP
20,	Robert Cunningham to I.E.Campbell by D.M.Hollaway JP
27,	Archer Robinson to Elizabeth Burks (col) by E.Cockrill MG
30,	J.W.Cole to Louella Dusenberry by T.D.Jones MG
May 2,	H.S.Rees to M.A.Pitts by A.P.Copeland MG

pg 52

18,	E.L.Jones to Sarah F. Miles by J.W.Jackson MG
22,	Martin Dunn to Martha E. Woodard by J.H.Smith JP
22,	W.H.Gibbs to A.C.Cheatham by J.B.Abernathy MG
29,	Alick Fulton to Ann Dodson (col) by Rev. J. Cephus
Jun 1,	J.M.Swanner to R.E.Wright by J.M.McAfee JP
1,	Charles T. Wicks to A.J.Davidson by S.L.Walker JP
3,	James S. Couch to Mary E. Shelton by J.T.Barker JP
4,	John Honey to Jane McAlister by E.W.Walker
10,	Starland Yowell to Jane Smith (col) by J.M.Dyer
11,	Samuel Stephens to Sallie J. McDougal by W.A.Gill MG

pg 53

11,	J.W.Hill to Oliva Emmons by D.M.Holloway JP
Jul 12,	W.M.Sanders to R.D.Jenkins by B.F.Hudson LE
Jun 15,	J.W.Wadkins to M.J.Cowan by E.H.Stedman JP
19,	W.J.Martin to Lucretia Satterfield by J.R.Abernathy
Jul 2,	Rufus Whirley to Nancy Johnson (col)
10,	J.C.Maynard to Eliza J. Hunter by J.W.Rawls JP
13,	Vance R. Mills to Virginia A. Jeffries by John Cary JP
13,	W.W.Edwards to Ann Rhoton by R.R.Davis JP
12,	N.B.Haskins to M.E.Payne
13,	J.N.W.Payne to M.H.Haskins

pg 54

15,	John Cronson to Elizabeth Hackles by J.R.Moores

1873	15,	Y. Tipps to Mrs. Sallie Hobbs by A.A.Williams JP
	20,	Thomas Hampton to Mattie Buchanan (col) by A.C.Martin JP
	20,	Willis Massey to Ann Buchanan (col) by A.C.Martin JP
	24,	Avary Hightower to Mrs. Lucy Ann Maddox by E.H. Steadman JP
	19,	James Webb to Annie Eslick (col)
	20,	Robert Rowland to Lucinda Pendergrass by R.N.Beavers JP
	24,	R.D.Palmer to Lou Pigg by B.B.Towry MG
	22,	Martin Dunaho to Mrs. Elvira Byner by J.R.Abernathy,M
	23,	E.A.Loyd to Mary A. Moore by J.B.Warren MG

pg 55

	23,	Henry Lay to Charlotte Raney (col) by E. Cockrill
	27,	E.G.Hodge to M.J.Renegar by L.L.Cole JP
	31,	Lee Nearing to Nancy Harris (col) by J.M.McAfee JP
	30,	W.B.Rosebrough to Jane Brown
Aug	2,	John R. Renegar to Mahala McClure (col) by B.B.Bradford
	2,	Jake Marbury to Elizabeth McDaniel (col) by John Cary JP
	3,	John H. Rees to M.B.Shofner by J.E.Frost MG
	5,	J.R.Rodgers to M.E.Payne by J.E.Alexander JP
	6,	Garland R. Oldfield to Sophronia A. Ford by Jacob Gray,M
	9,	Wesley Shaw to Huldy Driskell by Wm. R. Martin JP

pg 56

	14,	E.T.Leatherwood to Ann C. Rowell by J.R.Abernathy MG
	14,	Smith Woodson to Rebeca Staton (col) by J.M.McAfee JP
	17,	Reuben Hays to Jennie Alfred (col) by Frank Kimbal
	13,	J.H.Huffman to Martha M. Bussey
	21,	Harvey Ray to E.C.Wells by F.R.McGaugh
	16,	William Dyer to Nancy Denshal (col) by J.K.Moores JP
	24,	Harrison Hedgepeth to Laura Sherrill (col) by Jerry Phelps
	20,	W.P.Coleman to R.J.Coleman by John Cary JP
	21,	W.F.Carter to Fannie Watson by Henry Bryson
	25,	Samuel F. Morris to Caldonia McAdams by J.B.Warren JP

pg 57

	28,	R.K.Locker to Alice A. Ventress by N.J.Wells JP
	28,	J.J.Dunston to Missouri Norton by W.T.Gill MG
	31,	Granville Edmiston to Lucy Groce (col) by L.C.Butler JP
Sep	4,	William Duncan to Martha J. King by Wm. Buntley JP
	1,	H.J.Hathcoat to Jane Wilkins by A.S.Sloan
	4,	Willis F. McGee to Cordelia Groce by M.R.Harp MG
	4,	Berry Whitaker to Mandy Vance (col)
	8,	William Culps to Martha J. Owens by J.H.Smith JP
	5,	R.P.Clark to M.E.Clift
	6,	Willis W. Scott to Susan A. Steed by J.B.Tigert MG

pg 58

	9,	F.P.Taylor to R.A.Whitaker by Elder T.G.Miller
	8,	Samuel Miller to Mrs. Nancy Garret by B.B.Bradford JP
	9,	Wm. M. Omohundro to Frances A. McElyea by J.B.Riley JP
	11,	Arch Clark to Sallie Halbert (col) by J.M.McAfee JP
	9,	Jefferson Mitchell to Mary Ford by J.K.Moores
	11,	W.D.Strain to Susie J. Blair by A.B.Coleman
	10,	Daniel McCombs to Sophia A. Gray by A.A.Williams JP
	11,	James M. Shannon to America V. Franklin by H.P.Turner,M
	11,	Joseph Story to Frances Bass (col) by J.K.Moores JP
	11,	Y.A.G.Murphy to Ella Bedwell by W.O.Price JP

pg 59

	13,	Charles Whitaker to Lucy Whitaker (col)
	17,	W.J.Hill to Maggie Eldridge by Rev. H. Smith VDM

1873 17,   J.C.Kelso to M.A.Philpot by J.R.Abernathy MG
     18,   T.P.Payne to Patsey A. Colston by J.K.Moores JP
     18,   John Boaz to Susan R. Largin by M.R.Harp MG
     20,   John W. Jackson to Virginia C. Hester
     21,   James Hill to Maggie Williams (col) by H.E.Bryant MG
     20,   John W. Cooper to Rebecca J. Cunningham by L.P.Myrick JP
     21,   Lewis Bonner to Manda McClure (col) by H.E.Bryant MG
     25,   W.J.McAlister to Mollie T. Crawford by E.W.Walker MG
pg 60
     26,   Tonie Stone to Nancy Wicks (col) by Daniel Whitaker MG
Oct 1,   Henderson T. Barnes to M.E.Ramsey by B.F.Hudson MG
Sep 28,   James A. Boggs to Arder Hays by J.I.Alexander JP
     28,   J.F.Watt to O.C.Dickey by J.B.Tigert MG
Oct 1,   Robert M. Thorton to Nancy J. Mullins by J.W.Corpier JP
      2,   James Clark to Katie Sullivan (col) by J.M.McAfee JP
      2,   Richard Boone to Rachel Staten (col) by J.M.McAfee JP
      6,   W.J.Collier to Eliza F. Tucker by W.B.Lowry MG
      6,   J.L.West to Sarah A. McFarland
      9,   Richard Vickers to Sarah Wooden by J.G.Stephenson MG
      6,   Calvin Alexander to Elizabeth Stone (col) by L.C.Butler
pg 61
      9,   William Clemmy to Nancy Bachelor by John Cary JP
      9,   T.B.Hardin to Drusie Smith by Wm. H. Dixon MG
      9,   F.R.Moorhead to Delia Alexander by Wm. Macks MG
      9,   E.J.M.Byers to S.F.Forbes by J.R.Abernathy MG
     15,   James M. Wilson to Kate Fulton by G.W.Mitchell MG
     15,   Daniel S. Snow to L. Ann Mitchell
     15,   Jack Dyer to Fannie Wilson (col) by J.K.Moores JP
     16,   L.L.Renfroe to Mollie J. Clark by J.B.Tigert MG
     16,   Bayless Johnson to Isabella Buntley (col) by L.L.Cole
     17,   W.S.Stroud to E.J.Hodge by J.R.Abernathy MG
     18,   Cornelious Barnes to Matilda Bright (col)
pg 62
     21,   F.M.Gilliland to Malinda Stephens
     22,   E.A.Barnes to Manerva Owen by T.W.Clark JP
     22,   Zachariah Haislip to Mrs. Mary J. Richardson by W.F.Cole
     23,   James Joins to Isa A. Clark by William Buntley JP
     23,   W.C.Brown to M.E.Johnson by M.R.Harp MG
     23,   J.T.Hines to M.J.Zimmerman by J.P.Osborn
     23,   J.W.Hall to Lizzie Gordon by A.S.Sloan
     25,   William Whitaker to Sara Hill (col)
Nov 2,   William Watt to Lucinda McDonald (col) by WM.R.Martin JP
Oct 28,   Charles Waddle to Lou May Gray by W.T.Gill MG
pg 63
     29,   Matthew Nipple to Rhoda Jackson by J.T.Barker JP
     30,   Thomas W. Rowell to Martha L. Jones by Wm. A. Gill MG
Nov 12,   W.P.Abernathy to Alice Petty by A.A.Allison MG
      1,   Stephen Massey to E.M.Buchanan (col) by David Whitaker
      1,   David Baxley to Caroline Clark (col) by David Whitaker
      2,   R.A.Rees to Ella May Whitaker by S.L.Sanford MG
      6,   William Wright to Martha Smith by J.C.Stevenson MG
      6,   Rufus M. Smith to Fannie A. Wright by J.C.Stevenson MG
      5,   Joseph M. McMullen to Josephine A. Polk by J.B.Moores JP
      6,   S.R.George to C.F.Sanders by A.S.Randolph JP
pg 64
      7,   Pat Buchanan to Josie Bright (col)
      9,   W.A.Martin to Mollie E. Smith by J.R.Abernathy MG
      8,   Thomas M. Harkins to Caledonia Simms by J.M.Dyer JP

1873 9,   M.H.Troup to Ada Woodard by J.M.McAfee JP
     10,   Jacob Lynn to Sarah Torsh
     29,   J.D.Yarbrough to Mary A. Ringo by Jacob Gray MG
     11,   James C. Lively to Sarah C. Claunch by J.P.Funk LD
     13,   Andrew J. Rees to Margaret A. Armstrong by D.L.Mitchell
     16,   Andy Smart to Polly Hobbs by J.K.Moores
     22,   Sandy Myers to Lydia McCrackens (col) by J.W.Corpier JP
pg 65
     18,   W.E.Woods to Belle Feeney by T.C.Miller,Elder
     20,   W.P.McCounts to Susan Williamson by J.M.Dyer JP
     20,   Nick Halbert to Lucy Ann Poindexter (col) by B.F.Hudson,M
     22,   Norris Henderson to Rebecca McKinney (col) by David
                                                        Whitaker
     22,   Eli Dunman to Caroline Miles by L.L.Cole JP
     26,   George N. Parks to E.M.Todd by B.W.McDonald MG
     27,   H.C.Smith to Harriet C. Tillery by J.H.Smith JP
     26,   Theo. Smith to Maggie Anderson by J.I.Alexander JP
     27,   Wm. Ashworth, Jr. to Mollie L. Templeton by W.A.Gill MG
     27,   Eli Story to Sarah Riddle by A.S.Randolph JP
pg 66
     27,   J.J.Brandon to Maggie Edmondson by A.P.Copeland MG
     30,   Alexander George to Mattie Harbin by J.W.L.Smith MG
Dec 7,   John Sweeney to Mrs. Margaret Smith by Eld. B.L.Thorn-
                                                            berry
     18,   L.C.Braden to N.A.Cole by D.M.Halloway JP
     10,   James F. Byers to Lizzie B. Baldridge by A.A.Allison MG
     11,   Caesar Pitts to Sucky Bonner (col) by S.R.Stonmont MG
     11,   Wm. B. Thompson to Sue A. Williams by Felix G.Buchanan JP
     14,   John J. Davidson to Josie Bradford by B.B.Bradford JP
     16,   William B. Nicks to Lizzie J. Gray by A.S.Sloan
     18,   J.N.Marcum to F.A.Emmons by B.F.Hudson MG
pg 67
     18,   John Green to Oma Malier (col) by D.M.Halloway JP
     18,   J.J.Maddox to Mattie Sherrell by J.R.Abernathy MG
     18,   W.S.Taylor to Martha A. Stubblefield by W.D.Moorehead Esq
     18,   A.J.McClain to Cordelia Alexander by A. VanHooser MG
     18,   John Allen to Mollie Griswell (col) by Lewis Neil
     25,   J.A.Christian to N.E.Smith by R.B.Riley JP
     20,   George Askins to Harriett Perkins (col) by S.R.Stonmont,M
     25,   Caesar Henderson to Caroline Clark (col) by A.B.Coleman
     21,   Fountain Halbert to Tooney Blake (col) by A.C.Martin JP
     22,   Rufus Massey to Adeline Swanner (col) by Jessey Philips
pg 68
     24,   John K. Hopwood to Jennie Martin by J.R.Abernathy MG
     28,   L.J.Anderson to Sallie Maddox by J.R.Abernathy MG
     24,   Humphreys Tug to Dora Blake (col)
     26,   H.H.Smith to Luticia March (col) by J.A.C.Martin JP
     24,   Mose Bonner to Mary J. Robinson (col) by Rev. Moses T.Wair
     25,   J.H.Surber to M.A.Pitts by A.P.Copeland MG
     25,   A.E.Brown to S.A.E.Ray
     28,   W.P.Worley to N.A.Alsup by J.M.McAfee JP
     28,   J.L.Mosley to M.J.Cothran by J.C.Stephenson MG
     28,   J.M.Strason to Mary J. McKinney by J.S.S.Smith JP
pg 69
     28,   Barney Hall to Isabella Grizard (col) by John M. Dickey
     30,   Robert W. Whitaker to HarrietHallum (col)
1874
Jan 1,   J.P.Vickers to Elizabeth Roper by J.R.Abernathy MG

152

```
1873
Dec 30,   David Carnes to Elizabeth Cathey (col) by J.M.McAfee JP
     31,   William Hensley to Belle Hines (col)
1874
Jan  1,   Jarred R. Taylor to Mollie A. Parkes by N.T.Powers
      1,   J.J.Gully to Martha J. Price by D.L.Mitchell MG
     --,   Dan Prosser to Candess Cox (col)
      3,   Lanson H.W.McAfee to Martha C. King
      3,   Charles Harrison to Mollie Brent (col)
      8,   Aleck Johnson to Susan Carty (col) by J.R.Marrs JP
      8,   John McCord to Catharine Bright (col) by H.E.Bryan
pg 70
      7,   G.W.Owen to Lou Drake (col)
      8,   Andrew B. Deford to Amanda Griffis by H.P.Copeland MG
      8,   W.F.Loyd to N.A.Nix by A.J.Whitaker JP
      8,   George Whitaker to Martha J. Scott by S.R.Stormont MG
     10,   J.C.Patton to Sarah E. McAdams
     13,   M.W.Parton to P.A.Wright by S.M.Emmons MG
     16,   William Pool to Gerimiah Maddox by J.R.Abernathy MG
     14,   J.W.Barnett to Julia C. Gorden by T.B.Fisher MG
     15,   Cicero Allen to Lily Bonner (col)
     15,   William Evans to Nancy Floyd by A.S.Randolph JP
pg 71
     16,   George McDonald to Mahala Dotson (col) by Barless
                                                     Johnson MG
     17,   Lewis Stone to Lou Thomison (col) by D. Whitaker
     19,   S.P.Carroll to Martha J. Willoughby by M.R.Harp MG
     22,   C.L.Clark to Susan E. Smith by Elder John Short
     19,   J.W.Stone to Mollie E. Robinson by Rev. N.D.Crawford
     20,   Aleck Meeks to Elizabeth McWhirter by J.W.L.Smith MG
     22,   G.W.Smith to M.E.Hale by W. Buntley JP
     22,   Wm. L. Rhodes to Rebecca Fortenbury by A.A.Allison MG
     23,   William J. Moore to Aratha McGee by M.R.Harp MG
     23,   James Luttrell to Mollie Wolaver by B.B.Bradford JP
pg 72
     25,   Cleyborn Dye to Lizzie Moore (col) by H.E.Bryant MG
     25,   Daniel March to Sarah Goodwin (col) by T.W.Clark JP
     27,   George Landenberger to N.E.Outon by E.L.Jones LD
     29,   B.M.McClusky to Alenia W. Jones by J. Hancock JP
     29,   Joe Whitaker to Eliza Hamilton (col) by D.M.Holoway JP
     29,   Adam C. Tallent to E.T.Locker by S.L.Walker JP
Feb  1,   Alexander Scoggins to C.A.F.Robinson by W.R.Martin
Jan 31,   Henry Cruse to Amy Pryor (col) by J.L.Jackson
Feb  5,   J.W.Mooney to S.E.Young by A.C.Martin JP
     14,   Joe Smith to Julia Simmons (col) by L.L.Cole JP
pg 73
      6,   Levy Halbert to Eve Palmer (col) by B.F.Hudson MG
     10,   R.H.Anderson to Sarah E. Kidd by A.S.Sloan
     12,   S.L.Reager to Mrs. Henrietta C. Gilliam by J.D.Floyd
     11,   William Boone to Lucy Sively (col) by B.F.Hudson MG
     12,   James S. Hollaway to Margaret Jane Roper by J.R.
                                                     Abernathy MG
     15,   Wm. E. Sexton to Louiza Maynard by J.H.Smith JP
     12,   Henry Desmukes to Belle Hickman (col) by S.R.Stormont MG
     12,   G.W.Davis to Mrs. Mat Sublett by J. Hancock
     15,   Henry Hill to Mrs. Nancy E. Cannon by J.S.Waddle
     18,   Marcus Bowlin to Nancy A. Pearson by S.M.Emmons MG
```

pg 74   1874

19,	J.H.Rich to Bettie George by A.A.Williams JP
20,	J.B.Pitts to C.T.Reese
25,	L.J.Phillips to Mary E. Merrell by Isaac Gatlin MG
25,	Christian Groth to Emily Phillips by Isaac Gatlin MG
24,	J.W.M.Wakefield to M.O.Woodard by J.R.Abernathy MG
Mar 1,	J.R.P.Buchanan to Amanda McCollum (col) by Eld. J.J. Short
Feb 26,	Clabe Griffis to Polly Grader (col) by S.R.Stormont MG
26,	J.W.Crane to Mattie E. Lane by William Buntley JP
Mar 8,	Morgan Scott to Lucretia Fanning (col) by W.D.Moorehead
3,	Silas Baker to Sarah Desmukes (col) by S.R.Stormont MG

pg 75

3,	Abe McGaw to Jennie Goodrich (col) by G.L.Jackson
9,	W.L.Metcalf to Harriett A. Harris by L.P.Myrick JP
12,	Robert F. Childers to Lizzie Bland by Felix G. McGaugh,M
12,	Abner Sebastian to Matilda Gregory (col) by H.E.Bryant,M
10,	Calvin Henderson to Ann Barnes (col)
15,	John P. Holman to Mrs. Sarah E. McDonegal by James Henderson JP
19,	James E. Runnels to M.J.Brady by J.H.Rawls
22,	William Gregory to Mary Bright (col) by Felix G. Buchanan JP
22,	J.A.Little to Elmira Hamblin by J.S.Waddle JP
25,	Charles Hatcher to Susan Todd (col) by G.L.Jackson

pg 76

26,	John Woodson to Manerva Cathey (col) by B.F.Hudson MG
26,	Thomas Clark to Mrs. Millie Ray by N.J.Wells JP
29,	James C. McCollum to Caroline Jester by A.A.Allison MG
31,	James Henderson, Esq to Mrs. Isabella Howard by S.M. Walker JP
Apr 2,	John H. Jackson to Sallie Scott (col) by S.R.Stormont MG
2,	J.B.Foster to S.A.Hudson
5,	Tilman Bates to Lou Phillips by Rev. M.R.Tucker
5,	Bob Bonner to Rebecca Wilson (col) by J.W.Corpier JP
9,	Robert Scott to Florina Marshall (col) by A.B.Coleman
12,	Sam Halbert to Hanah A. Stephens (col) by J.M.McAfee JP

pg 77

16,	George K. Turner to Elizabeth Sergent by B.F.Hudson MG
20,	J.W.Trantham to Georgia Ann Parks by J.M.McAfee JP
17,	William Howell to Rebecca Campbell (col) by D. Whitaker,M
24,	Preston Riggs to Hettie Bonner (col) by H.E.Bryant MG
24,	Thomas Powell to Martha A. Thorton by Samuel Bond JP
24,	W.L.Stewart to Mrs. Orpha Ware by I.J.Towry JP
29,	R.F.Laws to J.A.Smith by William Buntley JP
29,	S.P.Hamilton to Josie R. Pitts by Elder G.A.Massey
30,	J.C.Satterfield to O.J.Woodard by W.R.Martin JP
May 2,	Ephraim Greer to Jane Griffis (col) by A.S.C.Bishop MG

pg 78

1,	J.W.Hobbs to Amanda A. Milliken by W.B.Towery MG
7,	J.J.Sullivan to Fannie McGee by W.F.Cole JP
9,	Sterlin Stone to Juda Moore (col) by J.W.Corpier JP
16,	Rufus Felps to Villa Holman (col) by H.E.Bryan MG
13,	Thomas S. Caldwell to Mary A. Cooper (returned, not executed, by J. Gill, Clerk.)
13,	E.M.Johnson to Mollie Alexander by T.J.Shaw MG
14,	James W. Maney to S.G.Campbell
24,	James Robertson to Susan Clark by T.M.Jackson

1874	31,	John Dosier to Amanda Wilson (col) by D.M.Holloway JP
	30,	Mat Johnson to Rina Maddox by J.R.Abernathy MG
pg 79		
	30,	Thomas Moore to Ella Dusenbery (col)
Jun	2,	Godwin Castleman to Lovenia E. Brents
	4,	J.W.McCullough to Mrs. Mary L. Pitts by J.B.Muse
	9,	N.A.Stale to A.E.Damron
	10,	James Lock to Lizzie Hill by N.J.Wells
	10,	Frank W. Carter to Susie J. Morgan by T.B.Fisher MG
	11,	J.W.Wheeler to Hettie S. Hopkins by A.J.Childress JP
	20,	Andy Buchanan to Sophia Norris (col)
	21,	J.A.Briscal to Mary E. Sullivan by Alexander Smith
Jul	13,	Joseph W. Johnson to Sarah Williams (col)
pg 80		
	5,	Pleasant Moore to Sarah Evans (col) by J.M.Dyer JP
Jun	24,	F.M.Jones to Mrs. Betsey Smith by J.R.Abernathy MG
	28,	Warner L. Morgan to Susan E. Orr by P. Hall
	30,	J.F.Payne to Mary A. Land by N.J.Wells JP
Jul	2,	Richard Hall to Mrs. Mary A. Cook by J.B.Riley JP
	12,	Alex. Patterson to Violet Douthat (col) by J.W.Corpier
	8,	Robert Steelman to Elizabeth Northcut by W. Buntley JP
	7,	C.G.Ramsey to Rosanna Ross by Charles Laxon
	12,	John Campbell to Sarah Morrison by J.K.Moore JP
	12,	J.F.Bledsoe to Susan A. Gunter by B.F.Hudson MG
pg 81		
	16,	George Creason to Prudence E. Faulkner by Wm.Buntley JP
	16,	R.A.Wagster to Nannie R. Foster
	19,	Allen G. Harrison to Phillis McDill (col) by A.S. Randolph JP
	18,	William Irvin to Amanda Gray (col)
	19,	Henry Haywood to Caroline Douglass (col) by J.L. Jackson MG
	22,	Zachary Taylor to Mary Pauline Whitfield by Rev. N.D. Crawford
	26,	R.A.Posey to Mattie A. Eaks by H.T.Childs
Aug	6,	Dan Robertson to Jane Henderson (col) by J.R.Abernathy
	1,	George W. Simms to Martha Ann Jones by Isaiah Hancock JP
	2,	T.J.Gill to M.V.Stewart by D.M.Holloway JP
pg 82		no page 82
pg 83		
Nov	2,	Ned Savier to Mary Whitaker (col) by A.J.Whitaker JP
Aug	4,	Jasper Buffalo to Elmira Malissa Hardin by T.W.Clark JP
	4,	Harry Landess to Mary Gracy (col)
	6,	M.A.Melson to Martha E. Holt by N.J.Wells JP
	6,	John W. McKinney to Sarah E. Bringar by J.W.Corpier JP
	9,	Willis Harrison to Lucy Allison (col) by J.M.McAfee JP
	9,	Cullin Campbell to Margaret Webb by J.M.Dickey JP
	9,	G.W.Brown to America Parker by M.R.Harp MG
	11,	James P. McGee to Sallie Pitts by J.B.Muse
	13,	William Andrew to Martha E. Lively by Hugh Parkinson JP
pg 84		
Sep	8,	William Christopher to Roda J. Davis by J.M.Dyer JP
	10,	James M. McNabb to Mollie Graham by A.A.Williams JP
	10,	James J. Smith to Mollie Hague by A. VanHooser MG
	10,	A.M.Hampton to Mollie Gant by Rev. J.B.Tigert
	10,	T.C.Largen to Mary Thomison by W.R.Harp MG
	15,	W.M.Houze to Icey Gill by D.M.Holloway JP
	13,	H.R.Williams to Frances A. Arnold by M.E.Carter JP

1874	17,	William Parks to Sarah Cashion by A. VanHooser MG
	17,	Thomas S. Caldwell to Mrs. M.A.Cooper
	20,	J.F.Tumms to Louisa Capps by B.B.Bradford JP

pg 85

28,	Giles Cavet to Eliza Harris (col) by M.R.Tucker MG
22,	Jasper Crumbley to Sarah Mason by D.D.Smith MG
22,	John Walker to Martha C. B------
24,	M.S.Seaton to Sarah F. Renegar by P. Hall
24,	M.C.Renegar to Emma Russell by J.K.Moore JP
24,	Alfred Hathcock to Dorah Griffis by J.W.Rawls JP
25,	Tom Shull to Manurvy Harris (col) by F.L.Ezell JP
27,	N. Hampton to Harriet Fowler (col) by H. Dunlap MG
Oct 1,	Thomas Davis to Margaret Bray by S.L.Walker JP
Sep 28,	John C. Walker to Sarah J. Tafts by J.K.Moores JP

pg 86

28,	Franklin Gautney to Sophronia Harrelson by Rev. B.T.King
29,	Robert L. Moore to Lucy F. Shofner by T.J.Shaw MG
Oct 1,	James T. Moore to Mary E. Crawford by Eld. G.A.Morning
1,	Brown Pinkerton to Sallie Armstrong by J.R.Rawls JP
3,	Reuben Thomison to Ann Higgins (col) by D. Whitaker MG
6,	John J.W.Rozell to Mary S. Beverly by D.D.Smith MG
26,	George Beaver to Polly Carty (col) by Alex. Smith MG
15,	L.S.Pitman to Sarah Pitman by J.R.Abernathy
15,	William M.L.A.Joins to B.C.A.M.Bradlie by J.T.Barker JP
12,	B.J.Myers to Sue Brown

pg 87

14,	James B. Morgan to Mary McElroy by J.B.Tigert MG
19,	James H. Williams to Martha L. Arnold by Rev. M.R.Tucker
22,	Zachariah C. Ivie to Mary J. Stephenson by S.L.Walker JP
21,	J.P.Thompson to Ella DeHaven by A.S.Sloan
21,	D.F.Myers to Ophelia E. Pitts by Silas W. Bruce MG
22,	Randol Perkins to Linda Hamilton (col) by J.K.Moores
22,	D.S.Clark to Hattie A. Kimes by J.B.Tigert MG
22,	W.A.Morrison to Mary Gilbert
22,	G.W.Winds to Fannie Brown (col) by L.C.Butler JP
25,	R.E.Sumners to Lula Walker by John Clark JP

pg 88

25,	J.W.McLemore to S.B.Smith by J.R.Abernathy
24,	Jas Martin to Lucinda Lictnum (col)
27,	A.E.Brown to Mary Wilson by M.R.Harp MG
31,	Samuel Hampton to Laura Webb (col) by J.K.Moores JP
29,	Lemuel Smith to Bettie Dyer by J.K.Moores JP
29,	James J. Holman to Julia Norman by J.T.Barker JP
30,	Wm. J. Brown to Martha J. Myers by M.R.Harp MG
29,	D.G.Bradford to Martha L. Fitch by T.S.Corder JP
29,	James McCollum to Amilda Beanland (col) by H.C.Bryant MG
29,	Charley Bell to Louiza Miles by E.L.Jones MG

pg 89

30,	John Sebastian to Harriet Moore (col)
Nov 4,	G.C.Chesser to Sarah D. Ray by B.F.Hudson MG
4,	John F. Luttrell to Rhoda E. Welch by J.T.Barker JP
4,	Jack Boyd to M.A.Monks by A.J.Childress JP
5,	Thomas J. Pitts to Anna Isom by Elder J.G.Woods
5,	J.E.Brown to Abigail Burton by E.W.Walker
12,	James O. Pickett to Josephine Cambron by A.J.Tant MG
12,	H.C.Duff to Rebecca Cunningham
12,	W.H.Ashby to America Whitaker (col) by S. Henderson
12,	George Bradshaw to Nannie Carter by W.A.Gill MG

pg 90   1874

15, J.T.King to Merriah Browning by J.R.Abernathy MG
14, John Jean to Sarah Neeld by S.D.Loyd MG
15, J.K.Mullins to Mrs. Matilda Ross by A.A.Williams JP
15, S.J.Millerford to Arlenia Braden by D.M.Holloway JP
15, John Hobbs to Lizie Crawley by F.L.Ezell JP
17, J.D.Williamson to Mattie C. Neely by J.B.Tigert MG
18, Jerry Brown to Angaline Halbert (col) by B.F.Hudson MG
19, James A. Frame to Sarah E. Davis by J.R.Abernathy MG
29, A.T.Davis to Martha L. Frame by J.R.Abernathy MG
19, A.S.Fite to Mrs. S.A.Childs by John J. Short, Elder

pg 91

25, John M. Davis to Mary S. Webb by Rev. A.J.Steele
25, William A. Walker to Mary V. Williamson by Rev. A.J.
                                                    Steele
24, Michell Smith to Mariah Greer (col) by D.L.Mitchell MG
24, Rev. David Tucker to Fannie A. Myrick by Rev. J.C.Mials
26, Wm. B. Crawford to Mary Ashworth by Smith L. Walker JP
26, Arthur F. Giles to L.T.Poindexter by N.P.Carter, Judge
27, John Malone to Tennie McCown by J.R.Abernathy MG
26, George Vaughan to Loutisha Robertson (col) by Harry
                                                 Dunlap MG

Dec 2, Perry Reese to Dona Whitaker (col)
pg 92

3,   M.M.Cass to M.M.Troop by L.C.Butler JP
3,   J.W.Turner to Martha J. Moyers by T.J.Jones MG
3,   Thomas Burks to Mollie Buchanan (col) by Caleb Thomas
6,   J.T.Winsett to Lou King by J.C.Elliott MG
6,   T.W.Harrison to M.E.Barnes by T.W.Clark JP
10, J.G.Pearson to M.E.Detson by J.F.Baxter JP
8,   A.P.Street to Josie Webb by Felix G. Buchanan JP
8,   James J. Mapp to Tennie L. Anderson by J.P.Smith JP
10, Lewis Lovelady to Mary Greer (col) by D. Whitaker MG
10, E.Y.McGregory to E.V.King by T.J.Towery JP

pg 93

9,   Robert W. Stewart to Mary E. Good by J.B.Muse
10, Ross Conger to Lou Isham (col)
10, Alfred Bonner to Delcie Ashby (col)
15, J.W.Rives to Virgie E.J.Hamlin by E.W.Walker MG
10, William March to Mary Mathews (col) by A. Smith MG
13, W.A.Curtis to E.J.Trantham by A.A.Williams JP
16, M.R.Hill to E.J.Bostick by David Jacks
15, Isaac Neeld to Adeline Sullenger by G.W.Jackson MG
16, Perry Yeates to Olla Whitaker (col)
17, James E. Bowlin to Anna Washburn

pg 94

17, L.A.Smith to T.J.Bledsoe by B.F.Hudson MG
17, John A. Moore to Ezella J. Buchanan by J.B.Tigert MG
17, Thomas J. White to V.C.Stone
20, James C. Walker to N.M.Quick by A.S.Moore JP
24, Dr. Ben S. Stone to Violet A. Sherrell by J.B.Anderson,M
22, R.D.Thorton to Mollie E. Kimes by J.B.Tigert MG
23, J.R.Childers to Sallie H. Whitaker by G.W.Carmichael,M
23, Thomas B. Reese to Mary J. Muse
24, Hard Smith to AlliceMcYearin (col) by A. Smith MG
24, S.H.McDill to Emma C. Taylor by A.B.Coleman

pg 95

24, John L. Washburn to Louiza Templeton by W.A.Gill MG

```
1874  25,   John Killmartin to Mattie Corpier by J.W.Rawles JP
      28,   Thomas J. Roden to Rebecca J. Abbot by J.W.McAfee JP
      28,   Isaac Cowley to Nancy Taylor (col)
      29,   Ben Olds to Harriet Wicks (col) by Caleb Thomas MG
      30,   William Snoddy to Fannie Clark (col)
      30,   Robert Robertson to Jennie Clark (col)
      30,   W.P.Paysinger to Eliza A. Roper by J.H.Smith JP
      31,   J.W.Foster, Jr. to Sallie Morrison by L.C.Butler JP
      30,   Ben Farrar to Mat Jones (col) by Caleb Thomas MG
pg 96
      31,   G.F.Isom to N.C.Barnes by F.R.McGaugh MG
      31,   Campbell Harris to Mattie Hobbs (col) by C. Thomas MG
      31,   P.T.Baker to S.A.Baker by J.S.Waddle JP
1875
Jan   3,   C.A.Rozell to Elizabeth Mullins by Charles Laxson
      2,   S.A.Ramsey to E.C.Campbell by G.W.Jackson
      2,   William Parks to Narcissa Thomison (col) by D.Whitaker,M
      2,   Hiram Perkins to Catharine Henderson
      5,   James H. Griffis to S.M.Clonch by N.J.Wells JP
      7,   J.R.McGee to M.E.Waggoner by S.L.Sanford MG
      7,   P.M.Bland to M.V.Jones by H.T.Childs JP
pg 97
      7,   Jo Childs to Flora Proctor (col) by S.R.Stormont MG
      7,   Ed Johnson to Lou Presley (col) by C. Thomas MG
      7,   John L. Buchanan to Mattie McElroy by Rev. J.B.Tigert
     10,   Isah Moody to Cornelia McDonald (col) by W.B.Martin JP
      7,   N.J.Sorrells to E.H.Armstrong by Rev. N.D.Crawford
      7,   James C. George to Emma C. Pinkerton by W.A.Gill MG
      7,   William Bright to Martha A. Ragins (col) by C. Thomas MG
     11,   Benjamin Snowden to Louisa Bagley (col) by C. Thomas MG
     14,   Jack Kercheval to Amanda Lamb (col) by A. Fulton MG
     19,   W.S.Smith to Mary E. Maddox by J.R.Abernathy MG
pg 98
     17,   R.M.Harrison to E.L.Jones by B.F.Hudson MG
     22,   James M. Copeland to Mattie Bray by J.T.Barker JP
     21,   W.M.Franklin to Amanda Renegar by G.M.Jackson MG
     20,   Abraham Conner to Claracy Newsom by M.F.Cole JP
     21,   Ennis Hill to Lou Clark (col)
     21,   W.G.Edmiston to Caldonia Thompson by John Cary JP
     24,   J.E.Brown to Mrs. M.J.Ashby by M.R.Harp MG
     25,   Taylor Kilpatrick to Emma Corn
     26,   J.W.Weaver to Sallie McMullin by D.M.Holloway JP
     26,   John W. Street to Mattie Reese by W.J.Collier
pg 99
     28,   J.W.Hourd to Mary Jackson by H.E.Bryant MG
Feb   4,   James Smith to Mrs. Eveline Brooks by T.M.Barnett JP
     10,   Leroy Williams to Martha Sumner by B.B.Bradford JP
      4,   Eliga Bonner to America Perkins (col) by S.R.Stormont MG
      4,   John Maddox to Mrs. Eliza J. Fox by L.L.Cole JP
      4,   Rufus Wells to Melinda Sparkman by N.J.Wells JP
      7,   Louis D. Williams to Loucinda Hogan by J.M.McAfee JP
      9,   Thomas Jones to Ann Cannon (col) by H.E.Bryant MG
      9,   James M. McFerrin to Minerva McFerrin by J.B.Muse
pg 100
      9,   John Holman to Emma Ashby (col) by H.E.Bryant MG
     11,   A.J.Pamplin to M.E.V.Pamplin by E.W.Walker MG
     11,   Albert Miller to Polly Williams (col) by Samuel Brooks,M
     11,   W.A.Hinkle to Mollie Bruce by A. VanHooser MG
```

187518,   Ike Bailey to Martha Whitaker (col)
18,   William Smith to Martha Talley (col)
18,   M.N.Benson to S.M.McKenzie by J.B.Tigert MG
18,   N.C.Harris to J.V.Giles by John L. Short Elder
21,   John E. Flynn to M.P.Jones by W.A.Gill MG
21,   R.M.Seaton to S.E.Seaton by Rev. William Seaton
pg 101
27,   Felix Pitts to Harriet Suggs (col) by H. Dunlap MG
25,   Jarrett Bailey to Jane Dusenbery (col) by A.J.Whitaker JP
28,   W.B.Burgess to Emeline Forrester by Wm. Buntley JP
Mar 2,   William Bright to Fannie Orrick (col) by Rev. C. Thomas
4,   Rufus C. McAfee to Sarah A. Barnes by B.F.Hudson MG
5,   James Read to Mrs. E. Ratliff by Samuel Bond JP
12,   Wash Thomason to Levy Talley (col) by D. Whitaker MG
14,   M.F.Turner to Bettie Laseter by H.F.Childs JP
14,   Pres. Hamilton to Sarah McCown (col) by Rev. C. Thomas
14,   D.W.Burgess to C.A.Corder by W.E.Carter JP
pg 102
18,   W.R.Pitts to Sue K. Laws by William Buntley JP
18,   Levi J. Langston to Mary E. Langston by J.B.Riley JP
22,   J.C.Phillips to M.E.Jackson by S.D.Loyd MG
23,   John E. Denson to Tabitha Hall by W.F.Cole JP
25,   S.P.Smith to M.S.McDaniel by John F. Baxter JP
24,   T.J.Cavitt to Lucy Brooks by A.J.Whitaker JP
25,   J.E.Snellings to R.L.Campbell by A.J.Whitaker JP
31,   Woodson Kimbrough to Lucy Moore (col)
pg 103
8,   W.M.Hunter to Mary Jane Cannon by A.S.Randolph JP
Apr 8,   Elias Dusenberry to Lucy Cooper (col) by S. Henderson MG
13,   W.B.Moore to E.J.Pigg by W.B.Towery MG
15,   Henry Jones to Julia Snoddy (col) by Rev. J.B.Tigert
18,   N.D.Counts to M.G.Pulliam by L.P.Myrick JP
17,   G.W.Whitaker to Cincinnatti Howard (col) by S. Henderson
22,   Lafayette Sisk to Elizabeth Waldon by T.W.Clark JP
25,   John W. Tally to Hariet Driver (col) by D.L.Mitchell MG
May 2,   Henry L. McGee to Mary R. Blackwell by A. Van Hoose MG
6,   James Donaby to Lucinda Word (col)
pg 104
10,   Warden M. Pope to Emma Hays by Rev. J.W.Wait
12,   W.G.Land to S.A.Cunningham by L.P.Myrick JP
12,   J.A.Floyd to Maggie Harrison by A. Van Hoose MG
16,   Benjamin P. Gibbs to Sarah J. Dunlap by S.C.McCollum JP
22,   George Bailey to Judy Whitaker (col)
24,   Riley Miles to Mrs. Josie Miles by D.M.Holloway JP
25,   Sam Sharp to Allice Clark (col) by B.F.Hudson MG
27,   Ferdinand Thomison to Mattie Waggoner (col) by A.M.
                                  Prosser
30,   Thomas White to Jane Simmons by J.T.Barker JP
30,   Wesley Whitaker to Martha McMullins (col) by L.L.Clark JP
pg 105
Jun 3,   Wm. B. Stevenson to Nelia R. Patterson by Rev. John H.
                                  Birdsong
6,   James R. Marshall to Mollie E. Summerford by Rufus Harris
5,   John L. Chisom to Lucy Chilcoat (col)
6,   James W. Cumberland to Nancy J. Phillips by G.W.Jackson
7,   John Smith to Dolly Smith (col) by Alex. Smith MG
8,   Nelson P. Carter to Orrer Lee Smith by A.S.Sloan
10,   Ervin B. Stegall to Fannie Alford by T.B.Fisher MG

```
187513,  Bunk Hague to Sarah Fannin (col) by J.M.Dickey JP
     15,  John D. Talley to Jennie P. Holman by J.E.Frost MG
     17,  W.L.Majors to Louella A. Parr by J.H.Smith JP
pg 106
     22,  Edward N. Grigsby to Fannie M. Whitman by A.Van Hoose
     29,  W.T.Talley, Jr. to Mattie E. Harris by W.H.Dixon MG
Jul  7,  Prunus Vaughn to Tery Pryor (col)
     11,  John L. Toole to Mary E. Smith by W.R.Martin JP
     17,  Calvin Wright to Julia Staten (col) by John Clark JP
     15,  Joseph G. Dickey to C.L.Farrer by W.H.Dixon MG
     22,  Cornelius George to Amanda Ross by A.A.Williams JP
     22,  I.A.Berrier to Julia A. Shelton
     22,  Leonard Durham to Maggie Buffalo by J.R.Abernathy MG
     27,  J.W.Hardin to M.A.Butler by G.S.Byrom MG
pg 107
     27,  T.B.Burnes to A.B.Foster
     29,  Wiley Sullivan to Martha Henderson (col) by Alexander
                                                     Smith MG
     29,  Thomas Parks to Eliza Smith (col)
     31,  Henry Vance to Annie B. Perkins (col)
Aug  3,  N. Gary to Tishey Walker by G.B.McKenzie JP
      3,  Isaac George to Martha Cunningham (col) by D. Whitaker
      4,  J.W.Etheridge to Sarah J. Thompson by J.T.Barker JP
      5,  A.J.Hale to Mattie A. Laws by W. Buntley JP
      4,  G.W.Solomon to D.C.Fanning
      5,  S.S.Downing to Mary C. Rowe by A.S.Randolph JP
pg 108
      5,  J.H.Myers to Susan Pentecost by F.L.Ezell JP
      7,  Stephen Ordway to Sarah Smith (col) by F.L.Ezell JP
      5,  John W. Dunn to Evaline Northcut by N.J.Wells JP
      8,  George Koonce by Elenora Smith (col) by Samuel Brooks
      8,  James M. Wright to Martha A. Mullins by F.L.Ezell JP
      8,  J.B.Wright to A.A.Hurley by John Clark JP
     15,  George Eddins to Emily Sheffield (col) by G.W.Puckett
      7,  Caleb Desmukes to Nancy Donalds (col)
     11,  David G. Douthat to Susie D. Bell by J.M.Bidwell MG
     12,  W.P.McDill to Emma J. Drennon by A.B.Coleman
pg 109
     12,  Ransom Crabtree to R.A.T.Mauldin by J.M.McAfee JP
     12,  H.S.McCauley to M.A.Forbes by J.B.Muse
     12,  William Smith to Ann Wilson (col) by John Clark JP
     21,  Jim Kelso to Catharine Thomison (col) by D. Whitaker MG
     16,  Joseph M.A.Brown to Martha J. Parker
     19,  Calvin Eddins to Jane Maddox (col) by G.W.Puckett
     19,  W.G.Furgerson to Ella Fowler by J.H.Smith JP
     18,  Robert Boyd to N.J.McElyea by G.B.McKenzie JP
     21,  George Jones to Nancy J. Foster
     22,  D.B.Armstrong to E.D.Cole by L.C.Butler JP
pg 110
     22,  A.J.Cowan to Mary J. Dollar by T.M.Barnett
     25,  J.W.Orrick to M.J.Wright by D. Tucker MG
     26,  Samuel George to Mattie Thompson
     26,  William Goosby to Mary E. Sawyers by J.B.Tigert MG
     27,  Anderson Tucker to Mattie Koonce by J.M.Dickey JP
     29,  Thomas E. Benson to Mollie H. Hardison by J.M.McAfee JP
     29,  Frank O. McCord to Ellen French by T.B.Fisher MG
     30,  Philander Perry to Mary Thompson by A.J.Whitaker JP
Sep  1,  S.B.Smith to C.L.Butler by Elder G.A.Morning
```

1875 2,   F.M.Bynum to A.S.Pate by L.P.Myrick JP
pg 111
   5,   J.M.Bostick to Sallie W. Bostick by J.F.Baxter JP
   7,   Emmerson Roberts to Jane Bates by W.F.Cole JP
   8,   John H. Fullerton to Lucinda Barnes by A.S.Sloan
   9,   W.S.Mount to Elizabeth J. Simpson by Rev. J.W.Wait
  12,   Barnham Garrett to A.J.Stanley by B.B.Bradford JP
   9,   T.E.W.Donaldson to America Foster by J.G.Woods
   9,   Robert Y. Gleghorn to Sallie Hampton by A.S.Sloan
   9,   Will White to Rebecca Wright (col) by Rev. C.T.Thomas
  12,   James R. Colston to Nancy Marlow by D.M.Holloway JP
  12,   Ira C. Cowen to Caldonia Colston by D.M.Holloway JP
pg 112
  14,   J.C.Hall to D.A.Nerren by M.R.Harp
  14,   John Allen to Lizzie Cole by A.P.Copeland MG
  16,   James M. Henderson to M.C.Campbell by A.L.Bates MG
  16,   R.F.Randolph to Mary H. Matthews by R.W.Rawls JP
  16,   James Epps to Addie Fox by J.M.Routt JP
  21,   W.J.Morrison to Martha S. Anderson by J.K.Moores JP
  22,   Robert Webster to Mary Taylor by D.M.Holloway JP
  23,   L.C.Cothran to Emily J. Hamilton by J.C.Stevenson MG
  22,   Thomas Russell to Lucy Bright (col) by C.T.Thomas
  23,   Thorton Russell to Emily Higgins (col)
pg 113
  26,   Elijah Smith to Loutisha Waggoner (col) by J.W.Smith MG
  26,   Green Harrison to Ann Beatie (col) by D. Whitaker MG
  30,   Thomas M. George to Mary D. Hughey by F.L.Ezell JP
Oct 3,   Thomas Fitzpatrick to Fannie Stricklin by A.S.Randolph JP
   4,   Sanford M. Buchanan to Pinkie M. Buchanan by D. Tucker MG
   6,   Jesse Langston to M.L.Walker by S.L.Walker JP
   7,   Jesse P. Butler to M.M.Smith by E.H.Holland MG
   7,   J.W.West to M.A.Sawyers by J.C.Stevenson MG
   7,   J.B.Bedwell to Mrs. R.E.Keith by Rev. N.D.Crawford
pg 114
   7,   Rufus N. Koonce to Mattie M. Bearden by W.A.Gill MG
  10,   William A.E. Pitts to Jennie B. Parks by J.G.Woods
  14,   J.H.P.Wallace to M.E.Butler by J.C.Wallace MG
  13,   D.L.Askins to Lou Caughran by A.S.Sloan MG
  14,   Samuel H. Colston to Amanda Hobbs by D.M.Holloway JP
  14,   M.M.Lineberger to Martha M. Watt by J.K.Moores JP
  14,   Wm. Clark to Mary F. Gray (col) by J.Wesley Johnson MG
  14,   Newman Edmondson to Clarisa Ellis (col) by J.W.Johnson,M
  17,   A.A.Dempsey to Emily Bradford by S.C.McCollum JP
  20,   Arthur Taylor to Polly Ann Jennings (col)
pg 115
  21,   John F. Monks to Katie Simmons by Isaiah Hancock JP
  21,   James T. Hardin to Eliza A. Sanders by J.M.Dickey JP
  24,   Henry Smith to Minerva Bonner (col) by G.W.Dunlap MG
  24,   Nathan Irvin to Mary Pigg by L.C.Butler JP
  26,   John J. Bryan to Martha Bennett by A.A.Williams JP
  28,   John Weaver to Jane Marshall by J.K.Moores JP
Nov 1,   J.H.Ray to C.A.Key by A.S.Randolph JP (4½ o'clock,pm)
   2,   W.J.Higgins to M.E.Duval by George Hall MG
   3,   J.H.Pitts to Fannie E. Cole by A.S.Sloan MG
   4,   William Clark to M.F.Harris by J.B.Tigert MG
pg 116
  11,   H.C.Martin to M.J.Smith by J.W.Rawls JP
  10,   John Jordon to Sallie Shoemake by L.L.Clark JP

1875 13, Travis Ashby to Caroline Ratliff by M.R.Harp MG
    18, J.A.Leatherwood to Nannie A. Rawls by J.B.Muse MG
    17, W.H.Fletcher to Dora Ellis by I.P.Osborne MG
    19, W.J.Bills to Sarah J. Harden by T.B.Fisher MG
    21, Henry Jordon to Mary F. Watts by George Hall MG
    21, John Jordan to Sallie A. Watts by George Hall MG
    24, G.A.Dorris to M.C.Owen by G.S.Byron MG
    25, C.T.Simms to Lou H. Dorris by G.S.Byron MG
pg 117
    24, Isaac Goodrich to Rutha Buchanan (col) by A. Fulton MG
    26, J.W.O.Scott to Ann Connell
    28, Presley Tillery to Angeline Patton by J.G.Woods MG
    30, A.J.Nichols to E.J.Land by J.M.Dyer JP
    30, D.L.Carmichael to Jennie Leatherwood by G.W.Carmichael,M
Dec 2, James Hays to Docia Pitts by J.W.Rawls JP
    5, W.T.Thompson to Mary P. Kent by S.C.McCollum JP
    2, Thomas Roland to Martha Ables by J.S.Waddle JP
    4, William Harris to Parthenia Pryor (col) by A.S.Randolph JP
    8, A.L.Corpier to M.M.Bledsoe by J.C.Stevenson MG
pg 118
    7, N.F.Harris to Stacie Smith by T.B.Fisher MG
    9, C.I.Hopper to N.A.Wright by B.F.Hudson MG
    10, A. Runnels to C.A.Reavis
    12, J.E.Harrison to Sophia Olliver by F.L.Ezell JP
    12, Green Harrelson to Violet Askins (col) by A.S.Randolph JP
    16, P.C.Carpenter to Martha J. Martin by J.B.Muse MG
    15, James A. Cole to Annie E. Bradford by G.S.Bynum MG
    16, Frank Moore to Dillie Wilson (col) by S.R.Stormont MG
    23, William A. Clardy to Martha Maddox by G.S.Bynum MG
    17, Newman Hays to Belle Curtis (col)
pg 119
    21, James Gawdy to Bettie Perkins by J.R.Barber MG
    19, F.E.Warden to Melissa Jeffries by Wm. Buntley JP
    19, Ezell Griffis to Vira Simmons (col) by A.S.Randolph JP
    21, A.L.Matlock to Mary F. Furguson by J.H.Smith JP
    28, Wyatt Smith to Malinda Read (col) by J.H.Smith JP
    28, James Read to Fannie Mack (col) by J.H.Smith JP
    21, Dan Sullivan to Nancy Sullinger by G.W.Jones JP
    21, James B. Kidd to Mary F. Dickey by A.S.Sloan MG
    21, Jacob R. Gillespie to Maud Cheatham by J.A.Woods MG
    22, A.N.Moore to S.I.Pylant by D. Tucker MG
pg 120
    23, J.W.King to K.T.Wynn by W.H.Dixon MG
    23, A.J.Renegar to Mattie L. Cowan by S.L.Sanford MG
    23, W.H.McClure to Julia Harper by J.T.Barker JP
    27, Oliver Bonner to Mattie Galloway (col) by Bailess Johnson
    26, James S. Thompson to Amanda Cowart by W.A.Gill MG
    28, William Kercheval to Sarah Clark (col) by John Cary JP
    28, Samuel Morrison to Lizzie Foster
    28, M.C.McMillen to Georgia Ann Spray by A.J.Childress JP
    29, James M. Webb to Bettie Johnson by M.R.Tucker MG
    30, J.A.Abbott to Eliza A. Reed by T.W.Clark JP
pg 121
    30, Austin McWhirter to Elvira J. Clift by T.W.Clark JP
    29, J.B.Bright to Mariah McPhail (col)
    30, W.R.Beard to Mary A. Moyers by T.J.Jones MG
    30, Anderson Branch to Susan Brooks by B.F.Hudson MG

162

```
1876
Jan   2,  Thomas Lawthorp to Nancy Little by G.B.McKenzie JP
      3,  John Branch to A. Hobbs by J.K.Moores JP
      4,  Henry Peterson to Gracie Jones (col) by Isaiah Hancock JP
      6,  F.F.Massey to Sarah Massey by L.C.Butler JP
      6,  T.S.Loyd to Mattie Howard by A.J.Whitaker JP
      6,  Felix Moore to Rachel A. Hatchett by Rev. Harry Dunlap
pg 122
      6,  John Beavers to Anna Scott by Alex. Fulton MG
      6,  P.Y.Newton to Olivia Milliken by John Cary JP
      6,  Benjamin Bailey to Sallie Reynolds by G.W.Jones JP
     11,  George Justin to Kittie Pryor (col) by Wyatt Dodson MG
      9,  C.C.James to Terrah Smith by John D. Hamaker MG
     10,  John Graves to Fannie Brooks by I. Hancock JP
     10,  William Goodson to Margaret Black by I. Hancock JP
     13,  Joseph N. Cole to Emily Moore by S.C.McCollum JP
     13,  John W. Franklin to Mary Copeland by J.T.Barker JP
     13,  James T. Boles to R.J.Williams by A.S.Moore JP
pg 123
     13,  Minus Cannon to Martha Smith by A.S.Randolph JP
     14,  Jack Johnson to Patsey McLear (col) by D.M.Holloway JP
     13,  John Edmonson to Sidney Hasty by William Buntley JP
     15,  Joe Scales to Jane Lay (col) by Lewis Neal MG
     19,  W.J.Hamilton to Mollie Hall by J.B.Warren MG
     20,  Eli Smith to Julia Huff by F.L.Ezell JP
     19,  John Pigg to I.B.Dyer by F.R.McGaugh LE
     20,  J.D.Dew to Bettie Menefee by B.B.Bradford JP
     20,  Ransom M. Jean to Rachel Fanning by A.J.Whitaker JP
     21,  W.R.Vickers to A.A.Vickers by G.S.Byron MG
pg 124
     20,  J.M.Jones to Emily Savage
     24,  W.R.Hamilton to M.J.Hardin by G.S.Byron MG
     20,  D.A.Hunter to Fannie Fite by B.F.Hudson MG
     21,  J.D.Griffin to H.E.Wood by B.F.Hudson MG
     23,  J.W.Maddox to Emma Eaton by J.W.Puckett
     22,  John Norman to Sarah Hill (returned not executed,Jan 31,187
     27,  John M. Maddox to Eva Fox by L.L.Cole JP
     28,  Lee Hedgepeth to Lucinda Bass (col) by J.K.Moore JP
     26,  A.W.Judd to Carrie R. McPhail by George Hall MG
     27,  A.E.Smith to Lizzie Kelly by W.E.Carter
pg 125
     30,  Henry Johnson to Fannie Desmukes (col) by D.M.Holloway
     30,  John H. Gunter to C.C.Emmons by A.A.Williams JP
Feb   3,  Gilbert T. Mosely to M.L.Harrison by J.C.Stevenson MG
      5,  W.P.Cole to Ann Green by N.B.Pearce MG
      3,  John Cowley to Emily Flynt (col) by Samuel Brooks MG
      3,  James Bonner to Dillie Vaughn (col)
      3,  J.A.Webster to Docia Dunivan by J.K.Moores JP
      3,  James N. Hariston to Jincie Sandlin by A.S.Sloan MG
      6,  Mc. Ramsey to Sarah Carland by T.B.Fisher MG
      9,  Libe McGee to Lizzie Colter by William Buntley JP
pg 126
      8,  E.S.Polk to A.A.Randolph by A.S.Sloan MG
     10,  Samuel M. Teel to Martha J. Adkins by H.T.Childs JP
     10,  George Webb to Maria Taylor (col) by John Moore MG
     10,  Harrison Flynt to Amanda Dickey (col) by John Moore MG
     10,  Charlie Edmondson to Caroline Kelso (col) by John Moore
     17,  Ben Young to E.H.Lock by J.H.Smith JP
```

1876 17,	J.E.Freeman to Florinda Brewer by S.C.McCollum JP
16,	James Jaton to Jennie Kenedy by A.S.Moore JP
17,	Thomas H. Harris to Delila Williamson by J.J.Short,Eld.
19,	J.W.Glidwell to A.A.Freeman

pg 127
20,	William O. Wilson to Mollie B. Thorton by T.B.Fisher MG
25,	R.F.Tucker to Sarah Eslick by A.J.Whitaker JP
27,	John Moore to Rosanah A. Brown by Wm. Buntley JP
28,	H.C.Street to Susan C. Golden by J.T.Barker JP
Mar 1,	Joel M. Harris to Lucy L. Johnson by J.J.Short,Eld.
2,	J.T.Loyd to Laura H. Renegar by W.D.Moorehead JP
9,	T.J.A----- to Mary E. Stephens by Rev. M.C.Beavers
8,	J.L.Smith to M.P.Ashworth by J.G.Woods MG
8,	S.H.Adams to M.J.Hodge by J.F.Baxter JP
9,	P.J.Freeman to Nannie Reese

pg 128
23,	Isom Cross to Mariah Sugg (col) by J.K.Moores JP
13,	Harry Dunlap to Lucinda Metcalf (col) by Lewis Neal MG
16,	James L. Stewart to Hattie Winburn by A.S.Sloan
23,	John Harper to Pink Sugg (col) by J.K.Moores JP
23,	Daniel Patterson to Sallie Wells (col) by B.B.Bradford
21,	B.M.Hopper to Sue E. Ennis by J.B.Tigert MG
23,	James J. Maddox to Sarah A. Smith by Wm. R. Martin JP
26,	Ed Jacobs to Amanda Buchanan (col) by H.T.Childs JP
Apr 5,	James H. Loyd to S.A.Thompson by A.J.Whitaker JP
8,	Andy Clanton to Josie McDonald (col) by Lewis Neal MG

pg 129
10,	Wm. M. Gray to Rachel Bachelor by J.B.McKenzie JP
12,	Mc. Haithcock to Susan Graham by J.W.Rawls
20,	William Crunk to Rosie Tallant by A.J.Childress JP
19,	Henry Day to Henrietta Morris by T.B.Fisher MG
25,	L.W.Hicks to Mattie P. Shuffield by J.B.Muse
25,	John Norman to Sarah Hill by J.K.Moores JP
27,	Calvin Sanders to Mary E. Dunivan by J.K.Moores JP
29,	John Hill to Sarah Wicks by J.B.Riley JP
May 14,	Will Goodrich to Orleana Goodrum (col) by B.F.Hudson,M
14,	John Bright to Cornelia Ann George (col) by D. Whitaker

pg 130
17,	J.H.Morrison to Mrs. E.M.J.Stephenson by L.C.Butler
25,	John A. Hamilton to Mattie F. Moore by F.L.Ezell JP
28,	Joe T. Robinson to America A. Hicks (col) by L.L.Cole JP
Jun 1,	J.A.Moses to Harriett L. Price by J.C.Stevenson MG
May 31,	G.G.Mitchell to Jennie Dusenberry by T.J.Shaw MG
31,	Robert Welch to M.E.Anderson by Rev. J.W.Wait
Jun 4,	Marion A. Cathcart to Margaret E. Page by B.B.Bradford JP
4,	William Jean to Betsey Ann Tucker by S.D.Loyd MG
10,	Isaac Drake to Lou Driver (col) by B.B.Bradford JP
15,	W.C.Copeland to Sallie B. Renegar by W.D.Moorehead JP

pg 131
16,	B.F.Herndon to Susan A. Chisum (col)
18,	B.F.Marshall to Joily Harston by J.G.Woods
23,	J.L.Simmons to Mary Bates by John Cary JP
29,	Robert F. Stiles to D.C.Franklin by W.D.Moorehead JP
Jul 3,	William R. Eddins to M.J.Majors by A.S.Randolph JP
6,	John Hays to Bettie Crawford (col) by John Cary JP
10,	Charles H. Commons to Ellen Turner (col) by J.B.Allison,M
13,	Henry R. Brown to Buena Vista Lane by Wm. Buntley JP

1876 13,   James L. Welch to Nissa Crabtree by J.M.McAfee JP
    20,   Thomas Eddins to Anna Vance (col) by G.W.Puckett
pg 132
    20,   W.M.Ray to M.S.Nelson by B.F.Hudson MG
    20,   Isaac A. Lincoln to Mrs. M.E.Deford by S.W.Bruce MG
    23,   J.C.Maynard to Sarah A. Dunivan by D.W.Holloway JP
    23,   W.D.Koonce to Mrs. Josie Williams by T.S.Corder JP
    23,   Z.M.Mansfield to Julia F. Porter by W.A.Gill MG
    23,   J.D.Latham to A.F.Gilliam by J.R.Abernathy MG
    23,   Dink Little to Martha A. Flax (col) by J.M.Dyer JP
    25,   A.L.Smith to C.R.Murrah by L.L.Cole JP
    24,   John S. Waddle, Jr. to Mrs. Mollie S. Diemer by T.B.
                            Fisher MG
    26,   Humphrey N. Petty to Susan V. Joins by A.B.Coleman
pg 133
    26,   Hiram Bright to Rebecca Hall (col) by J.W.Johnson MG
Aug 3,   Charley Foster to Margaret Clark (col) by D. Whitaker MG
Jul 26,   W.L.Alexander to M.C.Warden by F.P.Fulton JP
    27,   Clement Wells to Louiza Wilburn (col) by J.W.Johnson MG
    27,   J.L.Eslick to G.A.Tucker by A.J.Whitaker JP
    27,   N.D.French to Mattie Lou Hoots by J.M.Groce MG
    30,   H.C.Gregory to Mollie Vickers by E.H.Holland MG
Aug 2,   Harry Landess to Catharine Henderson (col) by Thomas
                            Diemer MG
     6,   John S. Britton to Mary E. Lock by J.R.Abernathy MG
   10,   David C. Bledsoe to Mary Jane Eddins (col) by G.W.Puckett
pg 134
   10,   John Caldwell to Sarah Robertson by L.P.Myrick JP
   10,   F.W.Tipton to C.B.Hambrick
   10,   Lewis Burke to Matilda Lamb (col)
   13,   William Elmore to Hannah Fagan by J.S.Waddle JP
   15,   J.C.Jennings to M.H.Caston by S.M.Parks
   15,   W.M.Roseborough to H.E.Thomas by J.J.Short, Elder
   17,   John J. Ramsey to Mrs. Caroline Jackson by G.B.McKenzie JP
   19,   C.J.Thorp to S.E.Russell by F.L.Ezell JP
   22,   William A. Loyd to Mrs. E.C.Cruse by J.T.Barker JP
   24,   D.B.F.Gunter to Loucinda Wells by S.M.Emmons MG
pg 135
   27,   J.A.W.Woodall to D.E.Putman by L.P.Myrick JP
   31,   Wesley Thompson to Jane Walker by D.M.Holloway JP
Sep 2,   Wm. J. Manley to Cornelia C. Renegar by T.S.Corder JP
    3,   John Colbert to Mary E. Gowers by W.D.Moorehead Esq
    4,   W.H.Marsh to Lizzie A. Butler by S.T.Sanford
   10,   Andy Bowers to Laura Harvey (col) by Howell Swinea MG
    6,   Guss Wells to Lizzie Edmonson (col) by W.C.Beaver
    7,   Henderson Thompson to Mattie Oaks by J.T.Barker JP
    6,   Martin H. Towry to Hannah Stephens
   10,   John T. Wicks to E.N.E.Keller by S.L.Walker JP
pg 136
    7,   Franklin P. Copeland to Mary E. Smith by William Jared JP
    7,   Charles B. Hughes to C.J.Noles by John Cary JP
   10,   William Gaines to Susie Mullins by W.A.Rhodes JP
   10,   Travis K. Howell to Martha Hanie by J.A.Hall JP
   10,   R.B.Cowley to Jocie Cooper by W.D.Moorehead JP
   11,   Josua Allen to Ellen Carty (col)
   12,   J.M.Bagley to M.S.Leonard
   14,   Wm. Price to Margaret J. Burget by D.G.Smith JP
   16,   Ben Finch to Betha Meaks by L.P.Myrick JP

1876 17,   James I. Pearce to Mary L. Cashion by S.L.Sanford MG
pg 137
     20,   Thomas M. Barnes to Addie Hopper by H.T.Childs JP
     21,   G.E.Wright to Amanda E. Davis by D.G.Smith JP
     29,   Wilson Gattis to Charity Campbell by S.L.Loyd MG
     24,   Jake Halbert to Minney Sladen (col) by A.S.Templeton JP
     28,   Babe Hopkins to Corinthia Moore by W.A.Gill MG
     28,   W.H.Warren to Fannie Taylor by A.J.Whitaker JP
     29,   Blanton Hill to Emma Lewis by G.B.McKenzie JP
Oct   5,   John Davis to Della Sullivan (col) by A.S.Templeton JP
      8,   J.J.Vickers to Nancy Smith by A.L.Bates, Elder
      3,   J.I.McCown to L.E.Caughran by A.B.Coleman
pg 138
      4,   W.P.Andrews to Mollie Hunt by W.D.Moorehead JP
      3,   Rev. C.P.Duvall to Belle W. Jones by S.D.Woods MG
      4,   George L. Rhoden to Martha A. Bynum by A.W.Sutherland,M
      8,   Book Holman to Polly Waggoner (col) by A. Smith MG
      7,   A.M.Smith to Mrs. Hellen L. Phillips
     10,   A.O.Battle to Eugenia Wright by J.D.Barbee MG
     11,   J.T.Sloan to Mary L. Parkison by A.S.Sloan MG
     12,   John Lindsey, Jr. to Mary Sloan by J.B.Muse
     12,   Harris Sullivan to Mrs. Eliza Owen by B.F.Hudson MG
     15,   Abe Barber to Julia McCollum by L.L.Clark JP
pg 139
     19,   Stephen Johnston to Jennie Moore by J.E.Frost MG
     18,   J.J.Sumners to N.A.Collins by Thomas Eason MG
     18,   G.L.Cambron to Mollie Robertson by J.T.Barker JP
     17,   J.L.Nelson to Lizzie Allen by George Hall MG
     20,   Julius Turner to Eliza Hutton by J.H.Smith JP
     19,   B.B.McWhorter to Sarah J. Kay by G.B.McKenzie JP
     20,   Columbus S. Weigart to Sarah E. McGee by E.M.Walker DM
     20,   John Hamilton to Julia A. Cambron
     21,   W.C.Childress to S.E.Clark
     26,   J.P.Mitchell to M.H.George by J.C.Harrison MG
pg 140
     26,   J.F.Faulkner to Tennessee Milstead by J.M.Noblett JP
     26,   Andrew J. Fletcher to Mary A. Kennon by J.F.Smith JP
     26,   H.L.Jones to M.E.Duffey by M.R.Tucker MG
     27,   George Smith to Ann Nelson (col) by B.B.Bradford JP
Nov   2,   J.N.Epps to Florence Cole by William Buntley JP
      1,   York Bass to Lizzie Hays (col) by H. Dunlap MG
      1,   L.G.James to Malinda Williams by W.A.Rhodes JP
      2,   J.A.Good to M.M.Jones by J.B.Muse
      5,   James W. Baits to Teresia Moore by William Buntley JP
      5,   M.C.Smith to S.C.Neal by J.B.Riley JP
pg 141
      9,   J.F.Mapp to Sallie A. Roper by J.R.Abernathy MG
     12,   C.M.Reynolds to Mary A. Patton by J.R.Abernathy MG
     11,   J.A.Cummins to Almeta E. Holt by B.F.King MG
     14,   W.M.Campbell to Mrs. N.R.Edwards by N.J.Wells JP
     16,   P.E.Farrer to A.J.Dickey by J.C.stevenson MG
     16,   W.C.Cathcart to Angeline Robison by D.G.Smith JP
     16,   Stephen Clark to Betsey Higgins (col) by L.N.Merry MG
     18,   Fran Dickerson to Mary Fullerton (col)
     24,   J.W.Austin to Fannie Epps by H.T.Childs JP
     23,   Wyatt Childress to Catharine Campbell by Rev. B.T.King
pg 142
     23,   Charlie Jones to M.M.Moores by T.B.Fisher MG

1876 25,   G.D.Ham to E.J.Nichols by W.H.Foster JP
26,   A.M.Ervin to N.A.Land by J.J.Short, Elder
26,   William Eslick to Mrs. Louisa Campbell by M.F.Jared JP
26,   John W. Warden to K.E.Keith by E.W.Walker DM
28,   F.M.Baldwin to Frances Melson by W.H.Foster JP
29,   Wade W. Shaw to Millie L. Jackson by Rufus E. Travis MG
30,   N.J.McClure to Mary E. Reed by J.T.Barker
Dec 3,   Sank Berry to Emily Smith (col) by J.W.Smith MG
1877
Aug 19,   Wilks Bryan to Millie Drake (col) by F.L.Ezell JP
pg 143
1876
Dec 2,   Bill Coppage to Nancy Pamplin (col) by A. Fulton
4,   Berry Crane to Ella Simmons by A. Washburn JP
6,   Robert Murry to E.L.Wright
7,   M.E.Whitaker to Ida Wood by Wm. H. Dixon MG
7,   M.A.Beard to Ollie T. Bratcher by T.J.Jones
7,   Thomas L. Norwood to Judith M. Bright by George Hall
10,   Spencer Smith to Mary March (col) by Alex. Fulton
10,   James Harris to Jane Harris (col) by A.H.Bishop MG
11,   William W. Pylant to Tennessee Idora Pitts by S.L.Sanford
14,   L.S.Barnett to Ann Franklin by J.R.Abernathy MG
pg 144
13,   H.G.Brown to S.F.Rutledge by William Buntley JP
14,   John W. Cunningham to Rebecca W. Land by L.P.Myrick,JP
14,   J.S.Routt to Amanda F. Curtis
14,   W.H.Cashion to Lizzie Monday by Wm. A. Gill MG
14,   M.M.Bearden to Susie J. Woods by J.G.Woods
19,   J.W.James to Martha F. Tillery by J. Franklin Smith JP
21,   James W. Gattis to Julia A. Riddle by W.F.Jared JP
17,   George Simmons to Ethiel McKee by Isaiah Hancock JP
20,   E.S.Bearden to M.E.Dickey by B.C.Chapman MVD
20,   Henry Raney to Mollie Scott
pg 145
21,   J.C.Anderson to Fannie Randolph by G.W.Jones JP
21,   H.B.Griffin to Mollie J. Jenkins by Levi Eslick JP
26,   Alfred Smiley to Mary Greer (col) by L.C.Butler JP
26,   Sam Wright to Mollie Halbert (col) by A.S.Templeton JP
24,   E.B.Merrell to Fannie E. Patterson by L.P.Myrick JP
24,   R.A.Smith to M.E.Scroggins by H.T.Childs JP
24,   A.J.Ventress to Isabella Renegar by M.R.Tucker MG
26,   W.H.McNelley to Ida M. Brazelton by George Hall MG
28,   J.H.Cox to Martha Smith by A.S.Templeton JP
28,   William McBride to Sallie Pitts (col) by J.H.Hamilton
pg 146
27,   Zadock Motlow to M.E.Anderson by J.G.Woods
27,   P.L.Wright to M.T.Sumners by D.G.Smith JP
28,   Andy Buchanan to Catharine Greer (col) by W.J.Hamilton
27,   Thomas Bledsoe to Nancy Harris (col) by W.H.Foster JP
28,   Joseph E. Sherrell to Pink Edmiston (col) by I.J.Towry
28,   London Woods to Amanda Halbert (col) by John Casey JP
28,   J.B.Hays to M.A.Hays by J.B.Muse
28,   Wm. Moores to Emma Commons (col) by Harry Dunlap MG
28,   George Bonner to Idella Robertson (col) by Samuel
                                      Brooks
28,   William McMurray to Mary Lay (col) by J.S.Waddle JP
pg 147
31,   Frank Ready to Mollie Pamplin by J.A.Hall JP

1877
Jan 1, Richard Webb to Lou Kelso (col) by J.B.Riley JP
     3, D.M.Perkins to Mrs. C.C.Everett by J.H.Smith JP
     7, John Richey to Jane Green by S.P.Graham JP
     3, G.B.Miller to Mary B. Gardner by H.N.McTyree
     4, Johnson Burnes to Sallie Alsup by D.G.Smith JP
     4, Henderson McDonald to Catharine Hairston (col) by J.
                                                 Johnson MG
    11, W.G.Rice to Mollie E. Hanaway by J.B.Warren MG
    11, Benjamin Miles to A.E.Merrell by S.P.Graham JP
pg 148
    14, J.B.George to D.J.Tate by L.L.Clark JP
    19, John Lay to Eliza Ervin (col) by J.T.Bright MG
    16, W.M.Roden to Fannie Park by D.G.Smith JP
    16, J.H.Taylor to M.M.Moore by Rufus E. Travis MG
    18, H.T.Woodard to C.A.Bryan by J.R.Abernathy MG
    16, W.A.Gill to M.A.Carter by Rufus E. Travis MG
    18, D.M.Smith to M.J.Wicks by D.D.Smith MG
    18, W.C.Warden to M.J.Isom by W.J.Collier
    18, M.C.Smith to L.C.Franklin by W.D.Moorehead JP
    18, S.E.Hunter to E.M.Gibson by G.S.Byron MG
pg 149
    18, James T. Moffett to L.N.Brown by Wm. Buntley, JP
    28, Henry Sunger to Fannie Hays (col) by B.B.
    28, Juber Clark to Mary Leatherwood by Rev. S. Brooks
Feb 1, R.E.Walker to F.C.Smith by J.B.Riley JP
Jan 31, W.M.Hopwood to Mrs. Mary E. Thorp by W.A.Franklin JP
    31, Sanford Wicks to Ellen Thomas by E.W.Walker DM
    31, R.W.Hicks to E.R.Smith by J.R.Abernathy MG
Feb 1, Robert Knowles to Julia Jennings (col) by J.B.Riley JP
     1, William A. Moore to M.H.Webster by L.L.Cole JP
     1, C.C.Hall to Eliza Forrester by William Buntley JP
pg 150
     1, Jacob Waggoner to Rebecca Sebastian
     4, C.N.Gunter to Calley Russell by D.G.Smith JP
     7, Joseph Pepper to Sarah C. Carpenter by W.R.Martin JP
     7, Stamp Alexander to Beadie Whitaker (col)
     8, E.C.Blankenship to Delia McMillen by A.J.Childress JP
     8, J.B.Moore to L.J.Walker by Rev. B.T.King
    13, J.T.Ratliff to S.C.Webb by S.D.Loyd MG
    13, S.H.Little to M.M.George by W.J.Collier
    14, M.D.Hampton to Callie Carter by N.T.Powers MG
    15, Frank McMullen to Mary McElroy (col) by G.B.McKenzie JP
pg 151
    18, S.A.Orr to Sarah Pickett by J.T.Barker JP
    18, Wiley H. Brown to Nancy Manerva E. Brown by E.W.Walker,M
    18, Silas Hopkins to Bell Webb by A.J.Childress JP
    22, Elisha England to Frances B. Summerford by A.P.Copeland,M
    28, W.N.Wicks to E.B.Lackey by S.L.Walker JP
    28, Charles N. Thomas to S.F.Freeman by John Abernathy MG
Mar 1, N.E.Abott to E.A.Spray by A.S.Randolph JP
     1, J.N.Welch to C.A.Hopper to W.W.Wilson JP
     4, A.J.Childress to Mary F. Moore by A.S.Randolph JP
     8, W.N.Roper to Donia Turner by J.R.Abernathy MG
pg 152
     8, A.B.D.Webb to Minerva Boggs by G.B.McKenzie JP
    13, Emanuel Carpenter to Mrs. I.E.Rowell by W.R.Martin JP
    18, Andy James to Sarah Fulton (col) by W.D.Moorehead JP

1877 15,   Thomas Hindman to Julia Marshall by J.W.Wynneger,Eld.

22,   Samuel Talley to Sarah Martin by W.H.Dixon MG

22,   James G. Brazier to Eveline E. Holloway by A.A.Williams

29,   Jarrod Simmons to Mrs. Henrietta Jones by W.E.Carter JP

29,   T.P.Whitaker to E.F.Sanders by S.C.McCollum JP

29,   Jeff Shelton to Caroline Scott (col) by W.D.Moorehead

29,   T.B.Pitts to Mattie L. Bradford by J.G.Woods Eld.

pg 153

Apr 15,   Richard Ellis to Sarah Bevill by Charles Laxon

4,   Henry Pitts to C.C.Blackwell by S.L.Sanford MG

12,   S.J.G.Davis to Bettie Perry by S.M.Emmons MG

12,   William Sowell to Rosie Tate by G.S.Byrom MG

12,   William Hays to M.J.Tucker by J.T.Barker JP

14,   Lem Whitaker to Nora Coppage (col) by Alex. Fulton MG

15,   Dick Boon to Eliza Wright by A.S.Templeton JP

27,   James Whitt to Anna Jenkins by W.A.Rhodes JP

18,   Marion Harbin to Nancy C. Holman by Levi Eslick JP

pg 154

19,   H.C.Gault to A.L.Tate by A.S.Sloan

22,   James S. Leonard to Rebecca A. Durham by J.A.Hall JP

22,   John Rigney to Lou Gillespie (col) by Alex. Fulton

26,   Leroy Bryant to Elnora E. Langston by J.B.Riley JP

25,   Lewis Moore to Anna Isom (col)

30,   Nelson Smith to Rytha Millhous (col)

May 3,   Green Buchanan to Amanda Proctor (col) by Arthur
                                          Nickerson

3,   James M. Phillips to Eliza L. Phillips by T.D.Griffis JP

3,   Thomas F. Casey to Mary M. Hays by J.T.Barker JP

8,   M.J.Farrar to W.M.Halbert by W.H.Dixon, Elder

pg 155

10,   L.M.Cothrum to M.J.King by J.M.Noblett JP

10,   Andrew Johnson Green to Betty Isabella Blake (col)

13,   R. Austin to Lou Hobbs by W.W.Wilson JP

17,   G.W.Campbell to Mrs. Rebecca Oldfield by S.L.Walker JP

17,   J.J.Lewis to Mrs. S.E.Frame by W.A.Rhodes JP

26,   S.L.Robinson to L.J.Lackey by W.W.Wilson JP

30,   Thomas H. Gray to M.E.Jarrett

30,   Allen H. Gray to Sarah King by F.L.Ezell JP

Jun 1,   James Lay to Harriett Buchanan (col) by L.N.Merry

5,   J.L.Patterson to L.A.Hill

pg 156

6,   James Leonard to Fannie Couch by J.B.Riley JP

10,   W.E.Hardin to N.J.Tooley by D.G.Smith

10,   C.H.Kelly to A.E.Miles by S.P.Grayham JP

11,   James M. Norman to Nancy C. Holman by J.P.Riley JP

13,   William Thompson to S.G.Kennemore by S.D.Loyd MG

13,   William Nevils to Julia Ann Thomas by L.N.Merry

13,   W.N.Whitaker to Mecca J. Holman by J.W.Holman MG

21,   W.M.Boyd to M.A.Anderson by G.B.McKenzie JP

22,   D.H.Groce to Sallie Buntley by J.M.Noblett JP

28,   Thomas Clayton to Ann Hazlewood by J.R.Abernathy MG

pg 157

Jul 2,   A.M.Bray to M.J.White

4,   G.W.Bruce to Fannie Sheppard by L.P.Myrick JP

10,   W.B.Hudson to Mattie F. Gowan by M.R.Harp

12,   James Tallant to E.D.Land by W.A.Gill MG

15,   John W. Brown to Nancy D. Wormack by G.W.Jones JP

15,   Austin Keller to Elmira Williams by J.B.Riley JP

```
1877 17,    John Green to Mollie Bonner (col) by S.R.Stormont MG
     18,    J.T.Russell to M.E.Steelman by B.B.Bradford JP
     22,    Jacob Pless to M.J.Woodard by J.H.Smith JP
Aug   2,    Alex Taylor to Retta Taylor (col) by J.T.Barker JP
pg 158
Jul  19,    Thomas W. Franklin to M.A.Hicklan by J.R.Abernathy MG
     19,    William Winkler to Julia Thompson by J.B.Riley JP
     22,    John M. McKinney to M.J.Rodgers by W.A.Franklin JP
     29,    F.P.Christian to C.C.Walker by J.B.Riley JP
     26,    Samuel Morris to Nancy Ross by J.T.Barker JP
     25,    R.C.Jones to W.C.Martin by J.W.Rawls JP
     26,    Charley Clark to Daney Freeman (col) by A.C.Martin JP
Aug  31,    Thomas B. Peoples to Mary Walker by F.L.Ezell JP
      1,    Warren Wallace to Jane Edmondston (col) by F.P.Fulton JP
      2,    Orange Eslick to Milly Reed (col) by W.D.Moorehead JP
pg 159
      2,    A.S.Parker to Sallie Taylor by J.T.Barker JP
      1,    M.L.Murray to M.C.Savage by W.H.Foster JP
      4,    E.B.Brown to M.E.Bradford by Wm. Buntley JP
      5,    Henry Dodson to Julia Corpage by John Casey JP
      7,    Joel Mullins to Nancy C. Cates by J.S.Waddle JP
     13,    Mack Jean to Clem Bates by M.R.Harp
      9,    Thomas F. Osborne to Sarah A. Edmiston by B.F.Hudson MG
      8,    T.J.Gaither to M.E.Jared by A.J.Whitaker JP
      9,    L.D.Crabtree to Susan Alexander by W.D.Moorehead Esq
     10,    Andy Harrison to Rose Sebastian (col) by A.J.Whitaker JP
pg 160
      9,    R.M.Armstrong to Rebecca Jane Crowley by J.F.Smith JP
      9,    J.E.Kent to L.P.Taylor by S.C.McCollum JP
      9,    Milton Bishop to Lutitia Pitts (col) by L.N.Merry
     12,    C.H.Cunningham to N.E.Zimmerman by J.H.Alexander MG
     12,    Ed Mosely to Hasty Griffis (col) by A. Smith MG
     11,    Pless Scales to Katie Greer (col) by L.C.Butler JP
     15,    George Taylor to Manerva Woodson (col) by A.G.Templeton
     12,    Thomas Horton to Ann Northcut by J.M.Routt JP
     14,    Samuel York to Mary Marshall by Rev. Isaac Gatlin
     16,    Samuel A. Dickey to Alice F. Pamplin by A.S.Sloan
pg 161
     19,    Rufus Sisk to Angeline Webb (col) by J.B.Riley JP
     19,    Mack Swinford to Lena Arnold by A.A.Williams JP
     20,    D.M.Foster to M.E.Counts by Rev. J.W.Wait
     19,    John Shofner to Amanda Zimmerman (col) by J.W.Rawls JP
     21,    Wm. G. Smith to N.E.Smith by S.M.Emmons MG
     21,    J.A.Myers to V.A.Smith by S.M.Emmons MG
     25,    Samuel D. Culen to Sarah A. Rowell by J.W.Rawls JP
     28,    John Washington to Mary Haley (col) by Rev. Wm.W.Hailey
     26,    John Alexander to Laura Childress (col) by B.F.Hudson,M
     26,    J.R.Pulliam to Nancy J. Luttrell by J.B.Riley JP
pg 162
Sep   6,    Columbus Dunlap to Mollie Hackett by W.A.Rhodes JP
Aug  30,    G.W.Luttrell to Mrs. Louretta Warren by Levi Eslick JP
     30,    Willis Green to Ellen Rosebrough (col) by N.J.Hamilton JP
Sep   2,    William E. Bryant to Sarah E. Langston by J.B.Riley JP
      4,    Jasper Harbin to Mary H. Harper by W.E.Carter JP
      4,    G.W.Davidson to S.A.Cast by L.C.Butler JP
      5,    A.J.Kingkade to Amanda Spray by G.B.McKenzie JP
      5,    J.C.McCown to M.C.Kenedy by A.B.Coleman
      6,    John Barnes to Susie Dyer by N.C.Sullivan JP
```

1877 6,   Benjamin Austall to Betsey Bonner (col) by L.N.Merry
pg 163
      6,   William Shull to Louretta George (col) by David Whitaker
      7,   John Sumners to Mary Harris
      7,   Edmond Drake to Cassena Benson (col)
      7,   Calvin Benson to Ceiley Douthit (col)
      9,   Jeff Oliver to Becky Moore (col) by A.A.Williams JP
     10,   J.H.Nichols to Mollie E. Hester by W.H.Foster JP
     13,   George Washington Melton to Lizzie Nichols by B.B.
                                              Bradford JP
     12,   James Arnold to Nancy Carpenter by A.A.Williams JP
     13,   John Simmons to Mollie Phillips
     13,   Henry Smith to H.C.Cannon by A.S.Randolph JP
pg 164
     13,   Edward Bonner to Fannie Woods (col) by Lewis Neal MG
     16,   Monroe Russell to Elizabeth Benson (col) by J.H.Smith JP
     16,   B.G.Stephens to Sarah M. Beard by A.J.Childress JP
     19,   Walter Sutton to M.A.Dixon by J. Franklin Smith JP
     20,   William Beech to Loucinda Gulley by F.L.Ezell JP
     20,   William Russell to Margaret Williams by F.L.Ezell JP
     24,   Edward Clark to Elizabeth Templeton by B.C.Chapman MVD
     23,   George Henderson to Sue Harper (col) by J.H.Smith JP
     24,   C.R.Burrum to Mary E. Rodgers by J.S.Waddle JP
     26,   H.M.Barnes to Mrs. Elizabeth Smith by H.T.Childs JP
pg 165
     27,   J.O.Luter to Margaret M. Thornton by W.A.Franklin JP
     28,   Willis March to Sallie Harben (col) by John Casey JP
     27,   Isam Price to Mrs. Bettie Maynard by J.H.Smith JP
     27,   J.M.Shelton to Frances C. Bray
     30,   J.F.Reed to Jennie Cashion by J.T.Barker JP
Oct   6,   J.M.Burnes to H.A.Solomon by A.J.Whitaker JP
      4,   John R. Stormont to Laura I. Tate by A.B.Coleman
      7,   Thomas J. Daniel to Josie Hannah by I.J.Towry JP
      6,   W.C.Meaks to Jennie McWhirter by L.P.Myrick JP
      8,   John S. King to Eliza Taylor by G.W.Puckett
pg 166
     11,   F.P.McMullen to M.E.Whitt by J.F.Smith JP
     11,   N.S.Smith to C.E.Paysinger by J.F.Smith JP
     10,   C.S.Knowles to C.I.Bryant by J.A.Hall JP
     11,   J.W.Wilson to S.A.Emmons by A.A.Williams JP
     10,   B.F.Kirkland to M.R.Gary by G.B.McKenzie JP
     11,   W.M.Terrell to Mollie Kirkpatrick by J.G.Woods Elder
     14,   W.H.Durham to Mary C. King by S.L.Walker JP
     18,   J.B.Bragg to B.E.Stanback by S.P.Grayham JP
     17,   John C. Bradley to Mary E. Vincent by A.D.McClure
     19,   George Martin to Ella Ousley by J.B.Tigert MG
pg 167
     18,   Asa Bradley to Nora Pates by J.B.Riley JP
     18,   John L. Smith to Beckey Clark (col) by L.L.Clark JP
     21,   J.N.Sanders to S.J.Gregory by J.H.Smith JP
     21,   C.W.Fackler to Katie Murray by W.W.Estill MG
     24,   Joseph Hackett to Eliza Bass (col) by H. Dunlap MG
     24,   Richard Simmons toManlda Mullins by J.S.Waddle JP
     25,   D.J.Jones to Nelly Dale by A.S.Randolph JP
     25,   Henderson Ellis to Mattie Wilson (col) by L.N.Merry
     26,   Charley Shelton to Mary Tolley (col)
     28,   T.J.Smith to Huldy Ward by W.D.Moorehead JP

pg 168   1877
    28,   Jasper Guyer to H.A.Pulliam by S.P.Grayham JP
    28,   Jerry Timmons to Caroline Todd (col) by L.N.Merry
Nov 1,   Milfred Eddins to Eggie Clark (col) by L.L.Cole JP
Oct 31,   Dick Carter to Eveline Patterson (col) by Harry Dunlap,M
Nov 4,   Toney Farquharson to Frances Bonner (col) by A.W.Williams
     5,   John Thomas Daniel to Clarinda C. Pitman by A.S.Randolph
     6,   J.W.Blair to A.E.Akard by J.G.Woods Elder
     8,   W.R.Wicks to G.A.Smith by S.L.Walker JP
     8,   James Moore to Delia Morris (col) by G.S.Byrom MG
     8,   W.G.Stephenson to Josie Morrison by W.H.Foster JP
pg 169
   13,   Joseph Boles to Henrietta Williams by S.L.Walker JP
   13,   D.C.Swiney to M.L.Hopper by H.T.Childs JP
   15,   R.A.Robinson to M.E.Wilson by Rev. Green P. Jackson
   15,   John W. Dyer to Sarah Jane White by W.D.Moorehead JP
   19,   Rev. G.A.Morning to Sarah M. Derrick by J.W.Weninger,Eld.
   15,   H.D.Smith to Fannie Madearis by J.M.Kidwell MG
   18,   Henderson Moore to Hannah Bledsoe by G.B.McKenzie JP
   18,   W.B.Wells to Elizabeth Sparkman by John M. Routt JP
   21,   Samuel Carter to N.E.Smith by J.L.Brown MG
   21,   Samuel Clinton to Sarah J. McKinney by J.F.Smith JP
pg 170
   22,   A.J.Smith to Mattie E. Merrell by J.W.Winiger, Elder
   22,   J.N.Stallings to T.R.Grayham by A.S.Randolph JP
   22,   Alf Taylor to Perlina Stovall (col) by Sam Brooks
   25,   F.M.Bonner to Fannie Foster by G.W.Nichols
   24,   Bud Wells to Emily Wells by J.B.Warren MG
   25,   James Vaughn to Julia Donald by J.C.Stevenson MG
   25,   John W. Ivy to Mary Alice Hill by Rev. Sandy Henderson
   26,   Wm. E. Buffaloe to Nancy E. Wilbanks by A.S.Randolph JP
   26,   Jim Scott to Lucy Smith (col) by Alex Fulton
   12,   Wiley A. Milam to Mary A. Commbs by J.R.Abernathy MG
pg 171
   27,   C.C.Powell to Catharine Posey by S.C.McCollum JP
   29,   T.J.Madray to Sallie Smith by J.H.Alexander MG
   28,   W.F.Street to M.E.Blankford by Rev. Green P. Jackson
Dec 5,   George W. Bond to L.R.Jackson by W.A.Franklin JP
Nov 29,   William Spray to Josie Satterfield by A.S.Randolph JP
Dec 1,   C.O.Phillips to Sallie Jones
     2,   Porter Bruce to Mary L. Coats by W.A.Franklin JP
     9,   Fred Hickman to America Walker (col) by Rev. Abner
                                         Johnson
     6,   F.R.Mitchell to Sallie O. Carter by Wm. B. Lowry MG
pg 172
   16,   W.J.West to Mollie Sawyers by J.C.Stevenson MG
    6,   Harvey Gill to Rusia George by F.L.Ezell JP
    7,   George Sebastian to Millie Murdock (col) by L.M.
                                       Massey MG
    5,   Ben Bright to Jennie Commons (col) by L.N.George MG
    6,   B.B.Thompson to Sarah H. Cowly by C.A.McDaniel JP
    9,   Ben Dyer to Harriett Barrett (col) by Alex Fulton
    8,   James Koonce to Adaline Clasberry (col) by Samuel Brooks
   11,   William Dyer to Sarah Buchanan by S.M.Emmons MG
   11,   W.R.Stallings to R.F.E.Haithcock by A.S.Randolph Esq
   11,   Andy Moore to Elizabeth Pylant by D. Tucker MG
pg 173
   13,   W.A.B.Rozell to V.L.Mason by Isaiah Hancock JP

1877 13,   C.M.Short to Ella Blakemore by J.J.Short, Elder
     16,   C.B.Koonce to M.J.Sanders by Elder J.G.Woods
     16,, John Griffin to Margaret Howard by Levi Eslick JP
     20,   Charley Drake to Celey Douthat (col) by J.H.Smith JP
     19,   James D. Scott to Mary E. Copeland by W.F.Jared JP
     20,   C.C.Sanders to F.C.Humphrey by J.C.Stevenson MG
     19,   J.G.Cummings to Ella E. Bledsoe by D.L.Mitchell MG
     20,   A.S.Woodard to Mrs. Nancy J. York by W.B.Lowry MG
     20,   Ben Whitaker to Frances Massey by F.L.Ezell JP
pg 174
     20,   James L. Dickey to Ann McClure by W.D.Moorehead Elder
     20,   Kenneth Stephens to Julia A. Sandlin by A.S.Sloan
     23,   W.L.Roper to T.C.F.Falkner by W.A.Franklin JP
     20,   H.B.Merrell to M.T.Merrell by E.H.Holland MG
     20,   John O. Boggs to Mrs. M.F.Walker by F.P.Fulton JP
     25,   J.J.Lasater to Mattie Nelson by F.L.Ezell JP
     24,   L.D.Sumners to E.C.Deford by W.H.Dixon Elder
     23,   J.B.Anderson to Rosana Murphy (col) by G.B.McKenzie JP
     25,   James Thompson to Elizabeth Smiley by W.H.Foster JP
     26,   Isaac B. Mason to Nancy E. Jones by J.B.Riley JP
pg 175
     25,   S.W.Whitt to E.A.Rodgers by E.H.Holland MG
     25,   J.S.Alexander to Nannie C. McClain by E.W.Walker MG
     25,   John M. Hulsey to Julia E. McClellan by J.B.Tigert MG
     24,   Bird Holman to Bell Whitaker (col)
     26,   Albert Sherrell to Sallie Nelson (col) by F.L.Ezell JP
     25,   James Gray to Ann Taylor (col) by J.T.Barker JP
     27,   L.L.R.Smither to E.A.Colman by J.R.Abernathy MG
     27,   Joseph Brown to M.J.Harrison by A.A.Williams JP
     26,   George Renegar to Frances Vaughn (col) by S. Brooks
     27,   Boat Reed to Amanda Gardner (col) by W.A.Franklin JP
pg 176
     27,   Thomas Nye to Ella Harston (col) by W.H.Foster JP
     27,   A.J.Cowan to Prescilla Clark by W.T.Gill MG
     27,   Louis McCollum to Lou Hill (col)
     27,   Washington Legg to Jennie Hall (col) by Wm. Buntley JP
     27,   James Vining to Mollie McKee by Isaiah Hancock JP
     28,   R.E.Freeman to Dillie M. Fitch by L.P.Myrick JP
     30,   G.W.Clark to Fannie Perry by S.M.Emmons MG
     30,   Brock Stone to Frances Simmons (col) by W.D.Moorehead Esq
     30,   Sol Perkins to Hannah Horton (col) by A.W.Williams
     30,   Bob Jennings to Fannie Webb (col) by J.B.Riley JP
pg 177
     30,   Dock Flynt to Amanda Clark (col) by H.T.Childs JP
1878
Jan 3,   G.J.Bates to Lucinda Phillips by Isaiah Hancock JP
     3,   Taylor Glasgow to Nellie Aynnett by E.M.Emmons MG
     3,   Lawson Smith to Annie Browning by J.F.Smith JP
     3,   B.C.Smith to Mattie Lineberger by J.H.Smith JP
     3,   A.C.Dunn to Mary Waggoner by J.M.Noblett JP
     3,   C.G.Abbott to Mary L. Milliken by A.P.Copeland MG
     3,   Thomas A. Rodes to Sarah P. McCree by T.C.Eason MG
     3,   Ben Gaines to Lou Bonner (col)
pg 178
     4,   Wm. S. Thurman to Leticia Hays by John Carey JP
     9,   Samuel H. Moyers to Rena Stephens
     10,   W.F.Dyer to N.J.Dyer by W.J.Hamilton JP
     10,   W.H.Tripp to E.J.Green by A.J.Whitaker JP

```
1878 10,   J.L.Waggoner to Sallie DeHaven by J.B.Muse & W.J.Collier
     13,   Sam Mullins to Jane Stinnett (col) by R.M.Woodard MG
     16,   John Caldwell to Mrs. L.A.March by W.B.Lowry MG
     16,   John L. Nelson to M.E.Ethridge by J.L.Brown
     17,   T.L.Owens to S.C.Gattis by W.F.Jarred JP
     17,   J.M.Ramsey to C.E.Barnes by H.T.Childs JP
pg 179
     17,   J.M.Biles to E.H.Beggerly by W.B.Lowry MG
     17,   J.J.Leatherwood to V.A.Henderson by W.B.Lowry MG
     17,   Miles Bonner to Sarah Solomon (col) by L.N.Merry MG
     17,   John Holman to Kate Neel (col)
     20,   J.W.Lively to L.E.Wells by M.H.Huston JP
     23,   James Blake to Ann Henderson (col) by Lewis Neal MG
     24,   J.A.Osborn to D.L.Blaylock by Wm. A. Gill MG
     24,   Samuel Wicks to Elvira Stone (col) by David Whitaker,M
     26,   Green Busby to Julia Haston (col)
     31,   L.A.Brady to M.E.Redd by B.B.Bradford JP
pg 180
     31,   L.E.Ramsey to M.A.Barnes by H.T.Childs JP
Feb  5,   R.P.Smith to Mattie Pulliam by J.B.Riley JP
      7,   W.M.Morrison to N.C.J.Pigg by A.C.Martin JP
      7,   W.G.Gray to Martha A. Holman by Levi Eslick JP
      7,   Francis Buchanan to Eliza Robertson (col) by L.N.Merry,M
      7,   Reubin Mapin to Katie Pamplin (col) by Sam Brooks
     11,   R.P.Lock to M.J.Cooper
     14,   Prince Wilson to Addie Green (col) by Arch Clark MG
     14,   Ross Conger to Henrietta Boyd (col)
     14,   William Woodard to Toke Peoples by F.L.Ezell JP
pg 181
     14,   W.A.Grable to Elizabeth Sanders by D. Tucker MG
     17,   John W. Wadkins to Mary E. Smith by W.A.Franklin JP
Mar 12,   McNelley Greer to Frances E. Bland (col) by W.J.Hamilton
Feb 19,   A.C.Bostick to M.J.Walker by Jacob Gray MG
     20,   Joseph Philpot to Nancy J. Harden by R.M.Woodard MG
     21,   J.M.Douthit to S.J.Holloway by Elder W.H.Dixon
     28,   L.E.Wilson to J.C.Kidd by A.B.Coleman
     28,   D.T.Rowell to E.V.Biles by Wm. R. Martin JP
     28,   Dave Singleton to Rosana Motlow (col)
Mar  3,   Ruben Thompson to Elizabeth Willbanks by W.E.Carter JP
pg 182
      3,   Joseph Pitcock to Ellen Counts by J.A.Hall JP
      3,   W.B.Sims to Peggy J. Pruitt by I. Hancock JP
      7,   John W. McGee to Stacy McGee by J.M.Noblett JP
      6,   Frank Wells to Mary Smith (col)
      7,   M.M.Renegar to N.C.Stevenson by S.L.Walker JP
     10,   J.P.Lesley to M.A.Hayes by W.D.Moorehead JP
     11,   James R. Furgerson to J.E.Clark by Rev. Wm. W. Hailey
     14,   J.W.Galloway to Cynthia Malear (col) by Arch Clark MG
     14,   Wm. H. Bright to Mattie Stonebraker (col) by Lewis Neal,M
     14,   Charles Harms to Sue Whitaker by Elder W.H.Dixon
pg 183
     14,   W.H.Sullinger to M.J.Jean by J.A.Hall JP
     14,   Isham Arnett to Ella Ratter (col) by W.A.Franklin JP
     14,   Clay Luster to Josie Conger (col) by Thomas Jones MG
     20,   F.A.Pitts to M.F.Hamilton by A.P.Copeland MG
     19,   John W. Gattis to Jennie A. Waggoner by A.J.Whitaker JP
     20,   J.L.Hayes to W.G.Bray by J.T.Barker JP
     23,   Hiram Pitts to Cynthia Sugg (col) by Harry Dunlap MG
```

1878	24,	Alex. C. Pamplin to Sallie Bagley (col) by L.N.Merry,M
	26,	J.M.Shannon to Mary E. Faulkner by W.A.Franklin JP
	28,	H.T.Trantham to J.S.Redd by D.G.Smith JP
pg 184		Blank
pg 185		
	31,	G.E.George to N.E.Hamilton by F.L.Ezell JP
	27,	John W. Prince to Sarah C. Brown by F.P.Fulton JP
Apr	6,	Harry Whitaker to Mollie Buchanan (col) by S.M.McCollum
	9,	J.M.R.Crawley to Lucy Sheppard by J.F.Smith JP
	14,	R.F.Noles to Laura Ann Arnold by J.B.Riley JP
	25,	Tom Stone to Alice Blake (col) by J.B.Tigert MG
	23,	Richard Moores to Puss Toon (col)
	29,	F.E.Brown to E.C.Prince by Wm. Buntley JP
	28,	M.M.Carlile to M.E.Herring by J.L.Brown MG
	29,	John Summers to Mary Harris by J.W.Rawls JP
pg 186		
May	2,	John H. Henderson to Mattie Moyers by S.L.Walker JP
	3,	Dewitt Johnson to Nannie Hamilton (col) by W.E.Carter JP
	5,	J.W.Duncan to Fannie Faulkner by J.M.Noblett JP
	5,	John Woods to Queen Whitaker (col) by Thomas Jones MG
	6,	G.R.Denton to R.C.Dollar
	7,	I.B.Whitaker to Mary Lou McDaniel by James A. Orman
	7,	James W. Adair to Virgie Gill by S.L.Sanford
	14,	Gustave Flemming to Mrs. Lizzie Zimmer by S.S.Burton
	15,	T.E.Power to Virginia Moyers by S.S.Burton
	16,	Willis Riggins to Mollie Flynt (col) by J.F.Humphrey,MG
pg 187		
	19,	J.E.Crawford to T.P.McNeel by Rev. B.T.King
	23,	Dr. J. Milton Stewart to Mollie E. McMillen by A.S.Sloan
	21,	John Kimbrough to Mary McGee (col)
	22,	Dave Rhodes to Christiana Sugg (col)
	22,	Wash Conger to Clara Whitaker (col)
	26,	W.B.Jennings to Sarah Arnold by E.W.Walker DM
	23,	Robert Patterson to Kit Crawley (col) by J.F.Smith JP
	26,	Henry Wright to Sallie McElroy (col) by Abram Johnson MG
	29,	W.H.Petty to E.E.Campbell by Rev. A.J.Steele
	29,	Dave Moore to Ella Jane Patton (col) by G.B.McKenzie JP
pg 188		
	29,	M.A.Pamplin to Nancy A. George by John Carey JP
Jun	2,	George W. Evans to Nettie Ashby by W.F.Jared JP
	1,	Ben Cannon to Sallie Cannon (col) by Abram Johnson
	11,	Alex. Ezell to Eliza Benson (col) by A.A.Williams JP
	5,	R.D.Warren to M.M.Gibson by B.C.Chapman MDV
	8,	William Moore to Cordelia Askins (col) by I.J.Towry JP
	13,	Joseph Brock to Cynthia Jean by John M. Routt JP
	13,	Tom Moore to Winnie Smith (col)
	13,	John Powers to Priscilla Roland by John S. Waddle JP
	16,	John Ashby to Mollie Keith by W.F.Jared JP
pg 189		
	18,	J.C.Edmiston to M.J.Webster by F.L.Ezell JP
	19,	John M. Dickey, Esq to Laura V. Kyle by Rev. M.R.Tucker
	19,	William Jones to Betty Harris (col)(not executed)
		P.D.Boyce,Clk.
	20,	J.M.Shelton to L.A.Wilbanks by J.J.Stevenson Esq
	24,	Richard Burwell to Mattie Studdard (col) by G.B.McKenzie
	27,	John Blake to Missouri Stone (col) by D. Whitaker MG
	30,	Henry Russell to Sarah A. Carpenter by W.W.Wilson JP
Jul	2,	James Ervin to S.A.Plexican by B.B.Bradford JP

1878	1,	William Jones to Bettie Harris (col) by L.C.Butler JP
	4,	John Wyatt to Alice I. McDill

pg 190

7,	J.M.Pool to Mahalie Culver by L.L.Cole JP
7,	Harry Porter to Nelly Webb (col) by John Tidbee MG
9,	H.W.McNeece to Martha T. Davis by S.M.Emmons MG
10,	Emanuel Kelley to Anna Stewart (col)
10,	A. Johnson to Nannie Renegar by G.B.McKenzie JP
12,	Arch Cashion to Caledonia Echols by J.A.Hall JP
14,	Thomas A. Mitchell to Julia Mosely by A.A.Williams JP
17,	W.T.Phillips to Victoria May Henderson
Sep 26,	Colman Halbert to Julia Childs (col) by B.B.Bradford JP
Jul 21,	John Seaton to Martha A. Slaughter by Rev. J.C.Mials

pg 191

23,	Berry Vaughn to Mary Heralston by L.L.Cole JP
23,	William Mullins to Mary V. Phillips by J.R.Abernathy MG
24,	John L. Washburn to Delia Blakemore by A.S.Randolph
25,	John W. March to Louisa Pitts (col) by A.C.Martin JP
25,	M.R.Groce to Hannah Ashby by W.F.Jared JP
26,	M.W.Pendergrass to Harriett Stephens
29,	J.P.Nunley to Lou Norman by John M. Routt JP
30,	Henry Horing to M.E.Matthews by Isaiah Hancock JP
Aug 1,	J.W.O'Neal to Fannie M. Smith by W.F.Franklin JP
1,	W.L.Bray to Kate Bradford by L.P.Myrick JP

pg 192

1,	J.B.Kidd to J.K.Stewart
2,	Charles Hale to Samantha Heath by Charles Kelley JP
1,	John L. Rudd to Mary Stewman by J.B.Riley JP
4,	James T. Hobbs to M.A.Watson by J.F.Smith JP
5,	J.S.Robertson to Kate Smith by J.W.Bragg
8,	James Joins to Bettie Coble by S.M.Emmons MG
8,	George Farrar to Julia Justice (col) by W.W.Wilson JP
11,	Jordan Sugg to Mariah Nelson (col) by J.H.Smith JP
8,	Moses Bright to Elizabeth Carter (col) by L.N.Merry MG
8,	G.B.Loyd to Lizzie Thompson by W.F.Jared JP

pg 193

11,	James Conaway to Catharine Taylor (col) by B.F.Hudson MG
13,	C.J.Hodge to Josie E. Lock by J.R.Abernathy MG
15,	D.A.Ramsey to Alla M. McCracken by David Strong
15,	George Walker to M.C.Haithcoat by J.R.Abernathy MG
18,	W.G.Hill to Mary L. Harris by J.H.Smith JP
18,	R.D.Whitworth to Willie E. George by J.J.Stevenson Esq
18,	W.G.(L) Brock to Elizabeth Meakes by J.J.Stevenson Esq
22,	G.A.Williams to Mary E. Renegar by S.D.Loyd MG
21,	Lewis Parks to Rosie Whitaker (col)
23,	Mat Thomas to Ceeny Benson (col) by Jery Philips MG

pg 194

22,	J.R.White to Doney Cowen by J.H.Smith JP
22,	R.P.McWhorter to -------- Epps by S.C.McCollum JP
25,	Janius Bonner to Kitty Wheeler (col) by J.F.Humphrey MG
28,	David Jester to Sarah Shanks by J.F.Smith JP
29,	J.M.Gilliam to V.L.Curry by Rev. G. Henderson
29,	E.L.Brotherton to M.J.Hampton by F.L.Ezell JP
28,	James Conry to Jennie P. Pearson by John Casey JP
29,	W.J.Fanning to F.L.Dies(Dyer) by W.D.Moorehead JP
Sep 1,	L.P.Ables to Susan Chick by J.S.Waddle JP
3,	M.M.Russell to Margaret Anderson by W.A.Rhodes JP

pg 195   1878
          5,   Charles Edmonson to Millie Hines (col) by W.J.Hamilton JP
          5,   W.T.Woodward to Julia Ann Curtis by S.M.Emmons MG
          4,   Peter Prosser to Nannie Blakemore (col) by J.F.Humphrey,M
          5,   J.H.George to S.C.Hamilton by G.M.Cherry
          5,   Thomas Keith to Ida Tucker (col) by W.D.Moorehead JP
          5,   H.D.Cowley to Sarah Thompson by W.D.Moorehead JP
          7,   T.J.Powell to Mary Lynn by Isaiah Hancock JP
          7,   John Warren to Lilla Gillespie (col)
          8,   Thorton Burkley to Mollie Timmons (col) by Rev. Thos.
                                                          Bright
         11,   J.W.Kinchum to R.J.Carpenter by S.M.Emmons MG
pg 196
         12,   James A. Birdsong to Susan Marion by I.J.Towry JP
         12,   G.E.Mason to M.A.Bell by J.G.Waddle JP
         12,   A.S.Foster to L.T.Blaylock by Isaiah Hancock JP
         15,   Tom Honey to Eliza Hall by J.G.Woods Elder
         15,   J.M.Summers to L.E.Smith by William Buntley JP
         18,   William M. Sneed to Ollie L. Mullins by Charles Kelley
         18,   Phillip Cooley to Nancy White by F.P.Fulton JP
         19,   G.M.Bevils to M.E.Brotherton by S.M.Emmons MG
         19,   Isaac C. Rutledge to Donie Hall by R.T.King MG
         19,   William J. Gibson to Bell Dyer
pg 197
         22,   C.C.Leatherwood to M.V.Abernathy by W.B.Lowry MG
         21,   Fenton Lockart to Mary E. Denton
         23,   C.C.Finley to M.E.Nunley by J.M.Routt JP
         26,   J.C.McKinney to S.F.Finley by T.C.Eason MG
         26,   M.C.Cathcart to Lauretta Robertson by B.B.Bradford JP
         28,   H.E.Denton to N.E.Dollar
Nov   2,   John L. Bingham to Eliza J. Faulkner by J.T.Barker JP
Oct   1,   W.R.Little to F.E.Isom by W.T.Gill MG
Sep 30,   Franklin Irvin to Hester Stone (col)
Oct   2,   John Chesser to Mary Griffin by B.B.Bradford JP
pg 198
          3,   David M. Rudd to Sallie Price by A.H.Bishop MG
          6,   Robert Williamson to Nannie Rees by G.W.Dolbey MG
         10,   M.F.Jacobs to Mary E. Sanders by A.H.Bishop MG
          7,   T.C.Taylor to Mrs. Clem. McClellan
         10,   Lawson Garrison to Amanda Price (col) by Jery Philips,M
         11,   Ben Henderson to Mary Henderson by S.L.Walker JP
         10,   A.B.Woodard, Esq to Maud Todd by J.H.Bryson MG
         10,   Thomas V. Hill to E.E.Pope by Elder S. Henderson
          9,   C.D.Curlee to Mourning Turner by J.G.Woods Eld.
         10,   Clint Woods to Rosana Kelso (col) by David Whitaker MG
pg 199
         13,   I.L.Adams to A.E.Brown by S.L.Walker JP
         13,   Edward Robertson to Anna Bagley (col) by L.N.Merry MG
         12,   Billie Todd to Lizzie Bonner (col)
         15,   Frances Preston to Mary Metcalf by Jacob Gray MG
         15,   T.B.Kilpatrick to Rena E. Pitts by A.S.Sloan
Dec 19,   G.F.Isom to Lizzie Keith by William Buntley JP
Oct 17,   W.E.Pitts to Emily Renegar by S.L.Sanford
         17,   Joel Parks to Mary Renegar by S.L.Sanford
         17,   J.T.Land to Mary F. King by L.C.Butler JP
         17,   William Gamble to Nerva Price by H.T.Childs JP
pg 200
         17,   P.G.Smith to Catharine Hale by G.B.McKenzie JP

```
1878  19,  W.A.Wagoner to Mattie Spencer by W.D.Moorehead Esq
      22,  W.A.Roach to N.E.Summerford by J.W.Holman MG
      23,  J.A.Sexton to Lucy J. Bond by W.A.Franklin JP
      23,  John T. Gordon to Sue A. Nix by Rev. Green P. Jackson
      27,  Charles McDaniel to Sarah Arney by W.W.Wilson JP
      31,  W.T.Cartwright to M.J.Ratican by W.F.Jared JP
      29,  E.B.Baldwin to Georgiana Dunber by S.M.Emmons MG
      31,  John Kimes to Louisa Allison by A.C.Martin JP
      31,  Allen Harrison to Milly Conger (col)
pg 201
Nov   4,  W.T.Baldwin to Sarah Stiles by S.M.Parks MG
       5,  J.A.Nelson to Katie C. Lynn by S.L.Walker JP
       7,  Bob Griffin to Sarah Staton (col)
       7,  T.N.Allison to Mollie Cordle by G.B.McKenzie JP
       7,  R.B.Turner to Jane McClain by A.S.Randolph JP
      10,  James M. Young to Willie M. Marshall by W.A.Rhodes JP
      12,  W.A.England to R.A.Good by W.B.Lowry MG
      11,  T.B.Bryant to M.A.Martin by S.L.Sanford
      14,  T.L.Furgarson to S.E.Coats by J.R.Abernathy MG
pg 202
      14,  J.W.Barnes to R.S.Owens by B.F.Hudson MG
      14,  J.M.Hinkle to Lou Waggoner by A.J.Whitaker JP
      14,  William L.Y.Keith to Loucinda Johnson (col) by David
                                              Whitaker MG
      14,  J.G.Fullerton to Mattie Merritt by L.R.Amis MG
      14,  R.G.Hayes to M.A.Leatherwood by J.B.Muse
      14,  J.A.Tripp to America Gattis by W.F.Jared JP
      14,  John Dobbins to Doney Hudson (col) by L.N.Merry MG
      16,  Green Webb to Jimmie Dunavan by G.B.McKenzie JP
      17,  J.H.Childers to Lizzie Phillips by A.S.Randolph JP
      20,  John C. Patterson to Sallie Rozell by W.H.Gill MG
pg 203
      21,  John F. Cole to C.C.Ray by W.H.Foster JP
      20,  J.G.Brazier to Nancy A. Woodard by J.H.Smith JP
      21,  H.L.Moore to Sue E. Stone by Rev. N.D.Crawford
      24,  L.F.Taylor to Elizabeth J. Smith by S.L.Walker JP
      25,  Ned Smith to Emaline Whitaker (col)
      27,  R.A.Renegar to A. Hague by W.J.Collier MG
      28,  W.J.Landess to May Boone by J.E.Frost MG
      28,  A.J.Anderson to C. Bartlett
      28,  P.W.Cunningham to Beuna Vista Harpe by L.P.Myrick JP
Dec   4,  John D. Thompson to Cordelia Ratekin by W.D.Moorehead
pg 204
       3,  J.W.Willingham to Mrs. F.H.McGahee by S.H.McCord JP
       5,  Milton Smith to Sarah A. Hall by J.W.Hilliard, Elder
       5,  J.M.Conine to Mary J. O'Neal by W.R.Franklin JP
      12,  J.B.Conine to Winnie Roper by J.R.Abernathy MG
       5,  G.A.Cole to M.J.Wisdom by A. Washburn JP
       8,  W.J.Stroud to R.C.Chapman by J.R.Abernathy MG
       8,  B.F.Luttrell to C.J.Bradford by D.G.Smith JP
      12,  Calvin Barnes to Sallie King (col) by W.G.Slatter MG
      12,  W.F.Smith to D.J.Smith by W.A.Franklin JP
      11,  Peter C. Braden to Lela M. Deford by G.Lipscomb MG
pg 205
      12,  Lewis Shipp to Liza Wherley (col) by L.L.Cole JP
      12,  W.H.Crawford to Lula Beard by W.W.Beard
      12,  Harvey Hoots to Susie Baker by C.A.McDaniel JP
      16,  Nathaniel Hopkins to Perina A.E.King
```

```
1878  18,   M.L.McMillen to Mollie L. Moore by J.B.Muse
      18,   W.E.A.Pitts to Parthena Roach by J.W.Holman MG
      19,   J.M.Menafee to M.C.Summerford by John J. Short,Eld.
      20,   B.S.Dobbins to Lizzie Jones by W.T.Gill MG
      22,   James Eddins to Loutitia McDonald (col) by W.A.Rhodes
      22,   Burrel Wright to Anna Wilson (col) by A.S.Templeton JP
pg 206
      23,   J.M.Hambrick to Mattie Layton
      24,   Joe Rosebrough to Fannie McMillen by J.J.Short Elder
      26,   Frank Mills to Louisa Marrs (col) by F.L.Ezell JP
      23,   Bill Fanning to Pink Clark (col) by W.E.Carter JP
      23,   Lee Sorrell to Bell Smith (col)
      26,   Dick Sharp to Sarah J. Wilson (col) by W.W.Wilson JP
      24,   G.W.Alexander to Delia Cashion by W.J.Collier MG
      24,   A.J.Jean to J.A.Thomison by E.W.Walker DM
      24,   James Isom to Sallie Thompson by W.T.Gill MG
      26,   I.(J)H.Porter to Mattie Jetton by S.L.Walker JP
pg 207
      26,   Nathan Bradford to Jane Porch by William Buntley JP
      27,   Samuel Bradford to Mollie Brown by William Buntley JP
      25,   Jim Patterson to Della Buchanan (col) by G.B.McKenzie
      28,   J.W.Baits to Dona Runnels by Isaiah Hancock JP
      29,   Hiram Fulton to Sue Gillespie (col) by Thomas Ward MG
      30,   J.E.Wicks to Ellen Pruitt
      30,   Nelson VinZant to Ann Stone (col)
      31,   Josiah Anderson to Mary Roden by J.H.Smith JP
1879
Jan  1,   J.F.Dickey to N.E.Timmons by John Carey JP
1878
Dec 31,   James Thomison to Irene Eddins (col) by Rev. W.S.Slatter
pg 208
1879
Jan  1,   R.C.Kercheval to Tommie Goodrich by G.B.McKenzie JP
      2,   Arch Green to Mollie Campbell (col) by J.B.Warren MG
      2,   O.I.Sebastian to Ellen Durham by W.J.Collier MG
      2,   R.D.Whitworth to M.F.George by John Carey JP
      2,   J.F.McClure to Elizabeth Gault by J.B.Riley JP
      5,   T.W.Warren to Elizabeth Steelman by W.H.Foster JP
      8,   Alexander Neely to S.J.Baker by J.B.Warren MG
      6,   N.H.George to Margaret Boggs
      6,   Phill Ragins to Catharine McGaw (col) by W.J.Young MG
pg 209
      7,   J.M.Cole to Mary Phillips
      9,   Alf Bonner to Belle Edmondson (col) by G.W.Jones JP
     12,   J.M.Sharp to M.F.Golden by M.E.Carter JP
     12,   Lafayette Tate to Elizabeth Haston by A.J.Parker MG
     12,   Jo McEwin to Mary Murphy (col) by Rev. M.S.Slatter
     16,   T.J.Copeland to M.J.Mitchell by A.J.Whitaker JP
     18,   James M. Wilson to Narcissa J. Thomison (col) by Dave
                                              Whitaker MG
     19,   J.J.Swanner to M.C.Weaver by W.W.Wilson JP
     19,   M.M.Renegar to Emily Lanier by Jacob Gray MG
     22,   M.R.Frame to S.E.Heath by S.M.Parks MG
pg 210
     22,   George Smith to M.R.McFerrin by J.B.Muse
     23,   L.D.Mullins to Susie Harrison by F.L.Ezell JP
     24,   W.J.Goosby to Lucy Shands J.F.Smith JP
     27,   Tom Sugg to Rosa Bonner (col) by Harry Dunlap MG
```

1879	25,	Joseph Smith to Babe Williams (col)
	26,	William Markham to Hannah Norris (col) by L.M.Merry MG
	30,	Z.J.Sawyers to M.C.Swinney by A.J.Whitaker JP
	28,	N.A.Pearson to Maggie Armstrong by John S. Waddle JP
	30,	M.R.Posey to S.L.Posey by J.J.Short, Eld.
Feb	2,	John W. Watkins to R.F.Watkins by J.F.Smith JP

pg 211

Feb	6,	Clark Pitts to Mattie Summers (col) by A.C.Martin JP
	3,	Baker Moore to Sarah Jane Sugg (col) by L.M.Merry MG
	4,	Josiah Herrell to Millie King (returned Apr 28th, not executed)
	6,	J.H.Beanland to Mary F. Sherrell by W.B.Towry MG
	6,	J.E.Moyers to Cordelia Marler by F.L.Ezell JP
	6,	A.C.Gleghorn to Sallie A. Hines by A.S.Sloan
	9,	William D. Sawyers to Callie Bearden by B.F.Hudson MG
	7,	Brad Cashion to Eliza Jolly by J.J.Stevenson JP
	8,	Elisha Green to Sarah P. Benson by M.F.Jarred JP
	9,	A.A.Parkes to Lizzie Steed by E.W.Walker

pg 212

	10,	G.W.Riddle to Jane Alley
	12,	W.H.Wilson to Lilly Brown by Rev. Green P. Jackson
	13,	Andy Hickman to Jennie Bonner (col) by Elder Abram Johnson
	15,	James Woodard to H.J.Kimes (col) by Wm. Buntley JP
	19,	John C. Warren to Susan M. Glazier by R.H.Johnson MG
	23,	E.M.Pamplin to Susan F. Brown by Wm. Buntley JP
	20,	Dave Summerford to Nannie Blakemore by J.J.Short Elder
	20,	S.B.Turner to M.D.Stotts by W.T.Gill MG
	23,	W.A.Steakley to Fannie B. Hill by Elder S. Henderson
	21,	Henry Evans to Sophrona Colter (col)

pg 213

	25,	James P. Terry to M.S.Tulley by J.E.Frost MG
	26,	A.M.Henderson to Rutha L. Laton by S.L.Walker JP
	27,	H.C.Sorrells to P.J.Renfroe by J.B.Tigert MG
Mar	2,	Joshua Bowden to Mary Mills by J.S.Waddle JP
	1,	J.R.Foster to T.A.Moore
	13,	J.M.Robertson to Mary C. Murphy by J.G.Woods Elder
	3,	Lum Smith to Ella Robinson (col)
	5,	John Cason to Becky Ezell by B.J.Marion
	8,	J.T.Goforth to Amanda Finley by B.A.Cornelius MG
	13,	Wm. Leatherwood to Maggie Sugg (col) by W.W.Wilson JP

pg 214

	13,	Robert Crutchfield to Emma Monday by Rev. Green P. Jackson
	19,	Wm. Buchanan to Fannie J. Ransom (col) by W.J.Young MG
	20,	George Russell to Eliza Townsend (col) by F.P.Fulton JP
	20,	Ed Cooley to Violet George (col) by W.E.Carter JP
	23,	W.C.Baits to Mrs. Mary Bray by I.J.Towery JP
	25,	J.F.Blair to Ex Leatherwood by W.B.Lowery MG
Apr	3,	Harrison Hickman to Joanna Fletcher (col) by Rev. Abram Johnson
	4,	William Jones to Sallie Clarke (col)
	9,	Robert Guy to Susan Hanvy by J.W.Rawls JP
	9,	C.A.Mullins to Florance Shamby by J.F.Smith JP

pg 215

	12,	John Wells to Martha Pryor (col) by W.E.Carter JP
	12,	Wiley Sullivan to Susie Henderson (col) by J.H.Smith JP
	27,	Elijah Bonner to Josie Moore (col)

1879	17,	J.K.Whitaker to Katie E. Sugg by W.H.Dickson MG
	22,	Samuel Dunn to Nancy Ryan
	29,	Pat White to Phebe Kelso (col) by L.M.Merry MG
	27,	Isaac Rowell to Viney Owens (col) by Harry Dunlap MG
May	1,	J.K.Mullins to Arminda Sanders by F.L.Ezell JP
	1,	William T. Thornton to Allie Pendergrass by G.B. McKenzie JP
	1,	Came Beatie to Lizzie Clark (col) by Alex Fulton MG
pg 216		
	1,	J.B.Arnold to Ane A. Hudson by W.H.Foster JP
	3,	L.H.Haston to Sallie C. Denton
	4,	Charles R. Prikard to Anna E. Crane (not executed)
	5,	Alex Edmiston to Z.A.Timmons by L.R.Armes MG
	8,	James McClure to Ninie Morris by J.B.Riley JP
	10,	J.R.Parker to Lucy Ann Durham
	18,	J.B.McKenzie to Dora Ramsey by F.P.Fulton JP
	29,	Dick Dunston to Mandy Bonner (col) by J.P.Humphrey MG
	28,	J.B.McFerrin to Olivia Phagan by J.B.Muse MG
	28,	J.W.Pinkerton to M.L.Banks by Levi Easlick JP
pg 217		
	29,	James Burrows to Pink Morgan by M.R.Harp MG
	31,	W.D.Cole to Mrs. Martha Hunt
Jun	1,	Frank Harris to Adeline Swanner (col) by J.H.Smith JP
	1,	J.M.Radford to Mollie O. Riley by Green P. Jackson MG
	5,	Alexander Thane to Ella Dunn by S.C.McCollum JP
	5,	J.D.Warden to Alice C. Hasty by William Buntley JP
	8,	Monroe Peyton to Mattie Bryant by J.B.Riley JP
	7,	G.W.J.Kay to R.B.McMinn
	9,	J.M.Stewart to M.H.Wilson (returned not executed)10th May
	12,	A.N.Ramsey to L.M.Fuls by H.T.Childs JP
pg 218		
	12,	J.W.Haney to Emma Brown by S.H.McCord JP
	19,	J.B.B.Shull to Louisa Hudson (col) by David Whitaker MG
	19,	H.W.Counts to Phebe Ann Crabtree by J.A.Hall JP
	19,	Aaron Bonner to Mary McMullin (col) by L.N.Merry MG
	22,	B. McDonald to Julia Henderson (col) by Jerry Phillips MG
	21,	Levi Winkler to Nancy E. Stewart
	25,	D.A.McCullick to Sarah Benson by W.E.Carter JP
	26,	John M. Moore to Laura M. Stewart
	26,	George Beavers to Margaret Buchanan (col) by Rev. M.S. Slatter
Sep	2,	A.J.Land to Avis Smith by J.A.Woods MG
pg 219		
Jul	9,	E.L.Cambron to Emily Gattis by J.T.Barker JP
	9,	W.R.McCollum to Sallie Tate by Elder J.J.Short
	9,	Jasper Dickey to Mary H. Kidd by A.S.Sloan
	10,	J.W.Danley to Cordie Bates by J.B.Muse
	18,	J.R.McMillen to Maggie M. Good by A.B.Coleman MG
	16,	Dr. J.B.Gorden to M.E.McCown
	16,	Judge Flack to Anna Mederis (col)
	17,	H.L.Zimmerman to Orlena Hughey by J.H.Smith JP
	17,	Marcus Bowden to Bettie Campbell by Green P. Jackson VDM
	20,	W.F.McGee to Sarah J. Faulkner by J.M.Noblett JP
pg 220		
	19,	C.F.Baitman to Mattie Epps by William Buntley JP
	20,	Walter Mills to S.J.Webb by G.B.McKenzie JP
	21,	George Chappell to Nellie Radford by G.P.Jackson VDM
	27,	T.F.Groce to Susan Wagoner by J.M.Noblett JP

```
1879
Aug  5,    Samuel C. Caudle to S.E.Scott by G.B.McKenzie JP
Jul 22,    George Koonce to Charity Bonner (col) by W.J.Young MG
    22,    R.T.Hoots to Franklin Thomison by J.W.Jean JP
    23,    Marcellus Spotswood to Susie Bonner (col) by J.F.
                                              Humphrey MG
    22,    Henry Tucker to Jennie Bonner (col) by W.J.Young MG
    25,    John Hale to Louiza Scrimpshire by S.H.McCord JP
pg 221
    28,    John W. Marcum to Henrietta Braden by S.M.Emmons MG
    27,    W.H.Young to Rebeca Wright (col) by J.F.Humphrey MG
    29,    H.G.Luttrell to Eliza Peyton by J.B.Riley JP
    31,    Moses Cathey to Emaline Sullivan (col) by A.S.Templeton JP
    31,    R.C.Templeton to E.A.Pitts by W.B.Lowery MG
    31,    George M. Bishop to M.M.Seaton
Aug  6,    P.L.Twitty to Mattie F. Thompson by D. Tucker MG
     4,    N.F.Wells to S.M.Rieves by L.C.Butler JP
     7,    J.T.Wilson to J.A.Hames by W.W.Wilson JP
     5,    J.Y.Burnes to S.M.Rives by G.B.McKenzie JP
pg 222
     6,    S.C.Hipsh to Tillie Nassauer by Rev. J.S.Golamer
     7,    Robert Ables to Mary Sisk by G.B.McKenzie JP
     7,    R.C.Smith to Mary E. Gibbs by W.A.Rhodes JP
    10,    R.H.Bryan to M.S.Woodard by L.L.Cole JP
    13,    Buck Petty to Mary Webb
    14,    Charley Bryson to Fannie Bonner (col) by L.N.Merry MG
    19,    Thomas Damron to Cora Sisco by J.T.Barker JP
    19,    William F. Payne to Jennie Howard by W.F.Jarred JP
    24,    John S. McDaniel to Bettie Metcalf by Charles Kelley JP
    24,    W.D.Mitchell to M.C.Mosley by L.W.Cherry MG
pg 223
    24,    Andy Greer to Adline Murphy (col) by W.S.Slatter MG
    23,    Henry Lamb to Ella Lamb (col) by Alex. Fulton MG
    27,    Jesse Tallant to Melia Roland by B.A.Cornelias MG
    24,    John W. Sanders to Susan F. Strong by J.B.Muse MG
    29,    G.L.King to L.E.Durham by Rev. B.T.King
    28,    P.D.Banks to K.A.Phillips by Levi Easlick JP
    28,    J.H.Cobb to L.E.Thurman by Levi Easlick JP
    28,    John Dyer to Mary Foster (col) by L.C.Butler JP
    28,    Ben Smith to Della Gilbert (col) by J.F.Humphrey MG
    28,    Abe Sebastian to Emily Whitaker (col) by A.J.Whitaker JP
pg 224
    28,    Dick Bonner to Leathy Robinson (col) by J.F.Humphrey MG
    31,    Charley Lay to Ellen Todd (col) by J.F.Humphrey MG
    30,    Spence Gustus to Mary Lamb (col)
    31,    J.B.Whitaker to Minnie McCollum (col)
Sep  3,    W.L.Bryant to Lou Hamby by J.F.Smith JP
     3,    W.L.Kilpatrick to M.H.Wilson by A.S.Sloan
     4,    Sewell Turner to Margaret A. Spray by W.A.Rhodes JP
     4,    W.D.Bennett to T.S.D.White by W.F.Jarred JP
     7,    James I. Odam to Nancy A. Stewart by B.A.Cornelius
     9,    George W. Johnson to Millie L. Puckett by Isaac Gatlin,M
pg 225
    11,    David McGee to Martha J. Canial by A.J.Parker MG
    11,    Eli Chasteen to Sallie A. Willeby by A.J.Parker MG
    12,    J.B.Leatherwood to Norah Pitts by W.B.Lowery MG
    12,    C.L.Street to Alice Dorris by W.B.Lowery MG
    10,    Eli Henderson to Mary Tallant by B.A.Cornelius
    11,    G.T.Bragg to H.J.Binum(Bynum) by Rev. B.T.King
```

```
1879  11,   Joe Pamplin to M.M.Whitworth by Wm. Buntley JP
      15,   Richard Taylor to Eliza Smith by W.E.Carter JP
      20,   R.L.Hamby to D.D.Laws by S.Washburn JP
      18,   Sam Smith to Rachel McGee (col) by J.D.Floyd MG
pg 226
      18,   W.T.Marshall to L.C.Revis
      18,   A.J.Nalley to Sarah Gulley by W.E.Carter JP
Oct 19,   John W. Smith to Mattie J. Metcalf by Charles Kelly JP
Sep 21,   Mack Bonner to Susan Street (col) by Alex. Fulton MG
      25,   H.L.Brown to Cordelia Mitchell by W.F.Jarred JP
      23,   W.C.Metcalf to Nancy E. Cole by D.L.Mitchell MG
      27,   Ned Sabra to Mollie Whitaker (col)
      27,   John McAllister to Maud Neely by W.T.Gill MG
      29,   John Farrar to Ellen Barkster (col)
Oct  1,   W.W.Pool to M.I.Pinkerton by A.S.Randolph JP
pg 227
       5,   R.F.Robison to M.C.Wilbanks by F.L.Ezell JP
       2,   J.B.Sanderson to M.A.Boland by J.F.Smith JP
       2,   Pleasant Snoddy to Delia Ashworth by Isaiah Hancock JP
       3,   Albert Pryor to Jane Jennings (col)
       7,   A.J.Burton to P.L.Randolph by A.S.Randolph JP
       8,   D.W.Thompson to M.E.Banks by W.E.Carter JP
Oct  9,   Lucius Clark to Mary Cole (col) (returned not executed)
      12,   Thomas Britton to Emaline Lynn by B.B.Bradford JP
      14,   J.J.White to E.T.Jean by C.A.McDaniel JP
      16,   G.W.Harvey(Hanvey) to A.F.Pamplin by A. Washburn
pg 228
      16,   W.J.M.Cole to E.C.Cummings by D.L.Mitchell MG
      22,   N.D.Woods to S.E.Birchenough by B.J.McNalley by C.Priest
      22,   T.J.Taylor to Ella Epps by L.L.Clark JP
      23,   Charley Edmondson to Fannie Taylor (col) by J.T.Barker JP
      25,   William Simmons to Mary Harris (col) by Levi Eslick JP
      25,   William Webb to Julia George (col) by M.D.Moorehead JP
      23,   W.T.Cowley to Mollie F. Lively by W.F.Jarred JP
      23,   W.J.Bradford to I.N.Commons by W.B.Lowery MG
      26,   O.G.Harrison to Ella Harrison by B.F.Hudson MG
      26,   R.A.Eddins to Leah Granlin (col) by Jery Phelps MG
pg 229
      25,   T.H.Gentry to Sarah T. Pool by J.W.Rawls JP
Nov  6,   C.G.Bates to Margaret W. Howard by S.W.Bruce MG
Oct 30,   William Ethridge to Mary A. Gaut by J.B.Riley JP
      28,   Henry Webb to Permelia Boggs by J.S.Waddle JP
      29,   George C. Gillespie to S.H.Gill by W.T.Gill MG
      29,   W.L.Sandlin to Medora H. McMillen by A.S.Randolph JP
      30,   George March to Julia Coppage (col) by A. Clark MG
      31,   J.C.Bullard to Nancy J. Shepard by B.A.Cornelius MG
Nov  2,   J.C.Coats to Alice E. Byers by W.B.Lowery MG
       6,   Sterling Brown to Sallie T. Downing by W.B.Lowery MG
pg 230
       4,   Samuel Hopkins to Hellen J. Caston by Rev. J.C.Wrals
       6,   George Dugger to Lissie Jester (col) by D.C.Sherrell JP
       6,   George Dunlap to Annie B. Vance (col) by S.W.Bruce MG
      16,   Thomas Wilson to Harriett Nelson (col) by D.C.Sherrell JP
      13,   A.J.Walker to Marietta Marlow by J.H.Smith JP
      13,   Isom Smith to Louiza Cannon by J.W.Rawls JP
      13,   I.B.Maddox to Rinda Cadon by R.M.Woodard MG
      13,   J.C.Wright to R.B.Street by W.B.Lowery MG
      13,   W.P.George to A.E.Bayless by I.J. Towry JP
```

1879	17, pg 231	Joe Simmons to Ella McAdams by A. Washburm JP
	20,	John Williams to Clara Phillips
	26,	A.J.Isabell to R.J.Pool by S.W.Bruce MG
	21,	John T. Moore to Mrs. Mary E. Berry by J.T.Barker MG
	24,	Rufus Buchanan to Icy George (col)
	30,	James M. Stone to Martha E. Turner by L.L.Clark JP
	27,	J.M.Moore to M.H.Moore by Rev. N.D.Crawford
	27,	Jess Waggoner to Sue McNeece by G.W.Mitchell MG
	30,	J.C.Koonce to M.O.Locker by J.J.Stevenson Esq
Dec	3,	John B. Bright to Kate Gill by W.T.Gill MG
	4, pg 232	Bob Mills to Mattie Harwell by G.B.McKenzie JP
	4,	S.D.Walker to N.L.Lamb by Isaiah Hancock JP
	11,	J.M.K.Jobe to M.E.Gault by H.T.Childs JP
	10,	Mart Douthat to Amanda Sugg (col) by J.H.Smith JP
	11,	Joe Minor to Sarah A. Maddox by W.B.Lowery MG
	13,	William Hawkins to Martha Ann McDonald (col) by L.L.Cole
	13,	Green Parks to Mary Buchanan (col) by J.F.Humphrey
	17,	W.A.Rhodes to M.E.Chapman by W.A.Franklin JP
	15,	Dawson Rozell to Emily Mason by Isaiah Hancock JP
	17,	John Gray to E.J.Cowan by D.C.Sherrell JP
	17, pg 233	H.H.Jarret to Celia Cowan by D.C.Sherrell JP
	21,	T.A.Story to S.N.George by F.L.Ezell JP
	17,	A.J.Rowe to Fannie L. Philpot
	17,	R.P.Smith to Nannie Hunter by A.S.Randolph JP
	18,	M.H.Wright to L.J.Duley by J.B.Tigert MG
	18,	George Summers to Ann Buchanan (col) by S.C.McCollum JP
	18,	J.S.Parker to A.D.Coats by W.B.Lowry MG
	20,	L.F.Austin to Mattie J. Hamilton by J.T.Barker MG
	19,	J.W.Watt to Sarah Holman
	20,	T.F.Mitchell to Mattie E. Brown by S.M.Cherry
	21, pg 234	James M. Posey to Elizabeth Posey by J.B.Tigert MG
	24,	F.P.L.Parr to Emaline Hazlewood by F.L.Ezell JP
	24,	Alonzo N. Hughey to Elenora Reese by Elder W.H.Dixon
	24,	John Strickland to Betty Merrell by S.M.Emmons MG
	24,	R.D.McAlister to S.A.Towry
	24,	J.B.Price to Della Robe by J.H.Smith JP
	25,	Thomas A. Beard to S.E.Crawford by T.J.Jones MG
	25,	Dr. F.R.Rawls to Jessie M. Lovelace by W.B.Lowry MG
	25,	Bill Zimmerman to Elizabeth Jane Wilson (col) by N.C. Sullivan JP
	28,	Tom Kelso to Lou Fulton (col) by W.B.Carter JP
	26, pg 235	Wyatt Vance to Jane Hampton (col) by John Cary JP
	25,	Lewis Bonner to Bell Robertson (col) by J.B.McKenzie JP
	25,	Hardy Beavers to Mariah Buchanan (col) by Arch Clark MG
	26,	W.C.Stubblefield to R.E.Solomon by W.E.Carter JP
	26,	Bob Millhouse to Louisa Rutledge (col) by Edward W. Halback
	28,	W.L.Hicks to N.A.Hobbs by R.M.Woodard JP
	30,	Wallace Henderson to Ann Clark (col) by A.C.Martin JP
	29,	Andy Bryant to Mary Langston by J.B.Riley JP
	29,	John Bonner to Mariah Clark (col)
	30,	James Easlick to Harriet Sebastian (col) by W.J.Young MG
	30,	W.T.Haggard to America Groce

pg 236 1879
   30,   S.A.Rosebrough to Jennie Greer (col) by W.J.Hamilton JP
1880
Jan 1,   John Jones to Mary A. Mullins by W.A.Rhodes JP
1879
Dec 31,   W.T.Cowan to M.A.Vance by W.T.Gill MG

LINCOLN COUNTY MARRIAGES EXTRACTED FROM NASHVILLE NEWSPAPERS

Henry Smith to Mary Hannah	Dec 30, 1820 NBNW
James G. Smith to Margaret Beard	May 27, 1826 NB
Isaac H. Wall of Huntsville,Ala. to Susan P. Smith	Apr 7, 1827 NBNW
Bezil Nelson to Mary Boyles	Nov 17, 1827 NBNW
Isaac Buchanan to Naomi Crawford	Oct 6, 1827 NBNW
Augusta Cannon to Eliza Jane Holman	Sep 8, 1827 NBNW
Charles Moore to Perlina,dau of Mark Whitaker	Sep 8, 1827 NBNW
Rev. Albert G. Gibson to Sarah Erwin, (mrd in Hazelgreen, Ala.)	Dec 13, 1828 NBNW
William D. Thompson,Esq. to Hetty E.K. Greer	Feb 2, 1828 NBNW
Elbridge G. Buchanan to Catherine Garner	Feb 26, 1830 NBNW
Hugh McKenzie to Rebecca C. Cole	Jan 29, 1830 NBNW
L.L.Stone to Eveline Drake (mrd in Madison County, Ala.)	Jun 3, 1830 NBNW
Joel Reece to Polly R. Leftwich	Jan 24, 1830 NBNW
James Sappington to Cynthia Norris	Jun 24, 1830 NBNW
John Park to Martha Parham	Jun 5, 1830 NBNW
Champion E. Smith to Mary Walton (mrd in Lawrence County, Ala.)	Apr 4, 1831 NBNW
N.B.Garner to Ann L. McConnell	Sep 28, 1831 NBNW
Col. Elliot Fletcher to Frances Hickman	Jan 24, 1831 NBNW
Maj. Thomas J. Dye to Eleanor Cocke (mrd in Maury County, Tn.)	Aug 8, 1831 NBNW
Lafayette Booker to Eliza Coffman	Feb 21, 1831 NBNW
Henry L. Brown to Laura P. Mosely (both of Alabama)	Jul 6, 1832 NBNW
N.C.Burford, of Giles County, Tn. to Ann A. Lesueur	Jul 6, 1832 NBNW
J.F.Callaway to Mary Cassander	Dec 31, 1832 NBNDA
Charles McKinney, Esq. to E. Howell	Nov 8, 1832 NBNDA
Thomas G. McGehee of Madison County, Ala. to Minerva Hunt	Oct 1, 1832 NBNDA
Samuel Talley to Lillian Short (mrd in Williamson County, Tn.)	Nov 29, 1833 NBNW
Jesse Oliver to Mary Ady	Dec 17, 1834 NBNW
Baker W. Ayres to Elizabeth West	Dec 6, 1834 NBNW
W.L.Berry to Nancy G. Wallace	May 12, 1834 NBNW
Mathew Martin to Margaret Bright, of Nashville	Apr 3, 1834 NRSG
Jacob Butts to Catherine Smith	Dec 6, 1834 NBNW
Samuel W. Carmack,Esq to Margaret Greer	Nov 26, 1834 NBNW

```
William Carty to Ann Russell                         May 12, 1834 NBNW
James D. Cunningham of Huntsville,Ala.
       to Sarah Turner                               Oct 20, 1834 NBNW
Gideon B. Cunningham to Mary R. Davis                Dec  6, 1834 NBNW
Asa Messer to Elizabeth Gibson                       Dec  6, 1834 NBNW
Joseph J.G.Gill to Angeline Moore                    Dec 17, 1834 NBNW
William A. Griffis to Mahala Johnson                 Dec  5, 1834 NBNW
William Harris to Eliza Old                          Dec 17, 1834 NBNW
Silas Hindman to Synthia J. Smith                    Dec  5, 1834 NBNW
Daniel Hughes of Logan County, Ky. to
       Nancy King                                    Nov 12, 1834 NBNW
Mark M. Lucas to Louisa Taylor                       Oct 17, 1834 NBNW
L.S.Quick to Tabitha McDougle                        Dec  6, 1834 NBNW
Mr. C. McFadder to Minerva Silvertooth               Dec  5, 1834 NBNW
Jesse Bain to Nancy C. McLain                        Dec  6, 1834 NBNW
William McMillen to Julia Moorehead                  Oct 17, 1834 NBNW
James Mangrum to Averille Williamson                 Nov 12, 1834 NBNW
Thomas Simpson to Nancy Rowark                       May 20, 1834 NBNW
Newton Whitaker to Frances Ann Wynn                  Jan 25, 1835 NR
John Watson to Launna Stewart                        Apr 20, 1835 NBNW
John M. Rowell to Lucinda Shuffield                  Jan  5, 1835 NBNW
John M. McDonald to Catherine M.
       McKenzie                                      Apr 20, 1835 NBNW
William Outon to Nancy Jones                         Apr 10, 1835 NBNW
Micajah P. Hedgepeth to Matilda Hays                 Jan 23, 1835 NBNW
George W. Stone to Mary Gillespie                    Jan  5, 1835 NBNW
Solomon Rutter to Elizabeth Elzy                     Jan 23, 1835 NBNW
John M. Donnohoo to Mary Ziverly                     Jan 23, 1835 NBNW
Doak McMillen to Madeline Davis                      Feb  5, 1835 NR
John Anderson to Margaret Kidd                       Apr 20, 1835 NBNW
John H. Bonner to Lucy Phillips                      Apr 20, 1835 NBNW
John C. Young to Ara C. Caruthers                    Apr 20, 1835 NBNW
Thomas B. Coleman to Maria E. Harper                 Jan 23, 1835 NBNW
William B. Crawford to Martha B. Moore               Jan  5, 1835 NBNW
Burgess Gray to Elizabeth Cunningham                 Jan 23, 1835 NBNW
William M. Old to Eliza Ann Edmiston                 Jan  5, 1835 NBNW
William H. Renegar to Arrena Miles                   Sep  8, 1835 NBNW
John Conally of Alabama to Frances Jones Jun 10, 1836 NBNW
John Weigart to Millberry Ann Jones                  Jun 10, 1836 NBNW
William McEwen,Esq. of Chulahoma, Miss.
       to Tabitha McKinney                           Jul 25, 1837 NBNW
James F. Drake to Mary A. Bright (mrd
       in Madison County, Ala.)                      Oct 27, 1837 RB
Byrd Douglass to Martha R. Bright                    Oct 23, 1838 NW
```

186

LINCOLN COUNTY MARRIAGES EXTRACTED FROM
LINCOLN COUNTY NEWSPAPERS
&
OBITUARY ITEMS

James Tucker to E.C.Tucker(obit.-mrd in N.C.)	Aug 14, 1814
Joel Commons to Sarah Gray (obit.)	1817
Alexander R. Kerr to Cynthia Campbell	Feb 20, 1823
Jesse B. Clements to Lucinda Norris	Mar 25, 1823
John J. Allen to Mary Ann Blake	May 15, 1823
Jonathan Frost to Eliza Caldwell of Bedford County, Tn.	Jul 14, 1823
Edward Sanderson of Sumner County, Tn. to Elizabeth Ann Holman	Jul 31, 1823
William Craig to Elizabeth Stringer	Aug 18, 1823
James McKinney to Tempe Rowe	Aug 27, 1823
S.E.Gilliland to Mary S. Fulton	Aug 28, 1823
Joseph Campbell to Rebecca Knowles	Sep 10, 1823
David A. Greer to Lucinda D. Wiley of Greenville, East Tn.	Nov 19, 1823
Robert S. Holmes to Minerva Norris	Jan 29, 1824
Maj. Andrew A. Kincannon to Agnes Garner	Feb 17, 1824
Ebenezer Hill to Mary Bryan	Feb 12, 1824
Pulaski Dudley of Tuscumbia, Ala. to Susan M. Bass	Feb 26, 1824
Charles Maze of McMinnville, Tn. to Nancy Hughes	Mar 25, 1824
Allen J. Kennedy to Agnes Harris of Huntsville, Ala.	Mar 30, 1824
Capt. Payton Wells to Mary Clift	Apr 22, 1824
Dr. Robert Martin to Melinda Conger	Jun 20, 1824
Maj. Robert Moore to Hannah Moores	Aug 18, 1824
James McCollum to Keziah Broilles	Sep 13, 1824
John H. Laird of Columbia, Tn. to Nancy G.Bryan	Nov 9, 1824
William E. Kennedy,Esq to Elizabeth O. Willis of Maury County, Tn.	Dec 16, 1824
Thomas J. Bryan to Angeline Davidson of Bedford County, Tn.	Dec 28, 1824
George Stonebraker to -------------(obit)	1825
William L. Petty to Mary V. Greer	Jan 4, 1825
John S. McAda to Jane Sanson	Jan 4, 1825
Robert Hannah to Melinda Jenkins	Jan 11, 1825
William Beverly to ----------------(obit)	1826
William Marsh to Clarissa Marsh	Apr 13, 1826
James Cunningham to Nancy Groce	May 4, 1826
John Beard to Rebecca Turner	May 2, 1826
Isom G. Smith to Margaret Beard	May 7, 1826
John Formwalt to Matilda Moyer	Jun 6, 1826
Natley Wilkinson to Peggy Richardson	Jun 20, 1826
Spruce McCoy to Hannah Barclay	Jul 13, 1826
Ambrose B. Gilbert to Sarah Wright	Jul 20, 1826
Capt. Thomas Hines of Fairfield District,S.C. to Mary R. Moores	Jul 27, 1826
George L. Lenard to Mary Gilbert	Jul 27, 1826
Joel Yowell,Esq to Mrs. Nancy Butler of Bedford County, Tn.	Jul 23, 1826
Capt. Cornelius Slater to Mary Ross	Aug 10, 1826
Eason Coulter to Jane Cunningham	Jul 22, 1826

Thomas Massey to Polly Rains of and mrd in Davidson County, Tn.	Aug 10, 1826
Eli Moores to Finetta Hines	Aug 31, 1826
John H. Clark to Rebecca H. Berry	Oct 1, 1826
John Ferguson to Eliza Woodroof	Oct 5, 1826
Henry Moore to Fanny Cole	Nov 9, 1826
Capt. Lee Smith to Elizabeth Clift	Dec 12, 1826
Sylvester Rife to Catharine Baker	Dec 12, 1826
Henry Smith to Mary Hannah	Dec 14, 1826
Joseph Wallace to Mary Harden	Dec 14, 1826
Mr. Allsup to Rachel Fitch	Dec 14, 1826
Fielding Parks to Caroline Davis	Dec 14, 1826
William Brown to Elizabeth Dorsey	Feb 15, 1827
Capt. S.S.Holden to Elvira Gullet of Maury County, Tn.	Feb 1827
John Gallegher to Fanny Blakemore	Feb 24, 1827
William Crawford to Nancy Garner	Feb 25, 1827
Capt. James Rorax to Parthenia Parks	Apr 1, 1827
James Griffith to Temperance Braden	May 4, 1827
Benjamin Berry to Fanny Ingle	May 3, 1827
Hillery Russeau to Lucretia Jennings(obit)	Sep 5, 1827
Alexander McNutt to Nancy Johnson	Aug 31, 1827
Leander Buchanan to Margaret Buchanan	Aug 30, 1827
Isaac Buchanan to Naomi Crawford	Sep 13, 1827
James Sweet to Mrs. Barbara Key	Oct 1, 1827
William Morton to Rachel Crawford	Oct 9, 1827
Thomas Short to Martha Kennon	Oct 10, 1827
Capt. Benjamin W.D.Carty to Catharine Bright	Oct 11, 1827
Bird Glidwell to Elizabeth Stinson	Oct 17, 1827
Maj. Richard Jones to Lucretia Ball	Oct 16, 1827
Bezil Nelson to Mary Boyles	Oct 25, 1827
Thomas B. Wyatt to Isabella Wham	Nov 1, 1827
William D. Thompson to Hetty E.K.Greer	Oct 17, 1827
Dr. William Bonner to Lucy Robertson	Jul 4, 1828
Augustus Cannon of Shelbyville, Tn. to Eliza Jane Holman	Aug 28, 1828
Charles Moore of Nashville, Tn. to Perlina Whitaker	Aug 17, 1828
Col. Davis Smith to Ruth Davis	Feb 7, 1828
Claiborne B. Worsham to Ellenor G. Bryans	Feb 10, 1828
John Porch to Nancy Maddox	Mar 9, 1828
Rev. Henry Bryson to Hannah -------	Nov 28, 1828
John C. Sloan to Elizabeth Morrow (obit)	1830
John Landess to Mary Stone (obit)	Apr 5, 1831
Robert Welch to Nancy Vaughn (obit.-mrd in Pa.)	Dec 27, 1832
McCager Pamplin to Lavina Frances -----(obit)	1832
Rev. W.A.Gill to E.F.----Gill (obit)	Jun 1, 1832
Abraham Noblett to Sarah Ann ---- (obit)	1833
James M. George to Mollie Sims (obit)	Feb 23, 1833
William R. Monday to Sarah K. Parsley (obit)	Apr 24, 1834
Josiah McCracken to Julia Curtis (obit)	Apr 30, 1834
Hugh T. Thomison to Elizabeth ------ (obit)	1835
Charles A. Franch to Olivia Neeld (obit)	Feb 12, 1835
Col. G.B.McKenzie to Matilda McKenzie (obit)	Jan 17, 1836
Abner Brady to Julian Gattis (obit)	Jan 7, 1836
W.M.Dameron to ---------- (obit)	1838

LINCOLN COUNTY MARRIAGES FROM MISCELLANEOUS
FAMILY RECORDS

A.J.Freeman to Polly A. ------	Dec 29, 1835
Thomas Boaz to Fanny Parks	Nov 22, 1814
John G. Broadaway to Elizabeth P.Boaz	Oct 18, 1831
Daniel Farrar to Nancy Caroline Shipp	Dec 25, 1830
Robert H. McEwen to Hetty M. Kennedy	Nov 14, 1815
John Downing to Elizabeth Lawrence	Mar 24, 1825
James Downing to Lydia Williamson	May 27, 1820
A. Downing to Elizabeth W. McClain	Jan 13, 1831
Alfred Bearden to Margaret Downing	Feb 24, 1831
Samuel Downing to Rebecca Williamson	Oct 12, 1831
Elijah Downing to Jane Clark	Aug 21, 1834
Johnson Downing to Nancy Goodwin	Feb 6, 1834
Thomas Downing to Elizabeth Cooper	May 17, 1835
William Stewart to Nancy McLain	Oct 12, 1831
Harmon Cummins to Dorcas Jones	Jul 21, 1825
James M. Spencer to Scicily Foster	Oct 29, 1829
George Waggoner to Jane Gattis	Dec 7, 1823
Alfred C. Dickey to Eliza Gibson	Jul 30, 1835
David R. Sowell to Mary M. Bingham	Jan 15, 1838
Joel Dollins to Mary(Polly) Armstrong	Jan 26, 1815
William Ingle to Sally Ingle	Oct 18, 1821
Robert N. McKinney to Elizabeth	
Crutchfield in Danville, Ky.	Jul 17, 1832
Robert Jones to Catharine M.--------	Feb 1, 1821
Thomas K. Warren to Elizabeth Ann	
Warren	Jul 2, 1835
Ephraim Washington McRady to Sarah M.	
Wingfield	Feb 15, 1826
Ephraim Washington McRady to Margaret	
White	Dec 18, 1839
Nathaniel Gattis to Mary Cate	Feb 10, 1824
E. Thomas George to Susannah Hobbs	Mar 13, 1823
Joseph George to Mary Margaret Colwell	Mar 26, 1822
Thomas George to Lilley Black	Apr 11, 1825
Needham B. Koonce to Burdotta Koonce	Jan 1, 1832
Joseph McMillen to Rachel Norris	Aug 18, 1814
James Loyd to Charity Pain	Feb 13, 1820
John S. Waddle to Nancy Shanks	Jan 27, 1837
William Thomas to Rebecca Lyon	Oct 19, 1814
M.L.Owens to Susannah Cowder	Feb 23, 1836
Richmond Campbell to Sarah S. Campbell	Dec 20, 1832
Thomas Conwell to Elizabeth Robertson	Mar 13, 1821
J.John Fullerton to Margaret Wyatt	Mar 17, 1811
Rhodes West to Elizabeth Wyatt	Dec 30, 1819
John Wyatt to Margaret Greer Hamilton	Nov 11, 1830
Alexander Morton,Jr. to Sarah Wyatt	May 3, 1832
William Wyatt to Sarah Breckenridge	Feb 18, 1834
Thomas Childs to Mary Meeks	Mar 7, 1822
Daniel Taylor to Arminta --------	1838
Harvey Gray to Emaline Gray	1836
W.M.Byers to Malina ---------	Mar 1, 1836
John H. Moore to Margaret H. Armstrong	1837
S.S.Alexander to Mary M. -------	Nov 8, 1827
Joseph Boyce to Martha J. ------	Jun 7, 1820
George Stewart to Harriett J.Woodward	Apr 7, 1836

Liberty Beasley to Mary W. Doak   1824
Isham Smith to Jimenter Olmer   Jun 22, 1837
Andrew Buchanan to Bethiah Lynn White   Feb 19, 1815
Washington Hunter to Sarah Hobbs   Mar 17, 1836
Simeon Nix to Sarah Taylor   1830

B., Martha C. 155
Bachelor, Nancy 150; Rachel
163
Baggett (Baget, Badgett),
John S. 81; J. R. 141;
Sack 106
Bagley, Ann 92,140; Anna
176; Ann Eliza 56;
Charley 143; Elisha 5;
Emeline E. 67; Harry 92;
J. E. 141; J. M. 164;
Louisa 157; Mary J. 124;
Mary O. 52; Rebecca W.
35; R. D. 113; Sallie
174; Sarah Jane 39;
Susan Jane 123; Thomas
141; William H. 35
Bagwell, M. J. 144
Bailey (Baily), Ann E. 98;
Arretter 50; Benjamin
162; Catharine B. 55;
Clarina M. 10; Cullen
73; Dianna 49; Elizabeth
117; Follin 139; Frances
M. 19; George 158; Ike
158; Isham G. 2; James
127,147; Jane 3; J. E.
79; Jarrett 158; Louisa
51; Louisa J. 19; Lucinda
126; Margaret 49; Martha
107; Mary Ann 78; M. C.
135; N. A. 69; Nancy M.
64; O. J. 115; Thomas
25; William B. 140;
William H. 36; Wilson
119; W. R. 124
Bain, Jesse 185
Baker, Catharine 61,187;
Eliza Ann 45; Eliza J.
24; Elizabeth 135; Enoch
G. 44; Ezekiel 16;
Frances A. 128; George
144; James M. 124; Jane
113; John 36; John P.
102; Joseph 39; Martha
E. 114; P. T. 157; S. A.
157; Silas 153
Balch, John T. 6
Baldwin (Baldin, Balden),
E. B. 117; F. M. 76.100,
166; Louvina Mrs. 107;
Sallie 120; William D.
40; William T. 77; W. T.
177
Baldridge, Lizzie B. 151
Ballard, Isaac 98
Bandy, Elizabeth 16; John
B. 35; Sarah 34
Banks, Elizabeth Jane 71;
F. M. 57; M. L. 180
Bankstone, W. L. 86
Banton, C. M. 80
Baptist, Sarah Ann 33
Barber, Abe 165
Barclay, Hannah 186
Barham, James M. 41,81;
Letisha C. 76; Martha
Jane 56; N. C. 129
Barker, Andrew 146; James
111; James T. 94; Lucy
A. 95; Martha 56; Mary
I. J. 52; Milly 80;
Susan M. 67
Barkster, Ellen 182
Barley, Ruth E. 78
Barnes (Barns), Ann 153;
Calvin 177; Catharine
103; C. E. 173; Corne-
lius 150; Decatur 45;
E. A. 150; Eli 6,78;
Emeline 73; Ezekiel L.
25; F. M. 101; Frances
C. 112; George E. 142;
Henderson 46;

Barnes contd.
Henderson T. 150; Henry
J. 34,121; H. M. 170;
Jacob 16; J. F. 147;
John 13,169; J. W. 177;
Lafayette F. 85; L. C.
142; Louisa C. 27; Lu-
cinda 160; M. A. 173;
Margaret C. 67; Margaret
Jane 118; Martha J. 113;
Mary C. 110; M. E. 156;
Mollie 145; Mollie E.
121; Nancy E. 35; Nancy
J. 126; N. C. 157;
Richard C. 23; Rodderick
29; Rutha 22; Sarah A.
158; Thomas M. 165; W. A.
113,130; W. H. 147;
William O. 19
Barrett, Harriett 171
Bartlett (Bartlet), James
137; John 100; Manerva
77; Mansel 8, Mary 131;
Ritty C. 69; William 79
Bass, Eliza 170; Frances
149; Lucinda 162; Susan
M. 186; York 165
Bateman (Baitman), C. F.
180; Henry 80
Bates (Baits), Alvin 57;
Anthony 35; Caroline 76;
Catharine 147; C. G.
182; Clem 169; Cordie
180; Edy 124; George 18;
George B. 127; George E.
80; G. J. 172; James 20,
29,59; James W. 165;
Jane 160; Jasper R. 37;
J. M. 64; John V. 96;
J. W. 113,178; Marlon
147; Martha E. 134; Mary
163; May 22; Nancy S.
110; Narcissa 11; Robert
112; Samuel 33; Sarah
C. 126; Sarah J. 73;
Tempsey 49; Tilman 153;
W. C. 179; William 130;
William C. 48; William
D. 41
Batt, Goodwin 116
Battle, A. O. 165; Judy
110
Baxley, David 150
Baxter, Archibald 1; Eliza-
beth K. 18; Hester 61;
John F. 44; Joseph H.
72; J. R. 124; Margaret
M. 46; Mary C. 36; Sarah
E. 142; Sarah J. 18;
William B. 26
Bayless, A. E. 182
Beach (Beech), Benjamin
A. 32; Elizabeth 118;
H. H. 82; James L. 55;
William 170; William D.
141
Beachboard, Elizabeth 16;
Susannah 16
Bean (Been), George 101;
James 58; Sally Ann 58
Beanland, Edward G. G. 2;
Jane Brown 131; J. H.
130,179; Mattie R. 127
Beard, Absolum 30,54;
Alexander 3; Benjamin A.
64; Charles M. 62,97;
Eliza Jane 42; Elizabeth
21; Elizabeth M. 59;
Francis M. 49; Ira W. 47;
Jacob B. 26; J. G. 87;
John 186; Lula 177; M.
A. 104,166; Margaret
184,186; Margret 27;
Martha 9; Samuel G. 47;

Beard contd.
Thomas A. 183
Bearden, Alfred 188;
Benjamin F. 13; Callie
179; Daniel H. 39;
Delia O. 102; Eliphaz 48;
E. S. 166; Eudonia D.
117; F. M. 20; John 1;
Josephine 45; L. A. E.
89; L. C. C. 59; Magde-
line 118; Maggie 118;
Mattie M. 160; M. M. 166;
M. V. 72; Nancy B. 52;
P. E. 88; R. M. 89; R. W.
120; William 6,36
Beasley, A. C. 114; Emeline
23; George W. 13; Henry
33; John W. 83; Liberty
189; Martha A. 82; Mary
8; Matilda 121
Beatie (Beatty, Beaty,
Batie), Ann 160; Came
180; Caroline J. 12;
Catharine V. 45; David
M. 20; Eliza 2; John M.
21; Madison 18; Marshall
44; Martha A. 24; Mollie
A. 145; Sallie E. 101;
S. J. 130
Beavers, A. J. 37; Asena
6; Betsey 6; Elizabeth
70; George 155,180; Hardy
183; John 162; Mary 59;
Pleasant W. 63; Priscilla
25; Sarah 30; Sarah P.
65; William 32; W. S. 106
Beck, Calvin 4; David W.
30; George L. 66; Henry
27; James C. 63; Louisa
47; Little Wilson 77;
Wilbourn 2; William P. 38
Becket, William 62; William
M. 61
Beddingfield, Alice M. 54;
Elizabeth 28; Mary 96;
M. J. 77; Nancy 119;
T. J. 96
Bedford, Alexander M. 37;
Ann 21; Benjamin 61;
B. R. 97; James S. 124;
J. L. 3; Marion M. 94;
Sarah Frances 5; Stephen
M. 30; W. H. 129; William
3; William R. 131
Bedwell, Elizabeth 83;
Elle 149; G. B. 111; J. B.
75,160; John B. 24; L. A.
J. 81; Louisa Jane 46;
M. J. 145; Rebecca 18;
Willis L. 52
Beeler, James C. 29
Beggerly (Baggerly, Bagerly),
E. H. 173; John B. 160;
M. A. 125; Mary 7; Mary
E. 30; Rena 95; Timothy
109
Bell, A. A. 43; A. B. 87;
A. H. 61; Annie M. 21;
Barthenia 24; Charley
155; Eliza 70; Elizabeth
104; Francis H. 60;
Henry H. 109; James M.
6,93; Louisa M. 14; M. A.
176; Martha A. 42; Mary
Catharine 79; R. F. 94;
Sarah 3; Sarah M. 11;
Susie D. 159; Thomas W.
7; T. M. 69
Benedict, Horace L. 42
Benington, J. T. 117
Benningfield (Benefield),
Mary J. 64; Thomas M. 45
Bennett (Bennet, Benet), A.
89; A. F. 100; Albert 31;

191

Bennett contd.
Caroline 110; Hicks 62;
John T. 68; John P. 122;
Joshua 135; Marion 85;
Martha 160; Nancy 80;
Robert 126; Thomas 115;
Thomas J. 80; W. D. 181
Benson (Bentson, Besson),
A. D. O. 141; A. J. 99;
Amanda J. 143; Ann 124;
Ben 106; Calvin 170;
Cassena 170; Ceeny 175;
Currin D. 26; Dore 128;
Elizabeth 170; Ella 121;
Faney 125; Fannie 130;
H. D. V. 85; I. A. 73;
I. B. 96; John 106; Levi
33; Lusina 104; Malinda
A. 111; Margaret 146;
Martha 113; Mary E. 68;
M. N. 158; Nancy 126;
Nepoleon 45; Sarah 180;
Sarah A. 127; Sarah P.
179; Thomas E. 159; Wil-
lis 120; Willis D. 80;
W. T. 131
Bentley, William 146
Benton, Arthur 93
Berch, H. H. 80
Berrier, I. A. 159; J. B.
102
Berry, Andrew J. 13;
Benjamin 187; Benjamin
H. 15; B. H. 67; B. H.
Jr. 101; E. A. 127; E. F.
43; George W. 125; G. W.
137; Henry 127; Jackson
4; Jane 1,127; John 122;
John W. 64; Josephus
121; Laura A. 122; M. A.
64; Mahala 120; Martha
116; Mary E. 44; Mary
E. Mrs. 183; Nath 126;
Rebecca E. 137; Rebecca
H. 187; Ruth Ann 128;
Sank 166
Best, Margaret 104
Bethany, Charles 19;
Charles H. 16; Polly 2
Bethune, Amilda 155;
Charles 16; Daniel 17;
John 2; Mathew 44
Beverly, Bascom 66; Eliza
116; E. R. 140; Margaret
122; Mary S. 155; William
186
Bevels (Bevil, Bevill,
Beavel, Bevell), E. G.
64; E. L. Mrs. 145; E. T.
121; G. M. 96,176; Green
22; James 75; Manerva
36; Mary Ann 23,57;
M. J. 127; Sarah 168
Bibb, Americus 128
Biggs, Josiah A. 63
Biggers, C. E. 43; David
L. 25
Biles, E. V. 173; J. M.
173
Billions (Billians,
Billins, Billings),
Anderson 13; Eliza 56;
Jane 56; Jason 91; Jas-
per 101; J. W. 106;
Nancy 73; S. J. 143;
William 28; Zilphey 63
Bills, W. J. 161
Bingham, John L. 176;
Margaret 74; Mary M. 188;
W. J. 111
Birchenough, S. E. 182
Bird, James 115; Sallie
P. 119
Birdsong, Angeline Mrs. 114;

Birdsong contd.
F. M. 114; James A. 176;
John C. 71; Mary 72;
Milage 81; S. S. 113
Birdthrone, Eliza A. 89
Birdwell, Margaret A. 97;
S. C. 95
Birmingham, Alfred O. 47;
Caswell 37; James C. 17;
James M. 8; Sarah 26;
Sarah C. 11
Bishop, Andrew H. 49;
George M. 181; Milton
169
Black, Agnes 113; Alice
120; Charlotte 31; John
F. 6; Lilley 188; Mar-
garet 162; Tillman 119
Blackamore, Daniel 17;
James J. 6; Sophia 5
Blackburn, J. C. 53;
William 133
Blackenship, Caladonia 135
Blacknall, George R. 112
Blackshear (Blacksher,
Blackshires), Anna 11;
David 14; Elizabeth 16;
Henry 146; Jesse 13
Blackwell, C. C. 168;
Charles F. 91; Eliza
Jane 55; James N. 39;
John 71; Margaret F. 49;
Martha W. 50; Mary Ann
65; Mary R. 158; R. C.
60; William C. 50; W. T.
84
Blades, Arnold 14; Cullen
C. 31; Edward 23; Sarah
Louisa 33; Solomon 19
Blair, Cassena 9; Eliza-
beth 61; Jane 113; John
M. 94; John W. 6,128;
J. F. 179; J. W. 98,102,
171; L. C. 70; Lewis C.
26; Martha E. 43; Mary
C. 109; Mary E. 97,130;
Nancy 25; Susan J. 149;
W. B. 95
Blake (Blakes), Alice 174;
Betty Isabella 168;
Catharine D. 50; Charles
95; Dora 151; Fannie 88,
132; George W. 51; G. W.
Dr. 110; H. E. 82;
James 173; John 174;
Margaret E. 58; Martha
A. 27; Mary Ann 39,186;
Mattie D. 114; Nancy 6;
Nancy E. 60; Sarah C.
30; Sarah E. 28; Susan
Ann 71; Susan M. 13;
Tennessee 85; Tooney 151
Blakemore, Chaney S. 37;
Delia 175; Elizabeth T.
32; Ella 172; Fanny 187;
Henry S. 37; Joseph A.
32; Maggie J. 116; M. D.
83; Nancy 176; Nannie 179;
Sarah C. E. 36; Sarah
E. 68; Sarah R. 6; Tho-
mas 56
Bland, B. J. 129; Catha-
rine 93; Elizabeth M.
39; Frances E. 173;
James M. 56; J. F. 144;
John 81; John W. 43;
Labrary 9; Lizzie 153;
Lucy J. 49; Martha E.
55; Mary 59; P. M. 157;
Sarah C. 38; Willis 93;
Z. Taylor 125
Blankenship, E. 2(2);
E. C. 167; Edward 81;
Martha Ann 81; Willis 73

Blankford, M. E. 171
Blanton, Benjamin M. 132
Blaylock, D. L. 173; L. T.
176
Bledsoe, Catharine 93; D.
97; David C. 164; Dru-
cillar Jane 44; Elizabeth
C. 76; Ella E. 172;
Fanie E. 100; George 108,
136; Hannah 171; Hills-
man 108; H. M. 77; Howell
H. 80; J. D. 144; J. F.
154; J. H. 109; J. L.
122; Mary Mrs. 109; M. M.
161; Parthenia 63; P. L.
125; Rebecca 67; Sarah A.
118; Sarah Ann 54; S. E.
96; Solomon C. 147;
Susan Ann 102; Susan F.
101; Tabitha 68; Thomas
134,166; Thomas H. 16,
54; Thomas N. 94,108;
Tillman 108; T. J. 156;
William D. 127; William
R. 131
Blue, Amanda 105; Jacob
53; John 18; Martha Jane
67
Blunt, Jane 107
Blye, W. M. 135
Blyth (Blythe), A. D. 136;
Alfred 6; James 38,97;
Mary 26; Pauline D. 38;
Sarah 7
Boaz, Doak 143; Edmond 7;
Elizabeth P. 188; John
150; P. L. 100; Thomas
28,188; W. N. 87
Bobo, Burrel 29; Ellen 92;
E. P. 113; E. S. N. 52;
I. F. 119; K. J. 120;
Lacy L. 125; Nancy H.
101; William L. 94
Boggs, Henry W. 129; James
A. 150; John O. 172;
M. A. 146; Margaret 178;
Martha 89; Minerva 167;
Permelia 182; Thomas J.
88
Bohannon, M. J. Mrs. 146
Boland, M. A. 182; S. L. 143
Boles, James T. 162; Job
K. 13; Joseph 171; Tho-
mas H. 66; William C. 128
Bolick, Philip 39
Bolten, May A. 22
Bonds (Bond), Bethenia 87;
E. J. 87; George W. 171;
John 11; Lucy J. 177;
Martha J. 37; S. A. 72;
Sarah 77
Bonepart, Henry 148
Bonner (Boner), Aaron 180;
Adam 93; A. G. Y. 90;
Alf 178; Alfred 156;
Alice 120; Allice 111;
Amanda 92,98,125; Ander-
son 81; Ann 118; Arch
125; Bery 139; Betsey
170; Bob 153; Cassanda
88; Charity 181; Charry
96; Coleman 93; Daniel
140; Dick 181; Dock 104;
Edward 170; Eliga 157;
Elijah 179; Eliza Ann
62,95; Elizabeth 123;
Elizabeth F. 66; Emily
91; Fannie 181; Fanny
128; F. M. 129,171;
Frances 115,171; George
166; Henry 116,146;
Hettie 153; Isaac 103;
Izarel 144; James 138,
162; Jane 93; Janius 175;

Bonner contd.
Jennie 101,179,181; John
57,183; John H. 124,185;
John Henry 121; John J.
65; Juda 93; Junurs 93;
Lewis 150,183; Lily 152;
Lizzie 176; Lou 172;
Louisa 143; Lucy 117;
Luddy 108; Lydia R. 52;
Mack 95,182; Mandy 180;
Manerva Jane 35; Marga-
ret 105; Martha 139;
Mary 141,148; Mary F. 77,
97; Mastin 142; Maud 145;
Miles 173; Millie A. 135;
Milton 136; Minerva 160;
Mollie 169; Molly 104;
Mose 151; Moses H. 4;
Nancy 91; Ned 139; Neeld
94; Neeley 126; Nelson
F. 112; Oliver 161; Percy
138; Pink 146; Rosa 178;
Sarah 140; Sarah A. 86;
Sucky 151; Susan 114;
William 91,114; William
Dr. 187; William R. 74;
Wyatt 111
Booker, Lafayette 184
Boone (Boon), A. S. 50,54;
Benjamin 46; D. C. 132;
Dick 168; Fanny A. 62;
Mary M. 25; May 177;
Nathan 57; Richard 150;
S. 79; Sarah 23; Susan
141; William 152
Booth, E. 86
Boren, Helen 66; Jenny 2
Borough (Burrough), Ella
100; Elvira 36; George
69
Bostick (Bostic), A. C.
173; Cynthia 29; E. J.
156; J. M. 160; Mary
Ann 33; Nancy E. 49;
Rose E. 123; Sallie W.
160; T. J. 135
Boteler, Thomas 21
Bowden, Henry 127; James
D. 140; Jesse 109; John
123,142; Joshua 179;
Marcus 180
Bowers (Bower), Andy 164;
Catharine 6; George 18;
Maggie A. 136; Susan 74;
Thomas 134; William S. 2
Bowles (Bowels), Caroline
Jane 54; Minerva A. 55
Bowlin (Bolin, Bowlen,
Bowling), Catharine 115;
George 70; Green 40;
James 43; James E. 156;
Marcus 152; Pinkney J.
28; Susan 76; William
122; William J. 129
Bowman (Boman), Lydy L.
58; Mary 104; Naomi 3
Boyce, Joseph 188; P. D.
139; Robert 33; Sarah A.
20; Susan J. 20;
William 141
Boyd, A. V. 105; Christo-
pher 22; Cyntha Caroline
77; Henrietta 173; Jack
155; Joseph 19; Mary 68;
Nancy 137; Nancy E. 101;
Robert 49,64,99,159;
Samuel 133; Sarah 67;
W. K. 113; W. M. 168
Boyles (Boyle), John
Colman 54; Mary 184,187;
Mary A. 118; Patrick 84
Bracken, Thomas G. 37
Braden, Anna 108; Arlenia
156; Henrietta 181;

Braden contd.
James W. 67; Jane 49;
John W. 60; J. W. 144;
L. C. 151; Lucinda C.
68; Nancy 5,6; Nancy A.
36; Narcissa 19; Peter
C. 177; Temperance 187
Bradford, Annie E. 161;
Charlotte 46; C. J. 177;
D. G. 155; Elizabeth 107;
Emeline 116; Emily 160;
James 116; Joanna 118;
Jocie 151; John 30;
Julia 98; Kate 175; King
David 13; Lucinda 82;
Margaret A. 142; Martha
144; Martha Jane 123;
Mary 133; Mary J. 52;
Mary Jane 74; Mattie L.
168; M. E. 169; Nancy
19; Nancy J. 116; Nathan
178; Nathaniel 11,127;
Pheby C. 132; Pheby E.
57; Rebecca J. 115;
Samuel 178; Sarah 35,99;
Sarah M. 127; Susannah
62; Wiley D. 138; William
E. 42; W. J. 182
Bradley (Bradly, Bradlie),
Asa 170; B. C. A. M. 155;
Clementine 13; David
131; Enoch N. 66; Fran-
ces E. 130; James 38; J.
C. 170; John 82; Martha
A. 147; Moses 2
Bradshaw, Arabella C. 66;
George 155; Harriet E.
38; Mary 36
Brady (Bradey, Braidy),
Abner 187; Alexander 1,
51; C. A. W. 70; Child-
ress 118; Elizabeth 29,
71; Elizabeth J. 43;
George W. 82; James 43;
James M. 67; Jerome B.
53; John 64; L. A. 173;
Martha 1; Mary 8; M. J.
153; Sarah 1
Bray, A. M. 168; Amanda
116; E. L. 79; Elijah
A. 52; Fannie E. 132;
Frances C. 170; James
134; James E. 63; James
H. 20; John H. 52; Lewis
W. 116; Margaret 155;
Martha A. 97; Mary Mrs.
179; Mattie 157; M. J.
89; Nancy A. 115; Sarah
J. 129; W. C. 63; W. G.
173; William 128; W. L.
175
Bragg, J. B. 170; Martha
65; Mary Elizabeth 127
Bramlet, James A. 140
Branch, John 135,162;
Samuel 139
Brancom, Jackson 4
Brandon, A. E. H. 57;
Benjamin B. 17; Catha-
rine 12; E. H. 112;
Jacob 112; J. G. 130;
J. J. 151; Lemuel 56;
Lucy 1; Martha 13; Ro-
bert 89; Solomon 94
Branham, Susan E. 68
Brannon, Benjamin 28;
Margaret 4
Branson, Franklin ;
John R. 125; Sarah Jane
46
Brantley, William C. 54
Brashier, J. D. R. 146
Brass, Mariah A. 60
Bratcher, Ollie T. 166

Brazel, Thomas 110
Brazelton, Daniel 29;
Ida M. 166
Brazier (Brasier), Ann M.
64; Emmarandi C. 107;
F. H. 143; James G. 168;
J. G. 177; Lucy H. 89;
Mary 32; Mary C. 111;
Polly 69; Sarah 129;
T. N. 108; W. J. 85;
Z. T. 135
Braxton, E. A. 121
Breast, John K. 125
Breckenridge, Sarah 188
Bresten, Wesley 39
Brents (Brent), John 58;
Lovenia E. 154; Mollie
152; Thomas W. 13
Brett, William 109
Brewer, Argile 108; E. H.
74; Elisha M. 16; Florida
163; George 55,67,142;
James R. 72; J. C. 145;
Joel S. 56,90; John F.
83; John H. 79; Johnson
147; Mattie E. 83; Mary
4; Mary E. 127; Rebecca
E. 108
Bridges, Elizabeth 31;
Elizabeth 116; Mary M.
16; Narcissa J. 25
Bridgeforth, J. W. 97
Briggs, Samuel 123
Bright, Alfred 98; Alson
134; Ann M. 123; Ben 92,
137,171; Catharine 152,
187; Charles 24,91,123;
Davy 112; Easter 89;
George 126; G. W. 140;
Hiram 91,164; Ike 97;
James M. 71; J. B. 161;
Joe 119; John 163; John
B. 183; Jorden 117; Josie
150; Judith M. 166; Laura
92; Lorra 137; Lucy 160;
Margaret 184; Mariah 103;
Martha 94,97; Martha E.
81; Martha R. 3,185;
Maria E. 14; Martin 94;
Mary 9,153; Mary A. 185;
Matilda 150; Milly 125;
Monroe 118; Moses 175;
Peter 148; Rebecca 91;
Robert 99,140; Susan 130;
Tom 89; William 131,157,
158; William B. 4;
William H. 173
Brimm (Brim), Mahala 39;
Mary Jane 36; Nancy 46;
Rebecca 37
Brinage, Sarah 35
Brine, Arnold 1
Bringer, Sarah E. 154
Briscal, J. A. 154
Bristen, William 31
Bristow, J. B. 5
Britton (Briton, Bratton),
George H. 78; G. H. M.
108; J. H. J. 145; J. M.
88; John S. 164; Thomas
182; W. A. 123; W. J. C.
82
Brock, Henry H. 88; James
105; Joseph 174; W. G.
(L.) 175
Brooks, Eveline Mrs. 157;
Fannie 162; Joseph 46;
Lucy 158; Martha E. 86;
Mary Jane 80; Susan 161
Broadway (Broadaway),
Agnes 4; Bettie 113;
Frances A. 5; George 18;
James 53; James W. 26;
J. E. 134; John G. 188;

Broadway contd.
Mary 29; Mary E. 114;
Nancy Ann 45; Peter 89;
R. A. 107; Rutha 8; Sarah
31; Squire 146; William
35
Broffett, Mary 139
Brother, George E. 148
Brotherton, Elizabeth 87,
145; E. L. 175; Lyda C.
66; M. E. 176; Sarah E.
79
Brown, ____ 4; Absolum M.
53; A. E. 151,155,176;
A. J. 82; A. M. 60(2);
Amy M. 28; Ann 136; Anna
57; Catharine E. 34;
Clarasa 52; Corilla 94;
David F. 57; Delila 23;
E. B. 169; Edward A. 21;
E. F. 87,120; Eli 67;
Elijah B. 64; Elisha 117;
Elisha S. 47; Elizabeth
14,18,52,60,93,100,139;
Elizabeth C. 14; Emariah
39; Emeline 28,34; Eme-
line E. 22; Emma 180;
Fannie 155; F. E. 174;
Frances 128; George W.
22,23,39; G. W. 154;
Harriet Ann 76; Henry
24,163;Henry C. 101,104;
Henry L. 184; Hezekiah
12; H. G. 166; Hillery
W. 84; H. L. 182; H. M.
100; J. 99; James 68,78,
104,116,145; James E.
23; James H. 132; James
M. 64; James R. 130;
James S. 49; James W. 22;
Jane 149; J. B. 79; J. C.
73; J. E. 155,157; Jerry
156; John 19,38; John C.
123; John E. 68; John L.
20; John M. 66; John N.
35; John W. 168; J. R.
88,126; Joseph 172;
Joseph M. A. 159; Joshua
D. 30; Julia A. 102;
J. V. 142; L. A. 134,
139; Laura 120; Leander
102; Lewis B. 83; Lilly
179; L. N. 167; Louella
136; Lucy A. 86; Mag
132; Malissa C. 138; Mar-
garet 83,138; Martha 39,
54; Martha C. 136; Mar-
tha J. 16,61,101; Martha
Jane 117; Mattie E. 183;
Mattie J. 119; Mary 10,
22,37; Mary A. 68; Mary
Ann 29,30,53,58; Mary F.
35; Mary Frances 2;
Mary J. 101; Mary M. 40;
Mary S. 50; M. F. 100;
Mollie 178; M. V. 82;
Nancy 60,63,66; Nancy H.
38; Nancy M. 46; Nancy
Manerva E. 167; Nelda J.
28; Patience E. 106;
P. R. 98; R. M. 72,114;
Rosanah A. 163; R. S.
20; Samuel D. 16,83,138;
Samuel R. 30; Sarah 30,
72,79,100,107; Sarah C.
174; Sarah E. 57; Sarah
E. Belle 130; S. D. 87;
Spence 120; Stephen P.
80; Sterling 182; Solo-
mon 29; Sopha R. 23;
Sue 155; Susan Catharine
77; Susan F. 179; Sus-
annah 88; Susannah W. 8;
Tabitha 16; Thomas O. 98;

Brown contd.
W. C. 150; Wiley H. 167;
William 29,80,187;
William A. 41,57;
William D. 39; William
H. 75,83; William J. 35,
155; William R. 74
Browning, Annie 172; Char-
les B. 69; Jane M. 1;
John A. 9; Martha A. 54;
Merriah 156; Ruth K. 6;
Samuel W. 67; Sudy D.
11; Susan J. 56; William
M. 38
Broughton, Joseph 99
Broyles (Broilles), John
E. 87; Joseph 27; Keziah
186; Malinda 19
Bruce (Bruice), G. B. 124;
G. W. 168; James W. 37;
Joel 31; Joel R. 40;
John A. 20,50; Margaret
Ann 60; Marshall 47;
Mary C. 116; Mary F. 95;
Mattie F. 124; Mollie
157; Nancy R. 8; Porter
171; Sarah 61; Susan C.
136; S. W. 132; William
117; Wormley 29
Brundrige, John W. 26
Bryan, A. E. 116; Angus
N. 59; Benjamin 16;
C. A. 167; Caladonia
148; Ellenor G. 187;
Ephraim B. 35,81; J. H.
130; John H. 67; John J.
29,160; Mary 186; Nancy
G. 186; Pleasant N. 80;
R. H. 181; Thomas J.
186; W. D. 116; Wilks
166; William H. 42
Bryant, Albert 14; Andy
183; Ann Moling 82;
Benjamin B. 11; C. I.
170; Cyntha 21; Docia
Ann 138; Elisha 44;
Eliza 67; Elizabeth 68;
Fannie 111; Frances M.
44; Jesse L. 25; J. O.
106; Joel P. 6; John 99;
John D. 89; J. S. 145;
Leroy 168; M. A. 115;
Mack 131; Malinda 81;
Martin 68; Mary 2; Mary
A. 57,66; Mattie 180;
Nancy 123; Permelia 96;
Reubin A. 142; Reubin G.
42; Sarah A. 74; Sarah
E. 137; Silas 42; Sus-
anah 73; T. B. 177;
William C. 11; William
E. 169; William H. 9;
W. J. 71
Bryson (Brysent, Brison),
Charley 181; Eddy 116;
Fanny 129; Henry Rev.
187; M. A. 98; Margaret
114; Martha 94,114; Mary
75; M. C. 102; Rebecca
93; Sarah 121
Byrum (Byrons), M. A. J.
96; Susan C. 75
Buchanan, Adaline 1;
Amanda 163; Andrew 188,
141; Andy 154,166; Anica
89; Ann 92,148,149,183;
Annie 140; Benjamin 30;
Cassan 89; Charlotte
94; Clarinda 146; Clar-
rinda 102; C. M. 127;
Cornelius 134; David S.
51; Delina 52; Della
178; Elbrady 104; El-
bridge G. 184; Ella 144;

Buchanan contd.
E. M. 150; Emily 22,49;
Ezella 156; Faney 106;
Francis 173; F. W. 112;
George W. 127; Green 168;
Harriet 92,168; H. C. 91;
Hesiah 134; Isaac 184,187;
Isabella 107; James 111;
James M. 19,131; Jane
114; John 103; John L.
157; John M. 16,50,56;
John W. 28; Joseph 21;
Josephine 134; J. P. 94;
J. R. P. 153; Julia 48;
Judith 35; Leander 187;
Lizzie P. 70; Louisa 13,
16,26; Louisa V. 98;
Maggie 126; Margaret 27,
37,68,100,180,187,49;
Margaret E. 42; Margret
34; Martha 3, Martha
J. 43; Mary 58,104,183;
Mary A. 16,53; Mary
Frances 79; Mary J. 62;
Mattie 149; Milton 5;
M. L. 107; M. T. 103;
Mollie 156,174; Moses 5;
Nancy 25; Nancy A. 65,
113; Nancy M. A. 28;
Pat. 150; Pinkie M. 160;
R. E. 77; Rebecca Ann 57;
Rebecca K. 18; Rena 103,
Robert 21; Rufus 183;
Rutha 161; Sally M. 86;
Samuel 147; Sanford M.
160; Sarah 11,51,171;
S. D. 4; Simpson 24;
Sinai A. 18; S. W. 97;
W. A. 129; Wesley 104;
William 71,76,93,128,179;
William S. 17
Budgett, Zack 135
Buffaloe (Buffalo), Burline
Genavia 105; Jasper 154;
Maggie 159; M. E. 146;
William 60; William E.
171
Bullard, J. C. 182; Martha
A. 143; Robert 143;
Washington 96
Bullock, William 16
Bunch, Joseph 25
Bunn, Eliza 66; Eliza E.
67; Fannie 134; Mary E.
67; M. E. 84; Nancy A.
65; Wiley 66,68; William
57
Buntley, Isabella 150;
Jacob 51; Louisa 5;
Louiza 143; Sallie 168;
William 48
Burford, Isabella 102;
K. H. 18; N. C. 184
Burget, Margaret J. 164;
Samuel 119
Burgess, B. F. 85; D. W.
158; J. L. 64; John 30;
Mary 130; W. B. 158
Burkley, Thorton 176
Burnam, James H. 89
Burnett (Bernet, Barnett),
James A. 5; James J. 5;
John W. 84; J. W. 152;
L. S. 119; Martha 5
Burrow (Burrows, Burow),
Benjamin G. 6; Charity
55; Freeman 52; James
180; Jarrel J. 3; J. L.
74; Lucinda 20; Susan 14;
Wiley G. 48
Burns (Byrns, Burnes, Burn),
Alex 96; Alford 108;
Andrew 35; Andrew J. 142;

Burns contd.
Charity 128; Eliza A. 73;
Henry 70,134; J. M. 170;
John 19; Johnson 167;
Joseph W. 143; J. Y. 181;
Louisa 67; M. F. 130;
Nancy 70; Nicholas 5,34;
Palmyrah E. 71; Rebecca
137; Sarah 89; Sarah J.
102; T. B. 159
Burr, Martha A. 41
Burrum, C. R. 170
Burrus, Elizabeth 15
Burk (Berk, Burke), Char-
lotte 131; Elizabeth
148; Hanah 131; Jesse
M. C. 28; Lewis 164;
Martha 111; Preston 2;
Sarah A. 71
Burt (Bert), Angeline 16;
J. G. 110; Joseph 4,122;
Lucy 112
Burton, Abegail 155; A. J.
182; E. G. 136; Eldender
H. 43; Frances L. 50;
J. A. 54; James 7,97;
James C. 30; James W.
116; Joseph S. 130; Mary
54; Nancy 109; Permelia
50; R. N. 86; Robert B.
16; Robert William 22;
W. R. 131
Burwell, Richard 174
Busbee (Busby), Elizabeth
Ann 42; Green 173; L. C.
141; Tabitha E. 125;
Vicy Jane 125; William
142
Bush, Jane 45
Bussey, Martha M. 149
Butler, Bethena 28; Boz-
well 141; C. L. 159;
David G. 54; Edward 6;
Fielding L. 31; James R.
46; Jesse P. 160; Julia
69; Lavina C. 107;
Lizzie A. 164; M. A. 159;
Manadora 83; Mary Ann 14;
M. E. 160; Nancy Mrs.
186; Nancy A. 124;
William 85; William W.
53; W. S. 87
Butts, Catharine W. 20
Byans (Byram), Jonas 1;
Lucy C. 19
Byers, Alice E. 182; D. W.
145; E. J. M. 150; James
A. 73; James F. 72,108,
151; Mary A. 113; M. E.
147; W. M. 188
Byner, Elvira Mrs. 149
Bynum (Binum), Ducinda 9;
F. M. 160; H. J. 181;
Rebecca L. 144

Caden, Rinda 182
Caldwell (Coldwell),
Eliza 186; J. E. 62;
J. H. O. 173; John 2,
164,173; Lucy Ann 75;
Louella 121; Mary Mar-
garet 188; M. M. 62;
Nancy 85; Sallie K. 72;
Thomas S. 153,155;
William J. 71
Calhoun, Anny L. 27; Car-
oline 2
Call (Cail), E. A. 54;
Eliza 71; Nancy A. 30;
Sarah L. 74
Callaway, J. F. 184
Callicott, W. C. 139
Calloway, Eli R. 81

Cambron, E. L. 180; F. M.
135; G. L. 165; J. A.
132; Josephine 155;
Julia A. 165; M. J. 135
Camel, Jennie 140; Mary 32
Cameron (Camron), James
122; James S. 110; Lewis
A. 40
Campbell, Albert 144;
Alexander 137; Bettie
180; Burchet R. 20; Cal-
adonia 147; Catharine
165; Charity 165; Cullin
154; Cynthia 186; E. C.
157; E. E. 174; Ellenor
1; Emeline 66; Emily 99;
Emmaline 109; Fanny 33;
Franklin A. 9; G. 92;
George 66,115; George W.
26; G. W. 168; Houston
108; I. E. 148; James 3,
24,143; James D. 41;
James H. 63,89,121; Jane
10; John 154; John D.
58; Joseph 186; Julia A.
15; Lilly 87; Louisa Mrs.
166; Margaret A. 129;
Marget S. 7; Martha A.
126; Mary 109; Mary Ann
16; Matilda E. 47; Matt-
hew H. 9; M. C. 160;
Mollie 178; Nancy 7;
Ollie 135; Parket 32;
Rebecca 153; R. H. 126;
Richmond 188; R. L. 158;
Sally 75; Samuel 110;
Sarah Ann 63; Sarah S.
188; S. C. 153; Tennessee
W. 53; Wesley 145; W. M.
165
Camper (Campers), James
L. 15; Julia Ann 67;
Sarah 50
Canada (Canady), Louisa N.
44; Mollie C. 116;
Virginia C. 108
Candiff, Calvin G. 81
Cannon (Connon), Amanda
90; Ann 157; Augustus
187; Ben 174; Dessa 55;
Drusilla 97; Elizabeth
E. 52; Hannah 106; H. C.
170; Jincy D. 33; Louisa
182; Lydia Hanna 102;
Maggie 121; Mandy 147;
Mariah 92; Martha E.
126; Mary Jane 158;
Minos A. 113; Minus 162;
M. T. 99; Nancy E. Mrs.
152; Sallie 174; Sarah
E. 120; William 77;
William W. 77
Carlile, M. M. 174
Carlin, Lizzie 144
Carloss (Carlos), A. J.
5; George 120; Lou 104;
Louisa 27
Carlton, John 115
Capps, Louisa 155
Carbo, James 1
Carden, David 14
Carey, John 117
Carithers, Fanny R. 1
Carmichael (Carmicle),
Daniel 40; D. L. 161;
John W. 45
Carnes (Corn, Carm),
Bryant 117; David 152;
Emma 157; John B. 109;
Margaret 5; Mary C. 62
Carrigan, Eliza J. 102;
H. M. 105; Joseph G.
73; Mattie 122; Sue 77;
Susan C. 64; W. H. 88

Carriger, J. S. 134
Carroll, S. P. 152;
Washington 102
Carpenter Emanuel 102,
167; Faney 144; Frances
62; Jane 73; J. W. 133;
Leroy 51; L. N. 106;
Logan 36; Mahala 66;
Martha A. 106; M. D. 45;
Morris 2; Nancy 170;
P. C. 161; R. J. 176;
Sarah A. 174; Sarah C.
167; Susan 66; W. F. 129;
William W. 22
Carpien, Thomas 115
Carrie, Susan 16
Carson, Frances 4
Carter, Ahaigy 31; Ann 126;
Callie 167; Caroline 95;
Crawford, 38; Cynthia A.
140; Dick 171; Eliza 30;
Elizabeth 14,100,175;
Ellen 126; Frank W. 154;
George 21,42; Hannah M.
108; H. M. 97; H. Y. 104;
John 21; John A. 39;
John C. 63; John D. 70;
Lucy G. 94; M. A. 167;
Malinda 144; Malinda C.
45; Martha 77; Mary 106;
Mathew 13; M. E. D. 81;
Morgan 78; M. W. 147;
Nannie 155; Nelson P.
158; Penny Ann 40; Robert
96; Ronald 128; R. M. 61;
Sallie O. 171; Samuel
171; Sarah 95; Sarah E.
40; Stephen 138; Thomas
J. 36; Thomas R. 67;
W. F. 149; William 79;
William B. 100; William
E. 28; Willis A. 40;
W. R. 137
Cartwright (Cartright),
Julianna 60; M. T. 143;
William T. 77; W. T. 177
Carty, Ann S. 32; Benjamin
W. D. Capt. 187; Catha-
rine 69; C. B. 60; E. C.
108; Ellen 164; Henry 58;
James B. 56; Lucy 145;
Mary E. 69; Polly 155;
Sarah E. 116; Sarah J.
98; Susan 152; William
185; William L. 61
Caruthers (Carrithers,
Carithers), Ara C. 185;
Lucinda C. 22; Lucinda
J. 75; Maulday O. 46;
Sallie 141
Carver, Samuel C. 90
Casey, Green B. 59; Henry
87; Isabella 17; Rebeciah
6; Joseph A. 45; Mary C.
59; Thomas F. 168; Unice
C. 57
Cash, S. N. 142
Cashion (Cashin), A. J. 99;
Anderson 18; Andrew 9;
Ann 55; Ann C. 94; Arch
126,175; Archibald 141;
Brad 179; Delia 178;
Dovey 38; Elizabeth 17,
36,136; E. T. 4; F. M.
80; G. L. 87; James 111,
146; Jennie 170; John W.
63; Joseph 51; Julia Ann
134; Letty 44; L. J. 110;
Louticia 9; Mary 13;
Mary L. 165; Millie 138;
Nancy N. 134; Richard W.
129; Sarah 155; Sarah E.
92; Sarah J. 140,113;
W. H. 166; William 5,28

Cast, Mattie 133; S. A. 169

Caskey, Martha 53

Cason (Caston), Hellen J. 182; John 179; M. H. 164; Sarah 55; Thomas 146

Cass, M. M. 156

Cassander, Mary 184

Castleman, Godwin 154; James H. 69; Nancy 25

Cates (Cate), Clementine 114; C. T. 51; Elizabeth 67; Mary 188; Nancy 76, 169; William Newton 132

Cathey (Cathy), Cyrus L. 55; E. C. Mrs. 115; Elizabeth 152; James F. 79; Jane 104; Manerva 153; Martha 117; Moses 181; Sallie 118; Wallace 130

Cathcart, Marion A. 163; M. C. 176; W. C. 165

Caton (Caten, Cayton, Ceton), Albert 61; Amandy C. 80; Camile 80; Mary M. 79; Smith 79; William A. 104

Caudle, Calledona 37; James 133; Julia Ann 100; Samuel C. 181

Caughran, Elizabeth 10; Harriet 124; H. P. 128; James 10,33; L. E. 165; Lou 160; Margaret 33; Margaret L. 101; Manson H. 48; Martha J. 145; Mary Ann 46; M. G. 144; M. J. 95; M. P. 90; Sara W. 47; T. W. 144; William P. 52

Causby, J. W. 72

Cavitt (Colvit, Cavet), Giles 155; Richard 30; Spicy 32; T. J. 158

Cavial, Martha J. 181

Cavin, Andy 30

Cebring, Susan E. 135

Chaffin (Chafin), B. J. 115; John H. 84

Chalk, Daniel 134; David 139

Chambers, Catharine J. 20; Daniel 79

Chamberlain, Ann 28

Channing, Virginia A. 11

Chambless, Emily J. 10

Champion, Jackson 10

Chapman, Benjamin B. 88; Hanah C. 79; Harriet 16; John 24,44; Martha 69; Mary Ann 20; M. E. 183; Nancy 30; N. R. 131; Sarah 52

Chappell, Freeman 103; George 180

Chasteen (Chastine), Eli 181; John 18; Thomas 35

Cheatham, A. C. 148; Elizabeth 148; Elizabeth R. 23; James 108; Mary Ann 147; Maud 161; M. E. 146

Chesser (Chesor), C. T. 70; G. C. 155; John 176; Mary Ann 45; Nancy E. 70; W. Y. 44

Chick, Angeline 77; Susan 175; William D. 51

Chilcoat, Ann 106; H. B. 88; James R. 65; Jennie 101; Lucy 158; Parthenia 66

Childs, Bennet W. 62; Henry C. 112; Jo. 157; Julia 175; Martha A. E. 28; S. A. Mrs. 156; Sarah A. 103; Thomas 8, 188; T. W. 126; William W. 60; W. P. 68

Childers, J. H. 177; J. R. 156; Robert F. 153

Childress, A. J. 41,167; Delina 21; Frances 116; James T. 8; Laura 169; Martha 145; Mattie J. 124; William T. 15; W. C. 165; Wyatt 165

Chiles, Alpha N. 77

Chilton, S. R. 119

Chisam (Chisum), Betsie 142; Sarah A. 163

Chitwood, Ann M. 17; Dillia E. 79; Frances M. 80; H. L. 102; James A. 102; Lucinda E. 61; Margaret 101; Martha 110; Mollie D. 119; Polly A. 42; Sarah Jane 45

Chrisman (Chism, Chisom), Andrew J. 147; Bill 134; John L. 158; Sarah Jane 146

Christian, Eliza 2; F. P. 169; J. A. 151; S. E. 101

Christopher, William 154

Chunn, William 136

Church, G. C. 80; George 58; Ruthy 40

Cimmons, William H. 21

Claiborn, Eliza M. 1

Clanton, Andy 163; Celia 93; John 36; Mary 93; Mary E. 8; William Thomas 79

Claresbery (Claresby), Indiana 103; Louisiana 128

Clark (Clarke), Abraham 91; A. J. 1; Allice 158; Amanda 91,172; Ann 90,183; Arch 149; B. A. 140; Beckey 170; Benjamin F. 78; Bolin 7; Calvin 119; Caroline 32, 150,151; Cezar 90; Charley 169; C. L. 152; Clemie 146; Cyntha 94; Davis W. 94; D. S. 155; Easter 91; Edward 170; Eggie 171; Elainor B. 38; Eliza A. 18; Elizabeth 123; Elizabeth B. 74; Eliza J. 44; Elizabeth M. G. 78; Emily 106; Fannie 157; F. S. 80; George 123; Gress 104; G. W. 172; Henry 95,130; Isa A. 150; J. A. 145; Jack 108; James 7,75,150; James A. 76; James C. 71; James D. 64; James H. 112; James T. 41; Jane 188; J. E. 173; Jennie 157; J. F. 94; John 32, 41,69,140; John B. 123; John H. 187; John L.77; John M. 13; John W. 43; Johnson 147; J. Porter 131; Joseph 3,22,109; Joseph S. 53; Juber 167; Kate 143; Lilburn L. 37; Liza 146; Lizzie 180; Lonie 134; Lou 157;

Clark contd.
Louisa 49; L. S. 103; Lucius 182; Lucinda 35; Lucy C. A. 59; Lucy L. 125; Margaret 164; Margaret B. 19; Mariah 183; Mariah L. 103; Mariah W. 72; Martha A. 98; Martin Van 76; Mary 21,94; Mary A. 61; Mary Ann 21; Mary Jane 57; Mary P. 108; Mary W. 29; Matilda 27; Micajah 1; M. O. 120; Mollie J. 150; Nancy 3; Nancy A. 107; Nancy E. 34; Narcissa 121; Obadiah 44; Phebe Elizabeth 75; Pink 178; Prescilla 172; Pryor 146; Rachel 106, 107; Rebecca 97; Rebecca E. 108; Rebecca M. 140; Rosannah 8; R. P. 149; Sallie 93,179; Samuel 68; Sarah 91,135,161; Sarah E. 147; Sarah Jane 121; Scula A. 127; S. E. 165; Simca 46; S. J. 116; Spencer 94; Stephen 165; Susan 153; T. H. 127; Thomas 32,90,106,153; Thomas H. 53; Thomas J. 64; Thomas W. 30; Virginia 102; Wiley 108; William 3,129,137,160(2); William A. 93

Clasberry, Adaline 171

Claunch (Clouch, Clunch), Elizabeth 40; Felix 59; James 49; Jenetta 7; Jesse 55; Letisha A. 79; Minerva 20; Nancy 77; Nancy C. 77; Sarah 13; Sarah C. 151; S. M. 157; William 49

Clay, Emiline 19

Clayborn (Claborn), John 130; Martha 39

Clayton, Amanda 11; Napoleon B. 14; S. M. 121; Thomas 168

Clements (Clemons), B. L. 83; George W. 19; Jesse B. 186; Wyatt 139

Clemmy, William 150

Clerckman, Will H. 108

Clift, A. P. 59; Elenor B. 1; Elizabeth 187; Elvira J. 161; Henry S. 65; James M. 75; James N. 59; J. B. 105; Joseph R. 84; Julia 75; Louisa J. 94; Mary 186; Mary J. 25; M. E. 149; M. M. 132; Nancy Ann 47; Sarah A. B. 25; Susan E. 39; Thomas B. 58; W. P. 119

Clifford, Artimesa 78

Cline, P. A. 140

Clinto, John 36

Clinton, Henry 28; Samuel 171; Susan 124

Clunn (Clun, Clem), Byran L. R. 50; Lucy 136; M. J. 61

Cluts, Mary E. 111; Susan M. 76

Coats, A. D. 183; Alexander 103; James M. 78; J. B. 96; J. C. 182; John H. 58; Louisa Jane 50; Mary L. 171; Orleany B. 89; S. E. 177

Cobb, George T. 99; James C. 64; J. H. 181;

Cowan contd.
Margret A. 36; Martha
A. 112; Mary A. 124;
Mattie F. 168; Mattie L.
161; May E. C. 100; M. J.
148; Oliver 121; Pris-
cilla 92; Sarah 146
Cowart, Amanda 161
Cowden, John F. 10; Martha
Jane 57
Cowder, Susannah 188
Cowley (Cooley, Cooly),
Benjamin T. 5; C. E. 85;
Ed 179; Henrietta 103;
H. D. 176; Isaac 157;
James 3; John 162; John
A. 90; J. H. 126; J. P.
114; Lucinda 139; Mathew
M. 35; M. W. 87; Nancy
C. 122; Phillip 176;
R. B. 164; Sarah 171;
W. T. 182
Cox (Cocks), Andrew J. 34;
Candess 152; David 123;
Elizabeth 68; Emeline
48; Frances E. 39;
James 51,89; J. H. 166;
John 140; John H. 75;
John T. 105; Lucinda
122; M. Ann 76; Mandana
E. 56; Marcia Ann 73;
Margaret A. 75; Marilda
66; Mary Jane 66; Nancy
63; Richard L. 11; Sarah
42; Sarah Ann 80; Sarah
C. 38; S. E. Mrs. 143;
Susan E. 46; Thomas B.
102; William 104
Crabtree, Elizabeth 84;
Ellen 124; F. F. 109;
Francis 86; G. W. 102;
Hannah 97; H. S. 145;
J. H. 117; John 11; John
C. 72; L. D. 169; Louisa
134; Martha 9; Mary E.
144; Nancy 37; Nissa
164; Phebe Ann 180;
P. J. 107; Ransom 159;
Samuel 19,57; Sarah
Jane 125; Susan 19;
William 51
Craig, David C. 55; George
A. 51; Henry 94; John
145; Matilda 10; Martha
75; William 7,186
Crammer, John 14
Crane (Cane), Anna E. 180;
Berry 166; Caroline 17;
E. D. Cane 82; Jane 58;
John 14; J. W. 153;
Mary A. 48; Spartin G.
18; Timothy 83; T. R. W.
53
Cravener, John 31
Crawford (Crafford,
Crofford), Adeline F.
112; A. L. 146; Anthony
36; Bettie 163; Charles
M. 10; Carter T. 14;
Dave 95; Elizabeth 31;
Elizabeth A. 16; Ellen
43; E. M. 131; Emily E.
40; E. N. 111; F. B.
125; Felix McP. 36;
George A. 29; George W.
140; Henry 93; Henryetta
8; James M. 22; J. E.
174; Jocie 144; John 28;
John G. 15; J. S. 141;
J. W. 119; Lucy A. 144;
M. A. 95; Manuel 93;
Margaret 21; Margaret A.
72; Martha A. 37; Martha
R. 45; Mary A. 119;

Crawford contd.
Mary E. 155; Mollie T.
150; Naomi 184,187;
Rebecca K. 49; Rachel
187; R. H. 109; Robert
39; Samuel 93; Sarah E.
70; Sarah S. 11; S. E.
183; W. H. 177; William
20,187; William B. 156,
185
Crawley, J. M. R. 174;
Kit 174; Lizie 156;
Nicey J. 76; Rebecca
Jane 169
Creacy, Elizabeth 48;
Mary 15
Crenshaw (Cranshaw),
Amanda 101; James S. 99;
Jennie 140; Margaret E.
130; Mary 26; Mary J.
54; Paskel 105; Samuel
T. 2; Thomas W. 100;
William T. 14
Creson (Creason), Eliza-
beth 52; George 154;
George MD 121; Margaret
98; Martha 81; Mary M.
78; Pamela 131; Susan
R. 131
Crichet (Crechit), Elephia
26; John 11
Criner, Thomas 1
Cronson, John 148
Crook, Eliza Jane Mrs. 98
Cross, F. M. 113; George
A. 114; Isom 163; Jane
96; William 59; W. M.
113
Croswait, James M. 31
Crowder, Elizabeth 24;
Isaac B. 181; Mary 4;
Mary A. 4; Mildred 17
Crownover, William 32
Crows, Mary L. 11
Crowson, Martha S. 128;
Nancy 11
Crouch, Jane 11
Cruise (Cruse), A. E. 80;
E. C. Mrs. 164; Eliza-
beth 17; Elvira 92;
Henry 152; Jacob 48;
Mary 72; Moses 7
Crumbley, Jasper 155
Crunk, A. J. 83; George
W. 27; John 88; Sarah
Ann 54; William 163
Crutchfield, Elizabeth
188; Robert 179
Culberson, James S. 2;
Nancy E. 59; Parthena 1
Culbreath, James 44
Culen, Samuel D. 169
Cullom (Cullum), A. B.
117; J. W. 67
Culver, Mahalie 175
Culps, William 149
Cumberland, George 45;
James W. 158; Jane 13;
Rebecah 1; Virginia 36
Cummins (Cummings), E. C.
182; Eliza M. 46; Har-
mon 188; Hessey 108;
H. D. 111; J. A. 165;
J. G. 172; J. J. 88;
Lucy E. 69; Mahala Jane
44; Martha J. 65; Mary
E. 60; M. E. 56; M. J.
113; Sarah Ann 60,71;
Thomas J. 32; W. T. 95
Cunningham, Abram 1;
Amanda M. 101; Ann 21,
98; Arriva 92; C. A.
169; Celia 48; C. H. 78;
Charles 66; Delphia 137;

Cunningham contd.
Demarcus P. 61; E. 95;
Elizabeth 21,38,185;
Eliza E. 53; Enoch 77;
G. 95; George 117; George
L. 34; George W. 117;
Gideon B. 185; James 15,
31,95,118,186; James D.
185; Jane 61,186; Jane
M. 38; Joel 44; John W.
76,166; John W. C. 16;
Joseph 80; Julia Ann 45;
Loucretia 81; Louisa V.
120; Lucy 35,117; Maggie
105; Maggie B. 145;
Malvira C. 36; Margaret
3,27,61; Mariah 14;
Martha 56,122,159; Martha
A. 18; Martha E. 78;
Mary 21,27,89; Mary D.
102; M. E. 136; Melissa
C. 88; M. G. 97; Nancy
A. 88; Nancy Jane 146;
N. C. 103; Peter 9,46;
P. W. 177; Rebecca 155;
Rebecca J. 150; Richard
85; Robert 148; S. A.
158; Samuel 27; Sarah A.
94; Tempa 96; W. H. 88;
Wiley 42; William 39
Curlee, C. D. 176
Currin, James T. 65
Curry, Isaac J. 5; James E.
3; James P. 40; Nathan
52; V. L. 175
Curtis, A. C. 117; Amanda
F. 166; Ann 114; Belle
161; Isabella 125; James
M. 63; John T. 14; Julia
187; Julia Ann 176;
Mollie 148; Moses 16;
Sophia 112; W. A. 156;
W. S. 75; William 14

Dailey, Thomas 114
Dale, Frances J. 112;
Hellen F. 126; James H.
121; John 23; Mary Eliza-
beth 123; Nelly 170;
Peter A. 18; Sarah 4;
W. T. 90
Dallas, Mary F. 46; Rhoda
2
Dalton, Laurana 81
Dameron (Damron), A. E. 154;
Celia E. 40; Elizabeth
19; Ellen 143; Ellender
121; Harvey 15; James G.
24; J. K. P. 116; J. W.
116; Lelia J. 58; Lindia
A. 80; M. A. 122; Marga-
ret A. 42; Mary 7,80;
Mary L. 120; Sarah 58,
81; Selia 63; S. L. 113;
Thomas 181; William 28,
112
Damsel, Hannah P. 23
Dance, James T. S. 25;
John W. M. 66; J. W. M.
36; Louisa 103; Martha
A. E. 15; Sally 115;
S. E. H. 64; Susan 57
Dandridge, J. W. 96
Dangerfield, Caroline 126;
Charley 123; Edmon 128;
Major 117; Maria 121
Daniel, Adeline 77; Benja-
min K. 18; Charlotta 74;
Catharine 29; Elizabeth
106; Elizabeth J. 84;
Fannie 99; George W. 88;
Hiram J. 90; James 43;
John B. 62; John T. 89;
John Thomas 171; J.W. 104;

Daniel contd.
Louisa 22; Maggie 141;
Margaret 67,145; Matilda
96; M. E. 77; Netie J.
119; Rena A. 143; Robert
25; Sarah 131; Sena 140;
Stephen 106; T. B. 138;
Thomas 73; Thomas J. 170;
T. L. 140; Wiley B. 95;
William 99,100
Danley, J. W. 180
Darnell (Darnal, Darnald),
C. 135; Emma C. 108;
James 4; James H. 67;
Martha E. 67; Mary Ann
12; R. F. 119; S. G.
141; Susan E. 98; T. L.
111; William T. 55
Daughtery, Jeremiah L. 35
Daves, Alexander 48; C. A.
98; Dotia Ann 27; James
47
Davidson, A. J. 148;
America E. 108; Andrew
22; Andrew J. 42; Carle-
ton 16; D. A. 82; Eliza-
beth 78; Elizabeth M.
72; George 124; Elizabeth
M. 72; George 124; George
W. 22; G. W. 169; James
16; John 105; John G.
86; John J. 151; Juliana
60; L. W. 104; Lucinda
143; Martha C. 102;
Martha E. 129; Martha
Jane 35,45; Mary 4,110;
Mary A. 81; Mary J. 61;
M. C. 123; Mildred 46;
M. V. 132; Nancy J. 115;
Nancy Virginia 122; N. C.
113; Robert A. 84; Tho-
mas 3; T. T. 139;
William 13; W. J. 79
Davis, Albin F. 27; Allen
10,49; A. M. 124; Amanda
E. 165; Anderson 36,77;
Ann E. 13; Archibald 74;
A. T. 156; A. W. 146;
Benjamin F. 120; Cale-
donia V. 85; Caroline
187; Catharine 98; Char-
lotte 32; David G. 24;
D. B. D. 121; Dorinda 8;
Elijah 5; Elizabeth 7;
Frances J. 110; Gabriel
43; Giles 50(2); G. W.
152; H. S. 67; J. A. 98;
Jackson C. 1; James J.
46; James M. 25,52,114,
James S. 2,45; James W.
23; Jane 45; J. B. 70;
John 27,83,165; John F.
104; John H. 86; John M.
156; Jonathan N. 19;
Josephine 55; J. W. B.
126; Laura 139; Louisa
B. 40; Lucretta I. 145;
Madiline 185; Margaret
136; Margaret E. 33;
Martha 31; Martha T.
175; Mary A. 13; Mary C.
40; Mary Jane 79; Mary
R. 185; M. E. 147; M. J.
94; Nancy 119; Nancy C.
70,117; N. N. 127; Nar-
cissa 2; Narcissa N. 25;
Parthenia E. 128; Rachael
70; Robert 54; Robert
C. 41; Robert M. 99;
Robert R. 115; Roda J.
154; Ruth 187; Sally 3;
Sarah A. 28; Sarah Ann
15; Sarah E. 156; Sisley
Ann 52; S. J. G. 168;

Davis contd.
S. R. 129; Tabitha J.
38; Thomas 155; Tillman
49; Washington 27;
William 9,22,102; William
H. 104; William M. 3;
William W. 3; W. S. 103
Dawes, Nancy Ann 27
Dawson (Dawston), Lebrew-
ster 123; William 78;
W. H. 136
Day, Henry 163
Deal, A. 99; Dillard 60;
John S. 54; Martha J.
98; Rachel E. 115; Riney
Ann 20
Dean, Alvin M. 9; Ann 15;
Eliza 19; Elizabeth 94;
Jane 76; J. M. 7; Joseph
66; Manning 85; Mary 95;
M. M. 137
Deavers (Devers), Henry L.
28; H. L. 116
Decker, Mary J. 48
Decoff, Calvin M. 89
Deford, James H. 55; M. E.
Mrs. 164; Nancy J. Mrs.
107; R. G. 94; Susan S.
81
DeHaven, Ella 155; Sallie
173
DeJarrett, Elizabeth 17
Dekins, George 91
Delap (Delapp), Astelia
90; William A. H. 116
Delaney (Delana), A. T.
71; Eliza 35; William
W. 8
Dellmon, Joseph O. 42
Delk, B. M. 109; J. J. 133;
John H. 102
Dement, J. W. 108
Dempsey, A. A. 160; Amanda
127; Catharine A. 51;
George 30; J. W. 144;
Priscilla Nancy Adaline
77
Denham (Dunham), Eli 151;
G. W. 126; John W. 122;
Lavonia 121; Margaret
E. 79; Sarah H. 130
Dennison (Denson, Denison),
E. C. 89; Emaziah 20;
John E. 158; Mariah 90;
Mary 109
Dennis, A. A. 60; B. F.
47; Emeline 3; Helen M.
62; Henry T. 9; Israel
P. 42; James 34; John D.
96; Lemuel P. M. 41;
Manerva 78; Martha J.
99; Mary 3; Mary A. 99;
Mary Ann 49; Nancy L.
108; Parthenia Ann 6
Dennwitt, Texas P. 100
Denshall, Nancy 149
Denton, G. R. 174; H. E.
176; Mary E. 176; Sallie
C. 180
Denver, Tim 106
Derrer, Aquellar 107
Derrick (Derick), John B.
70; Sarah M. 171
Deshaser (Deshager), Eliza
39; Nancy 22
Desmukes (Dismukes), Bet-
sey 93; Bob 93; Caleb
159; Elisha E. 15; Ellie
128; Fanny 162; Henry
152; I. P. 11; Jack 93;
Robb 120; Sarah 153;
Sarah E. 113; Sarah Jane
120; William 120
Devins, Mary Ann 138

Dew, J. D. 162
Dewoody, John A. 6
Dick, Ann G. 4
Dickey, A. J. 165; Alfred
C. 188; Amanda 162;
Caroline 71; Elizabeth
17; Elizabeth L. A. 65;
Ella 124; E. M. C. 136;
James L. 172; Jasper 57,
180; J. F. 178; John M.
174; John S. 53; Joseph
G. 159; Martin L. 144;
Mary F. 161; M. E. 166;
Nancy K. 45; Newton 55,
115; O. C. 150; Samathia
E. 135; Samuel A. 169;
Thomas 75
Dickinson, F. A. 35
Dickson, Adaline 72; Alex-
ander G. 10; Henry C.
11; Joseph D. 31; Mary
M. 14
Diemer, C. A. 65; Charles
89; Frances 110; Isaac
115; Julia 127; Mollie
M. Mrs. 164; Sidney L.
136; Susan 89; Thomas
143; W. V. 145
Diggins, Nancy 132
Dildine, Jonathan B. 7;
Minerva 53
Dillard, Henry 116
Dilleha, Mary 127
Dillender (Dellender),
Amanda 16; Charles 20;
James B. 4
Dillingham, Brice 52;
Dianna 133; H. B. 104;
John 53; Sarah P. 62
Dillon (Dillen), F. M. 49;
Mary E. 57; Minerva 41;
Virginia A. 119
Dixon, M. A. 170
Doak, Mary M. 189
Dobbs, Fernando R. 110;
J. H. 74; John 77,97;
John W. 3; L. 75; Marga-
ret A. 116
Dobbins, B. S. 178; Jane
J. 9; John 93,177; Lottie
94; Nancy A. 17; Rebecca
32; Rebecca D. 38; Sally
14,16
Dockins, G. A. 109
Dodd, Marion 19
Dodson, Ann 148; Daniel B.
142; Harriett 104; Henry
169; Jane 127; Mariah
126; Rufus 115; Silas M.
132; Spencer C. 73
Dollar, Calvin 145; Cul-
purna 125; Duncan 12;
Elijah 11; Eliza A. 116;
Hiram 132; J. B. 129;
Joel T. 84; Mary Ann Ruth
9; Mary J. 159; Mary R.
82; M. H. 109; N. E. 176;
R. C. 174; Samuel J. 120;
Silas 86; William 8;
William P. 124
Dollins, Andrew A. 40;
Bob 91; David B. 19;
Eliza J. 144; George 132;
Hugh A. 131; James D. 33;
Joel 188; Joel M. 19;
Julia A. 97; Lizzie 131;
Margaret J. 43; Martha
91; Mary Jane 29; Nancy
Jane 58; Sallie (Donkins)
145
Dollinson, William J. W. 35
Donald (Donalds), Nancy
159; Sarah M. 104; J. R.
(P.) 90; Mary E. B. 104;

Edmondson contd.
Mary A. 94; Nelson 120;
Newman 160; Noah 133;
Rosala 145; Susan A. 27;
Thomas M. 81
Edwards, A. O. 141; Cyrus
90; Eliza M. J. 38;
James P. 131; Martin 118;
Sallie C. 98; Sarah 119,
131; W. J. 83; W. W. 148
Elam, Evaline 82; Eveline
80; Nancy A. 31; Nancy
Catharine 55
Eldridge (Etheridge), J.
W. 159; Leander 143;
Maggie 149; William 182
Ellerson (Ellison), A. C.
143; Joseph 3,142; Tho-
mas H. 146
Elliott (Ellet), Archibald
122; S. E. W. 56
Ellis, Clarissa 160; Cles-
bey 14; Delila 61; Dora
161; D. W. 89; Elizabeth
39,70; E. W. 60; Hender-
son 170; Irene 4; Jacob
108; James 4,96; James C.
62; James W. 87; Jasper
49; Josiah 35; J. P.
100; Margaret Ann 31;
Mary 27; Mary F. 52;
Nancy 23; Narcissa 15;
Peter 52; Pleasant M.
13; Richard 168; Sarah
Ann 55; Sarah E. C. 34;
S. D. 60; Stacy 58;
Wiley B. 102; Wiley C.
1; William H. 53
Ellison, Edmon 114; N. A.
139
Elmore, Mollie 109;
William 164
Elston, Allen 68; Sobra 10
Ely, James A. G. 2; Mary
T. 123
Elzy, Elizabeth 185; J. M.
D. 146
Emery, Mary 67
Emmons, A. M. Mrs. 83;
A. O. 108; Catharine 32;
C. C. 162; E. A. 73;
F. A. 151; James J. 89;
John 3; L. F. 108; Mary
M. J. 92; M. M. 99;
Oliva 148; S. A. 170
Endsley (Endsly), Alexan-
der M. 26; E. C. 125;
J. P. 75; Margaret E. 41
England, Elisha 167; W. A.
177
English, James E. 33; Jane
89; Montgomery 3; Samuel
L. 24; W. B. 108
Ennis, F. 52; John C. 35;
Sue E. 163
Enochs, C. A. J. 116;
Caroline A. P. 26;
David S. 15; G. W. 116;
Jane 31; J. E. M. 140;
John G. 6,49; Mary M.
5; Rebecca E. 33; Sarah
E. F. 78; Sarah S. 25;
Susan G. 6
Epps, ____ 175; Dariah
123; Elizabeth 6,59;
Elizabeth C. 110; Ella
182; Fannie 165; Fanny
126; Francis D. 72;
Hiram 7; Hugh Mc. 6;
James 160; James C. 79;
James N. 79; J. N. 165;
John N. 138; Joseph 147;
Juley Ann 118; Lary F.
101; Louisa J. 26;

Epps contd.
Margaret Jane 8; Mattie
180; William 72
Ervin, A. M. 166; B. S.
107; Eliza 167; Ezekiel
H. 34; James 174; J. J.
139; John F. 25; John
H. 139; Lucinda 22; Mil-
ton 70; Nancy 23
Erwin, J. H. 123; Lavoy
17; Sarah 184
Eslick (Easlick), Annie
149; Austin 35,43,55;
Caledonia 105; Caroline
26; Harvy 20; Isaac H.
84; Isaac N. 63; James
183; John 105; John G.
13; John J. 125; J. L.
164; Loucinda 4; Mahala
18; Martha 58; Mary 120;
Mary E. 125; Mathew 100;
M. C. 103; Nancy 17;
Orange 169; Phoba C. 129;
Polly 1; Rhoda 48,66;
Roda 33; Sarah 24,163;
Sophronia 56; Thomas 43;
William 30,165; W. M. 95
Estill, Mary R. 14; S. H.
110
Estes (Estus), J. S. 129;
Rebecca C. 133
Evans, Alfred 7; Carrol
24; Dessey 12; Eli 44,
56; Frances C. 133;
Felix R. 103; Green B.
116; Hanah D. 117; Har-
riet 9; Henry 179; Isaac
69; James 61; James D.
67; John 25,136; Lucinda
10; Martha 44; Martha
A. E. 144; Martha E. 134;
Mary Ann 70; Mary E. 62,
73; Melissa 26; Nicholas
69; Nicholas M. 35; R.
F. 62; Ruth E. 125;
Salina 10; Sarah 41,154;
Sarah A. 135; Sarah H.
86; S. C. 85; Sebron 52;
Susannah 20; Turner 130;
William 152; William E.
130; William J. 125;
William R. 59; William
S. 16
Everett, C. C. Mrs. 167
Ewing, Elizabeth Jane 61;
Eliza M. 51; J. C. 65,66
Ezell, Alex 174; Alexander
104; Beckey 179; F. L.
64; John 92; Manerva A.
37; Micajah 33; Willie
E. 77

Fagan, Hannah 164; R. T.
143; S. W. 142
Fanning (Faning, Fanon),
America 52; Andrew J.
55; Benjamin 63; Benja-
min F. 71; Bill 114,178;
D. C. 159; Delpha Ann
56; Elizabeth 7; Fran-
cis M. 51; George 43;
James 23; John W. 41;
Lucretia 153; Malissa
A. 84; Martha J. 45;
Nancy J. 141; Phebe 26;
Rachel 162; Samuel 4,
31; Sarah 159; Thomas
86; William C. 35;
W. J. 175
Farmer, Stephen M. 25
Farnsworth, J. W. 88
Farquharson, Robert 71;
Toney 131,171
Farrar (Farrer), Ben 157;

Farrar contd.
C. J. 104; C. L. 159;
Daniel 3,188; David 51;
E. C. 88; Elmyra A. E.
22; George 175; James T.
104; Jane 17; Jennetta
M. 112; John 182; Lucy
A. 81; Mary E. 73; Mary
J. 47; M. J. 168; Nancy
A. 94; Nancy Jane 77;
P. E. 165; Samuel T.
102; Sarah 91; Silva 93,
145
Farris, Fanny 79; Mary 137;
Matilda S. 114; Samuel
R. 24
Fason, Henry T. 54
Fauch, H. H. 82; Margaret
102
Faulkenberry (Faulkenbury,
Faulkinboro), Jeremiah
M. 46; Lura 95; Nancy E.
110; Sarah E. 51; William
R. 56
Faulkes, Eliza A. 86
Faulkner (Forkner, Fautner,
Fortner, Falkner,
Faulkiner), Anna 45;
D. E. 109; Elizabeth 144;
Eliza J. 176; Fannie
174; James H. 60; Jane
80; J. F. 165; J. P.
120; L. H. 60; Mary 13;
Mary E. 174; Prudence E.
154; Sally 95; Sarah J.
180; T. C. F. 172;
William 16,50; William
B. 96; William W. 48
Fears, Thomas W. 108
Fearson, William 103
Feeney (Feenney), A. W.
114; Belle 151; James R.
98
Felips, Rivey 126
Felps, Alexander 11; Alfred
11; Caroline 67; Eliza-
beth 7,47; Emily 148;
Jane 34,112; Jasper N.
35; John 33,54; Josie
136; Mary 14; Riley 141;
Rufus 153; Sarah 14
Fennel, Lucinda 147
Ferguson (Furguson,
Furgerson), Alexander D.
46; Augustus 12; James
R. 173; John 187; Joseph
H. 137; Mary F. 161;
T. L. 177; W. G. 159;
W. T. 107
Ferrell, Isaac 137
Ferrin, Sarah 126
Fielder, Enos T. 113
Fielding, Louisa Virginia
85
Fife, Samuel 23; William
10
Fight, J. M. 145
Finch, Ben 164; Ellen 86
Fincher, A. J. 107; John
83; Mary 22; Sarah J.
74; T. W. Mrs. 107
Findley (Finley, Fenley,
Finly), Amanda 179; C. C.
176; Clabren A. 114;
Jackson C. 48; James S.
39; Jane 121; Martin 7;
Newton W. 76; Rachel 31;
Sarah E. 112; Sarah L.
98; S. F. 176; W. W. 110
Finney, A. A. 98; David
C. 26; James J. 34;
Nancy 28; Sarah J. 145;
S. M. 113
Fisher, Jonathan 11

Galloway contd.
William P. 145; W. J. 34
Galtna, Mary Ann 121
Gamble (Gamell, Gambil,
Gammels, Gamill,
Gammill), Elizabeth 34;
J. J. 128; Joshua P. 81;
Julia 132; Lucy 41;
Martha 24; William 176
Gamblin, John H. 23
Gant, Charles 89,143;
George 17,36,37; Mary
M. 112; Mollie 154
Gardner, M. A. 103; Mary
B. 167; Spencer 107
Garland, Sarah 162; S. B.
135
Garman (Garmon), Ann 27;
Hariet 28; Robert P.
19,50
Garner, Agnes 186; Ben
93; Catharine 184; Eliza
Ann 17; Harriet P. 24;
James 95; N. B. 184
Garrett (Garret), Barnham
160; Bartley 142; Mollie
P. 130; Nancy Mrs. 149;
William T. 103
Gary, M. R. 170; N. 159
Gassaway, John J. 41
Gates, H. G. 145
Gather, W. M. C. 86
Gatlin, E. P. 111; Francis
M. 70; Isaac T. 99;
Isaac V. 112; John W.
111; Martha A. 147; Mary
27; N. G. 145; Robert
100,120; William 95
Gattis, Amanda M. 51;
America 177; Benjamin
77; D. B. 89; Elizabeth
5; Emily 28,180; George
F. 65; George W. 56,
102; G. C. 80; Green C.
17; Isaac N. 9; James
20; James W. 166; Jane
188; J. N. 138; John T.
89; John W. 173; J. T.
136; Julian 187; Martha
Ann 71; Martha E. 141;
Mary Jane 72; Nancy C.
17; Nathaniel 188; Ro-
bert F. 59; Sallie 141;
Sally Ann 25; Sarah
Catharine 62; S. C. 173;
Susan E. 62; Thomas 24;
William 54,63; William
H. 50; Willis 19
Gault (Gaut), Elizabeth
178; H. C. 168; Henry
C. 9; Henry S. 125;
Hugh C. 30; James J. 30;
Martha F. Mrs. 133;
Mary A. 182; M. E. 183;
Samuel B. 90; Sarah A.
146; W. T. 133
Gauthy (Gautney, Gauthney),
Franklin 155; Sarah
Elizabeth 117; W. S. 145
Gavin, Matilda 21; Nancy
9; William W. 21
Gawdy, James 161
Gay, Judia L. 79
Gentry, Lucius 139; R. A.
129; T. H. 182
George, Alexander 151;
Bettie 153; Bettie S.
134; Caroline 18; Casenia
116; Cornelius 159;
Cornelia Ann 163; Daniel
E. 5; David 64; Docia
136; E. A. 129; Esther
104; Esther H. 8; E.
Thomas 188; Franklin A. 37;

George contd.
G. A. 131; G. E. 174;
Harriet 143; H. P. 139;
Icy 183; Isaac 159;
James A. 61; James C.
157; James M. 17,187;
James N. 38,117; James
S. 13; Jane 51,133,146;
Jane F. 85; J. B. 167;
J. C. 116; Jesse M. 71;
J. H. 82,176; J. M. 100;
J. M. M. 148; John 4;
John H. 71; Joseph 37,
50,188; Joseph N. 83;
Julia 182; J. W. 142;
Keziah A. 9; Lizzie 98;
Louisa 15; Louretta 170;
Malinda 101; Manervy
147; Margaret 41,143;
Margaret Ann 59; Marga-
ret J. 53; Margaret V.
56; Martha J. 41; Mary
7,98; Mary Ann 57; Mary
Jane 20,127; Mary T. 40;
M. F. 178; M. H. 165;
M. M. 167; Nancy A. 174;
Nancy H. 115; Nannie E.
120; Needham 51; N. H.
178; Permelia T. 69;
Presley O. 109; R. A.
113; Rachel E. 82;
Rebecca A. 86; Robert B.
30; Rusia 171; Samuel
159; Sarah 68; Sarah E.
143; Sarah J. 119;
Solomon 35; Susan Ann
76; Susan F. G. 49;
Susannah 52; S. N. 183;
S. R. 150; T. F. 118;
Thomas 11,188; Thomas
M. 160; Thomas P. 96,
111; Unstead 9; Violet
179; William 31,50;
William B. 65; Willie
E. 175; W. P. 182
Gerelds, James 14; Mary
A. 86
Germley, Manerva 28
Gess, Manerva 30
Gibbs, Benjamin P. 158;
E. P. 72; Mary E. 181;
Miles 13; W. H. 130,
148; William E. 7
Gibson, Albert G. Rev.
184; A. M. 73; Elizabeth
185; Eliza 188; Eliza-
beth E. 35,107; E. M.
167; Emeline 35; Fran-
ces E. 73; G. L. 138;
Jane 93; J. B. 108;
Joseph 16; Lizzie E.
107; Lucy A. 89; Ma-
halia J. 135; Mahala
S. D. 14; Manerva 68;
Margaret 25; Margaret
M. 77; Martha 32,48;
Martha A. E. 53; Mary
Jane 41; Mary Susan 136;
M. M. 174; Nancy A. 39;
Nancy R. 20; Nathan F.
34; R. B. 55; W. H. 137;
William H. 8; William
J. 176
Gilbert, Ambrose B. 186;
Calvin 71; Della 181;
Maggie 142; Malinda C.
14; Martha 106; Mary
155,186; P. G. 62;
W. A. 94; W. W. 108
Giles, Arthur F. 156;
J. V. 158
Gill, A. A. 120; Abram
91; A. H. 76; Alexander
H. 8; Betty F. 49;

Gill contd.
E. F. 187; Hardy 123;
Hezekiah 100; Icy 154;
James B. 17; John Y.
63; Joseph J. G. 185;
Kate 183; M. A. 144;
Mark L. 139; Martha A.
48; Mary C. 100; Mollie
Ann 64; Rebecca 133;
R. O. 135; Robert 113;
Sallie G. 109; S. H. 182;
T. J. 154; Virgie 174;
W. A. 167; W. A. Rev.
187; William D. 49;
William S. 10; William
T. 76; W. W. 7
Gillespie, Caroline 134;
George C. 114,182; Jacob
69; Jacob R. 161; Lilla
176; Lou 168; Martha E.
74; Mary 185; M. M. 82;
Robert 58; Samuel 107;
Sue 178; Vadora E. 125;
Wright 142
Gilley (Gillery, Gilly,
Gulley), A. J. 60; Eliza-
beth C. 148; George 145;
Hardin J. 62; James 86,
125; James J. 83; J. J.
65,152; John J. 131;
Loucinda 170; Lucinda 60;
Mary A. C. 76; Mary F.
78; Nancy E. 61; O. C.
127; Peter 14; Sarah 69,
75,182; Solomon 23; T. C.
83; William 106,143
Gilliam (Gillam, Gillum,
Gilham), A. F. 164;
Henrietta C. Mrs. 152;
Henry A. 15; John A. 46;
John D. 32; Joseph S. H.
67; Martha E. 50; Mary
Ann 56; Nancy S. 34;
R. J. 82; R. L. 116;
T. P. 100
Gilliland, Margaret 99;
Margret J. 26; Martha
48; R. E. 76; S. E. 186;
S. J. 66,88
Gillmore, A. J. 40
Givens, Harriet 94; Nar-
cissa 29; William 9
Clasgow, Taylor 172
Glasscock, George W. 31;
Jane C. 60
Glaze, A. L. 100
Glazier, Susan M. 179
Gleghorn, A. C. 179; An-
drew C. 36; Elihu 37;
Elijah 6; Elizabeth B.
53; Johnson J. 42; Mary
Ann 9; Nancy P. 33;
Robert Y. 160; Sarah S.
106; S. W. 106,125;
William 6
Glenn (Glen), Emily E. 65;
Mary W. 68; Washington
99
Glidewell (Glidwell), Aron
84; Bird 187; Drucilla
14; John G. 24,35; J. W.
163; Martha A. 52; Martha
Ann 20; Nancy 36; Thomas
H. 2
Glover, Rachel 97
Gobble (Gobbell), Edward
19; Jacob C. 24; John L.
11
Goff, Elizabeth 23; Sally
Ann 3
Goforth, Haslip 9; J. T.
179; Sabra 25
Gold, James M. 38; Manerva
46; Noah 34; Thomas 36;

Gold contd.
William 60
Golden, J. J. 121; M. F.
178; Ruben 62; Sarah A.
134; Susan C. 163
Goode (Good), Della C. 32;
Elizabeth 63; Hetty 9;
J. A. 165; John 48;
Joseph H. 75; Maggie M.
180; Margaret 29; Mary
E. 156; Sarah Ann 48;
William 31
Goodin, Arthur A. 17
Goodwin, A. F. D. 58;
George 120; James W. 125;
M. A. 95; Nancy 188;
Sarah 152
Goodrich, Ann 142; Bonner
114,137; Isaac 161; J.
C. 68; Jennie 153; J. F.
93; Lou 131; Mary E. 61;
Mollie 131; Tommie 178;
W. C. 131; Will 163
Goodrum, Charles L. 21;
Orleana 163
Goodson, William 162
Goosby, Elizabeth 110;
J. J. 141; William 130;
W. J. 178
Gordon (Gorden), J. B. Dr.
180; John T. 16; Julia
C. 152; Lizzie 150; Mary
132
Gordy, S. A. 133; W. F.
145
Gore, Elizabeth 80; James
91; Jemima G. 18; John
E. 38; Martha 100; Mary
68; Mary C. 54; Nancy C.
119; Rebeccah 7; Sarah
41; Sarah J. 125;
William L. 142
Gowan (Gowen), Daniel H.
12; Frances 126; Hamil-
ton 73; James D. 141;
Mathew P. 42; Mattie F.
168; Nancy Ann 61;
Samuel E. 74
Gowers, Mary E. 164
Grable, Dave F. 113; W. A.
173
Grace, E. F. M. 76
Gracey (Gracy), Calvin 122;
Elizabeth A. 54; Hetty
104; John A. 74; Mary
154; Tranquilla R. 71
Grader, Polly 153
Graham (Greham, Greyham,
Grayham), Calvin 40;
Eliza J. 14; Ewing 25;
John J. 67; Manerva 42;
Mary 15; Mary Lou 133;
Mollie 154; Sarena 42;
Susan 163; T. R. 171
Grammer, A. H. 123; Alvin
M. 122; Isaac 60; J. 87;
James M. 97; Jesse L.
74; Millford 74; M. M.
124; Nancy C. 83;
William 50
Grant, C. C. 87; Charlotte
3; Clarence 57; E. M. J.
67; Louisa 23; James 1;
John S. 119; Sarah E.
124; William 76
Grantland (Grantlin,
Granlin), A. E. 108;
Cornelia S. 37; Fannie
A. 140; Leah 182; Vio-
let 103,126
Graves, Arabiam 30; C. C.
142; Elema 137; Eliza-
beth A. 44; Isaac S. 27;
Jesse 33; John 162;

Graves contd.
Lucy M. 29; Mary J. 86;
Robert R. 6
Grau, Clus 148
Gravet, Mary R. 114
Gray, Allen H. 168; Amanda
154; Brice P. 16; Bur-
gess 185; Catharine 70;
Charles 85; David L. 6;
David M. 49; D. L. 119;
D. N. 136; Elizabeth 4,
18,27; Emaline 188;
Elinor T. 106; Emily 2;
George 28; Harvey 188;
Isaac H. 70; James 172;
James H. 5; James P. 86;
James T. 94; Jane 140;
J. H. 107; John 95,183;
John B. 78; Joseph W. C.
28; Joshua D. 47; Julia
Ann 2,14; J. W. N. 97;
Lizzie J. 151; Lou May
150; Lucy 141; Mahaley
14; Margaret 105; Margaret
Ann 14,55; Martha C. 46;
Martha Jane 28; Mary 35,
112; Mary A. W. 55;
Mary F. 160; M. F. 104;
Nancy 106; Rebecca 34;
R. W. 127; Sarah 186;
Sarah Ann M. 8; Sarah
E. 50,127; S. M. 128,
129; Sophia A. 149; T.
A. 86; Thomas 22,100,
132; Thomas H. 168;
W. G. 173; W. H. 130;
William C. 21; William
M. 163; Wilson 8
Green, A. C. 104; Andrew
Johnson 168; Angeline
59; Ann 162; Arch 178;
Edwin 132; E. J. 172;
Elisha 179; Elvina J.
51; Emily 33; Felix 120;
Flenn 127; Frank 124;
Harvey 33; Isaac 8;
James 115; James C. 42;
James E. 77; Jane 167;
Jemima E. 44; John 29,
151,169; John A. 133;
John D. 137; Lizzie 103;
Lucy 136; Mary 126;
Mary D. C. 137; Mildred
H. F. 72; Richard 99;
Rebecca J. 65; Sally S.
47; Sophronia C. 105;
Susan E. 58; Thedosia
O. 81; W. C. 105; William
T. 143; Willie 169
Greer, Alexander A. 29;
Andy 181; Anna 111;
Catharine 166; David A.
186; Drucilla 14; Eliza
131; Ephraim 153; Flenn
100; Gracy 107; Hetty
E. K. 184,187; Jane C.
7; Jennie 184; John 137;
John A. 46; Joseph H.
32; Julia E. 62; Katie
169; Margaret 184; Ma-
riah 156; Martha P. 55;
Mary 156,166; Mary E. 5;
Mary V. 186; McNelley
173; M. Lula 122; Sarah
Jane 130; Vedora Ann
137
Griffith, James 187; S. M.
90
Griffin, Ann 86; Bailey
128; Bob 177; Elizabeth
22; H. B. 166; James
138; J. D. 162; John
172; John J. 131; Louisa
Jane 57; Lucinda 97;

Griffin contd.
Martha R. 95; Mary 176;
Nancy 49; William B. 39
Griffis, Addie 136; Amanda
152; B. F. 131; Clabe
153; Dorah 155; Dunkin
103; Elizabeth 72; Ezell
161; George 143; Hasty
169; H. D. 129; James H.
157; Jane 69,153; John
147; J. W. 138; Lizzie
121; Lucy A. 103; Martha
C. 27,122; Nancy 20;
Oliver P. 12; Prince 95;
Robert T. 105; Susan 88;
Susan D. 15; T. D. 98;
William A. 185; Wilson
165
Griggs (Gregg, Gragg),
Elizabeth 44; Eliza Jane
26; Henry A. 40; Jane
39; John W. 16; Joseph
M. 81,86; Margit 4;
Mary M. 121; Samuel B. 40
Grigory (Gregory), Brown
14; Elizabeth 31; Ephraim
H. 141; H. C. 164; John
3; John F. 72; Louisa
31; Martha 57; Mary 14,
94; Matilda 153; Ned 95,
146; Ruth A. 63; Sarah
13; Sarah E. 121; S. J.
170; William 153; William
D. 29; William T. 30
Grills (Grill), Elizabeth
V. 59; Eveline P. 73;
James A. 45; Mary A. 46;
Sarah C. 48; William J.
45,76
Grimes, Margaret 119; P. G.
115; P. J. 126
Grinnette, Mathew N. 60
Grisby, Edward N. 159
Griswell, Mollie 151
Grizzard (Grizard, Grisard),
Isaac W. 81; Isabella
151; Lucy A. Mrs. 92;
Margerett V. 73; Marion
139; Mary C. 60; N. J.
114; Sarah F. 27; Susan
E. 52; Wiles A. 15
Groce, Alexander P. 36;
America 183; Bettie 103;
Cordelia 149; D. H. 168;
Elizabeth 83; Joanna 96;
Lucy 149; Martha 83;
Martin V. 80; Mattie Lou
147; M. R. 175; Nancy
186; Thomas 78,131; T. F.
180
Gross, F. M. 113; Martin
R. 105; Mary S. 84; Wiley
90; W. M. 113
Groth, Christian 153
Groves, C. C. 100
Grubbs, Eliza J. 72; Martha
E. 99; Nancy C. 65,66;
Sarah F. 69; Z. H. 101
Guerin, W. M. 90
Guest, Lou 136
Guinn (Guin), Claskey Jane
45; David B. 9; Elizabeth
29
Gullett (Gullet), Elvira
187; James 64
Gunter, Alvessa 30; Caldonia
136; C. N. 167; D. B. F.
164; D. J. 105; Dyca J.
99; Eliza 24; Franklin
24; G. W. 140; H. W. 103;
J. A. 141; James R. 67;
John H. 162; John W. 26;
Lucy A. 116; Martha 1;
Mary E. 127; Rebecca 24;

Gunter contd.
Sarah Ann 49; Susan E.
130; W. F. 108; William
4; William H. 88; W. J.
102
Guslay, Kissiah A. M. 24
Gustus, Dealie 125; Nar-
cissa 148; Spence 181
Guthrie, Samantha J. 72
Guy, Abner 5; Annie 140;
Robert 179
Guyer, Jasper 171; Thomas
139; Warren 137

Hackett, Joseph 170;
Mollie 169
Hackles, Elizabeth 148
Haggard, Ruth 21; William-
son 11; W. T. 103,183
Hailey (Haley), Elizabeth
C. 11; Hester D. 79;
Lewis 148; Mahala 115;
Martha 6; Martha E. 39;
Mary 169; Mary Jane 58;
William F. 112,137;
W. W. 94
Hair (Heirs), Amon 42;
James 32; Margaret 57;
Norah 57
Hainey, John 135
Haislip, Zachariah 150
Hall, Alexander 99; Amanda
M. 141; Anderson 108;
Barney 151; Berry 85;
C. 11; Hester D. 79;
C. C. 167; Clinton 93;
Constantine A. 18;
Darcus Mrs. 92; David
C. 34; Donie 176; E.
Jane 117; Eliza 176;
Elizabeth 75; Eliza J.
27; Elzada 78; F. J.
138; G. W. 130; Hannah
24; Harriet 131; Henton
25; Ida L. 122; Isaac
C. 7; James M. 144;
J. C. 160; Jennie 172;
John D. 12; J. W. 150;
Lucinda 2; L. Z. 79;
Malinda 1; Martha 115;
Martha Ann 60; Mary Ann
108; Mollie 162; Nancy
22,122,124; Nancy M.
144; Napoleon 98; Para-
lee 83; Phillip J. 28;
Rebecca 164; Richard 84,
86,154; Ruben 111; Sam-
uel 57,68; Samuel H. 18;
Sarah 124; Sarah A. 177;
Sarah F. 38; Sarah R.
40; Selina A. S. 40;
Tabitha 158; Tennessee
142; Thomas 147; W. C.
133; William 14,141;
William H. 11,23
Halflack, John 62
Hallam (Hallum), Andrew
J. 21; Harriet 151;
James R. 10
Hallaway (Halloway, Halo-
way, Halaway), Adolphus
B. 45; Davis M. 43;
D. M. 75; Eveline E.
168; G. D. 113; Harris
114; Henry 50; Jack 106,
118; James S. 152;
J. P. 147; Laura Eliza-
beth Sandlin 100; Sarah
J. Mrs. 142; S. J. 173
Hames, J. A. 181
Hamby, Chesley 30; Gideon
J. 54; Harriet M. 125;
Lou 181; Martha 143;
Mary 83; Mary Ann 36;
R. L. 182

Hamilton, A. J. 57; A. L.
73; Alexander 56; Barbery
27; C. C. 118; David R.
152; Eliza 152; Eliza-
beth 21,122; Elizabeth
S. 54; Eliza C. 53;
Emily J. 160; Emily Jane
130; Enoch 20; Evicy T.
66; Francis M. 34; G. W.
110; Harriet 96; Harriet
M. 97; Henry 97,98;
Henry C. 45; Hester Ann
139; Isaac 21; Jacob 84;
James 9,69; James G.
109; James M. 112; James
P. 113; J. H. 100; John
2,32,165; John A. 163;
John R. 74; L. 81;
Linda 155; Lucretta B.
101; Mahala 27; Margaret
Greer 188; Malinda 25;
Mary Ann 107; Mary E.
54,101; Mary Jane 122.
127; Mattie J. 183;
M. F. 132; Nancy A. 46;
Nannie 174; N. E. 174;
Neil S. 119; Newton 54;
Peter 45; Peter J. 11;
Pres. 158; Preston 134;
Prudence 8; Rebecca Ann
32; R. F. 105,112; Ro-
bert A. 12; Sallie 88;
Samuel P. 81; Sarah A.
84; Sarah B. 37; Sarah
Elizabeth 82; Sarah J.
81; S. C. 176; S. P.
128,153; Susan A. 54,
96; Susan C. 66; Teny
G. 24; W. B. 69; W. H.
135; William 10,68;
William F. 99; William
G. 1; W. J. 162; W. R.
162
Hamlin (Hamblin), Elmira
153; Harriet 18; Henry
W. 75; H. W. 66; James
H. 65; Martha 33; S. P.
130; Virgie E. J. 156;
William T. 8
Halbert, Amanda 95,166;
Angeline 156; Colman
175; Desina 23; Eliza-
beth 130; Emaline 130;
Fountain 151; Frances
J. 2; Hettie 137; Jacob
103; Jake 165; James C.
73; J. H. 113; Levy 152;
Margarett J. 45; Mariah
93; Martha 2; Martha E.
61,69; M. J. 82; Mollie
166; Naomi 121; Nick
151; Peter 147; Pleasant
49,115; Pleasant W. 101;
Rose A. 109; Sallie 149;
Sam 153; S. G. 130;
Susan 111; W. H. 130;
W. M. 168
Hale (Hail), A. J. 159;
Burrel 4; Catharine
176; Charles 175; Fanny
Jane 79; George W. 90;
Jane 83,138; John 181;
Mary Ann 120; M. E. 152;
Parthenia 5; Sarah 121;
Thomas 73; William 4,23
Hambrick, C. B. 164; Isham
12; J. M. 88,178; J. S.
63; Mahala 3; Mary E.
87; M. M. V. 85; Nancy
P. 136; Ruth 60
Hamlet, Ben 102; John H.
25
Hammonds (Hammons), Jas-
per P. 15; M. H. 144;

Hammonds contd.
Thomas 23
Hampton, A. M. 154; Asbery
J. 26; Berrel 93; C. S.
123; Elizabeth B. 12;
E. T. 139; Hardin 35;
Henry 128; Henry W. 125;
H. L. 137; Isham 109;
James D. 130; James H.
142; James W. 94; Jane
183; Jane Mrs. 84; Joe
135; John W. 77; M. A.
99,140; Maggie E. 105;
Margaret 38; Mariah 136;
Martha 37; Martha C. 64;
Mary A. 9; Mary E. 98;
Mary M. 94; M. D. 167;
M. J. 92; N. 155; Pres-
ton 2; Reuben 141; Sallie
160; Samuel 155; Scott
104; S. F. 101; Susan E.
9; Theodosia 9; Thomas
19,149; Wade 126; W. W.
117
Hananaday, Robert R. 98
Hanaway, J. R. 135; Mollie
E. 167
Hanby, M. D. L. 85
Hancock (Handcock), Benja-
min D. 1; Benjamin 39;
Isaah 39; John 21; Martha
4; Nancy E. 22; Sarah C.
49; William G. 32
Hanes, George 46; James E.
105; Lucy C. 31
Haney (Hanie), J. W. 180;
Martha 164; Samuel 65
Hanks, Clarissa H. 34;
Delila 13; Harrison 51;
James M. 43; John C. 52;
Lucy 12; P. S. 67;
William 25
Hankins, Caroline 45;
Milly R. 98
Hannah, Josie 170; Mary
184,187; Mary E. 104;
M. F. 99; Robert 186
Harber, Mirah 144
Harbin (Harben), Alexander
134; Andrew M. 72; Enoch
E. 46; Hannah 73; Jasper
169; John 15,147; Marion
168; Martin 21,82; Mary
E. 50,125; Mattie 151;
Millie A. 95; Nancy Ellen
132; Nelly E. 62; Ruth
J. 73; Sallie 170; Sarah
E. 33; T. A. 146; William
24
Hardeman, Mary Lucinda 75
Hardin (Harden, Hardens,
Harding), A. Caroline
23; Amanda 133; Ann E.
129; Derinda 83; D. G.
117; D. T. 124; Edward
27; Elmira Malissa 154;
Epp 43; Eppey 8; Gar-
brell 129; George 140;
Harry 91; Jack 132;
James T. 160; James W.
80; J. D. 71; J. H. 121;
Jonathan 6; Jose 123;
J. T. 100; J. W. 94,159;
Lovel C. 51; Martha Ann
146; Martha E. 143; Mary
4,187; Mary E. 78;
Mattie 115; Minney 35;
M. J. 162; Nancy J. 162;
Nathan P. 3; Penelope
33; R. D. 82; Robert D.
51; Sarah E. 109; Sarah
J. 161; T. B. 150; W. E.
168; Wiley K. 15; William
21; William M. 37

Hardison, Mollie H. 159
Hardy, Julia Ann 49;
   Martha J. 49; Mary 42;
   W. T. 139
Harkins (Hankins), B. F.
   81; C. D. 113; Easter
   C. 21; Jane E. (Haskins)
   70; Margaret C. 63; Mary
   107; Susan 107; Susan
   A. 27; Susan E. 83,138;
   Thomas M. 72,150; T. M.
   87
Harmon, Cornelius 24
Harms, Charles 173
Harpe, Beuna Vista 177;
   Parmelia Ann 100
Harrel, Ive Jefferson 37;
   Josiah 179; Julia A. 33
Harrington, H. D. F. 142
Harris, Agnes 186; Amanda
   24; Annie Jane 116;
   Bettie 175; Betty 174;
   Caleburn 69; Calvin 56;
   Campbell 157; Catharine
   20; Clasbourn 32; David
   L. 129; Dick 136; D. L.
   66; E. C. Mrs. 99; Edna
   92; Eliza 155; Emma 119;
   Fannie V. 97; Frank 180;
   Hannah 16; Harriett A.
   153; Henderson 19; Henry
   91; James 13,26,166;
   Jane 166; J. L. 113;
   J. M. 118; Joel M. 163;
   John 136; John B. 45;
   John D. 67; Lizzie 121;
   Lou 113; Manurvy 155;
   Martha 10,19; Mary 170,
   174,182; Mary Ann 71;
   Mary E. 13; Mary L. 175;
   Mattie E. 159; M. C. 87;
   M. F. 160; Milly 112;
   Nancy 149,166; Nathan
   120; N. C. 158; N. F.
   161; Rebecca Jane 32;
   Ruffus 60; Rufus 71;
   Susan 14; Tabitha 42;
   Theophelus 34; Theophi-
   las 18; Thomas B. 90;
   Thomas C. 137; Thomas
   H. 106; William 31,161,
   185; William E. 123;
   William J. 78; William
   S. 52
Harriston (Harrison, Hair-
   ston, Harston, Harstin),
   Allen 177; Allen G. 154;
   Amanda 29; Andy 169;
   Ann 115; Catharine 167;
   Charles 152; Daniel 53;
   Delilah 93; Eliza Jane
   67; Ella 172,182; Ellen
   123; Eveline 139; George
   132; Green 160; Harriet
   49,101; James 4,87;
   James G. 3,33; James H.
   43; James N. 162; J. C.
   86; J. E. 161; Jodie
   138; John 114; Joily
   163; Julia Ann 141;
   Kennelen T. 40; Lethe
   8; Lorenzie 30; Maggie
   158; Manly M. 18; Mary
   19; M. J. 172; M. L. 162;
   M. M. 70; Nancy D. 84;
   O. G. 129,182; Perry
   108; R. M. 157; Robert
   P. 101; Susie 178; T. W.
   156; William 78,139;
   Willis 154
Hart, Eliza 106; S. A. M.
   4; Sarah A. 47; Simon
   49; Sinia S. 27; Step-
   hen 45; Thomas 77;

Hart contd.
   Viana 83,138
Harshaw, Thomas A. J. 117
Hartgrass, Nancy J. 58
Harper, Celia Ann 120;
   Daniel 143; Douglas 16;
   Elizabeth 49; Henry 111;
   Henry J. 84; Jane 103;
   John 7,163; Julia 161;
   Lenzy C. 15; Maria E.
   185; Martha E. 53; Mary
   H. 169; Mary L. 29;
   M. E. 123; P. J. 123;
   P. M. 139; Sarah 100;
   Selina 122; Sue 170;
   Thomas C. 29; Thomas M.
   123
Harvey (Hanvey, Hanvy),
   Chesbey 63; Erwin 111;
   Grandville 107; G. W.
   61,182; J. J. 121; Laura
   164; Manuel 106; Maud
   my 102; Susan 179
Harwell, E. J. 101; Mattie
   183; Robert M. 4
Harvin, Ann E. 65
Hasket, Frances 123;
   Henry 133
Haskins (Hoskins), Eliza-
   beth M. 70; Jane E. 70;
   John S. 66; Lou 122;
   N. E. 147; Robert C.
   123; Susan F. 62
Hastin (Haston), Elizabeth
   178; Julia 173; L. H.
   180; Mary S. 145; M. H.
   148; N. B. 148
Hasty (Hastie), Alice C.
   180; Allie M. 148;
   James A. 125; Mathew 7;
   Sidney 162; William L.
   134
Hatcher, Charles 153;
   Ida Lou 138; O. R. 147
Hatchett (Hatshet), Arm-
   stead 84; James 131;
   James W. 60; Rachel A.
   162; Sarah A. 55,86
Hatley, James 109
Haugh, J. E. 124
Hawes, Rebecca L. 29
Haywood (Hawood), Benja-
   min 8; Henry 154; John
   F. 120; Sarah Ann 128
Hawkins (Hawkings), Daniel
   10; E. D. 127; Elizabeth
   R. 59; Henry 25; Matilda
   10; Moses H. 61; Samuel
   2; William 183
Hawkwood, Martha 58
Hayes (Hays, Hay, Hayse),
   Abraham M. 114; Arder
   150; Charles B. 30;
   Ed. 144; Elizabeth 39,
   48,141; Emma 158; Fannie
   167; F. O. 101; Frances
   M. 8; Isaac 52; Jacob
   8; James 161; James D.
   8; James G. 9; J. B.
   166; J. L. 173; John
   163; John B. 10; Leti-
   cia 172; Lizzie 165;
   Lucinda C. 114; M. A.
   145,166,173; Margaret
   76; Margaret M. 140;
   Martha 145; Martha L.
   6; Mary Ann 39; Mary E.
   70,142; Mary M. 168;
   Matilda 185; Milly F.
   96; Narcissa E. 26;
   Nedd 89; Newman 161;
   Rebecca 2,8; Reuben
   149; R. G. 177; Sallie
   148; Sarah 114;

Hayes contd.
   Sarah E. 101; T. R. 147;
   William 168; William S.
   104
Hazelwood (Hazzlewood,
   Hazzellwood, Haiselwood,
   Haizlewood), Ann 168;
   Emaline 183; George W.
   98; John W. 76; J. W.
   114; Levi W. 55; Lucinda
   67; Martha L. 72; Mary
   147; Mary Jane Elizabeth
   96; Nancy 17; Nancy A.
   74; Thomas A. 54; William
   H. 23
Hazzard, Martha J. 28;
   Thomas 28
Hazzelett, W. H. 129
Head, Mary J. 103
Heals, Sallie 116
Heard, J. S. 116
Heart, Bird 111
Heath, E. H. 128; George
   W. 126; Nancy 24; Pris-
   cilla E. 63; Samantha
   175; Sarah P. 45; S. E.
   178; Sophia E. 29
Heathcock (Hathcoat, Hath-
   cock, Haithcock, Health-
   Coat), Alfred 29,155;
   Angeline 106; Anna 144;
   Bartin W. 33; Caroline
   87; Casanda 105; Eliza
   95; Elmira 56; Henry 25;
   H. J. 149; John F. M. 71;
   Lavina 58; Lavina J. 88;
   Louisa J. 56; Lucy Ann
   71; Mahaley 32; Mary 47;
   Mc. 163; R. F. E. 171;
   Samuel 47; Wiles J. 30;
   William 56; W. J. 141
Hedgepeth (Huddspeth),
   Charlott M. 43; Cornelius
   88; E. J. 76; Elviry
   Jane 30; Harrison 149;
   Lee 162; Lucinda L. 43;
   Lydia E. 14; M. 103;
   Manerva C. 37; Mary Mrs.
   114; Mary J. 121; Mica-
   jah P. 185; Minerva 38;
   M. L. 89; Narcissa 75;
   N. P. 55; Sam 104;
   Samuel M. 13; S. J. 115;
   W. B. 78
Hedrick (Hendrick), Andrew
   6; James A. 63; J. B.
   107; Joseph C. 48;
   Martha Jane 61; Sarah 119
Heflin, Frances C. 88;
   Joab 24; John H. 20;
   Samantha 21
Helms, John 113
Helton, John N. 77; Lizzie
   137; S. P. 137
Hemphill, Martha Jane 18
Henderson, A. M. 179;
   Amanda 113; Ann 173; Ben
   176; Caezar 151; Calvin
   153; Catharine 157,164;
   Cezar 114; Doncilla 92;
   Eddey 29; Eli 181; Eliza
   131; Elizabeth 147;
   Ella 148; Ellen 127;
   Elza 93; Fanny 134;
   George 132; Henry 70;
   J. A. 124,144; James 21,
   33,62; James, Esq. 153;
   James M. 160; Jane 154;
   John H. 174; Julia 180;
   Lucy 104; Martha 159;
   Mary 176; Norris 151;
   Sandy 24; Sarah Ann 68;
   Sarah E. 96; S. J. 132;
   Susie 179; V. A. 173;

Henderson contd.
Victoria May 175; Wallace
183; William M. 60;
W. T. 114
Henry, Carrol 106; Eliza-
beth 2
Hensley (Henslee), Eliza-
beth 68; Frances 66;
Isa 66; Louiza 72; M.
118; Susan 73; William
152
Henson, Archibald 95
Heraldson (Heralson,
Heralston, Herelston,
Harralson, Harston),
Alsy 92; Enoch 92; E. S.
90; Fred 92; Green 161;
James H. 69; M. A. 89;
Mary 31,175; Nora 92;
Sophronia 155; William
27,87; Willis S. 105
Hereford, Robert S. 127
Herndon, B. F. 163
Herren, Guss 119
Herring (Herrings), James
S. 116; M. E. 174
Hess, August 46; William
S. 38
Hester, Caroline 115,126;
Easter 92; Edmond E. 91;
Elizabeth 48; Elizabeth
Jones 50; Elizabeth L.
71; James W. 60; J. W.
68; Louisa O. 123; Mar-
anda C. 53; Mary Eliza
20; Mollie E. 170;
S. A. 117; S. J. 124;
Virginia C. 150; William
H. 63,82
Hiat, Ellen 33
Hickland (Hicklin, Hicklan),
Caroline 145; John 26;
M. A. 169; Sarah J. 121
Hickman, Andy 179; Belle
152; Bettie Ann 116;
Frances 184; Fred 171;
Harrison 179; Josephine
23; Mariah 133; Sam 92;
William 148
Hicks, America A. 163;
Edward M. 50; Elisha
69; G. M. 148; James
108; Lucy J. 80; L. W.
163; Martha L. 28; Mary
Ann 16; Mary F. 126;
M. H. 95; R. W. 167;
Thomas B. 45,75; W. L.
183
Hickson, Malinda 59
Higgins, Ann 155; Ann
Jane 32; Betsey 165;
Dennis 92; Emily 160;
Fannie E. 73; George W.
41; G. W. 77; H. C. 119;
Joel C. 26; Johnson 132;
Mariah 35; Martha D. 61;
Mary H. 26; Morgan H.
28; Nancy J. 84; Nancy
Y. 6; Samira 103; Sarah
L. 51; Susan E. 58;
Virginia 142; Willis C.
28
Hightower, Avary 149;
James 12
Hiles, Walton 90
Hill, A. J. 116; Albert
105; Benjamin 24; Blan-
ton 165; Cintha 21;
Clarissa 76; D. J. 68;
Ebenezer 186; Eliza 32;
Elizabeth 14,88; Eliza-
beth L. 59; Eliza V.
140; Emily E. 124; Ennis
157; Fannie B. 179;

Hill contd.
Fannie Catharine 77;
Frederick 141; Hattie
N. 73; Henry 152; Hilton
85; Houston 49; Hunter
66; James 16,128(2),150;
James B. 118; James S.
110; Jane 71; J. H. 117;
J. M. 138; John 57,78,
124,136,163; John M.
20; John W. 148; L. A.
168; L. H. 77; Lizzie
154; Lou 172; Lucy A.
38; Malinda Jane 60;
Mary Alice 171; Mary Ann
130; Mary E. 122; Mary
Elizabeth 72; Mary J.
114; Mary W. 26; M. R.
156; Nathaniel R. 26;
Richard 6,12; R. K. 66;
Robert 44; Samuel 69;
Samuel A. 122; Samuel M.
87; Sarah 150,162,163;
Sarah J. 139; Susan 65;
T. D. 63; Thomas V. 176;
W. G. 175; Wiley 8;
William J. 44; W. J.
149; Z. C. 70
Hilliard, Eliza J. 110;
G. W. 99
Hilton, Dinah 129; Marga-
ret 1; Sady 7
Hindman, Bartlett 49;
Peggy 3; Silas 185;
Thomas 168; William W.
60
Hines (Hine), Belle 152;
David 7; Finetta 187;
Henrietta Mrs. 134;
J. S. 84; J. T. 150;
Martha B. 28; Martha E.
90; Millie 176; Nancy
113; Sallie A. 179;
Sarah Ann 137; S. D. Dr.
108; Thomas Capt. 186;
W. A. 145
Hinds, Eliza 13
Hinebaugh, Peter 142
Hinkle, A. R. 127; Bryant
38; Caroline 1; E. A.
90; J. M. 177; Mary W.
7; Morgan W. 4; M. W.
96; Sarah 10; W. A. 157
Hinson (Hintson), Jones
H. 130; J. R. 77
Hipsh, S. C. 181
Hise, William 63
Hitchcock, Joseph 19
Hitt, Mary 142
Hobbs, Alexander 84;
Amanda 160; Andrew T.
148; Berry 8; B. H. 91;
David F. 12; David S.
24; Eliza 128; Eliza-
beth 7; Emeline 10;
James T. 175; Jesse W.
15; J. N. 137; John 10,
143,156; John W. 75,
96; Josiah 91; J. S.
147; J. W. 153; Lou 168;
Margaret J. 87; Martha
Caroline 9; Martha P.
24; Mary 48,91; Mary L.
133; Mattie 141,157;
N. A. 183; Nancy 6,42;
Nathaniel 38; Pleasant
130; Polly 151; Polly
Ann 144; Sallie Mrs.
149; Sarah 189; Susannah
29,188; Thomas B. 106;
Wiley A. 52,97; William
P. 71; W. W. 98,135
Hobson, J. Y. 127
Hodge, Calvin L. 25;

Hodge contd.
Charles W. 48; C. J. 175;
E. G. 149; E. J. 150;
Eli L. 27; Frances A.
95; James C. 108; Joseph
B. 12; Margit J. 13;
Mary G. 43; M. J. 163;
N. C. 119; Sallie E. 136;
Sarah 5; W. M. 101
Hogan, Elizabeth 96;
James L. 34; John A. 100;
Loucinda 157; L. P. 114;
Mary Jane 105; Maving A.
112; Samuel 10; Wennie
E. 129
Hogue (Hague), A. 177;
Amanda 144; Bunk 159;
Catharine T. 21; Cordelia
J. 115; Eugenia C. 61;
Eugine C. 62; James C.
84; John R. 57; Keziah
M. 27; Margaret Ann 26;
Mary C. 21; M. E. 99;
Mollie 154; Nicey 1;
Robert M. 36; Sarah R.
106
Holder, Mary Ann 74;
Wilson 98
Holden (Holdin), Mary 91;
S. S. Capt. 187
Holland, J. E. 146; Thomas
H. 25
Hollensworth, Vicey 143
Holly (Holley), B. F. 74;
Catharine 95; Davidson
11; Frances 87; Jane 59;
John 36,74; Margret 47;
Mary 72; Shadrack 76;
Susan A. Mrs. 103;
Thomas 63; William M. 89
Holman, Andrew 125; Anna
E. Mrs. 95; Archy 97;
Bird 172; Book 165;
Daniel 14,126; D. W. 141;
Eliza Ann 1; Elizabeth
Ann 186; Eliza Jane 184,
187; Hannah 130; Hardy
C. 28; Isaac J. 29;
Isaac M. 69; James H. 93;
James J. 131,155; James
P. 41; Jasper S. 53;
Jennie P. 159; John 157,
173; John P. 38,153;
Joseph 19; Julia Ann 136;
M. A. 141; Marion 143;
Martha 147; Martha A.
173; Mary B. 32; Mary
Frances 121; Mecca J.
168; Nancy C. 168(2);
Permelia A. 60; R. A.
144; Rachel 33; R. L. 73;
R. M. 143; S. A. 73;
Sallie M. 127; Samuel C.
45; Sarah 183; Sophrona
J. 86; Sue 97; Thomas 9;
Thomas 43,143; Villa 153;
W. D. 106; William 135;
William H. 26; William
P. 81; William T. 147;
Willis 145; Willis M. 61
Holmes, Oliver C. 8;
Robert S. 186
Holt, Alfred 65; Almeta E.
165; Ambrose 64; Andrew
M. 117; Anna 128; Augus-
tus A. 82; Catharine 34;
Eleanor 39; James M.
121; Jordin C. 42; Joseph
55,56; Lucinda E. 64;
Margaret M. 86; Martha
A. 88; Martha E. 154;
Mary 21,61; Michael 15;
Patrick 126; Rebecca E.
59; Samuel 72; Sarah 26;

Holt contd.
S. F. 127; Virginia 89;
William 25,113
Honea, A. W. 144; Solomon
101
Honey (Honney), James 84;
James Henry 134; John
78,148; Louisa 107;
Nancy 79,115,137; Robert
8; Ruth 25; Sarah 23;
Sarah E. 92; Tom 176;
William R. 123
Honeycut (Honnicut),
Hiram T. 36; Winfield
S. 34
Hood, D. 87
Hoots, Doke 40; Elizabeth
7; Eliza Jane 135; Har-
vey 177; John 73; Louisa
54; Mattie Lou 164;
R. T. 181
Hope, Nancy A. 128; Samuel
D. 46
Hopewood (Hopwood), John
K. 151; M. M. 129; W. E.
147; W. M. 167
Hopkins, Babe 165; Bedford
3; Candis 103; E. 105;
Elizabeth 86; Florinda
87; Hannah 116; Hettie
S. 154; James 125,144;
Lewis 116,144; Mahaley
123; Mollie 139; Nathan-
iel 177; Newton 136;
Olla 140; Rebeccah B. 5;
Samantha 27; Samuel 182;
Sarah Ann 134; Sarah
Jane 120; Silas 167;
Wiley 139; William J. 4
Hopper (Hooper, Hoper),
Addie 165; B. M. 132,
163; C. A. 167; C. I.
161; Elen P. 40; Eliza-
beth 45; Enoch 106;
G. W. 76; John 10; John
M. 39; Joseph 50; Joseph
T. 44; Lucy C. 101;
Martha 42; Martha J. 59;
Mary E. 122; M. L. 171;
Nathaniel 38; Reid 13;
Richard O. 53; Sarah
110; Sarah A. 128;
Shady D. 28; William A.
35
Horing, Henry 175
Horton, Hannah 172; M. A.
77; Thomas 169; Thomas
M. 105; W. A. 70
Hosch (Houch), Amanda 76;
Jacob 2; Martha C. 26
Hough, Randolph 20
Hourd, J. W. 157
House (Houze), Nicholas
J. 42; W. M. 154
Houston, Elizabeth 36;
Martha 13; Mary V. 36;
Patience O. B. 13
Hovis, Ephraim 85; Mary
87; W. H. 128
Howard, Benjamin 72;
Cincinnatta 35; Cin-
cinnatti 158; Eliza A.
123; Faner 77; Frances
141; Hulda N. 108;
Isabella Mrs. 153;
James 72; Jane 58; Jen-
nie 181; John W. 71;
Josephine 117; Julian
33; Lucy A. 109;
Margaret 172; Margaret
W. 182; Martha 66;
Martha G. 77; Mattie
162; Nancy 77; Sarah 9,
95;

Howard contd.
William 23,34,125;
William J. 50; W. J. 95
Howe, John E. 106
Howell (Howel), Altaritha
C. 57; Amerrilda M. 26;
Charles S. 15; Clark
134; E. 184; Elizabeth
78; Hyson M. 69; James
P. 87; Martin V. 78;
Nancy R. 48; Newton W.
43; Pearce 131; Samuel
J. 46; Susan 33; Thomas
49; Travis K. 164;
William 153; William J.
121
Hubble, William R. 89
Huckabee, John H. 25;
Manda 74; Martha Ann
148; Nancy 35
Hudlow, Andrew 80; William
R. 41
Hudson, Ana 48; Ane A.
180; Benjamin F. 38;
B. V. Rev. 140; Caroline
136; Doney 177; Eliza-
beth 32; Eveline 84;
Francis 60; Isaac 99;
James P. 84; Jane K. 33;
Joseph L. 74; J. W. 146;
Louisa 180; Margaret
Jane 3; Mary C. 90;
Nancy J. 53; N. S. 87;
S. A. 153; Sallie E.
127; Susan P. 54; Thomas
M. 23; W. B. 168
Huey, John 14
Huff, Doct. Earley 27;
Julia 162; Thomas 9
Huffman, J. H. 149; Sarah
A. 114; Sarah E. 116
Hughes, Charles B. 164;
Cornelius 24; Daniel
185; Nancy 41,186;
Nancy A. 36; Russell 13;
William J. 36
Hughey (Hughy), Alonzo N.
183; Elizabeth D. 8;
Elvira Jane 30; Franklin
A. 72; G. L. 94; Harri-
son H. 12; Margaret 16;
Martha H. 85; Martha L.
75; Mary 34; Mary D.
160; Mary Elizabeth 72;
Orlena 180; Parthenia
35; Robert 64; Sarah E.
101; W. H. 97; William
D. 121
Hughlin, Manerva 148
Hulme, W. F. 135
Hulsey, Betsey 6; Catha-
rine 7; Frances 2;
John M. 172; Martha Jane
34; William 111;
William J. 42
Humphrey (Umphrey), F. C.
172; J. E. 56; Sarah
Ann 58
Hunt (Hunts), Elizabeth
70; George W. 106;
G. W. 95; James A. 90;
John 31; Louisa 17;
Malinda 7; Martha Ann
53; Martha E. 28;
Martha Mrs. 180; May J.
89; Minerva 184; Mollie
165; Robert 122; Sarah
C. 36; Susan 55
Hunter, D. A. 162; Eliza
J. 148; Fanny 106;
Hamilton 113; Henry 133;
H. H. 75; Inda 127;
James D. 134; John D.
136; Julia Ann 73;

Hunter contd.
Mary E. 76; Nannie 183;
Sarah E. 77; S. E. 167;
Shepard 61; Tilda 136;
Washington 189; William
E. 27,55; W. M. 158
Hurley, A. A. 159; F. A.
138; William R. 22
Hurst, Mortimor 19
Hurt, Burnetta 6; John 6;
Marget 6
Husband, Caladoni 1;
Elvira 9
Hutcherson (Hutchison,
Hutchinson, Hutcherson),
John H. 61; John M. 62;
J. T. 116; Mary F. 27;
M. D. 102; Nathaniel 120;
W. H. 126
Hutson, Jerry 127
Hutton, Eliza 165

Imessan, Alfred 97
Ingle, Benjamin B. 53;
Mary Ann 71; Susan F. 59;
William H. 79
Inman, Elizabeth 43; Lucy
T. 113; Nancy 19
Irvin, Ansel W. 25; Frank-
lin 176; J. C. 55;
Martha Jane 52; M. J. 55;
Nathan 160; William 154
Isaacs, Adeliza 19; Agatha
2; Samuel 2; Samuel J. 13
Isabell (Isabel), A. J.
183; Mary M. A. 135
Isham, Ann 28; Caroline
47; Claborn 17; Lou 156;
Malinda Ann 9
Isom, Anna 168; Edward A.
32; Eliza 42; Elizabeth
69; F. E. 176; G. F. 56,
157,176; H. C. 136;
James 92,178; Mary B.
67; Mary F. 90; M. J.
167; Rachel 17; Sarah
45; Valentine C. 32;
W. P. 94
Ivie (Ivy), A. J. 59;
Zachariah C. 155

Jackson, Ann 14; B. A. 74;
Caroline Mrs. 164; Eldo-
nia 147; Elizabeth 76;
Emma 86; Isabella 20;
Isiah R. 10; Jennie E.
119; John 114; John A.
107; John H. 153; John
Henry 136; John N. 99;
John W. 150; Joseph-A.
85; L. R. 171; M. A.
128; Mary 61,122; M. E.
158; Millie L. 166;
Nancy 86; Nulen T. 108;
Priscilla 77; Rhoda 150;
Rosanah A. 47; Sarah 92,
103; Sarah Ann 48;
Virginia E. 60
Jacob, Ed. 163; Edmonds
110; Henry 43,53; M. F.
176; Robert 33,43
James, Abraham 33; A. C.
62; Adam 142; Ambrose
34; Andy 167; Ann 56;
C. C. 162; Fanny P. 122;
James 106; Jane B. 1;
Julia 106; J. W. 166;
Lewis G. 74; L. G. 165;
Malinda 50; Martha 98;
Martha E. 30; Newberry
7; R. M. 77,125; Susan
J. 50; William M. 15;
W. W. 74
January, Hiraim 2

Jarnett, James D. 11
Jarred (Jarret, Jared,
Jarrett), Caroline 31;
H. H. 183; Manda Jane
142; M. E. 168,169;
Sarah A. 19; William F.
46
Jarvis, Arletia 36; Gus-
tavus A. 122
Jean (Jeans), A. J. 178;
Calvin 39; Cyntha 174;
David 68,106; David A.
131; David C. 64; Eliza-
beth 75; E. T. 182;
Francis M. 11; James
104; Jesse L. 37,77;
John 67,95,156; John W.
32; Joseph 59; Mack 169;
Martha A. 41; Mary 49;
Mary Ann 118; Mary Ann
Elizabeth 74; M. J. 173;
Nancy 50; Ransom M. 162;
Sarah 27,74; Thomas 62;
Wiley 67,80; William 4,
163; William F. 147;
Wyatt 73
Jefferies, Melissa 161;
William J. 60
Jeffers (Jeffiers), Benja-
min 12; Eliza 85; Leah
A. 73; Linda 131; Sarah
A. 84; Thomas N. 126,
144; William 20
Jefferson, Louisa A. 59
Jenkins, Anna 168; Daniel
M. 125; Elizabeth 50,
117; Eliza J. 38; John
F. 35; Lou 142; Loutenny
147; Lucinda J. 64;
Mary 55,56; Mary A. 129;
Mary Ann 76; Mary J.
104; Melinda 186; Mollie
J. 166; N. M. 65; R. D.
148; Sarah 68; Thomas
11,97
Jennings, Bob 172; Char-
lotte M. 39; Elizabeth
16; Jane 182; Jane M.
40; J. C. 164; Julia
167; Lucretia 187; Lucy
107; Margaret 121;
Martha Jane 70; Melinda
87; Polly Ann 160;
Samantha 102; Sarah Ann
44; Susannah P. 2; W. B.
109,174; W. Z. 76
Jester, Caroline 153;
David 175; Lissie 182;
William N. 41
Jeter, Emeline P. 76
Jetton (Jaton), James
163; Mattie 178
Jewell, James 48; Martha
A. 43; Nancy Jane 46;
Walter E. 5
Jibb, E. J. 87
Jobe, J. H. 51; J. M. K.
183; John H. 33; Samuel
A. 124
Johnson, A. 175; A. B.
115; Agnes D. 53; Alfred
139; Angus A. 112; Arch
A. 37; Archibald 53;
Bayless 150; Benjamin
67; Bettie M. 98;
Caroline 41; Cornelius
16; Cyntha M. 23; De-
witt 174; Duke 124;
Ed 157; Edward G. 15;
Elizabeth 22,63; Ellen
140; E. M. 153; Epsey
22; George W. 122,181;
Henderson 107; John A.
7; John C. 107;

Johnson contd.
John M. 63; John R. 56;
Joseph W. 154; Larkin
29; Loucinda 177; L. P.
41; Lucy L. 163; Marga-
ret 33; Martha 30,60,
131; Martha J. 102;
Mary 91,144; Mat. 154;
M. E. 107,150; Molly Ann
67; Nancy 187; Nelson
112; Permelia 9; Pru-
dence E. 26; R. A. 71;
R. B. 134; Samuel 100;
Sarah 84,125; Walker
133; William W. 47
Johnston, Allen 11; Cat-
harine 7; Harriet 83;
Joseph 4; Julian 8;
Lucy 105; Margaret 3;
Mary 5; Orpha 57;
Robert 113; Stephen 97,
165
Joiner, Frances 53; Sarah
C. 86
Joins, Elizabeth 87; James
150,175; Mary Ann 47;
Susan V. 164; William
M. L. A. 155
Jolly (Jolley), Eliza 179;
Fany 106; Frances E. 95;
James 76; Jane 84;
Margaret E. 84; Margaret
Mrs. 99; Sarah A. 103
Jones, Alenia W. 152; Al-
len C. 47; Amanda 101;
Andrew J. 46; Asa 2;
Belle W. 165; Charlie
165; Charlotte 7; Clar-
risa 12; Cynthia 18;
David 38,144; D. J. 170;
Dorcas 188; Edmond C.
62; E. L. 148,157;
Eliza A. 147; Elizabeth
Mahala 8; Enoch F. 99;
F. M. 154; Frances 185;
George 159; Gracie 162;
G. W. 73; Henrietta Mrs.
168; Henry 33,158; H. L.
165; Isaac M. 39,104;
James 106; James A. 115;
James H. 43; James P.
143; Jane 15,84; Jasper
114; Jesse L. 58; J. M.
162; Joel J. 38; John
68,107,122,124,184; John
L. 49; John N. 99; Jo-
seph 59,112; Josephine
105; Julia 122; Lavina
19; Lee A. 123; Lizzie
178; Lorenzo D. 10;
Malinda 64; Malissa 86;
Margret 42; Martha 28;
Martha A. 42; Martha
Ann 154; Martha E. 62,
63; Martha L. 70,150;
Mary 3,140; Mary Ann
46; Mary E. 64; Mary F.
130; Mary Louisa 75;
Mary S. 79; Mat. 157;
M. E. 137; Millberry Ann
185; Millie A. 147; M. M.
165; Morris 104; M. P.
158; M. V. 157; Nancy
64,185; Nancy A. 27;
Nancy E. 172; Nancy G.
79; Nathan 122; Polly
12; R. A. 103; Rachel
12; R. C. 169; Rebecca
20; R. L. 109; Richard'
Maj. 187; Robert 188;
R. S. 129; Rufus 139;
Sallie 171; Sallie Ann
116; Samuel 12; Sarah
6,95,112; Sarah C. 81;

Jones contd.
Sarah E. 65; Sarah H. 63;
T. D. 68; Thomas 29,157;
W. D. 104; Wiley 134;
William 25,174,175,179;
William H. 93
Jordon (Jorden, Jordin),
Henry 161; James L. 60;
John 161; Mary 101;
Sarah P. 44
Juber, Thomas 138
Judd, A. W. 162
Judy, Henry C. 34
Junior, Tempy Elizabeth
114
Justice, Julia 175; Nancy
115

Kavanaugh, Lillian 59
Kearn, Nancy 5
Keda, Nancy J. 105
Keith, Amanda F. 29;
Charlotta 26; James L.
19; James S. 66; John
P. 78; K. E. 166; Lizzie
176; Margret A. 41; Mary
56,126; Mary A. 83;
Mollie 174; Presley A.
84; R. E. Mrs. 160; Sarah
11; Sarah E. 83; Selia
132; Solomon E. 75; Tho-
mas 176; William F. 84;
William L. Y. 177
Keller, Austin 168; Emeline
25; E. N. E. 164; G. B.
53; Isaac 60; Jacob A.
6; Lauret 56; Laurett 56;
Mary E. 110; Nancy M. 32;
Susan T. 121
Kelly, C. H. 168; Eliza
Jane 81; Emanuel 175;
Jaala 147; John 129;
John W. 79; Lizzie 162;
Lucy C. 108; M. A. 135
Kelso (Kelsoe), A. D. 101;
Andrew 134; Carol 93;
Caroline 162; Celia 93;
Dana 117; Dick 93; Elzira
107; Emeline 93; Emily
93; Fanny 114; Florence
137; Hardy 95; Isaac 18;
J. C. 150; Jim 159;
John 98; J. R. 110; Kaye
K. 145; Mariah 95; Mary
122; Milly 93; Nancy 93;
Newton 117; Patsey 90,
93; Phebe 180; Polly 93;
Reuben 141; Rosa 96;
Rosana 176; R. W. 141;
Sarah 16,95; Thomas 18;
Tom 183; Zachariah 20
Kemp, Westley 128
Kennard, Joseph H. 133
Kennedy (Kinney, Kenedy),
Abigail 2; Allen J. 186;
Hetty M. 188; Hugh T.
29; Jennie 163; John W.
13; Lucretia 144; Matilda
B. 17; Mattie A. 138;
M. C. 169; Perlina Eliza-
beth 137; Sarah A. 50;
T. H. 127; William E.
186
Kennemore, S. G. 168
Kennon, Celia A. 4; Els-
worth R. 33; Martha 187;
Mary A. 165; Matilda G.
16; Sarah E. 40;
William 13
Kensley, Elizabeth 35
Kent, Eliza Jane 117;
J. E. 169; J. M. 115;
J. P. 77; Mary P. 161;
Thomas W. 117

Kerbo, Malinda 21
Kercherval, Harrison 90;
Jack 157; R. C. 178;
William 161
Kernal, Delitha 15
Kerr, Alexander R. 186;
Gilford 103
Keton (Katon), Mary 48;
Sarah 86
Key (Kye, Kay), Angeline
90; Barbara Mrs. 187;
C. A. 160; C. G. 97;
Elizabeth 127; G. W. J.
180; Maggie 120; Nancy
Ann 137; Sarah J. 165;
Thomas F. 127; Virginia
91
Kidd, James 139; James B.
161; James H. 34; J. B.
175; J. C. 173; J. T.
111; John L. 146; Mar-
garet 185; Mary H. 180;
Sarah E. 152; Sarah Jane
85; William 4,19
Killingsworth, Mary 146
Killmartin, John 157
Killpatrick (Kilpatrick),
Eliza Jane 41; E. R. 82,
97; Margaret M. 37; Mary
M. 53; Sarah 118; Taylor
157, T. B. 176; W. L.
181
Kimbro, Adelia 105
Kimbrough, John 174; Kate
94; Lizzie C. 93; Nanny
80; Sarah A. 68; Woodson
158
Kimes (Kymes), Aleck 134;
Alice 95; Barton 95;
C. M. 145; Cynthia J.
28; David J. 56; D. J.
94; Eliza Ann 7; Eliza-
beth E. 56; E. J. 82;
Fannie E. 87,140; George
121; Hattie A. 155; H.
J. 179; Isola A. 102;
John 13,20,124,145,177;
Kiah 92; Louisa 124;
Martin 115; Mary A. 101;
Mary L. 68; Minerva L.
11; M. L. 145; Mollie E.
156; Nelson 93; P. J.
91; Sallie 132; S. H.
52; Susan 94,134
Kincaid (Kincade, Kinkade),
A. J. 169; Louisa 137
Kincannon, Andrew A. Maj.
186
Kinchum, J. W. 176
King, Albert G. 22; Andrew
7; Andrew J. 4; Arch 93;
Caroline 49,66; Charles
N. P. 31; Dicey 24,43;
Dock 109,146; E. J. 101,
143; Eleanor M. 18;
Elizabeth A. 75; Eliza-
beth M. 61; Eliza J. 26;
Ellen 28; Ephraim C. 39;
E. V. 156; Eveline F.
5; Garrison 143; George
17; G. L. 181; Hiram W.
14; Isaac W. 25; Isaiah
7; James C. 41; Jane M.
50; Jasper 137; J. E.
135; J. H. 125; John 25;
John S. 170; John W.
41,111; J. R. 104; J. T.
156; J. W. 161; Letha
57; Lou 156; Malinda 8;
Martha 4,23,103; Martha
C. 152; Martha E. 33,
79; Martha J. 149;
Martha Jane 118; Mary 3;
Mary C. 170; Mary E. 176;

King contd.
Mary F. 136; Mary Jane
41; Millie 179; M. J.
168; M. V. 142; Nancy
185; Olley Ann Mrs. 137;
Perlina A. E. 177;
Permelia Ann 81; Sallie
177; Sarah 8,168; Sarah
A. 116; Shaddrick A. 9;
Susan 19; Susan K. 36;
Thomas H. 31; William
J. 60
Kinnells, William 145
Kirk, Eliza Jane 133
Kirkland (Kirklin), B. F.
170; George 34; James
74; Mary 123; Matilda
142
Kirkpatrick, Henrietta
139; James 45; Mollie
170
Kirsey, John T. 107
Knight, William 71
Knowles, Benjamin W. 143;
C. S. 170; Rebecca 186;
Robert 167
Koonce, Bertha 59; Burdot-
ta 188; Calvin 13; C. B.
172; C. T. 137; Eliza J.
104; Eliza N. 82;
Emaline 120; Emeline 42;
George 159,181; Hickman
M. 62; James 143,171;
James M. 80; J. C. 183;
Letty C. 122; Lewis 89;
Mattie 159; Martha Ann
47; Martha E. 76; Martha
P. 18; Mary F. 117;
Nancy C. 77; Needham B.
188; Robert 139; Rufus
N. 160; Sophia A. 24;
W. D. 164
Kyle, Edward H. 108;
Laura V. 174
Kyser (Kiser, Kizer),
Amanda 121; Harrison W.
18; Mary H. 22; Mary M.
78; Nancy E. 78

Lackey, Bedford 82; Beriah
44; E. B. 167; Eli A.
42; Elizabeth 61; Eliza-
beth Y. 22; L. J. 168;
Louvenia 50; R. P. 104;
Temple 48; Thomas B.
55; William D. 7; William
S. 29; William Y. 66;
William Young 142
Lacy, Wilson 136
Laird, John H. 186; Mar-
garet E. 11; Nancy A. 28
Lamb, Allen 93; Amanda
157; Aron 92; Daniel 94;
Ella 180; Fanny 93;
Henry 181; James B. 66;
Martha 93; Mary 180;
Matilda 164; Molly 98;
Newton 102; N. L. 183;
Thomas 127; William 125
Lambert, H. C. 89; Isaac
R. 111; Joseph 122;
Lucinda 68; Martha 99;
Mary 45; Mary Jane 68;
Mollie 138
Lancaster (Lankester),
James M. 143; Susan 145
Land, A. J. 180; Ann 58;
Benjamin M. 20; Drury
P. 48; E. D. 168; Edie
Mrs. 84; E. J. 161;
Elizabeth 7,8; Emaline
126; Emaline D. 132;
Fred 148; James 56;
James G. 59; Joseph T.27;

Land contd.
Josiah J. 62; J. T. 176;
Mahala H. 96; Malichi B.
54; Margaret 13; Martha
52; Martha E. 134; Mary
A. 154; Mary Jane 147;
N. A. 166; Nancy 24,101;
Rebecca W. 166; Robert
61; Sarah J. 96; Sarah
Jane 132; Terresa C. 57;
Vienna Ellen 140; W. G.
158; William P. 29
Landenberger, George 152
Landers, Elizabeth 102;
Mary R. 42; Nancy 9;
Sarah T. 53
Landess, Adam 71; Berrill
145; Burrell 104; Cynthia
58; E. G. 52; Fannie E.
141; F. G. 49; G. E. 19;
Harry 92,154,164; Jeff-
ries E. 42; J. H. 133;
John 187; Joseph T. 26;
Maria R. 122; Martha 143;
Mattie 111; Milly A. 57;
Robert 92; Sarah J. 143;
Susan F. B. 25; W. J. 177
Landis, Josephine 134
Landman, George P. 75
Landreth, Elizabeth 41;
Hardin H. 24; Mary S. 26
Lane, Bailey E. 44; Beuna
Vista 163; Elizabeth 87;
Ely 84; C. W. 127; John
H. 63; Louisa 9; Mattie
E. 153; Robert 142; Tho-
mas M. 52
Langly, Peter 104
Langston, Delilah 37; Eliza
Ann 139; Elizabeth 127;
Elmira 12; Elnora E. 168;
James 85; Jesse 160;
Johnathan 41; Levi J.
158; Mary 183; Mary E.
158; Sarah E. 169; Sarah
L. 128; Wiley 65; William
20; William W. 127
Lanier, Emily 178
Lankford, Martha S. 97
Largen (Largin), H. M. 83;
Margaret A. 116; Susan
R. 150; T. C. 154
Larson, Margaret 87
Larwood, Edmond D. 37;
Thomas 30
Lasater (Laseter), Bettie
158; J. J. 172
Laten (Layton, Laton),
James W. 52; Mattie 178;
Ruth L. 179
Latham (Lathaim), Elizabeth
2; J. D. 164; John 18;
Levi 88; Susannah 17;
William 16
Lathrop (Lawthrop), Ruel
29; Thomas 162
Lauderdale (Lodderdale),
Ann 27; Eliza 23; Fannie
E. 112; John W. 87;
Margaret E. 90; Mary E.
82; Mary P. 40; Robert
12; Samuel T. 114; Sarah
J. 69; William T. 47
Laughinghous, Joseph W. 81
Laws, David 62; David A.
119; D. D. 182; J. A.
19; Mattie A. 159; M. C.
109; R. F. 153; Spencer
M. 29; Spencer N. 29;
Sue K. 158
Lawrence, Elizabeth 188
Lay, Charley 181; Harriet
89; Henry 103,149; James
89,168; Jane 162;

211

McAlister (McAllister,
McCalister, McCollester),
James 38; Jane 148;
John 182; Margaret 3;
Martha A. 142; Nancy 28;
Nancy E. 107; Nathan 45;
R. D. 183; Samuel 66;
S. M. 131; William M.
31; W. J. 150
McAnn, Daniel B. 53; El-
mira 146; Martha A. 83;
Thomas 128
McAteer, H. D. 140
McBay, Edward 13,128; Mar-
garet 51; Sam 120;
Sarah 29
McBray, Philip 44
McBride, James 50; Jane
34; Lucinda 11; Margaret
62; William 166
McCalla, H. B. 87; John
G. 58; Martha A. 25;
Mary Ann 29; Nancy J.
40; Samuel Y. 28; S. Y.
84
McCalley, Mariah N. 110;
T. G. 107
McCan (McCann), Daniel B.
57; Elizabeth 32; James
J. 72; Jane 12; Mary 15;
William H. 82; William
L. 45
McCants, William 87
McCanless (McCandless),
James S. 140; Julia 116
McCarry, R. M. 148
McCartney (McCartey),
Charles 46; James 57;
Nancy 33; William 40
McCarver, George J. 40;
John S. 18; Mary Jane
40,144
McCastney, Zany 31
McCaudless, L. J. 136
McCawley (McCauley), B. M.
132; H. S. 159; Isabellia
E. 79; J. T. 111
McChristian, Fanny Ann 62
McClain (McClane), A. J.
151; Elizabeth W. 188;
George C. 1; Henry R.
148; Jane 177; Nancy 140;
Nannie C. 172; Rebecca
131; Susan 37
McClaren (McClarren),
Louisa 131; Laura 142
McClelland (McClellan),
Ann 143; Carrie B. 141;
Clem Mrs. 176; Eliza J.
10; Elizabeth M. 127;
James C. 30; J. C. 143;
John G. 10,47; Joseph
D. 64; Julia 127; Julia
E. 172; Mary 93(2); Mary
Ann 14; Susan Ann 136;
William A. 38; W. W. 118
McClenny, John W. 102
McCloud, W. W. 69
McClung, James W. 5
McClure, Amanda M. 54; Ann
172; Caroline 146; Cat-
harine 66; David M. 18;
Elisha M. 77; Elizabeth
1,20,60; Franky 25;
James 29,180; Jane 15;
Jesse 15; J. F. 178;
John 55; John W. 63;
Lydia 20; Mahala 149;
Mark 3; Manda 150; Martha
80; Mary J. 113; Nancy
33; Nancy Ann 67; N. J.
166; R. N. 51; Samantha
J. 110; Sarah 38,45;
Sarah A. 81; Sarah J. 64;

McClure contd.
Sarah J. 64; Susan E.
68; Susannah 13; Thomas
14; Thomas B. 44; W. H.
161; William 46; W. M.
133
McCluskey, Benjamin 9;
B. M. 152; David 19;
Hannah E. 99; Isom
Newton 140; William 41
McCollum, A. J. 53; Amanda
153; Daniel 25; James
155,186; James C. 153;
Julia 144,165; Louis
172; Louisa J. 144;
Margaret J. 43; Mariel
19; Mary B. 25; Minnie
181; Neil 35; Neill 32;
Ruhama 32; Samuel C. 57;
Sarah 20; Sarah R. 28;
W. R. 180
McCombs, Daniel 149;
John R. 51.
McConnico, Garner M. 31
McConnell (McConnel), Abe
92; Ann L. 184; Mary E.
44; Sarah T. 28
McCord, Eliza H. 110;
Frank O. 159; Gabrilla
L. 122; John 152; Mar-
tha 118
McCormack, Elizabeth 61;
Mary Ann 39; Rebecca J.
5; William 5
McCounts, W. P. 151
McCourt, L. L. 146
McCowley, James 7
McCown (McCowen, McCowan),
Abram 131; A. J. 101;
Cordelia 109; Elizabeth
39; Eliza J. 41; Ema-
randa 124; H. B. 81,121;
Henry B. 61; Hettie V.
108; Isaac W. 20; James
C. 98; James P. 71;
Jane 53; J. C. 169; J.
H. 110; J. I. 165; John
4; John L. 22; John R.
72; Lavina 25; Lewis C.
9; Louisa 39; Lucrettia
Jane 79; M. A. 129;
Margaret R. 88; Martha
133; Mary Ann 76; Mary
E. 85; Mary M. 128;
M. E. 180; Miles H. 28;
Miles H. 5; Paullina
Jane 80; Sarah 85,158;
Sarah L. 84; S. S. 81;
Susan S. 124; Tennie
156; Thomas W. 98;
William H. 86
McCoy, Candass D. 8; Eliz-
abeth 60; Elizabeth
L. A. 31; James 55;
John L. 71; Margaret L.
81; Mary F. 47;
Sallie 105; Samuel C. 9;
Spruce 186; Winney 13
McCracken (McCrackin),
Alla M. 175; Amanda S.
85; Ann 100,140; Bettie
127; F. F. E. 102; James
B. 90; Josiah 187;
J. W. 108; Lydia 151;
Mary J. 64; Samuel 83;
Sarah A. 82
McCrary (McCary), Cammilla
111; Nancy C. 113
McCree (McCary), Elizabeth
43; Joanah 79; Sarah P.
172
McCurdy, Elizabeth 11
McCulley, Sarah 128

McCullough (McCollough,
McCullick), Alexander 24;
Ann 131; D. A. 180; Eli
K. 34; Elizabeth 34;
John 9; J. W. 154; Samuel
P. 40
McCurry, Jonathan 120
McDaniel, A. 106; Aaron 88;
Agness B. 17; Amos 91;
Ann 127; Archibald V. 42;
Ben 122; B. J. 146; C. A.
68,99; Cardine 6; Catha-
rine K. 6; Charles 177;
Charlot 103; Elias 7;
Elizabeth 63,149; George
O. 41; Henry 90,113;
Henry B. 59; Jane 33;
John 86; John S. 181;
Joshua 33; L. M. 69;
Lucinda 12; Lucy A. 118;
Lydia 48; Maria 11; Mary
36; Mary J. 97; Mary L.
56; Mary Lou 174; M. S.
158; Polly 102; Richard
J. 107; Sarah A. 96;
Sarah C. 111; Sarah L.
62; Susan 119,122; Vio-
let 102; William H. 121;
W. T. 112; W. W. 66
McDill, Alice I. 175; J. A.
71; Margaret L. 98; Mary
E. 100; Phillis 154;
Sarah Ann 82; Savanah 133;
S. H. 156; W. P. 159
McDonald, Alford 92; Amy
92; Andy 92; B. 180; Bob
145; Caroline 123; Cass
91; Charles 125; Cornelia
157; Daniel 92; Delda 92;
Emily 93; Esek 93; Essex
115; Fanny 91; F. H. 100;
George 152; G. W. 92;
Henderson 167; Hugh 91;
Joanna 137; Joe 104;
John M. 185; Josia 163;
Julia 91; Kenney 125;
Loutitia 178; Lucinda 150;
M. A. 138; Margaret 92;
Mariah 92; Martha Ann
183; Mary 91,92(2); Mary
J. 109; Melia 92; R. A.
75; Robert 93,148; Robert
S. 11; Sarah 139; William
118
McDougal (McDugal, McDougle,
McDougall), Aaron 15;
Daniel 140; David F. 138;
George L. 122; J. W. 86;
Mary 9,139; Nancy E. 119;
Nancy L. 59; Sallie J.
148; Sarah 6; Sarah E.
Mrs. 153; Tabitha 185
McElroy (McLeroy), Addie
148; Allen 38; Cintha A.
42; David 122; Elizabeth
12,44,53; Elizabeth A.
49; Emily B. 93; Isaac
92; J. C. 36; John 148;
John A. 95; Martha J.
32; Mary 13,155,167;
Mary J. 40; Mattie 157;
Micajah L. 79; Pat. H.
140; Robert 92; Rufus C.
60; Sallie 174; Sarah
Ann 34; S. G. 41; Stan-
ford M. 22; Thomas B.
67; Wesley 109
McElvany, Robert 48
McElvy (McElvie), Noah H.
69; R. L. 72
McElyea, Elizabeth C. 81;
Frances A. 149; H. P.
77; Isaac F. 73; Nancy
A. 103; N. J. 159

McEntire, R. U. 77
McErin, Frances 98
McErvin, Susan F. Mrs. 110
McEwen (McEwin), Calvin
81; Jo 178; M. A. 125;
Margaret Carmack 131;
Martha 79; Robert C. 5;
Robert H. 188; William,
Esq. 185
McEwing, John 119
McFadder, C. Mr. 185
McFarland (McFarlin),
James M. 20; Mary J. 18;
Sarah A. 150
McFerrin (McFarin, McFer-
ren), Cassena 52; James
M. 157; J. B. 180; John
M. 16,54; J. P. 143;
Mary A. 84; Mary J. 94;
Minerva 157; M. R. 178;
Susan 142; Thomas 126
McFreeman, James M. 94
McGaugh, Abe 99; Caroline
1; Elizabeth S. 9;
Felix Grundy 2; Sally 1;
Thomas H. 36
McGaw, Abe 153; Catharine
178; George 146
McGee, Abner S. 51; Alpha
A. 41; Aratha 152; C. H.
120; David 181; Eliza
A. 47; Fannie 153; Henry
L. 158; James P. 109,
154; Jane 44; J. C. 90;
John 12; John P. 44;
John W. 173; J. P. 82;
J. R. 157; Libe 162;
Louisa E. 82; Manurvy
105; Martha E. 61; Mary
174; Mary E. 58; M. J.
130; Mollie 80; Rachel
182; Rufus A. 52; S. A.
96; Sarah E. 165; Stacy
173; Stephen 118; Susan
23; Thomas 147; Tilman
L. 45; W. F. 180; William
48; William A. 128;
Willis F. 149
McGeehee (McGhee, McGehee,
McGehey), Catharine 57;
Elihu 21; Elvira A. 75;
F. H. Mrs. 177; Frances
R. 106; Jane 120; Jesse
P. 19; John L. 84; J. T.
128; L. N. 96; Lucinda
20; M. A. 115; Margarett
S. 57; Martha A. 114;
Mary E. 85; Middleton
67; Rinah 16; Robert 47;
Susan 132; Thomas B. 67;
Thomas G. 184
McGowen, William 35
McGrath, Mikel 87
McGraw, Silas 123
McGregory, E. Y. 156
McGuire, Cordelia 110;
Elizabeth J. 124; James
S. 112; J. T. 68; J. W.
124; L. L. 126; Lucinda
C. 95; M. P. Miss 83;
Nancy H. 38; Narcissa
140; Sarah L. 29
McHaffy, Francis M. 50;
T. M. 53; William E.
54,55
McIntosh, Charles 13
McKay, Alcy 130
McKee, Ethiel 166; H. 75;
Mary F. 42; Mary R. E.
59; Mollie 172; Susan E.
55; William 139; William
B. 49
McKelvy, Samuel Sr. 138
McKennon, Mary F. 39

McKenzie, Catharine M. 185;
Frances C. 46; G. B. Col.
187; H. C. 83; Hugh 184;
J. B. 180; K. A. 58;
M. A. 73; Margaret A.
38; Matilda 187; Ronia
91; S. M. 158; William
B. 64
McKeon, John 129
McKinney (McKennie, Mc-
Kenney), Abe 136; Amanda
136; B. C. 116; Caroline
6; Charles, Esq. 184;
C. J. 56; Easter 89;
Elizabeth 82; Ellen 98;
Ellen C. 112; Emeline
88; Emily 146; Ethelvin
109; Frances 142; Galen
A. 50; H. C. 134; India
134; Isabella 64; James
186; James A. 113;
James H. 10; J. C. 176;
Jennie F. 138; John 96;
John M. 87,169; John V.
67; John W. 154; Julia
Ann 15,47; J. V. 117;
Kate W. 139; Leonard H.
7; Lucinda C. 17; Martha
Cordelia 75; Mary 17;
Mary A. 37; Mary J. 151;
M. E. 59; Nancy Eliza-
beth 79; Nancy J. 58;
Rebecca 151; Robert N.
188; Sarah J. 73,171;
Sarah T. 140; Silvester
41; T. A. 98; Tabitha
185; William 7; William
D. 11; William E. 101
McLain (McLean), Laura A.
107; Louisa I. 147;
Martha M. 58; Nancy 188;
Nancy C. 185
McLaughlin, Agnes A. 87;
Bettie C. 107; E. C.
114; Elijah C. 47;
Harrison 128; L. 113;
Lucretia 64; Mary E. 75;
M. B. 112; Mollie 134;
Sarah Glen 79; Susan
51; Susan A. 138;
William B. 27
McLear, Patsey 162
McLemore, Ann 123; C. C.
137; Elizabeth 115;
Eliza J. 5; Josephine
129; J. W. 155; Sterl-
ing 12
McLin, Eliza 8; Martha E.
60; Susan K. 36
McMillen (McMullen, Mc-
Millin, McMilican),
Constant T. 9; Delia
167; Doak 185; Eliza
123; Elizabeth A. 28;
Ellen 1; Fannie 178;
Joseph 188; Josephine
T. 30; J. R. 180;
Louisa 70; Mary J. 12;
M. C. 161; Medora H.
182; M. L. 178; Mollie
E. 174; R. D. 69; R. D.
C. 77; Rebecca J. 15;
Robert 59; Robert H.
51; Robert M. 40; Sarah
M. 94; L. J. 58; Susan
C. 40; William 185;
William B. 54; William
L. 27; William M. 12
McMinn, Joseph S. 81;
R. B. 180
McKnight, Wade 107
McMullin (McMullen),
Agnes 94; F. P. 170;
Frank 167; Jo 94;

McMullin contd.
John 143; Joseph M. 150;
Lunna J. 83; Martha 158;
Mary 180; S. A. 124;
Sallie 157; Susan 102;
William 103
McMurray, William 166
McNabb, James M. 154
McNatt, Ermine 135; James
37,119; John 31; Marion
111; Mary 3; Nancy 19;
Richard 2; Samuel 67;
Sarah 45; Sophia 2
McNeece (McNeace), Angeline
78; Elizabeth A. 44;
George J. 81; Henry 65;
H. W. 175; Lucinda 43;
Sue 183
McNeely (McNelly), W. H.
166; William W. 17;
W. W. 74
McNeil (McNeel), Angeline
85; Mary A. O. 34; Nancy
R. 43; T. P. 174
McNutt, Alexander 187
McPhail, Ann 109; Anna
109; Caroline 132; Carrie
R. 162; John A. 12;
Mariah 161
McPhearson, Ross 126
McQuary, Mary 120
McQuiddy, Newton 17
McQuiston, Thomas 27
McRady, Ephraim Washington
188(2)
McRee, Carroll 28; Delina
E. 52; Elizabeth 16;
Emily R. 28; John 8;
Mary A. 16; Nicholas H.
28; Rachell 83; S. B.
145
McVay, Hettie 19
McWhorter (McWhirter), A.
E. 117; Austin 161; B. B.
165; D. A. 100; Eliza
A. 38; Elizabeth 12,85,
86,152; Esther E. 32;
George 12; Hugh B. 23;
Jane E. 115; J. E. 58;
Jennie 170; John D. 139;
John E. 17; Mandy 145;
Margaret 16,112; Moses
19; Nancy C. 40; Prudy
68; Richard A. Dr. 135;
Robert 84; R. P. 175;
Samuel 100; Sarah 53;
Verlenia 31; William 89
McWright, Daniel V. 122
McYearin, Allice 156

Maben, Nancy E. 76
Mabry, N. H. 103
Macberry, Berry 79
Mack, Fannie 161
Mackey, William G. 18
Madison, Matilda 3
Maddox (Madox), Daniel 39;
E. F. 133; Gerimiah 152;
I. B. 182; Isaac B. 105;
Isaac N. 107; James J.
163; Jane 135,159; J. J.
151; John 157; John M.
162; J. W. 162; Loucinda
108; Lucy Ann Mrs. 149;
Malinda Ann 90; Martha
161; Martha J. 70;
Mary E. 125,157; Mary L.
96; Nancy 187; Rina 154;
Sallie 151; Sarah A.
183; Sarah W. 22; Thomas
A. 77; W. C. 132; W. G.
132
Majors, Anna 7; Elijah 12;
Elizabeth 57; Isaac 57;

Merrell (Merril, Merrill),
A. E. 167; Betty 183;
Charles 5; E. B. 166;
Elijah 31; Fredonia E.
85; Garrett 48; G. W.
79; H. B. 172; James S.
79; Jane 21; John 52;
Lucy A. 136; Mary E.
153; Mary J. 54; Mattie
E. 171; M. T. 172; N. A.
108; Nancy 4; Salina J.
16; Samuel 25; William 3
Merritt (Merrett), Barrett
96; Bennett B. 63; Bolen
72; Burrick 139; Jane
137; John W. 133; Mattie
177; S. A. 83; W. H.
129; William 145
Merry, Cuff 120
Messer, Asa 185
Metcalfe (Medkiff, Medcalfe,
Medcalf), Amanda M. 4;
Bettie 181; Charles B.
74; Elizabeth C. 46;
Henrietta 51; Judith A.
38; Lucinda 163; Mary
176; Mattie J. 182;
Sarah Ann 32; Sophy A.
74; Thomas L. D. 48;
W. C. 182; William 46;
William H. 84,107;
William R. 69; W. L. 70,
153
Michael, Elizabeth 37;
Elly 10; Floddle 44;
Jesse 40; John 1,29;
John W. 22; Levi 74;
Martha 25; Mary Jane 85;
Nancy E. 42; Silas 24;
William 68
Middlebrooks, John T. 114
Middleton, A. J. D. 115
Milam (Miliam), David 125;
Elizabeth F. 129; John
G. 21; Lucinda 2;
Malinda G. 27; Martha P.
7; Wiley A. 171; Wiley
G. 55; Willis M. 27
Milambes, Milley 144
Miles, A. E. 168; Ann 41;
Armacinda 64; Arrena
185; Benjamin 167; Cal-
vin A. 144; Caroline
151; Elizabeth 70; G. D.
116; Green 12; James L.
138; J. P. 144; Josie
Mrs. 158; Josephus 78;
Louiza 155; Martha 78;
Mary E. 97; Nancy 57;
Riley 158; Samuel C. 8;
Sarah F. 148; William
123,133; William A. 103
Millard, Cynthia 69; Docia
28; John G. 85; Marga-
ret 13; Mary Jane 69;
Sarah 30
Miller, Albert 157; Annie
H. 135; Charles 36;
Columbus 136; Elizabeth
127; Emily 41; Frances
Louisa 134; G. B. 167;
James 35; John 58;
Lafayett 115; Louisa
119; Mary 82; Mary J.
93; Mary M. J. 53;
Michael 40; Samuel 149;
Sarah 70; Serena 84;
Sidney Miss 112; Susan-
nah A. 6; William J. 60
Millerford, S. J. 156
Milliken (Millikin), A.
65; Abe 92; Amanda A.
153; George W. 21,53;
James A. C. 67;

Milliken contd.
J. H. 73,113; L. A. 121;
Mary L. 172; Olivia 162;
Polly Ann 13; Sarah 71
Mills, Annie B. 139; A. V.
49; Bob 183; Caroline
116; Eliza 13; Elizabeth
A. 37; Frank 178; George
24,136; Hannah 14; Henry
P. 49; James 14; James
E. 87; James W. 49; John
5,51; John C. 78; John
H. 5,52; Margaret A. 37;
Martha 83; Mary 179;
Nancy 6; Narcissa C. 41;
Nathaniel 59; Sarah 9;
Vance R. 148; Walter
180; W. C. 83; Win J. 87
Millhouse (Millhous),
Bob 183; Rytha 168;
W. A. 97
Milstead, Elizabeth C.
96; George 5,95; Polly
1; Tennessee 165
Milton, Bettie 102; James
95; Mary 72; Mattie 126;
Pearson 35
Mims, Drury M. 68; James
61; Mary Ann 7
Minatree, A. J. 61
Minger, John 73
Minor, Joe 183
Mitchell (Mitchel), Char-
les 17; Cordelia 182;
David C. 27; D. F. 86;
Elizabeth 15; Elizabeth
R. 77; Ephraim 94;
Eveline 3; F. R. 171;
Franklin 133; Franklin
F. 93; G. C. 163; G. M.
81; Harriet E. 46; Iba
(Ida) 89; Ibby 4; Jack-
son O. 69; Jacob 78;
James 124; James L. 111;
James W. 62; J. B. 142;
Jefferson 149; John 40;
John D. 15; John L. 51,
92; J. P. 165; L. Ann
150; L. C. 88; M. A.
141; Martha 8; Martha
J. 91; Mary 122; Mary A.
3; Mary I. Mrs. 146;
Mary Jane 56,132; Mat
133; M. C. Mrs. 96;
M. J. 178; M. M. 143;
Nancy E. 109; Rebecca
D. 63; R. H. 53; Rufus
119; Sarah 56; Sarah Ann
142; Sarah C. 64; Sarah
E. 98; T. F. 67,183;
Thomas A. 175; Thomas
F. 29; Tullilon 21;
Vina C. 142; W. D. 181
Mock, Amy 136
Moffett, Eliza 7; Elliot
27; Elliot F. 32; James
T. 167; Judith 5;
Margaret 18; William
Jr. 18
Monday, Emma 179; Lizzie
166; Melissa 5; William
R. 187
Monks, James 16; John F.
160; M. A. 155; Mary 33;
Mary J. 96; T. J. 144
Monney, Sallie 134
Montgomery, Andrew S. 37;
C. W. 19; Elizabeth 40;
John 48; John F. 76;
Joseph 17; Robert 31;
William 43
Moody (Moodey), Bettie
118; Isah 157; Sarah T.
74; William 122

Moon, O. F. 19
Mooney, Hugh P. 9; J. W.
152; Martha M. 108;
Mary 14; George P. 37
Moorehead (Moorhead).
E. C. 100; Elizabeth 47;
F. R. 150; James L. 56;
John N. 48; Julia 185;
Malvina F. 136; Mart.
121; Martha A. 90; Mary
6,100; Nancy A. 28; Reu-
ben 112; Sarah F. 11;
William D. 4
Moores (Moore, Moors),
Abner 118; A. E. 38,97;
Alvelena 32; Alzney 48;
A. N. 161; Andy 106,171;
Angeline 185; Ann 5;
Anna 65; Ann J. 97; A. S.
88; Anthony 123; Baker
179; Becky 170; Belle
119; C. A. 127; Charles
78,101,147,184,187;
Charles F. 27; Corinthia
165; Dave 174; D. F.
116,126; E. A. 31;
Easther H. 74; Eli 4,187;
Elizabeth 32,40; Eliza-
beth K. 15; Elizabeth L.
42; Elizabeth M. 27;
Ellender E. 119; Emily
162; Esther 39; E. W.
45; Fannie R. 112; F. E.
139; Felix 162; F. R. 5;
Frances 120,148; Frances
N. 19; Frances R. 39;
Frank 161; George W. N.
33; Gilbert 107; Green
95; Hannah 186; Harriet
155; Harrison 94; Hender-
son 171; Henry 24,143,
187; Hiel A. 105; H. L.
177; Hugh 39; Isaac B.
113; Isabel Josephine
147; Jacob W. 36; James
171; James A. 62; James
H. 144; James K. 65,145;
James M. 19; James P.
135; James S. 38; James
T. 155; Jane 18,88,125;
Jane E. 19; J. B. 167;
Jennie 165; J. F. 90,
117; J. Knox 139; J. M.
183; Joab 35; John 78,
110,163; John A. 156;
John D. 75; John H. 188;
John K. 18; John M. 180;
John R. 26; John T. 183;
John W. 67; Joseph 85,
143; Joseph L. 53; Josie
179; Juda 153; L. A. 139;
Laura 101,105; Lewis
168; Lizzie 152; Louisa
J. 47; Lucinda E. 147;
Lucy 158; M. A. 117;
Margaret 133; Margarett
B. 59; Margaret Ann 30;
Martha 22,140; Martha
A. L. 35; Martha B. 185;
Martha J. 76; Martha Mrs.
145; Mary 37,40,69,105,
127; Mary A. 149; Mary
Ann 33; Mary E. 112;
Mary Ele 83; Mary F. 167;
Mary J. 31; Mary L. 2;
Mary M. 99; Mary R. 186;
Mattie F. 163; M. C.
118; M. H. 183; Milton
J. 42; M. J. 97; M. M.
165,167; Mollie L. 178;
M. V. 61; Nancy A. 28;
Nancy C. 105; Nancy V.
78; Nathan 73; Otho H.
27; Phireba J. 28;

215

Moores contd.
Pleasant 154; Polly 5;
Prisilla Ann 43; Rachel
6; Rachel E. 109; Ric-
hard 105,174; Robert 29,
93,145; Robert L. 155;
Robert Maj. 186; Sally
98; Sarah 93; Sarah F.
43; Sarah Frances 72;
Sarah J. 117; Sarah Jane
39,61; S. M. 95; T. A.
179; T. C. 79; T. D. 79;
Teresia 165; Thomas 14,
21,103,154; Thomas B.
111; Thomas F. 61; Thomas
H. 14; Tom 174; T. R.
144; W. B. 158; W. D.
57; W. H. H. 118;
William 166,174; William
A. 17,167; William D.
98; William E. 75;
William G. 82; William
H. 5; William J. 152;
William N. 30; William
P. 34; William S. 65;
William W. 1
Morgan, Andrew 53; Austin
19; C. J. 68; H. B. 118;
James B. 155; J. M.
134; John M. 144; Lewis
13,27; Millie 122; M. J.
84; N. M. 88; Peter W.
20; Pink 180; Susie J.
154; Warner L. 154;
W. H. 113; William 91;
William A. 4
Morning, G. A. Rev. 171
Morris, A. H. 129; Caroline
32; Delia 171; Henrietta
163; Henry M. 39; Isreal
3; James R. 38; Jane D.
1; Malinda 48; Martha M.
36; Mary Ann 70; Mary
Jane 33; M. M. 115;
Minie 180; Samuel 13,
169; Samuel F. 149;
Sarah 112; Sceny 10;
Unice 14
Morrison, A. W. 49; Cal-
donia 140; George 139;
James P. 108; J. H. 163;
John H. 45; Josie 171;
Margaret 146; Mollie V.
141; R. A. 140; Robert
A. 46; Sallie 157;
Samuel 161; Sarah 154;
W. A. 155; W. B. 84;
William A. 42; W. J.
160; W. M. 173
Morrow, Elizabeth 187;
John 147; Nancy Jane 128;
Samuel S. 19; Susan 102
Morton, Alexander Jr. 188;
Isaac 90; John S. 84;
Martha 10; Martha J.
64; Mary 29; Mary B. 55;
Sarah 88; William 187
Moses, J. A. 163
Mosley (Mosely, Moseley),
Alfred N. 39; Bettie M.
90; Ed. 169; Eliza J.
122; Gilbert T. 162;
Harrison 101; H. H. 145;
Hillory 66; Jane 78;
J. L. 151; Julia 175;
Laura P. 184; Martha
29; M. C. 181; Nancy
29; Sarah H. 29; William
48; William T. 51
Moss, Drucilla 8; Nancy
7; William F. 147
Motes, Marcus D. 73
Motlow, Elizabeth V. 27;
Ellen 100; Emily G. 4;

Motlow contd.
Felix 119; Felix W. 106;
Harriet 15; J. L. 78;
John 51; John A. 51;
Katie 134; Lauret M. 64;
Mary 20,124; Mary B.
101; Milly 131; Nancy
A. 26; N. J. 38; Rosana
173; Sue V. 113; Susan
B. 95; William G. 50;
Wilson 99; Zadock 101,
166
Mount, W. S. 160
Moyers (Moyer), Archibald
L. 44; Bryant 49; David
C. 46; Francis M. 62;
George 58; George W.
24,37; Hetty F. 64;
Isaac L. 34; J. E. 179;
John V. 68; Leoma 112;
Louisa 91; Margaret E.
48; Margaret J. 43;
Martha 43; Martha J.
156; Mary 43; Mary A.
161; Matilda 186; Mat-
tie 174; Nancy F. 45;
Samuel H. 172; Sarah R.
77; Vinetta 80; Virginia
174; William 78; William
T. 54
Mulder, Emily 86; Zebuda
41
Mullins, A. J. 64,115;
Amanda Ellen 146; Betty
119; C. A. 179; Catha-
rine 23; Cinda 140;
Elizabeth 37,157; George
81,100; George W. 105;
George Washington 127;
H. W. 101; James 141;
J. B. 121; Jefferson
28; J. K. 156(2),180;
Joel 169; John 14; J. R.
104; J. W. 123; Kiser
19; Leoma 42; Lewis
123,140; L. D. 178;
Louiza 20; Manda S. 22;
Manlda 170; Martha A.
20,159; Mary 20,84,105;
Mary A. 184; Mary Ann
124; Mary Jane 76;
Mathew 23; Melinda J.
64; Milly 25; Mollie A.;
Nancy J. 150; Ollie L.
176; Pleasant 18; Sam
173; Sarah 39,122; Sinda
108; Susan 19; Susie
164; Viannus 10; Vincen
84; Vincent 15; William
78,175; William R. 132;
William W. 35
Murdock, Amanda C. 129;
Cynthia A. 89; Delpha
141; Isabelle 56; Louisa
37; Mary Ann 48; Millie
171; Minerva A. Mrs.
105; Nancy C. 33; Sam-
uel R. 79; S. J. 142;
William C. 75
Murphy, Adline 181; Ben-
jamin W. 61; Fanny 145;
Jane 51; Lewis 147;
Mary 178; Mary C. 179;
M. D. 119; Rosana 172;
Sallie 106,108; Sarah
16; William 21; William
S. 31; Y. A. G. 149
Murray (Murry, Murrah),
C. R. 164; George W.
55; John 147; Katie 170;
Mary Ann 4; M. L. 169;
P. T. 68; Robert 166;
Sarah 139; William A. 5

Murrel (Murrell), Jemima
1; Mary 74
Muse, Bazel 22; J. L. 114;
John R. 130; J. W..65;
Mary J. 156; Nancy S.
89; S. A. E. 144; Thomas
W. 26; William H. 21
Musgraves, S. M. 129
Myers (Miers), Abigail 138;
B. J. 155; D. C. 112;
Denoah 42; D. F. 155;
Elizabeth 32; J. A. 169;
J. H. 159; Luvena 40;
Margaret 99; Maria 119;
Martha J. 155; Missouri
123; Nelson 100; Sandy
109,151; Sarah L. 120;
William H. 76; W. P. 112
Myrick, Amanda M. 75;
Caroline 33; Fannie A.
156; L. P. 124; Martha
87; Mary 23; Mary Ann 12;
Minerva 16; Sarrah C.
117; Susan E. 44

Nabers (Nabors), B. E. 146;
Benjamin D. 3
Nalley, A. J. 182
Nance, John 23
Napp, Rebecca 52
Nash, Nancy Catharine 79
Nassaurer, Tillie 181
Nave, Eleanor A. E. 64;
William F. 65
Neaves (Neive), Martha Ann
63; John 9
Neece, Barksdale 46; Eglen-
tine 53; H. H. 87; Hul-
dar 85; James K. 117;
Jesse 125; Joel R. 65;
John E. 54; L. L. C. 95;
Mary Jane 119; Rebecca
103; Sarah E. 99; Sarah
E. T. 81; William F. 70
Neeld, Anna E. 106; Bettie
126; Etna 125; Green
131; Ida 137; Isaac 156;
James Irvin 23; J. D.
123; John 92; Louisa J.
86; Margaret M. 36; M.
Annie 70; Mary Elizabeth
144; Olivia 187; R. A.
142; Sarah 156; Thomas
J. 98; William P. 10;
W. T. 114
Neeley (Nealy), Alexander
178; Angeline 81; Elias
22; Elizabeth 7,97;
Joseph N. 112; Marget 4;
Mary 77; Mattie C. 156;
Maud 182; Nancy 3;
Sally 137
Neese (Nees), Craven W.
47; H. H. 5; Huldah 63;
James 16
Neil (Neal, Neill, Neel),
Caroline 14; Eliza 35;
Jefferson 132; Joab 55;
Kate 173; Lewis 92;
Marcus 91; N. A. 64;
Newton F. 34; S. C. 165;
Washington 92
Nelson, A. B. 106; Abraham
128; A. H. 119; Ann 165;
Antney 126; Antoney 89;
Barney 80; Bezil 184,
187; E. 130; E. J. 139;
Ellen 133; Emily F. 73;
Harriett 182; J. A. 177;
J. L. 165; John 140;
John L. 173; J. R. 39;
J. W. 69; Lucinda 18;
L. W. 135; Margaret E.
116; Mariah 106,175;

216

Nelson contd.
Martha M. 70; Mary 35; Mary Jane 63; Mattie 172; M. S. 164; Nancy 92; Nancy A. 9; Permelia 16; Robert B. 35; Sallie 172; Sarah A. 101; Susan 15; Susanah 115; T. R. 69; V. T. 71
Nerrin (Nearin, Nearrin, Nearen, Naring), Benjamin 44; D. A. 160; D. L. 146; H. A. 107; Jane 111; Lee 149; Mary E. 88; Thomas C. 115
Nevels (Nevils), E. B. 134; Lewis 120; Sarah 115; William 168
Newman, J. A. 117; J. C. 130; J. J. 118; J. M. 130; Mary E. 138; M. E. 135; Nannie E. 145; R. L. 102; T. D. 140; Thomas M. 16; W. H. 130; Wiley C. 2; Wiley M. 24
Newsom, Claracy 157; James W. 73; Lacy 139; Lewis 80; Martha 96; Mary E. 75; Rowlin 74; Sarah A. 109
Newton, G. W. 120; P. Y. 162; Sarah 104; William G. 99
Nicar, Sarah C. 25
Nicholas, Betsey 1
Nichols (Nichol), Alfred 21; A. J. 47,161; Briggs 71; E. J. 166; Green W. 60; Greenwood 7; Henry 41; Jane 26; J. H. 170; John 41,85; John W. 18; Joseph R. 75; Lizzie 170; Louisa C. 52; Lucinda 93; Manerva S. 69; Martha 65,108; Mary E. 33; Mary F. 132; Nancy A. 105; Susan Savannah 121; Thomas 62; William 34,124
Nicks, A. Y. 46; Dave 132; Editha 41; Elizabeth 80; Elizabeth E. 65; Henretta 36; Joseph A. 58; Margaret Elizabeth Ann 5; Martha A. 63; Martha J. 113; Samuel T. 14; William B. 151
Nickson, Narcissa 19; Willford 13
Night, Martha 22
Nipp, Rosnell 24
Nipple, Matthew 150
Nix, A. C. 135; Bettie 132; Christiana 21; N. A. 152; Rebeccah 7; Sanders T. 90; Sarah 144; Simeon 189; Sue A. 177; Susan 69; William Y. 54
Nixon, Alfred 7; Elizabeth 11; Polly M. 6
Noah, Alexander G. 24; John 57; Nancy K. 77; Nancy P. 12; Pleasant D. 61; T. A. 129; Thomas J. 99; William 124; W. R. 112
Noble, Alford 111; James 138
Noblin, Elizabeth 38; Nancy 39
Noblett (Noblet), Abraham 187; Canada 82; D. J. 79; Mary A. 109

Noe, Frances 58; Sarah E. 17
Noles, A. M. 89; Benjamin 55; Caroline 84; Catharine 111; Charity J. 51; C. J. 164; Cynthia 13; Emeline P. 88; Frances A. 67; Henrietta 137; Julia 136; Malissa 55; Martha E. 55; M. T. 67; R. F. 174; Sarah A. E. 35; William 68
Norman, Berry 18; Daniel T. 72; Elijah 18; Elizabeth 24; James M. 168; Jane 86; Jesse 4; John 162,163; John J. 134; Julia 155; Kelly 69; Lou 175; Malinda 7; Mary E. 95,96; Sarah 73; Selina 30; Thomas 51; William 10,75; William C. 97
Norris, Allen 109; Amanda S. 42; Benjamin Westly 80; Cynthia 184; Dan 91; Hannah 179; Josiah A. 43; Lucinda 186; Margret E. 26; Minerva 186; Rachel 188; Sallie 143; Sophia 154
Northcut, Ann 169; Elizabeth 154; Evaline 159
Norton, Missouri 149; R. C. C. Beall 76
Norvill (Norvell, Nevels), M. E. 145; Robert 36; William 122
Norwood, Elizabeth 39; G. A. 139; John A. 43; Josiah M. 4; Margaret S. 22; N. A. 131; Pheobe C. 56; Thomas L. 166
Nowell, Sarah 8
Nowlin (Nowlen), Bluford P. 2; Margaret 19
Nunley, J. P. 175; M. E. 176
Nye, Thomas 172

Oakly, William 129
Oaks, Mattie 164
Odell, Benjamin F. 59
Odom (Odam), James I. 181; Mary 134
Ogletree, A. C. 5
Old (Olds), Ben 157; Eliza 185; Mary K. 61; Mattie 137; William M. 185
Oldfield, Garland R. 149; John 37,99; Rebecca Mrs. 168
Oldham, Rhoda Ann 69; Samuel 131; W. R. 116
Oliver (Olliver), Asa 53; Benjamin 32; Betsey 8; C. 130; C. B. 68; Charles B. 32; Dan 140; Elsey 2; George 10; James 27; Jane 117; Jermima 12; John P. 119; Lucinda 136; Martha 116; Mary 142; Narcissa 75; Pleasant 9; Rebecca 2; Rosanna 133; Rufus 100; Sarah 9; Sophia 161; William 24,31; William F. M. 75; W. P. 119
Olmer, Jimenter 189
Omohundro, William M. 149
O'Neal, Jane 106; Julia M. 77; J. W. 175; Mary J. 177

O'Quinn (O'Quin), Catharine 8; Josiah 9; Mary Ann 61
Ordway, Stephen 159
Orr, B. T. 120; Cyntha C. 117; D. C. 143; S. A. 167; Sample 13; Susan E. 154; Terrissa 105
Orrick (Orick), Elizabeth D. 84; Fannie 123,158; J. T. 138; J. W. 159; Sarah 49; William 28,81
Ortner, Daniel 16; Jesse 67
Osborne (Osborn), J. A. 173; Thomas F. 169
Ostrander, Jackson 89
Ousley, Ella 170; E. M. 85
Outon, N. E. 152; William 185
Overby, Robert B. 40
Owden, Talitha 6
Owens (Owen, Owings), Amanda M. 88; Arrena 43; Eliza 126; Elizabeth A. 44; Eliza Mrs. 165; G. W. 47,152; James J. 33; James M. 108,147; Jeff 170; Jesse 184; John 60; John N. 12; Josephus 139; Logan 50; Manerva 150; Manervia 141; Martha J. 149; Mary A. 89; Mary J. 95; M. C. 161; M. L. 188; Nancy 8; Nancy E. 71; Nancy F. 27; Nancy Jane 51; Narcissa 9; O. P. 65; R. S. 177; Sarah 66; Thomas A. 22; T. L. 173; Viney 180; William 112; William S. 140
Owensby (Owenby), Caroline R. 58; Elizabeth A. 44; Pantha R. 75; Pheby S. 59; Sarah C. H. 73
Oxoudine, Elizabeth 136

Pace, Dempsey 6,13; James C. 8
Pack, Amanda 26; F. M. 99; James H. 140; Nancy 13
Paddie, James D.
Page, Margaret E. 163
Painter, Mary 62
Palmer, Ethelbert 75; Eve 152; R. D. 149
Pamplin, A. F. 182; A. J. 157; Alex C. 174; Alice F. 169; Armstead 1; B. W. 83; Cynthia E. 106; Delinda L. 78; Elijah 40; Eliza 20; Elizabeth 141; E. M. 179; Emily H. 53; F. M. 84; Frank 94; Henry J. 75; Isham 129; Jacob 93; James H. 29; James W. 56; Jane 96,145; Joe 182; Joel K. 58; John A. 80; John Thomas 98; J. T. 87; Katie 173; Lucinda 60; M. A. 174; Martha 45; Martha Jane 125; Martha L. 59; Martha M. 49; Mary 129; Mary Amanda Frances 60; Mary M. 83; McCager 187; M. E. V. 157; Milton 118; Mollie 166; Nancy 93,166; Nancy Ann 56; Nancy R. 56; Roda 101; S. 84; S. A. E. 62; Sallie 143; Sarah J. 77; Sarah L. Caroline 98; William 12
Pannaqula, John 103

Panter (Panther), Elizabeth
44; James A. 64; John 62;
Mahala 72; Malinda 80;
Mary 42; Sarah A. 114;
Selena 128
Paradice, Margret E. 80
Pardon, Nancy J. 51
Parham, Margaret 86; Mar-
tha 184; Jefferson 6;
Thomas J. 40
Parker, Allen 40; America
154; A. S. 169; David
52; Elijah 45; Eliza-
beth 7,24; John 10;
J. R. 180; J. S. 183;
Mariah 13; Martha J.
159; Mary 23; Nancy 31;
O. A. 123; Parthenia E.
29; Sarah Jane 46;
William A. 39
Parkerson, Brown 59;
Catharine B. 28; Hugh
33; John 29; Thomas W.
32
Parkinson, James 74;
L. C. C. Mrs. 113
Parkison, Mary L. 165
Parks (Park, Parkes),
A. A. 179; Aaron 78;
A. J. 100; Allen 14; Dr.
Allen 110; Amanda 15;
Ambrose L. 38; Ann 78;
Annice M. 40; Ann S. 9;
Benjamin T. 3; Catharine
51,118; Charley 106;
David L. 136; Elisha J.
91; Elizabeth 39,128;
Emily 18; Fannie 167;
Fanny 91,188; Felix G.
26; Fielding 187;
Frances A. 11; George N.
151; Georgia Ann 153;
Green 183; Henry 91;
Isaac 10,18; Ivson 139;
Jennie B. 160; Jesse W.
47; Joel 176; John 184;
Lewis 175; Lilly 119;
Lizzie C. 135; Louisa E.
36; Margaret 126; Martha
D. 18; Martha F. 73;
Martha J. 51; Martin L.
38,50,121; Mary 15,91,
142; Mary C. 15,133;
May 91; M. E. 103;
Milton 47; M. N. 102;
Mollie A. 152; Moses 13;
Nancy 141; Parthenia
187; Susan 28; Susan C.
31; Susan F. 48; Tennie
142; T. H. 122; Thomas
159; Thomas L. D. Jr.
34; Van 91; William 38,
155,157; William W. 24
Parr, F. P. L. 58,84,183;
Jane 11; J. C. 62;
Louella A. 159; Sarah J.
104; William M. 51;
Zebulon 63
Parrish (Parish), Barbary
56; Emeline 62; Emily
30; James 15,20; Lydia
A. 22; Mary Ann 3; Mil-
ley 40; Sarah 2; Susanah
47
Parsley, Sarah K. 187
Partin (Parton), Alfred
J. 36; Elizabeth 75;
Mary Ann 41; M. W. 152
Pate (Pates), A. S. 160;
Nora 170
Patillo, L. A. 79
Patrick, Andrew J. 65;
Eliza A. 110; J. T. 82;
Margaret E. 5;

Patrick contd.
Margret R. 78; Sarah E.
42; Susan 80; Susan A.
82; William 59
Patterson, Alex 154; Buck
106; Daniel 160; David
S. 23; D. M. 67; Easter
105; Elizabeth S. 68;
Eveline 171; Fannie E.
166; Hannah 8; Henry
124; Hugh L. 123; J. 86;
Jim 178; J. L. 168;
John 13,96,141; John C.
177; John K. 65; John
M. 6; Joseph M. 141;
J. W. 95; Lillian 45;
L. M. 65; Louisa 85;
Martha E. 43; Mary L.
82; Mary O. 97; Mary S.
123; Milly Ann 133;
Nancy 13; Nelia R. 158;
Nelson 133; Nelson A.
125; P. F. 142; Robert
45,174; Robert C. 138;
Sally 1; Sarah 69,79;
Sarah E. 126; Stephen
45; Susan 34; Thomas
93; Vincy 147; William
H. 129
Patton (Paton), Angeline
161; A. R. 97; E. L. 75;
Ella Jane 174; Fulton
98; Harriet 127; J. C.
152; Mary A. 165; Mary
L. 69; Mary M. 46
Pattie, M. E. 127
Paul, R. K. 140; William
147
Paysinger (Pasinger),
Barshaby 28; B. E. 124;
C. E. 170; Henry 16;
John J. 89; Julian 35;
Martha J. 70; Mary 26;
Nancy A. 82; Rhody 57;
Thomas A. 16,85; W. P.
157
Payne (Pain, Paynne),
Caroline 67; Carrol E.
138; Charity 188; Dianna
5; E. V. 138; George B.
109; George W. 104;
James M. 110; J. F. 154;
J. N. W. 148; John L.
114; Maria 77; Mary E.
111; M. E. 148,149;
Parthenia 112; Sarah E.
107; Susan 13; T. P.
150; William F. 181
Peach, A. A. 116; Eliza-
beth 32; Ella D. 129;
Sue E. 114
Pearson (Pierson), Bettie
L. 71; C. M. 101; Jennie
P. 175; J. G. 156; John
A. 8; John M. 109;
K. J. 88; Manson G. 11;
Mary J. 83; Meredith 5;
Milley 110; Milly 24;
N. A. 179; Nancy A. 142,
152; N. J. 81; Selina
135; Sidney 113; S. J.
69
Pebby, Mahulda 15
Pegram, Martha C. 56
Pemberton, Eliza A. 45
Pendergrass, Allie 160;
Lucinda 149; M. W. 175
Penick, Kesiah Jane 4
Pennington, Emily 63,65
Penny, Hugh P. 55; Marga-
ret 7
Pentecost, Robert 142;
Silva 109; Susan 159

Peoples (Peebles),
Emeline 98; Priscilla L.
78; Thomas B. 169; Toke
173
Pepper, Joseph 167; Theo-
phelus 73
Perdue, John H. 136
Perkins (Purkins), Amanda
106; America 157; Annie
B. 159; Bettie 161;
Charles 94,120; D. M.
147,167; Drury M. 4,50;
Edith 96; Elmira H. 110;
George 126; Harriett 151;
Hiram 157; John H. 147;
J. W. 113; Margaret 113;
Polly 113; Randol 121,
155; Sol 172; Solomon
113
Perry, Bettie 168; Eveline
35; Fannie 172; George
40; G. F. 121; Isham 5;
James 126; James W. 25;
Jasper N. 69; J. W. 59;
Louisa J. 75; Martha 127;
Martha J. 50; Mary 43;
Mary Ann 64; Nancy 10;
Nathan 3; Philander 159;
Rhodica 40; Samuel 42;
Susan Caroline 80;
William 15
Perryman, Eliza Jane 115
Peterson, Henry 162
Pettitte, H. T. 47
Petty, Alice 150; Buck
181; Catharine A. 85;
Elizabeth 58; Emeline 64;
Florinda J. 141; Hannah
Ritta 2; Humphrey N. 164;
Jane M. 6; John 64; Jo-
seph 25; L. V. 145;
Martha Jane 60; Narcissa
13; Nathan 36; Ralph 16;
Susan D. 55; W. H. 174;
William 34,42; William
L. 186
Peyton, Eliza 181; Margret
J. 26; Monroe 180; Nancy
E. 49; William H. 47
Phagan, Catharine 145;
Elizabeth A. 23; Fenica
J. 121; Georgia Ann 114;
James H. 68; John 82;
Margaret 2; Mary A. 105;
Mary G. 18; M. J. 95;
Nancy V. 129; Olivia 180;
Philip T. 34; Sarah E.
94; Thomas P. 84;
William M. 78
Pheares, John 124
Phelps, Anna 92; Elija
89; Jane 99; Jefferson
51; M. J. 90; Nancy 64;
Patience 132; Ruben 109
Phillips (Philips), Arena
12; Cintha A. 22; Clara
183; C. O. 171; Cressy
16; E. J. 63; Elizabeth
38,49; Eliza L. 168;
Elvira 101; Emily 153;
Feriby 2; George W. 27;
Hellen J. Mrs. 165;
Hester 112; James 48;
James Calvin 115; James
M. 168; J. C. 158; J. H.
114; John T. 59; Joshua
47; K. A. 181; Letty 12;
Lizzie 177; L. J. 153;
Lou 153; Lucinda 172;
Lucy 185; Margaret T.
125; Martha A. 22; Mar-
tha A. D. 54; Mary 178;
Mary J. 129; Mary M. 39;
Mary V. 175; Mollie 170;

Phillips contd.
Nancy J. 37,158; Peter
100; William A. 41;
William M. 34; W. T. 175
Philpot, Alexander 10;
Elizabeth 45; Fannie L.
183; Henriette A. 106;
James 61; Joseph 86,173;
L. E. 133; M. A. 150;
Margaret A. 52; William
37
Pibus, Sarah J. 20
Pickett (Picket), Andrew
J. 15; Ebenezer 15;
G. W. 128; Henson 23;
James M. 124; James O.
155; Louisa 7; Louisa J.
66; Margaret A. 121; Mark
H. 10; Mary E. 62; Sarah
167; Thomas R. 117
Pickle, Nancy Ann 52; Nancy
J. 65; Squire 10,82
Pierce (Pearse), A. E. 81;
Ambrose H. 16; C. C. 104;
F. A. 54; James 50; Ja-
mes F. 121; James I. 165;
Jesse 32; Josiah W. Dr.
137; Kate 142; Louisa A.
134; Malinda 41; Martha
35; Nancy 113; N. B., M.
G. 56; Polly 78; Sarah
46; Simon A. 44; William
49
Pigg, Anna 4; Delia E. 35;
Edmond 103; E. J. 158;
Eliza 88; Elizabeth 61;
James 68,76; James B.
64; James J. 5; Jennett
53; Joel J. 75; John
162; John N. 54; Joseph
H. 78; Lou 149; Martha
67; Martha C. 73; Martha
E. 94; Mary 160; Mary
Ann 66; Milley 128;
M. L. 114; Nancy 11;
Nancy D. 62; Rebecca S.
67; S. A. L. 139; Sarah
J. 65; William 77
Pilot, Cassa Ann 134
Pingram, George 43
Pinkerton, Brown 75,155;
Elizabeth L. 31; Emma
C. 157; James 81; J. P.
70; J. W. 180; Martha
48; Martha P. 75; Mary
74; M. I. 182; Thomas
U. 129; Y. U. 108
Pinkney (Pinky), John M.
103; Sylvester 64
Pitcock, Elizabeth 78;
Elizabeth B. 70; Fran-
ces A. 77; Jacob B. 58;
John 136; Joseph 173;
Lewis 138; Mary Ann 69
Pittman (Pitman), Cla-
rinda C. 171; Dave H.
118; L. S. 155; Sarah
49,155
Pitts, Almedia D. Y. 65;
Ann 143; Bethune 56;
Caesar 151; Caroline
122; Cinthia E. 84;
Clark 179; Cynthia E.
71; Docia 161; E. A.
181; E. B. 81; Eliza A.
109; Elizabeth Ann 24;
F. A. 173; Felix 158;
Frances O. 132; George
92,135; Henry 168;
Henry P. 67; Hiram 173;
Isaac R. 50,55; James
C. 99; James J. 74;
J. B. 107,153; J. C.
134; J. H. 160;

Pitts contd.
Joel A. 103; Joel J.
84; John L. 32; Josie
R. 153; Louisa 175;
Lutitia 169; M. A. 148,
151; Manerva 115; Mary
E. 123; Mary L. Mrs.
154; N. C. J. 173;
Norah 181; Ophelia E.
155; Pamphilla 126;
Rachel 144; Rachel A.
57; Rachel E. 108; Rena
E. 176; Riley W. 49;
Robert H. 109; Robert K.
35; Sallie 154,166;
Sallie A. 130; Samuel
95,134; T. B. 168;
Tennessee Idora 166;
Thomas B. 38,101; Thomas
J. 155; W. E. 176; W. E.
A. 178; W. J. 122;
Wiley J. 51; William A.
69,119; William A. E.
160; W. R. 158
Pless, Jacob 169
Plexican, S. A. 174
Pluss, Melvina 99
Poindexter, L. T. 156;
Lucy Ann 151; M. L. 125
Polk, E. S. 162; Josephine
A. 150; Sallie 3;
William 20
Pollard, Becky Ann 59;
Elizabeth 12
Pollock, Boyers 62; Joseph
H. 62
Polly, David 7; Jefferson
96,123; Leafly 23;
Lucinda 35; Lyddia 75
Polston, Manda 115
Pool, Allen 5; A. Y. 86;
Fanny 9; James F. 42;
J. M. 175; John 38,120;
J. R. 183; Matilda 27;
Sarah T. 182; William
152; William J. 25;
W. W. 182
Poorstone, Margaret Ann
89
Pope, Alphia P. 66; E. E.
176; James H. 34; Mar-
tin V. 64; Surfrona 72;
Warden M. 158
Porch, Jane 178; John 187;
John A. 37; Mary Ann 33
Porter, D. S. 141; E. L.
A. 146; G. W. 110;
G. W. D. 127; Harry 175;
Hugh 113; I. H. 178;
Isaac S. 3; Jarmon 132;
John 70; Julia F. 164;
Lucie 129; Mariah 112;
Martha 69; Mary E. 117;
Stephen 13
Posey, Catharine 171;
Elizabeth 183; E. M. 70;
Emory M. 16,69; George
W. 48,63; James M. 183;
M. R. 179; Polly J. 89;
R. A. 154; S. L. 179;
William 26,68
Potter, Mary 35
Potts, Judia 103
Powell (Powel), C. C. 171;
Henry M. 59; James N.
40; Mary E. 81; P. R.
116; Sarah A. F. 73;
Thomas 153; T. J. 176
Powers (Power), Elvira
75; Frances R. 132;
Holloway 11; John 174;
Martha 13; Matilda 130;
Sebra 47; T. E. 174
Pratt, A. E. 82;

Pratt contd.
Cordelia A. 42; F. M.
60; Martha M. 37
Presley, Lou 157
Presswood, W. R. 76
Preston, Frances 176; Jesse
9; Lucinda 81,85; Nancy
142
Prewitt, Elizabeth R. 24;
William C. 24
Price, Amanda 176; Ann R.
30; E. J. 105; Elizabeth
10; Emily 36; Emily P.
41; George 124; George
T. 55,80,82; Harriett L.
163; Isam 170; James 51;
James B. 54; James M.
61; J. B. 183; Jesse J.
55; John 61; John H. 37;
Joshua Y. 119; Martha J.
152; Mary C. 88; Mary E.
74,99; Matthew 18; M. J.
99; Nancy 89; Nancy H.
38; Nerva 176; Polly 128;
Rachel 41; Rebecca 32;
Redorick 42; Sallie 176;
Samuel 74; Sarah 38;
Sarah E. 60,66; Thomas
86; Thomas J. 111; W. D.
85; William 7,164
Prince, E. C. 174; Gedion
34; George W. 103; Jere-
miah 68; John W. 174
Prints, William 123
Pritchard (Prikard),
Charles R. 180; Levi 12
Pritchett, Drury 1; Jamima
38; Theodore J. 61
Proctor, Amanda 168; Flora
157; Frances A. 129;
Robert T. 34; Wesley 112
Prosser, A. M. 43; Anny
113; Dan 152; Fannie M.
94; Frances 73; George
133; Groce 115; Hessey
79; James A. 35; James
M. 82; Jesse 61; J. G.
56; Jonathan E. 22;
Louisa 37; M. A. 74;
Martha Jane 70; Mary E.
74; Peggy Jane 3; Peter
176; P. G. 50; Priss 46;
Sarah 47; W. B. 95;
William 52; William D.
45; W. M. D. 85; W. P.
114
Pruitt, America 50; Cansada
C. 88; Catharine 20,85;
Ellen 178; Emily 38;
John P. 137; Lucillar
47; Mahala 142; Mary 81;
Nancy P. 50; Peggy J.
173; Polly 6; Samuel D.
51; Sarah 143; Thomas
147; William A. 9;
William W. 5; Wilson C.
15
Pryor, Albert 182; Amy 152;
Ann R. 105; Elizabeth H.
141; Flora 114; Flora D.
128; Kittie 162; Kitty
120; Martha 179; Parthe-
nia 161; Tery 159
Puckett, C. E. 112; George
W. 30; Martha A. 122;
Mary J. 68; Millie L.
181; Patrick H. 85;
Sarah J. 108
Pullen, Joseph G. 50
Pulliam (Pullam), Eliza A.
129; Frances E. 47;
H. A. 171; John W. 12;
J. R. 169; Margret 44;
Mattie 173; Maudana M. 12;

Pulliam contd.
M. G. 158; Thomas 124;
W. B. 101
Pully, Celia 33; Elizabeth
24; Mary 52
Purdom, Mark 53
Purdy, Samuel Jackson 137
Pursin, Calvin 122
Puryear, Elizabeth 3
Putman, D. E. 164
Pylant (Pilant, Pilate),
Casey 128; Casey Ann 77;
Elizabeth 171; Felix G.
G. 110; Gabriel 22;
Gabriel M. 129; George
W. 42,107; Gray J. 67;
Green A. 31; Green A. F.
109; James C. 52,114;
John L. 45; John M. 106;
Louisa A. 84; Luther M.
52; Margret A. 29;
Martha A. 109; Mary 87;
Mary F. 140; Nancy Ann
122; P. C. 131; Penina
19; Rebecca 63; S. E.
161; William 7; William
G. 61; William W. 166

Qualls, Minerva 22
Quarles, Irena L. 19
Quick, J. A. 97; L. S.
185; N. M. 156; Stephen
L. 124; T. M. 96

Raby, Ann E. B. 119;
Hilliard 118; James K.
139; J. R. 124; Martha
E. 81; Molly J. 95;
P. A. 96; T. A. 138
Radford, J. M. 180;
Nellie 180
Radican (Radiken, Radigan,
Ratican), A. J. 89;
Cordelia 177; Frances
E. 105; Martha A. 132;
Mary 24; Mary C. D. 138;
M. J. 177; Permelia 73;
Sarah Ann 72
Ragin, George 119; Martha
A. 157; Phill 178
Ragsdale, Charlotte 144;
W. F. 85
Rainey, Elizabeth 36;
Febe Jane 43; James 43;
Jane 37; Nancy 25;
Sarah 34; William J. 43
Rains (Raines), Baily 41;
Earl 10; Emily A. 47;
Frances 69; James 108;
Polly 187
Rambo, James R. 136; R.
M. 76
Ramey, Benjamin 7; Mary
A. 18
Ramsey (Ramsy), A. N.
180; Ann 59; C. G. 154;
D. A. 175; David 4;
D. C. 130; Dora 180;
Elizabeth 5,34; Eliza
Jane 10; Ellen 78;
Elzira 19; Hardy F. M.
22; J. B. 133; J. M.
173; John 40; John J.
164; L. E. 173; Martha
A. 39; Martha J. 125;
Mary 54,138; Mary E.
50; Mc. 162; M. E. 150;
Mial 11; Penuel 20;
Reubin B. 17; S. A.
157; Sarah 11; Sarah A.
4; S. B. 130; S. K.
115; T. M. 74; W. T.
124
Randall, Elizabeth 105

Randolph, A. A. 162; Ade-
line 96; Amandia C. 43;
Barbary A. 21; C. C. 91;
Fannie 166; F. L. 71;
Hugh 2,86; James E. 60;
J. W. 79; L. A. 131;
Loucinda 82; Lucinda 80;
Lucretia H. 35; Martha
A. 87; Martha S. 38;
Mary 74; Mary B. 15;
Mary C. 131; M. E. 86;
Nancy A. 9; P. L. 182;
Pleasant A. 75; R. F.
160; Rilla T. 48; Sallie
99
Raney, Casena 133; Catha-
rine 13; Celia 64;
Charlotte 149; Cynthia
Ann 1; F. M. 85; Harriet
59; Harriett 51; Henry
166; James 123; J. C.
95; Joel B. 63; J. W.
57; Martha J. 18;
Mary Jane 79; Matilda
85; Nancy 33,41,46;
Polly Ann 53; Ruth 147;
Sarah 97; W. J. 94
Ransom, Caleb 142; Fannie
J. 179; John R. 37
Ratley, J. R. 144
Ratliff, Caroline 161;
Catharine 84,135; E.
Mrs. 158; Elizabeth 76;
J. T. 91,167; M. C. 73;
Newton 139; William
115,137
Ratter, Ella 173
Rattler, Olive 120
Rawles (Rawls), Calvin
83; F. R. Dr. 183;
Hanah 123; James W. 88;
J. J. 118; Lucinda 17;
Mary Ann 30; Mary Jane
45; Nannie A. 161;
Thomas H. 48
Rawson, Rutha Jane 121
Ray, Ann E. 100; C. C.
177; G. H. 72; Harvey
149; J. F. 108; J. H.
160; John 8; J. S. 90;
Logan 140; Maggie E.
148; Margaret 125; Mary
F. E. 122; Millie Mrs.
153; Milton S. 67;
Patrick 68; Permelia
28; Robert H. 111; S. A.
E. 151; Sarah D. 155;
Smith 143; Thomas C.
57; W. G. M. 96; William
78; William C. 51;
W. M. 164
Rayburn (Raiburn), Eliza-
beth 10; Mathew 36
Raymond, Lettitia L. 53;
Martha S. 9; Mary E.
43; William S. 40,142
Rayerster, Charles 41
Read, James 158,161; John
M. 21; Malinda 161;
Mary F. 112; May Ramsey
77; W. O. 120
Reed (Reid), Absolom M.
2; Auline C. 101; Boat
172; Caroline 53; Cat-
harine E. 53; Eliza A.
161; Eliza E. 88; Eve-
line 11; George 12;
J. D. 54; J. F. 170;
John 17; John H. 4;
John W. 143; Loisa
Josephine 79; Maggie J.
120; Mahaly 21; Martha
J. 16; Martha S. A. 79;
Mary E. 166; Merdica 126;

Reed contd.
Milly 169; Nathaniel 120;
Richmond P. 4; S. E. 56
Ready (Reedy), C. M. 134;
Frank 166; Levin G. 23;
Martha J. 117; Mary Ann
3
Reagor (Reager), S. L.
152; William 95
Reaves (Reevis, Reives,
Reeves, Reavis, Rieves;
See Rives & Revis),
Angeline 111; C. A. 161;
Eliza 42; H. A. 80;
Hardy 52; Henry H. 25;
J. A. 130; James L. 22;
John A. 75; J. T. 137;
Letty 45; Margaret 12;
Martha Ann 8; Mary 124;
Mary L. 142; Miles J.
69; Morgan 37; Nancy 48;
N. S. B. 144; P. H. 67;
Sally 5; S. M. 181;
Susannah 25; Susannah L.
11; Victoria J. 108;
W. A. 146; Willis 29
Redd, Christianna T. 81;
John F. 73; J. S. 174;
Martha A. 85; Martha H.
67; M. E. 173; Susan E.
99
Reddick, Jania 31
Redick (Reddick), Anderson
92; Asa S. 52; Jane 92
Redings, Elizabeth 115
Redman, Reuben Thomas 131
Reece, Benjamin F. 81;
Booker 141; F. B. 87;
James 112; James C. 41;
Joel 184; Lutitia 89;
Martha 47; Mary 42;
Mary Mrs. 90; Nannie 85;
Nettie 140; P. O. 141;
Sarah 98; Sarah E. 114;
Thomas M. 85
Reed (see Reed, Read)
Rees, Andrew J. 151;
Charles A. 71; Charlotta
A. 82; Cyntha 24; George
W. 109; H. S. 148; Jake
148; James O. 62; Joel
135; John H. 149; Lizzie
P. 109; M. A. 129;
Martha J. 107; Martin V.
100; Mary 65; Mary F.
75; Minerva A. 75;
Nannie 176; N. S. 76;
Phebe E. 70; Phillip
103; R. A. 150; Sofa
103; W. H. 68; Wilkerson
W. 25; William 14;
William H. 2
Reese, Artenia 64; Charles
T. 35; C. T. 153;
Elenora 183; Eliza 36;
Elizabeth 33,57; Elvira
55; Fannie 146; Fanny
B. 60; George W. 24,42;
Hiram H. 64; Jackson
131; James R. 33; Joel
7; Joel L. 8; John 8,66;
M. A. 125; Manerva 8;
Mary Jane 118; Mattie
157; Milly 4; Nancy K.
42,51; Nannie 163; Pa-
lina A. 72; Perry 156;
Pertesia Ann 44; Robert
68; Sallie 129; Thomas
B. 156; Thomas J. 44;
Virginia 47; Wilkinson
58; William H. 49;
William W. 2; William W.
23
Remington, C. H. 52

Renegar, A. J. 54,161;
Amanda 157; Belinda 15;
Catharine 9; Cornelia
C. 164; Cyntha M. 143;
David 51; Eliza M. 122;
Elizabeth A. 83; Ellis
23; Emily 176; George
172; George F. 18; Henry
M. 126; H. J. 69; Isa-
bella 166; Jackson 128;
Jacob 56; Jane 118;
Jasper 62; John M. 37;
John R. 149; John T. 70;
Joseph H. 38; Joseph N.
141; J. T. 124,144;
July Ann 15; Laura H.
163; Lottie C. 103;
Louisa 124; Martha 62;
Mary 2,10,84,176; Mary
E. 175; Mary Jane 62;
M. C. 155; M. J. 149;
M. M. 173,178; Nancy N.
104; Nannie 175;
Nicholas 25; R. A. 177;
Sallie B. 130,163; San-
ford 32,85,105; Sarah
51; Sarah F. 155; William
H. 185
Renfro (Renfroe, Renfrow,
Renfor, Ranfro), Caro-
line 128; Druline 59;
G. H. 76; James F. 39;
L. L. 150; M. A. 123;
Mattie J. 138; P. J.
179
Revis (see Reaves), David
J. 52; John W. 87;
L. C. 182; Mary J. 98;
Mattie S. 129; Nancy
A. 4
Reynolds, Cicero 145;
C. M. 165; E. F. 88;
J. C. 147; Jesse 66;
J. H. 88; Nancy J. 102;
Sallie 162; S. R. 77
Rhea, Benjamin 132;
Elizabeth Ann 34; James
M. 50; Jefferson L. 39;
John J. 72; Margaret
23,115; Margaret Jane
32; Mary M. B. 12;
Nancy E. 57; Phebe An
24
Rheyer, Mary A. 121
Rhoden, George L. 165
Rhodes (Rodes), Dave 174;
Eliza 58; Jane 73;
Lemuel 12; Mary Ann 55;
Mollie Ann 119; Rebecca
5; Sarah 17(2); Simeon
10; Thomas A. 172; W.
A. 183; William A. 54;
William L. 152
Rhoton (Rhoten), Ann 148;
Ann E. 118; B. W. 117;
Elizabeth A. 18;
Mary Ann 48
Rhyme, Vardy M. 11
Rhyne, V. M. 56
Rice, Emmy E. 40; Green
P. 33,55; Isaac 88;
James 141; John 93;
Mary Elizabeth 78;
Othneil 14; Sue Ann
114; W. G. 167
Rich, Henry J. 40; Jane
13; J. H. 153; Joseph
M. 57; Martha Ann 58;
Thomas J. 76; William-
son 35
Rife, Sylvester 187
Richardson, Drury 52;
Jackson 67; Joel 81;
Martha 33;

Richardson contd.
Mrs. Mary J. 150;
Parmelia G. 137; Peggy
186; Ritta C. 8; T. J.
137; William 33;
William T. 117
Richerson, Frances 72
Richeson, James 62
Richey (Richy), John 167;
Sarah C. 73
Rickets, Diana 52; Martha
83; Mathias 52
Rickey (Richie), Martha
Ann 139; Mary J. 83;
Mary Jane 139
Ricks, Ann Roberta 34
Riddle (Riddell), Alex-
ander 76; Betsey 7;
Ephraim 6; G. W. 179;
Harmon 6; Johnson 90;
Julia A. 166; Manuel
113; Martha P. 79; Mary
67; Milly 120; M. V. 67;
Nathaniel M. 94; Sarah
151; Stephen 8; William
17; W. M. 102
Ridings, Elizabeth E. 107
Riggins, Willis 174
Riggs (Rigg), Elizabeth
10; John 6; Preston
105,153
Rigney, Elvira 136
Riles, Elizabeth 55
Riley, A. F. 106; Eliza-
beth 11; George M. 133;
Mary J. 141; Mollie 0.
180; Nancy 84; Sacratus
145; Sarah C. 71; Tho-
mas R. 80; W. H. 68
Ringo, Inez 115; Joseph
H. 74; Mary 52; Mary A.
151
Rison, William R. 70
Rives (see Reeves, Revis),
Alexander S. 14; A. R.
104; B. W. 112; B. W.
L. 68; C. H. Mrs. 112;
Jane 51; J. W. 156;
Martha 18,100; R. C.
82; Sallie 107; Sarah
74; S. M. 181; Sue E.
72; T. J. 116; Virginia
Mrs. 111; Willis G. 27
Roach (Roch), Cyntha 30;
Elizabeth 15; John 18;
Martha C. 30; M. E. 118;
Parthenia 178; Sarah E.
82; Susan J. 18; W. A.
177
Roan (Roane, Rone, Rhone),
Caroline T. 9; Haisting
39; James 50; John 22;
Margaret A. 41; Mary
54; Nancy 58; Rebeccah
7; Samuel 17; Samuel H.
63; Samuel H. A. 48;
William Henry 133
Robe, Della 183
Roberts, Andrew 17;
Annie E. 108; Clementine
J. 18; Emmerson 160;
Manuel 2; Mary A. 61;
M. H. 65; Nancy J. 57
Robertson, Amanda J. 13;
Anderson 50; Anna 103;
Ann F. 4; Bell 183;
Catharine 10; Dan 154;
Edward 176; Eliza 37,
173; Elizabeth 188;
Eliza C. 32; G. A. 73;
George 136; Hannah A.
E. 44; Idella 166;
James 153; J. M. 179;
John F. 42; Joseph M. 39;

Robertson contd.
J. S. 175; Lauretta 176;
Loderick 6; Loutisha
156; L. T. 61; Lucy 187;
Malinda M. 24; Martha
80; Mary 7,12; Mary A.
M. 30; Mollie 165; Nancy
10; Penina 12; Robert
157; Sarah 164; Sopha A.
78; Starkie 10; Sue 120;
S. W. 89; Tallafar 17;
W. F. 112; William 129;
William A. 50; W. P. 89
Roberson, Chaddy 148;
Louisa J. 142; Polly 43;
Robert 148
Robeson, Elinor M. 57
Robinson, A. H. 73; Archer
148; C. A. F. 152;
Catharine 144; Charles
A. 42; Celian 144; Daniel
93; Delia 3; Ella 179;
Elzira 10; Emmaranda J.
47; Eunicey 5; Frances
D. 24; Harriet E. 100;
Henry 17; Hulder G. 86;
James 126; Jenial P. 32;
Joe 108; Joe T. 163;
John 104,146; Julia 146;
Julia A. 97; J. W. 104;
Leathy 181; Leona 93;
Lodrick 83,138; Lucy Ann
140; Margaret F. 51;
Mary J. 151; Mollie E.
152; Molly 99; R. A.
171; Sarah 1; Sarah J.
126; S. L. 168; Susan
91; Thomas R. 37; Wells
91; W. S. 144
Robison, Angeline 165;
Eliza A. Mrs. 101; James
C. 42; Mary E. 89; R. F.
182
Rochelle (Rochele, Rochel),
Elizabeth 86; Georgia E.
142; Jesse 76; W. A. 135
Roden (Rodin), Albine 65;
James 78; John H. 49;
L. C. 118; Mary 178;
Mary M. 87; Mrs. S. J.
108; Thomas J. 157; W. M.
167
Rodgers (Rogers, Roggers),
Coleman 75; E. A. 172;
Eliza 125; Elizabeth 32;
Jackson 14; James 142;
James P. 102; James R.
10; Jane 130; J. L. 112;
John 4,20,67; John C.
26; J. R. 149; L. B.
123; Mary E. 63,64,170;
M. J. 169; Rebecca 41;
Shepard 48; Spencer G.
38; Washington 21; Wil-
liam J. 65; William W.
60
Roper, Bracken 119; Eliza
119; Eliza A. 157; Eliz-
abeth 151; Emily 118;
G. T. 87; James 86;
Julia 13; Margaret Jane
152; Martha 84,106;
Milly J. 83; Mollie 132;
Sallie A. 165; William
D. 13; Winnie 177; W. L.
172; W. N. 167
Rorax (Rorex), Agness 71;
David 2; James Capt.
187; Louisa 24; William
105
Rose, Thomas 134
Rosebrough (Roseboro,
Roseborough), Charity C.
98; David D. 9;

Rosebrough contd.
Eleanor Eveline 20;
Ellen 169; Emeline 36;
Janie 127; Joe 178;
John L. 22; Joseph G.
124; S. A. 184; Samuel
B. 65; Samuel M. 1;
Sarah 126; W. B. 149;
William B. 65; William
H. 32; W. M. 164
Ross, A. C. 31; Amanda
159; Elizabeth 75; E. M.
125; Josephine 98; Mary
186; Mary F. 100;
Matilda Mrs. 156; Mattie
G. 135; Nancy 169;
Robert 12; Rosanna 154;
Silas C. 9; W. S. 135
Rossen, Isabella 146
Rosson, Martha 6
Roter, Emeline 3
Roughton, C. D. 89; James
M. 44; Mariah 111;
Rachael 50; Sarah 83,
138; Sarah M. 124;
Tennessee C. 87; Thomas
P. 53; T. M. 123;
William B. 47,56
Roulin, Mary A. 97
Roundtree, Ann 7; William
G. 31
Rousot, Florida M. 24
Rousseau (Russeau), C. C.
72; Hillery 187
Routt, James R. 59; John
M. 64; J. S. 166;
Richard 142
Rowark, Nancy 185
Rowe (Roe), A. J. 183;
Anna 95; Benjamin 41;
Cyntha 6; Elizabeth M.
67; James A. 85; Jasper
44; John T. 118; Joseph
128; Joseph S. 73;
Lucinda 71; Martha Ann
75; Martha J. 54; Mary
C. 159; M. C. 81; Nancy
105; Rachel T. 79;
Sally 11; Samuel 90;
S. E. 142; Susan 122;
Tempe 186; Thomas 28;
William 63
Rowell, Amanda S. 66;
Ann C. 149; D. T. 173;
Eliza J. 6; H. P. 109;
I. E. Mrs. 167; Isaac
180; James M. 73; James
T. 141; Johnathan W. 65;
John J. 72; John M. 185;
Louisa Jane 76; Manson
E. 73; Martha Caroline
2; Martha J. 81; Mary
Ann 65; Milton N. 114;
M. J. 146; P. E. 68;
Samuel M. 9; Sarah A.
169; Sarah E. 102,104;
Thomas M. 79; Thomas
W. 150
Rowland (Roland, Rowlin,
Rolin), Elizabeth 68;
Fennetta 68; Frances
144; James 57; Jesse
M. 19; Malinda 59;
Mary 124; Mary A. 68;
Mary J. 80; Mary L. 5;
Melia 181; Priscilla
174; Rachel L. 94;
Richard M. 1; Robert
149; Solomon 66; Susan
80; Thomas 42,161;
William 79
Rozell (Rozel), C. A.
157; Dawson 183; J. B.
116; John J. W. 155;

Rozell contd.
Madison 46; Sallie 177;
W. A. B. 171
Ruckers (Rucker), Preas-
ley 3; Presley 19;
William R. 141
Rudd, David 36; David M.
176; Elizabeth 78;
George W. 65; John L.
175; Nancy Ann 71;
W. B. 98
Runnells (Runnels), A.
161; Absolom G. 24;
Coleman 14; Dona 178;
Edmond G. 41; Elijah J.
107; Emanuel 47; Jacob
C. B. 63; James E. 153;
J. E. 75; Martha 14;
Martha C. 104; Mary E.
131; Reuben 49; William
T. 34; W. J. 100
Russ, James 11
Russell, A. H. 99; Ann
185; Calley 167; C. E.
60; E. C. 60; Eliza 55;
Emma 155; George 179;
Green B. 4; Henry 174;
Jane 34; John 139;
Margaret J. 22; Mar-
garett A. 75; Mary 34,
58; Mary E. 5; Mary G.
60; M. E. 129; M. G.
112; M. M. 175; Monroe
170; M. P. 77; Robert
101; Safronia M. 22;
S. E. 164; Thomas 160;
Thomas J. 123; Thornton
96,160; T. J. 69,169;
William 170; William
H. 5
Ruth (Ruthe), Darah 125;
Elizabeth 3; Eliza P.
22; Harriette 106;
Mary K. A. 94
Rutledge, Ann Rebecca 26;
Charles S. 104; Cor-
delia A. 109; Elizabeth
109; Harriet E. 35;
Henry 79; Isaac 16,71;
Isaac C. 176; James 3,
34(2); Louisa 183;
Margaret 78; Martha
Emily 62; Mary A. 90;
Mary Jane 67,145; Phebe
16; Pheby E. 109;
Rebecca A. 106; Ruth
5; Samuel 22; Sarah
Jane 44; S. F. 166;
William A. 90
Rutter, Solomon 185
Ryals, Mary Ann 16
Ryan, Nancy 120

Sabra, Ned 182
Samson, Thomas L. 2
Sanders, Adeline 117;
A. H. 129; Arminda 180;
Calvin 163; C. C. 172;
C. F. 150; Cordelia
129; Daniel 117;
Daniel W. 57; Dave M.
102; David 57; David
S. 97; E. F. 168; Eliza
A. 160; Elizabeth 12,
114,173; Elizabeth S.
52; Emeline 26; George
20,40,114; George W.
48; Hardy 19; Henry
32; Jacob 126; James
48,101; James H. 56;
James M. 130; Jane 147;
J. N. 170; John 20;
John S. 72; John W.
181; Joseph 88;

Sanders contd.
Julia 117; Julina 19;
Louisa 36; Lucinda 84;
Luzanna A. 62; Margret
Jane 79; Martha 49;
Mary Ann 6; Mary E. 176;
Mary W. 135; Medora M.
101; M. J. 172; Nancy 9;
Nancy A. 114; Nancy E.
143; Nancy L. 61; N. J.
143; Sallie 121; Sarah
29; Sarah A. 37; Sarah
Ann 138; Sarah Jane 44,
78; Selome 78; Smith 80;
Thomas L. 116; W. H. 64;
William 19,123; William
B. 1; William C. 33;
William F. 13; W. M. 148
Sanderson, Edward 186;
Emily 8; J. B. 182;
Lewis G. 11; Mary Ann
56; Nancy M. 121; Sarah
A. 68
Sandlin (Sandland), Anne
S. 25; Jincie 162; Jona-
than 58; Julia 172;
Lewis 78; Martha 99;
Nancy 48; Nicholas 68;
Polly 20; W. L. 182
Sanford, A. 41; Asa L. 27;
James B. 57; James T.
83
Saint, John C. 22
Saintclair, Frances M. 28;
Mary Ann 37
Sanson, Jane 186
Sappington, James 184
Sartin, John 106
Satterfield, B. M. 97;
Caroline 54; Elizabeth
147; Fannie V. Mrs. 146;
James 45; J. C. 153;
John 12; Josie 171;
Lucretia 148; Martha 131
Saunders, George 66; James
C. 80; Malinda 14; Mary
Ann 45; M. E. 143;
Joshua 61; Sarah A. 12
Savage, Emily 162; M. C.
169
Savier, Alexander 23; Ned
154
Savish, Allice 94
Sawyers, A. G. 51; Amanda
125; Eli 122; E. O. 74;
George W. 32; G. M. 58;
Isaack 86; James K. 134;
James M. 98; John 89;
Judea 103; Louisa 44;
Louisa J. 90; M. A.
160; Mary Ann 69; Mary
E. 159; Mollie 171;
Pheba T. 78; Rebecca E.
58; Rebecca N. 101;
R. H. 94; S. A. 52;
Stephen 68; Susan E. 97;
Thomas 104; William D.
179; Wilson P. 35; Zero
68; Z. P. 179
Scales, Carrie 99; Joe
162; John 23; Joseph 111;
Julia 118; Lousa 102;
Pless 169
Scivally (Sively), C. L.
80; D. W. 81,124; Eliz-
abeth Ann 11; Esther
105; Leah Jane 38;
Lucy 152; Martha Jane
128; Mary E. 90; Mary
Frances 75; Nancy C.
32; Ruth C. 97; Susa A.
111; W. E. 116; William
M. 36

Scoggins (Scroggins, Scrogins), Abner 11; Alexander 58,152; Elizabeth 120,121; Jesse 26; Leah C. 48; Lizzie 136; Mary E. 57; M. E. 166; Rachel A. 94; Smith 39; William J. 63; W. J. 125

Scott, A. B. 67; Angeline 13; Angeline O. 69; Anna 162; Charley 129; Caroline 168; Catharine 45; Della Margaret 67; Elias M. 101; Elinor 104; Elizabeth 39; Elizabeth M. 108; George 132; George W. 33; Harriet 82; Hetty S. 25; Irena 31; James D. 172; James K. 110; Jane 55; Jensey 48; Jim 171; Jocie 145; Jo Celia 114,137; John 27, 119; John H. 45,76,135; John L. 16; Joseph 21, 36,37; J. W. O. 161; Lucinda 40; Margarett 129; Martha 44; Martha J. 152; Mary Ann 60; Mary S. 128; Mollie 166; Morgan 153; Nancy J. 124; Polly 145; Rachael J. 46; Rebecca 120; Robert 153; Sallie 104, 153; Sarah E. 51; Sarah J. 87; S. E. 84,181; Susan 106; Susan C. 90; Tempa 101; Temple 58; Thomas 115; Thomas J. 50; William 74,114; William M. 57; Willis W. 149

Scrimpshire, Louiza 181

Scruggs, Nancy 131; Sarah 107; S. S. 105; T. J. 142

Sea, Julia 135

Seagraves, Michael 14; Sarah 18

Seal, Julia Ann 107

Searcey, Robert 57

Seaton, A. F. 110; Emaline 117; Endora 141; George B. 139; James 7; John 175; M. M. 181; M. S. 155; R. R. 158; S. E. 158; William G. 82

Sebastian, Abe 181; Abner 125,153; Amanda 133; Annie 96; George 171; Harriet 183; John 155; Joseph 67; Laura C. 139; Mattie 132; O. I. 178; Rebecca 167; Rose 169

Seeth, Josiah 105

Sergent, Elizabeth 153

Setliff (Sutliff), A. 76; Absolum 26; Ann 94; Lewis L. W. 48; Louisa 117

Sewell (Sewal), Mary 14; Mary Ann 25; Nancy J. 21

Sexton, Charles 96; Eliza P. 66; J. A. 177; John D. 57; John J. 12; Joseph 16; Lewis 6; William E. 152; William G. 56

Seymore (Seamore, Seamoore) Eponetus 30; James E. 10; Mary E. 29; Reuben 57

Shackleford, Margaret Ann 66

Shaddy, John Francis Marion 102

Shamby, Florance 179

Shands (Shand), Jesse A. 47; Lucy 178

Shanks, Ann 87; Nancy 188; Sarah 175

Shannon, James M. 149; J. M. 174

Shapard (Shepard, Shappard, Sheppherd), Avarilla E. 50,54; C. C. 128; Fannie 168; John 26,143; Lucy 174; Martha 140; Mary C. 63; Nancy J. 182; Parelee 139; Rosena 49; William 59

Sharp, Barthena E. 42; Dick 178; Eliza 4; Elizabeth H. 11; J. M. 178; Martha J. 59; Mary E. 74; Sam 158; William 128

Shaw, Ann 17; Betsey 7; Elizabeth 107; George 107; H. C. 76; James H. 27; J. B. 133; Jennie 112; John M. 62; Joseph 29; Mariam 119; Mary E. C. 94; M. S. 131; Nancy S. 76; Paul A. 23, Robert A. 62; Sarah Jane 66; Susan 96; T. J. 126; Wade W. 166; Wesley 149; William R. 36

Sheffield, Emily 159; M. L. 132

Shelton, Ben A. 88; Brice D. 10; C. A. P. 105; Catharine 10; Charley 170; Elifus G. 69; Eliphas 4; Elisha 45; Eliza 136; Elizabeth 28,47,131; E. L. M. 70; Frances J. 142; Grif 104; Henderson A. 95; Henry 44; James 50,129; James R. 116; Jane 35; Jeff 168; Jesse 7,139; J. M. 170,174; John 121; John F. 7; Julia A. 159; Leah 44; Martha Ann 69; Mary 4,23; Mary E. 86, 148; Matthew M. 85; Nancy 13; Peter 11; Richard 101; Robert M. 36; Rosannah 30; Samuel 42; Thomas J. 24; William E. 147; William H. 59; W. L. 56

Sheriff (Sherriff), A. C. 142; M. C. 137; Nancy Jane 134; Sallie M. 123

Sherley, Calaway 85

Sherrell (Sherell, Sherrill), A. J. V. 103; Albert 172; Ann E. 64; Arch 96; Ella 106; Hary 93; Henry 113; John 35; Joseph E. 166; Laura 149; Mariah H. 50; Mary F. 179; Mattie 151; Miles R. 11; Violet A. 156; W. S. 69

Sherwood, Mary A. 145

Shields, Daniel B. 29; Maurning Ann 64; Thomas 116

Shinalt, Mary 25

Shipman, Martin 30

Shipp (Ship), Austin A. 34; Elizabeth 43; H. N. T. 100; Lewis 12,177; Louisa P. 23; Mary E. 65; Nancy C. 3; Nancy Caroline 188; Orlena B. 78; Sarah 12,74; Susan 35

Shires, Elizabeth 52; James 74; John P. 67

Shoemake, James A. 75; Sallie 160

Shofner, A. E. 73; Allice R. 138; Amanda 25; H. Bettie 133; James C. 90; John 169; L. M. 142; Lucy F. 155; Martha 56; Martha E. 125; Martin K. 5; Matilda 5; M. B. 149; M. L. 93; Nancy A. 17; P. L. 100; Wilson P. 20; W. M. 140

Shook, Elizabeth M. 34; Mary A. 69

Shores, Mary J. 54

Short, C. M. 172; Easter 127; James M. 89; Jo. 121; John J. 101; J. W. M. 130; Lillian 184; Mary 96; Thomas 187; William 113

Shuffield, A. B. 129; Ann 22; Arthur B. 32; Crecy 146; H. W. 39; John J. 82; Lucinda 185; Lucretia 19; Luveney 116; Mattie P. 163; Zerilda E. 128

Shull, Amanda 79; D. B. 51; Elizabeth N. 45; J. B. B. 180; Joseph L. 43; Martha Jane 55; M. R. 45; Sue 80; Tom 155; William 170

Sikes (Sykes), A. J. 57; A. T. 109; Cincinatta 30; Elizabeth 49; James 31; Lemuel T. 21; Singleton 1; William C. 25

Siler (Syler), George W. 102; Isaac N. 39; Jacob 17

Silvertooth, Amanda 126; James A. 37; John A. 14, 66; M. F. 104; Minerva 185

Silvester (Sylvester), Nancy M. 107; Thomas H. 74; T. M. 98; W. L. 87

Simmons (Simons), Abetha 22; Abraham 71; A. P. 121; Catharine J. 14; Charlotte 39; Eli 71; Elizabeth Catharine 63; Ella 166; Frances 172; George 166; Hannah 48; Henry F. 138; James 20, 35,107,122; Jane 158; Jarrod 168; J. L. 163; Joe 183; John 170; Julia 152; Katie 160; Lethe A. 2; Lucinda 7; Mahala F. 76; Margaret 125; Martha 21; Mary Ann 74; Mary E. 82; M. S. 86; Nancy 71; Richard 170; Sarah 20,143; Sarah Eliza 80; Sarah Tabitha 144; Susan 23; Susan Ann Jane 63; Vira 161; William 28,111,182; Winney 107; Zachariah 7

Simpson, Elizabeth J. 160; Hester R. 57; Joseph 71;

Simpson contd.
Nancy Ann 53; Rachel M.
38; R. J. 144; Sarah J.
38; Thomas 185; William
K. 11
Sims (Simms), Caledonia
150; C. M. 87; Cordelia
106; C. T. 161; David
59; Elizabeth 97; Eliza-
beth D. 124; Fannie 106;
Frona 116; George W. 52,
154; Hampton 2; James
83; James M. 44; J. M.
112; John 34,63; Julia
141; Mary 3; Mary Ann
66; Mary E. 148; M. B.
136; Milley 119; Mollie
187; Rachel 15; Thomas
D. 129; W. B. 173; W. H.
117; William H. 3
Singleton, Dave 173; J. R.
141; J. T. 125
Sinkton, Sarah 31
Sisco, Cora 181; Fleming
J. 72
Sisk, Daniel 116; Lafayet-
te 158; Mary 117,181;
M. L. 99; Rufus 169;
S. B. 53; Solomon B. 30
Slack, Frances N. 32
Sladen, Minney 165
Slater, Cornelius Capt.
186
Slaton, John 84
Slaughter, Martha A. 175;
Mary E. 144; S. A. 56;
Samuel A. 39
Sledgepeth (Hedgepeth),
Isaac N. 12
Sloan (Slone), Amanda C.
R. 63; Ann Jane 28;
Archibald S. 37; Eliza-
beth J. 37; Emily 91;
Grissilda B. 32; Jane
91; John C. 187; Jose
124; J. T. 165; Lucinda
E. 33; Martha A. 87;
Mary 165; Newton 91;
Nora 145; Rachael 47;
Samuel H. 25; Sarah J.
32; S. H. 148; Thomas M.
112; Thompson 145;
William A. 76
Small, A. C. 9; Amos 29,
78; Burrel 134; Cisa
Ann 22; Elizabeth H. 19;
E. P. 101; G. 91; George
20; George E. 136;
Henry 103; J. R. Sr.
111; Lucy E. 4; Margret
E. 80; Robert J. 138;
Susannah J. 3; Syntha
93; T. F. 132
Smallman, William 50
Smart, Andy 151; Wiley 145
Smiley, Alfred 166; Eliza-
beth 172; J. S. 110;
Mary M. 81
Smith, Abel R. 42; A. D.
75,89; Adaliza T. 27;
A. E. 143,162; A. J.
171; A. L. 164; Alex-
ander 54,90; Alexander
P. 27; Alfred 12; Alfred
R. 47; Alfred W. 47;
Allen 3,43; A. M. 165;
Amanda 101; Amanda A.
60,112,137; Amanda J.
35; Amilla 23; Andrew J.
14; Angeline 93,147;
Asa 10,40,50; Austin G.
8; Avis 180; B. C. 101,
172; Bell 178; Betsey
Mrs. 154; Ben 181;

Smith contd.
Benjamin 96; Benjamin
B. D. 148; Benjamin C.
97; B. F. 52; B. W. 120;
Caleb 28,71; Calvin 55;
Caroline 132(2); Casey
P. 10; Catharine 184;
Champion 74; Champion
E. 184; Charles 69;
Charles L. 10; Charles
W. 71; C. L. 71,116;
Cleresia 68; Cyntha A.
55; Dick 91; David 48;
David B. 1,115; David
G. 63,87; David H. 101;
David L. 52,88; David
M. 57; Davis 57; Davis,
Capt. 187; D. F. 53;
Dinah 147; D. J. 177;
D. M. 167; Dolly 158;
Drury J. 15; Drusie
150; Edmon 146; Edward
55; Elenora 159; Eli
162; Elijah 160; Eliza
11,31,32,127,159,182;
Eliza Ann 17; Elizabeth
30,43,50,57,65,104,111,
127; Elizabeth A. 79;
Elizabeth C. 48; Eliza-
beth D. 40; Elizabeth
J. 98,177; Elizabeth M.
58; Elizabeth Mrs. 170;
Elizabeth Searcy 141;
Ella H. 138; Ellen 137;
Ellen J. Mrs. 139;
Emma L. 140; Emily 4,
166; E. R. 167; Fannie
104,142; Fannie M. 175;
F. C. 167; Fennetta T.
11; F. J. 100; Florinda
119; Frances 94; Frances
A. 65,145; Frances E.
43,67,74; Frances M. 74;
F. M. 115,143; Fred 110;
F. W. 139; G. A. 171;
George 140,143,165,178;
George F. 38; George W.
6,27; Green D. 2; G. W.
97,152; Hard 156; Hardy
H. 12; Harriet M. 69;
Harris 128; Harrison
16; H. C. 151; H. D.
171; Henretta 48; Henry
29,118,147,160,170,184,
187; Henry J. 145; Henry
L. 3,54; Hester Ann 17;
Hezekiah 8; H. H. 134,
151; Hugh M. 17; Isaac
J. 79; Isham 2,189; Isom
182; Isom G. 186; I. V.
144; J. A. 136,146,153;
Jack 105; Jackson 54,
78; James 84,157; James
D. 2,59; James E. 41,
184; James F. 81; James
H. 59; James J. 154;
James M. 42; James R.
35; James W. 53; Jane
42,148; Jane E. 122;
Jane R. 26,60; J. B.
106; J. F. 141; J. H.
100; J. L. 163; Joe 152;
Joe B. 48; Joel 52;
John 10,41,53,79,129,
158; John B. 82,122;
John C. 113; John D.
139,142; John H. 112;
John L. 170; John M. 41,
44,54,58; John P. 92;
John R. 38,41,143; John
W. 70,108,131,182;
Jonathan 43; Joseph 128,
179; Joseph G. 10,21;
Josephine 54; Joshua 7;

Smith contd.
Josia A. 110; J. R. 76;
J. T. 141; Julia 20,105,
124; Julia A. J. E. 42;
J. W. 144; Kate 175;
L. A. 156; Larkin A. 58;
Lavina 42; Lawson 172;
L. E. 176; Lee 44; Lee,
Capt. 187; Lemuel 155;
Lera 10; Levi 20; Lizzie
103; Louisa 1,52,98;
Louisa A. 22; Lucinda 9,
30,34; Lucinda C. 65;
Lucy 104,129,141,171;
Lum 179; Malinda 91;
Marcus L. 102; Margaret
40,137; Margaret J. 51;
Margaret M. 67; Margaret
Mrs. 151; Margaret S.
132; Martha 19,134,137,
150,162,166; Martha A.
50,53,130; Martha Ann
43,55; Martha C. 38;
Martha J. 31,90; Martha
V. 115; Martin 57,66;
Mary 10,20,44(2),112,
124,130,173; Mary A. 22;
Mary A. C. 21; Mary Ann
37,69,70; Mary Ann E. 80;
Mary C. 83,126; Mary E.
14,44,59,72,89,93,118,
133,159,164,173; Mary
Frances 79,144; Mary J.
25,87; Mary Jane 86,130;
Mary S. 26; Mary V. 116;
Matilda 41; Maulda P. 54;
May C. 138; M. C. 165,
167; M. E. 86; Michell
156; Milton 97,177; M. J.
160; M. L. 65; M. M. 160;
Mollie E. 150; Nancy 43,
80,165; Nancy A. 65;
Nancy Ann 24,60; Nancy
Jane 128; Nancy M. 46;
Nancy M. 73; Nancy O.
135; Nathan 96; N. E.
151,169,171; Ned 177;
Nellie 131; Nelson 168;
Newton 137; N. J. 78;
N. M. 77; N. P. 120;
N. S. 139,170; Octava
107; O. G. 138; Orrer
Lee 158; Parthena P. 4;
Patsey 77; Permelia 42;
Permelia S. 56; Peter
94,112; P. G. 109,176;
P. H. 138; Polly 93;
Presious G. 12; R. A.
166; Rachel 6; R. C.
181; Richard 30,45,130;
R. J. 74; Robert 133;
Robert P. 102; Robertson
124; Roling 2; R. P.
173,183; R. S. C. 68;
Rufus K. 57; Rufus M.
150; Rutha 100; Sallie
139,171; Sam 182; Samuel
56; Samuel P. 46; Samuel
S. 42; Sarah 69,76,112,
118,133,159; Sarah A.
22,99,163; Sarah A. E.
104; Sarah Ann 71,102;
Sarah Bersheba Lucinda
134; Sarah E. 21; Sarah
H. 74; Sarah M. 116;
Sarah Morgan 72; Sarrah
115; S. B. 155,159; S.C.
121; Sebra 93; S. H. 98;
Simon 144; Sinthey S. A.
36; S. J. 83,138;
Solomon 72; Solomon B.
32; S. P. 158; Spencer
166; Stacie 161; Stephen
C. 39; Susan B. 2;

Smith contd.
Susan E. 152; Susan P.
16,184; Susan R. 64;
Susan Young 70; Syntha
O. 72; Synthia J. 185;
Synthy E. 60; Taylor
81; Tempy 140; Terrah
162; Theo 151; Theodore
61; Theodore G. 53;
Thomas W. 111; T. J.
170; Unice C. 84; V. A.
169; Victoria 114;
Virginia F. 56; W. B.
74; Wesley 24,128; W. F.
177; William 16,24,34,
43,52,68,129,158,159;
William B. 12,23;
William C. 28; William
F. 4; William G. 169;
William H. 42; William
M. 42,58,78; William P.
24; William R. 26,55,
76,82; William T. 34;
Willis M. 101; Wilson
17; Winnie 174; W. M.
117; W. R. 83; W. S.
157; Wyatt 161
Smithers, L. L. R. 172
Smoot, Daniel 17
Smotherman, Martha Ann
Mrs. 126
Smyth, David R. 7
Sneed, Ann E. 46; John R.
110; John S. 22; Susan
J. C. 123; William M.
176; William W. 101
Snellings, J. E. 158
Snoddy (Snoody), Charlotte
120; Elizabeth 30,41;
Eliza J. 66; F. M. 77;
Julia 158; Martha 26;
Mary 20; Mary A. 47;
Mary C. 65; Pleasant
182; Price M. 120;
William 50,157
Snow, Daniel S. 150;
Edmond 144; Edward 36;
Emily C. 125; Henry 1,
41; Mahala 48; Margaret
Elizabeth 127; Nancy 14;
Patrick 74; Sarah 55;
W. H. 126
Snowden, Benjamin 157
Solomon, Andrew J. 37;
Ben 97; Benjamin F. 38;
Bennett 23,30,63,84;
Caladonia 139; Eliza
35; Elizabeth 78;
Elizabeth D. 21; Eliza-
beth V. 29; E. P. 109;
E. Y. 70; F. E. 103;
G. W. 159; H. A. 170;
Harriett 21; James W.
44; Levina Ann 44;
Lizie A. 139; Lucy A.
88; Mary A. 84; Mary
Ann 15; Mary L. 9; R. E.
183; Samuel 15; Sarah
125,173; William C. 49,
51
Soroniphear, Elizabeth 35
Sorrells (Sorrels),
Adaline 74; Elizabeth A.
34; H. C. 179; Isham 19;
James 2; James M. 63;
Jane 62; John A. 116;
Lee 178; Malinda 41;
Margaret 94; Mary J.
129; Nancy C. 100;
Needham 29; Nelly 74;
N. J. 157; Sallie J.
129; Sarah C. 88; Susan
C. 51,53; W. H. 84;
William 18; William Y. 81

South, Sarah 85
Southern, Robert B. 12
Southworth, J. H. 73,105;
Louisa 60
Sowell, David R. 188;
William 168
Spain, William G. 1
Sparks, William H. 45
Sparkman, Elizabeth 171;
Melinda 157
Speck, Albert 13; Amos
111; Amy 75; Henderson
70; John Wesley 130;
Leander 8; Martha 72
Spelch, Thomas 61
Spence, Arminta M. 82;
Elizabeth 78; Hannah B.
109; James L. 39,90;
Margaret J. 138; Martha
50; Mary A. G. 54; Nancy
36; Nancy M. 54; Sarah
J. 75
Spencer, Adaline 89; Al-
fred M. 30; Allen 109;
Benjamin E. 23; Caroline
132; Catharine 23; E. M.
63; Hannah 138; James
F. 88; James M. 13,188;
J. E. 71; John C. 87;
John E. 60; Jonathan E.
55; Martha L. 85; Mary
72,56; Mary C. 118;
Mattie 177; Nannie C.
138; Stephen F. 51;
Thomas J. 50,79; Tilda
136; William A. 107;
William M. 36,72
Spillman, C. G. 64
Spotswood, Marcellus 181
Spray (Spry), Amanda 169;
Amanda J. 146; America
11; E. A. 167; E. F.
106; Georgia Ann 161;
Henry 22; James 30;
Jane 11,96,142; J. L.
137; John 48; Lewis 56;
Margaret A. 181; Wiley
61; William 171
Springer, William 11
Spur, Jocie 134
Spurlock, E. D. 124; John
H. 144
Stacy, John C. 53; Judy
111
Stafford, Leambrose 28;
Nancy 76; Samuel 38;
William 12
Stale, N. A. 154
Stallcup, Samuel 73;
Sarah 72
Stallings, J. N. 171;
W. R. 171
Stamps, George 136
Standback, B. E. 170;
Nancy 137
Stanford, Persona 4; S. M.
87
Stanley, A. J. 160; E. K.
113; Eliza 60; Josephine
132; Mariah 57; Martha
E. 60; Mary 10; Nancy
Ann 49; Prescilla Jane
77; Sarah 13; William
42,58
Starnes, W. P. 110
Staton (Staten), Amanda
4; Cary Ann 103; Charles
111; Cyntha 133; Elvira
13; Isham 108; Julia
159; Leann 135; Nancy
147; Polk 111; Rachel
150; Rebecca 149; Sarah
96,177; William 21;
William T. 26

Steadman, E. H. 59; G. W.
86; Mary E. 47; M. L.
102,116; N. R. 103;
Thomas R. 105
Steakley, W. A. 179
Steber, Nancy M. 23
Stedford, James D. 71
Steed, Augustus 8; Jesse
96; John 98; Lizzie 179;
Mary Ann 39; Naomi 20;
Nathaniel 1; Susan A.
149; Syntha 19; Tabithia
139; William F. 39
Steele (Steel), G. M. 7,
63,75
Steelman, Cynthia Ann 46;
Elizabeth 34,54,178;
George W. 72; H. A. 99,
102; Halifax A. 45; James
75; James R. 49; Jane 18;
Joel 64; John H. 20;
John L. 77; J. R. 117;
J. W. 101; Margaret 120;
Mary 77; Mary A. 82;
M. E. 169; Rebecca M.
97; Robert 154; Sarah F.
58; William 41,52
Stegall, Ervin B. 158;
J. B. 93; Margaret M. 7;
Matilda 51; Sarah Jane
34
Stennett, Ruffin C. 18
Stephen, Allen 96; A. P.
124; B. G. 170; Catharine
130; Cyntha 76; Daniel
120; Elizabeth E. 71;
Enoch 118; Ervin 3;
George P. 57; Hannah 164;
Hanah A. 153; Harriett
175; Jerry 116; J. M. 99;
John 26,116; Joseph C.
79; Kenneth 172; Lettie
140; Malinda 150; Maria
96; Mary Ann 43; Mary E.
163; Mary Jane Mrs. 140;
M. M. 137; Nancy 45; Nancy
Jane 53; Nelson 119;
Peter 119; Rena 172;
Richard 9; Ruth 113;
Samuel 148; S. E. 130;
William 1; William J.
44; Willis 76
Stephenson, Charlotte 57;
Dulsena 45; Elsina J.
34; E. M. J. Mrs. 163;
F. M. 116; Frances A.
75; G. W. 59,79; James
M. 41; J. C. 125,135;
John C. 29; Mary J. 155;
N. H. 118; Sarah A. 68;
Sarah Ann 24; Silas 46;
T. U. 21; W. G. 171;
William H. 44; W. M. 92
Stevens, Martha C. 122
Stevenson, Allen 39; B. A.
105; F. E. B. 74; Frank-
lin 39; James 22; James
R. 90; J. J. 86; N. C.
173; Robert 50; S. T.
135; William B. 158
Stewart, Angeline 72; Anna
175; Anna D. 20; Avery
13; Catharine 32; E. A.
98; Eliza E. 34; George
188; Green 136; Hesterpas
72; James L. 163; J. B.
124; J. K. 175; J. M.
180; J. Milton Dr. 174;
John 7; John D. 21; John
H. 34; John P. 76; Joseph
4; Laura M. 180; Laur-
anna 185; M. A. C. Mrs.
148; Margaret 13; Marga-
ret Ann 145; Martha 68

Stewart contd.
Martha F. 65; Mary A.
73; Mary E. 81; M. C.
123; M. J. 96; M. V.
154; Nancy A. 181; Nancy
E. 180; Nancy L. 64;
Robert A. 142; Robert W.
156; R. W. 128; Sarah
Ann 55; Sarah Jane 63;
Sophia 114; Sophia A. E.
13; T. A. 84; Thomas P.
132; William 188;
William C. 103,122;
W. L. 153
Stewman, Mary 175
Stiles (Styles), Elizabeth
E. 36; George W. 125;
J. A. 77; Jane 10;
John A. 111; Margaret A.
76; Martha C. 69; Mary
J. 139; Robert F. 163;
Samuel 13; Sarah 23,177;
Seaborn 113; William
110; Young 114
Stinnett, Jane 173
Stinson, Elizabeth 187;
Naomi E. J. 72
Stockstill, Eliza 75;
W. F. 73
Stockston, William J. 18
Stone, Abegail 37; A. F.
62; Alexander 87; America
F. 49; Ana 147; Ann 178;
Anna 62; Ben S. Dr. 156;
Bill 147; Brock 172;
Calvin 10; Dolphus A.
42; Eliza 21; Elizabeth
33,92,124,150; Elvira
173; Emily 36,102;
Ephraim 95; E. W. 68;
Fanny A. 119; George W.
185; Hester 176; Isaac
130; James A. 4; James
B. 46; James D. 80;
James M. 183; Jane 94;
John 143; J. W. 152;
Lewis 152; Louisa 135;
L. L. 184; Maranda 18;
Maria 91; Martha J. 84,
100; Mary 34,187; Mattie
135; Mike 91; Missouri
174; Narcissa 57; Polly
91; Reubin J. 70; Sarah
L. 41; Sarah P. 63;
Selina 25; Sterlin 153;
Suiah 96; Tom 174; Tonie
150; V. C. 156; W. H.
130; William 41,92
Stonebraker, Caroline E.
47; Catharine 130;
Frances 134; George 186;
G. J. 103; Mary A. 64;
Mattie 173; Mattie J.
73; Sarah Jane 122
Stoneman, Frank 114
Stormont, John R. 170
Story, Daniel G. 64;
E. C. 84; E. F. 101;
Eli 151; Elizabeth 62;
James E. 31; Jane 97;
Joseph 149; M. C. 65;
M. M. 68; Moses S. 72;
Nancy 9; N. L. 85;
Samuel M. 100; Sarah 31;
S. N. 78; Syntha 50;
T. A. 183; Thomas M.
35; W. A. 120
Stotts, M. D. 179
Stovall, A. D. 141; Al-
fred D. 74; Assena H. 3;
Frances 130; George 84;
Gilbert 68; James P.
134; Littleton M. 2;
Martha 86;

Stovall contd.
Nancy Jane 68; Perlina
171; Sarah 132; Thomas
54; Thomas J. 63;
Willis B. 7
Strain, W. D. 149
Strand, Martha 132
Strason, J. M. 151
Straton, William R. 31
Stray, Mary 21
Street, A. P. 156; Asa
110; Calvin 38; Caroline
25; C. C. 107; C. L.
181; Eliza 117; Emily
60; George W. 30; H. C.
163; John 60; John W.
157; Joseph G. 122;
Julia A. 77; Lizzie 110;
Louisa 60; Mary 106;
Nancy E. 26; Oliver 79;
R. B. 182; Susan 182;
Victoria 93; W. F. 171;
William 75
Stricklin (Strickland),
Fannie 160; John 70,183;
Manda 131; Ruffin 14
Stringer, Elizabeth 186;
William W. 56
Strong, Alexander 104;
Catharine 55; Dorthaney
42; E. A. 129; Edith
134; Eliza 40; Elizabeth
M. 40; Fannie P. 67;
George M. 59; Isabella
73; Jacob 106; John R.
127; Margret Jane 29;
Martha A. 68; Mary 4;
Matilda Ann 66; Paralee
Jane 54; Robert S. 7;
Samuel C. 40; Susan F.
181; Thomas B. 77
Stroud, Andrew W. 17;
Joshua 6; Littlebery 21;
Sarah A. 101; S. C. 134;
W. J. 177; W. S. 150
Stuart, Harriet E. 10;
James C. 78; Martha 70
Stubblefield, Harriet C.
134; Hester M. 65;
J. C. 122; John 79;
Joseph 31; Louisa 69;
Lucinda 70; Manson 117;
Martha A. 151; Martha
E. 128; M. M. 88; Nancy
38; Nancy P. 63; Susan
J. 66; Susan Jane 65;
Thomas B. 117; Vincy
89; W. C. 183; William
77
Studdard, Mattie 174
Stuman, Ruben 38
Sublet (Sublett), James
127; Mrs. Mat. 152
Sugg, Amanda 126,183;
Anthony 136; Jane 94;
Christiana 174; Cynthia
173; Edd 105; Elizabeth
H. 5; Harriet 158;
Henry H. 74,89; H. H.
61; James 92,140; Jordan
175; Katie E. 180;
Lemuel D. 61; Luther
126; Maggie 179; Mariah
163; Mary 95; Mollie E.
139; Pink 163; Prince
98; Sarah Jane 179;
Tom 178; Washington 102;
William C. 71
Sullinger (Sullenger,
Sulenger), Cordelia 100;
Emily 121; James 26;
John H. 40; Susan 71;
Thomas 120; Thomas C.
133; W. H. 173;

Sullinger contd.
William A. 77
Sullivan (Sulivan), Ade-
line 156; America 43;
Benjamin 39; Cincinnatta
F. 42; Cincinnatti 111;
Dan 161; Della 165;
Elizabeth 20,35; Emaline
181; Epps 26; Fanny 116;
George 133; H. A. 134;
Harris 165; Henry 7;
H. H. 144; Isaac W. 113;
James 42; Jeremiah 2,8;
J. J. 153; J. N. 87;
Joannah 72; John B. 110;
John H. 132; Katie 150;
Martha 39; Martha Eliza-
beth 75; Mary Ann 41;
Mary E. 154; Mary L. 43;
Michal 72; Nancy 32,161;
Parmelia 98; Ruth 7;
Sallie 139; Sarah 46;
Sarah C. 19; Sarah Jane
53; Silvannes 72; Susan
68; Thompson 22; Wiley
159,179; William 100
Sulser, Henry 85
Summers, A. H. 85; D. M.
123; Eliza C. 21; Fannie
Ann 133; George 183;
George W. 60; J. M. 176;
John 174; John C. 27;
Mattie 179; Thomas P. 18
Sumners, Adaline K. 140;
Charles 133; Elijah D.
140; Eliza 46; George
W. 66; James S. 55; J. J.
165; John 170; L. D.
172; Martha 157; Martha
A. 19; Mary A. 67,133;
Molly 125; M. T. 166;
Nancy M. 39; R. E. 155;
Sallie 127; Sallie E.
128; Thomas 133; Thomas
P. 79; William 50
Sunger, Henry 167
Surber, J. H. 151; John
24; Joseph 49; Julia A.
61; Mary 42; Rachel P.
12
Sutherland, William 89
Suttle, Francis 16; George
E. 81
Sutton, Tenny 140; Walter
170
Swain, Josiah, Judge 135
Swann (Swan), Elizabeth
58; J. T. 142
Swanner, Adeline 151,180;
J. J. 178; J. M. 148;
J. W. 128; Lafayette 86;
Letty B. 41; Mary 2;
Mary B. 40; Obediah 22;
Rutha 69
Sweaton, Moses 2
Sweet, James 187
Sweden, Lewis 86
Sweeney (Swinney, Sweanea,
Swiney), D. C. 171;
James J. 121; John 8,151;
Louisa Jane 82; M. C.
179; Sarah 18; W. F. 130
Swinebroad (Swinebro),
Amanda M. 48; Dona E. D.
63; Donnda 120; George
W. 26; Henry Green 57;
Manerva L. 59; Mary 30;
Parthena C. 58
Swinford, Amanda J. 31,95;
Harriet 106; James H.
147; James M. 143; John
8; Lydia 22; Mack 169;
Martha Catharine 77;
Mary E. 55; Nancy J. 90;

Vickers contd.
Richard 150; S. J. 137;
William 43; W. R. 162;
Zebulon 20
Vines, Benjamin 81
Vining, James 172; John
32; L. T. 142
Vincent, A. 3; James 2;
Mary E. 170; Sarah 15
Vinson (Venson), Abraham
22; Amanda Jane 56;
Eliza A. 97; Lucy Jane
123
Vinzant, Nelson 178

Waddle, Charles 150;
John S. 188; John S. Jr.
128; Rebecca 128
Wade, C. J. 71; Elijah F.
17; Ellen J. 80; Emeline
17; Francis M. 31,100;
James 116; John 98;
Mary 121; Mary J. 52;
Rebecca 14; Sarah M. 49;
Sulthany 46; W. D. 94;
William 88; William H.
37
Wadkins, Fannie 146;
George 61; Harris J. 80;
Jacob 109; John 50,147;
John W. 173; J. W. 148;
Peter 144
Waggoner, A. J. 73;
Alexander 6,58; Allen
G. 11; Alley J. 60;
Anderson 133; Andrew 6,
61,73; Ann 132; Caroline
138; Catharine 17,43,
84; C. E. 130; Charles
L. 63; Cynthia 90; Dan
N. 94; David 34; Dick
103; D. J. 118; Elijah
128; Eliza 24; Eliza-
beth 16,17,47; Emily
127; Felix 15; F. M.
118,120; Frances L. 59;
Frederick 87; F. W. 59;
George 188; George H.
78; George W. 71,72;
Henry 2,8; Henry A. 69;
Jacob 38,167; Jacob L.
29; Jane 42,111,130;
Jennie A. 173; Jesse
183; J. G. 95; J. J.
120; J. L. 173; John
39; J. R. 139; L. 104;
Lou 177; Louisa 24;
Loutisha 160; Lucy C.
23; M. A. 70; Martha
J. 16,64; Martha Mrs.
101; Mary 172; Mary E.
48; Mary J. 120; Mary
M. 56; Mary T. 23;
Mathew 17; Mattie 158;
M. E. 157; M. G. 66;
Mollie E. 105; Moses
136; Nancy 6; Nancy Ann
55; Nancy C. 39; Ned
126; Orpha 134; Peggy
Ann 1; Polly 165;
Rebecca J. 103; Revy
76; R. F. 133; Sarah
125; Sarah A. 37,42;
Sarah E. 80; Susan 3;
Susan 19,102,125,180;
Susan A. 90; Susan E.
95; W. A. 177; William
139; William R. 28;
William S. 32
Wagster, Elizann 62;
Martha 58; R. A. 154;
Sarah E. 135
Waid, C. W. 141

Wakefield, Andy 106;
Bettie 142; Delia A.
54; Elizabeth 7; James
H. 80; J. F. 70; John
B. 131; Joseph N. 57;
J. W. M. 153; Mary A.
84; Mary J. 122; Nancy
E. 85; Samuel J. 49;
Sarah E. 58
Waldrop, Martha Jane 62
Wales, Dink 99
Walden (Waldon), Barbara
119; David A. 136;
Elizabeth 158; Ella J.
139; Jane 115
Walker, A. J. 182; A. L.
92; Alfred 66; A. M. 73;
America 171; America
Jane 40; Anna 48; C. C.
169; Celina A. E. 101;
Charles L. 14; Cynthia
M. 10; David B. 17;
D. G. 125; E. A. 122;
E. E. 112; Elijah W.
109; Eliza Ann 64; Eliz-
abeth 10,23; Frances C.
120; George 175; Harret
29; Harriet A. 44;
Humphrey 135; Isham J.
9; J. A. 98; James A.
20; James W. 18; Jane
26,164; J. H. 76; John
155; John C. 70,155;
John H. 76; John W. 46;
J. R. 117; Laura Ann
53; Laurret 6; Lewis S.
104; L. J. 167; Louis
113; Lula 155; Malinda
66; Martha 12,66,119;
Martha A. E. 65; Mary
34; Mary Ann 136; Mary
J. 86; Mary Martha 146;
M. F. Mrs. 172; M. J.
173; Milton 11; M. L.
160; N. A. 128; Nancy
24; Nancy C. 52; Nancy
M. 38,70; Peter T. 26;
R. E. 167; Rebecca J.
26; R. S. 121; Samuel
92; Samuel H. 123; Sarah
1; Sarah Ann 87; Sarah
E. 90; S. D. 183; Serena
121; S. J. 132; S. M.
96; Smith L. 66; Sophia
E. 42; Stephen A. 32;
Susannah M. 33; Susan
L. A. 143; Tishey 159;
William A. 30,54,77,
134,156; William B. 15;
William D. 59; William
M. 65; Zachariah 27
Wallace (Walace), Anna
S. 12; Caroline 12;
F. R. 121; H. B. 105;
H. L. 97; Hugh B. 46;
J. H. P. 160; Joe 132;
Joseph C. 62; Josiah
P. 47,119; Mary E. 52;
Nancy G. 184; N. O.
59; R. A. 80; Sarah
129; Sarah P. 23; Susan
81; Thomas Y. 55;
Warren 169
Waller, W. H. 113
Walls (Wall), B. F. 112;
Isaac 184; James 107;
Mary 101,148
Walter, Bob 142
Walton, Mary 147,184;
Mary C. 45; Peter W. 23
Walworke, Joseph 122
Wanslow, Eliza 20; Eliza-
beth A. 3; Joseph 30;
Joseph W. 48; Mary E.90;

Wanslow contd.
Narcissa 25; Patrick H.
14,18
Ward, Catharine 72; Daniel
B. 8; Elizabeth 54;
E. M. 113; Emaline 39;
Erasmus 3; Huldy 170;
John 118; John F. 146;
Lutitia 120; Margaret
12,76; Martha 23; Mary
J. 87; Mary M. 105;
Mary S. 124; Nancy 13,77;
N. C. 57,142; Rebecca
25; W. H. H. 117; William
126; William C. 77;
W. J. 119; W. L. 110
Warden, Bethiah E. 87;
Daniel 52; Emily 20;
F. E. 161; Franklin 81;
Hardin 22,56; James 97;
J. D. 180; John 32,61;
John W. 166; Malinda J.
92; Mary Jane 125; M. C.
164; Nancy 45; W. C. 167
Warner, Mary 5; William R.
10
Warnick, H. H. 107
Warren, Andrew J. 101;
Benjamin 18; Bettie 131;
Caroline 35; Daniel 47,
77,140; Eglentine 100;
Elijah 36,110; Eliza
112; Elizabeth 37,50(2);
Elizabeth Ann 188; Eme-
line 34; Enoch 45; Hanah
106; Henry 9; James A.
33,123; James K. 115;
Jane 76,89; Jesse 18;
John 25,47,58,127,176;
John C. 179; Johnson 62;
John W. 115; Louisa E.
115; Louretta Mrs. 169;
Margaret E. 63; Mariah
100; Martha 42,48,68;
Martha Ann 36; Mary 1,
40; Mary E. 131; Mary
J. 119; Nancy 64; Nancy
Jane 82,130; N. D. 82;
Peter 49; Rachel 90;
Rebecca 54; R. D. 174;
Robert 15; Samuel 45;
Sarah 20,51; Starlin A.
33; Susan 4; Susan E.
113; T. H. 146; Thomas
21,106; Thomas K. 188;
T. W. 178; W. C. 94;
W. H. 165; William 1,15,
86; William H. 101;
William R. 18
Washburn, Abraham 8; Anna
156; Arthur 43; John 11;
John L. 156,175; Jane
74; Mary 53; Mourning
70; Nancy 95; Susan A.
84; Thomas 29
Washington, Ford 132;
John 169
Waterman, Henrietta M.
104; Sarah L. 65;
William 45
Waters, Harriet V. 124;
Martha 21; Roena J. 110
Watkins, Annanias 118;
Green 28; John W. 179;
R. F. 179
Watson, Anne E. 111;
Charlotta 76; Daniel J.
50; Eliza 18; Elizabeth
66,75; Fannie 149; G. A.
112; Harriet Ann 134;
Henry W. 110; Hugh 1;
James 45; Jane 67; John
185; John H. B. 22;John
W. 58; Lucentha 5;

Watson contd.
Lydia Ann 10; M. A. 175;
Margaret J. 82; Martha
J. 102; Mary M. 49;
Matilda 19; Milly 2;
Nancy 124; Nimrow W. 15;
Rebecca B. 29; Rebecca
J. 51; Rutha 70; Samuel
81; Sarah C. 25; Turner
B. 30; W. F. 141,143;
William 8; William A.
59; William F. 56;
Wright H. 43
Watts (Watt), J. F. 150;
John W. 29; J. W. 183;
Martha M. 160; Mary F.
161; Mary Jane 57;
Nancy J. 120; Sallie A.
161; Sarah E. 69;
William 150
Wear (Ware, Weare), Eliza-
beth A. 23; Jane H. 31;
Nancy M. 31; Orpha Mrs.
153; Sarah N. 11; Wiley
1
Weaver, A. M. 123; David
K. 15; Dozier T. 54;
Eliza 109; Ephraim 19;
Fenetta 7; John 40,160;
J. T. 113; J. W. 157;
Mc. 178; Nancy E. 37,50;
Peter 3; Piety 60; R. F.
74; Samuel 41,82; Sarah
E. 72; William 116,127
Webb, Abb 107; A. B. D.
167; Angeline 169; Bell
167; Caleb Z. 41; Cla-
rinda C. 43; Cynthia H.
89; Elizabeth 116;
Elizabeth Mrs. 96;
Fannie 172; George 6,
135,162; George T. 132;
George V. 37; Green 177;
Henry 182; James 149;
James H. 104; James M.
161; Jessie C. 86; J. F.
76; J. G. 117; J. M. 82;
John 1; John W. 52;
Josiah T. 26; Josie 156;
Julia Ann 33; L. A. 135;
Laben A. 29; Laura 155;
Lou S. 99; Lucretia 19;
Margaret 154; Mariah
B. 37; Martha A. 90;
Martha J. 69; Mary 181;
Mary S. 156; M. C. 91;
M. W. 147; Nancy 6;
Nancy B. 31; Nancy C.
23; Nancy J. 110; Nelly
175; Richard 167; Rosana
80; Samuel 36; Sarah 41;
Sarah Elizabeth 143;
Sarah F. 72; S. C. 167;
S. J. 180; Thomas 33;
Virginia A. 78; William
27; William B. 182;
William H. 37; William
N. 139
Webster, Absolum 62; Ann
Eliza 22; Elizabeth 60;
J. A. 162; Joseph D.
75; Lucy H. 45; Martha
35,64; M. H. 167; M. J.
174; Nancy J. 75;
Peter C. 19; Reubin 75;
Robert 160
Weeks, Alfred 147; George
121; Isaac 25; Margaret
M. 121; M. J. 131;
Sarah E. 96; Thursa A.
115
Weigart, Columbus S. 165;
Daniel 94; George Ann
68; John 185

Welch, James L. 164; J. N.
167; Margaret A. 117;
Martha C. 87; Mary 89;
Mary E. 125; M. B. 109;
Nicholas N. 6; N. M.
136; Rhoda E. 155;
Robert 163,187; Sarah
Ann 82
Welder, Elinor P. 14
Wellman, Icy Dora 143
Wells, Argyle 9; Benjamin
136; Bud 171; C. A. 100;
Clement 164; Coleman
13; Drewry 55; E. C.
149; Elizabeth A. 20;
Elizabeth Ann 59; Eliza-
beth J. 30; Eliza E.
21; Emily 171; Francis
12; Frank 173; Guss 164;
Harrison 2; Hill E. 112;
Isam 60; Isham 49; Isom
99; James M. 64; Jocie
C. 106; John 118,179;
John D. 117; John G. 14;
Josiah 35; Julia Ann
61; L. E. 173; Loucinda
164; Margret A. Mrs.
128; Martha 120; Martha
E. 59; Martha Jane 3;
Mary A. E. 41; Mary E.
114; Mary J. 59; Minerva
J. 98; Nancy 57; N. F.
181; N. J. 70; Perry 3,
98; Peyton, Capt. 186;
Rachel 11; Rebecca 66;
Reuben W. 61; Rhodia A.
122; Rufus 157; Sallie
163; Sarah A. 75; Sarah
Ann 148; Thomas J. 30;
Virginia 57; W. B. 171
Wersham (Wisham), Eliza-
beth 26; Margaret E. 26
Weshshown, Lucinda 31
West, A. J. 124; Alfred
5; Amanda 50; Andrew J.
97; Cena 9; E. J. 127;
Elizabeth 44,117,184;
Elizabeth C. 42; Eliza
C. 65; Emily 19; Frankey
18; Hetty 11; Isabell
C. 72; James M. 20; Jane
29; J. L. 150; John C.
71; John S. 10; Joseph
C. 101; Josephus 62;
J. W. 160; L. J. 125;
Lucy Anabella 143; Man-
erva J. 62; Rhodes 188;
Richard W. 7,125; Sarah
C. 120; T. A. 125;
William C. 40,107; Win-
ney 18; W. J. 171
Westbrooks, Robert 102
Westerman, Daniel 21;
Leotha 29; Newton B.
28; Siambra 15; Sintha
29; Wilson L. 24
Westmoreland, C. W. 33
Wham, Isabella 187; John
W. M. 32
Wheeler, Albert C. 45;
A. M. 125; Caroline 26;
Drury C. 44; Emily 3;
J. W. 154; Kittie 175;
Robert H. 31; Sarah 19
Wherley (Wherey, Whirley),
Amery 128; Liza 177;
Rufus 148
Whitaker, A. J. 58; Allis
117; Amanda 136; America
155; America W. 55;
Anderson 122; Andy 126;
Beadie 167; Bell 172;
Ben 172; Benjamin 15;
Bennet 31,74; Bettie 109;

Whitaker contd.
Berry 149; B. F. 65;
Caroline 105; Charles
149; Charles H. 9;
Clara 174; Cordelia Mary
11; Doctor John D. 47;
Dona 156; E. A. 54;
Easther 133; Edmon 126;
Edmond 103; Eliza 51;
Elizabeth 35,73; Ella
May 150; Emaline 177;
Emily 139,181; Fanny
116; Fenetta 22; George
32,152; G. W. 158;
Hailey 147; Harey 105;
Harry 174; H. C. 62;
Henry 126,133; Hettie
143; I. B. 174; Jack 95;
James 137,144; Janie 108;
Jane V. 94; Jasper 125;
J. B. 181; Jennie 114;
Jesse 103; J. K. 180;
Joe 152; John 141; Jordon
116,138; Joseph C. 39;
Judy 158; Julia 134;
Julia F. 63; Lem 168;
L. J. 90; L. L. 62;
Lossen P. 26; Louisa 63;
Lucy 149; M. A. 64; Mar-
garet 139; Mark 184;
Martha 79,126,158; Martha
A. 12; Mary 154; Mary
Jane 49; Mary M. 2,110,
111; M. E. 166; Minerva
Jane 2; M. L. 106; Mollie
182; Moses 118; Murina
25; Nancy H. 38; Nancy
J. 144; Nannie S. Mrs.
108; Nathaniel H. 110;
Nelson 143; Newton 185;
Olla 156; Perlina 187;
Queen 174; R. A. 149;
Robert N. 37; Robert W.
151; Rosanna 143; Rosie
175; Sallie C. 88; Sallie
H. 156; Sarah 132; Sarah
Ann 7; Sue 173; Susan 134;
Susan E. 15,50; Thomas
56,136; Thomas J. 27;
T. P. 168; V. 109;
Wesley 158; William 126,
150; William B. 80; W. N.
168
White, A. L. 135; Alfred
89; Amanda 135; Anthony
94; Bethiah Lynn 189;
Brasley 80; C. B. 75;
Cyntha 25; D. F. 145;
Eliza B. 31; Eveline 8;
F. M. 130; George 98;
G. W. 132; Hamilton 66;
H. F. 102; J. J. 182;
John 61; John D. 48;
John R. 68; Joseph A.
103; J. R. 175; Julia F.
133; Lizzie 106; Lucinda
122; Manuel 94; Margaret
188; Margaret S. 63;
Martha 8,133; Martha J.
130; Martha M. 70; Mary
49; Mary J. 19; M. J.
168; Nancy 59,176; Nancy
A. 89; O. A. 145; Pascal
41; Pat 180; Rebecca
S. C. 111; Samuel M. 26;
Samuel N. 26; Sarah 18;
Sarah C. 36; Sarah Jane
171; S. M. 66; Stephen
A. 42; Thadeus 65;
Thomas 158; Thomas J.
156; Thomas M. 91;
T. S. D. 181; Will 160;
William C. 6,18; William
F. 72; William M. 49;

White contd.
William P. 65; Willis
66
Whited, Louisa A. 88
Whiteman, Elizabeth 85
Whiteside, Manerva Ann 36
Whitfield, B. H. 118;
Fannie 95; Mary Pauline
154
Whitlock, Jackson 70;
Kate S. J. 117; Nancy
F. S. 30; Octavo 22
Whitlow, Mary C. 39;
Sarah E. 127
Whitman, Fannie M. 159;
Mary E. 47
Whitt (Whit), A. B. 82;
David 56; Eliza 129;
Frances Ann 137; James
168; M. E. 170; S. W.
172; Wesley 90
Whittenburg (Whittenberg),
Norman H. 36; Peter L.
142
Whittington, A. H. 63;
Daniel J. 12; Lucinda
27; Mary Jane 131; Nancy
27; Nannie 104; Sarah
P. 143
Whitworth, A. M. 77; C. H.
98; George W. 77;
Hannah 15; H. C. 145;
J. A. F. 115; Jaily 41;
John 19; John A. 110;
Lydia E. 78; Martha J.
60; Mary R. 115; M. M.
182; R. D. 175,178; R. L.
76; Sarah E. 56; Thomas
B. 63; Thomas J. 60
Whorton, James 135
Wickers, Martha J. 134
Wicks (Wickes), Charles
T. 148; G. D. 146;
Harriet 157; James M.
39; J. E. 178; John A.
123; John T. 164; Levina
A. 124; Martha 22; Mar-
tha A. 34; Mary E. 112;
Mary S. 40; M. J. 167;
Nancy 150; Robert F. 70;
Samuel 173; Sanford 167;
Sarah 163; Virginia 109;
William 143; W. N. 167;
W. R. 171
Wiggins, Catharine B. 62
Wilbanks (Willbanks),
Elizabeth 173; Jacob
101; L. A. 174; M. C.
182; Nana E. 171; Visna
E. 101
Wilburn (Wilbur), C. O.
118; Daniel T. 52;
James 52; Louiza 164;
Mariah 109
Wiles (Wyles), Celia 7;
Charles 14,17; Mary 1;
Minerva 120; Nancy J.
43; Polly Ann 69;
Rachel 22; Rosannah 31;
S. J. 138; Stephen 96;
Stephen L. 37
Wiley, Bob 148; E. C.
109; Elizabeth Jane 81;
Frank 93; G. M. D. 100;
James 5; Joseph C. 47;
Lucinda D. 186; Lu-
venia M. 114; Margaret
9; Martha J. 66; Mary
140; Mary E. 55; Mary
T. 33; Miriah L. 49;
Nancy 1; Reevis B. 145;
Susannah J. 37
Wilhoit, John W. 32; Mary-
an A. 29; Sandy 141

Wilkerson, Caroline 35;
Eliza 49; Elizar 18;
Margaret 15; R. A. 114;
Sarah 1; Temperance 15
Wilkins, Caroline 46;
Edy 2; Elizabeth 23;
George W. 31; Jane 52,
149; John F. 42; Martha
20,65
Wilkson, Natley 186;
Sarah Ann 2
Wilks, Elizabeth 106
Willis, Elizabeth O. 186;
Margaret 86; Sarah 66
Willett, Eliza L. 3; John
83,138; Sarah Ann 2
Williams, A. E. 90; Alex-
ander 17; Alfred 55;
Alfred W. 45; Amon A.
40; Ann 133; Artemicia
106; Babe 179; Berry
122; Carrell 76; Char-
lotte M. 93; Clarinda
30; C. W. 87; D. Adaline
140; Edy 147; E. L. 144;
Eldrige S. 37; Elijah
T. 23; Elizabeth 15;
Eliza J. 37; Elmira 168;
F. M. 117; Francis M.
63; G. A. 175; G. W.
87; Henrietta 171; Henry
66,93; Henry F. 123;
H. R. 154; Isaac 121;
James 14,91; James H.
155; James R. 51; James
T. 144; Jane 90; Jane
E. 120; Jasper 63; J. C.
101; Jerome B. 78; John
3,105,113,122,183; John
N. 90; John R. 70;
Joseph T. 15; Josie Mrs.
164; J. P. 64; Keziah
26; Leroy 157; Lorlesa
Ann 75; Louisana 50;
Louis D. 157; Lucinda
17,64; Maggie 150;
Malinda 165; Margaret
16,19,170; Margaret A.
27; Marion 98; Mary 38,
104; Mary A. 18; Mary
Ann Adaline 49; Mary
Jane 141; Mary M. 108;
M. G. 49; Minerva 50;
M. R. 21; Nancy 100,
135; Nancy A. 28; Nancy
Ann E. 39; Penina E.
41; P. J. 54; Polly 157;
Reece 66; Richard 124;
R. J. 162; Sarah 2,8,
16,154; Sarah E. 140;
Sarah Jane 131; S. E.
139; Spencer 20; Sue A.
151; Susan 7,20; Susan
D. 44; Susan K. 55;
Tempey 6; Thomas F. 119;
W. A. 102,121; W. F.
129; William 66,76,88,
135; William F. 52
Williamson, Ann E. 142;
Averilla 185; Bob 132;
Delila 163; Eliza J.
56; Hawley 16; H. E.
145; Holly R. 55; Isaac
69; J. D. 156; Lewis C.
37; Lydia 188; Manerva
71; Martha 4; Mary V.
156; Parmelia 88; Per-
melia 50; Rebecca 188;
Richard S. 62; Robert
176; Robert W. 74; Rosa
111; Sarah Emma 135;
Susan 151
Willingham, J. W. 177

Willoughby (Willoby),
Martha J. 152; Sallie A.
181
Wilson, Adeline 120; Allice
140; Amanda 154; Andrew
M. 17; Ann 159; Anna 178;
Betsey A. 4; Burnetta
20; Charles 127; C. M.
62; Creasy 103; C. S. 82;
David M. 64; Della 94;
Eillie 161; Dora I. Mrs.
145; E. H. 6; Elizabeth
34; Elizabeth A. 144;
Elizabeth G. 38; Eliza-
beth Jane 183; Elizabeth
M. 32; Elizabeth T. 23;
Ellen 80; E. S. 68,87;
E. S. 68,87; Fannie 150;
Frances A. 16; Galen P.
60; Gilbert 94; Hantipic
127; Harrison S. 22;
Henry 113; J. A. 124;
Jack 131; Jackson 95;
James 125; James A. 47;
James B. 64; James M.
150,178; James M. D. 145;
Jane 10; Jane Mrs. 146;
Jasper N. 142; John 78,
88; John T. 13; Jones L.
27; J. R. 94; J. T. 181;
J. W. 62,170; Kasiah 143;
Larza 115; L. E. 173;
Lottie 102; Lou 106;
Lucy 97; Margret M. 29;
Mariah 6; Martha Ann 57;
Martha B. 17; Martha
Elizabeth 81; Martha J.
29; Martha Jane 24; Mary
24,89,155; Mary Ann 143;
Mary E. 61; Mary F. 111;
Mathew 39; Mathew T. 30;
Mattie 170; M. E. 171;
M. H. 181; M. T. 85;
Oliva 42; Prince 173;
Rebecca 153; Robert M.
139; Robert W. 72; Rosa
127; Samuel 89,133; Sam-
uel L. 35; Sarah 13;
Sarah A. 102; Sarah E.
41; Sarah J. 178; S. C.
6; Sintha A. 63; Stephen
B. 39; Thomas 182;
Thomas A. 101; T. M. 140;
Urias A. 32; Washington
34; W. C. 110; W. H. 179;
Wiles 115; William 32,
147; William O. 163;
William T. 5; William W.
36
Winburn (Windborn), Hattie
163; Mattie J. 115
Winds, C. W. 155
Winford, B. F. 105;
Caroline 110
Winfred, Nannie 141
Wingfield, Sarah M. 188
Winkers, Hiram 107
Winkler, Henry H. 46;
Jennie 134; Levi 180;
William 169
Winkley, Hiram 135
Winsett, J. T. 156; Susan
P. 135
Winstead, John M. 21;
Luretha A. 54; Mary S. 31
Winters, Cynthia 2
Wisdom, Jessie L. 115;
J. M. 126; M. J. 177
Wise, David 99; David M.
4; James W. 78; Martha
8; Mary 78; Matthew 97;
William 141
Wiseman, Elisha 99; J. F.
82; John S. 60; L. M. 77;

231

Wiseman contd.
Mary 95; Mary J. 127;
William 10
Wishon, Jane 42
Wisner (Wisener), E. O.
Mrs. 105; M. A. 74;
Martha M. 68(2)
Withers, Catharine 37;
Harriet 11; Sarah A. H.
24
Witt, David 93; Eliza 14;
Euticia 23
Wofford, Lucy 37
Woodall, Eliza 41; James
24; J. A. W. 164; John
A. 37; Leroy W. 24;
Louisa A. 123; Malissa
76; Nancy M. 77
Woodard, A. B. 176; Ada
151; Alfred 144; Amanda
J. 97; A. S. 172; B. A.
130; C. C. 138; Dilly
Ann 132; Eliza C. 67;
Elzira 7; Frances E. 61;
H. F. 127; Hials 6; H.
T. 167; James 179; J. H.
86; J. R. 104; J. S.
144; J. W. 98; Lenizetta
A. 114; Lucy Ann 41;
Margaret E. 95; Marriah
116; Martha 141; Martha
E. 148; Mary 107,119;
Mary E. 96,147; Medora
A. 118; M. J. 169; M. O.
153; M. S. 181; M. W.
138; Nancy A. 177; Nancy
L. 109; Narcissa J. 66;
N. J. 65; O. J. 153;
Rhoda 147; S. A. 104;
Sarah A. 118; Sarah E.
116; Sina 91; Susanah
68; W. A. 139; William
173; William M. 73;
Wilson 3; W. S. 109
Woodbay, Liza J. 21
Wooden, Sarah 150
Woodly, Charley 137
Woodruff (Woodroof),
Bettie 67; Eliza 187;
George G. 24; Matilda
40; Nancy 27; Wyatt T.
88
Woods (Wood), Addie 125;
Alex 120; C. C. 141;
Clint 176; Eliza A. 114;
Fannie 170; George W.
23; H. E. 162; Ida 166;
James G. 20,99; J. H.
104; John 9,58,174;
John R. 25; Landen 144;
London 166; Mary S. 71;
Matt 93; Mattie A. 103;
N. D. 182; Nick 115;
Oscar 122; Robert 1;
Stephen 147; Susan 121;
Susie J. 166; W. E. 151;
William 16; William C.
20; W. P. 61
Woodson, Crawford 137;
John 153; Manerva 169;
Smith 149
Woodward, Abner S. 32,71;
Frances E. 51; Harriet
J. 188; James 7; James
S. 124; James T. 62;
Lucy E. 53; Mary M. 52;
Mitta C. 73; Robert S.
17; Samuel McDonald 25;
Sarah M. 52; William M.
44; William S. 8;
William W. 29; W. R.
123; W. T. 176
Woodwin, George 94

Woody, J. Charles N. 27;
Rachel 19
Wooley, Joel 13
Wolaver, Mollie 152
Womack (Wamack, Wormack),
A. B. 86; Arch 116;
Archa 129; Benjamin F.
58; Charles W. 80;
D. S. 135; E. 56;
Elisha 56; Elizabeth
Ann 62; Eliza J. 51;
F. M. 102; Frances 128;
Green 131; Harriet 128;
H. P. 128; Lewis 1;
Lucy A. 86; Malinda C.
105; Mary 78; M. H. 78;
Nancy 55; Nancy D. 168;
N. C. 44; Rachel J. 32;
Rebecca E. 39; Sarah
66; Sarah Ann 32; Sarah
E. 70; S. M. 130;
Solomon 22; Susanah 68;
William 11,112,127,130,
134; William R. 55;
W. J. 54
Word, Lucinda 158
Workman, Isaac N. 102;
James T. 122
Worley (Whorley), James
141; Jarrett 145; Wiley
22
Worthy, C. E. 85
Worsham, Clairborne B.
187
Wray, Harrison C. 121;
Martha E. 118
Wright, A. A. 109; Adaline
77; A. J. 98; Amanda
122; Amanda J. 76;
Amanda M. 81; A. N. 135;
Andrew J. 69; B. L. 132;
Burrell 178; Catharine
7; Calvin 125,159;
Caroline 136; Edde Eme-
line 63; E. L. 166;
Eliza 168; Elizabeth 7;
Elizabeth S. 57; Ely
104; Emily C. 41; Emily
E. 90; Ervin 135; Esther
14; Eugenia 165; Fannie
A. 150; Frances E. 67;
Francis M. 27; G. E.
165; George S. 70;
George W. 31; Harriet
144; H. D. 117; Henry
174; H. P. 119; Isaac
N. 8; Jacob R. Jr. 52;
Jacob T. 35; James 5;
James H. 50; James M.
159; Jane M. 46; J. B.
159; J. C. 182; J. M.
148; John B. 25; John
M. 138; John W. 16;
Joseph 9; Loumanda P.
34; Luvina 19; Mag 108;
Magie 134; Malinda 33;
Margaret E. 122; Martha
55; Martha E. 116;
Martha J. 50; Mathew M.
137; Martin 2; Mary
Elizabeth 67; Mary J.
58; M. H. 183; Mira 95;
M. J. 159; N. A. 161;
Nancy J. 106; Nancy R.
105; N. V. 139; P. A.
152; P. L. 166; R. E.
148; Rebecca 160,181;
R. H. 104; Richard 108;
Sam 166; Sarah 186;
Sarah A. 69; Silvester
H. 48; S. M. 96; Susan
A. 60; Susan N. 99;
W. A. 66; William 3,15,
150; William B. 121;

Wright contd.
William D. 80; William
N. 58; William P. 58
Wyatt, Elizabeth E. 68;
Isabella J. 23; James B.
61; John 175,188; Maggie
J. 81; Margaret 188;
Mary E. 86; Sarah 188;
Thomas B. 187; Turnie
113; William 188; William
R. 84
Wynn (Winns, Wynne), Drury
M. 68; E. W. 5; Fannie
W. 98; Frances Ann 185;
K. T. 161; Ridley B. 5

Yant, C. H. 70; Cynthia E.
58; E. S. 78; Mary L.
84; Moses W. 67; Rebecca
87; Travis A. 60; W. D.
72
Yarbrough, Amanda 65;
Elizabeth 26; James N.
97; James W. 141; J. D.
151; Jeptha 15; Julia
63; Mary Ann 78; Mary E.
141; Nancy 98; Nelson
53; R. J. 92; Sarah 21;
Sarah J. 97; Solomon S.
28; William 115
Yarley, William 117
Yates, Benjamin 111; James
38; Joshua 20; T. B. 87
Yaunt, Charles J. 127
Yeates, Amanda F. 62; John
65; Margaret F. 40;
Perry 156; William C. 74
Yell, Elizabeth 52; Jane
37
Yergen, James A. 30
Yerger, Maria E. 37; Mary
C. 31
York (Yorke), Caroline 76;
Laura A. 108; Nancy J.
Mrs. 172; Pharaba 36;
Samuel 169; Zekiel 109
Young, A. J.87; Ben 162;
Dewitt C. 98; Drucilla
Ann 61; Elizabeth A. 71;
Elizabeth Ann 37; Eliza
P. 25; Gabriel 74; John
127; John C. 185; Marga-
ret J. 146; Mary Ann 5;
Mary Ann J. 139; Mary
Jane 37; M. M. 64; Robert
B. 44; Sarah 26,115;
Sarah Isabella 81; S. E.
152; S. E. J. 94; Susan
A. 12; William N. 77
Youngblood, William L. 59
Yowell, Joel Esq. 186;
Sallie E. 89; Starland
148; Sue 129

Zimmer, Lizzie Mrs. 174
Zimmerman, Amanda 169;
Berry 93; Bill 183; H. S.
105; Joe 131; Julia 147;
Manerva 132; Marinda 93;
N. E. 169; Sallie 145;
Susan 72
Ziverly, Mary 185
Zolicofer, Terry 125

www.ingramcontent.com/pod-product-compliance
Lightning Source LLC
Chambersburg PA
CBHW021900020426
42334CB00013B/418